CW00924797

The Palgrave Handbook of Disabled Children's Childhood Studies

Katherine Runswick-Cole • Tillie Curran
Kirsty Liddiard
Editors

The Palgrave Handbook of Disabled Children's Childhood Studies

palgrave
macmillan

Editors
Katherine Runswick-Cole
The School of Education
The University of Sheffield
Sheffield, UK

Tillie Curran
Department of Health and Social Sciences
University of the West of England
Bristol, UK

Kirsty Liddiard
The School of Education
Sheffield, UK

ISBN 978-1-137-54445-2   ISBN 978-1-137-54446-9   (eBook)
https://doi.org/10.1057/978-1-137-54446-9

Library of Congress Control Number: 2017955062

© The Editor(s) (if applicable) and The Author(s) 2018
The author(s) has/have asserted their right(s) to be identified as the author(s) of this work in accordance with the Copyright, Designs and Patents Act 1988.
This work is subject to copyright. All rights are solely and exclusively licensed by the Publisher, whether the whole or part of the material is concerned, specifically the rights of translation, reprinting, reuse of illustrations, recitation, broadcasting, reproduction on microfilms or in any other physical way, and transmission or information storage and retrieval, electronic adaptation, computer software, or by similar or dissimilar methodology now known or hereafter developed.
The use of general descriptive names, registered names, trademarks, service marks, etc. in this publication does not imply, even in the absence of a specific statement, that such names are exempt from the relevant protective laws and regulations and therefore free for general use.
The publisher, the authors and the editors are safe to assume that the advice and information in this book are believed to be true and accurate at the date of publication. Neither the publisher nor the authors or the editors give a warranty, express or implied, with respect to the material contained herein or for any errors or omissions that may have been made. The publisher remains neutral with regard to jurisdictional claims in published maps and institutional affiliations.

Cover illustration: Book cover artwork by Sara Ryan

Printed on acid-free paper

This Palgrave Macmillan imprint is published by Springer Nature
The registered company is Macmillan Publishers Ltd.
The registered company address is: The Campus, 4 Crinan Street, London, N1 9XW, United Kingdom

To Connor Sparrowhawk
Ginger Bread Figures JusticeforLB

Foreword

The Palgrave Handbook of Disabled Children's Childhood Studies brings together a rich, international, collection of work by disabled children and adults, family members, carers, staff, doctoral students and leading academics in various fields. It represents a range of different perspectives and areas of focus which are woven together to produce a deeply committed, textured, important and, in many ways, celebratory text.

At the heart of this collection are stories of humanity. Stories of growing up about those labelled as different, and who are often denied opportunities others typically experience, are presented. Stories of taking part in participatory research, of children's experiences in the classroom, of being the parent of disabled adult children and of being silenced are also presented. The authors are deeply immersed within their research and writings, and the boundaries between public and private, personal and professional, activism and research are blurred, shaped and reshaped in innovative ways.

Drawing on a range of methodological, political and theoretical frameworks, the authors offer challenges and make visible the intricate ways in which certain children and adults are excluded from and across different processes and contexts. The contributions not only touch upon silencing, abuse, intersectionality, surveillance, neglect, ethics and discrimination but also on identity, activism, resistance, resilience, defiance, passion, determination, friendship, playfulness, enjoyment, relationships and love. The breadth of the contributions means that *The Palgrave Handbook of Disabled Children's Childhood Studies* can be read as a whole or dipped into thematically or just randomly.

Ideas, strategies and methods are offered, equipping the reader with the tools to do things differently as well as think differently. The key strength of this book, however, is the imagination it both evokes and demands. The denial of an imagined future has, for too long, been the default position for too many people.

Sara Ryan

Acknowledgements

We would like to thank all the chapter authors for their engaging, challenging and thoughtful contributions to this volume and their commitment to Disabled Children's Childhood Studies.

We would like to acknowledge the support of our research centres: The Research Centre for Social Change: Community Wellbeing, Manchester Metropolitan University; the School of Education at the University of Sheffield; and the Faculty of Health and Social Sciences, University of the West of England.

We would like to thank all those people who made the gingerbread figures on the cover of the book. Each ginger figure represents a different child, young person or adult, celebrating all their differences and diversities.

We would like to thank Sara Ryan for writing the preface for this book and for her tireless campaigning for disabled children, young people and adults to imagine their lives otherwise.

Contents

List of Figures

List of Tables

Introduction

The Purpose of the Book

The purpose of this Handbook is to provide a global account of disabled children's childhoods bringing together contributions from children, young people, family members, activists, practitioners and academics (both established and early career researchers) in the field. The Handbook offers a unique and comprehensive guide to disabled children's childhood studies.

The Background and Approach

Until recently, disabled children have been discussed through medical concepts of disability rather than concepts of childhood (McLaughlin 2008). Western concepts of childhood have defined disabled children against child development 'norms' and have provided the rationale for segregated or 'special' welfare and education provision (Burman 2008). Paradoxically, research shows that the focus on medical diagnosis has contributed to a lack of attention to the lives of disabled children as they are marginalised or excluded from 'the expectations, opportunities and aspirations afforded to the so-called typically developing children' (Goodley et al. 2015, p. 6). Sadly, it is still the case that disabled children, and their families, are likely to experience greater levels of inequality in all areas of life (Read et al. 2006).

How disabled children and young people are viewed, of course, has a significant impact on their lives and the lives of those closest to them. In the preface to this Handbook, Sara Ryan describes the 'denial of imagined futures' for disabled children and young people. As an academic and activist, Sara has campaigned tirelessly alongside disabled children, young people and adults to end the discrimination that haunts their lives in the hope of re-imagining their futures. Sara launched the #JusticeforLB campaign following the death of her son Connor Sparrowhawk (known affectionately as Laughing Boy—LB) who drowned in the bath in a National Health Service Assessment and Treatment Unit in England on 4 July 2013. An inquest found that Connor's death was preventable and was contributed to neglect.

The campaign for justice for Connor led to an investigation into the unexpected deaths of people with learning disabilities and/or mental health issues in the health trust in which Connor died. The report found that hundreds of unexpected deaths went un-investigated (Green et al. 2015). Sadly, Connor's death and the scandal that his death revealed are not isolated issues. Disabled children, young people and adults continue to experience discrimination and disadvantage across the globe. Their voices are not heard. This Handbook makes a small contribution to challenging such injustice by foregrounding the experiences of disabled children, young people and adults from across the globe, celebrating their lives and offering possibilities for change.

The Handbook brings together 37 chapters from 65 contributors including young disabled people, family members, activists, practitioners and academics based in Europe, Canada and America, Africa, Australia and New Zealand.

The chapters in **Part I Experiences and Building Understandings** provide the call of the book. Authors write from their own experience and illustrate how they have stepped out of the normative shadows to create counternarratives to the stories of vulnerability and passivity about disabled children and young people. In **Part II Research Studies, the chapters** describe the lives of disabled children and young people across the globe. There are also a number of studies written by researchers who are also parents of disabled children, young people and adults who provide powerful insights and discuss key ethical concerns that arise from that experience. **Part III Ethics and Values** offers reflections on the complex ethical issues of working with children and families, focusing on the contentious issues of voice and ethical participation. In **Part IV Theory and Critical Ways of Thinking,** authors reflect critically on constructions of disabled children's childhoods as 'other' and seek to expose and to challenge the practices of marginalisation. Finally, in **Part V Changing Policy and Practice,** authors point to ways in which change is needed and discuss how change for children and young people can be brought about.

In the concluding chapter, we review the themes that cut across many of the contributions and highlight the changes called for. We also discuss the differences between authors' perspectives and phases of action and relationships as part of continuing change. We end with our reflections on how far the studies presented help us to respond to Sara Ryan's call for change. We offer a number of research questions that are based on social justice, rights, equality and on the ethical principles produced in the Handbook.

The Aims of the Book

The chapters in this book discuss the intimate everyday experience of disabled children and young people seeing disabled children as active, creative and productive. The Handbook aims are focused on change in public understanding, policy and professional practice. This Handbook builds on the 2013 collection of studies (Curran and Runswick-Cole 2013) that introduced disabled children's childhood studies as a distinct domain founded on three key principles:

1. They take a very different starting point from other studies of disabled children by moving beyond the discussion of impairment, inequality and abuse to enable disabled children to step out from under the shadows of normative expectations that have clouded their lives.
2. Disabled children's childhood studies demands an ethical research design that seeks to position the voice and experiences of disabled children at the centre of the inquiry.
3. Disabled children's childhood studies seeks to trouble these practices in their local, historical and global locations (Curran and Runswick-Cole 2013).

The Handbook begins with disabled children's lives and locates their childhoods in context. The studies include disabled children and young people's experiences at home and in their communities and discuss experiences of services and of parents and carers. Authors locate their identity, the policy context and the global context in which they are located. Their questioning seeks to open out thinking about disabled children's childhoods, rather than taking a fixed position. Disabled children's childhoods involve everyone and the Handbook is of value to all involved directly and with direct impact on policy, practice and ultimately disabled children and young people's lived experiences.

References

Burman, E. (2008). *Deconstructing Developmental Psychology*. Hove: Routledge.

Curran, T., & Runswick-Cole, K. (2013). *Disabled Children's Childhood Studies: Critical Approaches in a Global Context*. Basingstoke: Palgrave Macmillan.

Curran, T., & Runswick-Cole, K. (2014). Disabled Children's Childhood Studies: A Distinct Approach? *Disability and Society, 29*(10), 1617–1630.

Green, B., Bruce, A.-M., Finn, P., Wright, A., Daniel, D., Povey, J., & Repper, D. (2015). *Independent Review of Deaths of People with a Learning Disability or Mental Health Problem in Contact with Southern Health NHS Foundation Trust April 2011 to March 2015*. Available online at: https://www.england.nhs.uk/south/wp-content/uploads/sites/6/2015/12/mazars-rep.pdf

Goodley, D., Runswick-Cole, K., & Liddiard, K. (2015). The DisHuman Child. *Discourse: Studies in the Cultural Politics of Education*. http://www.tandfonline.com/doi/full/10.1080/01596306.2015.1075731

McLaughlin, J., Goodley, D., Clavering, E., & Fisher, P. (2008). *Families Raising Disabled Children: Enabling Care*. Basingstoke: Palgrave Macmillan.

Read, J., Clements, L., & Ruebain, D. (2006). *Disabled Children and the Law: Research and Goods Practice*. London: Jessica Kingsley Publisher.

Part I

Sharing Experience and Building Understandings

Disabled children's childhoods are introduced in Part 1 through accounts of personal experience. Many of the authors are people who have contributed to the annual Child, Youth, Family and Disability conferences initiated in 2008 at Manchester Metropolitan University and which have since been hosted by the University of the West of England (Bristol) and the University of Cardiff. A common thread running through the chapters is children and young people's accounts of having to manage the reactions of, usually non-disabled, others to their lives.

In contrast to popular images of disabled childhoods that represent disabled children as passive recipients of care, the authors powerfully convey the assertive and reflective approaches they have developed over time to shape their own experiences of childhood, youth and adulthood. In so doing, they challenge the reader to reflect on their own understandings of disabled children's childhoods in their local and global contexts.

The chapter "The Texting Project" is a texting project between **Blair Manns** and **Sarah Manns**, son and mother. Blair texts his mother about his views on his life for this chapter, finding text the easiest way to communicate, both his personality and his thoughts. The use of text provided Blair with control over what was in his account and, as importantly, what was not presented. Sarah identifies that this medium of communication enabled, supported and gave Blair the power to present his own views. The text is a full, unaltered account.

Jennifer McElwee, David Cox, Tony Cox, Rosemary Holland, Thomas Holland, Theresa Mason, Chloe Pearce, Caroline Sobey, Julie Bugler, Andy James and Beverley Pearce are disabled young people, parent carers and staff in a multi-disciplinary health team for young people with learning disabilities in England. In the chapter "The Tree of Participation: Our Thoughts About Growing a Culture of Participation Between Young People, Parents and Health Team Staff", they share their experiences of using participatory approaches to inform the development of local health services. By using the metaphor of a tree with roots and branches, they explain the growth and development of their participation and the service over time.

In the chapter "What Can I Say?", **Wendy Merchant** begins with the ethics of writing together with her son, Jamie. Jamie made a short animation about what he wished to do during his school summer break, including attending the local play scheme. In response Wendy composed a drama to convey her experience of trying to find him a play scheme. Wendy works as a researcher in disability studies and, had she found a welcoming and accessible play scheme for Jamie, this volume would include a chapter drawing on Wendy's research into the experiences of mothers with disabled children in hospital wards in England. As Wendy was unable to access childcare, that chapter was never written. This chapter, instead, reveals the impact of inadequate childcare on mothers of disabled children. Despite the fact that this issue is recognised in the United Kingdom in government, law and policy, Wendy proposes a number of further strategies needed to address the hostility and barriers encountered by parents and their children, including advocacy, networks of support and co-production in research.

In the chapter "The Heaviest Burdens and Life's Most Intense Fulfilment: A Retrospective and Re-understanding of My Experiences with Childhood Liver Disease and Transplantation", **Sophie Savage** also reflects back on her childhood as she explores the messages she was given as a child. Sophie's story focuses on her survival and messages about her future as someone living with liver disease, and then life after liver transplantation. In order to do this, she reworks a metaphor of 'burden' to turn the weighty everyday pressures put on her into sources of insight and determination. Her passion for learning and her personal creativity weave a story for us to time travel with her from childhood to adulthood where she now mentors young people facing similar interventions but with growing understanding and networks of support.

Rebecca Whitehead shares her journey as a sister to Beth in the chapter "My Sister, My World: From Second Mum to Nurse". The world of professional labels and interventions came into her home in ways that either over-involved her or ignored her as a sibling. She develops her own understanding of her sister's feelings to retain and build a close reciprocal relationship. She invites the reader to get to know young people with learning difficulties and explains how her experience has made her who she is now – a trainee nurse for people with learning difficulties.

Jo Skitteral tells her story of becoming a mother in the chapter "Being a Disabled Woman and Mum: My Journey from Childhood" Jo's story began in childhood when she received powerful messages that motherhood would not be part of her future or those of her friends in the special school she attended. Although Jo's story is one of defiance, she tells us how difficult it is for a disabled woman to access maternity services in England and to manage the hostility shown to her by others. In a disabling context, it is also difficult for Jo to share her concerns as a thoughtful parent. Jo shares the ways she has shaped motherhood and how she and her child enjoy many aspects of difference together and with others close to them. Her account challenges readers to reflect more broadly on their understandings of mothering.

In the chapter "Going 'Off Grid': A Mother's Account of Refusing Disability", **Kim Davies** gives a critical account of negotiating possibilities for her son by refusing 'disability'. In the chapter, Kim explains her reasons for refusing her doctor's recommendation that her child should have an appointment with a psychiatrist. Writing from Australia, in a context in which the psy-professions have a strong grip, Kim's account boldly challenges understandings of 'normality' and 'inclusivity' in the search for alternative subjectivities in-between 'ability' and 'disability'.

As we outlined above, the authors in this section offer personal accounts. They do not seek to represent the lives of others, but their concerns are echoed in the chapters that follow where we see how the dominant norms of the Global North also impact the Global South. The strategies discussed here are not presented as universal answers but are illustrations of everyday activism generated and shaped by young disabled people, groups and communities and grounded in specific contexts.

The Texting Project

Blair Manns and Sarah Manns (son and mother)

So, what is the thing that is currently important to you? xx

I'm not sure xx

B. Manns • S. Manns (✉)
Independent contributor, University of the West of England, Bristol, UK

© The Author(s) 2018
K. Runswick-Cole et al. (eds.), *The Palgrave Handbook of Disabled Children's Childhood Studies*, https://doi.org/10.1057/978-1-137-54446-9_1

What is a thing that makes you laugh?

Music, art and comedy

Which music makes you laugh?

Songs that are about exs and stuff

If you could tell your younger self one thing...
what would it be?

You will grow up to be yourself in a few years.

What would you tell the younger me? x

Laugh every day... just like you do. X What would you have told the younger me? x

Don't be afraid to take risks and enjoy life x

What makes you angry inside?

Pretty much everything, tv ads and my generation ...

It is...   its mission impossible

Wow. It's sounds hard to be you.

What can we, mum and son, do to make it mission possible in our lives?

I just have to live like this and let it take control unless I get meds or something

Which is the one thing you want people to know about you?

I don't know   thats a good question   what you do you think?

Ignore it then. What would you like to ask me.

No   I won't   tell me

What would you like to tell people about being 21 in this day and age?

Wow umm not too sure

What is it about horses that you are so attracted to?

They are calm and don't judge you

Can you tell me about what you mean about being judged?

Ok everything about me. My clothes my hair my stammer and my music

Thanks for sharing. Is there any last message? Anything you would like us to all hear and remember?

No   nothing just what I have said is enough

Your welcome

Blair Manns describes himself as a 21-year-old drummer with a wicked sense of humour.

Sarah Manns Blair's mother, is described by Blair as a caring creature whose calmness lasts forever.

The Tree of Participation: Our Thoughts About Growing a Culture of Participation Between Young People, Parents and Health Team Staff

Jennifer McElwee, David Cox, Tony Cox,
Rosemary Holland, Thomas Holland, Theresa Mason,
Chloe Pearce, Caroline Sobey, Julie Bugler, Andy James,
and Beverley Pearce

Key Points

- This chapter is written by a group of young people, parent carers and health service staff and is about our experiences of participating in and contributing towards the development of health services.
- We use a 'tree of participation' to help us think about what makes 'participation' work and how it can help services to develop from the roots upwards.
- The chapter emphasises young people at the heart of thinking and presents a strong argument for collaboration and mutual respect between young people, their families and staff.

The scene: An interdisciplinary community-based learning disability mental health service for children and young people and their families

J. McElwee (✉) • D. Cox • T. Cox • R. Holland • T. Holland • T. Mason
• C. Pearce • C. Sobey • J. Bugler • A. James • B. Pearce
The Specialist Service for Children with Learning Disabilities Participation Group,
Bristol, UK

© The Author(s) 2018
K. Runswick-Cole et al. (eds.), *The Palgrave Handbook of Disabled Children's Childhood Studies*, https://doi.org/10.1057/978-1-137-54446-9_2

The Cast

Young people:	*David, Chloe and Tom*
Parent carers:	*Tony, Caroline, Rose and Theresa*
Barnardos (children's charity) participation worker:	*Bev*
Health team staff:	*Julie, Andy and Jeni*
Team manager (moved to a different job, good at baking):	*Mr Cupcake*

Introduction

We are a group of people who join together in different ways to facilitate active 'participation' in the day-to-day running and development of health services in a city in the south-west of England. In this chapter we draw upon our ideas and experiences as young people, parent carers and staff to create our story of participation. Central to this narrative is the premise that young people and their families bring with them a host of expertise and experience. As partners, they are viewed as catalysts for change in services, not 'patients' in need of support from services.

We begin this chapter by describing what we mean by the term 'participation'. We then introduce the 'tree of participation' as a framework for thinking about how to promote a 'participation' culture through putting into place the roots (values, beliefs and ideas), trunk (systems, structures and people) and leaves and flowers (actions and outcomes seen when 'participation' works well). We finish the chapter with key messages for a successful participation group.

We hope that readers will draw on our experiences and ideas to create their own 'participation' journeys, and in so doing, challenge any system-held beliefs that staff are the most expert in knowing what is best for 'patients'.

Conversations About Participation

Jeni: *This group has changed and developed over the years, whilst staying true to the values that guide it. People have had different levels of input to the group and through the group into bigger systems. My role within this chapter has been that of interested listener and note taker within conversations about 'participation'. I have spoken with people both individually and collectively and threaded these conversations into a collective narrative in order to present you with this book chapter. All participants have commented and agreed the chapter as a whole.*

What Is Participation?

Chloe: *Participation means to join in with conversations or activities.*

Caroline: *We deal with words in the group. You have to be careful with words and think about what you say. In the group we try to spot words and make them make sense. It doesn't have to be long winded. We first got together and there was no pressure. It's like being on a soft cloud or bubble and it's ok. It's like with some people you have a conversation then you leave then the next time you meet again and the conversation just continues. It's like a reunion all the time – a good reunion.*

Andy: *It's part of our culture, I'd say. It's a constant loop of feedback so when we are with a family or a young person we are looking for their comment about that particular session or the overall service they're getting and we're listening to what they have to say and then hopefully adapting our service to improve it for them.*

Julie: *I get such a buzz from it and I can only ever think about really positive words like wonderfulness, which isn't a word! Well, we have regular meetings with a mix of formal and informal discussions. We have pieces of work to do at those meetings like critiquing service leaflets and consultation documents. We mix that with discussions around new ways of working and being creative. We also provide training in 'participation' for other health teams. We got involved with 'participation' training for the whole Health Partnership because we believed that the service user's voice was an equal and fundamental part of the 'participation' process. In this training we use participant feedback to enable us to change and function better – a perfect reflection of the feedback loop involved when 'participation' is put into practice.*

Tony: *We hold meetings approximately every six weeks. The meetings are friendly and informal but also very productive. One very important feature is that everyone brings food to share, which encourages a more relaxed and productive atmosphere. When the group was formed four years ago it was originally just to deal with one small task of reviewing and re-designing a leaflet that the service had been using for some time. Since then it has grown into numerous other activities and projects. When we started four years ago nobody involved in the group had any idea that it would develop the way that it has.*

Bev: *When I first started in this job I thought, 'am I capable of doing that?', 'participation' can feel scary, but actually if you break it down it's quite simple, it's about listening and taking on board everyone's views and doing something with it.*

Rose: *I want professionals to understand that it's important for us to be involved because they can learn from our experiences and hopefully do it in a different way with people. Don't be negative because small steps happen and they are better than a big step. When professionals say an offhand comment maybe they don't realise what us parents take away. My son has achieved so much and I was told he wouldn't achieve anything.*

These definitions of 'participation' are drawn from experience, rather than from a textbook, and this means that everyone has a slightly different idea about what it is to 'participate' in health service development. There are common ideas related to *tasks* associated with 'participation', such as attending meetings and designing leaflets, as well as more *process*-oriented ideas around sharing food and developing meaningful conversations.

Our Tree of Participation

We wanted to think of a way of representing our thoughts about 'participation' and how it has grown from the seed of an idea (redesigning a service leaflet) into a cultural shift for all involved. Thus we present the values and ideas that we believe drive successful 'participation' in terms of the roots of a tree that provide the foundations of a cultural shift. The systems, structure and people that promote 'participation' are thought of as the strong, yet flexible trunk of the tree. The actions and outcomes of successful participation are represented by leaves and flowers (Fig. 1).

The Roots

The roots represent values, ideas and beliefs that drive 'participation'

Tom: *I am very nice. I like going out though I sometimes get worried about where I am going and not knowing other people's reactions. I like meeting new people and chatting with them and finding out about what they do. I like to look after other people and think about what they might need. I carried my Nan a glass of water.*

Fig. 1   The tree of participation (Illustration: Andy James)

Tony: *As a parent member of the group, I feel privileged to be part of it. It is a place where parents and young people can have a genuine influence on the way the service is provided. Where else do you get this kind of opportunity? If you feel something could be done better, in a different way, or correspondence could be worded more appropriately, there is the opportunity to discuss it within the group and try to get it changed. It is also a place where the health staff are fully committed to the process and fully open to change where it is agreed within the group.*

Andy: *It's important in my job to be totally family focussed so that every-thing we do is for the benefit of the family and the young person. Although we work under time pressures I think it's important to build a relationship with a family and evolve the relationship – you can't force these things. I think it was the same with the participation group, it wasn't forced it took time. Also if you speak with parents about what they want from the service they just want to be treated as if they are people rather than a number. I believe that people with learning disabilities are often not treated equally and that obviously affects their families and part of our role is to try to address some of these inequalities. If 'participation' can get people's voice heard then that can help.*

Julie: *I think that 'participation' can be used to support a person to reach their potential, rather than what those around them think they should achieve.*

The Trunk

The trunk represents systems, structures and people that promote participation

Andy: *We have a core group of parents who attend the group on a very regu-lar basis. They give their own time and energy which we are very grateful for. The fact that they feel listened to and their ideas are implemented encourages them to keep coming. Some parents are more outspoken than others, others have been quieter, but all have opinions.*

Theresa: *To get a parent's point of view about someone with learning dis-abilities is better than reading it out of a textbook. You need to be hands on because every single young person is different. If you have parents involved then they can explain things better than anyone else because they know their child the best. That's why I wouldn't give up with my daughter because I knew what she needed. You just know.*

Tom: *It's good for the kids to be part of this because they can go to school and tell their friends and teachers what they've done. It would be a shame if no kids were involved. It's all well and good the professionals talking to the parents but sometimes the parents don't really under-stand what's going on.*

Bev: *A lot of staff might feel if their managers are not on board then they can't do anything but sometimes you can start from the bottom and change your service and it doesn't always take money and can save time in the long run. What I've learnt is to try and start small and notice what you are already doing because you can't change the structures and cultures straight away. Our team help staff to work in a different way because they bring in experience so people don't have to feel on their own. This allows staff to be creative and think about 'participation' as a way of life rather than as an add on and something else to do.*

Caroline: *It's like building blocks – everybody building on each other's ideas. You can't do it on your own. We give each other support. Having Julie and Andy has been like winning the lottery. They've got the gift of listening and taking it away and doing stuff with it. It's unfortunate we lost 'Mr Cupcake'. He was a manager but he showed that you can be at any level but it doesn't matter in the group – what everybody says is important. We're all human.*

The Leaves

The leaves represent actions and outcomes that can be seen when participation works well

Chloe: *I've been taking part in games. I played the X-ray game, I think it's called 'Operation'* [a board game in which participants take it in turns to remove body parts without a buzzer going off]. *I designed a t-shirt for Mother's Day. Every so often we do an activities day. You can have your nails done (my mum did that!) and put icing on biscuits. I designed a mug with my name on it. I had my face painted but I didn't like that. The best bit about going to the 'participation' group is the pizza – my favourite is vegetable pizza.*

Tom: *Me and mum did our first interview in August last year. Another parent helped us because it was our first time. I read a question then mum read a question. We had a laugh doing the interviews because we got them to do a game. At the end of the day we all met together with the professionals and said what we thought. When we did training we had a laugh because they didn't have a clue what they were doing! When I left school I had to go for an interview for college – it was good. They said I'd done really well. I wasn't worried about it.*

David: *I've done interviews, training days, conferences, part of a DVD and a story in a leaflet. I feel happy and proud to do all this and I feel I have gained in confidence. It has helped me because I had to have an interview to get into my work experience at 'Horseworld'* [a local charity providing a home for unloved horses]. *I gave full sentence answers and I galloped in. Since then I have done another interview answering questions on some footballing experience and made a couple of speeches. It has always been fun and educational at the same time and I loved getting out of school!*

Chloe: *We did 'Young People Friendly'* [an accreditation scheme for health staff teams] *with Julie. We made a poster and there were questions on it. We said what would make a good team member. We said what we thought Julie should do and it was the same as what she thought she should do! It was good fun! I just like being part of it.*

Theresa: *Maybe I'm vocal about what is needed, maybe Julie thought I'm a bit of a chatterbox! I went with Julie to the university. I was in front of students and they asked me questions. I talked about my daughter's life. How I had to deal with things. I was alright about it. I think if it helps people then that's ok.*

Rose: *The interviews are really interesting because you find out about what people are about. I was a governor at my son's old school so I had some knowledge of the interview process. You get a feel for people when you do a few interviews. You get a sense that you know people will be right. When I interviewed for the team I thought about the post and whether the person would get on with the team*

Andy: *What the group says is fed back and it has changed services, for example when we 'jargon bust' standard letters so they are more user friendly they are changed immediately. It's not just lip service things are carried through. We added photos of ourselves to our letters and compliment slips and now other services are using that idea. Our ideas have spread through the Health Partnership like a domino effect and everyone is taking on our ideas and putting their own twist on it.*

Julie: *I never felt comfortable talking in big groups before but running the participation training of large groups of staff alongside the young people and parents made it easy for me and that gave me the confidence to go for the lecturing job at our local university I wouldn't*

*have gone for that otherwise. There's no way I would have stood up
in front of groups of people talking, no way, but each time the groups
got bigger and it was just easy. The young people and parents just
talked about their lives and it was so amazing and that made it
easier to talk about anything to do with 'participation' because it
always goes back to them. Whether we are talking about a service or
a process they are at the heart of it.*

Tony: *Parents, young people and health team staff members have all agreed
that being involved in the group has boosted our own confidence.
Standing up at conferences, helping to run training courses, talking
to a hundred students at the university, all would have seemed very
scary prospects four years ago and maybe things we would have shied
away from. We now know we can do these things and we can make
a difference in the process.*

Andy: *I think it's the overall way that participation has been established in
our team rather than the individual things that we've changed that's
been important. I like the knock on effect of how the young people
have become more confident through being more involved in the
interview process and the training and how the parents have been
challenged and have met the challenge every time and their confidence has grown. And we have won awards. Really we accepted that
with a bit of tongue in cheek, but I was happy for the parents to have
their hard work acknowledged. It was fun to run around London
with a posh suit on.*

Caroline: *It's hard to meet other parents when you have a child with special
needs. The group has been a lifeline for me because it has given me a
purpose. The main thing is being heard on your child's behalf. Being
a parent, things can change all the time but the group's always here.
It's nice to give something back and to know and to see what we've
done in the leaflets and suchlike. When we leave it just gets dealt
with. It's a journey that won't end because there is always something
to do.*

Our tree started out as a tiny seed of an idea, brought into reality by a small
group of staff and parents. As it has grown it has weathered a few storms in
the form of unhelpful higher management decisions and pressures on time
leading to difficulty in attending. We believe it has been nurtured by the
sharing of good food and fun and the sense that we can make a difference by
hearing and valuing what *everyone* has to say.

Our Key Messages for a Successful Participation Group

1. *Everybody bring food and share it.*

Bringing and sharing food allows people to make a contribution and feel valued and creates a sense of community, breaking down some of the barriers between 'expert' staff and parents as 'patients'.

2. *Use clear tasks with tangible outcomes.*

Clear tasks create a focus for the group and a sense of achievement as each task is completed.

3. *Think big, start small.*

Have faith that what the group says is important and will have an impact on much wider systems, but start with a small manageable task, such as creating or changing a service leaflet, in order to gain confidence and momentum.

4. *Mix informal style with formal purpose.*

Be warm, enthusiastic, have fun, whilst taking views seriously and acting on them.

5. *Share experiences and translate them into action.*

People coming to the group have often experienced services as a place where they come for advice on problems, but this is not the purpose of the group. Listen to both positive and negative experiences and then use them to influence service development.

6. *Give positive feedback.*

Let the group hear how what they say has impacted positively on the service and regularly express appreciation.

7. *Be flexible and think laterally.*

Be stoical about what can and can't be achieved, then take a 'can do' attitude and try something different.

8. *Let the group grow organically.*

Don't force a framework onto people. Use facilitators who want to be part of the group, take note of what fires people's imaginations and work with motivation.

Jennifer McElwee The specialist service for children with learning disabilities participation group contains people of different ages and backgrounds, who share a common goal of developing and improving health services.

"What Can I Say?"

Wendy Merchant and Jamie Merchant

Key Points

- This chapter is about a child's desire to participate in play activities. The child, who happens to be disabled, needs his mum to fight his corner to be able to join in.
- It uses a play script to show the barriers that prevent the child from fully joining in these play activities.
- It discusses the ability of disabled children in the UK to access play activities and the impact this has upon the ability of their parents to access employment.
- Finally, the ability of disabled children to easily access both play and childcare activities is considered within the political context of the UK in 2016.

Introduction

This chapter is based on a paper for "There is no them!" 7th Child, Youth, Family and Disability Conference, in England (Merchant 2015). The presentation was produced by me, Wendy and Jamie, my son. It was written from our joint experiences of the barriers we faced when trying to gain access to play, out-of-school activities and childcare for Jamie. My current research is a doctoral

W. Merchant (✉) • J. Merchant
University of Bristol, Bristol, UK

© The Author(s) 2018
K. Runswick-Cole et al. (eds.), *The Palgrave Handbook of Disabled Children's Childhood Studies*, https://doi.org/10.1057/978-1-137-54446-9_3

study looking at what it is like for mothers of disabled children looking after their children on wards when they are admitted to hospital. When I first heard about the conference, I was very excited and hoped to share some of the mothers' experiences. However, the difficulties I faced, trying to get Jamie into play activities during the school holidays so firstly, he could play and secondly, so I could do my research were so overwhelming and time consuming that I decided to make these disabling practices my focus for the presentation of this chapter. It has been very surprising how difficult it has been trying to get adults who run play activities to agree to Jamie coming along. I assumed that because The Equality Act 2010 (gov.uk) set out an imperative for "reasonable adjustments" to be made to include disabled children that this would have been widely adopted and Jamie would have been welcomed. In contrast to equality, I encountered adults who referred to other legislation such as The Children and Family Act 2014 (gov.uk) around safeguarding to "trump" the requirements of The Equality Act 2010. It is this experience we would like to talk about in this chapter.

Writings from disabled children and their family's experiences and the ethics involved are key principles of disabled children's childhood studies, a relatively new area of study (Curran and Runswick-Cole 2013). This means asking disabled children's permission to talk about their experience of childhood and listening to their voice and not an adult's interpretation of it. Many writings from a disability studies perspective choose not to repeat the dominant methodologies associated with the medical model of disability that has arguably given rise to and perpetuated negative views of disability (Oliver 1991). Play leaders and public in general, as we will show, see concerns around impairments before disabled children's full identity. I chose to use a film and a play, a film made by my son and a play written by me, to portray the adult practices. By adopting a different approach, in a small way maybe I could be seen as engaging with Lorde's (1984: 112) contention that "the master's tools will never dismantle the master's house."

I will first explain the approach taken to present Jamie's voice and the ethics involved. I then present his "play list" film about his wishes for summer play time. The next section sets out the method used for my story and presents a play dramatising the disabling practices I experienced. The discussion section puts our experiences in the wider context of disabled children's childhoods in England.

Our stories are not a large study or even a small one, but using film and drama art forms we present an exemplar that illustrates the layer upon layer of disabling practices that require deep change. Within our story we try to make links to research and policy that shows that our situation, like many others, is unlawful, commonly experienced and difficult to change. The strengthened mandate from both equality and children's legislation (Equality Act 2010; Children and Families Act 2014) in England offers opportunities for successful challenges but given the level of change needed, I end with a number of strategies and "solutions" that might be effective at the deeper level and one of these is about our own strength.

Jamie's Story

After my son Jamie was born, it became clear that he had a range of needs that meant he needed a bit of extra "looking after." Now, Jamie describes himself as "I'm disabled, my disability is Autism. I'm Autistic!" In the past eleven years Jamie has gone to numerous nurseries, pre-schools and primary schools. Accessing both education and recreational activities has required the completion of forms, the sharing of personal information, meetings, negotiation and being required to stay to support the people working in these settings. This additional "invisible" work was surprising as I thought, from my previous experience as a children's nurse, that we now lived in a more inclusive society and people were ready to accept disabled children without question.

Jamie created a cartoon so he could tell everyone at the conference all the fun things he would like to do over the summer school holidays. I first asked Jamie if he would like to tell everyone at the conference all about what he would like to do over the summer. I explained that lots of different people who were interested in improving disabled children's childhoods would be there and would want to listen to his view. Jamie agreed this was a good idea, so we both made a list of things he wanted to do. I opened a "PowToon" account (a free online digital film-making website) and he did the rest. I think his cartoon film was brilliant! This is what Jamie said:

> *"What I'd like to do in the summer..."*
> *This summer I would like to go the park with my friends and family.*
> *I would also like to go to my local summer sports camp.*
> *I'd like to play video games with my friends.*
> *When I go on holiday I'd like to do fencing.*
> *I hope you all have a great summer holiday. Bye…*

I talked to Jamie about what he felt about including his experiences of trying to join in activities and go away on camp in the conference and also as a chapter in this book. These experiences form part of Jamie's childhood; my role as his mother is to facilitate the best experiences I can. Once published and presented, the information is "out there" so I could not do it unless he gave his permission. Jamie thought it was "great" that lots of adults would watch his cartoon film and listen to what he said. He did not want them to hear his voice so he would not come to the conference. Jamie thought that if adults learned how to make it easier for "boys like me" to join in, that will be "great." I said that all we can do is hope that adults listen, try and understand what it is like and then try and change things. He said that was "ok."

Wendy's Story

For the conference I wrote a short play called "What can I say?" Jamie's access to recreation and inclusive childhood was also a matter of my inclusion in employment, my being a postgraduate student at university and my ordinary family life. The following story was so challenging that I began by wondering "What can I Say?" In what way can I convey the repeated experience and to what end?

In the play a mother of a disabled child has a phone call with the organiser of a local holiday sports camp to try and get their child a place. The play is a composite of three or four phone calls I had made in the preceding three years in an attempt to access play activities for Jamie. I chose a play as it seemed the simplest way to convey the barrage of differing reasons I had been given as to why my son could not be included in various activities. I also wanted to share my struggles to answer these questions whilst not upsetting the activity leaders who held the decision-making power.

The use of drama is recognised within the field of visual sociology as a means through which researchers may represent themselves reflexively expressing their thoughts and reactions (Harper 2012). I tried to make it sound funny, for impact; in reality it was not funny. I became angry, more angry than I have ever been, frustrated and then sad, very sad. Through the lens of a play it was possible to project these experiences and emotions and engage the audience in the lifeworld of a disabled child. Here it is:

Conversation Between Mother and Holiday Sports Camp Organiser

Mother: "Hello is that the summer sports camp? I wanted to talk about booking my children in for some days in the summer holidays…"

Play worker: "Oh yes have you got one of our forms, you just need to fill that in really…"

Mother: "Yes I picked one up at the Library it was just the bit about having a child with special needs…"

Play worker: "Special needs … oh … what sort of special needs?"

Mother: "Well it says on your form that … 'subject to the availability of appropriately trained staff and resources we try to ensure that no child is turned away because of special needs. However it is vital that we are fully informed of the needs concerned…'"

Play worker: "Yeah well we're just volunteers like and we haven't had no training…"

Mother: "Oh yes I understand it must be very difficult for you…"

Play worker: "And there's Health and Safety to think about you know…"

Mother: "Oh yes it's very complicated isn't it, I was just hoping to get some child care so I can finish working on my research study…"

Play worker "Oh and Ofsted [the official inspection body in England] wouldn't like it if we were giving more attention to your child we've got to think about the other children you know…"

Mother: "Yes of course it's such a difficult job for you to do I was just hoping to get some child care so I can do some work…"

Play worker: "Have you thought about the disabled sports camp they run in Clacton. I heard that's very good you know for those disabled kids…"

Mother: "Oh yes I have heard of it but that's 6 miles away and they charge twice as much per day as you do. Henry wants to be with his friends and they are going to your sports camp…"

Play worker: "Have you thought about working in a school? Then you wouldn't have to worry about the holidays. That's what I do and we've adapted our life so we don't have expensive holidays…"

Mother: "Work in a school? No I hadn't thought about that, I trained as a nurse and was just hoping to finish my research project…"

Play worker: "Oh Henry … Didn't we send you a letter about him?"

Mother: "Oh yes that was last year you had a special committee meeting and sent me a letter saying you were pleased to tell me you would accept him on to the sports camp as long as I provided, trained and funded a one to one support worker…"

Play worker: "Oh did I?"

Mother: "Yes we sent Simon but as he was 17 years old you weren't happy for him to help Henry change his pants if he wet himself…"

Play worker: "Safeguarding issues, I can't let someone come if I'm worried about safeguarding … Jimmy Saville and all that you know…" [sex offender in the UK who was a TV celebrity]

Mother: "No of course, Jimmy Saville that was terrible … but the Disabled Children's Team at the Council trained and provided Simon to come along to sports camps like yours…"

Play worker: "Well the committee said that your one to one needs to take full responsibility for Henry, can a 17 year old do that?"

Mother: "Well, no, but what if I work from home, promise not to go out and if there are any problems at all you ring me and I'll be there … I'm only 5 minutes away…"

Play worker: "Well, we'll have to discuss it at the next committee meeting…"

Mother: "Oh, thank you so much! That means a lot. When is the committee meeting?"

Play worker: "It's in September when we start planning for next year's sports camp…"

Mother: "Oh couldn't you meet before then so Henry can come along this year … I was just trying to finish my research…?"

Play worker: "You must realise we all work, you know, and have our own families to look after, there simply isn't time until September…"

Mother: "No, of course, you are all fantastic for arranging the sports camp … what do I need to do for my daughter Alison to attend the sports camp?"

Play worker: "Is she special needs?"

Mother: "No…"

Play worker: "Oh just fill in the form and bring it with a cheque on the day…"

End

Discussion

The first thing that struck me was the contrast between getting my daughter a place compared to my son. My daughter is not "disabled" and for her I am required to complete the sports camp a form and write a cheque to the organisation. This is not the case for my son. At various times I have been (1) asked for a letter detailing all of his impairments, (2) asked to wait while a special committee meeting discussed whether a sports camp can take him or not and (3) sent a letter saying the organisers were pleased to tell me they would accept him on to the sports camp as long as I provided, trained and funded a one-to-one support worker. Like many mothers of disabled children, I receive a small amount of "Direct Payments" from the government as part of their commitment to the provision of "short breaks" for families with a disabled child (Breaks for Carers of Disabled Children Regulations 2011). This gives us a sum of money to pay a one-to-one support worker to assist Jamie at mainstream play activities throughout the year. However, if Jamie were to attend for the duration of the sports camp (2½ weeks), it would use 70% of the annual amount of direct payments we receive. As Jamie's mum it is my aim to fulfil Jamie's play list, but he cannot attend the whole of the sports camp (his sister can) as we cannot afford to pay his one-to-one worker. It is also my job to tell him that he can only go for a short time. At times Jamie requires a little extra care, but above all he needs understanding and if the sports camp providers were willing to listen, learn and adapt their structure, an additional worker would not be needed. The disabling practices of the activity providers are getting in the way of managing Jamie's impairments.

Secondly, it struck me as unusual that the provision of one-to-one workers, which is established by the Local Authority Disability Social Care service for disabled children, is questioned by providers of play activities. Our Local Authority provides two systems to access a one-to-one worker: the direct payments scheme (as above) and/or the provision of a "buddy." The "buddy" is usually a young person aged 16–18 years, in full-time education, who is provided with some training to work alongside a disabled child. In return, the young person receives a small amount of pocket money and the experience of working with a disabled child. The role of the "buddy" is to accompany a disabled child to play activities to provide extra support. The concern of the activity leaders focused upon the suitability of a "buddy" to adequately care for Jamie as the local authority does not allow the "buddy" to engage in personal care. However, at the same time, the activity leaders would not take full responsibility for his extra care needs. Over the phone, "safeguarding" concerns following the negative publicity regarding well-known celebrities' child abuse crimes and the subsequent convictions were offered as reasons for both the buddy and the staff not being suitable to provide personal care and that decision prevented Jamie's inclusion.

Finally, it was the lack of awareness by members of our local community that The Equality Act 2010 which stipulates the need for "reasonable adjustments" applies to them and their activity. I was met with ignorance. Making adjustments to include a child with autism goes beyond the practical and visible adjustments such as widening doors, having a ramp and installing an accessible toilet. I was met with surprise when I suggested that smaller groups, a space for quieter games and slightly more supervision may help include my son (and others). I was met with indignation, when I politely asked for change to comply with the law. The barriers we encountered arose from deeply entrenched disabling practices, and the consequence was exclusion for Jamie and myself.

So, where does this leave Jamie and his play list? He is having some time at the local sports camp and is satisfied with this as that leaves him more time to stay at home to play video games. We can visit parks in the late afternoon/early evening when they are quieter, and with planning, we can take a friend too. I am still searching for somewhere he can "do fencing."

In order to understand these experiences, it is important to put them into the wider context of disabled children's childhoods in England. I suggest that most parents who access out-of-school play activities for their child are aiming to give their child new experiences and to give themselves time to pursue "other" activities such as employment. Much has been said by the current Conservative Government of the need to support "hard working families" (Marsh 2015). However, it is currently very difficult for parents of disabled children to join the ranks of the "hard working" due to the amount of invisible work they are required to do to obtain access to childcare or play activities for their child.

In 2014 the Parliamentary Inquiry into Childcare for Disabled Children was published. The foreword to the report includes a quote from the Children's Commissioner for England, Maggie Atkinson, who suggests that disabled children are missing out on opportunities to socialise with other children, play and have fun. Consequently, this is a breach of the United Nations Convention on the Rights of the Child (1989). It is also important to consider the impact of this upon the parents' ability to undertake paid work. The 2014 Inquiry found that 16% of mothers of disabled children were employed compared to 61% of mothers of non-disabled children. If a parent or parents are unable to work due to a lack of childcare, they will have no other choice but to claim social security benefits. The Inquiry found that families with a disabled child were 2½ times more likely to have no parent working more than 16 hours a week. The Inquiry was chaired by two MPs, Robert Buckland and Pat Glass, and they suggest:

> No parent should be excluded from the opportunity to work. It makes no sense for disabled children to be included in mainstream education but excluded from mainstream childcare. (2014: 5)

My experience leads me to challenge the assumption that disabled children are included in mainstream education. Much of mainstream provision for disabled children involves teaching in corridors or small groups away from the classroom, and those children considered too disruptive are routinely excluded. However, it is good to see the absurdity of the childcare situation acknowledged.

The Parliamentary Inquiry highlighted a number of differing reasons that saw disabled children excluded from mainstream childcare provision. These included the high cost of childcare; some parent-carers reported paying £12–£14 per hour, with some up to £20 per hour, compared to a national average of £3.50–£4.50 per hour (figures from 2012/13). Alongside this 33% of parent-carers reported not using childcare as the staff did not have the right experience, whilst 8% reported the staff had told them their child posed a health and safety risk. The number one recommendation of the Parliamentary Inquiry was:

> The Government should develop a cross-departmental action plan and funded programme to ensure that all disabled children and young people can access affordable, accessible and appropriate childcare. (2014: 8)

Access to childcare for disabled children has been formally identified as a "problem," and the report clearly identifies the extent of the problem and alludes to the impact upon families of disabled children. The experience discussed above suggests that at the heart of the problem are the entrenched disabling attitudes and practices that pervade social attitudes and professional practices. Seven years on from The Equality Act 2010 and it is still too easy to exclude disabled children by citing vague health and safety concerns—who is at risk or safeguarding issues in terms of being unable to support a child needing help with toileting. These complex layers of disabling practices are cemented by what I also see, as a researcher, is an apparent fear of disabled children. It is a lack of will and education that allows these practices to continue. I conclude by considering a number of strategies and solutions to tackle these practices and bring about change.

Concluding Thoughts

It is clear that disabling practices that prevent the inclusion of disabled children in play activities and usual childcare opportunities need addressing on many different levels. In order to affect change, solutions need to address professional ethics and practices, policy, service design and the law. In this way, the inclusion of disabled children within all play activities should, eventually, become the norm. However, the challenge to these disabling practices and the exclusion of disabled children has to come from individuals: individual disabled children, young people, their parents or carers, health and social care professionals, teachers, play workers and allies. When faced with exclusion we all need to ask "Why?" My own research demonstrates the ability of mothers of disabled children from varied backgrounds to challenge when needed. They show strength, energy, patience and drive. If we question these disabling practices and allow ourselves to be questioned, change will happen.

Curran and Runswick-Cole (2015) captured the subject area "Disabled Children's Childhood Studies" from a groundswell of injustice and anger they encountered within their practice and personal lives and hearing other accounts of childhood that were productive and creative. Listening to the challenges we face navigating a disabled child's access to childhood activities is the start of change. The next step for each person who hears our story is to question their practice, their activities and their attitudes. In this way we can co-construct access to play that each disabled child wants. There are advocacy organisations such as SCOPE, Contact a Family and the National Autistic Society supporting families and activist academics such as Clements (www. LukeClements.com) who are providing support and legal advice. It is however very difficult to challenge one's own "community"; other children's parents who are volunteers for instance. The use of the arts can assist understanding and build confidence to ask a parent to come along and try out best approaches to start with as part of a positive welcome.

The scenario discussed clearly includes gender, disability and class, but further layers of inequality are also relevant. How do parents from ethnic minority groups risk challenging their community leaders when the community as a whole may be marginalised? How do parents with learning disability navigate the relentless demands of service providers? Future research might therefore want to draw on the arts and action research to generate impact. Co-production of research is key given the likelihood that the "problems" are individualised as a matter of parenting capacity and that can become internalised. Staff capacity to care needs to be invested in and that is also a matter of "community" change. Some fun inclusive pop-up events might for example be an approach to research the possible.

Meanwhile, another summer approaches and Jamie is drawing up another list of fun activities that he would like to do. I will continue to help him try to access them and will work on my research project when I can...

References

Curran, T., & Runswick-Cole, K. (Eds.). (2013). *Disabled Children's Childhood Studies. Critical Approaches in a Global Context*. Basingstoke: Palgrave Macmillan.

Curran, T., & Runswick-Cole, K. (2015). There Is No Them! in Disabled Children's Childhood Studies. In *"There Is No Them!", Child Youth Family and Disability Conference*. Bristol: University of the West of England.

DfE. (2011). *Children and Young Persons England: The Breaks for Carers of Disabled Children Regulations*. London : Department for Education. http://www.legislation.gov.uk/uksi/2011/707/made. Last accessed June 2015.

Glass, P., & Buckland, R. (2014). *Parliamentary Inquiry into Childcare for Disabled Children. Levelling the Playing Field*. London: The Stationary Office.

Harper, D. A. (2012). *Visual Sociology*. London: Routledge. Retrieved from http:// uwe.summon.serialssolutions.com/2.0.0/link/0/eLvHCXMwbV3dS8MwED_ 2AeKTbtO6TaFPog_rR5Z12aNMR8Hhg8oQX0a6JjDQbq4dw7_ Nf85L0pahe2lJmnLh6N2ld_n9AtAnjtf74xMojyR-O9QnC1XrFNJj CyI9OeBepGpZ5iC6aUjH74OwAj8FNEbtsjTlQ7HhJrmkNOfmJAYid s1TzS-YcLTm4k21fkpQq852V8CyVvyDu58i4xr2FaPXLbcE_RMTi_ Xa3ejdxHvCCmZm9y5SiYhFNluKnfuiWHyIqgOTYNivQpVpF_H0HJTZ HnWeF6Uj9VtYDszpf8q2jm5iL7pNTqEuFOShARWRNKFtELt2bvWpfZ NTU982oVPiW-xrOx9niEa-W3AyW6Zb7EiLMWfQnTy8jsMeCpzneaI5R- c1pAHrn0MtQU1YUJdoAnjHsGThlCw4ehtN71n4ODbNRtF0Ug0Rc74y- C6OgtqBe4AwvwJZx5HMm4wHzBfU4w9WPGHmUxr4fEby2oXVoDp3D3V04 xgULMSmQS6hlm6240mr7BRxxs3E.

Legislation.gov.uk. (2014). *Children and Families Act 2014*. [online] Available at: http://www.legislation.gov.uk/ukpga/2014/6/contents/enacted. Accessed 1 June 2015.

Lorde, A. (1984). The Master's Tools Will Never Dismantle the Master's House. In A. Lorde (Ed.), *Sister Outsider: Essays and Speeches* (pp. 110–114). Berkeley: Crossing Press.

Marsh, D. (2015, March 20). Welcome to the Election. But Only If You Are a Hardworking Family. *The Guardian*.

Merchant, W. (2015) What Can I Say? In *7th Child, Youth, Family and Disability Conference*, University of the West of England, Bristol, 7 and 8 July 2015.

Oliver, M. (1991). *The Politics of Disablement*. London: Macmillan.

The Equality Act. (2010). [online] Chapter 2 (2010). *Legislation.gov.uk*. Available from http://www.legislation.gov.uk/ukpga/2010/15/contents. Accessed 18 July 2015.

United Nations. (1989). *Convention on the Rights of the Child*. London: HMSO.

Wendy Merchant is a mother-activist and researcher whose interests include parenting, disability and interactions with education, health and social care services. Wendy is married to Mark and they are the proud parents of Jamie and Abbie. Wendy works in the Norah Fry Centre for Disability Studies at the University of Bristol.

Jamie Merchant is eleven years old and a committed video gamer. He is the proud owner of an extensive range of new and retro gaming consoles. Jamie's ambition is to establish his own video game company, and he hopes to produce a new generation of games.

The Heaviest Burdens and Life's Most Intense Fulfilment: A Retrospective and Re-understanding of My Experiences with Childhood Liver Disease and Transplantation

Sophie Savage

Key Points

- This chapter presents a personal reflection on my childhood with liver disease, including thoughts on going to school with chronic illness, my family and undergoing transplantation.
- The chapter is presented under the framework set out at the beginning of the chapter regarding burdens as fuel, and under that framework is a narrative retelling of childhood illness and new understandings of those experiences through reflection and consultation with literature.
- Changes suggested include more engagement between medical and educational staff that work with children and their families who have chronic illnesses and better training for teachers who have chronically unwell pupils, so they are prepared to support them appropriately. Much lower tolerance in schools for any sort of bullying and effective protocols for dealing with bullying are also suggested.

The heaviest of burdens is therefore simultaneously an image of life's most intense fulfilment. The heavier the burden, the closer our lives come to the earth, the more real and truthful they become. (Kundera 1984: 5)

S. Savage (✉)
University of the West of England, Bristol, UK

© The Author(s) 2018

K. Runswick-Cole et al. (eds.), *The Palgrave Handbook of Disabled Children's Childhood Studies*, https://doi.org/10.1057/978-1-137-54446-9_4

41

Academic work can be seen as a theoretical and factual world separate from personal experience; however, there are notable academics who draw from their personal lives and use research methodologies that are based upon their subjective experience. For example, Sacks (2010), a neurologist and popular author, uses evocative language whilst exploring a variety of neurological conditions. When he explains his own bewildering experiences of living with prosopagnosia, a condition which is also known as face blindness (Harris and Aguire 2007), I was instilled with the fears he shared of not recognising my loved ones or getting lost outside my own home. I found his evocative language to be very moving and I felt I could empathise with his situation. I found Sacks' (2010) account of having eye cancer to be incredibly honest as he shares his vulnerability, whilst being factual about his illness. He provides the reader with the opportunity to understand his learning process and to experience something of his emotional ordeal. Similarly, within the realm of social science, Petrov (2009) demonstrates the use of autobiography as a valid research method. It allowed him to present his experiences with mental health care reform in Bulgaria in the post-communist era in a creative way that conveyed a greater understanding of mental health through autobiography as a professional developing services with ownership of what services can really mean to people.

Such accounts communicate to the reader a multitude of emotional landscapes and these insightful personal narratives emphatically demonstrate the value of learning from others' lived experience.

I choose to begin my account with Kundera's (1984) quote from his inspiring novel *The Unbearable Lightness of Being* where he explains that the heavy burdens we carry are the ones from which we can draw the most meaningful purpose. When the word 'burden' is used, I consider what I carry with me each day. This includes my responsibility for my health concerns, the long-term impact my health concerns have had on my family, the ways in which my health affects my daily life and my awareness of suffering and loss of life for many within the paediatric liver transplant community. My experience of 'burden' is something that I hold on a personal, familial and communal level. This is not something that is simplistically connected to my diagnosis but something that I believe many may carry from a variety of different social and health circumstances. I imagine the burdens as coal that is carried on my back; it is very heavy but fuels my motivation to effect positive change. Although these burdens can at times weigh me down, they provide me with the ongoing determination to explore issues that affect the quality of life for those with similar diagnoses, in an attempt to gain a greater understanding of my own experiences and identity. I hope that my work may work towards improving the lives in comparable circumstances to my own.

When beginning this chapter about my experiences, I was aware of the limitations of my memory and began to research my past through different sources. I applied for my medical notes from my local hospital in the south-west of England. These notes act as a timeline for prominent medical events from my childhood and provide detailed descriptions of my biomedical and developmental progression. I consulted my close family for their stories and studied my photo albums for visual recollection. Relevant literature was used for medical explanations. Throughout my life, the Children's Liver Disease Foundation (CLDF) has been a constant source of good-quality, accessible resources for families affected by childhood liver disease. Their current online resources explain clearly how the liver works and what happens when it does not. As I am currently a student, I also endeavour to make appropriate academic connections to this discussion. This story is not a strict retelling of events as I am reflecting on events and speculating upon my own development with the knowledge I have of the person I am now as a 27-year-old master's degree student living independently in Bristol. My medical notes are not only a record of my condition and treatment but exist as an extensive compendium of the complexities of my childhood. The stories shared between me and my family members provide our family cohesion; however, accessing these memories is an act of self-reflexivity that allows me to create and tell my own stories.

I was born in the summer, the first child of a machine shop engineer and a radiography secretary by the seaside in England, where my parents still live. I was born a little late but seemingly healthy initially. I was diagnosed with jaundice, according to correspondence, (Medical Notes 1989a), when I was three weeks old, and after a variety of tests, scarring was observed on my liver. A crucial function of the liver is to produce bile for the digestion of fat; the biliary system transports bile to the gut through ducts (Children's Liver Disease Foundation 2013). My biliary system was not functional and I was diagnosed with biliary atresia, whereby the bile ducts had developed inflammation that restricted the flow of bile, subsequently leading to scarring also known as fibrosis of the liver (Children's Liver Disease Foundation 2013). The damage from the scarring is irreversible. I went to the operating theatre for the first time when I was six weeks old to have a Kasai portoenterostomy (Medical Notes 1989a, b). This is a procedure used to re-establish the flow of bile by attaching part of the gut to the underside of the liver (Children's Liver Disease Foundation 2013). My parents were informed that I had a moderately severe liver disease and that there was a high likelihood of increasing problems and an uncertain prognosis (Medical Notes 1989a, b).

Stories repeated by my parents and grandparents, photographs and medical correspondence tell different stories of birthday parties with balloons, family members looking happy in photographs and tales of my curiosity. The letters between my paediatrician and liver specialists tell a different story again reporting ongoing infections, hospital trips and increasing amounts of medication.

Like others with chronic illnesses, according to Nabors et al. (2008), school provided a number of both social and academic challenges. Children were for the most part incredibly cruel. I can of course now rationalise their behaviour towards me and understand that perhaps I was an outlet for their own frustrations. I was perceived as being different which was enough in their determinations to warrant their negative behaviour towards me. I suffered from jaundice to varying degrees, with ascites which presents as a very extended abdomen due to an accumulation of abnormal fluid, my arms and legs were thin and a considerable contrast to my main body-my physical differences were very obvious. I am sure my class just thought I was some sort of alien. I remember some events in particular. At five years of age, I was given medication by my teacher in front of a packed dining hall. Looking back, this could have just been done because it was the allotted time when the teacher was available, but at the time, it felt like a singular event that began the divide between me and the rest of the school. When I was six years old, after a long hospital stay, I returned to school to find my work had been ripped up in my drawer and my brand new dictionary, which I really loved, had been torn up. When I was seven, I recall being loudly told off for disrupting class due to my excessive nosebleeds caused by continuous internal bleeding. I felt like I was despised by teachers and pupils and that school provided no allies. Bullying of one kind or another is not disease specific and we also know that children who are bullied may have diagnoses of 'invisible illnesses' (Cavet 2000).

On reflection, I felt there was a sense of anxiety from the teaching staff surrounding how best to deal with my ongoing health concerns during school time. Roux (2009) explored the attitudes of teachers towards pupils with chronic illness and found that many teachers do not have a clear understanding of the health conditions that pupils may have and reported feeling both ill equipped and resistant to deal with acute medical issues when they arise in the classroom. An amalgamation of these factors, Roux (2009) concludes, can lead to negative attitudes towards chronically unwell pupils. Nabors et al. (2008) echo this finding, adding that a lack of confidence to address such issues is felt by many teachers especially since they may feel responsible for the needs of the child during school time and may lack accessible knowledge about the conditions that a pupil may have. When I was a child, there was much less information about biliary atresia and my doctors and teachers to my knowledge had very little in the way of communication with one another.

Information about biliary atresia is now available from CLDF for teachers and parents. Online guidance is provided for parents who are preparing to send their children to school (Children's Liver Disease Foundation, 2012) discussing what to expect, how to access additional support and signposts to further resources (see http://www.childliverdisease.org/Information). These resources outline assessment of educational needs and describe a few of the ways that a parent might be supported by state provision. Hopkins et al. (2014) point out that despite major changes made to support families in these circumstances, the practical reality is often less than ideal. Communication issues tend to arise when a variety of individuals from different networks are responsible for the educational welfare of a child. Hopkins et al. (2014) found that those that lived in smaller communities had more favourable outcomes due to greater collaborative efforts in engaging the child or young person with the family, clinicians and teachers. Schools that demonstrated best practice were those that worked in a holistic fashion, responding to the needs of the child and also their family. As I come from a small seaside town in the south-west of England, it is possible that with all of the changes made since I was in school, a child now with a similar diagnosis might have a very different experience and may feel well supported throughout their journey through primary and secondary education.

In regard to bullying, CLDF publishes specific resources for children and young people about bullying (Children's Liver Disease Foundation, n.d), explaining how it can be recognised and addressed. CLDF provides a system of support that is in place and their officers visit wards and clinics in addition to being available online. This means that if a child is bullied, they hopefully already have a positive supportive relationship to share that directly or online. Children and young people might also be a part of the CLDF young persons' forum where they are able to chat online to other young people in a similar position. There is a much greater emphasis on community support, from both the voluntary sector and within healthcare systems, with the introduction of additional psychological support staff and the newly introduced mentoring service for those in transition between child and adult care (Hunt et al. 2014). So hopefully, there is a decreased likelihood in bullying going unaddressed or young people being unsupported when they are bullied.

Despite these challenges at school, I loved learning. I just didn't like the environment but I enjoyed the work I was doing. I was always reading. My mother kindly took me to the library to get new books often, and at birthdays and Christmas, books were always requested. I was finding new ways to escape into these stories and making connections with new and different characters in unfamiliar environments with fantastic concepts like magic. Reading became a safe place for me to escape my reality. I found reading comforting and it challenged my literacy skills and nurtured my imagination without the pressures of socialisation with other children of my age.

Clark (1998) shows insight into the different ways children with chronic illnesses cope with the reality of their situation by referring to the work of Winnicott (1971) and his theory of transitional phenomena and spaces. Children, she explains, may escape from their reality through their imagination. Winnicott's transitional space is a space between a person and their environment, an intermediary between inner and outer life (Crociani-Windland 2013). Looking back, I saw reading as a space that was convenient and did not require others for access. My imaginary life grew to become a rich and colourful place where I connected environments from different stories and borrowed characters for entertainment. This form of comfort became a primary coping technique. I had minimal success with attempted friendships in school and those in the hospital were often short-lived. I often felt that a great deal of pressure was placed upon me to try and engage in 'healthy' normative relationships (Schaffer, 2004) with peers, who were, for the most part, incapable of understanding the challenges of my life, which was not their fault.

The exception to this was the schoolroom at both my local and specialist hospital in London. In both cases, the schoolroom teachers were very aware of what I may or may not be able to manage, they were strong advocates for ensuring I kept up with my education and spoke with my mother often and kept her well informed with any communications they had with my school. The schoolroom at the hospital in London had computers, an art space, somewhere you could cook and a small collection of resources for most subjects. I don't remember a time when I felt unwelcome at all. They would make me sit next to a child with pins in their legs and opposite a pupil with a drain in their head and the topic of discussion would be the favourite colour of a felt-tip pen. I wished school was always this way, with a focus on learning and enjoying yourself, rather than simply struggling through each day.

This inner world and transitional space are known only to me though. Throughout my childhood, I was referred to child psychology and psychiatric teams for assessments, research and investigations. These investigations were not interested in how I felt or how I coped but about what my parents could expect. My parents were advised to lower their expectations in regard to my developmental progression, physical stature, academic achievement, mental cognition or emotional capacity as I was likely to be stunted in all of these areas. When I was a very young child, and throughout my childhood, there were very few children surviving with liver disease and/or had undergone transplantation. The expectations in regard to all developmental aspects for this group of children were very low and the liver team rarely had experience with grown-up children. For this reason, my mother reports she pushed me much harder than she might have done if she had not been given this news.

When I started walking and talking, it was observed that I was quite a bright and curious child and some of the anxieties regarding academic capabilities subsided. My mother was sent to see a psychologist herself on only one occasion. There was some concern from ward staff in regard to her ability to cope and it was suggested that swimming might be helpful, but as my mother was 'stuck on the ward', there was really no way to implement this suggestion and there was no further advice given and there were no attempts to examine or support her relationship with me.

The judgements that were made in regard to my developmental capabilities were not, I believe, made maliciously; however, it was troubling to determine limits for all that a child may achieve, communicate to the world or become at their very beginning. The story created by this forewarning practice effectively diminishes all of that child's potential and foretells the likelihood of a dismal future. I was occasionally present while these statements were made about me but often learnt second-hand from my parents often years later. I paid very little attention to them—they seemed to be for the benefit of the medical staff and concerned my parents. I wasn't interested in how much of a disappointment I was supposed to be, but my mother and I still had to carry this professional idea of me as a doomed person that is present in my medical notes.

I learnt so very much from these experiences that were supposed to be about the limits of my progression and capabilities. I began to feel the weight of the coal and value the intensity of relationships that, though unsupportive, provided me with insights and lessons. These lessons included being patient, empathising with others, listening very carefully and asking important questions. It now seems archaic to press upon a family a probable dystopian personal future without room for hope.

I am aware that the liver team is now a department with an entire multidisciplinary team that includes a specialist social worker, clinical nurse specialist, specialist child psychologist, paediatric liver family services worker and adolescent care specialist with transition service. There is also a growing body of literature exploring the quality of life of this population that details how good life might be in comparison to other children and other disease groups, and it also seeks to understand some of the complexities of such a life for both the child and their family (Taylor 2008). If my family had access to the services that are now available, I believe that blanket statements regarding my development would not have been given and my family's well-being would have been supported. As previously discussed, there are few children that survived childhood transplantation to the age I am now and those who have survived are considered pioneers (Lowton 2011). In order to shape services around a population, you must first understand the needs of the said population and at the time this was not established.

I reflect on Kundera's (1984) quote (above) and consider the perspective of my mother at this stage, a woman who is at times struggling to cope with the complexities of my health, the systems that exist within the hospital and her own well-being. My mother might have accepted that I was a child who was unable to attend to academic pursuits, and would have great difficulties emotionally, mentally and physically, and had taken that idea to heart. This is not what happened and she seemed to utilise this knowledge; it seemed to fuel her determination that I would have the same opportunities academically as my peers, which certainly influenced my relationship with education. 'Burden' to me equals fuel for determination and this burden seemed to be one that was shared by my family, fuelling our determination throughout my childhood.

On the Christmas of my eighth year, my health deteriorated significantly. In my medical notes, there was a letter from my paediatrician to the liver team which reads that all current treatment I was receiving was no longer effective but was only managing my symptoms (Medical Notes 1996). In the notes, it states that my father expressed his hope to my paediatrician that I may be considered for transplantation. My medical notes did not simply provide the timeline of medical events. I found that reading this letter was very moving and different to my childhood perspective about my father. As a child, I remember my father was always at work and I didn't see him much so I think I thought he didn't like me as he did not have time to play with me. Reading this letter confirmed quite the contrary.

I remember the night it happened, my transplant. My father was out with friends (as it was a Friday night), my little brother was asleep in bed, as was I, and my mother had taken a dose of night nurse medication as she was not feeling well. The call came late at night. My brother was whisked off to our grandma's house, and an ambulance collected my parents and me to be taken to the specialist paediatric hepatology centre, King's College Hospital in London. The paramedics were very patient with me; they explained how everything in the ambulance worked and let me play with the sirens when we were on the motorway. They came into the hospital and stayed with us until I was taken for an x-ray. This relationship we had with the paramedics, although brief, was important, as this journey could have been an incredibly difficult, anxious and emotional one, however, this is not how I remember it. This intense period of time was greatly eased by their care, support and attention.

At the hospital, my mother had to bathe me so I was ready for the operation. This was the last time we were alone together before I was taken to the theatre. The anaesthetist came to the ward, the lights were off and the ward was quiet. I feel like this was a fixed point in my timeline. I remember wishing the anaesthetist good luck before being anaesthetised. I have borrowed the terminology 'fixed point in time' from the much-loved television programme Doctor Who (BBC One 1963), where it is a concept that refers to a point in time that must happen or the very fabric of reality may be compromised or obliterated. I have used this term because I feel like from that moment on, my identity has been very much framed around being a transplant recipient. This has provided me with a sense of purpose and direction in life, especially when I needed it the most. This is fitting as amongst all the burdens I might carry around, the liver is physically the heaviest organ in the body and here is where the physical meets the metaphorical. The heaviest burden also provides me with a large amount of fuel to persevere when life has been particularly difficult.

Liver transplantation, Samyn (2012) explains, is not a cure for liver failure, but it is the exchange of a terminal condition for a chronic one. I think that I understood that a liver transplant did not make everything better as I knew children on the ward that were still in and out of the hospital after their transplant. I understood what the transplant procedure was going to be because I was given a model almost like a board game, whereby you stick down a plastic illustration of a girl to a cardboard bed and can stick on all of the different tubes that the girl might have immediately after the operation.

There wasn't any discussion about the donor of my liver, although I knew there was one and there wasn't allotted time to discuss the more ambiguous side of transplantation with me or my parents. Everything discussed was very practical and mechanical much like the 'surgery of spare parts' described by Shildrick et al. (2009). The biomedical model towards healthcare has such a focus on the visceral reality of transplantation (Shildrick et al. 2009) that I was never given the opportunity to think about what it might be like to carry around an organ that originated in someone else's body or how I would process what that might mean as I was growing up. A popular dialogue in regard to organ transplantation is that of the 'gift-of-life' (Shildrick 2015) which I have recently unpicked a little. Mauss (2002) explains the components of a gift relationship which is the giving, receiving and reciprocation. In the case of transplantation, it is quite impossible to reciprocate. This is perhaps why I (and many other transplant recipients (Shildrick 2015)) feel that there is a weight to carry. This is another one of Kundera's (1984) burdens, that I carry, knowing that my life is dependent upon such an overwhelmingly incomprehensible gift.

I cannot give anything to an unknown stranger who has died, and due to anonymity, I couldn't pay anything back to the loved ones of the deceased.

Even if I could, nothing I could ever give would equal the value of the organ that keeps me alive. I try my very hardest to be what I think a good person is and to live a moral and ethical life, which, after the hard work of my family and the various healthcare professionals, along with the fiscal investment into my bodily existence, is the least that I can do to respect time and hard work that I have been afforded. This feeling is in the context of continuous media coverage of costs to the health service, decisions regarding responsibility for the provision of my care by different area providers and the impact this kind of discourse has on my day-to-day life as another burden of which I am constantly reminded—I am very expensive!

The hospital trips, medication and time away from home and school did not decrease after my transplant. Complications occurred as a result of the immunosuppressive medication I was prescribed, and time passed inside hospital beds, waiting rooms and my bedroom. My immune system began waging war upon itself and my liver. When I was 12, it was found that I had de novo auto immune hepatitis, which, as Mieli-Vergani and Vergani (2009) explain, requires large doses of steroids to treat. This resulted in further side effects, my face resembled the shape of a moon and no amount of sleep ever addressed the ongoing fatigue. A little over a year later, puberty began and I noticed a lump on the back of my head, lower right, just below the occipital ridge. I recall they were doing a refit of the children's ward at my local hospital and the first junior doctor we saw looked very tired and overwhelmed and asked me if it was a part of my head. It wasn't, I was rushed up to the liver unit at King's College Hospital and they prepared me for lymph node biopsy. They said they were going to shave my head, a horrifying prospect at this age. When I awoke, I was pleasantly surprised they had opened my armpit instead of my head for their sample. I had cancer, post-transplant lymphoproliferative disorder, a serious complication that can afflict transplanted individuals and which behaves similarly to a form of aggressive lymphoma (Lymphoma Association, 2016). My parents never mentioned cancer, no one did, but I knew what it was that they were treating. I was growing tumours and breasts at the same time. I had a Hickman line placed, which is a port of venous access in the chest which was used to deliver my intravenous treatment (Nuffield Orthopaedic Centre NHS Trust 2006), and I was trained how to use it. Treatment was very unpleasant and it took months to find one that was effective. Life was exhausting, keeping up with my education and my health concerns, all whilst trying to find out what sort of person I was. It seemed like an endless cycle of escaping and trying to cope.

I really wanted to have some friends when I was a young teenager, and with little previous experience of how to establish connections, I never really felt like any of my friendships were 'successful'. I did not understand the many desires of young teenagers as I was accustomed to speaking with adult health professionals in a format that allowed them to communicate effectively with me. I spoke with teachers when necessary and I watched a lot of sci-fi films and television programmes and of course I read. Although friendships were quite difficult for me, I considered the play leader, on the ward in the hospital in London, to be a trusted companion. I knew that it was his job to play with, entertain and support all the children on the ward, but I truly believed my connection with him was special. He was tall, with a shaved head and tattoos, he wore big boots and dirty jeans most of the time and I think his outward appearance may have been intimidating to some but I adored him. This wasn't a superficial crush, I truly believed he was my friend, he shared my love of sci-fi and he would wind me up no end. This very key relationship I had in hospital was, I believe, pivotal in my upbringing and social development and I will always remember him fondly.

My father worked long hours in the machine shop making materials for aircraft. My mother was my carer and constant companion, and my younger brother was often left with my grandma. My family never had a social worker and it took a long time for my parents to even be subsidised for all the travel costs incurred taking me to and from the hospital in London. I had a home tutor for a brief time after my transplant. My brother was never offered additional educational support. My mother became an absolute expert in navigating health care systems; she became familiar with all the relevant medical terminology along with a fierce determination that I was going to receive excellent care and that all my questions were going to be answered. My grandparents provided a safe haven for me and my brother growing up, a place for play. My mother's parents set up games in the garden, model train sets with our own named train stations and we had endless hours of board games. My father's mother cooked warming meals for us on the weekend and we would play in her garden and make friends with her pets. We became a highly adaptive unit, and we all supported each other in the best way we could.

Along the edges of childhood and into adolescence, I amassed the kind of questions that were particularly difficult to answer. This curious nature has continued growing which is why I have such an important relationship with learning. When reflecting upon my childhood, I have become increasingly aware of the impact my circumstances have had upon my family, both negative and positive.

My academic journey has been a peculiar one. I think most children will tell you fantastic stories of what they wanted to be when they 'grow up' and initially I wanted to be a paediatric liver transplant surgeon because I wanted to be what I thought a 'hero' was I suppose. I wanted that job until I realised what it would involve. My love for sci-fi led me to believe that I wanted to make costumes for television and film, which was followed by wanting to make the films themselves. Something changed as I was turning 20. I moved to a new place and studied FdSc Complementary Health Therapies where I was introduced to the idea of holism. Holism in the domains of healthcare means that the 'whole' person must be considered—physically, mentally, emotionally, socially, culturally (Greenwood 2010). Understandably, I found this idea very attractive, having myself viewed as a whole person instead of just a collection of poorly functioning parts. I made another transitional move from aiming to be the medical hero, to escaping to sci-fi film making and to then situating my life and my experience in a holistic health perspective.

I became engaged with holism, and with the academic work that came with it, because it gave me the opportunity to explore some of the grander questions I had about life in a more unboundaried way than in the school curriculum. I followed the complementary therapies work with a BSc Professional Studies (Health) and then to my current MSc Psycho-Social Studies. Psycho-social studies is an emergent academic field of inquiry that challenges many issues, including those pertaining to health by observing the psychological, social, cultural and historical contexts which engage in subjective experiences (Association for Psychosocial Studies 2017). It is a way of thinking that seeks to challenge and engage complex systems (in my case, healthcare and educational systems) so that we can attain new and different understandings. It is important within psycho-social work that the subjective experiences of the researcher be immersed within the work. Unconscious communications structure the understanding of the reality that the researcher inhabits (Crociani-Windland 2009). Ultimately, I have an area of academia that encourages me to use my experiences to shape my work. This allows me the opportunity to seek out new answers to the great questions I have held since I was a child.

I consider myself to be an expert by experience—terminology that has been contested because there are no clear guidelines as to who qualifies for this title (McLaughlin 2007). The meaning of such terminology, The Health Foundation (2011) reports, can depend a great deal on a person's relationship with their diagnosis, with the services they use and how their health affects their emotional well-being. As I have discussed and illustrated with Kundera's (1984) concept of burdens, I see my experiences as a chronically ill person and a very unwell child as a source of continuing motivation and direction for my future. For several years, I have been volunteering as a mentor with the liver transition team at the hospital where I was a patient as a child. I have returned to what I know in order to exist in this space but to serve a different function.

My role includes providing a listening service to those who are between child and adult care and providing support outside of the healthcare service and setting. The eligibility for application to this role required my lived experience as a previous patient who had a diagnosis of childhood liver disease (Hunt et al. 2014) and a new commitment to the community I belong to.

Some Final Thoughts

The way that I have presented my life as a series of burdens that drive me forward could be interpreted as leading a life of guilt and obligation, but I close this chapter by talking about choice. I chose to continue my education, even though there were plenty of opportunities to leave and pursue other prospects. I have chosen to bring my lived experiences into my work in order to explore them.

Why did I choose to boldly go into academia? Probably because I felt like the only thing I was ever good at was being a student. I knew that there would be allowances for absences, extensions for missed deadlines and that I might have an interesting perspective to offer. In the wider world, where I could have made costumes for sci-fi films, or tried to capture intriguing moments on film, you are relied upon and accountable. There is so much uncertainty in my life that holding onto the feeling of disappointing people is a burden I choose not to carry.

It is my hope that my reflections and interpretations of my childhood may provide one story of the life of a child with chronic ill health. Complexity is tangled throughout this chapter, considering the different roles I have played, the characters, bodies and systems I have engaged with. I am still trying to navigate my healthcare, and now, during a time of national systemic vulnerability due to the ongoing challenges of living in a period of austerity, I am finding my way through academia and doing my utmost to maintain my well-being and live an ethical life.

These hopes I have about my contributions feel important, like I have chosen a path that not only engages with being an activist, an expert by experience, a student, a service user researcher but also contributes to my own holistic well-being and sense of self.

It was very difficult as a child feeling like I did something awfully wrong and I somehow deserved the things that happened to me. I will probably spend the rest of my days unlearning this but I choose to use these experiences as an opportunity to be involved in psycho-social, service user research and inquiries and to share my particular perspective to illuminate some of the ways we might think about children and their families addressing childhood liver disease and other chronic illnesses.

> the absolute absence of burden causes man to be lighter than air, to soar into the heights… become half-real. What then shall we choose? Weight or lightness? (Kundera 1984:5)

I have chosen weight and a life more fulfilling than I could ever have imagined.

References

Association for Psychosocial Studies. (2017). Association for Psychosocial Studies. Available from: http://www.psychosocial-studies-association.org/about/. Accessed 17 July 2017.

BBC One. (1963, November 23). Doctor Who [TV]. *BBC One*.

Cavet, J. (2000). Children and Young People with a Hidden Disability: An Examination of the Social Work Role. *British Journal of Social Work* [online], *18*, 619–634.

Children's Liver Disease Foundation. (2012). *Going to School some thoughts....* 30 December 2015.

Children's Liver Disease Foundation. (2013). *Biliary Atresia*. 11 November 2015.

Children's Liver Disease Foundation. (n.d.). *Bullying*. 1 May 2016.

Clark, C. D. (1998). Childhood Imagination in the Face of Chronic Illness. In J. de Rivera & T. R. Sarbin (Eds.), *Believed-In Imaginings: The Narrative Construction of Reality* [online] (pp. 87–100). Washington DC: American Psychological Association.

Crociani-Windland, L. (2009). How to Live and Learn: Learning, Duration and the Virtual. In S. Clarke & P. Hoggett (Eds.), *Researching Beneath the Surface: Psycho-Social Research Methods in Practice* (pp. 51–78). London: Karnac.

Crociani-Windland, L. (2013). Old Age and Difficult Life Transitions: A Psycho-Social Understanding. *Psychoanalysis, Culture and Society, 18*(4), 335–351.

Greenwood, J. (2010). Holism [online]. In M. Baldwin & J. Woodhouse (Eds.), *SAGE Key Concepts: Key Concepts in Palliative Care*. London: Sage UK. Available from: http://search.credoreference.com/content/entry/sageukjlcz/holism/0. Accessed 19 Jan 2016.

Harris, A. M., & Aguire, G. K. (2007). Prosoganosia. *Current Biology, 17*(1), R7–R8. Accessed 11 Nov 2015.

Hopkins, L., Green, J., Henry, J., Edwards, B., & Wong, S. (2014). Staying Engaged: The Role of Teachers and Schools in Keeping Young People with Health Conditions Engaged in Education. *Australian Association for Research in Education* [online], *41*, 25–41. Accessed 11 Dec 2015.

Hunt, J., Hames, A., & Malan, J. (2014). *Young Person Mentoring Handbook*. London: The Institute of Liver Studies and Kings College Hospital.

Kundera, M. (1984). *The Unbearable Lightness of Being*. London: Faber and Faber.

Lowton, K. (2011, November 11). *Adult Survivors of Childhood Liver Transplantation* [News on webpage]. Available from: http://www.kcl.ac.uk/sspp/news/newsrecords/lowton.aspx. Accessed 30 Dec 2015.

Lymphoma Association. (2016). Lymphoma Association. Available from: https://www.lymphomas.org.uk/about-lymphoma/types/post-transplant-lymphoprolif-erative-disorder-ptld. Accessed 17 July 2017.

Mauss, M. (2002). *The Gift: The Form and Reason for Exchange in Archaic Societies.* London: Routledge Classics.

McLaughlin, H. (2007). What's in a Name: 'Client', 'Patient', 'Customer', 'Consumer', 'Expert by Experience', 'Service User'—What's Next? *The British Journal of Social Work* [online], *39*(6), 1101–1117. Accessed 10 Jan 2016.

Medical Notes. (1989a). The author can be contacted through the editors regarding these sources, as they are private hospital notes and not publicly available.

Medical Notes. (1989b). As above.

Medical Notes. (1996). As above.

Mieli-Vergani, G., & Vergani, D. (2009). Auto Immune Hepatitis. In F. J. Suchy, R. J. Sokol & W. F. Balistreri (Eds.), *Liver Disease in Children* [online] (3rd ed., pp. 447–458). Cambridge: Cambridge University Press. Accessed 17 Dec 2015.

Nabors, L. A., Little, S. G., Akin-Little, A., & Iobst, E. A. (2008). Teacher Knowledge of and Confidence in Meeting the Needs of Children with Chronic Medical Conditions: Peadiatric Psychology's Contribution to Education. *Psychology in the Schools* [online], *45*(3), 217–266. Accessed 17 Dec 2015.

Nuffield Orthopaedic Centre NHS Trust. (2006). *What Is a Hickman?* [online]. 1 May 2016.

Petrov, R. (2009). Autobiography as a Psycho-Social Research Method. In S. Clarke & P. Hoggett (Eds.), *Researching Beneath the Surface* (pp. 193–213). London: Karnac.

Roux, A. L. (2009). *Examining Teacher Knowledge and Attitudes About School Issues for Children with Epilepsy: A Mixed-Method Investigation.* PhD. University of Florida.

Sacks, O. (2010). Face Blind. In O. Sacks (Ed.), *The Mind's eye* (pp. 82–110). London: Picador.

Samyn, M. (2012). Optimising Outcomes for Pediatric Recipients. *Liver Transplantation, 18*(s2), s34–s38. Accessed 24 Sept 2015.

Schaffer, H. R. (2004). *Introducing Child Psychology.* Oxford: Blackwell Publishing.

Shildrick, M. (2015). Staying Alive: Affect, Identity and Anxiety in Organ Transplantation. *Body and Society* [online], *21*(3), 1–22. Accessed 1 May 2016.

Shildrick, M., McKeever, P., Abbey, S., Poole, J., & Ross, H. (2009). Troubling Dimensions of Heart Transplantation. *Journal of Medical Humanities* [online], *35*(1), 35–38. Accessed 26 Jan 2016.

Taylor, R. M. (2008). *Health-Related Quality of Life in Young People After Liver Transplantation.* PhD. Kings College London.

The Health Foundation—Inspiring Improvement. (2011). *Can Patients Be Teachers? Involving Patients and Service Users in Healthcare Professionals' Education.* Available from: http://www.health.org.uk/sites/default/files/CanPatientsBeTeachers.pdf. Accessed 11 Jan 2016.

Winnicott, D. W. (1971). *Playing and Reality.* London: Tavistock Publications.

Sophie Savage is an MSc Psycho-Social Studies student at the University of the West of England. Sophie is also a peer mentor for the liver transition team at King's College London, which is where she had her liver transplant as a child. She plans to continue her studies with a PhD, in the hope of having a career in academia as a psycho-social/disability studies researcher and writer. Sophie enjoys reading, cooking and watching sci-fi films at her home in Bristol with her partner Jan.

My Sister, My World: From Second Mum to Nurse

Rebecca Whitehead

Key Points

- Professionals need to listen to families.
- Keep going—times get really hard and you might want to give up but you can't.
- Try to include enjoyable experiences for all family members as disability is about the whole family.

Introduction

It is a challenge to write my story in a way that respects my sister's privacy as she cannot give informed consent and it did not feel right to talk about her without her permission. I have chosen to use Beth as a pseudonym to remind me to respect her confidentiality. I am not sharing the stories of my other family members as I wish to focus in my own story as Beth's sister. We can all misunderstand and upset someone, but this story shows that if professionals label 'behaviour', it can stop us from trying to understand the meaning behind the behaviour. The story shows how I began to understand my sister's behaviour and what she might mean and how I started to think about how best to be her sister. I have shared this story with health care students

R. Whitehead (✉)
University of the West of England, Bristol, UK

© The Author(s) 2018
K. Runswick-Cole et al. (eds.), *The Palgrave Handbook of Disabled Children's Childhood Studies*, https://doi.org/10.1057/978-1-137-54446-9_5

as I want people to know about young people with learning disabilities. As a Learning Disability Nurse student now, my learning relates to my practice and hopefully it is useful to others.

My Story

In 1997, I found out, aged seven, that I was going to have a baby sister and I was full of joy and excitement. I would often find myself daydreaming about all of the things we could do together as adults: go for coffee, be there for each other during a messy break up, go shopping for wedding dresses and be aunties for each other's children. Those nine months went very slowly. The day came when Beth was born. I remember going to the hospital after school to visit her for the first time. It was just magical. I had a beautiful healthy baby sister who was born with an auburn triangle of hair standing up on the top of her head, bright blue eyes and a heart-melting smile. I loved to do things like change her nappy and mum showed me how. Now I question these 'ordinary expectations' and I am more aware of the many different ways life can be. This is one of the important lessons I have gained from being a sister to Beth.

Beth was described as being slightly 'behind' when the health visitor would come to the house and carry out the 'milestone tests'. Now I know that health visitors assess how a baby is developing (sitting, crawling, walking and talking and so on) and check this against the average for that age to see if their development is reaching the 'normal' milestone. At the time, I didn't think anything of it. I had the perfect little sister but I remember that she didn't cry very much. Around the age of two years, Beth was rushed to hospital as she was having epileptic seizures and she was hospitalised for two weeks. This was a difficult time for the whole family as mum spent the two weeks in hospital with her and Dad was working, so my brother and I often found ourselves cared for by various family members. I did not get to see my mother or Beth very much during this time but my first hospital visit was an occasion that sticks in my mind and probably always will.

Beth was required to have a lumbar puncture procedure. My mother and I went into a small room on the ward with two nurses. They laid Beth on a bed and asked me to assist them in holding Beth still as the nurses said this would be 'a very painful procedure'. I was ten years old and I felt awful pinning down my baby sister as I did not want her to be in pain. I thought I should protect her. The worst part of this experience for me was that Beth didn't even flinch. She couldn't feel the needle in her spine. I didn't want to see her in pain but then it worried me even more that she couldn't feel it. The nurses did not explain what a lumbar puncture was or why it would be helpful. The nurse should have explained Beth needed to be still so she would NOT feel any pain. Why did the nurses put me into a distressing situation and why were they not thinking about what that was like for me? Why did she not ask me what I understood and if I was ok or preferred to wait outside with someone? Looking back, I think that the nurses wanted me involved to help my sister feel safe, but this has stood out for me and now I would think hard about asking a sibling to do this role. I would also be aware that the sibling had been without their mother and I would ask them how they are feeling.

This first hospital visit was the first of many. After further investigations and over the years, Beth was diagnosed with many terms: 'severe learning disabilities', 'global delay', 'complex needs', 'autistic traits', 'speech and language delay', 'dyspraxia', 'epilepsy', 'challenging behaviour' and 'a rare genetic disorder'. As a family, we were new to the field of learning disabilities. I was a child. I had no idea what they were talking about. My mum tried to explain it to me and she would read books or research the different words that were being thrown at us. I remember feeling sad for Beth. She wasn't born wanting to be different or wanting to be in hospital but it just happened. But as her sister, I knew I would be there for her no matter what. The labels that Beth was given had a great impact on us, sometimes negatively. I wanted to learn and be at the meetings to help Beth in any way I could, but it was like someone had given me a foreign dictionary and told me to learn it overnight. There were different professionals coming to my home and I didn't know who they were. Some had really long job titles that I couldn't even pronounce. They would talk to my mum and used big words that I assume they thought we could understand; however, I just couldn't. I was only a child. Instead, I would sit there and smile, pretending I understood. So I was treated as quite grown up, expected to understand professional speak and take part in Beth's treatment, and at the same time, I was treated as a young child or as if I was not there. I think about how I might use professional terms and how I could use easy to understand language when talking with other family members. I think about how it is for families when lots of professionals start to arrive in their home, asking the same questions over and over and how that could be a more positive and supportive experience.

As Beth grew older, she began to walk. I found myself helping her with things other children her age could do independently such as eating, dressing, washing and personal care. She could never be left alone as she had no awareness of danger. Beth began to talk a few words but it was hard to understand what she meant as her pronunciation wasn't clear, and when she was misunderstood she became upset and angry. My story over those years was very much about Beth's story—what happened at nursery, schools, play schemes and later with carers at home was generally about how she expressed her feelings, and services were usually withdrawn or she was excluded. As a family, we did not exclude her but kept trying to understand. I learnt to help Beth as much as possible to calm her down and remove her from an upsetting situation; however, I cannot predict every situation. It took me a long time to recognise that she wasn't being intentionally unkind or 'naughty'. This was actually her communicating to us about how she was feeling, as she probably didn't understand what her anger felt like to us. This is a very important thing that I learnt as a child. Someone can act in one way, but there could be a different meaning behind it from what might first be understood.

Over time, I learnt how to recognise what might upset Beth and to plan ahead to avoid that, but it is not possible to make all plans go smoothly. One year, when I was 22 years old, I took Beth to a zoo for a special Christmas event for just two of us. Sometimes, Beth likes to go out in a wheelchair as she feels much safer, and I know she doesn't like ending enjoyable experiences and usually becomes distressed so I thought we would leave Father Christmas for just before home time as a good way of being able to leave peacefully. We got in the queue 30 minutes before the event ended. I had pre-warned Beth that we would see Father Christmas and then it would be home time. A member of staff came to us and said 'sorry the queue is closed'. Those words cut me like a knife. I knew how upset Beth would be and I could have cried for her as she could not express verbally how she felt. I promised she could see Father Christmas and I broke that promise. We normally get together as a family and discuss what happened and we learnt very quickly to never promise to go somewhere or see something as you cannot always guarantee it will happen, and some things are just out of your control. We tried to pre-warn Beth but not everything goes to plan, and I felt so guilty, like it was my fault, but I had done everything I could for her to have a nice time. Beth needs to be safe and secure and know exactly what is going to happen. I am also upset when promises are broken. If professionals make promises and don't keep them, we as a family are upset! Now I can explain the sadness to people and they can better understand. The professional words like 'high anxiety' or fear of 'transitions' are used to describe behaviour or explain it, but I find it helps to think about what Beth is trying to let me know.

I had to leave my social and sports clubs and try to keep up with school work, sometimes so tired I could hardly stay awake due to my caring responsibilities. At times, professionals did offer help but it sounded as though we were not managing and that brought more stress. Beth settled into having short breaks away and that gave me time with my mother, which we both enjoyed. Mum and I would go out for food together or watch a film and that was our special time together. It really helped our relationship as it allowed us to let go of our responsibilities and roles as carers and we could have fun together without having to worry as Beth was in safe hands. Now, as a professional, I would gradually introduce the options and not suggest that a family was not coping. I would discuss the positive opportunities like time with each other, time to recharge batteries and most importantly give the message that it is an opportunity for the young person to have life away from the family home as they need a break too.

Beth Is 17 Now

She is very aware of my emotions and can often tell if I have had a good or bad day. She will say, 'You OK, Bec?', and I normally give her a hug and that instantly makes me feel better if I have had a rubbish day. When we spend time together, it normally involves lots of giggles, singing and dancing and generally being silly. We go shopping, to the cinema, swimming, have girly sleepovers with popcorn and a DVD and go to fun fairs. I think of other people of my age and if they have teenage siblings, some of those wouldn't have the type of relationship I do with my sister, in comparison with a typical teenager. Although it may sound like a typical relationship, going to the cinema, for example, involves lots of pre-planning, getting to the cinema without too much time involved in sitting around as Beth would get bored, giving Beth plenty of warnings about our plans so she is prepared and reminding her how to behave in the cinema. All of these added strategies are put in place so we can try to have an enjoyable experience as sisters together.

At Beth's nursery, there were many children with different needs and professionals talking with their hands and using pictures to communicate. I remember reading a book with a four-year-old boy who taught me the Makaton sign for frog. For my school work experience, I spent a week in my sister's school which gave me an insight into what a day in the life of Beth was like, and I decided I wanted to work with children with learning disabilities so I owe her a lot as she has made me who I am and has shaped my career path. She has made me very passionate about people with learning disabilities and I stand up for them and voice my opinions whenever I can because people with learning disabilities are now a big part of my life, and they have rights and should be heard.

After graduating in Early Childhood Studies (BA Honours), I was lucky enough to work for the Children with Learning Disabilities Team based in a hospital. I was a community support worker and worked alongside community nurses, clinical psychologists and a consultant psychiatrist. Within this job, I have spoken at training sessions, conferences and have been a guest lecturer at university health courses talking about my experience for students to learn and be more aware of how they can engage positively with a family. I am now in my second year of Learning Disability Nursing (BSc Honours). I have first-hand experience of what a good professional is and what a not-so-good professional is. For me and my family, we didn't want someone coming into our home and talking 'textbook'. We are real people and a real-life family. We would take on board everything that was thrown at us as we really did want to improve Beth's happiness and our own family life.

Writing this chapter has brought back so many memories for me and my family. Everyone is an individual and it is helpful to not generalise. Just because two people have autism doesn't mean they are going to be the same. I think it is really beneficial to get to know the person and find out what they want. Remember who is in the centre of the discussion and think from their perspective. In my experience, family members are such a great resource for information. Listen to them. A number of professionals haven't listened to us but have listened to someone who has a few letters after their name and has only met Beth a few times. I am thankful that I have had the opportunity to have my eyes opened to the way Beth is and the joy that she brings me. Although over the years there has been blood, sweat and tears (literally!), I would not change Beth for the world. She is who she is and she has made me who I am.

Rebecca Whitehead is a student on the (Graduate Diploma) Learning Disability Nursing Programme at the University of the West of England. She has ten years of experience working with children with learning disabilities and their families. Rebecca is also the president of the students living at home society within the university for students that live at home rather than in student accommodation.

Being a Disabled Woman and Mum: My Journey from Childhood

Jo Skitteral

Key Points

- This chapter discusses a disabled woman's personal quest to be a mother.
- It illustrates how messages towards motherhood were missing in childhood so there was no expectation to be a parent.
- The chapter identifies valued support and offers learning for professionals.

Introduction

This chapter is about my childhood, growing up and finally being a mum. It includes messages for people who support men and women to become parents and who enable disabled children and young people to choose those aspirations. In the chapter, I discuss the so-called norms of embodiment, gender, sexuality and family in terms of culture and environment. I set out the problems other people present in their initial responses to meeting me. I also describe the buildings that expect me to have wings!! I show how practitioners and relatives develop their understanding and confidence to support disabled people to meet their parenting aspirations.

I describe the moments in which my future as an adult seems to be disregarded or ignored by people around me but, at the same time, the same people

J. Skitteral (✉)
Social Worker and Independent Trainer, Somerset, UK

© The Author(s) 2018
K. Runswick-Cole et al. (eds.), *The Palgrave Handbook of Disabled Children's Childhood Studies*, https://doi.org/10.1057/978-1-137-54446-9_6

left me with adult responsibilities. As a child, I was expected to undertake caring responsibilities for others' children, and at the same time, I was not ever expected to become or want to become a mother.

In conclusion, this chapter does not speak about the 'right' way to support disabled people to become parents but shares one journey. My story reveals that I needed the opportunity to explore, talk about, weigh up and prepare for becoming a parent So, I share my story to illustrate the difference those opportunities make to me being supported as a full and playful mother.

First Messages at School

At the residential school I attended, we were all told about reproduction—that is, frogs' reproduction. I was lucky that I was able to check things out at home with my mother, and I had a sibling too who also shared this kind of information. Many of the other children were boarders living at the residential school weekly. We knew that staff were having relationships. They were very young, not much older than us—I went there when I was 12. We knew little about the lives of the staff but our intimate information was there for all to see. There was a record card system of open clear pockets where everything personal was there for staff to see. The record cards were available on a stand in the public space open to everyone, including visitors, to see. The young people could look at each other's private information too, but I don't think anyone dared to.

So staff did not share their relationship world (though we knew anyway) but they did think they could share our worlds—or what they thought they knew about our worlds. Our lives were made public. It was the same for changing clothes or using the loo—no walls or cubicles—all open, boys and girls. The school had quite a few boys with Duchenne muscular dystrophy—a boy's progressive impairment. So, under the professional gaze, impairment was gendered but not our identities. Our identities were genderless. I've talked about genderless, sexless schools before (see Skitteral 2013). Gender and sexuality was not seen as negative, it was just seen as nothing at all; it was missed—there was no expectation that anyone would have a relationship. We were told about sex in a bizarre way—you only have sex if you are married and you only have sex to have children. But, we got the message—this is not about *you*, *you* won't be having children and *you* won't be having children like *you*.

I don't ever remember a home corner or that kind of imaginative play. I had dolls at home, a pram, but I don't ever remember thinking at school one day that I would have a baby. It never entered my head. Imagining my future family life was missing.

Messages Kept on Coming!

At the secondary stage of 'special' school, I began to question the message that we would not be parents. I demanded to know: 'Well why not?' As I was told I shouldn't, I said, 'why shouldn't I?' and 'Why not me?' I was labelled rebellious. Staff were getting pregnant and so were my friends' parents and my friend had a younger sister. Despite being 'the rebel', at school, I became a pseudo care assistant—I looked after the young children, gave them physiotherapy exercises and helped them to eat their lunch. It was my choice. They were five or six years old. One boy would only walk with me, other than using his frame, and would call out for 'Jo Bananas!'—his nickname for me. I used to know how to prop him up and support him, the young boy at school, how he liked to lie and not tip over. It was just presented by staff silently as a woman's role to care.

Men were few and far between in the school, but there were a couple of male staff somewhere in the teenage unit. My friend and I had single-parent mothers. Her mother had little expectation for her future—my friend had a thing for one of the male carers. School went up to 21 but I never heard of anyone getting pregnant. Relationships were discouraged. I only remember heterosexual relationships, if there were any at all. I don't remember any gay staff or young people—no one came out.

I made many friends when I first went to college and went to gigs and stuff. Many friends were in relationships. I think I was the only one who wasn't. At school, I did not have an established friendship group. There was very little time—just break time. There was a regime where we were expected to rest after lunch rather than socialise. Socialising was not a priority for any staff, though perhaps the boarders did have more of a peer group. At home—it was too late in the evening once home and at weekends I did not know anyone— just a few boys who were my brother's friends, not mine. I spent a lot of time thinking about it on my own, and it's not for my mother to know and get involved is it? At college, I had to learn how to socialise and became more confident and assertive.

Such regimes are common, and in my job later on, I worked to make sure a young man with Duchene could ask and plan for a full university life and that included possibilities for relationships and sex. We have to make it happen as otherwise, it's missing.

So Am I a Young Person or Am I Growing Up? Mixed Messages

I had to communicate a lot in the adult world; we often become experts in our own life, need to be assertive and our parents too learn not to be browbeaten by professionals because 'I'm a social worker' or 'I'm a paediatrician'.

I was in a prevocational course, though I was doing standard exams for 16 year olds. No one else in my group could read and I was expected to tutor them. It was before the 'inclusion' agenda in school! My tutor followed me around, and my friend would ask me, 'who is that following you behind the bush?' 'Oh it's my tutor'. I had to tell the tutor to step back and let me have time to go or not go to classes. Another tutor I had would say 'oh I just want to lift you up'—I'm 17 at this point. My friends were musicians and played in bands.

Giving the Messages Back and Moving Forward

It was when I was 29 and living in a new area that I asked my new consultant about my body and about having a baby. She offered me genetic screening. She found that I had the 'wrong' diagnosis—at 29, my diagnosis was confirmed—and it would be more likely to be inherited. I said it makes no difference to me and she said it is probably more problematic for me if I had a child who did not have the same condition—the child would be bigger. At her colleague's surgery, the receptionist asked me how many weeks pregnant I was. I was not pregnant then, but it made me think I could be. So I think time was ticking, and I knew I wanted to be a mum. I was in a relationship and she had two children. I was looking into it, I suppose. With this consultant, I thought it worth having the conversation—I hadn't with the previous doctors as I already knew their perspective.

Messages for Others

There were no 'disabled parking' spaces at the hospital maternity unit where I attended appointments so I could not drive to appointments. So did that mean that there were no disabled staff, disabled visitors, disabled mothers, fathers or grandparents? The first midwife called my name and then saw me. I saw her see me. Her jaw dropped and she was lost for words. The last midwife was very different. She was very experienced; she treated me as a pregnant woman. She arranged for me to visit, before I gave birth, the neonatal intensive care and also the post-operative ward to see what equipment was needed.

She showed me breast-feeding, and she showed the staff how to support me. She had organised my visit to the hospital, planning and preparing. She was a generic midwife, she did not or need not have 'special' knowledge; it was about her values and her readiness to get things in place.

To have my baby was a 13-year journey—plans and preparations were in place. I had the obstetrician ready for a no-battle approach. I had established trust, though plans can change and she was off sick when I was pregnant. She was not there to get the accessible parking space she had promised if I became pregnant! The sonographer was at first perhaps taken aback, and on our first meeting, I went alone to process the information myself and chose to tell exactly what to who myself. When I was pregnant and we first met, she painted the worst-case scenario—it is not for others to hear, I decided, especially those closest to me, so I filtered the discussion.

Mostly, initial professional responses are full of panic. 'You should not be doing this!' And then a process all about risk takes over. Firstly, it was about the danger of my baby having the same condition as me. Why was that their concern? I had done ok, hadn't I? So it's shock, it's negative—'oh you will die' and 'he will come early' and 'the baby could have all these problems'—and a list of problems. Then, when they get to know my baby is planned, that I have family and a close network of support, they change. The respiratory consult said, 'Do not ever get pregnant' and then when I was pregnant, he was holding his breath until I had my baby. He came to see me there and said how well I looked. He said he wished more of his patients were like me—'get up and go, doing so well, baby doing so well!' So it's a shock—professionals don't expect me to cope, my baby to thrive us to fail—mostly that it would not happen! So again, let's see the person and not jump to conclusions about impairment. It gets rational then—starting with the person, using talking and respecting own experiences. The professionals are also on a journey.

Norms, Culture and Environment: Getting to Know My Baby and Me?

We are in a culture where health care people work on morals and are deemed risky to the child in the following ways. The 'baby's book' is used to keep the care plan and any information the practitioners want to put in. I would have wanted to decide what information is in my baby's 'best interest'. It's not public information, yet my personal records are made freely available. What happened to my 'right to private family life'? And surely, if my baby *was* at risk, professionals would not just write that down in a book!

It's no good for professionals to say they have seen 'someone like me' either; another person would not be like me! Even after my son's birth, I have to have 'the conversation' and say 'no, you have not seen someone like me!' If I had asked them about their experience of supporting anyone with my needs, that would be a different starting point. Practitioners could think outside the box—disabled men and women often want children and they should not be deterred but supported. Some may manage to become parents without intervention, but are we made more vulnerable if we need to avoid professional intervention? I'd like to explore my own concerns, and I'd have liked to have messages that it's likely I might want to be a parent and have my ideas nurtured and not squashed. Becoming a parent as a disabled person can take time. We have waited to be turned down for adoption as 'not physically fit'. We may struggle to afford treatments that are not provided free by health services. No one knows the outcome of an early birth—there are statistics but no one can know. I felt pain free when I was pregnant and I enjoyed it. I would have another baby if I had more resources.

A counsellor told me that any child I would have would be disadvantaged because I was a disabled parent and she implied that my child would have to be my carer. I said she needed to think about what she had said. She could not explain what she meant. I complained about her but I have no idea what happened.

I had my baby. Midwives in hospital encourage parents to 'get on with it immediately' which is good, but how do I reach the handtowels? Old-style midwives helped me have a wash, while others did not. It took six days to have a shower—by 7 pm, someone was found to assist me (after several names were identified). I've had an operation. I can't bend or reach my feet, but it was not in her domain, not nursing, so it felt like no one wanted to do it. My mother was unwell, but she came in when she was better for two days and helped me have a shower. Am I a child again? My mother supports me, but should she do my personal care? There were no choices. I just have to be so resilient, assertive, know what I want and be in control of my destiny and not to settle for what you've got or feel grateful.

And the Messages Still Keep Coming and We Keep Giving Them Back

At some play spaces, you can't take the baby's buggy. At a children's centre, it's ok to stay with younger children, and as my baby was born early he is doing similar things. Also, I keep thinking, when do I face children who will ask 'why' when they see me? Will I be knocked off my feet when they run about just excited? At one place, the play leader said that a couple of parents had said to her that they don't know how to help me. 'Help me with what, why?', I asked. 'They don't know what to say'. 'Why?'

So Can I Have Any Worries? And Support? And Trust?

This chapter is not about my baby—that is his story. I will just say that he knows me; he knows I sit with him on the floor to play and we use the stair lift and so on. He knows his grandparents do things differently and he does too. We work around things. We have fun. When he was born, he was in very poor health and needed help to breathe at points. We spent the first 11 weeks in hospital so I was pretty anxious then, caring for him with the nurses—two regular nurses who were really good. Having him home was fairly scary; at home, we had watched the resuscitation DVD for premature babies. A year and a bit on, I still have his breathing pad, a pad that has a sensor to sound an alarm if his breathing stops. He frightened the life out of me once when the alarm sounded—he was lying across the top of his cot!! Next, he is moving into his own room. Not having a night's sleep is par for the course, but for me my pain is worse from breast-feeding and my mobility has reduced. Lifting and carrying takes its toll. Having a practitioner whom I can trust, that gives supportive feedback, likes the job and with whom I can talk through ordinary worries is just what I need.

Childhood to Motherhood

In childhood, as a disabled child, I had the dual experience of being disregarded as a future adult (and parent), and, at the same time, I was being left with adult responsibilities. I had to travel alone without the expectations of being the ideal mother that others might have (and may wish to reject). At the same time, I had to see professionals' perspectives and learn how to challenge them. This is a childhood/adulthood paradox. As a disabled young woman, I was expected to take for others' children at school at the same time that I was never expected to become or want to become a mother. At school, we were to understand and agree that a child like us should not be brought into life. Once expecting a baby, the same fear was expressed by looks and comments to question of how a disabled person could look after a child if they are not able to look after themselves. If you get to know me, you will see I do look after myself in as many ways as most people might, mostly by myself and partly with family.

The second paradox, the paradox of health as a disabled child, occurs when others' concerns about my health are uppermost in their responses to me and at the same time that their support is not forthcoming. These paradoxes structured my motherhood experience. If we really think about parenting and non-disabled parents, we tend not to attribute good parenting simplistically to their body or learning ability. The comment that a child of a disabled parent will become a carer and be disadvantaged is made without knowing me and without knowing my child.

Now, my little boy is two-and-a-half years, full of life and energy, and growing up fast, and I can see myself in him. He definitely has my attitude and determination that I hope will continue into his adult life. I have always been determined that he will never be my carer as I'm his mummy and he is my son.

References

Skitteral, J. (2013). Transitions? An Invitation to Think Outside Y/our Problem Box, Get Fire in Your Belly and Put Pebbles in the Pond. In T. Curran & K. Runswick-Cole (Eds.), *Disabled Children's Childhood Studies: Critical Approaches in a Global Context* (pp. 22–29). Basingstoke: Palgrave Macmillan.

Jo Skitteral has worked in social care settings with disabled children and young adults since 1992 and is qualified as a social worker. Jo is passionate about equality and diversity and has led in learning and development in voluntary sector organisations.

Going 'Off Grid': A Mother's Account of Refusing Disability

Kim Davies

Points of Interest

- A mother's account of negotiating identity possibilities for her son by refusing 'disability'.
- An account of how refusing 'inclusive' schooling and psychiatric intervention also amounted to refusing disability.
- Theorisation about how refusing disability links to emerging forms of human possibilities.
- Provides an example of how unbecoming 'disabled' enabled resurgent health and wellbeing.

Introduction

This is an account of a mother's efforts to refuse 'disability' for her son. As an aestheticized accounting of person-in-relational experiences and as an attempt to tell the sociocultural stories involved in the reproduction of 'disability', I have deliberately used depersonalised terms like 'mother' and 'mother's son' to disorient the reader and shift their gaze away from any anticipated individualised disability narrative even though I draw on family experiences to construct this historically accurate account of becoming 'disabled'. In this

K. Davies (✉)
School of Education, Deakin University, Burwood, VIC, Australia

© The Author(s) 2018
K. Runswick-Cole et al. (eds.), *The Palgrave Handbook of Disabled Children's Childhood Studies*, https://doi.org/10.1057/978-1-137-54446-9_7

account, I work to re-present 'disability' as a sociocultural category materialised through intersubjective encounters, and my writing, including my choice of nominals, is a continuation of this larger project of refusing disability. Part of the refusal of disability is my refusal in this account to use the names of the particular individuals involved, although I can assure the reader that this account was written with the informed consent and active involvement of those involved.

Specifically, this account reproduces a letter the mother wrote to her family doctor trying to explain her reasons for not following through on the doctor's recommendation to arrange an appointment for her son with a psychiatrist. The mother's efforts to refuse disability are contextualised historically in terms of the family's engagement with disabling discourses as well as theoretically in terms of an attempt to refuse disability along the lines of the anti-social 'radical passivity' demonstrated by queer activists like Jamaica Kincaid (Halberstam 1998). This chapter recounts a mother's act of unbecoming, as she struggles to renegotiate the grounds of her son's healthcare outside of an ableist disabling paradigm whilst also seeking to secure a way for him (and her) to count outside of 'disability'.

Explaining the Metaphor

Where I come from, going 'off grid' is a colloquialism referring to disconnecting your domestic residence (your 'home') from mainstream, commercial electricity suppliers. The power lost through this disconnection is usually replaced by alternatively sourced electricity, typically solar or wind power generators, located at the point of domestic need. Sometimes the alternative power generated is surplus to needs and can be fed back into the *mainstream* grid, generating an unexpected, bonus income. In the context of this article, going 'off-grid' refers to this mother's attempts to position her son outside of disabling ableist discourses and generate alternative, safer sources of power and subjectivities closer to home.

History, Briefly: Becoming 'Disabled'

The mother's son was born in 1993, amidst the autism 'epidemic' that swept the global north for the following couple of decades. His geopolitical location—his mother was a well-paid, educated professional living in Australia—and gender —he was identified as male—placed him precariously in relation to the crisis of 'bad boy's behaviour' that popular media reported was affecting our schools in alarming proportions (Harwood 2006). Despite the dangerous discourses afoot, the child met the 'normal' developmental milestones and successfully attended several different childcare facilities, avoiding any labels of deviance or disability. It was only when he attended preschool, in preparation for his first year of mainstream school, that his preschool teacher initiated his entry into 'abnormality' by describing his social behaviour as problematic and citing his resemblance to another boy in her care the previous year who, captured within and framed through her (neuro)developmental gaze, had subsequently been diagnosed with Asperger's Syndrome.

This teacher's intervention instigated a diagnosis of Asperger's Syndrome for this mother's son as well, and there followed a decade of unsatisfying and unremitting negotiations with educational authorities to have her son 'included' in mainstream school without trading off or sacrificing his academic development and/or wellbeing.

Her efforts were marginally successful at best and 'good days' at school, from either her son's or his teacher's perspectives, were increasingly infrequent. His elementary education, especially after he left the play-based, self-directed pedagogies of early childhood behind, was very patchy, with him spending so much time away from school that he was eventually enrolled in 'school' via distance education.

He returned briefly to elementary school in an attempt to negotiate his re-entry to mainstream high school. This proved equally fraught and ultimately unsuccessful, and following an incident where the mother witnessed the high school principal disciplining (via lunchtime detention) a group of students for failing to wear 'the correct' (i.e. mandated) sort of uniform socks, she un-enrolled her son from mainstream school for the final time. Strangely, it was this witnessing of disciplinary power, not the decades-long experience of it trying to reconcile her 'normal' out-of-school child with her son—who-has-Asperger's-Syndrome-at-school child—that finally enabled her to realise just how ludicrous and dangerous a place 'school' can be.

By the time he left mainstream school for the last time, the mother's son was anxious and depressed and keen to leave the frustrations and injustices and 'madness' of school behind. He reports that his abiding memories of school are of enjoying the company of his friends but of being misunderstood by his teachers and policed by his teacher aides. He subsequently re-enrolled in secondary school, again via distance education, and now has a flexible relationship with his previous diagnosis of Asperger's Syndrome, occasionally identifying with it retrospectively to offer support to friends but usually preferring to identify himself in other ways, for example, as a gamer. The availability of alternative subjectivities and his removal from the disablement effected by deficit discourses and school practices of 'inclusion' have enabled a strong sense of self and wellbeing. Tensions remain, however, in relationship to 'schools', 'schooling' and 'teachers', and he is sometimes still angry and upset when recalling and recounting these experiences. Thankfully, his different beyond-school subjectifications now locate these strong emotions outside of schooling's pathologising frames and, as a consequence, he is more frequently positioned to be a fully feeling person—justifiably 'angry' and simultaneously 'human'. His mother also feels angry and upset when recalling these experiences of 'inclusion', although she additionally feels guilty and ashamed for her complicity in the processes that made her son so vulnerable to unhappiness and ill health.

From the mother's perspective, 'Asperger's Syndrome' was a double-edged sword, appearing to promise some sort of protection and/or access to special services that never actually eventuated. It seemed to be what was expected of her, the required way for her to demonstrate that she was a 'good mother' to her 'disabled' son. On reflection, it was the diagnosis of disability itself that was disabling, since it set into motion the misrecognition of her son and his abilities exclusively through the lens of Asperger's Syndrome and necessitated, from the system's perspective, the provision of his 'special learning needs' as a student diagnosed with an autism spectrum disorder. This service, described as 'inclusion', amounted to his literal (i.e. removal to a special education unit) or metaphorical (placement at an individual desk on the periphery of the classroom space) separation from his peers and his unequal access to a quality academic curriculum. After his preschool diagnosis, her son ceased to exist as a human being, becoming instead an instance of a category of convenience for convenience schooling. The mother regrets that it took her so long to 'see' and respond to the damages done to her son by disabling discourses, especially those taken up in 'inclusive' school contexts. She failed for too long to clearly count the costs of having her son counted as disabled.

Refusing Disability, Theoretically

Following Titchkosky (2012), this chapter represents this mother's account as an account of refusing disability by centring disability in its location in culture (Bhabha 1994). Through her account, the mother realises the pedagogic possibilities of her son's 'disability', in the end, refusing the disablement of 'disability' in order to try to secure for her son more sustaining sorts of subjectivities beyond 'disability' and 'inclusion'. Through her account, the mother comes to realise that her son was disabled by 'disability' itself and that whatever what problematic did not inhere in him as an individual but rather in the 'between-ness' (Titchkosky 2012, p. 84) of the relations involved in the sociocultural politics of schooling and the deficit discourses of difference that are taken up there through mandated policies like 'inclusion'. Interpreted in this way, the mother's account of her son's experiences of *being schooled in being disabled* recounts 'the social accomplishment of difference' (Titchkosky 2012, p. 89). Using Ahmed's (2006) metaphor of the table to describe how we organise and orient to the spaces of apprehension between us, Titchkosky (2012) writes:

> If we think nothing of what lies between our actual encounters with others, we might not come to know about the actual work we are involved in, work that makes up the meaning of people. True enough, as the saying goes, 'stuff hap-pens'…because of the particular tables we find between us, and how we orient ourselves to this in-between *makes the difference*. (p. 89 italics in original)

By finally removing her son from mainstream school where he was required to be disabled by Asperger's Syndrome and reorienting him through discur-sively reconfigured spaces, she both refused disability, got off the ableist dis-ability grid and put new, more sustaining tables between herself, her son and others, furniture that has allowed different subjectivities for them both, self-affirming and life enhancing.

> The meaning of bodies, minds and senses are formed from our relations – from the in-betweens of histories, politics and cultures through which and against which we perceive each other…What lies between us are the grounds that orga-nise our perceptions of self and other…Attending to what lies between the per-ception of human limits and possibilities, such as oppressive power relations, allows us to learn about the social character of perception instead of re-enacting the ground of perception as if it is natural or unquestionably good. (Titchkosky 2012, p. 91)

According to the mother's account, despite her regrets about how long it took her to attend to what lay between herself, her son and their school, she finally realised that getting off the disabling ableist grid was possible by turn-ing the tables on schooling. As she recounts it, eventually she did learn that 'evaluations of bodies are places to reconsider how we make up the meaning of human limits and possibilities' (Titchkosky 2012, p. 92). The change she made to her son's education by refusing the disablement of mainstream 'inclusion' opened new subjective possibilities and allowed a return to health and wellbeing for both herself and her son.

Queer-ying Becoming

I also represent this account as a refusal of becoming (disabled), along the lines of the radical passivity that Halberstam (1998) cites in her critique of the anti-social turn in queer studies. Halberstam (1998) describes radical passivity as an act of unbecoming, signalling 'the refusal to quite simply be' (p. 150) as 'a way to witness the willingness of the subject to actually come undone, to dramatise unbecoming for the other so that the viewer does not have to witness unbecoming as a function of her own body' (p. 151). The vicarious other effects of this mother's account of unbecoming by refusing disability are yet to be played out. What, if anything, will feed back into the mainstream ableist grid, remains uncertain. What follows now, however, is a subsequent and recent effort to turn the tables again and renovate the space between herself and her family doctor by refusing to follow through on this doctor's recommendation to make an appointment for her son with a psychiatrist.

Refusing Disability, Practically: The Letter

Dear Doctor,

I am writing to you to explain why I have chosen not to follow through on your recommendation and make an appointment for XXXX to see a psychiatrist.

As you are aware, XXXX was diagnosed in preschool with an autism spectrum disorder and struggled with both anxiety and depression throughout his time in mainstream school. He was happiest and healthiest away from this school environment and since leaving school has regained his sense of self and his health and wellbeing. After many years, he now knows himself to be a good and capable person, with strengths and weaknesses and much to offer his friends and family.

I know that you are well intentioned and act in what you believe to be XXXX's best interests, but I don't think that you understand what it is that disables XXXX. Within our family and our various communities, XXXX thrives and currently he is both happy and healthy. You seem to think though that because he is neither employed for money nor on some form of income support, that his life is restricted and that he is disabled. I disagree.

XXXX is young and still working out for himself how he wants to live his life. I intend to support him as he works through his options and considers various possibilities. I honestly do not believe he is either unwell or disabled as he currently lives his life. Engagement with psychiatry is therefore unnecessary. I am not prepared to risk his wellbeing by re-engaging with a system that has failed us and harmed him in the past.

I thank you again and hope that you will understand my rationale.

I ask that you place this letter on file so that it is included with his medical history.

Yours sincerely,

XXXX's mother*

Concluding: Refusing Disability and Turning Tables?

In turning the tables by not arranging the psychiatric appointment recommended for her son by the family doctor, this mother is refusing (again) to have her son counted as 'disabled'. Her account draws attention to the places in culture where her son is and isn't disabled. Whether the family doctor attends to this act of unbecoming, by witnessing it as a performance of pedagogic possibilities, remains to be seen. The risk is that by turning the tables and reconfiguring the space between herself, her son and her doctor, she may make herself, as mother, vulnerable to other sorts of disciplinary interventions. But these are the risks of trying to count as human beyond the ableist grid. Unbecoming may be tolerated under certain circumstances, like in this instance of an affluent mother prepared to shelter and protect her son's becomings within the affordances of her own privilege. But what of people less capitalised who wish to count as human? How can we count their human becomings beyond the ableist grid?

Afterword: Problematising (Even More) the Ethics of Researching 'Disability'

Researching disability is a subjectifying process. Typically, depending upon one's identifications, for example, one is seen to be 'disabled' or 'non-disabled', with epistemic privilege and ontological validity afforded to standpoint and first-person perspectives of 'disability'. There are problems that attend to such either/or positions and complications knotted through the politics and discursive mediation of experience-based standpoints. I have no answers to these intracabilities but instead wish to respond to and begin a conversation about an ethics of researching and writing *in-between* 'dis/ability' locations, or, rather, the locations and encounters where 'dis/ability' is made and experienced, of working through person-in-culture frames to draw out some of the accountabilities for disablement. This is part of my efforts to understand disability as a dialogical experience, as an intersubjective process of relational un/becomings, within specific, historicised sociocultural contexts and in defiance of the individuated diagnosis of pathology that constitutes neo-liberalised versions of 'inclusive schooling'.

In my chapter, I have tried to account for what happened in-between 'the school', 'the teacher', 'the doctor', and 'my son' and 'my-self-as-mother' and

how, at the times and in the places when and where 'it' happened, 'it'—
disablement—was actually understood as 'inclusion'. To do this, I have drawn
upon my own recollections as well as my son's recounts of these events but,
strangely, and contradictorily and most emphatically, I am not validating or
legitimising my arguments through a personal frame and/or because I shared
these experiences. I seek no special authority as 'mother' or 'mother of son
diagnosed with Asperger's Syndrome' but rather wish to posit a different
accounting of disability as something that was socially produced and discursively materialised as 'my son' and 'I' were hailed as 'disabled' and 'mother-of-
disabled' and so constituted through our encounters with mainstream
schooling throughout the 1990s and early 2000s in the state of Queensland,
Australia. While I have sought to spotlight these encounters in-between 'ability' and 'disability' by drawing upon and re/accounting for my son's experiences, I am trying to tell a cultural-in-personal story so that some of the
sociocultural and relational machinery that creates the experience of 'disability' can be heard, smelt, felt and seen; so that, as Titchkosky (2012) suggests,
the tables between us can be discursively re-materialised (Butler 2004), even
if it is just so that we can turn them over and/or dismantle them. This seems
an important and difficult project to me, although it may be self-evident to
you. I don't know. What I am beginning to realise, however, is that it is seemingly impossible to write of and research 'disability' without being subjectiv-
ised by it. This may be because our ethical frameworks are tied to notions of
individual persons—that we can only understand people and make them
intelligible as individuals with experience as a privatised event for which we
are personally responsibilised, and that disability politics still connects so
strongly with impairment categories and *self*-advocacy in the face of *social*
injustices. My chapter is a fraught exercise in going 'off-grid', of considering
some of what is possible when the usual tables are turned. It represents an
attempt to tell the sociocultural stories that narrate personal accounts and to
acknowledge how seemingly impossible but necessary this work is. What are
an ethics of the in-between and how can we constitute and conduct ourselves
ethically there without reinscribing and reproducing 'disability'?

References

Ahmed, S. (2006). *Queer Phenomenology: Orientations, Objects, Others*. Durham:
    Duke University Press.
Bhabha, H. K. (1994). *The Location of Culture*. New York: Routledge.
Butler, J. (2004). *Undoing Gender*. New York: Routledge.

Halberstam, J. (1998). The Anti-social Turn in Queer Studies. *GJSS Graduate Journal of Social Science, 5*(2), 140–156.

Harwood, V. (2006). *Diagnosing 'Disorderly' Children: A Critique of Behaviour Disorder Discourses*. London: Routledge.

Titchkosky, T. (2012). The Ends of the Body as Pedagogic Possibility. *The Review of Education, Pedagogy and Cultural Studies, 34*(3–4), 82–93.

Kim Davies is concerned with the sociocultural politics of schooling. Her teaching and research focus on critical engagement with theories and practices of 'difference', 'diversity', 'disability' and 'inclusion', and their implications for educational policies and teaching practices. She works at Deakin University as a Lecturer in Education (Special Education).

Part II

Research Studies: the lives of disabled children across the globe

This section is split into two parts: first, research with disabled children and young people, and second, research with disabled children, their families and allies.

Research Involving Disabled Children and Young People

In this section, the authors reflect on their experiences of involving disabled children and young people in research in different local and global contexts. The authors reflect on the challenges of engaging disabled children and young people in research, as well as the opportunities for creative disruption that these encounters provoke in terms of research methods, ethics and analysis. In exploring and problematising everyday practices, the contributors encourage the reader to imagine things otherwise for disabled children and young people.

In the chapter "The Social Relational Model of Deaf Childhood in Action", **Kristin Snodden and Kathryn Underwood** discuss early childhood education and inclusion discourses as they pertain to deaf childhoods and deaf culture. Using the social relational model of deaf childhood (Snoddon and Underwood 2014), the chapter explores the inherent connections between inclusive education practice, early childhood education and care, as well as how inclusion principles may be better applied in the case of deaf children. Snodden's (2015) research on developing an intensive American Sign Language (ASL) curriculum for parents of young deaf children is discussed as a means through which a social relational model of deaf childhood can be put into action, with a view to extending the capabilities of parents and, by extension, their children. Access to sign language instruction for deaf children, as well as for their families and members of their extended communities, is central to an inclusion strategy. On the other hand, separate deaf schools and spaces are critical as sites for active cultural participation and production. These sites provide the cultural structure that informs deaf education for all children who are part of the deaf community.

Dawn Pickering shares accounts of disabled young people in her research about their experiences of recreational activities and explains her research methods designed to facilitate their voice in the chapter "'The Embodiment of Disabled Children and Young People's Voices About Participating in Recreational Activities': Shared Perspectives". Dawn identifies limitations of the dominant medical definition of health found in physiotherapy in terms of lack of outcomes evidence. It follows that the basis of judgements regarding the child's best interests, benefits and harm is contested. Dawn promotes the more holistic concept of wellbeing that includes the participation and enjoyment identified by disabled children. The stories illustrate that when activities are made accessible, adults' expectations are challenged. Young people also see themselves differently to the labels they were given or that they imposed upon themselves, making wellbeing much more than the measurement of physical function.

In the chapter "Making Space for the Embodied Participation of Young Disabled Children in a Children's Centre in England", **Heloise Maconochie** focuses on the embodied participation of disabled young people in the context of early years provision in England. Heloise questions traditional ideas of democracy that seem to valorize neutral, rational, verbal forms of participation. Drawing on the stories of three young children, Heloise seeks to foreground the young children's multi-modal communicative practices to make space for more inclusive forms of participation and understandings of the voice of the child.

Karen Watson focuses on the 'inclusion' of children with medical and/or psychological diagnosis in 'mainstream' early education in New South Wales, Australia, in the chapter "Interrogating the 'Normal' in the 'Inclusive' Early Childhood Classroom: Silence, Taboo and the 'Elephant in the Room'". Presenting the data from an ethnographic study in three early years classrooms, Karen draws on a post-structural framework to make visible the ways in which the children themselves produce and maintain the category of 'normal' in the classroom. For Karen, the 'elephant in the room' is the awkward silence that emerges as a result of the struggle for social order and the 'normal' in the classroom. Her aim is to problematise everyday practices and under-standings in order to imagine things 'otherwise' in the context of early years education.

In the chapter "The Kids Are Alright: They Have Been Included for Years", **Ben Whitburn** takes us to Spain to examine issues of voice and qualitative interviewing in disabled children's childhood studies. He explores the limi-tations of incitements to 'voice' in the lives of disabled children and young people. He explores 'silences in interviews' and how these might be under-stood in terms of circulating power relations in schools and within interviews themselves.

Debby Watson, Alison Jones and Helen Potter jointly author the chapter "Expressive Eyebrows and Beautiful Bubbles: Playfulness and Children with Profound Impairments" exploring playfulness in the lives of children with profound impairments. As researcher, mother and family support worker, respectively, the authors bring together their individual perspectives on play in the life of Thomas, a young child with complex impairments. The chapter concludes by arguing that levels of playfulness were not determined by levels of impairment but by focussed, sensitive support by those around them who value play in all children's lives.

In the chapter "My Friends and Me: Friendship and Identity Following Acquired Brain Injury in Young People", **Sandra Dowling, Roy McConkey and Marlene Sinclair** explore the identity work that young people have to engage in following an acquired brain injury (ABI). The study was based in Northern Ireland, and uses qualitative approaches working with nine young people who created 'narrative collages' to represent their experiences of friend-ship following injury. The young people's accounts reveal the importance of friendship in the teenage years and the crucial role it plays in identity re/construction.

In the chapter "Thinking and Doing Consent and Advocacy in Disabled Children's Childhood Studies Research", **Jill C. Smith** explores the ethics and politics of disabled children's childhood studies, a body of research which, she argues, requires specific ethical considerations in design, methodology, proce-dure and, perhaps most significantly, everyday practice. Jill uses the chapter to think through the thinking *and* doing of disabled children's childhood studies research. She highlights the ethical issues inherent in research, particularly in relation to advocacy and consent, which she maintains are necessary in devel-oping, delivering and writing an ethical project.

The Social Relational Model of Deaf Childhood in Action

Kristin Snoddon and Kathryn Underwood

Key Point Summary

- Early childhood education and care discourse on inclusion and 'supports' presents parents of young deaf children with false options regarding language learning that are not in the best interests of deaf children.
- The authors argue that the social relational model of deaf childhood can account for differences in children and their communities.
- The first author's research, presented here, describes the process of developing an intensive American Sign Language (ASL) curriculum for parents of young deaf children. This curriculum is aligned with the *Common European Framework of Reference for Languages* (CEFR; Snoddon 2015).
- The research shows how the social relational model can be put into action for the parents of different deaf children.

K. Snoddon
School of Linguistics and Language Studies, Carleton University,
Ottawa, ON, Canada

K. Underwood (✉)
School of Early Childhood Studies, Ryerson University,
Toronto, ON, Canada

© The Author(s) 2018
K. Runswick-Cole et al. (eds.), *The Palgrave Handbook of Disabled Children's Childhood Studies*, https://doi.org/10.1057/978-1-137-54446-9_8

Background

In the current context of universal neonatal hearing screening and follow-up early intervention services, parents of deaf children frequently face competing discourses surrounding signed and spoken languages, and what it means to be deaf. Both deaf studies scholars and disability studies scholars have cited the hegemonic medical/pathological identities that have been imposed on children and have offered counter-narratives that for deaf studies position culture, language, and ethnicity as central to deaf identity (e.g., Ladd 2007; Lane 2005). However, medical discourses continue to dominate deaf childhoods. In Ontario, Canada, the Ontario Infant Hearing Program has frequently not supported access to American Sign Language (ASL) services for families of children with cochlear implants (Snoddon 2008). This is due to the philosophy of auditory-verbal therapy practitioners, who have often placed operational policy restrictions on deaf children's access to learning sign language (Snoddon 2008). As in other countries that have established universal neonatal hearing screening programs, a large proportion of young Ontario deaf children and their families do not access sign language programs or services (Komesaroff 2008; Small and Cripps 2011).

As outlined in this chapter, the social relational model of deaf childhood is suggested as a guiding framework for professionals and educators working with deaf children, as well as for parents and caregivers of deaf children. The social relational model attempts to account for the complexities and diversities inherent in the lives of deaf children who, alongside their parents and family members, negotiate their emergent plurilingual identities in the face of competing discourses surrounding language and inclusion. The term *plurilingualism* signifies multilingualism at the level of the individual and recognizes the different purposes, domains, and types of competence that the individual social actor may have in their use of two or more languages (Coste et al. 2009). Plurilingualism is fundamental to the Common European Framework for Reference for Languages (CEFR), which is based in conceptions of the second-language learner as a social agent who develops general and particular communicative competences while achieving everyday goals (Council of Europe 2001). As we have argued elsewhere, owing to its focus on dynamic individual capabilities, plurilingualism thus bears special relation to the social relational model of deaf childhood (Snoddon and Underwood 2014).

The next sections of this chapter discuss how our thinking has progressed in relation to disability, inclusion, and deaf culture discourses. The social relational model is then discussed in further depth with reference to the first author's study of developing a parent ASL curriculum aligned with the CEFR. In this way, this chapter illustrates the social relational model of deaf childhood in action.

Medical Models and Social Models, and Deaf Childhoods

Disability studies as a theoretical field has been interested in disrupting medical discourses that categorize individuals as being other than normal. Disability studies instead present the argument that 'we are not disabled by our impairments, but by the disabling barriers we face in society' (Oliver 2013, p. 1024). The social model of disability was first introduced in the 1970s and has undergone intense debate and maturation as a theory, which 'became the vehicle for developing a collective disability consciousness and helped to develop and strengthen the disabled peoples' movement' (Oliver 2013, p. 1024).

The social model and the subsequent field of disability studies have been closely aligned with the political movement for inclusive education. Inclusive education, as a political and social movement, has also undergone intense scrutiny and has developed from the early demands for placement of children with disabilities in classrooms that were designed for children who did not have disability labels, to a more complex understanding of how the institutions of education construct disability in order to exclude (Underwood 2008). The language that marks early discourses of inclusion points to its problems: for example, inclusion that is defined as placement in a 'regular' class, or with 'typically developing' peers, as was often cited in early definitions, continues to reinforce the idea of normalcy (Slee 2011). In his defense of the theory that he helped to author, Mike Oliver notes that while the social model was instrumental in collective social action, since that time, 'the hegemony of special education has barely been challenged in schools' (Oliver 2013, p.1024).

The deaf community has long resisted its labeling and positioning as a community of disabled people due in good part to the impact of the inclusion movement in terms of closing and/or limiting access to schools for deaf children (Carbin 1996; Siegel 2000), which are sites of linguistic and cultural transmission (Hoffmeister 2008). Rather than bringing about systemic changes in deaf education to ensure that access to sign language is provided from early childhood, as advocated by deaf communities and researchers (e.g., Humphries et al. 2012; Snoddon 2008), inclusion has often worked to limit deaf children's contact with other deaf adults and children, and has often failed to provide adequate practical or policy support for sign language learning (Snoddon 2009). The World Federation of the Deaf (n.d.) writes:

> Sign language should be recognized as the first language of a deaf child. The sign language used with the child must be the national sign language, i. e. the language of the adult Deaf community of that specific country. It is important that deaf children have early exposure to sign language and have the right to be educated as bilinguals or multilinguals regarding reading and writing because sign language is the only language that a deaf child can acquire without someone specifically teaching it.

The inclusion movement and the disability movement overall have often failed to recognize the distinct linguistic and cultural identity of the deaf community (Kauppinen and Jokinen 2014). Moreover, the social model has overlooked how the deaf community's cultural-ethnic identity (Valente 2011, p. 647) can lead to a focus on collective goals that are more properly seen as the domain of language planning than accessibility accommodations.

The Social Model Under Scrutiny

Other criticism of the social model has included concerns that it does not acknowledge the personal experience of disability, that is, one's relationship to self, which positions social and systemic relations as more relevant than personal experience (Morris 1992; Oliver 2013; Tregaskis 2002). Terzi (2004) argues that the social model limits its own achievement by presenting a partial and somewhat flawed understanding of the relation between impairment, disability, and society, since the social model 'conceptualizes disability as unilaterally socially caused' (p. 141). Terzi outlines three main limitations of the social model: (1) over-socialization of aspects of impairment and disability, (2) failure to notice effects of impairment, and (3) rejection of 'normality' (the sense of average human functioning). However, she argues that the social model's simplistic views on disability and the oppressive nature of certain social arrangements are the powerful core value of the model. For example, the dominant culture's focus on deaf identity as impairment has caused disability to be constructed for deaf children in myriad ways. Because a majority of deaf children are denied access to sign language, they run a significant risk of linguistic deprivation and subsequent cognitive, social, and psychological effects (Humphries et al. 2012). In other words, the disabling conditions produced by society can in turn produce a real experience of impairment or restriction of capabilities in deaf children that will affect their individual educational and social relationships.

The social model has also been critiqued for not acknowledging the difference among those who are labeled as disabled. Kliewer et al. (2006) map the historical roots of identifying poor, racialized communities as being impaired and applying this thinking to the work of segregating and reforming children. This understanding of the roots of special education, and the history of inclusion discourse, has contributed to a more mature inclusion discourse, which calls for an overhaul of education systems as a whole in order to ensure that the diversity among learners is fostered, acknowledged, and celebrated (Slee 2013). The new inclusion discourse asks for comparable expectations for learning for all students (Kliewer et al. 2006) and challenges a binary discourse, where a separate system is organized for children deemed disabled (Ferri and Bacon 2011). It is this last argument that has itself been challenged directly by the deaf community owing to the closure of deaf schools in the guise of implementing an inclusion agenda. As Kauppinen and Jokinen (2014) argue, 'education of the deaf is not special education but education in one's own language and culture' (p. 136).

The World Federation of the Deaf (2015) advocates for a renewed understanding of inclusion where 'Bilingual education is not seen as special education but as a form of education within the inclusive education system' (p. 3). This understanding of inclusive education for deaf children entails recognition of the limitations of accommodations such as sign language interpreters in the general education system (Kauppinen and Jokinen 2014). Not only does reliance on interpreters limit deaf children's participation and accessibility in educational situations (Kauppinen and Jokinen 2014) but also a mediated education via interpreters can compromise deaf students' access to the curriculum and thus to a quality education (Russell and McLeod 2009). For full inclusion to take place, accommodations, such as interpreters and notetakers, must be accompanied by opportunities to study with other deaf students and with teachers who are themselves fluent in sign language, by the provision of bilingual learning materials and by opportunities to study sign language as a school subject (Kauppinen and Jokinen 2014).

Disability Culture, Deaf Culture, and Inclusion

Hall (2002) details the 'core values' and characteristics of a disability culture and notes its importance in providing a place of belonging and representation of individual and collective identity. Hall (2002), like deaf studies scholars, believes that the inclusion movement has neglected the identity development of individual children, particularly in the context of school. Disability culture is not shared with other groups, and children recognize 'corporeal and psychological distinctness' from their nurturers (Gilson et al. 1997; cited in Hall 2002, p. 145). For this reason, Hall (2002) claims that special education classes have been the site of important opportunities to interact with other children with disabilities but notes that this has been limited in current placements. Because inclusion impacts the social relationships of individuals and their relationship to their society, Hall (2002) argues inclusion can be analyzed in a policy framework; inclusion can and has led to a sense of alienation among children with disabilities.

Deaf cultures are defined by sign languages and deaf spaces, which have supported the social, political, and representative components of a fully realized cultural group. Barnartt (1996) has argued that the disability movement is more likely a collective consciousness than a culture; however, more recent cultural production from disability communities has been a global trend. These unique cultural groups (which are themselves pluralistic) are quite distinct; however, politically, these movements have some alignment. The inclusion movement is based in a rights discourse that promotes the right of all children to high-quality education, which promotes full participation in society as a whole, as well as in one's own cultural communities.

Placements that focus only on physically keeping all students in regular classrooms do not meet the criteria of inclusion for any student, including deaf students. Inclusion is the right to participate in all public institutions, including schools, and to reach one's potential within those settings. Deaf schools and their surrounding communities of sign language users support bilingual and bicultural education and identities, and they are therefore important sites of cultural production for deaf communities. Deaf children who are educated in mainstream settings should likewise have the right to sign language instruction and opportunities to learn with other deaf children and adults, in addition to accommodations such as interpreters and notetakers. Ideally, deaf schools can function as a resource to support inclusion in other schools with deaf students.

Deaf studies provide a useful lens for understanding the shortcomings of both early childhood special education models and the discourse of inclusive education (Brennan 2003). A fundamental tension is evident in the struggle for children (and as the primary actors, their parents) to gain access to education and early intervention services (Underwood et al. 2012; Reindal 2008) as human rights under the United Nations Convention on the Rights of the Child and Convention on the Rights of Persons With Disabilities. Theories of inclusive education, originally focused on access to universal programs, have been informed by disability theory and now recognize the shortcomings of approaches that define inclusion in ways that do not recognize the cultural production of disability (Ferri and Bacon 2011).

However, there are limitations in comparing disability theory and deaf studies. With its linguistic and historical base as a cultural group, deaf communities as cultural entities are not analogous to disability communities, nor are the 'deeper needs' (Ladd 2003, p. 15) of deaf communities met by a disability model alone. As Ladd (2003) writes, a more comprehensive model 'requires that Deaf communities are seen as intrinsic "dual-category members"—that is, that some of their issues might relate to issues of non-hearing, whilst others relate to language and culture' (p. 16). In seeking to bridge this divide, the United Nations Convention on the Rights of Persons with Disabilities calls on state parties to recognize and promote sign languages (Article 21), facilitate learning of sign language by deaf students and promote the linguistic identity of the deaf community in the education system (Article 24). The World Federation of the Deaf took a leading role in drafting the Committee on the Rights of Persons with Disabilities (CRPD) and in seeking the 'right to be different' as fundamental principle (Kauppinen and Jokinen 2014). This is seen in Article 3(d), which recognizes 'Respect for difference and acceptance of persons with disabilities as part of human diversity and humanity' as a general principle of the Convention.

Superdiversity and the Deaf Community

Superdiversity is a term coined by Vertovec (2007) to recognize the 'diversification of diversity' in present-day societies, where focus on single aspects of identity such as ethnicity proves to be a 'one-dimensional' approach (p. 1025). Superdiversity instead captures the interplay of variables 'such as country of origin, ethnicity, language, immigration status (and its concomitant rights, benefits and restrictions), age, gender, education, occupation and locality' (Vertovec 2007, p. 1044). Just as deaf communities present an important facet of difference within the disability community, there is broad diversity within deaf communities themselves. The diversity among deaf children, as observed by Snoddon and Underwood (2014), is an important underpinning of the social relational model of deaf childhood. This diversity encompasses not only etiology and types of hearing loss and other disabilities but also the broad range of variables outlined by Vertovec (2007).

At the same time, the enjoyment of other human rights and achievement of capabilities hinge on a fully accessible first language and culture for deaf children (Kauppinen and Jokinen 2014). With the advent of universal infant hearing screening programs that has been accompanied by a rapid increase in referrals to cochlear implant clinics (Komesaroff 2007), and with the overwhelming numbers of individual deaf children attending local schools where sign language is generally not in use (Small and Cripps 2011), this ability to access sign language within the deaf community appears increasingly constrained. Yet the available evidence suggests that most deaf individuals will eventually come to adopt sign language as a primary language (Akamatsu et al. 2000; Karchmer and Mitchell 2003; Piñar et al. 2011) and come to join the deaf community as 'active participants' (Ladd 2003, p. 16). This evidence is strengthened by data from the first author's study that show parents of deaf children with cochlear implants actively seeking opportunities for improved communication via sign language (Snoddon 2015). It is, therefore, critical to ensure access to sign language and deaf culture in the early intervention and education systems as a whole.

The Social Relational Model of Deaf Childhood

As it is framed by this chapter, the social relational model of deaf childhood has the capacity to shed unique insight into the situation of deaf children and their parents in an early intervention context. This is so because in addition to the collectivist cultural—linguistic and social—political aspects of deaf identity, the individual effects of disabling pedagogy (Komesaroff 2008) are acknowledged. A capability approach that is at the heart of the social relational model seeks to support deaf children's freedom to achieve their full potential as contributing members of deaf and hearing communities (Sen 1999; Snoddon and Underwood 2014). The social relational model of deaf childhood also acknowledges individual diversity and, in Ladd's (2003, p. 3) words, 'reflects different interpretations of Deafhood, of what being a Deaf person in a Deaf community might mean.'

Previous work identified the ASL learning needs of hearing parents of deaf children as a central focus for supporting deaf children's capabilities (Snoddon 2012; Snoddon 2014; Snoddon and Underwood 2014). Yet there has been a lack of formal ASL curricula and learning initiatives for this group of learners, who have unique learning needs with regard to developing ASL communicative competences while achieving everyday goals (Snoddon 2015). The present study's aim of developing a CEFR-aligned parent ASL curriculum has both theoretical and practical underpinnings in terms of supporting inclusion for deaf children. Parents of deaf children, rather than children themselves, are participants in the curriculum project. This is so because inclusion is 'not…something that we do to a discrete population of children, but rather…something we must do to ourselves' (Allan 2005, p. 293). Along with parents, this work is led by deaf community members as teachers and researchers. As Allan (2005) writes, '[t]he success of the ethical project of inclusion will depend on how far all of the people involved allow themselves to hope, accept their responsibilities, and are prepared to do the necessary work, which starts, of course, with oneself' (p. 293).

The Study Design and Rationale

The first author's two-year study uses an action research design (Kemmis 2001; Heron and Reason 2001) to qualitatively and collaboratively document steps leading up to the development and field-testing of a pilot parent ASL curriculum and assess the impact of this curriculum on parents' ASL learning, using CEFR proficiency descriptors (Snoddon 2015). Observational data was collected via field notes and video recording from two one-week curriculum development workshops taking place between August 2014 and May 2015, and a 14-week parent course during fall 2014/winter 2015 that met for 2.5 hours each session. This data was supplemented by a document review of the teaching materials developed in the form of teacher and student guides, video clips to support parent learning and retention of vocabulary taught during class, and videotaped assessments of parent learning progress at the end of the first course.

The CEFR descriptors are a series of 'can do' statements scaled to levels A1-C2, which involve six levels to describe learners' language proficiency from basic user (A1-A2) to independent user (B1-B2) to proficient user (C1-C2) (Council of Europe 2001). The 'can do' statements are presented across a grid of understanding, production, and interaction (Council of Europe 2001). In the case of sign languages, understanding activities consist of real-life and pre-recorded receptive sign language exercises (Leeson and Byrne-Dunne 2009). To date, work taking place in Toronto, Canada, in collaboration with Dutch practitioners has focused on developing curriculum materials and teaching one course aligned with A1 (beginner) proficiency descriptors.

The inspiration for using a CEFR design in developing a parent ASL curriculum comes from pioneering work by Oyserman and de Geus (2013, 2015) in developing CEFR-based parent courses for teaching the sign language of the Netherlands, or *Nederlandse Gebarentaal* (NGT). The rationale for using this design rests on several factors. For one, a CEFR approach means that the learning of sign languages has the same gravitas as the learning of spoken languages (Snoddon 2015). This point is important since the CRPD requires countries to establish sign language training on par with spoken language training (Greiner-Ogris and Dotter 2012). Moreover, the CEFR proficiency descriptors provide both parent learners and teachers with clear assessments of learning progress and motivate them to continue. This rigorous approach to teaching sign language to parents of deaf children stands in contrast to existing initiatives, which to date consists mainly of informal teaching and discussion via home visits from deaf consultants or mentors (Snoddon 2008; Watkins et al. 1998; Young 1999). In Foucault's (1998) words, this rigor was needed in order 'to place at the disposal of the work that we do on ourselves the greatest possible share of what is presented to us as inaccessible' (cited in Allan 2005, p. 293).

Participants

Participants in the study included two Dutch practitioners who originally developed CEFR-aligned parent NGT courses and four Canadian ASL instructors. This group participated in the study's first one-week curriculum development workshop in August 2014. Participants in the 14-week ASL course during fall 2014/winter 2015 included 17 parents of deaf children aged from 18 months to 7 years and two ASL instructors from the first workshop. The latter instructors, both deaf adults in their 60s who had attended the same residential school in Ontario, also participated in the second curriculum development workshop in May 2015 along with the Dutch practitioners.

Parent participants were recruited via service agencies and home visiting teachers who shared information about the classes with parents. Parents reported that their children attended both deaf schools and mainstream schools, or that they faced a choice of which type of school their children would attend in the future. While demographic information was not collected directly from the parents, during the study, it was evident that the superdiversity described by Vertovec (2007) was present, as a range of ethnic, cultural, and spoken-language backgrounds were observed among parent participants. The ways in which this superdiversity was taken up by and engaged with during the parent course are described further below.

Inclusion Starts with Oneself

The parent participants all stated that they had been led to our ASL classes because of their deaf children. The need for inclusion at the level of the family was expressed alongside comments about the scarcity of existing resources for parents to learn ASL. One couple, Dolores and Juan, had four other children besides their deaf three-year-old son and were expecting a sixth child. These parents stated an urgent need for their child's siblings to also have opportunities to learn ASL as, for example, a school subject. Although many of the parents reported that their children wore cochlear implants, sign language was seen as needed and beneficial: Dolores stated that ASL was probably going to be her son's primary language, as it was difficult for him to communicate in spoken English. Another couple, Tom and Elizabeth, described their frustration in communicating with their two-year-old deaf son and that sign language helped ease the parents' frustration. Another father, Jian, who came to class on his own, described how he and his wife were unable to communicate with their three-year-old daughter before she wore her cochlear implant. ASL was seen as a needed means to improve communication.

Basim, a mother of a three-year-old son who came to class accompanied by Maliha and Amir, another couple who had an 18-month-old boy, told us on several occasions about her initial resistance to learning sign language. As she stated at the end of our class:

> I came here with no sign; I just knew the sign for 'shoes.' My son is hard of hearing, and I didn't know sign and I didn't want him to sign. I wanted him to talk, not sign. But [my son's teacher] told me, he needs it. So I came to this class, and it was very helpful for me. I understand more about sign now. I watch videos on Youtube with my son, 'ASL Kids.' And we sign to each other a bit, not too much.

Similarly, Maliha reported at the end of the sixth class that her biggest takeaway from the course was learning how to be inclusive with deaf people and how to include her child in dinner table conversations. She cried as she mentioned the two ASL instructors' role-play activity during the fourth class, where they illustrated how deaf children are left out of family conversations when only spoken language is used.

Just as the parent participants came to meet the ethical project of inclusion as learners, the ASL teachers learned to stretch the boundaries of Canadian deaf cultural norms in order to accommodate the diversity among parent participants. This was evident during our fifth class when the parents learned about attention-getting behaviors used by deaf people. It came to light that Amir was not comfortable with tapping Basim's shoulder for attention. At first, one instructor expressed his opinion that deaf cultural norms should prevail over norms from other cultures, and the other instructor added that there should perhaps be a woman-only class for Basim. But there was evidence of reflection and revision on the instructors' part, as when during the seventh class Basim was uncomfortably paired with Michael, the father of a seven-year-old girl, for an ASL rhyme activity involving touching a partner's arm. Observing Basim's discomfort, the first instructor told Mahin, the mother of a five-year-old boy, to switch places with Michael so that she would partner with Basim for this activity. The mothers were then able to practice the ASL rhyme using sign language. There was further evidence of relaxation of norms for ASL classes when the instructors allowed the parent participants to converse with each other using spoken language during breaks. Although it was a desired goal for the ASL classes for parents to practice signing at all times, there was also recognition of parents of deaf children's need to meet with each other and share experiences. Our class further provided this opportunity for inclusion.

Conclusion

In Snoddon and Underwood (2014), we wrote of Sen's view of the capability approach, where individual development is intrinsically linked to larger structures of social justice (Walker 2005). Deaf community leadership of early intervention initiatives supports both the flourishing of individual deaf children and the freedom of the adult deaf community to guide provision of programs and services to deaf children and their parents. The findings from the study described above illustrate how the social relational model of deaf childhood can be put into action, with a view to extending the capabilities of parents, and, by extension, their children. Access to sign language instruction for deaf children, as well as for their families and members of their extended communities, is central to an inclusion strategy. On the other hand, separate deaf schools and spaces are critical as sites for active cultural participation and production. These sites provide the cultural structure that informs deaf education for all children who are part of the deaf community. As we have argued in this chapter, the social relational model of deaf childhood is closely tied to reenvisioning inclusion for deaf children and the radical diversity involved therein; this 'will inevitably remain a work in progress' (Allan 2005, p. 293).

References

Akamatsu, C., Musselman, C., & Zweibel, A. (2000). Nature Versus Nurture in the Development of Cognition in Deaf People. In P. Spencer, C. Erting, & M. Marschark (Eds.), *The Deaf Child in the Family and the School: Essays in Honour of Kathryn P Meadow-Orlans*. Mahwah: Lawrence Erlbaum Associates.

Allan, J. (2005). Inclusion as an Ethical Project. In S. Tremain (Ed.), *Foucault and the Government of Disability*. Ann Arbor: University of Michigan Press.

Barnartt, S. N. (1996). Disability Culture or Disability Consciousness? *Journal of Disability Policy Studies, 7*(2), 1–19.

Brennan, M. (2003). Deafness, Disability and Inclusion: The Gap Between Rhetoric and Practice. *Policy Futures in Education, 1*(4), 668–685.

Carbin, C. (1996). *Deaf Heritage in Canada: A Distinct, Diverse and Enduring Culture*. Toronto: McGraw-Hill Ryerson Ltd.

Coste, D., Moore, D., & Zarate, G. (2009). *Plurilingual and Pluricultural Competence: Studies Towards a Common European Framework of Reference for Language Learning and Teaching*. Strasbourg: Language Policy Division.

Council of Europe. (2001). *Common European Framework of Reference for Languages: Learning, Teaching, Assessment*. Strasbourg: Language Policy Unit. Retrieved from http://www.coe.int/t/dg4/linguistic/source/framework_en.pdf.

Ferri, B. A., & Bacon, J. (2011). Beyond Inclusion: Disability Studies in Early Childhood Teacher Education. In B. S. Fennimore & A. L. Goodwin (Eds.), *Promoting Social Justice for Young Children* (pp. 137–146). New York: Springer Science+Business Media B.V.

Foucault, M. (1998). Practicing Criticisms. In L. Kritzman (Ed.), *Michel Foucault: Politics, Philosophy, Culture*. New York: Routledge.

Gilson, S. F., Tusler, A., & Gill, C. (1997). Ethnographic Research in Disability Identity: Self-Determination and Community. *Journal of Vocational Rehabilitation, 9*, 7–17.

Greiner-Ogris, S., & **Dotter, F.** (2012). SignLEF: Sign Languages Within the European Framework of Reference for Languages. In *International Conference ICT for Language Learning* (5th ed.). Retrieved from http://conference.pixel-online.net/ICT4LL2012/common/download/Paper_pdf/72-CEF01-FP-Greiner-Ogris-ICT2012.pdf.

Hall, P. J. (2002). Narrowing the Breach: Can Disability Culture and Full Educational Inclusion Be Reconciled? *Journal of Disability Policy Studies, 13*, 144–154.

Heron, J., & Reason, P. (2001). The Practice of Co-operative Inquiry: Research 'with' Rather than 'on' People. In P. Reason & H. Bradbury (Eds.), *Handbook of Action Research: Participative Inquiry and Practice*. London: Sage.

Hoffmeister, R. (2008). Language and the Deaf World: Difference Not Disability. In M. E. Brisk (Ed.), *Language, Culture, and Community in Teacher Education*. New York: Erlbaum.

Humphries, T., Kushalnagar, P., Mathur, G., Napoli, D. J., Padden, C., Rathmann, C., & Smith, S. R. (2012). Language Acquisition for Deaf Children: Reducing the Harms of Zero Tolerance to the Use of Alternative Approaches. *Harm Reduction Journal, 9*, 16.

Karchmer, M., & Mitchell, R. D. (2003). Demographic and Achievement Characteristics of Deaf and Hard-of-Hearing Students. In M. Marschark &

P. Spencer (Eds.), *Oxford Handbook of Deaf Studies, Language, and Education*. New York: Oxford University Press.

Kauppinen, L., & Jokinen, M. (2014). Deaf Culture and Linguistic Rights. In M. Sabatello & M. Schulze (Eds.), *Human Rights and Disability Advocacy*. Philadelphia: University of Pennsylvania Press.

Kemmis, S. (2001). Exploring the Relevance of Critical Theory for Action Research: Emancipatory Action Research in the Footsteps of Jürgen Habermas. In P. Reason & H. Bradbury (Eds.), *Handbook of Action Research: Participative Inquiry and Practice*. London: Sage.

Kliewer, C., Biklen, D., & Kasa-Hendrickson, C. (2006). Who May Be Literate? Disability and Resistance to the Cultural Denial of Competence. *American Educational Research Journal, 43*, 163–192. https://doi.org/10.3102/00028312043002163.

Komesaroff, L. (2007). Introduction. In L. Komesaroff (Ed.), *Surgical Consent: Bioethics and Cochlear Implantation*. Washington, DC: Gallaudet University Press.

Komesaroff, L. (2008). *Disabling Pedagogy: Power, Politics, and Deaf Education*. Washington, DC: Gallaudet University Press.

Ladd, P. (2003). *Understanding Deaf Culture: In Search of Deafhood*. Clevedon: Multilingual Matters.

Ladd, P. (2007). Cochlear Implantation, Colonialism, and Deaf Rights. In L. Komesaroff (Ed.), *Surgical Consent: Bioethics and Cochlear Implantation*. Washington, DC: Gallaudet University Press.

Lane, H. (2005). Ethnicity, Ethics, and the Deaf-World. *Journal of Deaf Studies and Deaf Education, 10*(3), 291–310.

Leeson, L., & Byrne-Dunne, D. (2009). *Applying the Common European Reference Framework to the Teaching, Learning and Assessment of Signed Languages, Report for the D-Signs Distance Online Training in Sign Language Project Consortium, UK/08/LLP-LdV/TOI/163_141*. Bristol: Centre for Deaf Studies, University of Bristol.

Morris, J. (1992). Personal and Political: A Feminist Perspective on Researching Physical Disability. *Disability, Handicap and Society, 7*(2), 157–166.

Oliver, M. (2013). The Social Model of Disability: Thirty Years On. *Disability and Society, 28*(7), 1024–1026. https://doi.org/10.1080/09687599.2013.818773.

Oyserman, J., & de Geus, M. (2013, July). Hearing Parents and the Fluency in Sign Language Communication. In *Poster Session Presented at the Theoretical Issues in Sign Language Research Conference 11*, London, UK.

Oyserman, J., & de Geus, M. (2015, July). Teaching Sign Language to Parents of Deaf Children. In *Poster Presented at the 2nd International Conference on Sign Language Acquisition*, Amsterdam, The Netherlands.

Piñar, P., Dussias, P. E., & Morford, J. P. (2011). Deaf Readers as Bilinguals: An Examination of Deaf Readers' Print Comprehension in Light of Current Advances in Bilingualism and Second Language Progressing. *Language and Linguistics Compass, 5*(10), 691–704.

Reindal, S. M. (2008). A Social Relational Model of Disability: A Theoretical Framework for Special Needs Education? *European Journal of Special Needs Education, 23*(2), 135–146.

Russell, D., & McLeod, J. (2009). Educational Interpreting: Multiple Perspectives of Our Work. In J. Mole (Ed.), *International Perspectives on Educational Interpreting*. Brassington: Direct Learned Services Ltd.

Sen, A. (1999). *Development as Freedom*. Oxford: Oxford University Press.

Siegel, L. (2000). *The Educational & Communication Needs of Deaf and Hard of Hearing Children: A Statement of Principle Regarding Fundamental Systemic Educational Changes*. Greenbrae: National Deaf Education Project.

Slee, R. (2011). *The Irregular School: Exclusion, Schooling and Inclusive Education*. London: Routledge.

Slee, R. (2013). How Do We Make Inclusive Education Happen When Exclusion is a Political Predisposition? *International Journal of Inclusive Education, 17*, 895–907. https://doi.org/10.1080/13603116.2011.602534.

Small, A., & Cripps, J. (2011). *On Becoming: Developing an Empowering Cultural Identity Framework for Deaf Youth and Adults*. Toronto: Ministry of Children and Youth Services.

Snoddon, K. (2008). American Sign Language and Early Intervention. *The Canadian Modern Language Review, 64*(4), 581–604.

Snoddon, K. (2009). Equity in Education: Signed Language and the Courts. *Current Issues in Language Planning, 10*(3), 279–295.

Snoddon, K. (2012). *American Sign Language and Early Literacy: A Model Parent-Child Program*. Washington, DC: Gallaudet University Press.

Snoddon, K. (2014). Hearing Parents as Plurilingual Learners of ASL. In D. McKee, R. Rosen, & R. McKee (Eds.), *Teaching and Learning of Signed Languages: International Perspectives and Practices*. Basingstoke: Palgrave Macmillan.

Snoddon, K. (2015). Using the *Common European Framework of Reference for Languages* to Teach Sign Language to Parents of Deaf Children. *Canadian Modern Language Review, 71*(3), 270–287.

Snoddon, K., & Underwood, K. (2014). Toward a Social Relational Model of Deaf Childhood. *Disability & Society, 29*(4), 530–542.

Terzi, L. (2004). The Social Model of Disability: A Philosophical Critique. *Journal of Applied Philosophy, 21*(2), 141–157.

Tregaskis, C. (2002). Social Model Theory: The Story So Far.... *Disability and Society, 17*(4), 457–470.

Underwood, K. (2008). *The Construction of Disability in Our Schools: Teacher and Parent Perspectives on the Experience of Labelled Students*. Rotterdam: Sense.

Underwood, K., Valeo, A., & Wood, R. (2012). Understanding Inclusive Early Childhood Education: A Capability Approach. *Contemporary Issues in Early Childhood, 13*(4), 290–299.

Valente, J. M. (2011). Cyborgization: Deaf Education for Young Children in the Cochlear Implantation Era. *Qualitative Inquiry, 17*(7), 639–652.

Vertovec, S. (2007). Super-Diversity and Its Implications. *Ethnic and Racial Studies, 30*(6), 1024–1054.

Walker, M. (2005). Amartya Sen's Capability Approach and Education. *Educational Action Research, 13*(1), 103–110.

Watkins, S., Pittman, P., & Walden, B. (1998). The Deaf Mentor Experimental Project for Young Children Who Are Deaf and Their Families. *American Annals of the Deaf, 143*(1), 29–34.

World Federation of the Deaf. (2015, April 8). *Presentation from the WFD Side-Event on 8 April.* 13th Session of the Committee on the Rights of Persons with Disabilities, Geneva, Switzerland, 25 March–17 April 2015. Retrieved June 22, 2015, from http://wfdeaf.org/wp-content/uploads/2015/05/WFD-side-event-presentation.pdf.

World Federation of the Deaf. (n.d.). Sign Language. Retrieved June 22, 2015, from http://wfdeaf.org/human-rights/crpd/sign-language.

Young, A. M. (1999). Hearing Parents' Adjustment to a Deaf Child: The Impact of a Cultural-Linguistic Model of Deafness. *Journal of Social Work Practice, 13*(2), 157–176.

Kristin Snoddon is an Assistant Professor at the School of Linguistics and Language Studies, Carleton University. Kristin's research interests are in applied sign language linguistics and sign language planning and policy, particularly with regard to deaf children's sign language rights in education. Kristin's research and professional experience includes collaborative work with deaf communities in developing sign language and early literacy programming for deaf children and parents.

Kathryn Underwood is an Associate Professor at the School of Early Childhood Studies, Ryerson University. Kathryn's research interests are in human rights and education practice, particularly with regard to disability rights and inclusive education. Kathryn's research experience includes work in family-school relationships, special education policy, and early childhood education and care policy, in both Canada and internationally. Recent research has focused on parent viewpoints of early years' services in early intervention, childcare, Full Day Kindergarten, Ontario Early Years Centres, and Parenting and Family Literacy Centres.

'The Embodiment of Disabled Children and Young People's Voices About Participating in Recreational Activities': Shared Perspectives

Dawn Pickering

Key Points

- This chapter describes two research projects carried out with disabled children and young people in the UK about what it means to the emotional wellbeing of disabled children and young people to join in meaningful recreational activities.
- It begins with the links between health, recreation and childhood regarding disabled children.
- The perspectives and stories by disabled children and young people presented illustrate the agency and fun enjoyed in recreation as well as relationships with others that includes issues of inclusion.
- Recreation is different to therapy and treatments in terms of functional goals, but this chapter suggests that some important goals of therapy and health can be met by recreation and importantly, the objectives of fun are added.
- Policy implications include the case for equality of opportunity for disabled children to play and participate in all activities, and to voice their experiences and ideas for future recreational activities.
- This chapter shows that a simple cost-saving objective for National Health Service (NHS) and Social Services needs caution as holistic care and participation requires investment if it is to be successful and have any real impact for disabled children.

D. Pickering (✉)
School of Healthcare Sciences, Cardiff University, Cardiff, UK

© The Author(s) 2018
K. Runswick-Cole et al. (eds.), *The Palgrave Handbook of Disabled Children's Childhood Studies*, https://doi.org/10.1057/978-1-137-54446-9_9

101

Introduction

This chapter describes research I carried out with disabled children and young people in the UK who spoke about their experiences of recreational activities. The first research project discussed was a pilot team project about adapted cycling. The second research project is my doctoral research examining participation as a construct and what it means to the emotional wellbeing of disabled children and young people to join in meaningful recreational activities. My background is in children's physiotherapy, and I am now a part-time doctoral student, engaging in literature about disabled children's childhoods, beyond the more familiar medical and physiotherapy discourses. This chapter questions current practices to explore how to move this participation and wellbeing agenda forward.

The chapter begins with the debates around health, disability and childhood and discusses how these influence the voice, opportunities and decisions for disabled children and young people. The ethics, methods and data described in the research sections below illustrate the ways that research is enabling the children and young people's voices to be shared within an ethical framework that seeks to embrace and not exploit their views. Stories of young disabled children's experiences are presented and discussed. The chapter highlights the embodiment of their lived experiences of participation in recreational activities in relation to their perceived benefits.

Childhood and Health: Recreation and Wellbeing

Childhood is a unique lived experience for everyone prior to adulthood; it shapes and forms us into who we are as people. The diversity of each disabled child's lived experience or their 'lifeworld' is unique; their family, culture, religion and age determine how this works out individually. This is for both their family and friends, and also for the education, health and social care professionals who teach, advise and offer treatments. Hopefully, these are provided within environments and professional cultures that promote equality, dignity and respect. Davis (1996) and Watson et al. (1999) revealed insights about disabled children and young people in educational settings. Davis (1996) highlighted cultural and gender differences with disabled children and young people affecting their sport's participation. Watson et al. (1999) revealed those with a learning disability often found social situations challenging with limited adjustments being made for their hidden disability. Taylor et al. (2015) looked at deaf and disabled children's experiences of safeguarding and found that the lack of professional interpreters increased their risk of not being listened to. Effective communication and teamwork with disabled children and young people is the key to all aspects of practice, education and research (Crombie in Pountney 2007).

Disabled children and young people have the right to and aspire to join in with the same opportunities as their non-disabled peers. Article 31 of the United Nations Convention on the Rights of the Child states that children have the right to rest, leisure, play and recreation and to take part in cultural and artistic activities (United Nations Children's Fund (UNICEF) 1989; UNICEF 2013). The challenge is the level of reasonable adjustments that can be made for disabled children and young people to be safe and enjoy participating in recreational activities (Equality Act 2010, gov.uk; Hart 1992). Learning how to have fun is part of growing up, and often friends make the experiences more fun as a sense of belonging is generated. Initially, children rely on their parents to build their networks and contacts that can lead to friendship development. As disabled children mature into adulthood, their aspirations to live independently, make and keep new friends, develop intimate relationships and become parents themselves are no different to any child or young person in the twenty-first century (Shakespeare 2014). It is clear, however, that there are some barriers to this being achieved, which are highlighted by the social model of disability, where the environment and people's attitudes can hinder these ambitions (Swain et al. 1993).

Conversely, the World Health Organisation's International Classification of Functioning framework (WHO-ICF 2001) has highlighted the need for holistic care. In holistic care, the additional social factors which impact on health outcomes both, body structure and function, are considered, as well as environmental and personal factors, where increased participation in recreational activities may improve both physical health and emotional wellbeing. The WHO ICF has been adapted to focus on children and young people's needs (WHO-ICF-C& YP 2012), and recent debates have suggested that quality of life and human development should be added in circles around this basic ICF framework to make this holistic care more transparent (McDougall et al. 2010). A more recent critique of the WHO-ICF model has proposed health as the ability to 'adapt and self-manage', suggesting that coping strategies and participation are more important than a full restoration of health (Huber et al. 2011). This approach could potentially reduce the care burden on the National Health Service (NHS) and Social Services, as expectations on professionals change and individuals living with long-term conditions become more autonomous. This is especially pertinent to children and young people with disabilities as they mature into adulthood.

Choices for disabled children and young people are often constrained by limited provision of activities that have made reasonable adjustments to be more inclusive. Activities can be provided in separate or integrated groups, but investment in these different groups is not always fairly distributed. This inequity of provision can vary according to where someone lives and what opportunities are affordable or accessible in their geographical region (Welsh et al. 2006). Some disabled children and young people and their families can only achieve increased choice to participate with additional financial support, such as Direct Payments to buy in the extra support staff they need. Direct payments are a government scheme for parents of a disabled child or those over 16 years to claim an additional allowance for their care and support needs (Direct Payments, gov.uk 2015). Some of this can be spent on recreational activities to benefit their health and wellbeing.

The physical health and emotional wellbeing benefits of joining in recreational activities are not always directly measured as outcomes from healthcare interventions. If disabled children and young people are given opportunities to try new recreational activities, they could be in a position to enjoy a fulfilling life which can improve their wellbeing. This can in turn reduce their health needs and dependency upon the NHS. If they wish to employ a personal trainer, then how can they go about this? Often those who are trained as personal trainers have limited knowledge of how to make activities accessible or adapt activities for the inclusion of disabled children and young people. Encouragingly, some educational training facilities for personal trainers are now developed and in place seeking to embrace inclusive principles (Oxford Brookes University 2011).

The objective within physiotherapy time, for example, may be to build capacity or maintain function, building children's confidence to try new activities. As the latter often happens outside the contact time of healthcare professionals, the transferable skill from the therapy may not be easily measured in terms of healthcare input. The lack of flexibility of environments where healthcare practitioners work makes this difficult, but it could be made more transparent by exploring community facilities and developing new activities (Taylor et al. 2004). It is not always possible to 'fix' a child's impairment or condition, and a balance needs to be negotiated with the child or young person, in consultation with their parents, about what level of function they are happy with (Mayston 2011). For example, with walking and talking, which are expected capabilities in typical childhood development discourse, different means of mobility and communication can be found with support. These may be more efficient to preserve children's energy and to aid their social and emotional development at a younger age (Rodby-Bouquest and Hagglund 2010). A sensitive way has to be found to navigate personalised aims, and to date, this 'normalcy' agenda has caused much emotional labour for parents and children (Ryan and Runswick-Cole 2008; Curran and Runswick-Cole 2013, 2014). Gibson et al. (2011) have called for a paradigm shift in physiotherapy practice, to stop reinforcing the norm, to manage this anxiety.

Medical research with disabled children about participation has often used questionnaire designs to gather numeric data hoping to demonstrate a change in participation levels (Welsh et al. 2006; Young et al. 2000, 2007). Additionally, there has now been some attempt to listen to their voices (Varni et al. 2005; Phelan and Kinsella 2013). Participation research evidence so far has suggested an increase in domestic participation such as activities around the home, with limited evidence of increased community participation such as recreational activities (Bjornson et al. 2013; Imms et al. 2009). An increase in participation in recreational activities has been shown to demonstrate improvements in health and wellbeing, but there is limited evidence that this is directly related to healthcare interventions (Shields et al. 2015). If healthcare professionals are to continue to offer services to disabled children and young people and their families, more consideration should be given to include emotional wellbeing by reinforcing their abilities (Hodge and Runswick-Cole 2013).

Voices of Disabled Children and Young People

To understand the 'lifeworld' of disabled children and young people better, a qualitative approach is necessary that actually asks the disabled children and young people about their views and experiences about participation in recreational activities (King 2013). As a child, they may not understand that these activities can have positive health outcomes. The best incentive for them is to enjoy the activity and to have fun. Whilst Rosenbaum and Gorter (2012) have proposed six 'F' words (Fun, Friendship, Fitness, Function, Family and the Future) in childhood disability rehabilitation, healthcare professionals are still strongly influenced by the medical model needing to quantify outcomes. The emphasis here would focus on functional outcomes not necessarily quality of life measures or emotional wellbeing. To date, the disabled child's voice has not directly influenced healthcare practice to demonstrate a change in participation outcomes such as enhanced emotional wellbeing. This is despite Carpenter and McConkey's (2012) suggestion that it is the healthcare professionals' *moral imperative* to listen to the voices of disabled children and young people. Kellet (in Clark, Flewitt, Hammersley and Robb 2014) suggests that voice and agency play a role in influencing change, so to enable disabled children to participate in this process requires adaptation and creativity, and more time. The next section expands upon the theoretical principles behind disabled children's childhoods.

Thinking Disabled Children's Childhoods

The complexity of a childhood has been described as a 'hybrid experience' where technology and prescribed drugs play an increasing role (Prout 2011; James and Prout 2015). This hybrid concept has relevance for disabled children, where this hybridity is often central to who they are. For example, using a communication aid or a wheelchair is part of their embodiment—their own lived experiences of how they live in the world. This has been termed their 'lifeworld' (Dahlberg and Nystrom 2008; Todres 2008), and research with disabled children and young people is only just beginning to gain insight into their real worlds (Simmons and Watson 2014).

Runswick-Cole (2011) celebrates disabled childhoods with photo-elicited stories affirming the positivity of their everyday experiences, promoting disabled children and young people's potential for creativity. Healthcare providers and policymakers may wish to demonstrate cost-effectiveness of the equipment and drugs provided; however, the disabled child wishes to 'be' a child first and is not necessarily concerned about what they may 'become' in their future self as an adult. The new sociology of childhood defines the opposing biosocial dualisms of 'being' and 'becoming', 'nature' versus 'culture' and 'agency' versus 'structure' (James et al. 1998; Prout 2011).

The debates about 'being' and 'becoming', medical and social discourse and the roles played by parents and professionals are pertinent within healthcare, as the lived experience of a childhood affected by a disability may be influenced by decisions made in the child's best interests for their future (Kehily 2009). For example, living with spasticity (a stiffness in the muscles) impacts on pain and function, and there is a good evidence base to aid decision-making to reduce the discomfort and loss of function this causes (National Institute of Clinical Excellence (NICE) 2012). The need to justify the cost-effectiveness of any intervention, sometimes measured in 'quality of life' adjusted years, can vary across the devolved countries of the UK: England, Northern Ireland, Scotland and Wales. This leads to a sense of unfairness and injustice for some families. A common coping strategy is to fund raise and seek treatment overseas (Collins 2014). Parents often make decisions on behalf of the disabled younger child, because with the child's growth, that opportunity for intervention will not present itself again, for example, with orthopaedic or neurosurgery. Some areas of practice have less certainty of long-term outcomes, for example, using splints or a standing frame, as there is no empirical research to date to support or refute their use although commissioned research is currently being undertaken (National Institute for Health Research 2015). Novak et al. (2013) have reviewed the evidence base and critiqued the low level of evidence to support the outcomes of many treatments currently offered, suggesting a traffic light system, where only the 'green' treatments that do have such evidence should be continued. Despite this lack of robust evidence base for the effectiveness of treatments, the value of supportive healthcare professionals has been reliably demonstrated by Measures of the Processes of Care (MPOC) (King et al. 2004; Pickering and Busse 2010). The attributes of professionals who listen, show respect and respond sensitively to the child or young person's needs are valued very highly. Professionals who solve issues in partnership with parents, children and young people are appreciated. However, the gap of professional's signposting families to recreational activities remains a weakness in service provision (McDowell et al. 2015).

Equality of Opportunity to Play?

Many disabled children and young people would like to have opportunities to try new recreational activities, and healthcare professionals are ideally placed to explore these possibilities as part of capacity building. Such opportunities are not likely to be based on hospital sites but in communities with their peers. A recent survey in Wales highlighted the geographical variation of available play opportunities for disabled children and young people (Bevan Foundation 2011). Activities highlighted in the more urban areas include cycling, swimming, horse riding and skiing clubs with adaptations for disabled children and young people. However, more rural areas offered fewer activities. Many have a sporting focus, and wider opportunities should be explored in order that the diversity of preferences for disabled children and young people can be catered for, such as art, craft, dance, drama and music, to name but a few.

Ethical Principles of Practice, Education and Research

When considering the four ethical principles of how to hear the disabled child's voice, a few challenges present (Beauchamp and Childress 1994). Firstly, the lack of empirical evidence for practice leaves practitioners, parents, and disabled children and young people with a dilemma of which route to follow. For example, if surgery could help increase function in some way or reduce pain and discomfort, surely is it essential to have it carried out? It must be doing 'good' (Beneficence). However, for some disabled children, if they realised the amount of hard work and commitment required for the rehabilitation period to optimise their function, they may choose otherwise. Often, they can be persuaded to try the intervention without being able to understand the implications through either immaturity or cognitive impairment. A lack of engagement with this rehabilitation process can do more harm (Non-Maleficence) than if no intervention had been carried out. Endeavours must be made to engage the child in the consent process and not only once, but assent must be ongoing as the disabled child matures, and their opinions change over time (Renold et al. 2008). If they are unable to understand what will happen to them, efforts must be made to make the information accessible using creative approaches where possible (Triangle 2010; Clark and Moss 2011).

The justice of equal opportunity in the NHS is based upon the clinical need, so choice (Autonomy) can come into the equation, but not always. This is particularly pertinent in diseases such as diabetes, cystic fibrosis or heart conditions where life-saving drugs or surgery is imperative. If the choice is not to accept these, then an early preventable death will be the outcome. Alternately, in long-term conditions, such as muscular dystrophy and cerebral palsy, there are a range of options to be explored which can impact on the disabled young person's quality of life. For example, the use of night-time ventilation that will reduce the unpleasant 'hung over' feeling in the mornings, for young men with muscular dystrophy, has a good evidence base (Eagle et al. 2002). On the converse, the neurosurgical procedure called selective dorsal rhizotomy (SDR) has a limited and conflicting evidence base for long-term outcomes in cerebral palsy (NICE 2012). So the decisions for all concerned are not easy and many exert a significant amount of emotional labour in deliberating over the best way forward, often resulting in a degree of uncertainty and risk with the outcomes.

The ethical approach for the research studies reported here seeks to bring out the voices of disabled children, to hear their own perspectives about recreational activities. The studies were approved by the School of Healthcare Research Ethics Committee at Cardiff University in 2009 and 2014, respectively. The creativity developed in the methods sought to represent children with a wider range of abilities including those using alternative and augmentative communication. All children chose a false name to protect their identity, however, when they wished their story to be told, and for them to be identified, a further level of consent was sought (Renold et al. 2008). In this chapter, although this permission was given by one child who made a digital story, they have not been made known, as she has the right to change her mind in the future, and it would not be possible to retract her identity once in print.

The next section highlights research methods used seeking to hear and listen to their experiences.

Methods to Capture the Voices of Disabled Children

The voices of disabled children and young people are now emerging in the literature with participatory and emancipatory methods being developed (Abbott 2012; Beresford 2012; Foley et al. 2012; Murray 2012; Ytterhus 2012; VIPER 2013). The author's research team began to ask disabled children about their cycling experiences adapting 'Mosaic' methods (Clark and Moss 2011; Pickering et al. 2012, 2013, 2015). Clark and Moss (2011) developed Mosaic methods with young children using a mixture of spoken words, mapping a nursery by photographs the children took and drawings they made of places important to them. Mosaic methods, for this study, involved the use of puppetry, pictures and drawing, engaging children in narratives about their recreational activities, including cycling, and they also kept a diary of their activities. Mosaic methods are based upon the principle of *unhurried listening* to seek out the child's voice (Clark and Moss 2011). Additionally, the non-verbal communication style for some children required further adjustments to be able to capture their 'voice' (Morris 1998; Minkes et al. 1994; Booth and Booth 1996).

A person familiar with the child's communication style was always present during the interviews to clarify the child's meaning for the researcher. Thirty-five children took part over a three-year period (2009–2012), taking part in two interviews, six weeks apart. Basil and Linda used Makaton signing (hand movements) to communicate, and Ian, Natalie and Suarez had dysarthric speech (difficulty saying the words for others to understand). The combination of the photographs, illustrations and narrative built up the Mosaic picture for each child, enabling their 'voices' to be heard. Basil engaged in eye contact with the glove puppet of a sheep in response to the questions asked, gesturing in Makaton to him (Makaton 2016). Makaton is the use of hand gestures to enable preverbal children to communicate. Diane, Husain, Lizzie, May and Natalie wrote their own diaries describing and illustrating some of the physical activities that they had participated in. The next section tells some of their stories.

Disabled Children and Young People's Cycling Stories

There are seven children's stories told below: Peter, Heather, Diane, Sally, Rachel, May and Ghost.

Peter aged 7 years said *I did cycling and it was wicked!* and his mother reported *This year we cycled from Bristol towards Windsor because we could hire the special trike....I think completely independently he cycled not far off 40 miles....* Peter's outstanding personal achievement was amazing, and he has continued with his cycling activities to date, now aged 14 years.

Heather, also aged 7 years, described her experiences of going on a tandem bike where her legs had to keep going round at her father's pace, but she preferred the tag along (added to the back of an adult bike) which meant she could pedal independently: *I hope that Dad doesn't get me on the tandem…on my tag bike I cycled 13 miles....* Heather later described that she aimed to cycle on a two wheeler at the velodrome, like her brother, when she was old enough.

Diane's (10 years) family has hired the bike for the whole six-week summer holiday at her parent's caravan park—this opened up a completely new social world for her. Diane wrote and illustrated her diary beautifully, revealing unique aspects about before and after having use of the bike. So when asked what it was like when she did not have her bike at the caravan? *I normally tag along, walk for a while, ponder my thoughts, get bored....The bike's great, easier to get around than walking. Clever, clever invention whoever invented it I want to thank them....* (Pickering et al. 2013).

Two children were unable to take part in the interviews; Sally (14 years) had limited verbal communication, and her mother expressed how she was able to show her enjoyment of cycling: *You can just see the joy in her face when she's on her bike yeah!....Um, I mean if it's straight, you know, you can virtually sort of let go and she'll just go by herself until she starts veering off course....But uh, yeah no she definitely enjoys it…*

And Rachel (8 years) attended a special school, and her support worker recorded in her diary: *Throughout the cycling sessions I feel that Rachel's confidence has improved. She is so happy when she is cycling and it gives her the freedom and independence she needs....* The adjectives used to describe these cycling experiences included *Fun, Enthusiastic, Wicked, Happy, Proud and Enjoyable.* These children's voices, as well as those who cared for them, demonstrate the enjoyment they had from one adapted activity.

May's (11 years) story stood out as both exceeding parental and mainstream school expectations. May's Mum said*: Cycling in itself is something that I didn't think May would ever achieve, not that I have ever told her that. But I actually* *applied for a grant from Cerebra for a trike, I didn't even know that trikes existed for…you know…for an older child…and it's really taken from there using the trike and getting her confidence….*

At the beginning of the interview, May showed a mobile phone video of her cycling a two-wheeler independently. May wrote in the diary herself about her up and coming *bike prefishinsiy test* (Pickering et al. 2015). So when asked about what she hoped that would lead to, she spoke about her difficult experience on a mainstream school cycle trip in year 5:

> *I want to get better and better at cycling…and go to the Hope Forest….I went before with school but I had to go on a 'stupid tandem' because my teacher kind of force me…another Dad pedalled…. [Mum: …It was sort of an ice cream basket on the back]…. I didn't do any pedalling at all…which was really, really, really disappointing…cos all my other friends were like riding a bike…and I was lonely….*

Observing on the mobile phone video that May was capable of riding a two-wheeler and was preparing for her bike proficiency test (a bicycle test to develop road safety and bikes' skills in the UK), this story was distressing as such a sense of disempowerment came over in the way she told it. The emphasis on the repeated word *really* showed how let down she felt and singled out as different and not being able to participate with her peers. It was clear May felt lonely, humiliated and not empowered; this was an undermining not affirming experience. It affected the researcher who reflected upon how in practice we do not always consider how our decisions affect how disabled children feel about themselves.

Ghost (8 years) had thought about cycling since the first interview where he has expressed concerns about being teased if he tried to ride a trike (a three-wheeler bike). He had considered the written information given: *Well, I looked at the photo of the thing, there's like a bike with three wheels….I'm thinking of hiring that one….*Mum: *I think we could attach this to his Dad's bike, like a tag along, so he could pedal at the back as much as he liked….*

After the research had ended, Ghost's mum wrote to say that although she *Didn't think he would ever be able to ride a bike*, Ghost had now learnt to ride a bike and was having one for Christmas.

'VOCAL' Research

In my doctoral study: 'VOCAL', the voices of disabled children and young people are being explored in a more in-depth approach using a method called Interpretative Phenomenological Analysis (IPA) (Smith et al. 2013). This method seeks to ask the disabled children and young people to tell their stories about what recreational activities they enjoy. Preliminary unpublished pilot data from two young people, Becky and Katie, are presented and discussed.

Becky was one of the children in the original cycling study who was aged 9 years at the time of the data collection. When the opportunity came to tell her story at a conference in 2014, Becky produced a digital story about her recreational activities *I can do it by myself.* 'Becky's' childhood story is framed around SDR, and at the age of nine years, the outcome is very positive, enabling Becky to participate in horse riding amongst other activities that she enjoys. The long-term outcomes are unclear, but they will change with the child's growth (Van Eck et al. 2008). But Becky's determination to succeed is shown in her words: *I can….Mummy said I can't…but I can, I can….* 'I can' was referring to playing the violin which she was able to pluck and play with the bow with one hand. So the 'being' of her childhood, attending a mainstream primary school, is varied and busy with many choices as a result of this SDR surgery. This surgery was not made available at the time by the NHS in Wales, and so fundraising took place for her to go to the USA. The emotional labour of this journey for all of the family has shown Becky's resilience. Becky's mother, interviewed now four years post-surgery, is convinced that without this surgery *Becky's hips would now be too stiff to get on a horse.*

This story has now been analysed using this IPA method to explore the descriptive, linguistic and interpretative perspectives. Two further interviews with Becky asked her about the meaning of this digital story to her to gain deeper insight into her 'lifeworld'. This approach uses the 'double hermeneutic' where the interviewer asks about the experience and then probes further to ask the participant if what the interviewer thinks it means, really is what the participant means. For example, at the end of the digital story, Becky is reading a book with a picture of a dragon on the front (Smith 2012). Here the dragon is used as a metaphor for spasticity (the muscle stiffness described earlier), so reading the book had helped Becky to understand that the surgery on her back had slain the dragon, and now the stiffness in her legs had gone away. In the first interview, Becky talked about the dragon story, in her own words *The dragon story is about Dr P…he did an operation on the boy…and it made the fires…that made my legs to cross, it flighted it away….* Using a puppet theatre and laminated cards, Picture 1 illustrates her activities:

The dragon was placed at the top by Becky's instruction, as he was flying away, whereas the horse riding, bike riding, swimming, reading and playing the violin were still important to her and fitted with the six 'F' words of Fun, Fitness, Family, Friends, Function and the Future. A second interview,

Picture 1 Puppet Theatre story

three months later utilised a 'sandbox' (Mannay 2015) for Becky to tell her story. Here, small figures were used including a dragon (Picture 2), however, as Picture 3 illustrates, Becky did not want the dragon in her story anymore:

The lived experience for Becky—attending a mainstream school, singing in the choir, playing in the orchestra, riding her bike, swimming and horse riding—do not sound that dissimilar to her peers. There is clearly 'fun' in her life as Becky learns to take turns and trot on the horse, developing a sense of group belonging with friends. However, to maintain her functional level and fitness, many individual activities take place in isolation. For example, the additional early morning exercises, treadmill training and personal trainer are different, as well as the time taken to walk and carry out everyday tasks such as dressing, washing and toileting. Before Becky even arrives at school, she has already exerted a significant amount of effort to maintain her level of function. Clearly, a supportive family enables this to happen. Becky also shows empathy for older people stating one of her future ambitions is to care for older people: *I'm just going to look after neighbours...and friends from my church...cos I'm going to make them happy cos they...erm ...they... it's very hard for them to walk.*

Picture 2 Figures offered to tell her story

In the diary, Becky had kept for three months, she had participated in a local Super Triathlon for disabled children and young people. The medal with the orange ribbon seen at the edge of the sandbox was one of her treasured trophies. The SuperTri can be viewed here not specifically with Becky in: https://www.youtube.com/watch?v=kE4oUW7FJN0. An opportunity to attend the SuperTri provided additional field notes with her father quoting: *It's amazing what difference a crowd cheering can do to Becky's motivation to walk* (400 metres around an athletics track with her walker). Becky was proud of her achievements, and the story reveals her resilience and self-determination to achieve her personal best, whilst being part of a group activity with the camaraderie and fun that it brings.

The final voice represented here is Katie. Katie is now 21 years of age and lives in a hall of residence at a University in the UK. Katie took part in two telephone interviews and kept an online diary for three months. Katie had

Picture 3   Becky's sandbox story

gone through two major orthopaedic surgical procedures in her early teens to improve her hip alignment. Katie was reflecting back to the age of 19 years and described herself as a *couch potato*, walking was difficult and a lot of effort for her, and she had become overweight. Katie described her lack of awareness of her disability as she was growing up:

> *No, I wouldn't have known I was disabled if it was up to my parents. I completely thought that I didn't have a disability. I only realised when I went to secondary school that – my mum said, put socks over your splints. I was like, why do I have to put socks over my splints? She was like, well you should do that. I don't know, and I used to hide my splints, thinking it was, why am I doing this? I was so freaked out....I never had a visual representation of myself. I didn't ever – I looked in the mirror but I didn't think, this is what I look like, is that bad or good, until I was like really old, like 13 or 14. Suddenly it's like, oh my God, I'm overweight. What does this mean?*

This is bad. Oh my God, I walk funny, this is bad. I don't think you get that, espe-cially if you don't see yourself, then you don't see how others see you until that time....

Here, Katie talks about the realisation that she was different in early ado-lescence and suddenly feeling this was 'bad'—although to this point she had not been aware that wearing splints was different or that she was overweight. After finding an activity, she enjoyed her perception of her capabilities was changed when at the age of 19 years an opportunity arose for Katie to try a new recreational activity called RaceRunning (www.RaceRunning.org). This changed her experience from being the *couch potato* into an athlete who trains for 15 hours per week:

It was an introduction to a cerebral palsy(CP) specific sport called RaceRunning...it was just so freeing, even though I looked ridiculous, despite everything it was just amazing! ....My activities previously were very short and staggered, I would never really raise my heart rate or get into an easy motor pattern.....Gravity and my CP is what made my walking pattern so disjointed- the need to stay upright against gravity with muscles which co-contract at the faintest hint that I might fall. So at first the RaceRunner gave me the experience of what walking must be like without cerebral palsy- using motor patterns which come naturally and easily.... What I can't do is think coherently when I walk, but I can when I RaceRun.

This new opportunity developed her self-confidence in a way that enabled her to try for additional responsibilities as illustrated by her time at the University: *...A soon as I started sport...not even any races, as soon as I started working out....it made me embrace the abilities I had and created new abilities-not necessarily physical.... I had more self-confidence, and I had more ability to deal with stressful moments in my life. In University, I went for the president of the faculty position; like an elected position you govern for a year in the univer-sity, I started doing quite a lot in my studies, I was so much more happy within myself....'*

Katie describes the emotional wellbeing benefits she found from becoming more active than before, revealing increased life choices. However, to reach the age of 19 years before such possibilities are opened up needs further question-ing. As practitioners, educators and researchers, are we taking the initiative to support disabled children and young people to develop their entrepreneurial skills to develop new recreational activities? By allowing exploration of new ideas, the boundaries can change and opportunities increase; however, are we so risk averse that we cramp any creativity for fear of whose responsibility it is?

The metaphors of the *dragon* and *couch potato* used by Becky and Katie have taken on a unique meaning for them. Katie describes not being able to think coherently when she walks, and yet practitioners are investing much rehabilitation time to achieve walking. Walking for most of us is an automatic activity; we do not need to think about it as we can balance and move limbs alternately. If disabled children and young people are exerting so much effort in walking, how is this affecting their concentration and creativity? As Gibson et al. (2011) have suggested, it is time to shift the paradigm of thinking to consider the social forces which underpin practice.

Further data with disabled children and young people will provide a deeper meaning to their 'lifeworlds'. This will help practitioners, educators and researchers to understand how we can support them to 'be' a child and enrich their lived experiences of participation in recreational activities as they mature into adolescence and adulthood.

Conclusion

These examples of disabled children and young people's voices are teaching us about what is important to them in terms of recreation and leisure participation. The 'being' of their childhood, towards adulthood, can be rich and varied as opportunities present themselves along the way. However, a few unanswered questions remain. How do health, education and research practitioners work in partnership with disabled children and young people to facilitate this process? Are policymakers for health and social care investing in the development of new recreational activities? As a society, there is a corporate responsibility as part of good citizenship to work together for doing good (Beneficence) and not doing harm (Non-Maleficence). As individuals, is there anything we can change to increase the choice of recreational activities for disabled children and young people to enrich their lived experiences? As Katie waited until 19 years of age before she found something that changed her experience, are there new as yet unconceived possibilities that could be developed? By listening to their voices, we are fulfilling the *moral imperative*. As the SuperTri vimeo asks—what have you done today to make you feel proud? The voices shared here illustrate the resilience developed through participating in recreational activities; this suggests that disabled children and young people can have realistic aspirations for future endeavours, but there remains a lack of choice of opportunities.

Acknowledgements The three-year study, 2009–2012, was funded by the Nancie Finnie Charitable Trust, now part of the Chartered Society of Physiotherapy in the UK.

References

Abbott, D. (2012). Other Voices, Other Rooms: Reflections on Talking to Young Men with Duchenne Muscular Dystrophy and Their Families About Transition to Adulthood. *Children and Society, 26*, 241–250. doi:10.1111/j.1099-0860.2012.00437.x.

Beauchamp, T. L., & Childress, J. F. (1994). *Principles of Biomedical Ethics*. Oxford: Oxford University Press.

Beresford, B. (2012). Working on Wellbeing: Researchers' Experiences of a Participative Approach to Understanding the Subjective Wellbeing of Disabled Young People. *Children and Society, 26*, 234–240. doi:10.1111/j.1099-0860.2012.00436.x.

Bevan Foundation. (2011). *Fair Play for Disabled Children and Young People in Wales*. Ebbw Vale: The Bevan Foundation. Available from: http://www.bevanfoundation.org/publications/fair-play/. Accessed 28 July 2015.

Bjornson, K. F., Zhou, C., Stevenson, R., & Christakis, D. A. (2013). Capacity to Participation in Cerebral Palsy: Evidence of an Indirect Path Via Performance. *Archives of Physical Medicine and Rehabilitation, 94*, 2365–2372. doi:10.1016/j.apmr.2013.06.020.

Booth, T., & Booth, W. (1996). Sounds of Silence: Narrative Research with Inarticulate Subjects. *Disability & Society, 11*(1), 55–70.

Carpenter, J., & McConkey, R. (2012). Disabled Children's Voices: The Nature and Role of Future Empirical Enquiry. *Children and Society, 26*, 251–261. doi:10.1111/j.1099-0860.2012.00438.x.

Clark, A., & Moss, P. (2011). *Listening to Young Children: The Mosaic Approach* (2nd ed.). London: National Children's Bureau.

Collins P. (2014). Wales on Line Newspaper. http://www.walesonline.co.uk/news/local-news/niamhs-dream-walk-without-pain-7906050. Accessed 28 Oct 2014.

Crombie, S. (2007). Chapter 2 Delivering Physiotherapy Services to Children and Young People. In T. Pountney (Ed.), *Physiotherapy for Children* (pp. 10–19). Edinburgh: Butterworth Heinemann/Elsevier.

Curran, T., & Runswick-Cole, K. (Eds.). (2013). *Disabled Children's Childhood Studies: Critical Approaches in a Global Context*. Basingstoke: Palgrave Macmillan.

Curran, T., & Runswick-Cole, K. (2014). Disabled Children's Childhood Studies: A Distinct Approach? *Disability and Society, 29*(10), 1617–1630.

Dahlberg, H., & Nystrom, M. (2008). *Reflective Lifeworld Research* (2nd ed.). Lund: Studentlitteratur.

Davis, J. (1996). Sport for All? PhD, Edinburgh.

Direct Payments. (2015). https://www.gov.uk/apply-direct-payments. Accessed 16 Aug 2016.

Eagle, M., Baudouin, S., Chandler, C., Giddings, D., Bullock, R., & Bushby, K. (2002). Survival in Duchenne Muscular Dystrophy: Improvements in Life Expectancy Since 1967 and the Impact of Home Nocturnal Ventilation. *Neuromuscular Disorders, 12*(10), 926–929.

Foley, K. R., Blackmore, A. M., Girdler, S., O'Donnell, M., Glauret, R., Llewellyn, G., & Leonard, H. (2012). To Feel Belonged: The Voices of Children and Youth with Disabilities on the Meaning of Wellbeing. *Child Indicators Research, 5*, 375–391.

Gibson, B. E., et al. (2011). Children's and Parent's Beliefs Regarding the Value of Walking: Rehabilitation Implications for Children with Cerebral Palsy. *Child: Care, Health and Development, 38*, 61–69.

Hart, R. (1992). *Ladder of Participation.* Available from http://www.algomapublichealth.com/UserFiles/File/Media/Youth%20Engagement/1616.pdf. Accessed 20 Aug 2015.

Hodge, N., & Runswick-Cole, K. (2013). 'They Never Pass Me the Ball': Exposing Ableism Through the Leisure Experiences of Disabled Children, Young People and Their Families. *Children's Geographies, 11*(3), 311–325.

Huber, M., van der Horst, H., Green, L., Alejandro, R. J., Leonard, B., Lorig, K., Smith, R., van Weel, C., Myan der Meer, J. W., Smid, H. C., & Bolk, L. (2011). Health How Should We Define It? *British Medical Journal, 343*, d4163.

Imms, C., Reilly, S., Carlin, J., & Dodd, K. (2009). Characteristics Influencing Participation of Australian Children with Cerebral Palsy. *Disability and Rehabilitation, 31*(26), 2204–2215.

James, A., & Prout, A. (2015). *Constructing and Reconstructing Childhood: Contemporary Issues in the Sociological Study of Childhood.* London: Routledge.

James, A., Jenks, C., & Prout, A. (1998). *Theorizing Childhood.* Padstow: Polity/Blackwell Publishers.

Kehily, M. J. (2009). *An Introduction to Childhood Studies* (2nd ed.). Maidenhead: Open University Press.

Kellet, M. (2014). In A. Clark, R. Flewitt, M. Hammersley, & M. Robb (Eds.), *Understanding Research with Children and Young People* (pp. 15–33). London: The Open University; Chapter 1.

King, G. (2013). Perspectives on Measuring Participation: Going Forward. *Child: Care, Health and Development, 39*(4), 466–469. doi:10.1111/cch.12083.

King, S., King, G., & Rosenbaum, P. (2004). Evaluating Health Service Delivery to Children with Chronic Conditions and Their Families: Development of a Refined Measure of Processes of Care (MPOC-20). *Children's Health Care, 33*(1), 35–57.

Makaton. (2016). https://www.makaton.org/. Accessed 16 Aug 2016.

Mannay, D. (2015). *Visual, Narrative, and Creative Research Methods: Application, Reflection and Ethics.* London: Routledge.

Mayston, M. (2011). From 'One Size Fits All' to Tailor Made Physical Intervention for Cerebral Palsy. *Developmental Medicine and Child Neurology* Editorial, 968. doi:10.1111/j.1469-8749.2011.04124.x.

McDougall, J., Wright, V., & Rosenbaum, P. (2010). The ICF Model of Functioning and Disability: Incorporating Quality of Life and Human Development. *Developmental Neurorehabilitation, 13*(3), 204–211.

McDowell, B. C., Duffy, C., & Parkes, J. (2015). Service Use and Family-Centred Care in Young People with Severe Cerebral Palsy: A Population-Based, Cross-Sectional Clinical Survey. *Disability and Rehabilitation, 37*(25), 2324–2329.

Minkes, J., Robinson, C., & Weston, C. (1994). Consulting the Children: Interviews with Children Using Residential Respite Care Services. *Disability and Society, 9*(1), 47–57.

Morris, J. (1998). *Don't Leave Us Out: Involving Disabled Children and Young People with Communication Impairments.* New York: Joseph Rowntree Foundation.

Murray, R. (2012). Sixth Sense: The Disabled Children and Young People's Participation Project. *Children and Society, 26,* 262–267. doi:10.1111/j.1099-0860.2012.00439.x.

National Institute for Clinical Excellence. (2012). Guideline 145. *Spasticity in Children and Young People with Non-progressive Brain Disorders. Management of Spasticity and Co-existing Motor Disorders and Their Early Musculoskeletal Complications.* Available from: https://www.nice.org.uk/guidance/cg145/resources/guidance-spasticity-in-children-and-young-people-with-nonprogressive-brain-disorders-pdf. Accessed 20 Aug 2015.

National Institute for Health Research. (2015). Health Technology Assessment—13/144/01: *Standing Frames as Part of Postural Management for Children with Spasticity. What Is the Acceptability of a Trial to Determine the Efficacy of Standing Frames?* Available from http://www.nets.nihr.ac.uk/projects/hta/1314401. Accessed 27 Aug 2015.

Novak, I., Mcintyre, S., Morgan, C., Campbell, L., Dark, L., Morton, N., Stumbles, E., Wilson, S. A., & Goldsmith, S. (2013). A Systematic Review of Interventions for Children with Cerebral Palsy: State of the Evidence. *Developmental Medicine & Child Neurology, 55*(10), 885–910.

Oxford Brookes. (2011). *Exercise Prescriptions for Long Term Neurological Conditions.* Available from: http://www.shs.brookes.ac.uk/clear/course. Accessed 20 Aug 2015.

Phelan, S. K., & Kinsella, E. A. (2013). Occupation and Identity: Perspectives of Children with Disabilities and Their Parents. *Journal of Occupational Science.* doi: 10.1080/14427591.2012.755907.

Pickering, D., & Busse, M. (2010). An Audit of Disabled Children's Services–What Value Is MPOC-SP? *Clinical Audit, 2010*(2), 13–22.

Pickering, D. M., Horrocks, L. M., Visser, K. S., & Todd, G. L. (2012, April 26). Adapted Bikes- What Children and Young People with Cerebral Palsy Told Us About Their Participation in Adapted Dynamic Cycling. *Disability and Rehabilitation: Assistive Technology,* Early Online 1-8 © Informa UK, Ltd.

Pickering, D. M., Horrocks, L. M., Visser, K. S., & Todd, G. L. (2013). 'Every Picture Tells a Story' Interviews and Diaries with Children with Cerebral Palsy About Adapted Cycling. *Journal of Paediatrics and Child Health.* doi:10.1111/jpc.12289.

Pickering, D. M., Horrocks, L. M., Visser, K. S., & Todd, G. L. (2015). Analysing Mosaic Data by a 'Wheel of Participation' to Explore Physical Activities and Cycling with Children and Youth with Cerebral Palsy. *International Journal of*

Developmental Disabilities, Early online: Available from http://dx.doi.org/10.117 9/2047387714Y.0000000038

Prout, A. (2011). Taking a Step Away from Modernity: Reconsidering the New Sociology of Childhood. *Global Studies of Childhood, 1*(1), 4–14.

Renold, E., Holland, S., Ross, N. J., & Hillman, A. (2008). Becoming Participant: Problematizing 'Informed Consent' in Participatory Research with Young People in Care. *Qualitative Social Work, 7,* 427–477.

Rodby-Bousquet, E., & Hägglund, G. (2010). Use of Manual and Powered Wheelchair in Children with Cerebral Palsy: A Cross-Sectional Study. *BMC Pediatrics, 10,* 10–59.

Rosenbaum, P., & Gorter, J. W. (2012 July). The 'F' Words in Childhood Disability: I Swear This Is How We Should Think! *Child: Care, Health and Development, 38*(4), 457–463. http://www.ncbi.nlm.nih.gov/pubmed/22040377#

Runswick-Cole, K. (2011, January 21). Celebrating Cyborgs: Photovoice and Disabled Children, Researching the Lives of Disabled Children and Young People, with a Focus on Their Perspectives. *ESRC Research Seminar Series,* The Norah Fry Research Unit Bristol University, Bristol. [Transcript of paper received 11.9.14].

Ryan, S., & Runswick-Cole, K. A. (2008). Repositioning Mothers: Mothers, Disabled Children and Disability Studies. *Disability and Society, 23*(3), 199–210. ISSN: 1360-0508 doi:10.1080/09687590801953937.

Shakespeare, T. (2014). *Disability Rights and Wrongs Revisited* (2nd ed.). London: Routledge/Taylor and Francis group.

Shields, N., Synnot, A., & Kearns, C. (2015). The Extent, Context and Experience of Participation in Out-of-School Activities Among Children with Disability. *Research in Developmental Disabilities, 47,* 165–174.

Simmons, B., & Watson, D. (2014). *The PMLD Ambiguity: Articulating the Life-Worlds of Children with Profound and Multiple Learning Disabilities.* London: Karnac.

Smith, R. G. (2012). *Sir Dr Park and the Dragon, Spasticity.* Available from: www. smittette.wordpress.com

Smith, J. A., Flowers, P., & Larkin, M. (2013). *Interpretative Phenomenological Analysis: Theory Method and Research.* London: Sage publications.

Swain, J., Finkelstein, V., French, S., & Oliver, M. (1993). *Disabling Barriers-Enabling Environments.* London: The Open University.

Taylor, N. F., Dodd, K. J., & Larkin, H. (2004). Adults with Cerebral Palsy Benefit from Participating in a Strength Training Programme at a Community Gymnasium. *Disability and Rehabiltation, 26,* 1128–1134.

Taylor, J., Cameron, A., Jones, C., Franklin, A., Stalker, K., & Fry, D. (2015). *Deaf and Disabled Children Talking About Child Protection.* Available from http://www. childprotection.ed.ac.uk/publications/database/k201503/. Accessed 19 Aug 2015.

Todres, L. (2008). Being with that: The Relevance of Embodied Understanding for Practice. *Qualitative Health Research, 18,* 1566–1573. doi:10.1177/1049732308324249.

Triangle. (2010). Two Way Street DVD and Booklet Resource. Available from http://www.triangle.org.uk/files/2015-12/communication-systems-2012.pdf. Accessed 3 July 2017.

United Nations Children's Fund (UNICEF). (1989). *United Nations Convention on the Rights of the Child.* http://www.unicef.org/crc/files/Rights_overview.pdf. Accessed 24 Feb 2016.

United Nations Children's Fund (UNICEF). (2013). *The State of the World's Children: Children with Disabilities.* New York: United Nations.

Van Eck, M., Dallmeijer, A. J., Voorman, J. M., & Becher, J. G. (2008). Skeletal Maturation in Children with Cerebral Palsy and Its Relationship with Motor Functioning. *Developmental Medicine and Child Neurology, 50,* 515–519. doi:10.1111/j.1469-8749.2008.03010.x.

Varni, J. W., Burwinkle, T. M., Sherman, S. A., Hanna, K., Berrin, S. J., Malcarne, V. L., & Chambers, H. G. (2005). Health Related Quality of Life of Children and Adolescents with Cerebral Palsy: Hearing the Voices of the Children. *Developmental Medicine and Child Neurology, 47,* 592–597.

VIPER: Voice, Inclusion, Participation, Empowerment, Research. (2013). A Literature Review of the Participation of Children and Young People in Decision Making [Online]. Available at: https://councilfordisabledchildren.org.uk/our-work/participation/policy/research-young-peoples-participation-local-decisions-viper. Accessed 23 Feb 2017.

Watson, N., Shakespeare, T., Cunningham-Burley, S., Corker, S., Davis, J., & Priestly, J. (1999). *Life as a Disabled Child: A Qualitative Study of Young People's Experiences and Perspectives.* http://disability-studies.leeds.ac.uk/files/2011/10/life-as-a-disabled-child-report.pdf. Accessed 18 Feb 2016.

Welsh, B., Jarvis, S., Hammal, D., & Colver, A. (2006). How Might Districts Identify Local Barriers to Participation for Children with Cerebral Palsy? *Public Health, 120*(2), 167–175.

World Health Organisation. (2001). *ICF. International Classification of Functioning, Disability and Health* (1st ed.). Geneva: World Health Organisation.

World Health Organisation International Classification of Functioning WHOICF Resolution. (2012). *Merger of ICF-CY INTO ICF pdf,* 311kb. Available from: http://www.who.int/classifications/icf/whoficresolution2012icfcy.pdf?ua=1. Accessed 28 July 2015.

Young, N. L., Williams, J. I., Yoshida, K. K., & Wright, J. G. (2000). Measurement Properties of the Activities Scale for Kids. *Journal Clinical Epidemiology, 53,* 125–137.

Young, B., Rice, H., Dixon-Woods, M., Colver, A. F., & Parkinson, K. N. (2007). Assessing HRQoL in Disabled Children. *Developmental Medicine and Child Neurology, 49,* 660–665.

Ytterhus, B. (2012). Everyday Segregation Amongst Disabled Children and Their Peers: A Qualitative Longitudinal Study in Norway. *Children and Society, 26,* 203–213. doi:10.1111/j.1099-0860.2012.00433.x.

Dawn Pickering is a former children's physiotherapist, and now a Senior Lecturer at Cardiff University in the School of Healthcare Sciences. Now as a part-time doctoral student, Dawn is exploring the choices for participation in recreational activities with children and young people with cerebral palsy. Dawn volunteers in Cardiff's RaceRunning Dragons Club.

Making Space for the Embodied Participation of Young Disabled Children in a Children's Centre in England

Heloise Maconochie

Key Points

- This chapter (re)-presents three stories and reflections on the perspectives of one young disabled child's experiences of participation in the context of a children's centre in England.
- Young disabled children are often excluded from participatory processes and are amongst the least listened to people in society.
- This chapter shows how to reflexively 'read' children's multimodal communicative practices and pay attention to the often taken-for-granted objects, routines and interactions of their everyday lives.
- To make space for a more inclusive theory of participation that embraces young, non-verbal disabled children, participation needs to be framed to incorporate embodied performances (including bodily gestures, acts of resistance, emotional tone), as well as voice.

Introduction

Some time ago I had the idea that I wanted to explore what very young disabled children's participation looks like, given that these children are often excluded from decision-making processes and are amongst the least listened

H. Maconochie (✉)
Indiana University Purdue University Fort Wayne, Fort Wayne, IN, USA

© The Author(s) 2018
K. Runswick-Cole et al. (eds.), *The Palgrave Handbook of Disabled Children's Childhood Studies*, https://doi.org/10.1057/978-1-137-54446-9_10

to people in society. Inspired by the new social studies of childhood and by emancipatory disability research, I didn't want to do research on young disabled children, rather I wanted to do research with them, and with those who care and work with them, including parents and early childhood practitioners. I knew that the endeavour would require considerable collaboration and trust if, as researchers, children, parents and practitioners, we were to build shared understandings of disabled children's perspectives. During the course of the study I also became aware that we needed to move away from a modernist mindset of trying to seek the 'truth' and evaluate the 'validity' of young disabled children's views, towards engaging in a process of reflexive meaning-making between people of different ages, abilities and social positions. The medium of narrative, both in sharing stories, and in storying other people's stories, became a key component in our meaning-making as we sought to recognise and valorise the everyday participatory practices of young disabled children.

I begin this chapter with a discussion of the notion of 'children's participation'. Next I outline the aim and methodological approach of the study, and then I offer three stories and reflections on the perspectives of one young disabled child's experiences of participation in the context of a Sure Start Children's Centre. Children's centres are multi-agency early years settings that aim to improve outcomes for children under the age of five, including at-risk children and their families. Although currently under threat due to funding cuts, they offer a range of services such as early education and childcare, employment advice, health and family support, as well as therapeutic services for children with impairments.

Disabled Children's Participation

In the global North, the notion of 'participation' is often associated with children expressing their views and participating in decision-making. Over 20 years ago, Hart (1992) referred to participation as 'the process of sharing decisions which affect one's life and the life of the community in which one lives' (p. 5). He went on to suggest that participation 'is the means by which a democracy is built'. Indeed, as the participation agenda has gained momentum over the last two decades, a series of legislative and policy measures have been introduced to ensure that children from birth, including disabled children, have a say when decisions are being made about their lives and communities. For example, the participation of young disabled children in expressing their views and making decisions in matters that affect them is a fundamental right enshrined in the United Nations Convention on the Rights of the Child (UNCRC 1989) and in General Comment 9 (UNCRC 2006).

In spite of this, young disabled children's views, everyday experiences and preferences are often missing in policy, practice and research. This may be due in part to prevailing attitudes that disabled children are too vulnerable, incompetent or dependent to be able to articulate an opinion or participate in decision-making. Indeed, research suggests that young children in general, and young disabled children in particular, are most at risk of being excluded from participatory processes (Clark et al. 2003; Pascal and Bertram 2009). Perhaps, this is unsurprising given that traditional notions of democracy valorise neutral, rational, verbal forms of participation (Young 2000). Indeed, the history of democracy over the last 150 years is one in which women, black and disabled people, children and other marginalised groups have been excluded from participatory forums on the basis of constructions that they exhibit emotional, dependent and irrational characteristics. Whilst many marginalised adults have struggled against these exclusions, today children in general, and disabled children in particular, continue to be excluded from many forms of participation through the use of a similar rationale, invariably in the name of their welfare (Cockburn 1998; Roche 1999; Moosa-Mitha 2005). However, as scholars from the fields of childhood and disability studies have argued, children with and without impairments are capable of communicating their views and preferences in a variety of multimodal ways, and do so from the moment they are born (Cavet and Sloper 2004; Flewitt 2005; Komulainen 2007; Franklin and Sloper 2009; Alderson et al. 2005; Tisdall 2012).

Young (2000) suggests that if democracy is to be deepened so that the participation of marginalised groups is recognised and respected, then inclusive communication is essential. She asserts that even when marginalised people are formally included in participatory processes, they may find that their claims are not taken seriously, since 'the dominant mood may find their ideas or modes of expression silly or simple, and not worthy of consideration' (p. 55). Although Young does not apply her argument to children, this type of exclusion is particularly apposite for young children, and those with impairments, who may find their modes of expression disregarded as stupid or irrelevant. Young argues that in order to deepen democracy and avoid exclusion, three important modes of communication should be recognised, alongside verbal, rational deliberation. She refers to these more inclusive modes of communication as 'greeting', 'rhetoric' and 'narrative'. 'Greeting' involves recognising others as included in the discussion, especially those who differ in terms of opinion, interest or social location. 'Rhetoric' refers to the variety of ways something can be said, including emotional tone, use of figures of speech, non-verbal and symbolic gestures. Finally, 'narrative' storytelling and situated knowledge should not be dismissed as 'mere anecdotes' since they are vital in enabling people to understand the experience of others and to develop a shared discourse. In this research study with young disabled children, the practitioners, staff and I sought to valorise these three important modes in order to build a shared understanding of what young disabled children's participation looks like in the specific context of an English children's centre.

Aim and Methodological Approach

This chapter (re-)presents three narrative observations I conducted of one young disabled child's experiences of participation. These narratives formed part of a larger ethnographic participatory action research project that took place with children, parents and practitioners in one children's centre in the north of England (Maconochie 2013). The overarching aim of the research was to generate contextualised understandings of what participation looks like for children, including disabled children, in this particular multidisciplinary context. There is a broad and ongoing base of research evidence that has sought to evaluate these centres from adults' perspectives and government agendas (e.g. DfE 2009–2015). However, the perspectives and everyday agendas of the children who participate in these services have been largely ignored. Given this gap in the research evidence, a voluntary team made up of a variety of practitioners, parents and children came together with a PhD student to explore the following questions: What does young disabled children's participation look like in a children's centre context, and how is it enhanced and constrained?

Ethnographic research takes place in the natural settings of people's everyday lives and involves direct observation over an extended period of time. It aims to offer an in-depth understanding of the way people live and work and the culture in which they do so by paying particular attention to the motives, emotions and perspectives of those studied. It is concerned with understanding 'the social meanings and activities of people in a given field' (Brewer 2000, p. 11). According to proponents of the 'new social studies', ethnographic methods allow children a 'more direct voice in the production of data' (James and Prout 1997, p. 8) than many other methods because children control what they do, when and with whom (Tudge and Hogan 2005). Furthermore, an ethnographic framework is particularly useful for research with young children and children with impairments who may not use verbal modes of communication (Flewitt 2005, 2006). Traditionally babies, children who communicate in non-verbal ways, and children with communication difficulties have been excluded from participation in research (Davis and Watson 2000, 2001; Corker and Davis 2000; Alderson 2008). By focusing on the range of strategies children use to express meaning, including talk, body movement, gesture and gaze, observational methods provide a means of challenging language-biased approaches to research by 'supporting multimodal expressions of meaning rather than "pathologizing"... silence' (Flewitt 2006, p. 46). Warming (2005) argues therefore that ethnography can be a powerful method for listening to what Malaguzzi (1993) has referred to as 'the hundred languages of children'. Throughout the yearlong fieldwork our aim was to adopt a reflexive approach, in order to recognise children's multimodal forms of expression, enhance their participation, and tell the everyday stories of their lives.

Three stories illustrating the participation of two-year-old Haniya are presented here, followed by an analytical discussion of the data. (Haniya is a pseudonym, as are all subsequent names of participants.) When I first met Haniya, the Special Educational Needs Coordinator told me that she has cerebral palsy with associated mobility, hearing, communication and learning difficulties. I sought the informed consent of all the adults involved in interactions with Haniya before we began the research. However, as Cocks (2006) suggests, the common understanding of informed consent, which relies on presentation of information by the researcher, followed by understanding and response by the participant, has inadvertently served to exclude particular children from research. I therefore sought the ongoing assent of Haniya, as a means of finding a more inclusive method of gaining consent. This required me to remain vigilant to Haniya's responses at all times, for example, being sensitive to her communicative practices, displays of emotions and lines of interest. Following this, a process of abductive reasoning took place in which I drew upon theories of democracy (Young 2000; Fraser 1999), disciplinary power (Foucault 1977) and ethics (Dahlberg and Moss 2005) to illuminate and inform the discussion of the narratives. In the stories that follow, I argue that Haniya's participation in expressing her views and in decision-making is enacted, not in the discursive space of the spoken or written word, but through a series of embodied performances in the physical, temporal and relational spaces of the children's centre. In the first story, Haniya's participation occurs through her relations with material objects within the physical environment.

Story 1: Material Matters

Haniya and her mother, Nasrin, arrive at nursery, at the start of the morning session. Nasrin sits Haniya on the ground. She scans the different toys in the room and fetches a scarf and an electronic ball that lights up and plays sounds as you move it. Nasrin rolls the ball to her daughter. Haniya bends over, placing her face next to the ball. She watches the lights closely until they stop flashing. Nasrin fastens stiff, fabric gaiters around Haniya's legs. For several moments Haniya repeatedly rubs her thumb back and forth against the fastenings. Then she picks up the silky scarf. She scrunches it, lets it go, strokes it with her fingers and then rubs her thumb against it several times. Nasrin picks up the material and throws it above Haniya's head. Haniya looks up, to track its flight. It floats and lands on Haniya's face. Haniya smiles and bounces up and down, vocalising 'ahh, ahh, ahh' in rhythm to her movements. Nasrin laughs. Nasrin repeats this activity several times. Both parties seem to be enjoying the experience. Haniya lies down on her side and rocks gently. 'Are you going to get up Haniya?' asks Nasrin. Nasrin sits Haniya up. Haniya tries to pull her new spectacles off her face. 'No Haniya', says Nasrin gently and firmly, as she moves Haniya's hand away from the spectacles. Haniya tries again to take off her specs and Nasrin intervenes. Haniya lets out a few whimpering noises as though she is protesting but then leaves the glasses alone. Sandra, the physiotherapist arrives: 'Hello Haniya. Oh, you've got glasses. We're going to do three exercises today'.

In this short episode, it seems that certain material objects are of particular importance and enjoyment to Haniya: The flashing lights, the fluffy fastenings, the silky texture of the scarf. Haniya looks, touches, rubs, strokes, scrunches, drops and tracks these objects of interest. The joy of experiencing the flashing lights and floating material is expressed in her body movements and gestures: She leans forward to watch more closely, she smiles, she makes noises and she bounces up and down. Of the plethora of toys and objects in the room, Nasrin seems to know which materials matter to Haniya. She carefully scans the room to select those objects that she thinks will appeal to her daughter, and Haniya responds with pleasure. Other objects and technologies carry significance too: For example, the new spectacles. They have negative associations for Haniya. Perhaps they are a source of discomfort or irritation. On the other hand, Nasrin wants Haniya to keep the glasses on because they will help her see better, which may increase her quality of life.

Reflecting on this observation later with Haniya's mother and the nursery practitioners we note that 'If children's participation involves ascertaining children's perspectives of matters that affect them, then this has to include recognition of the everyday material objects that affect and matter to them' (Maconochie 2013, p. 143). In young children's ever-widening circle of physical space (carer's arms, floor, home, children's centre, park, neighbourhood) material things, however seemingly mundane, are fundamental to their everyday experiences and perspectives. Therefore, for those interested in ascertaining disabled children's perspectives, this means that there is much to learn from the things that matter to children, as well as the things they discard. This includes the little things, the ordinary, everyday, taken-for-granted objects that mean something to children. As Latour (2002) argues, 'Consider things, and you will have humans. Consider humans and you are by that very act interested in things' (p. 20).

Of course, we cannot presume to know just what Haniya's perspectives of these objects are and what they mean to her, because, even if we could talk to her about them, there would always be slippage between what she communicates and how we interpret and represent those meanings. However, we might infer that these objects have particular value for Haniya. She demonstrates particular preferences. The objects are imbued with emotions and meanings, not in disembodied, cognitive ways, but in practical and haptic relations (based on the sense of touch) within and between bodies, both human (between Haniya and Nasrin, and/or other carers and children) and non-human (between Haniya, material things and her surrounding environment). Therefore, as a research team we conclude that since children's participation is practised through their relations with everyday objects and other bodies, this requires that we pay close attention to the importance of these materialities in children's everyday lives. Over the coming weeks, we sought to enhance Haniya's participation in decision-making further by working with her to develop a treasure basket containing some of her favourite items.

In summing up this story, I wish to situate these 'findings' within broader political arguments. If, as the UNCRC suggests, children's participation involves ascertaining children's perspectives of matters that affect them, this has to include recognition of the everyday material objects that are important to them, followed by incorporation of these materials into our provisions and practices with children. However small or seemingly ordinary, certain material artefacts matter profoundly to children and therefore carry political significance. I suggest, therefore, that attention to the importance of these materialities in children's everyday lives is part of what Fraser (1999) refers to as a 'politics of recognition and redistribution'. In other words, for practitioner-researchers seeking to enhance disabled children's participation, this involves cultural recognition of their material preferences as well as resource distribution that takes these preferences into account.

In the next story, Haniya's participation occurs not through the spoken word, but through her bodily protest against the temporal routines of daily physiotherapy.

Story 2: Resisting Routines

All the children in the nursery have been taken outside to play in the outdoor area, except Haniya who has to stay behind for her daily physiotherapy. Sandra, the physio, demonstrates some new exercises that Haniya needs to learn, to Nasrin, Haniya's mother, and Jo, her keyworker. Sandra explains, 'We're going to do three new exercises: 'four-point kneeling', 'high kneeling' and 'standing up', which you need to do with her each day'…

After finishing the first two exercises, Sandra places Haniya in a sitting position. Haniya stops making moaning noises, suggesting that she is more comfortable in this position.

Sandra to Haniya:	Time out. Are you happy now?
Sandra to Jo:	Give her two minutes rest.
	Haniya lies down for a while and then sits up to look at a musical ball that Sandra is rolling back and forth.
Sandra to Haniya:	Are you ready for the next exercise now?
	Sandra places gaiters on Haniya's legs and Haniya watches quietly.
Sandra to Haniya:	Good girl.
Sandra to Jo:	She needs to be stood at a surface, or at a wall, or against you. She needs holding and standing because she can't participate with her legs with the gaiters on.
Jo to Sandra:	About five minutes?
Sandra to Jo:	Yes. Little and often.
	Sandra places Haniya in a standing position so that Haniya's back is against Sandra's chest. She places an arm across Haniya's chest to support her. Haniya cries. Jo tries to distract her with a toy but Haniya drops her head and continues to cry.
Sandra (singing):	Haniya standing tall, Haniya standing tall, one, two, three, four, five, Haniya standing tall.

	Haniya throws her head to the side, as if in distress. She is crying loudly now. She throws herself back against Sandra and moans.
	Sandra picks up Haniya. Her cries subside. Sandra carries Haniya over to the wall.
Sandra to Jo and Nasrin:	I'll just show you the 'standing against the wall' position.
	Haniya bends her body over to the side so that Sandra is unable to stand her against the wall.
Sandra to Haniya:	You're not having any of it today.
Sandra to Jo:	If she doesn't want to do it she won't.
Sandra to Haniya:	OK poppet, you're telling me quite clearly that its time to stop.

Unlike her non-disabled peers, Haniya is excluded from outdoor play so that the adults have time to conduct physiotherapy. Time penetrates Haniya's body 'and with it all the meticulous controls of power' (Foucault 1977, p. 151). This is seen in the cyclical pattern of exercise ('*About five minutes*', '*Little and often*') and rest (*Time out*', '*Give her two minutes*') and the expectation that these exercises will be performed as part of Haniya's daily routine at home and nursery. Power also circulates through physical manipulation of Haniya's body, and through the use of toys as technologies of distraction/coercion. Here the disciplinary practice of physiotherapy functions ambivalently: in one sense imposing limits and constraints on Haniya's body and her participation ('*she can't participate with her legs with the gaiters on*'); and in another sense increasing her bodily capacities which, in turn, enable her to participate through bodily resistances ('*dropping her head*', '*crying loudly*', '*throwing herself back*', '*bending*'). The manipulation of Haniya's body places her in a passive position, and yet Haniya is also active in resisting the exercise routines, through moaning, crying and changing her body posture.

As I reflect on the above episode, it occurs to me that whether children like Haniya are seen as participants, exercising agency through practices of resistance depends on the reflexive capacities of the people interacting with them, in this case the physiotherapist. Sandra 'reads' Haniya's resistances as an indication that Haniya wants the exercises to stop ('*OK poppet, you're telling me quite clearly that its time to stop*'). Her reflexive interpretation of Haniya's body language also seems to suggest that Haniya participates by shaping the temporal domain of her life ('*You're not having any of it today*'; '*you're telling me... its time to stop*'). As Davis and Watson (2006) argue 'For resistance to be read as meaningful, cultural exchange has to occur between the participants in a social setting' (p. 165). If this does not happen, young disabled children's participatory behaviours can be seen as lacking meaning and can therefore be ignored by the adults caring for them.

Haniya's participation is embodied, in the sense that her views and decisions are expressed though her bodily resistances. An embodied conceptualisation of participation challenges the Cartesian dualistic separation of mind and body which arises from the maxim 'I think therefore I am'. Indeed it questions prevailing conceptions of participation, which value verbal, cognitive and rational forms of thinking and decision-making above corporeal experience. Here Haniya's participation is enacted through emotional tone and bodily action. Indeed, as Alderson (2001) argues, respecting young children's rights to participate depends on accepting that all human beings are bodies as well as minds. As I reflect on this, it occurs to me that children's bodies are almost entirely absent within research accounts and theories of children's participation. Studying young children in their spatial domains helps to throw light on the important role of inter-corporeality in participation. Indeed, a closer appreciation of the somatic details of children's lives gives us a richer insight into how participation is embodied in practice.

Time and routine shape children's participation, but children also participate in shaping the temporal patterns of their lives. As this story suggests, young disabled children are capable of communicating preferences about the duration of their therapeutic routines through their embodied performances. However, if children's participation in temporal processes is to be enhanced, then these performances and acts of resistance need to be reflexively 'read' by the adults caring for them. It also requires that practitioners are flexible in the process of managing children's daily routines.

The final story highlights the importance of the relational space for supporting young disabled children's participation.

Story 3: Encountering Care

Haniya has been at nursery for half an hour with little interaction with other people or toys. She has been placed in the middle of the room and is unable to reach any of the resources that are situated around the perimeter, since she is not yet mobile. As a consequence, Haniya spends her time alternating between sucking her thumb, making quiet whimpering noises, staring at the ground between her legs or into the middle distance, playing with the fastenings on her gaiters, rolling onto her side and sitting up. I get the impression that she is bored. On one occasion a practitioner calls to Haniya from across the room but then resumes her conversation with the adults. Haniya does not register the greeting, perhaps because she can't hear it. On another occasion a practitioner rolls a ball in her direction, but it stops short of Haniya and therefore she does not see it. Whenever adults and children walk past her, Haniya looks up at them, or reaches out, but this goes unnoticed.

After 30 minutes a practitioner asks where Haniya's treasure basket is. A reply is given, but then the practitioner explains that Haniya will need her tilting table in order to use the basket. The practitioner leaves the room to search for the table. Another ten minutes pass.

In the meantime, Kamal (aged 2) is playing in the area just behind Haniya. He is playing with a small plastic horse and a rainmaker. Haniya turns her head to listen to the rainmaker. She smiles at Kamal. Kamal walks over to her. 'Haniya, Haniya, Haniya', he chants tenderly in her ear. Then he strokes the horse gently across the back of her head and sits down next to her. 'Haniya, Haniya, Haniya', he repeats, as he passes the rainmaker to her. Haniya rubs her thumb back and forth against the rubber bands around the rainmaker. Haniya pauses for a moment to look at Kamal. Then Kamal walks away and Haniya returns her attention to the rainmaker.

During this time, the practitioners take a custodial and functional role in caring for the children: All the children are safe and seemingly occupied, whilst the adults fold laundry, prepare snack, change nappies and mop up paint. Perhaps, because Haniya is relatively quiet and they are busy talking, they are unaware of her whimpers and bodily cues that seem to indicate a lack of stimulation and boredom. Haniya's participation is restricted to 'passive participation' (Boyden and Ennew 1997), in the sense that she is physically present in the room and taking part in some sort of activity (*sucking her thumb*', '*playing with the fastenings*', '*rolling onto her side*). However, unlike the other children, Haniya is unable to participate in a more active way, such as being able to decide what she plays with, on account of the disabling environment she finds herself in (*she … is unable to reach any of the resources that are situated around the perimeter*). On a few occasions, practitioners momentarily acknowledge Haniya by calling across the room, by rolling a ball in her direction and by searching for her treasure basket and table. However, it is impossible for Haniya to respond, given the physical remoteness of these actions.

Haniya tries to affect her experience of nursery through '*whimpering*', '*looking up*' and '*reaching out*'. However, the lack of awareness of this by the staff, and their focus on the functional rather than more responsive and relational aspects of care, constrains Haniya's ability to participate in influencing the situation. In spite of her seeming desire to engage with others ('*whenever adults and children walk past her Haniya looks up*'), her embodied views go unrecognised until Kamal arrives. Here we see Young's (2000) notions of 'greeting' and rhetoric' beautifully exemplified. Haniya's attention is grabbed by Kamal's physical proximity and the sound of the rainmaker. She greets Kamal by *'turning her head'* and *'smiling'*. Kamal reciprocates by *'walking over to her'*, *'whispering her name tenderly'*, *'stroking her head'*, *'sitting next to her'*, *'repeating'* her name and *'passing the rainmaker to her'*. Thus, Kamal's actions exhibit aspects of both emotional and functional care. His care for Haniya is sensitive (he speaks *'tenderly'* and acts *'gently'*), emotionally supportive (he sits next to her, he calls her name) as well as practical (he gives her a toy to play with).

Dahlberg and Moss (2005) link participation, not just to political ideas of citizenship and decision-making, but also to ethical ideas of care and encounter. An ethic of care and of encounter is built on welcoming and hospitality of the Other and trying to listen to the Other from his or her own position and experience. It is characterised by a non-instrumental relationship founded on an openness and responsibility to the Other. Kamal's interaction with Haniya is characterised by openness and proximity. This means he is able to listen to the tacit soliciting of care that is the call of the Other. Thus he responds to the call of Haniya's face through embodied acts of recognition and care. In this Haniya becomes an active participant, able to initiate interaction and influence action, rather than simply a custodial object. Moreover, this is a reciprocal relationship of care and recognition: Haniya welcomes Kamal with a smile and *'pauses for a moment'* to look Kamal in the face before he ends the 'dialogue' and walks away.

Based on this episode, and the others above, I would suggest that young disabled children's participation need not be essentially rational or verbal, but is always intersubjective and intercorporeal, evoked when encountering the face of another. It occurs in relational spaces, characterised by an ethic of care, proximity and openness to the call of the other. However, young disabled children's participation can be constrained by the unresponsiveness of adults and their focus on the functional rather than the dialogical in care relationships. Consequently, if children's participation is to be enhanced, then adults must move beyond the functional-custodial towards the relational-ethical. This means that caring relationships should not only provide for and protect disabled children but should also take responsibility for the 'call of the other'. Hence, they must also allow for the participation of children. Children can only ever become active participants if the relationships that precede their speaking and embodied actions are taken seriously. Thus, it is in the context of responsive, caring relationships, characterised more by dialogue than functional-technical relations, that children's participation is most likely to take place.

Conclusion

During this chapter I have critically examined what disabled children's participation means and looks like in the particular context of a children's centre. I have suggested that if we are to gain a greater understanding of how young disabled children's participation is enhanced and/or constrained, then we need to pay attention to the 'small things': the often taken-for-granted objects, routines and interactions of everyday life. Making space for the participation of young disabled children requires attention to the physical/material, temporal and relational domains of their lives.

Underpinning this chapter is the idea that if we are to have a more inclusive theory of participation that embraces young, non-verbal disabled children, participation needs to be framed to incorporate embodied performances (including bodily gestures, acts of resistance, emotional tone), as well as voice. We also need to appreciate that children's participation does not occur in individual children's isolated performances, but through reciprocal, interdependent caring relationships.

The medium of narrative helps us to develop a shared discourse in which children's participation is recognised as a micropolitical process of embodied performance in space and not simply as a cognitive discursive activity of children expressing their views and making decisions. These understandings have significant implications for broadening current conceptualisations of participation to make them more inclusive of young, disabled children's perspectives.

References

Alderson, P. (2001). Young Children's Health Care Rights and Consent. In B. Franklin (Ed.), *New Handbook of Children's Rights: Comparative Policy and Practice* (pp. 155–167). London: Routledge.

Alderson, P. (2008). *Young Children's Rights: Exploring Beliefs, Principles and Practice* (2nd ed.). London: Jessica Kingsley Publishers.

Alderson, P., Hawthorne, J., & Killen, M. (2005). The Participation Rights of Premature Babies. *International Journal of Children's Rights, 13*(1), 31–50.

Boyden, J., & Ennew, J. (1997). *Children in Focus: A Manual for Participatory Research with Children*. Stockholm: Rädda Barnen.

Brewer, J. D. (2000). *Ethnography*. Buckingham: Open University Press.

Cavet, J., & Sloper, P. (2004). Participation of Disabled Children in Individual Decisions About Their Lives and in Public Decisions About Service Development. *Children and Society, 18*(4), 278–290.

Clark, A., McQuail, S., & Moss, P. (2003). *Exploring the Field of Listening to and Consulting with Young Children*. Nottingham: DES Publications.

Cockburn, T. (1998). Children and Citizenship in Britain: A Case for a Socially Interdependent Model of Citizenship. *Childhood, 5*(1), 99–117.

Cocks, A. (2006). The Ethical Maze: Finding an Inclusive Path Towards Gaining Children's Agreement to Research Participation. *Childhood, 13*(2), 247–266.

Corker, M., & Davis, J. M. (2000). Disabled Children—(Still) Invisible Under the Law. In J. Cooper & S. Vernon (Eds.), *The Law, Rights and Disability* (pp. 217–237). London: Jessica Kingsley.

Dahlberg, G., & Moss, P. (2005). *Ethics and Politics in Early Childhood Education*. London: Routledge Falmer.

Davis, J. M., & Watson, N. (2000). Disabled Children's Rights in Every Day Life: Problematising Notions of Competency and Promoting Self-Empowerment. *International Journal of Children's Rights, 8*(3), 211–228.

Davis, J. M., & Watson, N. (2001). Where Are the Children's Experiences? Analysing Social and Cultural Exclusion in 'Special' and 'Mainstream' Schools. *Disability and Society, 16*(5), 671–687.

Davis, J. M., & Watson, N. (2006). Countering Stereotypes of Disability: Disabled Children and Resistance. In M. Corker & T. Shakespeare (Eds.), *Disability/Postmodernity: Embodying Disability Theory* (pp. 159–174). London: Continuum.

Department for Education (DfE). (2009–2015). *Evaluation of Children's Centres in England (ECCE)* [online]. https://www.gov.uk/government/collections/evaluation-of-childrens-centres-in-england-ecce. Accessed 20 May 2016.

Flewitt, R. (2005). Is Every Child's Voice Heard? Researching the Different Ways 3-Year-Old Children Communicate and Make Meaning at Home and in a Preschool Playgroup. *Early Years, 25*(3), 207–222.

Flewitt, R. (2006). Using Video to Investigate Preschool Classroom Interaction: Education Research Assumptions and Methodological Practices. *Visual Communication, 5*(1), 25–50.

Foucault, M. (1977). *Discipline and Punish: The Birth of a Prison*. London: Penguin.

Franklin, A., & Sloper, P. (2009). Supporting the Participation of Disabled Children and Young People in Decision-Making. *Children and Society, 23*(1), 3–15.

Fraser, N. (1999). Social Justice in the Age of Identity Politics: Redistribution, Recognition and Participation. In L. Ray & A. Sayer (Eds.), *Culture and Economy After the Cultural Turn* (pp. 25–52). London: Sage.

Hart, R. (1992). *Children's Participation: From Tokenism to Citizenship*. Florence: UNICEF.

James, A., & Prout, A. (Eds.). (1997). *Constructing and Reconstructing Childhood* (2nd ed.). London: Falmer.

Komulainen, S. (2007). The Ambiguity of the Child's "Voice" in Social Research. *Childhood, 14*, 11–28.

Latour, B. (2002). Morality and Technology: The End of Means. *Theory, Culture and Society, 19*(5/6), 247–260.

Maconochie, H. (2013). *Young Children's Participation in a Sure Start Children's Centre* (Unpublished PhD Thesis) [online]. http://shura.shu.ac.uk/7437/. Accessed 20 May 2015.

Malaguzzi, L. (1993). For an Education Based on Relationships. *Young Children, 49*(1), 9–17.

Moosa-Mitha, M. (2005). A Difference-Centred Alternative to Theorization of Children's Citizenship Rights. *Citizenship Studies, 9*(4), 369–388.

Pascal, C., & Bertram, T. (2009). Listening to Young Citizens: The Struggle to Make Real a Participatory Paradigm in Research with Young Children. *European Early Childhood Education Research Journal, 17*(2), 249–262.

Roche, J. (1999). Children, Rights, Participation and Citizenship. *Childhood, 6*(4), 475–493.

Tisdall, E. K. M. (2012). The Challenge and Challenging of Childhood Studies? Learning from Disability Studies and Research with Disabled Children. *Children and Society, 26*(3), 181–191.

Tudge, J., & Hogan, D. (2005). An Ecological Approach to Observations of Children's Everyday Lives. In S. Greene & D. Hogan (Eds.), *Researching Children's Experiences* (pp. 102–122). London: Sage.

UNCRC (United Nations Committee on the Rights of the Child). (2006). *The Rights of Children with Disabilities, General Comment 9*. Geneva: OHCHR CRC/C/GC/9. 27 February 2007 [online]. http://www.childrensrights.ie/files/CRC-GC9_Disability06.pdf. Accessed 22 Sept 2009

United Nations. (1989). *Convention on the Rights of the Child*. Geneva: United Nations.

Warming, H. (2005). Participant Observation: A Way to Learn About Children's Perspectives. In A. Clark, A. T. Kjørholt, & P. Moss (Eds.), *Beyond Listening: Children's Perspectives on Early Childhood Services* (pp. 51–70). Bristol: The Policy Press.

Young, I. M. (2000). *Inclusion and Democracy*. New York: Oxford University Press.

Dr Heloise Maconochie is a visiting scholar at Indiana University–Purdue University, Fort Wayne, USA. She has worked as a Senior Lecturer in Early Childhood Studies and Teacher Education at Sheffield Hallam University, UK, and as an early years coordinator and primary school teacher. Her research interests include early childhood care and education, disabled children's childhoods, children's rights and participatory methodologies. She is also a Court Appointed Special Advocate for abused and neglected children.

Interrogating the 'Normal' in the 'Inclusive' Early Childhood Classroom: Silence, Taboo and the 'Elephant in the Room'

Karen Watson

Key Points

- Problematising the notion of 'inclusion' and the 'truths' that inform policy and practice.
- Turning the focus of 'inclusion' towards the discursive constitution of the un-interrogated 'normal' and its effects on subjectivities in the classroom.
- Making visible how silences operate as discursive practices to exclude the Other.

Introduction

The 'inclusion' of children with a medical and/or psychological diagnosis into the 'mainstream' early childhood classroom has become common policy and practice in Australia and other countries. Research in the field for the most part has focused on the child with a diagnosis and their transition and 'inclusion'. More recently an alternative view has argued the need to turn the interrogatory gaze away from the child with a diagnosis towards the so-called mainstream or normal children in the classroom. This perspective questions the power and knowledge of the diagnosis and the disciplines that produce it. The notion of the constructed 'normal', against which all children are explicitly and implic-

K. Watson (✉)
School of Education, University of Newcastle, Callaghan, NSW, Australia

© The Author(s) 2018
K. Runswick-Cole et al. (eds.), *The Palgrave Handbook of Disabled Children's Childhood Studies*, https://doi.org/10.1057/978-1-137-54446-9_11

itly measured, is challenged and destabilised by this view. In this chapter, I present some of the data created in a six-month ethnographic study in three early childhood classrooms in New South Wales (NSW), Australia (Watson 2017). Using a post-structural framework and analysis, I make visible the multiple ways that children produce, reproduce and maintain the category of the 'normal' by taking up the discursive practices of silence. I argue that this produces a 'taboo' around the discursively positioned Other, the child with a diagnosis. The 'taboo' becomes part of the struggle to conserve social order and sustain the 'normal'. The 'elephant in the room' emerges as the prevailing discourses create an awkward silence.

Troubling the Concept of 'Inclusion'

Over the past decades, in early childhood education in Australia and other countries, there has been a move towards 'inclusion' and the mainstreaming of children with a diagnosis into settings with children who do not have a diagnosis (Warming 2011). The Australian Government's 'Early Years Learning Framework' (Australian Government Department of Education, Employment and Workplace 2009) supports the idea of 'inclusive learning communities' (p. 15), where ability and disability are viewed as aspects of diversity. However, research undertaken in 'inclusive' education underscores the challenges of such a policy, and the inclusion approach in the early years has been described as 'far from ideal' (Grace et al. 2008, p. 18).

As others have argued before me, 'inclusive' education, for the most part, has failed to interrogate the normative assumptions that shape it (Allan 2008; Graham and Slee 2008). 'Inclusive' education practices continue to operate within the framework of 'special education', drawing on knowledge that focuses on pathologising the individual child while measuring and comparing their difference from the norm. The ideology that underpins the concept of 'inclusion' has not yet taken the same 'leap forward' as the children's physical relocation (Slee and Allan 2001), and the medical model of disability for the most part continues to inform 'inclusive' education practice and educational research.

Graham (2006) warns us to be mindful of the many different ways in which the term 'inclusion' can be understood. We cannot assume that there is a shared or generalised meaning of 'inclusion' or a 'benign commonality' (Graham and Slee 2008), as this can hide competing and alternative discourses. Furthermore, discourses of 'inclusion' imply that there is a 'need' to include (Graham and Slee 2008), that there is somewhere to be included, and that there are those who are already included and those who are perhaps not, but in need of it. Who is included and why are others 'naturally' excluded and in need of including? Slee (2013) argues that trying to define inclusion is merely a distraction, and the need to further examine, understand and dismantle exclusion as it is present in education is the real challenge. Who are the already included groups and how do they create themselves and others?

In this study, silences are made visible, in particular how they operate in the production, reproduction and maintenance of the 'normal' or the already included group. Using a post-structural framework, I turn the traditional special education gaze away from the pathologised child, towards the 'normal', the automatically included, and focus on how the nuanced 'silences' of the children and their teachers produce particular inclusive and exclusive effects.

The 'Inclusive' Classrooms

I present in this chapter data from my doctoral study, which was created in a six-month post-structural ethnography in three early childhood classrooms in the Newcastle region of NSW, Australia. In all, 75 children and 12 teachers participated in the study. I visited each classroom for eight weeks, two mornings a week, for about four hours. While each centre was somewhat different, they all provided for the most part what might be described as a 'standard' preschool experience in Australia. A 'child-centred' pedagogy operated in all classrooms with adult planning, daily schedules and orchestration, all managed for the most part by the teachers and staff. To participate in the research, the classrooms needed to have a child with a diagnosis attending. As it turned out, they each had several children with a diagnosis enrolled. Overall, in the three classrooms there were ten children with a diagnosis in the study. I do not include any commentary on the children's diagnostic labels. Making no mention of the diagnosis is one way of disrupting acknowledgement of it, the merit of which might become apparent in the reading of this chapter.

In my research, I grappled with the many terms used in the field to describe children. In my writing I use the terms: 'child with a diagnosis', 'marked child' or the 'not normal' child, and alternatively, 'child without a diagnosis', the 'unmarked child' or the 'normal' child. To disrupt the work of diagnosis-as-usual, I use these terms to underscore the ways a diagnosis positions the child in the setting (Watson 2017).

In the field, other terms are more often used, such as 'special needs child', 'child with special needs', 'child with additional needs', the 'disabled child', 'child with a disability'. The term often changes, but it seems the epistemology remains firmly the same. These more commonly used labels, however, locate the 'problems' associated with inclusive practice *in* the child. The words 'with a diagnosis' best describes for me, how the child is *marked* by medical and psychological discourses. These terms I believe confer a certain 'truth' about the child which has effects for the 'inclusion' process.

In the creation of my data, observations and conversations with children, and sometimes the teachers, were recorded. I also took photographs of the children in the classroom to stimulate conversations about the child with a diagnosis. To enable my data generation, I paid attention to the unmarked children's encounters with and around each other and the marked child. Although not the focus, the child with a diagnosis was conceptualised as a catalyst and a way of observing inclusive and exclusive processes. In looking reflexively at this strategy, I do acknowledge my complicity in re/producing these limiting binaries and my regrettable, but unavoidable, further contribution to the child's marked positioning (Watson 2016). This was a useful strategy, nevertheless, as it helped to make noticeable the work being done by the unmarked children, as they maintained the borderlands of the 'normal'.

My focus was to explore ways to trouble the knowledge or 'regimes of truth' (Foucault 1977) that produce and privilege the 'normal', the already included, by asking the following: What is the 'normal'? How it is produced, reproduced and maintained in the classroom and what are its effects?

Conceptualising the 'Normal'

Foucault (1977) describes the norm as 'the new law of modern society' (p. 184) as it exercises power and gives muscle to a homogeneous social body. The norm has the power to impose uniformity, while at the same time individualising and making it possible to measure the gaps or the difference. Foucault proposes that the norm is fashioned via techniques of surveillance, where 'inspection functions ceaselessly. The gaze is alert everywhere' (Foucault 1977, p. 195). He identifies three mechanisms of surveillance that can be observed to shape the subjectivities of the children in the classroom: hierarchical observation, normalising judgements and examination. Hierarchical observation allows for the surveillance of the classroom at all times, a perfect disciplinary apparatus for monitoring and controlling, a view from everywhere as the norm supervises the surveillance of oneself and others.

Children in the classroom become objects under observation and scrutiny, but they also are capable of scrutinising others (Watson 2017). In the classrooms, I examine how the power of the norm is exercised *on* the children but also *by* the children as they encounter others who may not conform. Young children are very aware of diversity and difference from an early age and are very capable of identifying what they understand as the 'normal' or the 'right' way to be (Robinson and Jones-Diaz 2006). Actively drawing on classroom understandings of the 'normal', they adjust their own behaviours and observe and scrutinise the behaviour of others (Robinson and Jones-Diaz 2006). They are continually making decisions about whether or not those around them are the same as them or different.

The construction of a 'developmental norm was a standard based upon the average abilities or performances of children at a certain age on a particular task' (Rose 1999, p. 145). It has generated in the early childhood classroom a desirable standard. These calculations have presented a picture of what is 'normal' and what 'normality' looks like, enabling the 'normality' of any child to be assessed (Rose, p. 1999). Psychology as a discipline in association with the norm, Rose (1999) argues, has the power to reshape subjectivity as we 'our selves are defined and constructed and governed in psychological terms' (Rose 1999, p. xxxi). The classroom is a place where psychological judgements and comparisons are made about children by their teachers and by children about each other.

Examining the Work of the 'Normal'

In analysing the children's construction of the 'normal', I utilise Foucauldian discourse analysis, along with positioning theory (Harré and van Langenhove 1999) and category boundary work (Davies 1989; Petersen 2004). These tools are interwoven, as the discourses provide the subject positions that the children take up or reject, and all the while the children, as positioned subjects, produce and maintain the category membership in their encounters with each other. As 'discourse make available positions for subjects to take up' (Harré and van Langenhove 1999, p. 16), one can position oneself within the available discourses and having taken up a position as one's own, a subject sees the world from that vantage point drawing on the position's storylines, images, metaphors and concepts (Davies and Harré 1999). In taking up a position as a member of a particular category, created within the discourses, the children work to become a particular kind of person who knows *how* to belong and *how* to be correctly located as a member (Davies 1993). Knowing how to belong, and how to perform as a member, and how to maintain oneself that way, involves category boundary and maintenance work. By examining membership categories and the sanctions and exclusions in the classroom effected on those who 'fail' to be the 'proper child', it is possible to recognise the significance of the constitutive force of the discursive 'normal'. It is also possible to recognise its relative delegitimisation (Petersen 2004) of others. How does the delegitimisation happen and what are the effects of the 'normal' category boundary and maintenance work on the subjects in the 'inclusive' classroom?

Silences Have Effects

As the 'normal' does its category boundary work on difference, silence is taken up by the children as a discursive practice in order maintain the 'normal'.

> *Silence itself – the things one declines to say, or is forbidden to name, the discretion that is required between different speakers – is less the absolute limit of discourse, the other side from which it is separated by a strict boundary, than an element that functions alongside the things said, with them and in relation to them within over-all strategies.* (Foucault 2008, p. 27)

These discursive moves of silence work to shape the category boundary of the 'normal', while at the same time are also the product of the category maintenance work. How do silences position subjects? In examining the silences, I do not wish to create a binary between speech and silence, that is between what one says and what one does not say, but instead theorising with Foucault it seems that:

> *we must try to determine the different ways of not saying such things, how those who can and those who cannot speak of them are distributed, which type of discourse is authorised, or which form of discretion is required in either case.* (Foucault 2008, p. 27)

When I started the process of analysing my field notes and transcriptions, looking for some meaning and understanding, the silences 'spoke' loudly (Watson 2016). Meanings can be masked, if as a researcher one only interrogates the spoken, the words, in the data. Silences can powerfully exclude and oppress those who do not 'speak' from the authorised discourse and in contrast, privilege those who do (Mazzei 2007b). I attempt here, in my multiple readings of the data, to explore how silences and their effects contribute to the creation of a separation between the marked and the unmarked children.

Silence: Moving Past

As I walked toward the preschool car park one morning I could see a woman getting out of her car with an infant on one hip and holding the hand of a crying preschool aged child. I recognised this child as I got closer as Hugo (a child with a diagnosis). He was crying loudly and resisting his mother's attempt to take him through the preschool gate. His mother persisted and dragged him into the preschool building with difficulty. As I followed them and moved into the foyer of the building I saw Hugo just inside the door lying sprawled out with a sheet covering him. He was now alone.

Another parent and child pair had followed me into the foyer and they stared down at Hugo as they moved around his body in the restricted space. As I stood in the foyer a teacher approached Hugo and tried to coax him further into the building but this was unsuccessful. As I moved down the hallway I could hear the mother discussing with the teacher her resolve to leave him at the preschool as she was sure that he should not "get what he wants if he chucks a tantrum". I did not hear what the teacher's response was.

The mother then returned to the foyer and picked up Hugo by the arms saying, "You can't stay here someone might trip on you and sue me."

The mother took Hugo to the classroom and left him on the floor but he immediately stood up and returned to the foyer crying loudly.

Many parents, carers and children were arriving through the front door during this encounter. The adults stopped briefly, looked and frowned, all the time holding the hand of their child. The children moved through the area, they glanced briefly at Hugo and then moved on. (Field Notes, 23/10/12, S3, p. 15) (Watson 2017)

Hugo was upset at the beginning of the preschool day, as children often are, and his actions make this position quite clear. As the unmarked children entered the centre, they moved quickly and silently passed him to reinforce their unmarked 'normal' category membership. They positioned themselves as being independent and not showing *their* emotions at the beginning of the preschool day. They seemed to disregard Hugo's loud wild crying. The teachers also appeared to take this position of ignoring Hugo. He was positioned as a child with a diagnosis and his actions reinforced the characteristics of this diagnosis. This diagnosis, *his* diagnosis, created him within a deficit discourse (Nutbrown and Clough 2009; Purdue et al. 2009) and a member of a homogeneous group of other subjects similarly diagnosed. *His* diagnosis described 'who he was', a unitary (Davies 1989) and a somewhat irrational (Rose 1999) being. Special education discourses provide strategies to remediate deficits, and leaving Hugo in the foyer and waiting for him to calm down might be one of those strategies. Hugo, as a pathological subject, is an individual of 'concern', who is in need of careful scrutiny. One reading of this scene via special education discourses would consider that Hugo needs extra support, patience and tolerance for his morning transition to preschool. From this perspective over time Hugo might be remediated and become more like the 'normal'.

Alternatively, by turning the gaze towards the 'normal', a different reading of this scenario could interrogate the actions of the unmarked children and teachers and the 'silent' way they move around Hugo's body sprawled across the foyer floor, noisy and unavoidable. If one's body does not seem to fit the 'normal', one is still produced in relation to the 'normal' (Cadwallader 2007). Hugo's body collapsed in the foyer does not 'fit' the 'normal'. The discursive 'normal' offers only limited possibilities for the body and the way it can 'be' or 'act'. In their shared silence, the unmarked children position Hugo as Other, the abject. The 'abject' is produced in the category boundary work; the 'abject' represents what it is not possible to be. The abjecting of another is thought to be a way of establishing an 'I'. Kristeva (1982) contends that in order to establish an 'I'—one's own subjectivity—there is a separation of a part of one-self that is considered the 'not-I'. They see and hear him because his presence is 'obvious', but they do not *see or hear* him, as recognition of him is 'taboo', since his behaviour at this time is 'scandalous'. Hugo as a discursive subject is 'the elephant in the room', very present, but carefully avoided by everyone. Evading Hugo's discursively produced being affirms and strengthens the definition to which his does not conform.

Hugo, in locating himself in the foyer and loudly expressing his 'unbridled' emotions, makes his position very visible to everyone as they arrive. This public space performance may have worked for him before. His actions were not attributed to his dislike of preschool, or an unsettled start to the day but were read as a characteristic of his diagnosis. His mother also positioned him in this way, drawing on the contextual discourses, as she entered the space of the preschool, seeking the assistance of the 'experts' to transition him into the classroom. She positioned herself as the mother of the Other, somewhat 'helpless/powerless', while positioning the teachers as the ones with the power to advise and help, and relieve her of the embarrassment of her son's actions. She conceivably wants to drop her son off in the same way that other mothers do, the 'normal' way. Hugo's mother joins in with the teachers, drawing upon the circulating discourses, that inform her of the need to 'correct and coerce' (Foucault 1977) and remediate Hugo.

Overall, there is a feeling of angst and awkwardness in the foyer on this morning. No one seems to know what to do. When Hugo's mother picks him up and moves him into the classroom, he goes back to the foyer so that his 'protest' powerfully remains on show. Hugo seems to understand the powerful effects of using this public space at this public time. As Laws and Davies (2000) contend, power acts on the subject, making the subject possible, the condition of its possibility and its formation. Additionally, power also acts as what is taken up by the subject and retold in the subject's own acting (Laws and Davies 2000, p. 207). The angst of the teacher and Hugo's mother could be explained by Hugo's power in lying in the foyer. They become positioned as unable to act, powerless, as Hugo's actions cannot be managed in a rational way, as he is subjected as irrational. Hugo's subjection is made possible in this context by the power of psychological discourses and by his own acting. Hugo's irrational behaviour is 'loud and large' in the foyer. Silence becomes the best way to contain this subject, as unreason must be curtailed and silenced (Foucault 2006).

Hugo's mother's comment, about him 'having a tantrum', is possibly an attempt to draw on 'normal' discourses about young children's behaviours. How would an unmarked child, acting in a similar manner in the foyer, be positioned? Would they be regarded as naughty or 'bad' and be disciplined? Would the adults have a rational discussion with the child? Hugo's diagnosis subjects him as 'not normal' and his tantrum is considered pathological rather than normative. As pathological behaviour, the tantrum is no longer normative but an act of the unreasonable.

This performance of silence 'speaks' and requires our attentiveness (Mazzei 2007a) as it is shaped by and shapes subject formation and discursive practice. Derrida (1992) affirms that silence is a strategic response and 'polite silence can become the most insolent weapon' (p. 18). The children do not say anything to Hugo, or say anything about his actions, as that is constructed as 'taboo'. In this scene, nothing was 'said' by the children as they made their strategic move (Mazzei 2007b) around Hugo in the foyer; moreover, it was the 'unsaid' that was shaping their subjectivities and Hugo's.

Douglas (1966) asserts that in any social system there is a fear of the marginal, and the precautions against the dangerousness of the marginal must come from the 'normal', as the marginal 'cannot help his abnormal situation' (p.97). If a person has no place in the social system, they become regarded as a marginal being and Douglas suggests that all 'cultures' have ways of dealing with anomalies. One way of dealing with difference is to 'avoid' it, which she asserts 'affirms and strengthens the definitions to which they do not conform' (Douglas 1966, p. 39). Moreover, Douglas contends that anomalies and the events that occur around them are often labelled dangerous as a way of dealing with them. Douglas (1966) concedes that individuals sometimes feel anxious when they are confronted with the anomalous, and that attributing danger to the anomaly is one way of putting it above dispute, again helping to enforce conformity (p. 40).

The unmarked children here do not say anything to Hugo, as they silently move on as they share the 'taboo' (Watson 2017). Foucault argues that 'people know what they do; they frequently know why they do what they do; but what they don't know is what what they do does' (Dreyfus and Rabinow 1982, p. 187). The children in their silence and actions 'do' something. From their vantage point, they do not acknowledge his way of being and acting. The children's embodied response and resistance to Hugo is made visible as they move around him. The marked child, as a discursively produced subject, is not spoken of, not spoken to or about, but nevertheless 'obvious' and present. The 'silent' performance in the foyer acts to protect the 'normal', to maintain the social order and to remediate the 'deviant'.

Sometimes the circulating discourses within the classroom provided no sanctioned way to speak about the Other, and in the following conversation, the shared 'taboo' is made obvious in the uncomfortable way the children respond to my questions.

Silence: No Way to Speak

A group of children Michaela, Spencer, Patrick, Ethan, Anna and Rachel (children without a diagnosis) have gathered around my computer to look at photos I have taken. The first photo I show them is of Oliver (a child with a diagnosis) in his wheelchair with two teachers either side of him. Oliver in his chair is in the centre of the photo frame.

> Me: "Let's look at this picture here."
> A child is coughing in the background so I ask again.
> Michaela: "Chris." (teacher's name)
> Me: "Can you tell me what's happening in this picture?"
> Long pause (in the picture the two teachers are standing either side of Oliver trying to get his headphones to operate)
> Patrick: "That's … Edith…ummmmm" (another teacher)
> Me: "What is happening in the picture Spencer?"
> (silence)
> Patrick: "I can see…ummmm…"
> (silence)
> Spencer: "Ummm… there's …umm I can see umm, I can see something citing." (exciting)(moving in his seat, not wanting to answer)

Me: "Who's in the picture?"
(silence)
Spencer: "Thomas."
Me: "Thomas? Where's Thomas?" (Thomas is not in the photo). "Who is in the picture Ethan?"
Ethan: "Chris."
Michaela: "And Edith" (a teacher)
Anna: "And not me I can't see."
Me: "No you're not there Anna. Who else is in the photo?"
Ethan: "Thomas, Thomas, Thomas." (pointing to a boy in a hooded jumper with his back turned to the camera).
Me: "I think that might be Lucas."
Patrick: "Where's Thomas?" trying to move the conversation on I ask.
Me: "And who's in the middle?"
Very long pause... (silence and children looking around the room)
Me: "Who is this in the middle do you know who that is Patrick?" (my direct question and pointing finally resulted in Oliver's identification)
Patrick and Michaela: "Oliver." (Field Notes, 25/5/12, S1, p.69) (Watson 2017)

The children in this conversation seemed to work hard to avoid identifying or saying Oliver's name. The discomfort created when asked to identify and name Oliver, at the beginning of this conversation, is palpable. The long pauses, the uneasy movement of bodies, the squirming in seats and the many 'ummm's' in the children's responses make visible the 'taboo' around the marked child. This child's name cannot be spoken. In between the silences, the children look in other directions, as I ask them to identify Oliver. Some look away from the computer screen and out into the room. Oliver's location, in the photo in the centre of the frame, is 'obvious', as his wheelchair is large and cumbersome. My questioning presented the unmarked children with an awkward brief. The physical signs of their discomfort took me by surprise. They tried to name everyone else in an attempt to avoid using Oliver's name. The children, it seems, do not have the words to talk about Oliver (Watson 2017). Things that are unsaid remain that way because in some ways they are forbidden (Foucault 2008). Naming Oliver was hindered by the available discourses, and possibly forbidden by the 'taboo', that surrounds the marked child in the 'inclusive' classroom. By remaining silent and not naming Oliver, but all the while naming everyone else in the photo, the unmarked children show, in this performance, that there are certain things that need to be left unsaid. Possibly they don't wish to mention Oliver, as they might be asked questions about him, that might be awkward and they cannot answer. If they name or address 'the elephant in the room', the 'taboo' would be broken and they would not know how to speak of it and so they avoid saying Oliver's name.

In this 'inclusive' classroom, the teachers refer to Oliver as 'a very disabled child'. His diagnosis and impairments define who he is, and what he does, and not only pathologise him, but also objectify and dehumanise him. The director and teachers on several occasions referred to him as 'the boy with cerebral palsy', before using his name (Field Notes, S1) (Watson 2017). This could explain, in some ways, why the children could not recall his name immediately in our conversation. Oliver is described by his pathology and via medical discourses, as an 'object of concern' and often as an 'object of sympathy'. The teachers often made comments such as 'the poor thing' and 'the poor family'. A discourse of personal tragedy is taken up by the adults in this classroom, particularly for this child, Oliver, but also for the other marked children. Comments such as 'I don't know how the parents cope' and 'Can't imagine what it must be like for his poor parents' (Field Notes, 4/6/12, S1, p.134) (Watson 2017) position the children within a tragedy discourse (Swain and French 2008). Comments about the marked child were usually not made quietly, or in isolation, away from the unmarked children. Perhaps, in line with developmental thinking in the classroom, there was a shared understanding among the teachers that young children are unable to comprehend adult interactions, their words, silences or body language.

Oliver is talked about mostly by the teachers in terms of the severity of his impairments and his need for specialised equipment and constant supervision. His subjecthood is created via a long list of deficits. The children use developmental and sanctioned discourses to describe Oliver, 'he can't walk', 'he can only talk like a baby' and 'he always cries'. In this classroom, there is not only an objectivisation of Oliver but also an infantilisation (Robey et al. 2006) of him by both the children and the teachers. The teachers respond to Oliver as one would to an infant. Oliver is four years old. They offer him food, a nappy change or they take him for a walk around the yard in his wheelchair to try and settle or stop his 'noises'. Oliver's 'noises', as Ethan in the previous scenario, produce a cause for concern among the 'normal' and stopping the 'noises' is a acted on as a matter of urgency. Oliver's 'noises' are not interpreted by teachers and children as a different way of communicating, perhaps worth exploring, but instead are attended to like the cries of an infant.

Oliver is also subjected by discourses that judge his embodied physical differences as a failing, incomplete and inferior and 'not so much for what it is but what it fails to be' (Shildrick 2005, p. 756). Shildrick (2005) argues that the anomalous disabled body represents an 'uncomfortable reminder that the normative, 'healthy' body, despite its appearance of successful self-determination, is highly vulnerable to disruption and breakdown' (p. 757). Shildrick goes on to say that as 'disability is viewed this way it is always the object of institutional discourses of control and containment' (p. 757). The 'normal' from this perspective feel threatened by Oliver's disabled body and the risk that a disabled body poses to their own 'normal' bodies. The disabled body exposes the 'normal' to its own vulnerability and its potential break down (Shildrick 2005). Thus Oliver is avoided by the children in their silence as they experience an uncomfortable anxiety around him as a discursively produced subject.

Discussion

As Foucault (2008) argues, 'There is not one but many silences, and they are an integral part of the strategies that underlie and permeate discourses' (p. 27). Silence as a discursive practice in the 'inclusive' classroom is taken up by the 'normal' as a mechanism of exclusion (Watson 2016). Those who are positioned in the sanctioned discourses as irrational or unreasonable are not addressed but nonetheless visible in this discursive context. For the 'normal', being silent and moving past or using only sanctioned ways to talk about the marked child, when there are no words to speak, are just some of the nuanced ways that silences operate in the classroom to position and reposition the 'normal.'

Silence conserves the social order. The silence is shared among the unmarked children and teachers as they sidestep interactions with the marked child. The notion of a 'taboo', so obvious and mutual, is created and enacted around the marked child as they remain often unacknowledged. The 'taboo' is adhered to via the social and discursive practices of the classroom creating an unaddressed anomaly, the classroom version of 'the elephant in the room'. Silence produces exclusion, a separateness and a divide between those created as with reason and those without reason.

In the 'inclusive' classroom, the acceptable and accessible discourses inform children, through a whole set of complex processes, that difference is difficult and oftentimes problematic and best to keep a distance from. Children are not passive in these processes. They do not merely imitate the adults around them, but instead actively draw on available circulating discourses to negotiate their social interactions. Children readily exclude peers based on their understandings of differences in their everyday interactions (Connolly et al. 2002). In taking up these discourses, the 'normal' work to maintain their recognisability and legitimacy as members of the category; however, in doing this, they also come to learn to *not* ask questions or protest or offer alternatives. The children learn to separate from, and ignore difference, and feel awkward discussing it, as they have no sanctioned way to talk about it. The 'normal' discourses create the 'natural' and 'right' way to be, that is so taken for granted, that other ways have no expression and no legitimacy.

Despite the efforts made by 'inclusion' policies and strategies for best practices, that have pushed for 'inclusive' early childhood classroom, it is still visible that 'difference', 'disability' and 'diagnosis' can only be addressed in particular ways, using the legitimated but limited discourses that dominate. Difference is at best tolerated and is often silenced and ignored (Watson 2017). What does the silence, avoidance and awkwardness around 'disability', expressed in these 'inclusive' classrooms, tell us about the classroom, and the possible effects of these discursive moves on the children's subjectivities?

By disrupting and interrogating the constitution of the 'normal' and understanding it as a social and cultural accomplishment that can take many shapes and forms, 'inclusive' early childhood education and practice might come to recognise that this separateness and distance that has been silently created is not 'inclusive' and is not sustainable. We need to shift the focus of 'inclusion' from the individual subject to the 'normal' group of subjects and trouble the way the discourses produce these subjects.

In undertaking my doctoral work, the motivation for me, was to find new ways of seeing, thinking and doing 'inclusion'. My own personal, educational and teaching experiences in early intervention and mainstream settings left me disillusioned. The field of special/'inclusive' education continues to view the diagnosed child as possessing a list of deficit characteristics that need to be remediated for successful 'inclusion'. For me, there is a desire to arrest 'inclusion's need to speak of and identify otherness' (Harwood and Rasmussen 2002, p. 5), as I see this working to shape and reinforce both the margins and a centre, privileging 'universal categories and a romanticised, universal subject' (Lather 2003, p. 260).

By problematising everyday practices and constructions *in* the classroom, there is a possibility for opening up different understandings and for thinking and acting 'otherwise'. Would it be possible to give up all references to things being 'normal' or 'natural'? For me there is promise if we can begin to shift the focus from the 'objectifying' of the subject towards a discursive understanding how 'human beings are made subjects' (Foucault 1982, p. 326) and begin to grasp how the operating power of the 'normal' creates effects for subjection. There is promise if we can come to recognise that we are all implicated and complicated in our own making as discursive subjects and also in the making of others (Watson 2017).

References

Allan, J. (2008). *Rethinking Inclusive Education: The Philosophers of Difference in Practice* (Vol. 5). Dordrecht: Springer.

Australian Government Department of Education, Employment and Workplace Relations. (2009). *Belonging, Being and Becoming: The Early Years Learning Framework for Australia.* Retrieved June 6, 2010, from http://docs.education.gov.au/system/files/doc/other/belonging_being_and_becoming_the_early_years_learning_framework_for_australia.pdf.

Cadwallader, J. (2007). Suffering Difference: Normalisation and Power. *Social Semiotics, 17*(3), 375–394.

Connolly, P., Smith, A., & Kelly, B. (2002). *Too Young to Notice? The Cultural and Political Awareness of 3–6 Year Olds in Northern Ireland.* Belfast: Community Relations Council.

Davies, B. (1989). *Frogs and Snails and Feminist Tales: Preschool Children and Gender.* Sydney: Allen & Unwin.

Davies, B. (1993). *Shards of Glass: Children Reading and Writing Beyond Gendered Identities.* Sydney: Allen & Unwin.

Davies, B., & Harré, R. (1999). Positioning and Personhood. In R. Harré & L. van Langenhove (Eds.), *Positioning Theory: Moral Contexts of Intentional Action* (pp. 32–52). Oxford: Blackwell.

Derrida, J. (1992). Passions: 'An Oblique Offering'. In D. Wood (Ed.), *Derrida: A Critical Reader.* Oxford: Blackwell.

Douglas, M. (1966). *Purity and Danger: An Analysis of Concepts of Pollution and Taboo.* London: Routledge.

Dreyfus, H. I., & Rabinow, P. (1982). *Michel Foucault: Beyond Structuralism and Hermeneutics.* Brighton: The Harvester Press Limited.

Foucault, M. (1977). *Discipline and Punish: The Birth of the Prison.* London: Penguin.

Foucault, M. (1982). The Subject and Power. *Critical Inquiry, 8*(4), 777–795.

Foucault, M. (2006). *History of Madness.* Oxon: Routledge.

Foucault, M. (2008). *The History of Sexuality: The Will to Knowledge Volume 1.* London: Penguin Group.

Grace, R., Llewellyn, G., Wedgwood, N., Fenech, M., & McConnell, D. (2008). From Ideal: Everyday Experiences of Mothers and Early Childhood Professionals Negotiating an Inclusive Early Childhood Experience in the Australian Context. *Topics in Early Childhood Special Education, 28*(1), 18–31.

Graham, L. (2006). Caught in the Net: A Foucaultian Interrogation of the Incidental Effects of Limited Notions of "Inclusion". *International Journal of Inclusive Education, 10*(1), 3–24.

Graham, L. J., & Slee, R. (2008). An Illusory Interiority: Interrogating the Discourse/s of Inclusion. *Educational Philosophy and Theory, 40*(2), 277–293.

Harré, R., & Van Langenhove, L. (Eds.). (1999). *Positioning Theory: Moral Contexts of Intentional Action*. Oxford: Blackwell Publishers.

Harwood, V., & Rasmussen, M. L. (2002). *Inspiring Methodological Provocateurs in Inclusive Educational Research*. Paper Presented at the American Educational Research Association, New Orleans.

Kristeva, J. (1982). *Powers of Horror: An Essay on Abjection*. New York: Columbia University Press.

Lather, P. (2003). Applied Derrida: (Mis)reading the Work of Mourning in Educational Research. *Educational Philosophy and Theory, 35*(3), 257–270.

Laws, C., & Davies, B. (2000). Poststructuralist Theory in Practice: Working with "Behaviourally Disturbed" Children. *International Journal of Qualitative Studies in Education, 13*(3), 205–221.

Mazzei, L. A. (2007a). Toward a Problematic of Silence in Action Research. *Educational Action Research, 15*(4), 631–642.

Mazzei, L. A. (2007b). *Inhabited Silence in Qualitative Research: Putting Poststructural Theory to Work*. New York: Peter Lang.

Nutbrown, C., & Clough, P. (2009). Citizenship and Inclusion in the Early Years: Understanding and Responding to Children's Perspectives on 'Belonging'. *International Journal of Early Years Education, 17*(3), 191–206.

Petersen, E. B. (2004). *Academic Boundary Work: The Discursive Constitution of Scientificity Amongst Researchers Within the Social Sciences and Humanities, (PhD)*. Copenhagen: University of Copenhagen.

Purdue, K., Gordon-Burns, D., Gunn, A., Madden, B., & Surtees, N. (2009). Supporting Inclusion in Early Childhood Settings: Some Possibilities and Problems for Teacher Education. *International Journal of Inclusive Education, 13*(8), 805–815.

Robey, K. L., Beckley, L., & Kirschner, M. (2006). Implicit Infantilizing Attitudes About Disability. *Journal of Developmental and Physical Disabilities, 18*(4), 441–453.

Robinson, K. H., & Jones-Diaz, C. (2006). *Diversity and Difference in Early Childhood Education: Issues for Theory and Practice*. New York: Open University Press.

Rose, N. (1999). *Governing the Soul: The Shaping of the Private Self* (2nd ed.). New York: Routledge.

Shildrick, M. (2005). The Disabled Body, Genealogy and Undecidability. *Cultural Studies, 19*(6), 755–770.

Slee, R. (2013). How Do We Make Inclusive Education Happen When Exclusion Is a Political Predisposition? *International Journal of Inclusive Education, 17*(8), 895–907.

Slee, R., & Allan, J. (2001). Excluding the Included: A Reconsideration of Inclusive Education. *International Studies in Sociology of Education, 11*(2), 173–191.

Swain, J., & French, S. (Eds.). (2008). *Disability on Equal Terms*. London: Sage Publications.

Warming, H. (2011). Getting Under Their Skins? Accessing Young Children's Perspectives Through Ethnographic Fieldwork. *Childhood, 18*(1), 39–53.

Watson, K. (2016). 'Silences' in the 'Inclusive' Early Childhood Classroom: Sustaining a 'Taboo'. In E. B. Petersen & Z. Millei (Eds.), *Interrupting the Psy-Disciplines in Education* (pp. 13–31). New York/London: Palgrave Macmillan.

Watson, K. (2017). *Inside the 'Inclusive' Early Childhood Classroom: The Power of the 'Normal'*. New York: Peter Lang.

Karen Watson is Lecturer in Early Childhood Education in the School of Education at the University of Newcastle, Australia. Her many years of experience in teaching in the early childhood classroom, and in early intervention, as a special education consultant, inspired her PhD research into inclusive practices. She is interested in how young children in the inclusive classroom actively negotiate inclusive and exclusive processes.

The Kids Are Alright: They Have Been Included for Years

Ben Whitburn

Key Points

- In this chapter, I examine complexities associated with voice and qualitative interviewing in disabled children's childhood studies.
- I argue that both are contextually specific and that the interviews that might appear on the surface to be unrewarding must be examined within the intricacies of their production.
- To demonstrate my argument, I work through my experiences of interviewing a group of 23 young people with disabilities who attended secondary schools in Spain. Of the group, only roughly a third responded to any extent to the questions I put to them.
- I conclude with a theoretical discussion of the role of voice and interviews in disabled children's childhood studies, noting in particular their limitations and implications for qualitative research.

Introduction

Undoubtedly you can relate to this. Twenty-three young people had sat down with me to participate in face-to-face interviews; each had willingly given his or her assent to join in; a similar line of questions was put to all—albeit in a

B. Whitburn (✉)
Deakin University, Melbourne, Australia

© The Author(s) 2018
K. Runswick-Cole et al. (eds.), *The Palgrave Handbook of Disabled Children's Childhood Studies*, https://doi.org/10.1057/978-1-137-54446-9_12

language different to my mother tongue; but less than half of the group had engaged to any extent in interviews. It was January 2014 and I had spent over a year in Spain conducting research with young people with disabilities about their experiences of inclusive schooling (Whitburn 2016) for my doctoral study. I was due to return to Australia to wrap up the PhD—though with what? Of that I was unsure, as I combed through numerous but seemingly sparse interview transcripts.

While studies in the tradition are put to work to reconceptualise the lives of children with disabilities via the complexities of their own perspectives (Curran 2013), the implications of voice in research are many and varied (Anderson 2015; Mockler and Groundwater-Smith 2015; St Pierre 2009) and the contexts of interviews are integral to its incitement (Abbott 2012; Youngblood Jackson 2009). To demonstrate some of the points raised, I discuss the different extent to which student participants of recent research engaged in "the interview"—focusing on the implications of their experiences of inclusive schooling on their loquaciousness or silences. Although this is not—and should not be read as a question of comparative enumeration, only roughly a third of the group ($n = 8$) engaged to any extent with the questions I put to them in interviews. While this might be discouraging to a researcher in the field, much can be inferred from silences (Humphry 2014; Miller et al. 2011).

Variations in interview engagement are examined to illustrate that the ways that students articulate their experiences of inclusive schooling are directly implicated in their constituted subjectivities. The chapter demonstrates the role of student discourse within disabled children's childhood studies to the analysis of inclusive education. That it does so by concentrating on the silences further exemplifies the significance of post-structural theory for analysing data collection in context about inclusive schooling (Whitburn 2014a).

Background to the Study

Having earlier lived and worked in Spain as a person with vision impairment, I noted that by and large, people with disabilities enjoyed a greater level of inclusion in the everyday fabric of Spanish society than they did in Australia— my country of origin and home. Many completed school at a similar rate as their peers; they held paid jobs and they received support from well-resourced and publicly recognised organisations that emphasised their users' strengths rather than their supposed deficits. I too benefited from the affirmative attitudes of employers in Spain, after having struggled to find work in Australia

(Whitburn 2015). The derogatory metanarrative of disability (Bolt 2012) appeared to have been rewritten for the Spanish context.

In my research, I aim to foreground the perspectives of young people who are at risk of marginalisation from education. I had conducted a prior phase of this study in an Australian secondary school in which I sought to learn from a group of students with vision impairment about their experiences of inclusive schooling (Whitburn 2014b). Together, a country's system of education and the way in which people with disabilities are treated offer insightful indicators of the social order in context (Slee 2011; Youdell 2006).

A comparative investigation in Spain would—I hoped—illustrate the inner workings of this alternate narrative. Young people who experienced schooling in inclusive settings in Spain might reveal what it is that facilitated their inclusion. I felt too that this would be welcomed, given some of the alarming experiences of current-day inclusive schooling that the young people in Australia had related, such as being quarantined by paraprofessionals (Whitburn 2013) and social isolation within the competitive school culture (Whitburn 2014b).

A substantial body of literature has emerged from Spain about including students with disabilities in both mainstream schools and educational research (Echeita et al. 2009; Moriña Díez 2010; Parrilla 2008; Rojas et al. 2013; Susinos 2007; Susinos and Ceballos 2012; Susinos and Parilla 2008; Verdugo and Rodríguez 2012). This fits within the larger European agenda of involving people with disabilities in all facets of research, in accordance with international disability rights conventions (Priestley and Waddington 2010). Consensus among this work is that education and educational research benefit inordinately from active membership of people with disabilities.

Young People's Voices in Disabled Children's Childhood Studies

To elucidate the discourses of inclusive education, not from above, but from the inside, epitomises the principal conviction of disabled children's childhood studies in the education sphere. Under this banner specifically, the views of children with disabilities are brought to the fore (Curran 2013). In a policy context, the United Nations Convention on the Rights of the Child (1989) and the Convention on the Rights of People with Disabilities (2006) together set out clear obligations of state parties to incorporate the views of children with or without disabilities in planning and evaluating service delivery. Active involvement of young people in the production of knowledge about schooling is a political move. One in which, as Mockler and Groundwater-Smith (2015,

p. 16) write, the objective is to discover "the ways in which power is exercised in the relationships between children, young people, and the adults with whom they engage, in particular … school settings".

To reconceptualise the life-worlds of children with disabilities via their own perspectives responds to a political imperative. Learning from what McRuer (2006) calls "Crip epistemologies"—an unconventional way of knowledge construction about the containment of the neoliberal imaginary—enables us to "access alternative ways of being" (p. 42) about living with disability, receiving special educational services, and expressing alternative possibilities for school inclusion based on embodied and mediated experience.

It is important, however, not to overstate the significance of student voice in research. Educators and researchers often utilise language that by default sets up a "bipolar dichotomy" (Mockler and Groundwater-Smith 2015, p. 40) of empowerment via the act of giving voice—enabling students to speak. Placing student voice on a pedestal in this way assumes that the incitement to speak will enable young people to express their "true" opinions, feelings, and experiences (Anderson 2015). Via voice, a glimpse into "a mirror of the soul, the essence of the self" (Mazzei and Youngblood Jackson 2009, p. 1) is made possible. In schools then, students will be allegedly free of oppressive power structures, as teachers adeptly incorporate the feelings of these informants into day-to-day practice. In turn, hierarchies of academic knowledge of present-day issues that impact inclusive schooling can be systematically overturned.

However, to imagine that one is able to speak of freedom is to take a view of power as a repressive force (Foucault 1978). Rather, the experiences that students' voices are mediated by the conditions in which they find themselves in context (Mockler and Groundwater-Smith 2015). Power, for Foucault, is exercised by all free subjects, and the "liberty to participate and speak out or have a voice is not the opposite of power, but the very vehicle through which power is exercised" (Anderson 2015, p. 135).

Students voiced testimonials therefore play witness to, mediate and are mediated by the situation under analysis (Clarke 2005). In turn, the significance of voiced experience to research is thrown into question (Anderson 2015; Mockler and Groundwater-Smith 2015). As St Pierre (2009, p. 225) writes, voice "structures the economy of conventional qualitative inquiry as it structures other humanist projects". It is appropriate, then, to draw on alternate theoretical strings to explicate how students' voiced interpretations of schooling contribute to an understanding of the effects of inclusive practices.

Methodology

My objective in undertaking educational research is not merely to represent students' views of inclusive practice—although I advocate that much can be learnt from these (Whitburn 2014c). Instead, I explore from the inside how discourse and material coalesce through modes of power to constitute "included" subjects in schools. In so doing, I decentre notions of students as knowing subjects and instead recognise the contingent landscape of student hood. As Besley (2007, p. 56) articulates, "Schools are institutions that clearly involve ... regulation and governance of the experience of their students. In turn, this constitutes the self." However, when the constituted self—the disabled self—is still considered anomalous, the goals of research in this frame become to critique the underlining causes to this end (Shildrick 2012).

I therefore employ a methodology that draws on post-structural theory for its capacity to engage both theoretically and politically with embodied experience. While Barnes (2012) critiques post-structural theorisation of disability for being "politically benign" (p. 22) in consequence of its emphasis on cultural and linguistic critique, the methodology I employ exposes instances of included subject hood through both schooling and policy discourses in specific contexts. Post-structural representation equips research with political teeth (Martin and Kamberlis 2013), and as Allan remarks, an "Incitement to discourse ... necessarily involves subversive research practices" (Allan 1999, p.124) and the lines between method and methodology are subsequently blurred (Miller et al. 2011).

Informed by constructivist grounded theory (Charmaz 2006) and situational analysis (Clarke 2005) for data collection and analysis, my purpose—closely aligned with disabled children's childhood studies—is to sort through the complexities of everyday schooling and the embodiment of impairment as a way of seeking a discourse of inclusive education that is affirmative towards disability. Via the constructivist framework, in this project I have systematically collected data via intensive interviewing (Charmaz 2006) focusing on emotional response and affect as well as the material aspects of life (Shildrick 2012) in the search of knowledge about students.

Anchoring analysis to the situation—inclusive schooling for students with diagnosed special educational needs—the inductive approach to data collection and analysis (Charmaz 2006) facilitates comprehensive illustrations of situated inclusive practice and the conditions therein that produce its effects on students (Whitburn 2014a). As Clarke (2005, p. 146) writes, "It is the combination of the groundedness of interpretation with the systematic handling of data that makes grounded theory and situational analysis robust approaches in qualitative research." After providing more details about participants, I introduce "The interview", which precedes a return to the theoretical discussion that leads me to examine the role of student voice in interviews and the critique of silences as signals of inclusion.

Participants

Written consent was obtained for 23 young people aged 12–19 years to participate in this phase of the study. Ethical clearance was granted from the Deakin University Human Research Ethics Committee. Of the participants, 13 were female while 10 were male. Among the group, the young people had varied medical diagnoses including sensory, intellectual, and developmental conditions and some had been identified as having behavioural disorders. Each received special educational support. Medical diagnosis was not the basis upon which young people were recruited to the study. However, the young people's embodied conditions have discursive significance to their constituted subjectivities (Shildrick 2012; Whitburn 2014a).

Participants were enrolled in one of the six secondary mainstream schools. Two of the schools shared affluent inner-city locations, while the others were situated in impoverished neighbourhoods. The two other schools were positioned in an urban and rural setting, respectively. From the list of schools, two catered to the secondary level of schooling only, while the other institutions had enrolments of students from the preparatory to post-secondary years, catering to young people aged 6–18. All six research settings were identified as local neighbourhood schools that had enrolments of young people with disabilities, who might be able to shed light on inclusive practice and provide the study with rich data.

The Interview

Wanting to utilise the same methodology that I drew on in the previous phase of this study, I aimed to conduct face-to-face interviews for the collection of data in Spain. My intention was to visit schools on at least two occasions to conduct interviews, and then to return on a final occasion to go through transcripts with each participant in order to verify their content and/or to clear up any errors in translations. All of these sessions were to take place in a room on school grounds. However, I held one major concern about this aspect of fieldwork. My mother tongue is English, and despite having a good level of Spanish, I was unsure I could communicate effectively with the participants; interviews were to be, after all, on the record. With the generous assistance of colleagues from The Autonomous University of Madrid, both sampling and translation was made easy as they both arranged and attended interviews with me throughout fieldwork.

With the exception of a hand full of occasions, each young person sat down with both me and the translator alone to conduct the interviews. This was important to the study because we intended to gather their contributions away from the presence of teachers or parents—figures of power—who might inadvertently coerce the young people's responses to questions. Only three young people requested the company of a teacher in interviews, while participants at another school attended these sessions in groups of two or three because their educators anticipated that they would be less willing to communicate freely without the support of their peers. Whether or not this was likely to be the case, we gladly took the opportunity to hold multi-participant sessions, figuring that impromptu group interviews might be productive. As it would turn out, we held group sessions on only three occasions in the same school.

With logistics taken care of, data collection commenced in early 2013. An ongoing consideration when undertaking qualitative research with young people is arbitrating their willingness to participate. As Connors and Stalker (2007) point out, consent becomes an ongoing process in which the researcher must frequently check for ethical approval to continue. All of the young people gave verbal assurance that they wished to participate in interviews—many expressed enthusiasm for being invited to speak about their experiences. This factor is a vital piece of the analytical puzzle when considering the extent to which the young people engaged in interviews—an issue that I return to later.

Although communication between myself and a majority of young people turned out to be possible with only occasional intervention from the invited translator, verbal interaction was not always easy. To enhance interaction with participants less able to communicate verbally, I later reflected that interviews would have benefited from other forms of interaction, such as online chat, electronic messaging, or alternative and/or supported communication. As it stood, some opportunities were regrettably missed to elaborate what on the surface appeared to be interesting stories about being well included from students who could be easily marginalised in other schooling contexts. Each of these young people indicated clearly that he or she made use of iPads and computers for recreation and school work, as well as for conversing with family and friends; indications are evident that by taking up alternate communication streams and technology with such ease, disability as a category "trouble[s], reshape[s] and refashion[s] traditional conceptions of the human" (Goodley and Runswick-Cole 2015, p. 243) through language and electronic-mediated relations.

The questions I put to all of the young people centred on their experiences of attending school; their emotional responses to particularities such as receiving special education support and/or studying from alternative materials to peers; the meanings and importance that they attributed to achievement; fitting in socially at school and in the local neighbourhood. Following the inductive techniques of data collection and interpretive analysis of grounded theory (Charmaz 2006), the young people spoke to what I came to regard as the five themes of significance to their experiences of inclusive schooling: the school community, resources, teacher pedagogy, support, and social cohesion (Whitburn 2016).

During fieldwork, a clear pattern quickly emerged. The participants—nearly a third of the sample—who expressed themselves the most in interviews were those who punctuated their stories of inclusion with alternate familiarity. Theirs were prior experiences of exclusion before transitioning to the research settings, and emotional accounts of a newly discovered sense of self-worth that now complemented their schooling. Relieved feelings of being fortunate to have transitioned to these schools was common among these young people, related alongside tales of less-advantaged peers from other schools who experienced marginalisation in one form or another.

Some of these participants related less-voluminous accounts of occasional relegation in their current schools. However, these were nearly always book ended with emphasis on being well included in the main, and an acknowledgement that their own actions were directly connected to their capacity to experience inclusion; evidence that the constituted included subject is directly implicated in the construction of inclusive schooling. As Youdell (2006, p. 42) explains, "Being such a subject s/he can also engage self-consciously in practices that might make her/him differently"—from subjugated on the margins, to an included member of the school community. However, it was the majority of the group who stayed largely silent in interviews, and it is to a discussion of the discursive formation of their reticences that I now turn.

Reticence to Speak in Interviews

Although they all expressed their enthusiasm to participate in interviews, the majority of young people who comprised the group said little, no matter how we—I and the invited translator—phrased and rephrased questions about their experiences. Questions were invariably responded to with a one-worded answer: a "yes" or a "no", a nod of the head or a shrug. These were young people who had been enrolled in the research settings since the beginning—or very early—in their schooling. While many adequately filled in the emergent themes of my constructive analysis alongside their more wordy peers—acknowledging community membership, appropriate resources and support, inclusive pedagogy and the significance of social interaction—there was little emotional status beyond general contentment. These were narratives of being included at school, feeling the need to apply themselves meticulously to their studies, and being integral members of strong relational networks with teachers, peers, and family members. When pressed for suggestions about how to change or improve their schools, these participants proposed little more than providing better food options for lunch and allowing for more free time on the school computers.

Special educational provision did not overshadow the young people's inclusion in the schools. Paraprofessional support in lessons, for instance, was shared among all attending students, rather than being tethered to a single participant—as was typically the case in the Australian phase of the study (Whitburn 2013). When asked about their interactions with paraprofessionals, these young people merely indicated that they were "good", "helpful", and "friendly". Further, given the use of varied resources in lessons among all students in the schools, participants were not made to feel uncomfortable for using assistive equipment such as visual aids, ebooks, or laptop computers. Again their use of particular resources was "good" and "helpful". When asked to consider the future beyond schooling, a couple of participants expressed disappointment that by receiving special educational services, they would be unable to graduate at the same rate as their peers. In the schools, inclusion was nevertheless attainable, and by describing fleetingly their full membership in the day-to-day education communities, these young people eloquently articulated included subjectivities.

Conceptualising the Interview

It might appear to some researchers that I have sorted these experiences of interviewing young people about their schooling into three broad categories: the verbose conversations, the quieter exchanges, and the opportunities lost—or the easy interviews, the tricky ones, and the "too bad" set. However, to categorise the fieldwork of this study objectively in this way runs the risk of hastening a superficial reading of the data. While opportunities were indeed missed to obtain rich interview data from all of the young people, each inter-action—no matter how expressive—presented a version of the truth uniquely accessible to every participant according to both his or her particular circum-stances and the questions I put to them in interviews.

In the remainder of the Chap. I demonstrate the reading of inclusive schooling that this analysis produces via a reconceptualisation of the inter-view, resourced by Foucault's (1978) notions of confession and silence along-side Butler's (2005) exploration of the act of giving an account of oneself. Although not specifically addressed at qualitative interviewing, the work of Foucault and Butler cuts across these contingent attributes of the method in instructive ways.

Seeking Confession, Constituting the Self

As a ubiquitous form of data collection in qualitative research, the inter-view is a technology of confessional interaction—itself, "one of the main rituals we rely on for the production of truth" (Foucault 1978, p. 58). In his examination of the production of the constituted subject, Foucault (1978) explores the development of confession as it has grown out of religious to secular institutional practices since the eighteenth century. Confession has become an everyday technology of truth production and subjectivity forma-tion that is entangled in relations of power. Interviews are routine forms of confession, in which the participant is asked to voice his or her subjecthood (Anderson 2015). At the intersection of disabled children's childhood stud-ies and educational research more specifically, the interview explores power relations that affect inclusive schooling in its constitutive capacity to produce subjects. In provoking confessions concerned with these impacts, interviews perform two interconnected roles: identification and constitution of the self.

When asked how particular events and practices impact them, the young people are encouraged to identify themselves—to speak freely of an "I" who experiences inclusive schooling. However, social norms are forever complicit in the accounting of self. As Butler (2005, pp. 7–8) writes, "When the 'I' seeks to give an account of itself, it can start with itself, but it will find that this self is already implicated in a social temporality that exceeds its own capacities for narration." In accounting personal experience then, social norms are omni-present, and in articulating their effects, "the task [of the interviewee] is to find a way of appropriating them, taking them on, establishing a living rela-tion to them" (Butler 2005, p. 9). The experiences that young people relate in interviews are thus a snapshot of how they negotiate their "selves" within the social fabric of their schools.

The interaction that takes place in interviews also has constitutive power. Asking young people to express their experiences of inclusive schooling, to describe their visceral reactions to receiving special education services, and to explore with them what appropriate inclusive schooling might look like is also to render participants particular subjects—students who are potentially included or marginalised. The interviewer caries a whole set of assumptions and modes of power; his/her role is to elicit the truth behind the participants' experiences of inclusion, and to validate them against supposed facts of what inclusive schooling should look like. Butler (2005, p. 11) writes "so I start to give an account … because someone has asked me to, and that someone has power delegated from an established system of justice". At the very moment of articulation, the truth is amenable to examination by the interviewer. As such, the interviewed subject is "authenticated by the discourse of truth he was able or obliged to pronounce concerning himself" (Foucault 1978, p. 58).

The contexts of interviews are highly relevant to the production of knowledge about the lives of participants (Abbot 2012; Youngblood Jackson 2009). Perhaps convenient to the current discussion, Butler (2005) examines the interaction between Foucault and his interlocutor in an interview entitled "How Much Does It Cost for Reason to Tell the Truth" (Foucault 1989). Butler notes that although asked to give an account of himself, Foucault's confession is illusive as he provides no causal justification for his actions. Instead he mentions some influences, but in doing so, he is constituted a particular subject at the time of articulation. As Butler (2005, p. 112) writes, "The account cannot be understood outside the interlocutory scene in which it takes place. Is he telling the truth about himself, or is he responding to the demands that his interlocutor imposes upon him?"

Extrapolating these questions to interviews conducted for the current study, and for that matter all qualitative inquiry, the truth elicited is highly contingent on the context of the discussion and the goals of the researcher. Power relations that circulate within the interview situation render both the interviewer and participants as subjects, who play a specified role in the production of truth.

Silences

But what of the silences that seemingly frustrated the interviews. To recap briefly, in "giving oneself over to a publicized mode of appearance" (Butler 2005, p. 114) via interviews, a majority of the group of participants of this study said little, no matter how many questions we put to them. This does not, however, indicate that these young people were holding back information, nor that they were wholly uninspired to speak.

In a study with teachers at an alternative school in the Australian State of New South Wales, Humphry (2014) writes of being confronted by "the pause"—moments of silences in interviews in which participants rearticulated descriptions of students. Through lengthy silences in interviews, participants used "careful, deliberate and purposeful choice[s] in words and phrasing" (p. 491) that enabled them to challenge deficit language, and to instead "establish a different truth" (p. 493) about their students who might otherwise be labelled as delinquents. Humphry's study demonstrates the constitutive influence of silences in interviews in a particular context, and the role of silence in the production of truth. As mentioned earlier, all participants of the current study expressed a willingness to take part in interviews, and a majority eagerly read—or listened to—his or her transcript when it was later presented back to the group for member checking.

Silence, for Foucault (1978, p. 27) describes the things one declines to say, or is forbidden to name, "[that] is less the absolute limit of discourse, the other side from which it is separated by a strict boundary, than an element that functions alongside the things said, with them and in relation to them".

This is not to say that silence is unproductive, but that it communicates a great deal about the speaker's subjecthood. Having attended the research settings for the entirety of their schooling, these young people had been included, insofar as it was possible to ascertain, since the beginning. Only those young people who knew otherwise about what marginalisation can feel like were motivated to speak. "Silence, then, goes beyond just existing as a passive, impotent state" (Humphry 2014, p. 492). It instead speaks volumes.

The divergent forms of "expressive power" (Butler 2005, p. 13) that the young people assumed when taking part in interviews were directly attributable to their prior experiences. Drawing on Nietzsche (1969), Butler (2005) demonstrates that we are able to become more aware of ourselves, and can therefore give an account of ourselves more applicably, only after having suffered injury. Those young people whose inclusion was never in question were not compelled to speak about it. Theirs were included subjectivities—as expressed in interviews—from the outset.

Conclusion

I have attempted in this chapter to problematise the role of young people's voices in the production of knowledge through interviews, as it is drawn on in disabled children's childhood studies. In doing so, I have worked beyond conventions of analysing transcribed data to explore the contexts of interviews of recent research in Spain with young people with diagnosed special educational needs on the efficacy of their inclusion in schools. I have demonstrated that the extent to which young people contribute to interview discourse is wholly contingent on their experiences, which is in turn conditional on the context of interviews. The interview opens a channel of communication in which the effects of power relations can be explored. For research of this kind, this refers to both circulating power relations in schools that affect its capacity for inclusion, and as well the context of the interview itself.

However, rather than to suppose that by interviewing young people about their experiences of inclusive schooling they are even able to voice their natural experiences, the exchange is grounded wholly in the present context. Youngblood Jackson (2009 p. 165) draws attention to the entanglement of "truth, power, desire and the subject/voice in certain acts of speaking of the present" in her analysis of the effects of interview data. She notes that the construction of truth is wide and varied when participants attempt to represent themselves to researchers (and to themselves). Youngblood Jackson draws on Foucault's (1990) fascination with Kant's reorientation of philosophical inquiry in his eighteenth-century text "What is enlightenment?" Foucault's thesis is that Kant moves analysis away from Cartesian philosophy, and instead centres focus on how our subjectivities are constituted in the present through examinations of historical discourses.

In other words, Kant reorientates the parameters of analysis. Taking this lead as inspiration, Youngblood Jackson (2009) subsequently reappropriates the question of qualitative inquiry: "What are research participants doing when they speak of their present?" (p. 166). By listening to young people's voiced experiences of school inclusion in interviews is to ask exactly that.

Acknowledgements I want to thank each of the young people who participated in this phase of the research for their contribution to the project, no matter how large or small. In addition, I extend my sincere thanks to Cecilia Simon, Gerardo Echeita, and Soledad Rappoport from the Autonomous University of Madrid for supporting my access to the field, and translation as required. Finally, I want to thank the editors of this volume—Katherine, Tillie, and Kirsty—for their important work in this space, and for having supported my development of the chapter.

Note

I adopt person-first language as a personal preference; however, at the same time, the Department of Human Services in the Australian State Government of Victoria (where I reside) recommends professionals use person-first representations for consistency when discussing disability in public discourse (see http://www.dhs.vic.gov.au/about-the-department/plans,-programs-and-projects/projects-and-initiatives/disability-services/reporting-it-right). For me, turning any condition—albeit race, colour, or creed—into an adjective that defines the person on the whole is to misappropriate their subjecthood.

References

Abbott, D. (2012). Other Voices, Other Rooms: Talking to Young Men with Duchenne Muscular Dystrophy about the Transition to Adulthood. *Children & Society, 26*(3), 241–250.

Allan, J. (1999). *Actively Seeking Inclusion: Pupils with Special Needs in Mainstream School*. Philadelphia: Falmer Press.

Anderson, A. (2015). Is Giving Voice an Incitement to Confess? In A. Fejes & K. Nicoll (Eds.), *Foucault and the Politics of Confession in Education* (pp. 133–145). Abingdon: Routledge.

Barnes, C. (2012). Understanding the Social Model of Disability: Past, Present and Future. In N. Watson, A. Roulstone, & C. Thomas (Eds.), *Routledge Handbook of Disability Studies* (pp. 12–29). London/New York: Routledge.

Besley, T. A. (2007). Foucault, Truth-Telling and Technologies of the Self: Confessional Practices of the Self and Schools. In M. A. Peters & T. A. Besley (Eds.), *Why Foucault? New Directions in Educational Research* (pp. 55–70). Oxford: Peter Lang.

Bolt, D. (2012). Social Encounters, Cultural Representation, and Critical Avoidance. In N. Watson, A. Roulstone, & C. Thomas (Eds.), *Routledge Handbook of Disability Studies* (pp. 287–297). London/New York: Routledge.

Butler, J. (2005). *Giving an Account of Oneself*. New York: Fordham University Press.

Charmaz, K. (2006). *Constructing Grounded Theory: A Practical Guide Through Qualitative Analysis*. Los Angeles/London/New Delhi/Singapore/Washington DC: Sage.

Clarke, A. E. (2005). *Situational Analysis: Grounded Theory After the Postmodern Turn*. Thousand Oaks: Sage.

Connors, C., & Stalker, K. (2007). Children's Experiences of Disability: Pointers to a Social Model of Childhood Disability. *Disability & Society, 22*(1), 19–33.

Curran, T. (2013). Disabled Children's Childhood Studies: Alternative Relations and Forms of Authority? In T. Curran & K. Runswick-Cole (Eds.), *Disabled Children's*

Childhood Studies: Critical Approaches in a Global Context (pp. 121–135). New York: Palgrave Macmillan.

Echeita, E., Simón, C., Verdugo, M. A., Sandoval, M., López, M., Calvo, I., & González-Gil, F. (2009). Paradojas y dilemas en el proceso de inclusión. *Revista de Educación, 349*, 153–178.

Foucault, M. (1978). *The History of Sexuality, Volume 1: An Introduction*. New York: Random House.

Foucault, M. (1989). *Foucault Live* (trans: Lotringer, S. & Honston, J. (Eds.)). New York: Semiotext.

Foucault, M. (1990). *Politics, Philosophy, Culture: Interviews and Other Writings of Michel Foucault, 1977–1984* (trans: Sheridan, A.). New York: Routledge.

Goodley, D., & Runswick-Cole, K. (2015). Thinking about Schooling Through Dis/ability: A DisHuman Approach. In T. Corcoran, J. White, & B. Whitburn (Eds.), *Disability Studies: Educating for Inclusion* (pp. 241–254). Rotterdam: Sense.

Humphry, N. (2014). Disrupting Deficit: The Power of 'The Pause' in Resisting the Dominance of Deficit Knowledges in Education. *International Journal of Inclusive Education, 18*(5), 484–499.

Martin, A. D., & Kamberelis, G. (2013). Mapping Not Tracing: Qualitative Educational Research with Political Teeth. *International Journal of Qualitative Studies in Education, 26*(6), 668–679.

Mazzei, L. A., & Youngblood Jackson, A. (2009). Introduction: The Limit of Voice. In A. Youngblood Jackson & L. A. Mazzei (Eds.), *Voice in Qualitative Inquiry: Challenging Conventional, Interpretive, and Critical Conceptions in Qualitative Research* (pp. 1–14). London/New York: Routledge.

McRuer, M. (2006). *Crip Theory: Cultural Signs of Queerness and Disability*. New York: NYU Press.

Miller, L., Whalley, J. B., & Stronach, I. (2011). From Structuralism to Poststructuralism. In B. Somekh & C. Lewin (Eds.), *Research Methods in the Social Sciences* (pp. 309–318). London: Sage.

Mockler, N., & Groundwater-Smith, S. (2015). *Engaging with Student Voice in Research, Education and Community: Beyond Legitimation and Guardianship*. Cham: Springer.

Moriña Díez, A. (2010). School Memories of Young People with Disabilities: An Analysis of Barriers and Aids to Inclusion. *Disability and Society, 25*(2), 163–175.

Nietzsche, F. W. (1969). *On the Genealogy of Morals*. New York: Random House.

Parrilla, A. (2008). Inclusive Education in Spain: A View from Inside. In L. Barton & F. Armstrong (Eds.), *Policy, Experience and Change: Cross-Cultural Reflections on Inclusive Education* (4th ed., pp. 19–38). Dordrecht/London: Springer.

Priestley, M., & Waddington, L. (2010). New Priorities for Disability Research in Europe: Towards a User-led Agenda. *ALTER, European Journal of Disability Research, 4*, 239–255.

Rojas, S., Susinos, S., & Calvo, A. (2013). 'Giving Voice' in Research Processes: An Inclusive Methodology for Researching into Social Exclusion in Spain. *International Journal of Inclusive Education, 17*(2), 156–173.

Shildrick, M. (2012). Critical Disability Studies: Rethinking the Conventions for the Age of Postmodernity. In N. Watson, A. Roulstone, & C. Thomas (Eds.), *Routledge Handbook of Disability Studies* (pp. 30–41). New York/Routledge: London.

Slee, R. (2011). *The Irregular School: Exclusion, Schooling and Inclusive Education.* London: Routledge.

St. Pierre, E. A. (2009). Afterword: Decentering Voice in Qualitative Inquiry. In A. Youngblood Jackson & L. A. Mazzei (Eds.), *Voice in Qualitative Inquiry: Challenging Conventional, Interpretive, and Critical Conceptions in Qualitative Research* (pp. 221–236). London/New York: Routledge.

Susinos, T. (2007). 'Tell Me in Your Own Words': Disabling Barriers and Social Exclusion in Young Persons. *Disability and Society, 22*(2), 117–127.

Susinos, T., & Ceballos, N. (2012). Voz del alumnado y presencia participativa en la vida escolar', Apuntes para una cartografíade la voz del alumnado en la mejora educativa. *Revista de Educación, 359*, 24–44.

Susinos, T., & Parilla, A. (2008). Dar la voz en la investigación inclusiva. Debates sobre inclusión y exclusión desde un enfoque biográfico-narrativo. *Revista Electrónica Iberoamericana sobre Calidad, Eficacia y Cambio en Educación, 6*(2), 157–171.

United Nations. (1989). *Convention on the Rights of the Child.* New York: Author.

United Nations. (2006). *Convention on the Rights of Persons with Disabilities.* New York: Author.

Verdugo, M. A., & Rodríguez, A. (2012). La inclusión educativa en España desde la perspectiva de alumnos con discapacidad intelectual, de familias y de profesionales. *Revista de Educación, 358*, 450–470.

Whitburn, B. (2013). The Dissection of Paraprofessional Support in Inclusive Education: "You're in Mainstream with a Chaperone". *Australasian Journal of Special Education, 37*(2), 147–161.

Whitburn, B. (2014a). Accessibility and Autonomy Preconditions to "Our" Inclusion: A Grounded Theory Study of the Experiences of Secondary Students with Vision Impairment. *Journal of Research in Special Educational Needs, 14*(1), 3–15.

Whitburn, B. (2014b). Voice, Post-Structural Representation and the Subjectivities of "Included" Students. *International Journal of Research and Method in Education.* doi:10.1080/1743727X.2014.946497.

Whitburn, B. (2014c). "A Really Good Teaching Strategy": Secondary Students with Vision Impairment Voice their Experiences of Inclusive Teacher Pedagogy. *British Journal of Vision Impairment, 32*(2), 148–156.

Whitburn, B. (2015). National and International Disability Rights Legislation: A Qualitative Account of Its Enactment in Australia. *International Journal of Inclusive Education, 19*(5), 518–529.

Whitburn, B. (2016). The Perspectives of Secondary School Students with Special Needs in Spain. *Research in Comparative and International Education, 11*(2), 148–164.

Youdell, D. (2006). *Impossible Bodies, Impossible Selves: Exclusions and Student Subjectivities*. Dordrecht: Springer.

Youngblood Jackson, A. (2009). What Am I Doing When I Speak of this Present?: Voice, Power, and Desire in Truth-Telling. In A. Youngblood Jackson & L. A. Mazzei (Eds.), *Voice in Qualitative Inquiry: Challenging Conventional, Interpretive, and Critical Conceptions in Qualitative Research* (pp. 165–174). London/New York: Routledge.

Ben Whitburn is Lecturer of Inclusive Education in the School of Education at Deakin University. Whitburn holds a PhD from Melbourne, Australia, and Madrid, Spain. Whitburn's thesis by publication works the intersection of disability studies and inclusive education research, by drawing on insider accounts of experience, and post-structural analytics.

Expressive Eyebrows and Beautiful Bubbles: Playfulness and Children with Profound Impairments

Debby Watson, Alison Jones, and Helen Potter

Key Points

- Playfulness
- Profound and Multiple Learning Disability (PMLD)
- Childhood
- Strengths

Yes, so he has got quite a lot of different expressions, very expressive with his eyebrows. He uses his eyebrows a lot. That would indicate he's enjoying something (Alison Jones, parent of Thomas)

Focussing on eyebrow movements may seem an unusual aspect of research, but this became an integral part of the Passport to Play study, conducted in the South West of England between 2010 and 2014 (Watson 2014). This doctoral study, funded by the Economic and Social Research Council, set out to discover how playfulness can be encouraged in children with profound impairments, including sensory, physical and intellectual. Playfulness, in

D. Watson (✉)
University of Bristol, Bristol, UK

A. Jones
Parent, Bristol, UK

H. Potter
Sense Children's Specialist Services Team, Bristol, UK

© The Author(s) 2018
K. Runswick-Cole et al. (eds.), *The Palgrave Handbook of Disabled Children's Childhood Studies*, https://doi.org/10.1057/978-1-137-54446-9_13

this context, can be seen as an emotional expression of pleasure, usually in response to a play activity or a playful exchange with another person, whereas play is broadly the manifestation of this playful response, where an object or other person is played with. Playfulness, having a stronger focus on inner processes than the wider field of play, is an appropriate focus for studying children with profound and multiple disabilities (PMLD) if an approach is taken which includes an acknowledgement that context and support issues are important to those processes. The subject of playfulness was therefore chosen for its potential to offer a way to reach the essential child, to look beyond impairments to look at character, preferences and strengths and to quantify what profoundly disabled children can do, rather than focussing on negative or medical aspects, as is too often the case in research in this field. This means that the children will be seen for what they are, as 'meaning makers' (Nind et al. 2010) rather than compared to non-disabled children or in terms of their deficits. The central tenet *of Disabled Children's Childhood Studies* (Curran and Runswick-Cole, Eds 2013), that disabled children should be viewed as having childhoods rather than having or being problems, is pertinent to this study. The aim of the study has been to focus on a fundamental aspect of childhood, playfulness, and it highlights strengths in children who are too often portrayed by their impairments or 'problems' surrounding their care. Impairments in profoundly disabled children cannot and should not be ignored as they inevitably have a significant impact, and to ignore them, as one participant in the study said, 'is to ignore the child'. However, this study has shown that impairment is certainly not the most important determinant of playfulness: attitudes of the people around them and the willingness to engage in playful interactions are more significant. For example, there were two instances where children had very different levels of playfulness at school and at home. Although acknowledging that different physical environments can have a bearing on a child's ability to access playful activities, their levels of playfulness changed considerably in these settings, and this can be attributed in large part to differing levels of expectations and opportunities for playfulness.

In this chapter, the Passport to Play study will be described, including a brief description of the theoretical background and methodology. Following this, contributions from the co-authors of this chapter, a mother of a child in the study, Alison Jones, and a senior family support worker from Sense, Helen Potter, are provided and interwoven with findings from the study which resonate with their contributions. This approach to authorship provides multiple viewpoints from people who have many years of first-hand experience of playfulness and children with PMLD as well as academic knowledge about the area. There are, however, some ethical concerns that the child who is mostly discussed in the chapter will be identified by those who know his mother. She requested that his real name be used, although his pseudonym has been kept in the 'mind map' in Fig. 3. As the subject matter is of a positive nature and no distressing or sensitive data has been used, it was considered by the authors that the benefits of having parental involvement in the chapter outweighed concerns about anonymity.

In children with profound impairments, playfulness can, as described below by Helen Potter, be as fragile as a bubble and can be expressed by as little as a movement of eyebrows but is nevertheless fundamental, as it is to all children. Several authors link play to well-being (Else 2009; Gleave and Cole-Hamilton 2012; Howard 2010; Hughes 2012; McConkey 2006; McInnes 2012), and the literature on child development suggests that early playful interactions may be the 'building blocks' of relationships (Rutter and Rutter 1993). This, as Helen Potter illustrates below, is just one of the reasons why the importance of playfulness, not only for people with profound impairments but also for those around them, should not be underestimated. It is therefore troubling that the Association of Play Industries (API 2011) states that England is lagging behind Scotland, Wales and Northern Ireland in realising Article 31 (the child's right to play) of the United Nations Convention on the Rights of the Child (UNCRC 1989). Read et al. (2012) confirm this view and express concerns about the current direction of policy that affects disabled children and play.

The Passport to Play Study

The study was conducted in three main stages. Initially, an initial online survey was undertaken via the PMLD Network (http://www.pmldnetwork.org/), which aimed to provide a picture of what current attitudes and practices were operating concerning playfulness and children with profound impairments. In addition, the respondents provided some knowledge about which sites to visit in the second stage of the study. This was where 11 visits to or interviews at sites in the UK were undertaken where there were professionals and families who were knowledgeable about playfulness and people with profound impairments. This stage involved spending time with several family members of disabled children and interviewing a range of professionals, including arts-based professionals from theatre and music backgrounds, academics, play therapists and intensive interaction practitioners. The final stage of the study, and of central importance, was observations of five children with PMLD, from three to seven years old, in three different settings: home, school and a play setting. Interviews were also conducted with the children's care-givers in these settings. In all, 27 hours and 58 minutes were spent observing the five children in the three settings, with minute-by-minute recording on an observation schedule devised for this study (see www.debbywatson.co.uk).

The theoretical basis for this study was necessarily complex and included four approaches to the broad themes of equality and connectedness. Critical realism was considered alongside current thinking in disability studies, childhood studies and psychological approaches, making it possible to carry out research with children with profound impairments that highlighted the importance of playfulness and the strengths that children with PMLD can demonstrate, whilst acknowledging their interdependence with others. Shakespeare (2013) argues convincingly that critical realism allows for complexity and the acceptance of an 'external reality'. Its emphases on the political, underlying mechanisms, analytical dualism, multi-levels, mixed methods and empowerment made it a useful basis for this study, when used alongside aspects of the approaches described below. Children with profound impairments, unable to speak for themselves, exemplify the need for a nuanced, multi-disciplinary theoretical approach that can capture their experience at three different levels: factors *within the child* such as personality, interacting impairments, strengths, preferences, characteristics, mannerisms and communication styles; factors *around the child* such as attributes in others that enable receptiveness to and messages for playfulness, physical and psychological issues (positioning, time, stress, etc.), preparedness and circularity; and factors *beyond the child* such as the permissiveness of the environment regarding playfulness, both in psychological and physical regards, communication between home, school and services, and positive attitudes regarding playfulness.

By developing a theoretical framework that incorporated notions of interconnectedness and interdependence whilst being mindful of the relative inequalities facing the child with PMLD, it was possible to examine playfulness and profoundly disabled children at three levels: a 'within child' level where they have profound impairments which make them almost wholly dependent on others to feed, clothe and nurture them and yet demonstrate playfulness, strengths and character; beyond that to their connections with those around them who enable them to be playful and interact with others; and also at a wider level where their social, emotional and physical environment, need for services and social development can be examined.

An important influence on this study was the work of Eva Feder Kittay (1999, 2005), a philosopher and parent of a young woman with profound impairments. She asserts that any approach towards equality has to include an appreciation of 'dependents', as there is a need to be realistic and accept that some in society will never achieve independence however effective the support given to them is. Indeed, as does Vorhaus (2013), Kittay acknowledges that to some extent, we are all dependent on others at some point in our lives. Kittay (1999) argues that we therefore need a connection-based equality rather than a 'rights-driven' approach. Vorhaus (2013) talks of the reciprocal nature of dependent relationships and how profoundly disabled people are often perceived to have an inverse relationship regarding their dependence and their ability to reciprocate. However, Kittay (1999) is clear that although she recognises the extent to which her daughter is dependent on others, she acknowledges that she also depends on her disabled daughter and would 'wither' without her. Within this study, one of the mothers spoke of how a 'whole world' had been opened up to her through her daughter, and it is important to acknowledge the contribution that profoundly disabled people make to the lives of those around them. Helen Potter, below, also acknowledges this aspect of reciprocity.

Alison Jones conducted an interesting exercise for a presentation (Jones et al. 2015) whereby she created a 'Word it Out' (permission granted by WordItOut: http://worditout.com/) picture using two very different documents. Figure 1 is a condensed view of a discharge report she was given on her son, Thomas, on leaving hospital:

Figure 2 is the result of the same exercise but of a report written about Thomas for the Passport to Play study:

The pictures have no overlap and show completely different aspects of Thomas. These pictures offer a stark reminder that if you focus on negatives

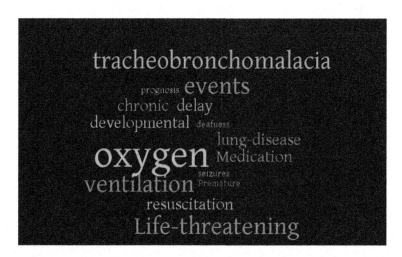

Fig. 1 Discharge report

Fig. 2 Thomas: Passport to Play study report

and medical aspects, that is the picture you get; if you look more positively at the child, you gain a very different view, one that incorporates eyebrows—those important indicators of playfulness!

Davis et al. (2008) suggest that by directly observing children, it is possible to avoid the 'pitfalls' involved in asking others to interpret their world. Interpretation is a key issue concerning children with profound impairments (Ware 2004; Grove et al. 1999; Lacey and Ouvry 1998) and although accepting that there will inevitably be some level of interpretation, an attempt to minimise this was achieved by combining detailed observation and referring back to those who knew the child well. In addition, where necessary, a parent, teacher or teaching assistant was asked for clarification about a child's behaviour. This is a similar approach to Beresford (2004), who suggests that it is useful to draw on a range of 'data sources' in reference to a particular child and relates to what is known as the Mosaic Approach, as described by Clark (2001). In addition, using an observation schedule allows for what is not said, an important aspect of 'listening' to disabled children. As Caldwell (2007) states:

> When we are with our non-verbal partners we are going to have to search at a micro-level for every flicker, every movement, every sound and rhythm – and also invest meaning in behaviour we might otherwise reject as just something they do. (p 19)

Caldwell (2012) suggests that we need to learn to 'listen with all our senses' and suggests that we need to look at what the person is doing, how s/he is doing it and where the focus is. The observation schedule developed for this study incorporated these aspects and covered the following aspects: time; context; communication and appearance; posture; mannerisms; influence and activity/comments. Care was taken not to interpret behaviours in isolation, even those as seemingly straightforward as a grimace, but to draw on contributory factors such as the child's body language, the context and the activities happening at the time.

Findings

The contribution by Helen Potter, below, highlights and echoes some important findings from the Passport to Play study, including the need to be child-led, attributes of supporters, the impact of the environment, joyfulness and the need to build on playful moments. The impact of the children's impairments has been touched on above and will not be reiterated here except to emphasise that the study clearly found that although physical impairments have obvious effects on functioning regarding playfulness, they can to a large extent be overcome. As a play therapist in the study said:

> I think physical disability obviously, you know, that's going to really limit you, the fact that you can't reach out and interact perhaps with your arms or move around, but I think those things can be overcome and that's when you need a sensitive approach to what that youngster needs.

The emotional state of the child was thought to be more significant, with issues around processing times also being relevant. However, these are factors that can be addressed by a sensitive 'play partner' and Helen's suggestions, below, for what makes a successful partnership are also reflected in the study's findings.

'Playfulness: Beautiful Bubbles' by Helen Potter

Learning to let the child lead is a crucial skill we need to have if we want to empower a child who is Deafblind or Multi-Sensory Impaired and only when we are able to let this happen will we help them to develop their playful personality, and also their play skills.

Yes, it is all about them, but crucially it is all about our role as the supporter as well. This interactive partnership is as difficult to create and as challenging to hold as a beautiful bubble. For many of our children that special moment of playful connection is, just like a bubble, sparkling and full of rainbow colours or when mishandled through lack of knowledge, gone and lost in a moment.

As a play partner you need to hone your observational skills. You must learn to be patient, learn about when is the right time to support the child and when it is the time to hold back. You have to keep your antenna twitching constantly for the optimum learning environment. The surroundings can impact negatively or positively on the way we achieve successful learning and play. We need to understand the impact of the environment and head off problems before they start impacting upon the child: the click of a door, the unwanted touch, the dog barking, the smell of dinner cooking, the washing machine clicking into spin cycle. So many things can impact and distract the child as they go through their day. But playful moments may happen when we sit on the washing machine as it spins, or feel the breeze of a door opening right next to us, or sit right by the cooker and smell the steam from cooking food. You have to know the child inside out and you also need to understand the impact the environment has upon the child as they learn to play.

You have to start where the child is by knowing their likes and dislikes. Observing the way the child tells you things through their body language, eye points, facial expression, their physical tension or their relaxed body language, the changes in their breathing patterns, and not forgetting their feet and legs as these are really important indicators of the child's happiness or otherwise. This is generally a good starting point.

Developing a friendship and a relationship with the child can be achieved simply by simply "hanging out" together. By using physical contact you can begin to judge the child's physical and emotional "voice". Being in close proximity to the child results in physical questions, such as: what is your best position for a successful conversation? What the child enjoys and who the child enjoys being with can become quite obvious if you get up close and personal! It is all about trust, pace and timing! You have to tell them what is happening without distracting them. It is a bit like walking a tightrope. Too much information overloads, too little can make the child scared or anxious. Too fast a pace can lose the child, too slow a pace can do the same thing. Letting the child's tiny "voice" be heard in playful, non-threatening call and response conversations can lead to so much trust because you learn to really listen to the child.

You need to work from an understanding that a child with Multi-Sensory Impairments will tell you more than you will ever notice. As sighted, hearing people we are used to a visual and auditory world where information comes to us through our distance senses, we filter it, pack away what we need to know and filter out the rest. Children who are Deafblind and Multi-Sensory Impaired have different priorities; their needs are unique to them. Their way of thinking and understanding the world is personal to them and sometimes distorted in a way only they understand. The child's exposure to new sights and situations are often limited because of their disability and how they process and integrate what they see, hear, taste, smell and touch. The child's expressive communication will often be fleeting, subtle and easily missed, so sometimes the child learns a message from our lack of skills that no-one listens and they give up.

But...when the conditions are just right you can hold that bubble in your hand, just for a moment and that moment tells you so much. That moment of playful connection offers you and the child a feeling of pure joy. It happens and then just like a bubble caught by the wind it goes away but because it happened you know it can be built upon, replicated and learned from. That's why play is important. Practice makes perfect and that practice, if you get it right, is just plain fun for everyone involved!

Parents and carers of children with profound impairments lead necessarily extremely full and busy lives. The extent to which this is dominated by contact with professionals and services is starkly illustrated in the 'Mind Map', written by Alison Jones to help to make sense of all the people in her life:

It is clear that very little time or energy is left for playfulness in this picture, and very few professionals are concerned with encouraging playfulness. Alison has written an account of life with Thomas, as a parent, who has very actively encouraged playfulness:

> As a family we spend lots of playful time together. Our son Thomas is 8 and loves being around people and joining in with fun activities. He loves riding fast in his trailer tagged on to the back of our bicycle because he can really feel the wind and see the world pass by. A trip to the cinema really gets his attention because he loves the bright screen and loud sound.
>
> However, Thomas spent a long time in hospital following his extremely premature birth and has profound disabilities as well as multi-sensory impairment. His discharge letter from the neonatal intensive care unit was full of medical terminology (see Fig. 1) and in those first few weeks at home we wondered how we were going to enjoy anything like a normal life. Medical equipment filled our house and we soon discovered the complex network of professionals involved with Thomas's health and development (see mind map, Fig. 3.). All these people made valuable contributions to Thomas's life but very few were there to help

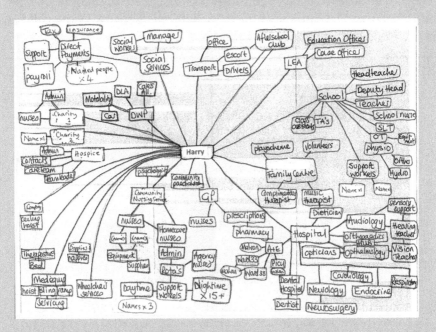

Fig. 3 Mind map

him have fun. At the same time as ensuring he stayed alive and well they made life with Thomas very complicated and regimented in a way that was not at all playful or enjoyable.

Thankfully, two or three of these people were able to help us understand Thomas and start to be playful with him. The professionals that did this the best were those that gave us the skills and confidence to encourage Thomas to be himself, have fun and interact with those around him. They taught us to follow his lead and give him plenty of time to respond.

Thomas is now described as a playful child, and the words from the Passport to Play report about his ability to respond to play (see Fig. 2) are a long way from the medical discharge summary from eight years previously.

From playful learning has developed more and more communication for Thomas.

He has even started to use Eye Gaze technology to play games and make simple choices. Thomas can do this independently of adult input which gives him a whole new freedom.

The phrase 'encouraging Thomas to be himself, have fun and interact' says a huge amount. The ability to see children with profound impairments as individual children, with particular likes, dislikes and preferences, is fundamental to changing perceptions of profoundly disabled children from children who are 'done' (Goodley and Runswick-Cole 2010) to children who *can*. The Passport to Play study identified 18 different strengths in the children that were observed, and Thomas demonstrated 14 of these:

Strengths demonstrated by Thomas
1. Makes choices (e.g. can choose between two toys)
2. Demonstrates sense of humour (e.g. laughs or smiles when something is accidentally dropped)
3. Draws people to him/her (e.g. gets attention by making eye contact)
4. Demonstrates intentional behaviour (e.g. deliberately presses switch)
5. Follows simple instructions (e.g. responds to request to strum guitar)
6. Responds to talk about past events/people (e.g. looks excited when favoured activity is mentioned)
7. Able to anticipate (e.g. looks excited when he sees a swing)
8. Able to concentrate (e.g. can sustain interest in a toy for prolonged period)
9. Shows signs of being 'naughty'/wilful (e.g. laughs when throws the toy on floor)
10. Able to indicate 'more' (e.g. rocks forward if the toy going to be taken away)
11. Able to indicate 'no more' (e.g. turns away from the person or the toy)
12. Plays without support (e.g. is able to sustain interest in toys when adult is no longer present)
13. Shows determination (e.g. makes several attempts to reach toys)
14. Enjoys risky/rough play (e.g. shows pleasure in being pushed high on swing)
15. Responds to praise (e.g. smiles when told 'well done')

Strengths are rarely documented in the literature on children with profound impairments, and yet it is these 'building blocks' that enable children with profound impairments to continue to lead what Kittay (1999) describes as 'a good life'. If playfulness is not actively encouraged, and children with PMLD are not actively involved, this study has been shown that playfulness will not thrive. The children's playful activities were divided into 'active' and 'passive' categories. Active playfulness describes activities where the children were actually involved in doing something, such as strumming a guitar. This type of activity was linked to a higher number of observed strengths and suggests that these types of activities should be particularly encouraged. Passive playfulness might involve watching something or being given an object to feel or smell. It was significant that the least actively playful child demonstrated the least strengths, particularly as he was not the child with the most physical impairments. A more detailed account of the findings from the study can be found in Watson (2015).

Conclusions

If a child with profound impairments can be playful despite finding it hard to communicate needs, often feeling unwell, needing frequent medical interventions and being unable to get up and run around or see too well, that must surely mean that playfulness is fundamentally important to all of us. The Passport to Play study has shown that the five study children were playful for an average of 67% of the time observed, with much of the remaining time being spent in physical and medical tasks or waiting for something to happen. This is where we need to acknowledge that childhoods differ for children with profound impairments: without focussed, sensitive support and a will to bring out playfulness, children with profound impairments can, as was found in one of the children in the study who experienced very low levels of playfulness, have lives that are dominated by mundane and medical interventions. A life that lacks a balance to these aspects veers far from the lives of non-disabled children. It has been suggested that levels of playfulness were not found to be determined by impairments but by the situations that the children were in and by those who were supporting them. We need to remember that, as one of the parents in the study said:

> We have made a promise to that child when we saved that child's life, to provide for that child...Saying you can have a bed and you can have a nursery chair and that is it, is just to me — we're talking about environments and what evokes playfulness and comfort and being able to access the toys, accessible toys.

Duffy (2013) estimates that people with the most severe impairments will bear the biggest burden regarding welfare cuts and that these decisions make us, a wealthy country, 'increasingly beginning to sound uncivilised' (p. 33). In order for playfulness to thrive under these circumstances, attention needs to be at three levels in 'mindful interdependency' (Watson 2015): within the child, noting their preferences and character; around the child, having people around them who can encourage their playfulness; and beyond the child to the wider environment, where playfulness is permitted and encouraged. Focussing on details, such as movements in eyebrows, our twitching antenna and the breeze from the door, will allow us to involve ourselves in mutually rewarding interactions and hold on to that beautiful bubble of playfulness just a little longer.

References

Association of Play Industries. (2011). Press release: Whitehall Falls Behind Rest of UK in Protecting Children's Right to Play. www.api-play.org/childrens-right-to-play. Accessed 10 June 2016.

Beresford, B. (2004). Developing an Approach to Involving Children with Autistic Spectrum Disorders in a Social Care Research Project. *British Journal of Learning Disabilities, 32*, 180–185.

Caldwell, P. (2007). *From Isolation to Intimacy: Making Friends without Words.* London: Jessica Kingsley Publishers.

Caldwell, P. (2012). *Listening with All Our Senses.* Brighton: Pavilion.

Clarke, A. (2001). How to Listen to Very Young Children: The Mosaic Approach. *Child Care in Practice, 7*(4), 333–341.

Curran, T., & Runswick-Cole, K. (2013). *Disabled Children's Childhood Studies.* Basingstoke: Palgrave Macmillan.

Davis, J., Watson, N., & Cunningham-Burley. (2008). Disabled Children, Ethnography and Unspoken Understandings: The Collaborative Construction of Diverse Identities. In P. Cristensen & A. James (Eds.), *Research with Children: Perspectives and Practices* (2nd ed., pp. 220–238). London: Routledge.

Duffy, S. (2013). *A fair society? How the cuts target disabled people.* The Centre for Welfare Reform/ Campaign for a fair society. http://www.centreforwelfarereform.org/library/type/pdfs/a-fair-society1.html. Accessed 10 June 2016.

Else, P. (2009). *The Value of Play.* London: Continuum International Publishing Group.

Gleave, J., & Cole-Hamilton, I. (2012). *A World Without Play: A Literature Review* Play England. http://www.playengland.org.uk/media/371031/a-world-without-play-literature-review-2012.pdf. Accessed 10 June 2016.

Goodley, D., & Runswick-Cole, K. (2010). Emancipating Play: Dis/abled Children, Development and Deconstruction. *Disability and Society, 25*(4), 499–512.

Grove, N., Bunning, K., Porter, J., & Olsson, C. (1999). See What I Mean: Interpreting the Meaning of Communication by People with Severe and Profound Intellectual Disabilities. *Journal of Applied Research in Intellectual Disabilities, 12*(3), 190–203.

Howard, J. (2010). Early Years Practitioners' Perceptions of Play: An Exploration of Theoretical Understanding, Planning and Involvement, Confidence and Barriers to Practice. *Educational & Child Psychology, 27*(4), 91–102.

Hughes, B. (2012). *Evolutionary Playwork*. London: Routledge.

Jones, A., Potter, H., & Watson, D. (2015, July 7–8) Playfulness in Children with Complex Needs: Three Perspectives'. Presentation at: There is no them! The 8th Child, Youth, Family and Disability Conference University of the West of England.

Kittay, E. F. (1999). *Love's Labor: Essays on Women, Equality and Dependency*. New York: Routledge.

Kittay, E. F. (2005). At the Margins of Moral Personhood. *Ethics, 116*(1), 100–131.

Lacey, P., & Ouvry, C. (Eds.). (1998). *People with Profound and Multiple Learning Disabilities: A Collaborative Approach to Meeting Complex Needs*. London: David Fulton.

McConkey, R. (2006) Realising the Potential of Play for ALL Children. *PMLD Link, 18*(3), Issue 55, 8–10.

McInnes, K. (2012). Opportunities for Playful Expressions of Wellbeing. In D. Watson, C. Emery and P. Bayliss with M. Boushel and K. McInnes (Eds.), *Children's Social and Emotional Wellbeing in Schools: A Critical Perspective* (pp. 143–156). Bristol: Policy Press.

Nind, M., Flewitt, R., & Payler, J. (2010). The Social Experience of Early Childhood for Children with Learning Disabilities: Inclusion, Competence and Agency. *British Journal of Sociology of Education, 31*(6), 653–670.

Read, J., Blackburn, C., & Spencer, N. (2012). Disabled Children and Their Families: A Decade of Policy Change. *Children and Society, 26*, 223–233.

Rutter, M., & Rutter, M. (1993). *Developing Minds: Challenge & Continuity Across the Life Span*. New York: Basic Books.

Shakespeare, T. (2013). *Disability Rights and Wrongs Revisited*. London: Routledge.

United Nations Convention on the Rights of the Child. (1989). UNICEF. http://www.unicef.org.uk/Documents/Publication-pdfs/UNCRC_PRESS200910web.pdf. Accessed 10 June 2016.

Vorhaus, J. (2013). Philosophy and Profound Disability: Learning from Experience. *Disability and Society*. doi:10.1080/09687599.2013.831749.

Vos, P., De Cock, P., et al. (2010). What Makes Them Feel Like They Do? Investigating the Subjective Well-Being in People with Severe and Profound Disabilities. *Research in Developmental Disabilities, 31*(6), 1623–1632.

Ware, J. (2004). Ascertaining the Views of People with Profound and Multiple Learning Disabilities. *British Journal of Learning Disabilities, 32*, 175–179.

Watson, D. (2014). *'Go-getters' and 'Clever Little Cookies': A Multi-Method Study on Playfulness and Children with PMLD*, Unpublished Thesis, University of Bristol, Bristol.

Watson, D. (2015). Turning to Playfulness: Findings from a Study on Playfulness and Children with Profound Impairments. *SLD Experience*, Issue 73, Autumn 18–23.

Debby Watson works as a social researcher for a charitable trust in Gloucestershire. She has a background in social work and was formerly a research fellow in the Norah Fry Centre for Disability Studies, University of Bristol. She has completed a PhD study on playfulness and children with profound impairments and has a keen interest in research ethics.

Alison Jones is a qualified pharmacist with a PhD in Pharmacology. She works part-time for the National Health Service (NHS) and as a trainer and educator in postgraduate pharmacy practice. She is the mother of two young children, one of whom has complex physical and sensory difficulties.

Helen Potter works for Sense, a national charity that supports children and adults who are deafblind, those with sensory impairments and those with complex needs. She is a specialist in multi-sensory impairment and works as a senior children and family support worker. Helen is a member of the Sense Children's Specialist Services team and is based at the Woodside Family Centre in Bristol. Helen has many years of experience playing with and encouraging children with sensory impairments and complex needs.

My Friends and Me: Friendship and Identity Following Acquired Brain Injury in Young People

Sandra Dowling, Roy McConkey, and Marlene Sinclair

Key Points

- Explores the role of friendship in redrawing identity following acquired brain injury (ABI) in young people
- Creative methods of collage and narrative approaches used
- Methodological developments enable participation and were endorsed by participants in advance of their engagement with the study
- The method enables ethical voice amongst participants
- 'Narrative collage' devised in the writing up of the study as a way of telling stories and maintaining confidentiality

The poet *Lynsey Calderwood* draws on her experiences as a survivor of Acquired Brain Injury (ABI) by producing an evocative voice that conjures vivid images, each conveying the acute discord and loss she experienced following ABI. She writes:

I am grateful to the young people and their families who took part in the research reported here. They were each generous and open in their engagement with the study in relation to sensitive memories and emotive experiences. The work was supported by a Vice Chancellor's Research Scholarship at Ulster University, Northern Ireland.

S. Dowling (✉)
University of Bristol, Bristol, UK

R. McConkey • M. Sinclair
University of Ulster, Newtownabbey, Northern Ireland, UK

© The Author(s) 2018
K. Runswick-Cole et al. (eds.), *The Palgrave Handbook of Disabled Children's Childhood Studies*, https://doi.org/10.1057/978-1-137-54446-9_14

191

My reflection
Hosts so many strange faces
Lost in the loneliness
I feel part of another species
(Calderwood 2003)

Tyerman and Humphrey (1984) describe ABI as a potentially devastating experience. ABI can have a significant impact on identity where a person can face such change that they lose a coherent or assured sense of self. The impact on teenagers may be particularly significant as they experience injury at such a tender time in their development; however, few studies have addressed this.

Hubert (1985) reports that on an average, every two hours, someone in the United Kingdom dies as a result of an ABI. This chapter draws on the experiences of nine young people who did not die. Their stories told, in part here, began with a single traumatic event, which for each produced enormous change in their lives and that of their families. A bedside vigil, taut in the hope of survival, gave way to fears of an uncertain future once survival was assured. As young people recovered from the physical impact of their injuries, they struggled to make sense of a new reality. The meaning they made of their sense of self and identity was newly surrounded by uncertainty, dissonance and oftentimes bewilderment. Strongly resonant of the picture drawn by Calderwood, and as one young person in the present study said:

I survived, that was a big step, now I have to learn to live (Patrick)

This chapter draws on doctoral research,[1] which sought to explore the reconstruction of identity in adolescence following ABI. The central theme of the chapter is the role of friendship in understanding the redrawing of identity amongst those young people who took part. Whilst the chapter concentrates primarily on the voice of the young people who took part in the study, some context is necessary. This begins with a brief synopsis of the common outcomes of ABI and consideration of the link between ABI, identity and adolescence, followed by exploration of the idea of evolving identity in young people generally and the role of friendship in the development of identity. A description of the methodological approach to data collection follows and precedes a description of the sample. A 'narrative collage' is presented with the aim of providing an aggregate lens on the experiences of the young people who were part of the research. This is followed by a detailed description of young people's reflections on the importance of friendship in relation to their sense of self following their injury. The findings presented draw on the words of young people and on images from collages they produced in the course of data collection (discussed below).

Outcomes of ABI

ABI can result from a wide range of events such as a fall, accident or assault or illness. Injuries differ in severity and impact, and conditions vary widely, are often subject to rapid change and have a potentially extensive impact which becomes increasingly apparent over time. Common sequelae include fatigue and lack of motivation, amnesia, poor memory and difficulties with concentration, changes in personality, inappropriate behaviour and impulsivity, problems controlling anger and difficulties reintegrating into previous family, social or educational situations (Andrews et al. 1998). Individuals often experience changes in their relationships, loss of prior status, emotional strain and depression as well as social isolation and marginalisation (Hubert 1985; Osborn 1998; Gracey et al. 2008). Whilst changes following ABI can be difficult to reconcile for affected individuals and those close to them, understanding within wider society can also be limited. Misinterpretation of outcomes combined with negative social attitudes can result in further disabling effects (Osborn 1998).

In young people, initial recovery is often more rapid than in the adult population (Hawley 2002). However, as young people mature and new challenges arise, a gradual but marked discrepancy between young people with ABI and their peers can emerge. Linden et al. (2005) report that the growing gap with peers is likely to impact on a range of social, emotional and psychological domains. Dixon et al. (2008) highlight the particular needs of young people with ABI, who although often physically resilient may experience increased risk of exposure to negative social, emotional and psychological outcomes due to the interruption in their development prior to maturity and as they are progressing towards independence and establishing the foundations for adult life.

Identity, Young People and ABI

Whilst theories of identity differ, they commonly recognise the adolescent period as crucial in the development of identity (see collection by Browning 2007). Typically, this period is characterised by the distancing of self from the limitations of the familial setting and the growing pursuit of self-interest, whilst also bringing together perceived needs within the perceived social context. Kroger (2004; 10) highlights the importance of the adolescent stage of development: *'adolescence encompasses one phase of heightened activity for most in this intra-physic and interpersonal juggling act.'* Whilst the adolescent years are noted to be a key site of identity development, McCabe and Green (1987) in their discussion of rehabilitation amongst teenagers following ABI state that: *'a severe head injury may profoundly undermine an adolescent's capacity to achieve the maturational tasks of adolescence in terms of adequate separation and individuation'* (p. 119).

Friendship and Evolving Identity

Friendship is crucial both during the developmental years and later. Companionship is not the only benefit of friendship, it also makes possible the development of social skills, such as building enduring relationships, taking part in competition and resolving conflicts (Crothers et al. 2007). Friendship can also enable young people to acquire life skills and knowledge to take forward to adulthood (Bedell and Dumas 2004). Young people tend to spend a lot of time with peers, either through daily contact in school or college or through other structured or purely social activities.

Inclusion and social participation have been found to be negatively affected following ABI (Boylan 2014). Crothers et al. (2007) reported that children and young people with impaired social skills were more likely to experience rejection and less likely to have friends. Rejection by peers can impose a serious detriment to development. Positive mental health is associated with friendship (Kupersmidt et al. 1990) whilst the risk of school drop-out has been linked to diminished peer status (Parker and Asher 1987).

Some outcomes of ABI may be misinterpreted and misunderstood by peers. These can lead to young people with ABI experiencing the loss of friendship and potential isolation from peers (Crothers et al. 2007). In addition, young people may experience increased reliance on parents and family networks and loss of opportunity to engage in developmental tasks of adolescence involving separation from parents and the carving out of an individuated sense of self.

The Child Brain Injury Trust (CBIT), a UK-wide voluntary organisation for children and young people who have experienced ABI, offers advice to help undermine this negative possible trajectory. Recognising the practical challenges, misunderstandings, strains on communication and various psychological difficulties experienced by young people following ABI, and these factors in interplay with peer relationships, they provide information through their website which aims to assist children and young people to positively negotiate peer relationships during their recovery. The information acknowledges the range of difficulties young people may experience and details steps they might take to undermine these. This more practical approach can be a leveller to the more psychologically experienced challenges and may be an antidote to the prescribed negative outcomes reported through the literature. Findings from the present study do resonate with existing literature, as is discussed below. However, it is important to acknowledge that challenging experiences can be managed and transformed and that organisations like CBIT, as well as therapeutic approaches to managing outcomes, can change trajectories and unseat adverse expectations.

The Study

The overall aim of this study was to examine through young people's self-report and self-reflection their reconstruction of identity following ABI. The objectives were:

- To consider young people's perspectives on the impact of their injury on their own lives and that of their family and the meaning this held for them in relation to identity
- To examine the interplay between perspectives on identity and young people's psychological well-being, emotional health and social membership

The study adopted a qualitative approach with the intention of listening to the views and perspectives of young people who had experienced an ABI. A bespoke approach to data collection was developed to facilitate the inclusion of young peoples' voices.

The study grew from the collision of a number of issues:

1. Adolescence is a key time in identity formation.[2]
2. Identity is disrupted following ABI.
3. Teenagers' views and perspectives are largely absent from the literature relating to ABI, although they are proportionally more at risk of ABI than any other group.

The study was approved by Ulster Universities Research Ethics Committee. As this research was focused on topics which were potentially sensitive, support from the CBIT was put in place for young people should they need to access it as a result of their involvement in the study.

Methodology

Data was collected using a qualitative approach that was devised in collaboration with the young people who took part in the study. Initially data was collected using semi-structured interviews. However, this proved to be of limited use with this group of participants who found it difficult to engage with the abstract concept of identity. Moreover, outcomes of their injury including fatigue, difficulties in concentration and challenges with recall militated against the usefulness of interviews.

In response to the challenges of using an interview approach, a focus group was convened comprising four initial participants. The aim was to discuss an alternative approach to data collection that might enable their participation more fully. Alternatives derived from creative approaches were presented and discussed. These included using a photo-elicitation method, using drama or story telling, or employing art or drawing as a means of engagement. Making a collage was also presented as an option and young people favoured that approach. They reported that this was something that they felt was possible and achievable, and that required no particular skill in art or drama but was something they could all do. Through engaging young people in devising the approach in which data would be collected, they developed greater ownership of the project and commitment to it.

Data was thus collected using a mixture of unstructured interviews mediated around the construction of a collage (Dowling et al. forthcoming). During collage construction, the interactions between the young person and the researcher were audio-recorded. In this way, the discussion of items which young people had chosen to place on the collage and the reflections that emerged in relation to these became part of the data collected. The collage provided a focus for the interview, enabling conversation to flow easily. Collages were constructed over a number of visits, with the time taken to construct them ranging from 4 to 23 hours depending on the individual. A trusting relation grew between the participant and the researcher as a consequence of repeat visits made in the course of the work. This method also was assisted with some outcomes of the young person's injury in that it:

- Helped to make more accessible the abstract concept of identity
- Facilitated concentration
- Aided recall for participants

- Assisted with fatigue
- Enabled continuity in repeat visits

In addition to data collected from young people, semi-structured interviews were carried out with a parent (in all instances the mother[3]). The purpose of this interview was to gather information about the young person's accident/injury and the outcome of it. Young people were uniformly unable to recall what had happened at the time of the injury, and many experienced amnesia in relation to months before and after their accident. A final piece of data was gathered when collages were complete. At this stage, young people shared their collage with their mother, discussing elements of it, the reason why particular items had been chosen for the collage and the meaning they held for participants. This aspect of the method emerged from the request of one of the young people. They wanted to share the collage with their parent (mother) to help them explain how they felt about certain things and how they felt about themselves. It was agreed that this could be recorded and form part of the data for the project. In this way, young people had an ethical voice in relation to their own story of their sense of self.

Data was therefore gathered at four levels of abstraction:

- initial interviews conducted with mothers
- interviews with young people (which ran alongside the construction of the collage)
- the collage
- the discussion that ensued when sharing the collage with the parent.

All spoken data were transcribed for analysis. The collage was the property of young people but was borrowed for a short period for analysis. With consent, photographic images of the collage were made in advance of returning it to participants.

Data analysis was approached using Interpretative Phenomenological Analysis (Smith and Osborn 2003, 2004). The different sources of data were housed in a matrix so that the interrelatedness and connections could be made drawing on superordinate and subordinate themes identified.

The Sample

The sample comprised nine young people with an acquired brain injury, three female and six male, aged 12–19 years. Participants were recruited through the CBIT. All but one of the young people had sustained a severe head injury as a result of a road traffic accident, either as a pedestrian, a cyclist or a car passenger. One of the young people had been injured following an incident of bullying at school. The severity of injury varied, but for each of the young people, it had led to a period of coma ranging between 10 days and 3 months with hospital stays between 3 weeks and 11 months. Two young people experienced physical impairment following the injury and were wheelchair users. Common sequelae, variously experienced amongst all of the young people, included fatigue, memory loss, difficulties with concentration, remaining focused and personality changes. Five of the young people returned to their former school following recovery, three attended a special school and one was not in education at the time of the study.

What follows is an extract from a ***narrative collage*** that was written as an amalgam of the experiences that the young people recounted. This method of 'story telling' was devised during the project on which this chapter draws, as a means of connecting readers to the experiences of young people who took part in the study, whilst maintaining the anonymity of individual tellers (Dowling 2009). The idea was inspired by the use of visual collage as a mode of data collection with young people in the project where a story is told through aggregate parts.

The narrative collage aimed to bring together elements of the storys' of each of the young people to draw a narrative around their composite experiences without compromising confidentiality and to use their words and expressions to deepen understanding of how they experienced and reflected upon their injury. This extract relates to what young people said about their friendships following their injury, and this is followed with findings from the study relating to friendship.

Me and My Friends

It's been a bit of a problem with my friends too. They are doing their best I think, but like they don't understand. They just see me looking like I did before, well obviously better and better looking as the years go by…ha ha! But there is nothing about me to say that I have had an accident. If you fiddle about in my hair you will find a scar where they opened up my head to let the pressure off my brain – ouch! But really I look like anybody else, so why they think, do I forget practically everything and why do I not always understand what they are talking about. Why do they have to be bothered to look directly at me when they speak or why do they have to keep stopping to make sure I understand what's going on? Why should they? They try but they are really losing interest now. Like I'll tell you a for instance, they wanted me to go to a club on Friday nights with them. They go, everybody goes, I used to go too. I went recently.

I hated it. I couldn't hear a thing, I couldn't understand what anybody was saying and the flashing lights and music gave me a killer headache for the rest of the weekend. So I stopped going and that has just made things worse 'cause now they have stopped asking me to go anywhere. So I just sit in here with my mum and dad like a pensioner. I sit here and watch my brother going out to work every day in his 2-door BMW, his first car and I'm stuck here watching. Like I get really angry. If I'd just looked where I was going…

Sometimes I think I feel depressed. Like I have no friends. How sad is that. I used to have loads of friends before this accident, I was really funny – always making them laugh and quick, you know witty. Now I am so crap. I had this accident and it took all the life out of me and left behind this shell that has just been left on the scrap heap. That's how I feel when I think about my friends. They are all doing loads of stuff – why would they bother with me. I can't even go on the computer – yeah headache – or watch TV – headache from hell – so I don't even have stuff to talk about to them. Mmmmm. You know what though, my mum always reminds me about this, they were brilliant when I first got hurt. They were always up at the hospital and like keeping me company and… you know when I was learning stuff again, like writing and reading, they helped loads, doing sort of homework with me and just getting me back into it. I was never lonely then…or when I got home they were always coming round and like they are really good friends. Then, like not now but before I really knew that they were there for me, they helped me put lots of pieces back together again. Now I think they have just had enough and because I have lost some of my pieces forever the whole me is different and they don't like it as much. Neither do I.

Some of them were there, like I said, when I had my accident. They saw it. We never talked about that you know…. (Dowling 2009, 4–5).

Findings

Consistently and throughout the data, young people raised the issue of friendship as a site of change following their injury. Interactions with their friends provided young people with a lens through which to view their sense of self. They described in their words during discussions and images within their collage how friendship played a crucial role in shaping how they viewed themselves post-injury. This is explored in more detail below.

Friendship and Loss

Friendship, although revealed as a critical issue for young people in terms of their sense of self and in reconstructing the narrative of their identity, was also the catalyst for feelings of sadness and rejection—many young participants' thoughts about their friends were accompanied by an overwhelming sense of loss. A number of the young people who took part focused a lot of attention on the disappearance and subsequent absence of their friends from their lives. For instance, Emma, who spent almost a year in hospital following her accident and subsequently went to a different school to the one she had attended prior to her injury, was emotional when recalling the friends she had before the accident:

> *I don't see any of them, not one, not anymore; I have no contact at all. It gets me really upset, no one really knowing how I am getting on. (Emma F, 18, P-RTA[4])*

While Emma made her collage, she played a tape that her old school friends had made for her when she was in hospital shortly after her accident. There were many messages hoping she would be better soon and saying how much they missed her; there was also some singing and laughing and then a recording of Emma and her friends' favourite songs. Emma has held onto this since her accident several years ago, saying she listens to it when she feels low and misses her old life; she said it still makes her cry. Prominently in her collage, Emma included photographs of herself messing around with her friends during her lunch break on the very day of her accident.

Emma continued in a more up-beat manner:

> *Now I'm not really fussed. I have got new friends now. They have all just moved on. (Emma)*

Whilst positive that she now has new friends, it was clear that Emma still felt the loss of her old friends as her sadness was readily evident when triggered by remembering.

Feelings of blame were for some young people associated with the loss of friends, and again the meaning that Jessica made of her experience was illuminating:

> Me and my friends have changed an awful lot. Before my accident I had two best friends, but now I don't really hear a lot from them, it's just all fell,[5] they just aren't the same as they were. I think that's because of me. Like they keep explaining, eh, not, they keep telling me what happened and I'm, like what? I'm a bit confused and that must annoy them. But before my accident I would know what they were talking about and would joke and make them laugh, but now I'm not able to do that, so they probably think I'm a bit annoying now. Like not understanding. I just think they are bored being with a person who doesn't talk and have craic. (Jessica F, 17, P-RTA)

In reconstructing her sense of self in the wake of the loss of important friendships, Jessica's perspective that she was at fault because she was not able to be the person that she was prior to her injury effected a negative perspective on her value, impacting on her confidence and self-esteem. Jessica reflected on the changes in friendships that had emerged over time:

> I can remember whenever I arrived home from hospital, they would have been ringing me all the time, but now I don't see them, I see them about once a month, so em, its gone down a lot. (Jessica)

This was typical of the experience of participants. Friends initially involved and sympathetic were soon tired. Some of the young people were at the age when there would be a natural separation through leaving school and moving onto university, jobs and a more independent life, away from family and old ties. However, whilst others move on, the injured person is likely to remain behind, their own plans depleted.

Being with Friends

When the opportunity came to spend time with friends, young people reflected on the different experiences they had. Jessica highlighted the contrasting experiences she had with two different sets of friends:

I just go back over to those friends from when I was small.... the craic⁶ is a bit better. They face me and explain a lot better, they include me in the conversation so they do. Like with my best friends, they speak to each other, like they don't talk to me, I just felt like I was someone spare there that they were trying not to talk to. I feel like a stranger when I am with them. I don't feel as if I am one of them I just feel like a very bad stranger. (Jessica)

Even though she was discerning about who she would rather spend time with, Jessica still yearned to be accepted and included with her two best friends as she had been before:

If I could change one thing it would be to have not got hit and not have a brain injury. Then I could be with them [friends], and off to New York for the weekend with them — like they didn't even ask me, my mum wouldn't have let me go, but it would be nice to be asked! (Jessica)

Some young participants talked of different kinds of experiences with their friends. Owen, while acknowledging the depleted relationship with one friend, also talked about one faithful friend who, in treating him as he always had, helped Owen feel both valued and more typical. With significant physical disabilities, Owen was getting used to life as a wheelchair user, as someone who was at times overlooked or treated differently; this friend appeared to see Owen first and the disability as a secondary consideration. Owen was bolstered by this and valued the friendship:

I have one friend he doesn't come round much, like maybe seven times in the last year, and another friend David, he comes every week. David, he doesn't see the wheelchair he just sees an average kid, except he has to push me up the road (chuckles). (Owen M, 16, PRTA)

Lorcan, likewise, talked about how he had the same friends as he'd had before his accident and that they were aware of his injury and treated him a little differently; at first, this seemed positive:

I still have the same friends but I think they know that I'm not as strong as I was before. They knew I had an accident, they were more gentle with me 'cause they knew I was definitely, well I was different and they knew my head was sore. (Lorcan M, 14, PaRTA)

However, as the interview progressed and during the making of the collage, Lorcan revealed a different perspective on his friendships:

I'd be a far more independent person now. I do have a lot of friends, but I'm very more of an independent person, I like to do things by myself. I used to be in a group, but now I'm more of a very independent person. Like if I was in school, I go about with people at break time, and I go about with people at lunch time, but like if I was doing anything I'd really want to be on my own, I wouldn't really be able to include other people, I'm very much independent. That's the way I want things. (Lorcan)

When asked to explain what he means by independent, Lorcan responded— 'it means on my own, I mean being alone.' Although Lorcan maintained that was the way that he wanted things and that he did have friends, he didn't include any reference to friendship, joint activities or photographs of friends on his collage.

Friendship as a Mirror on the Self

Participants talked about what they felt like when they were with their friends. One young person gave two contradictory statements—firstly:

I feel most like myself when I am with my friends 'cause it makes me feel like the old Jessica. (Jessica)

Followed by:

I feel least like me when I am with my friends, but I do try to push myself. (Jessica)

It was not uncommon for this dilemma to present. It did, however, illuminate the way in which friendship could act as a mirror on the self. Young participants saw themselves reflected through interactions with their friends. Friends were unlikely to understand as much as close family did about the consequences of an ABI and were thus more likely to expect the injured person to slot back into their previous role in the group. This led participants to be treated in a way that makes them feel more like they did—more like their 'old self.' Then, because of a desire to fit in and be accepted, young participants revealed how they were likely to make more of an effort when they are with their friends; however, the changes in themselves and the difficulties they find with joining in were also magnified through the lens of friendship.

Jessica's responses and others like them revealed the importance of friendship in young people's lives in relation to their sense of self and reconstructed identity. This contextualised the difficulties that many of them faced in their relationships with friends, following their injury and the depth of loss they felt when close friendships dissolved in the wake of their accident.

Friendship and Expectations

Some participants talked about friends in a way that revealed their own diminished expectations from friendship. Bill contradicted what his mother had said; she had reported that her son had no friends at all, was completely alone and isolated. During his interview, Bill talked about his friend—Daryl. With probing, the extent of his friendship became clear:

> Well there is a friend Daryl who I would get a phone call from out of the blue when you least expect it, like he called last year one day when I wasn't even expecting it. And he drives, and maybe I would see him driving about in his car and he always waves if he sees me. That's it, that's really it. (Bill M, 17, PRTA)

Bill went on to talk about his difficulties in making friends, also illustrated in an excerpt from his collage where he described feelings of self-consciousness, a lack of confidence and 'no social skills':

> I have problems in social situations, I am just very confused and I just don't know how to react. (Bill)

These images (as all that were included in young people's collages) were selected by the young person themselves. In between meetings with the researcher, this young person spent time on the computer seeking out images which represented points that they wanted to make using their collage. All collages were completely produced by young people; the researcher did not supply any images for or format to their work.

Bill described how his confidence was damaged in part because of some teasing he experienced following his accident:

Some people played on my outbursts to get a laugh for their own entertainment and that would make me angrier, it was perfect timing for them. (Bill)

He went on to say:

There was no one to stick up for me, well my friends seemed to be laughing too and I didn't know how to react and....I don't know. (Bill)

Bill was not alone in his experience of being bullied since his accident. Matthew too had been victim to bullying. Matthew revealed that his two friends, who are his only friends, sometimes called him names and pushed him around:

They push and punch me and laugh at me [...] I don't care 'cause they are my friends ...no one else wants to be. (Matthew M, 12, Fall)

This excerpt (above) from Matthew's collage also shows him with his 'friends'; with a protective glow around him, he looks happier than his unprotected bullies. However, this masks the reduced expectations that he has from friendship, and the fact that these boys want to spent time with him is, he thinks, better than being on his own:

It is ok. We have a laugh, they want to be my friend, they call round my house for me. They can't hurt me. (Matthew)

Discussion

The social world of young people changed following their injury. It was common for there to be a narrowing in the circle of friends and acquaintances and a greater focus and dependence on familial relationships. For all young people, relationships with friends had altered significantly. Through these altered friendships, young people construed information about themselves. Messages, perhaps unintended, were interpreted by young people and, as they report, were internalised as a representation of their self. Negative experiences were attributed to young peoples' perceived negative aspects of themselves. They held themselves to account.

The losses and changes in friendship were found to be critical components of young peoples' redeveloping sense of self. Their interpretations of the changes in their relationship with friends and of the actions of their friends were apparent in their evolving sense of self, as they absorbed and incorporated their reflected image, as they perceived it through the expressions and actions of others. Therefore, if friendships waned and young people had less contact with their friends, the interpretation of this situation was invariably that friends no longer wanted to be with the participant and no longer liked, valued or were able to relate to them in the same way as before. This experience was translated into young people regarding themselves as less likeable, valuable or worthwhile. Feeling abandoned or let down by friends, as was the experience of several, was read by young participants as being their fault. That is, because they were themselves changed as a result of their accident—and in their view negatively so—it was not at all surprising to them that their friends no longer wanted to be with them. The damaging meaning they made of this unwanted situation was in this way attributed to the self.

Young participants did not seem to recognise other potential explanations for depleted friendships, although mothers, in their interviews, did identify other possibilities. For example, the natural change in relationships that occurs over time may have accounted for relationships diminishing. The impact that the injury had had on friends themselves, some of whom had witnessed the accident or were experiencing seeing their friend cope with the repercussions of their injury was also identified by mothers as a potential rationale for changes in friendships. For young participants however, a refracted view of reality filtered through their redrawn lens meant that the impact on their sense of self (amongst those who had experienced the loss of friendship) was overwhelmingly negative.

In part, identity is formed through a reflection of self in interaction with others. As Shrauger & Schoeneman put it: *'One's self-concept is a reflection of one's perception about how one appears to others.'* (1999:54). Identity shaped negatively through unhelpful interactions with others, particularly those with whom one has or has had a close relationship, is likely to lead to challenges in emotional well-being and difficulties in redrawing a positive sense of self for young people following ABI.

There are two important caveats to this chapter. Firstly, there are many influences on the reconstruction of identity amongst the young people who took part in this work. Friendship was only one element, though one which did prove particularly challenging for participants, as has been demonstrated. This chapter has presented a fairly negative view of self through the prism of depleted friendships, however, not all of the findings of the study are of the same sentiment. A pathway towards redrawing a sense of self following the kind of changes accompanying ABI is an uneven one but the picture is not wholly negative. Secondly, there is a need for further research to explore the relationships young people have with their friends following ABI. A study which included the views and perspectives of friends as well as young people would perhaps be illuminating. The aim would be to improve pathways to positive friendship experiences for young people, following ABI, perhaps in terms of the kind of information that friends could have to enable them to include their friend or information for schools to support and nurture social relationships for young people returning to school after a brain injury while being alert to the potential for isolation or risk of bullying.

Friends are of great importance in teenage development and perhaps even more so for the young people in this study for whom positive reinforcement, inclusion, shared experiences, fun and laughter could have been central in drawing a strong, resilient sense of self in life after ABI. As one young person said:

> …the times when I am with my friends can still be great sometimes. If we are having a chat or a laugh and I feel in it and part of it then, you know, it is like, it is like, well it feels great to be me again. (Jessica).

Notes

1. This work was supported by a Vice Chancellor's Research Scholarship at Ulster University, Northern Ireland<!--Northern Ireland (NI)-->.

2. Whilst this view is perhaps embedded in present Western cultural perceptions of the teen years, there are numerous examples in cultures around the world of conceptualisations of adolescence as a time of change or 'coming of age,' with emotional change, alterations in social status and thus identity coinciding with the physical changes associated with puberty. Historically, within Western cultures, the idea of adolescence as a discrete phase of development has held greater prominence since perhaps the 1950s. It is beyond the scope of this chapter to explore these ideas further, except to say that the concept of adolescence is one which is variously recognised as a time of transition, but as a defined developmental stage, it is a relatively recent construction.

3. In five of the nine families, the mother was a single parent and their son/daughter resided with them. In the remaining four families, the mothers were not employed outside the family home and some had ceased employment following their child's injury. Mothers made themselves available for participation in the study, and fathers were not present in the home when data collection was taking place.

4. Unique identifier code—M/F to indicate gender and age in numbers; P-RTA—pedestrian in a road traffic accident; Pa-RTA—car passenger in a road traffic accident; fall—fall resulting in head injury and CA—cycling accident.

5. 'It's just all fell' is colloquialism, meaning that friendships altered/ended.

6. Irish colloquialism for 'fun'/'enjoyment.'

References

Andrews, T. K., Rose, F. D., & Johnson, D. A. (1998). Social and Behavioural Effect of Traumatic Brain Injury in Children. *Brain Injury, 12(2)*, 133–138.

Bedell, G. M., & Dumas, H. M. (2004). Social Participation of Children and Youth with Acquired Brain Injuries Discharged from Inpatient Rehabilitation: A Follow-Up Study. *Brain Injury, 18(1)*, 65–82.

Browning, D. L. (Ed.). (2007). *Adolescent Identities: A Collection of Readings*. London: Routledge.

Boylan, A. M. (2014). Social Inclusion Following Childhood Acquired Brain Injury (ABI): A Qualitative Exploration. *Brain Injury, 28(5–6)*, 824.

Calderwood, L. (2003). *Cracked: Recovering After Traumatic Brain Injury*. London: Jessica Kingsley.

Crothers, I. R., Linden, M. A., & Kennedy, N. (2007). Attitudes of Children Towards Peers with Acquired Brain Injury. *Brain Injury, 21(1)*, 47–52.

Dowling, S. (2009). *It's Like Two Different People But Me: Identity Following Acquired Brain Injury in Young People*. PhD Thesis, Ulster University.

Dowling, S., McConkey, R., & Sinclair, M. (forthcoming). Collage as Method in Qualitative Research. *Paper submitted for publication*.

Dixon, R., McLellan, D. L., & Morgan, J. (2008). Review of Services for People with Traumatic Brain Injury in Northern Ireland. www.dhsspsni.gov.uk/acquired_brain_injury_review.pdf. Accessed July 2017.

Gracey, F., et al. (2008). 'Feeling Part of Things': Personal Construction of Self After Brain Injury. *Neuropsychological Rehabilitation, 18(5/6), 627–650.*

Hawley, C. A. (2002). Behaviour and School Performances After Brain Injury. *Brain Injury, 18(7),* 645–659.

Hubert, J. (1985). *Life After Head Injury; The Experiences of Twenty Young People and Their Families.* Avebury: Brookfield.

Kroger, J. (2004). *Identity in Adolescence: The balance Between Self and Other.* London: Routledge.

Kupersmidt, J. B., Coie, J. D., & Dodge, K. A. (1990). The Role of Poor Peer Relationships in the Development of Disorder. In S. R. Asher & J. D. Coie (Eds.), *Peer Rejection in Childhood* (pp. 274–305). *Cambridge*: Cambridge University Press.

Linden, M. A., Rauch, R., & Crothers, I. R. (2005). Public Attitudes Towards Survivors of Brain Injury. *Brain Injury, 19(12),* 1011–1017.

McCabe, R. J. R., & Green, D. (1987). Rehabilitating Severely Head-Injured Adolescents: Three Case Reports. *Journal of Child Psychology and Psychiatry, 28(1),* 116–126.

Osborn, C. L. (1998). *Over My Head: A Doctors Own Story of Head Injury from the Inside Looking Out.* Kansas City: Andrews McMeel Publishing.

Parker, J. G., & Asher, S. R. (1987). Peer Relations and Later Personal Adjustment: Are Low-Accepted Children at Risk? *Psychological Bulletin, 102, 357–389.*

Shrauger, J., & Schoeneman, T. (1999). Symbolic Interactionist View of Self-Concept: Through the Looking Glass Darkly. In R. F. Baumeister (Ed.), *The Self in Social Psychology.* London: Psychology Press.

Smith, J. A., & Osborn, M. (2003). Interpretative Phenomenological Analysis. In J. A. Smith (Ed.), *Qualitative Psychology: A Practical Guide to Research Methods.* London: Sage.

Smith, J. A., & Osborn, M. (2004). Interpretative Phenomenological Analysis. In G. M. Breakwell (Ed.), *Doing Social Psychology Research.* Oxford: BPA Blackwell.

Tyerman, A., & Humphrey, M. (1984). Changes in Self-Concept Following Severe Head Injury. *International Journal of Rehabilitation Research, 7, 11–23.*

Sandra Dowling is Lecturer in Disability Studies at the Norah Fry Centre for Disability Studies, University of Bristol. She is a social anthropologist by training and has been working in the field of disability research for the past 20 years. She has a particular interest in childhood disability. Her work has focused on issues of identity, friendship and social inclusion and as well as children in families, looked after children and safeguarding. She has developed methodological approaches to facilitate inclusive research with disabled children. Sandra co-ordinates the UK Disabled Child Research Network.

Roy McConkey is Emeritus Professor of Developmental Disabilities at Ulster University and a visiting professor at Trinity College Dublin and the University of Cape Town. He has worked in the field of intellectual disability for over 40 years and has authored, co-authored and edited over 15 books and published nearly 200 book chapters and research papers in learned journals. He has acted as a consultant to various United Nations agencies and international NGOs. This work has taken him to some 25 countries in Eastern Europe, Africa, Asia and South America.

Marlene Sinclair is the first Personal Chair for Midwifery Research in the island of Ireland and is the head of research at the Maternal Fetal and Infant Research Centre at the Institute of Nursing Research. She is a registered midwife and nurse with almost 30 years of research experience including the management of over 30 research projects, 250 published outputs. She has been a successful collaborator in obtaining over €15 million in research funding, and four of these partnership projects have received European Union funding. In addition, Sinclair established the International Doctoral Midwifery Research Society with funding from the Northern Ireland Research & Development Office. This research forum acts as a major platform for support and dissemination of research findings. She is the founder and editor of the Royal College of Midwives, *Evidence Based Midwifery* journal, distributed to over 42,000 midwives.

Thinking and Doing Consent and Advocacy in Disabled Children's Childhood Studies Research

Jill Pluquailec

- Disabled children's childhoods have been absent in broader work around participatory research with children.
- Research with disabled children and their families involves distinct ethical considerations and different ethical starting points.
- Ethics in disabled children's childhood studies requires a resistance of narrow conceptualisations of participation and consent.
- Researchers must work with children and families around ethics in research which values their everyday lives in and of themselves.

This chapter contributes to the growing body of work in disabled children's childhood studies which requires specific ethical considerations in design, methodology, procedure and, perhaps most significantly, in everyday practice. I use the chapter as an example of the thinking *and* doing (i.e. the methodology *and* analysis) of disabled children's childhood studies research. The chapter explores ethical issues inherent in research, particularly in relation to advocacy and consent, which are necessary in developing, delivering and writing an ethical project.

I use this chapter to explore, in storied form, the ethical encounters from one particular research project working with disabled children and their families (Smith 2016b). What began as an ethnographic project spawned into something inherently auto/ethnographical due, in part, to the significant

J. Pluquailec, PhD (✉)
Sheffield Hallam University, Sheffield, UK

© The Author(s) 2018
K. Runswick-Cole et al. (eds.), *The Palgrave Handbook of Disabled Children's Childhood Studies*, https://doi.org/10.1057/978-1-137-54446-9_15

ethical dimensions within which I felt entangled as a researcher. *Being* a researcher, *doing* research, with disabled children and their families was a blurring of traditional researcher/researched relationships as I was invited into family homes, family lives and children's everyday worlds. There are ethical imperatives at the heart of any work that puts the everyday, embodied lives of disabled children at the front and centre.

My research and this chapter sit within dis/humanism, part of dis/ability studies (Goodley and Runswick-Cole 2014; Goodley et al. 2016). The slash (/) of both dis/ability and dis/humanism brings to attention 'the meaning making of either side of the disability-ability binary and the messy stuff in the middle. Dis/ability is also a moment of contemplation: to think again what it means to be dis/abled and what it means to be human' (Goodley 2014, p. x). Where dis/ability in its slashed form enters, we are invited at once to the *ability* complex of dis/*ability* and to question its form and power. Dis/humanism, as dis/ability, also takes the prefix 'dis' from dis/ability and from the colloquial verb 'to dis' as in to dis-respect (Goodley and Runswick-Cole 2014). *Dis*/humanism, in this sense, is ambivalent to the modernist conception of the human, independent, rational and contained, as it so often is incongruent or exclusive of those who experience dis/ability (ibid). Dis/human (Goodley and Runswick-Cole 2014), and more recently DisHumanism (Goodley et al. 2016), acts as somewhat of a heuristic of dis/ability, which invites complexity, invites relationships and invites humanity to a commitment of dis/ability politics. This turn in Critical Disability Studies is 'ambivalent about the human because too often it represents only a minority and bypasses the empirical human world' (Goodley and Runswick-Cole 2014, p. 10). Instead of, as Titchkosky suggests is the case, 'detaching' disability from what it means to be human, dis/ability and the dis/human allow us a way in to renegotiate humanism to consider 'how we value the human and what kinds of society are worth fighting for' (Goodley and Runswick-Cole 2014, p. 4). In bringing in the 'dis' to humanism, Goodley and Runswick-Cole (2014) ask that whenever we speak of the human, a politics of dis/ability should not be far behind. In more recent writing, developing this compelling challenge of 'the human', Goodley, Runswick-Cole and Liddiard introduce us to the DisHuman child—the demand 'to think in ways that affirm the inherent humanness in [disabled children's and young people's] lives but also allow us to consider their disruptive potential' (Goodley et al. 2016, p. 777). This is a call to a new ethics in our research with disabled children, a different starting point, one which in both theory and practice affirms the humanity of a claim to childhood whilst recognising and disrupting its ableist, exclusive boundaries.

The children I worked with all had labels of autism; they were living within bodies that were discursively constituted as both 'child' and 'autistic'.

Traditional conceptualisations of disordered childhood, such as those labelled with autism, ruminate on a particular ghostly spectre of ableism; the child with an autism label deviates from an imagined normative developmental trajectory. Research centred around this developmental deviation does not see an ethical imperative to value the lived, embodied childhood associated with this disordered cognition. From a different starting point, one of dis/ability and more specifically dis/human, we are able to shift our ethical gaze away from the disembodied disordered mind of a child and towards a politics which disrupts, and contributes to, what it means to be a valued child and a valued human (Goodley and Runswick-Cole 2014; Goodley et al. 2016).

So what does this shift in our ethical gaze mean, and why does it require distinct thinking and doing? Ethics here is not merely procedural, an adherence to social research or university ethical *codes;* it is a commitment to ethical *values* (Homan 1992). Ethical here means understanding and valuing the everyday lived experiences of children and their families as valuable in and of themselves; to challenge the dominant discourses of medicalisation, pathologisation and psychologisation that stalk disabled children's childhoods; to value and speak to their childhoods and their humanity and to trouble discourses and practices that do otherwise. To be ethical is to interrogate the risks and potentialities of moral implications, both implicit and explicit, in the designing and doing of a project. 'Ethics' do not exist in a vacuum and take place in the social (Bulmer 2008), that is, the commitment to ethical research takes place *with* the participants, not simply before or around them.

It is with this commitment to ethics that I now turn to some of the most pertinent considerations embedded within this project's conception and undertaking—consent, advocacy and valuing embodiment. What follows are a number of stories and reflections upon them about some of the poignant ethical moments I encountered in the thinking, doing and writing of this project. I focus on a conversation about consent and advocacy with Kate, a mum of five children with autism diagnoses, pertinent reminders of risk from two of Kate's children, Max and Joe, and a brief example of the embodiment of consent with another child, Zac, which took place on a community allotment.

Consent and Advocacy

Billington (2006, p. 8) asks us, as professionals working with children, to question, 'How do we speak of children?' I extend this to the work we do in research with disabled children: how do we speak of disabled children?

It became apparent very early in meeting each of the parents in this particular project that advocating on behalf of their children was a familiar and well-worn path. I was to be one of many 'professionals' that had come before, and would come again, into their family lives in the complex relation to dis/ability and their child. I write about the complexity of the ethical process in a formal sense of gaining informed consent from both the parents and the children and the enmeshment of advocacy woven throughout parents' conversations with me throughout the process. Parents, in their talk of their lives, children, autism and dis/ability, narrated the stories of other lives too, their other children, their partners, teachers, professionals and more. In recognising how stories seep into one another, spreading from one life to another, let's consider some of the ethical possibilities inherent in such leakage: 'the familial relation is not a simple one; it is an embodied relation and as such it is a messy, tangled nexus of love, hope, grief, anger, disappointment, joy and, always, always more' (McGuire 2010, p. 1).

I had originally developed an extended period of consent to be undertaken with the children in my project. This was to include a period of discussion with the parents, including sharing of ideas and materials (photographs, favourite TV characters, music, hobbies) to be developed into an interactive, personalised consent form on an iPad. This was designed to explain the purpose of being introduced to the children in a way that recognised the need to make such a process personal and meaningful for the child. However, for a number of reasons, some of which I go on to explore, this digital process of personalised consent didn't happen with any of the families. Instead, parents gave written consent and the consent with children was established verbally and on a moment-by-moment basis.

I turn here to the ethnographic story I wrote after a conversation with one mum about how I should be introduced to her son and what I would or should mean to him and him to me:

> We had an interesting conversation about how Kate should 'pitch' me to Max. She remarked that however she pitches me will effect whatever experience I am able to share with him and that I needed to know what that was manufacturing. Am I Kate's friend who is interested in stuff to do with autism? Am I a researcher? Am I from the university? Or am I someone that likes to play with Lego? I very much wanted Kate to take the lead on this and talked about how I was never quite sure of how comfortable how much families had to 'give' to be part of research.
>
> We talked about consent and the assumptions and potential for 'overdoing' it. I explained my plans for the super-personalised digital consent and had to concede that, knowing Max as she does, Kate was probably right in suggesting I could just talk to him instead, negotiate a deal. She laughed as she said she didn't have a problem consenting for him, she does it all the time anyway. Perhaps it's because we as parents think we have ownership over our children – Kate reflected. Her one reserva-

tion was about how much time I spent with Max and how he might become attached and then distressed after I stopped the research. We need to talk about this more.

This story had the hallmarks of conversations I have had with the parents about consent for their child's participation in numerous projects. Each in one way or another, as Kate reflected, seemed happy to claim 'ownership' over their child that if they said something was fine, the child would accept it was fine (or have to accept it). This varied from 'oh, there's no point trying to explain it to them. They won't get it anyway' to 'she'll let you know if she doesn't want you around. Trust me!' These responses to the consent process aren't unique to this project or perhaps even specifically about parents referring to their child's communication or comprehension skills, in particular, but more a common discourse around parent-child decision-making. Within the sociology of childhood, there has been an active move to counter the discourse that reifies children as passive in an adult-led world, submitting (or being without) agency in their decision-making because of their lack of adult competency. Developing research projects with children's active participation in the ethical consent process has been front and centre of such a move (James and Prout 1997; Danby 2002; Christensen and O'Brien 2003; Christensen and James 2008). This paradigm shift brought with it research aimed at increasing the participation of children in their childhood (Clark 2005). Traditional representations of the child as 'unreliable and developmentally incomplete' (Mayall 2008, p. 110) were replaced. This progressive research agenda strove for the recognition of the diversity and non-universal experience of childhood and was undoubtedly hugely successful in redressing the positivist imbalance. I would suggest, as have others (Watson 2012; Davis 2012; Curran and Runswick-Cole 2014), that the participatory research agenda has somewhat sidestepped or bypassed disabled children in an overly homogeneous conceptualisation of childhood agency and participation that doesn't account for differing embodiments or communicative modes. As participatory methods with children developed, it became apparent that disabled children (in their diversity), who may enact their agency and autonomy in ways that were not normatively visible, remained at the margins of such research (Watson 2012). The beginnings of participatory methods were often framed around ableist conceptualisations of 'participation', the autonomous child's 'voice' being predetermined by a literal voice or observable social competencies (Davis et al. 2008). Disabled children, particularly those who didn't use spoken language as their primary mode of communication, remained marginal to, or excluded from, research which aimed to recognise and value the diversity of childhood experience. Those critical of such exclusion of disabled children challenged researchers to recognise that enacting 'voice' in non-normative ways did not equate to not having anything to say (Beresford et al. 2004; Rabiee et al. 2005). In turning to a more critical conceptualisation of participation, the centring of ableist, normative markers of autonomy, agency and voice can be destabilised (Curran and Runswick-Cole 2014; Watson 2012; Davis et al. 2008).

In drawing together an ethic of disabled children's childhood studies which recognises ableist approaches to conceptualising participation, I spent time considering how best to recognise agency and value communicative intent for the children I envisaged taking part in my project. I felt at times that I was becoming over-reliant on narrow cognitive conceptualisations of competencies associated with autism and communication that were pushing me towards a deficit approach, reifying children's passivity in the process, for example, wondering how to 'compensate' for children who didn't use language. In drawing back from such a slippery slope, I returned to the sociology of childhood's framing of agency whilst resisting its normative stance. In de-prioritising spoken language, I turned my attention to a more visual and personalised presentation of what my project could mean to the children participating. This drew loosely on communicative strategies supported by autism theory such as the Picture Exchange Communication System, which recognises the value of personalised, visual information. Where I would caution against the homogenisation that is latent within such assumptions about autism and communicative preferences, the adoption of techniques that at least offered creative inroads to the complex process of consent was welcomed.

It was within such a move that I had gone to such lengths to develop a creative consent procedure for the children that drew on notions that recognised their ability to communicate intent and make decisions. I stand by such an intent but also recognise its limits. I needed to be mindful not to undermine parents' expertise about their children, whilst ensuring that my consent process centred around children as active in the process. In a similar quandary, Davis et al. (2008) wrote of their ethnographic study with disabled children at school in which the children were homogeneously positioned as incapable of understanding the consent process, with the power to 'access' remaining firmly in the staffs' hands. It seems possible that, perhaps not knowingly on either side, I was becoming re-socialised by the parents and their constructions of their children by changing my original plans for consent. How was I to value the parents' expertise about their children (a central call of the project) whilst simultaneously remaining mindful of what/who is conceived when parents advocate for their disabled child (McGuire 2010)?

I am reminded here of the ever-pertinent words of who heeds us to 'read our readings and watch our watchings' of how we come to speak of disability in particular ways. Building on this, McGuire (2010) cautions that we need to be mindful of the 'we' being conceived when 'we' (parents and allies) seek to speak of 'living with' the disability of another (in this case the child). Taking Butler's (2004) notion of 'unknowingness', the distance between you and I is at once what binds and separates us (McGuire 2010, p. 5); it is not a natural space but a negotiated one that happens at once between the parent and child, researcher and family. McGuire contests the 'we' of those 'living with' disability and reminds us to be ever-mindful of the seamless leaps that are often presented as natural when describing our interpretation of another's life. The temptation to gloss over the power exerted when a parent speaks of their child, or *for* their child, is not a site for moralising parents' knowing of their child, but a site to interrogate how the 'other' is always already being reconstituted through such a storying, even within intimate family relations. To 'live with' the other, to speak the 'we', is always to be at risk of relating to the other violently (ibid). However, this risky space may also be an opportunity to re-enter the story that 'we' are telling and to tell it differently (ibid., p. 14).

The ethics of such a power imbalance and its complex facets were at the heart of this project and remained a cautionary tale in my research with families, my writing of the stories and the analysis of the 'we' (the child, parents and I) that I speak of. As I saw it, for this project to be ethically grounded, it had to be done with a commitment to not prioritise the parents over the children and to continually problematise the 'we' that was being conceived by myself, in interactions with parents and children. Without problematising this 'we', the project was at risk of further perpetuating the dominance of research that is carried out around disabled children's lives that is actually exclusive of their experience and focuses only on the experience of their parents.

There was tension within this; was the project becoming more about the parents at the expense of the experience of the children? I felt quite strongly that the process I had developed was conceived recognising the children's participation actively in the consent process. So, despite moments of reservation, I had to trust each of the parent's advocacy of their child's consent in the first instance and work on a range of verbal and embodied sharing of my project's intentions and the children's consent as I met them. This is not by any means to suggest that once the formal consent had been handed over by the parents that I assumed the children's participation.

Consent as Embodied and Ongoing

As I explained, I began by relying on relatively traditional tenets of ethical codes in a *procedural* sense, with a consent 'form' that perhaps was still overly reliant on markers of participation that favoured normative participation, spoken words and active agency demonstrated through a literal 'voice'. In *practice*, the process of consent was very much embodied and enacted in a shared moment-by-moment becoming of participation. It was undoubtedly 'assent' that I sought rather than informed consent. This was not because I believed the children's consent to be unimportant or that I believed them to lack the agency or competency to give consent, rather that I problematise the ableism of the individualising concepts themselves. It would be problematic to suggest that the children participated in something that could be called informed consent by traditional definition: (1) presentation of information, (2) understanding and followed by (3) a response where consent is either given or withheld (Morris 2003; Morris 1998). Significantly, this was not exclusive to the children but speaks to more general issues around informed consent in research. I spent many hours conversing with parents about my project, its everyday workings and its potential outcomes and dissemination and would still contend that many did not give fully informed consent relating to either their understanding or my presentation of information. On one occasion, long after the formal consent process and several visits with the family, one of the dads said, 'Are you still wanting to do your study? When are you going to start?' Somewhat taken aback, I realised that despite information sheets, consent forms and conversations explaining what the project would 'look' like, there was still an expectation somewhere that I would be *doing* some kind of formal *studying* of the children. There I was, digging away in their community allotment, chatting to a parent about school, the children pottering around me, *doing* my research, or so I had thought. The dad, however, was seemingly still waiting for me to *do* something with his children. That my research didn't involve testing, requiring the children to *do* something *for* me, undid much of the negotiation of informed consent. This is an important lesson for those of us interested in research with disabled children about their childhoods, the expectation that we will be *studying* their impairments is a powerful one with a long history of pathologisation and medicalisation. The distinctiveness of disabled children's childhood studies lies within the challenge to this expectation, a valuing of research about everyday lives, not impairments (Curran 2013). Part of the role of disabled children's childhood studies is in changing these starting points and redressing expectations. Part of the challenge is the reminder that this needs to involve ongoing conversations with those we research about what 'research' is and what it looks like.

So, instead of somewhat unreflexively assuming informed consent, I sought to understand children's assent to my presence. This valued embodiment as a way of knowing and a process of meaning-making (Hackett 2014, 2015). With the children at the allotments, this was often just a 'checking in' as I arrived at the site, a wave from a distance, a crouch to say hello or a shared plot of soil to dig alongside without the need for any direct interaction. I was never the only 'stranger' at the community site and the children seemed as indifferent to my presence as to any other adult who pottered and dug around their play for the most part. The children had the space to be far removed and out of site from mine or anyone else's 'gaze' as much as they pleased, and I made a conscious effort not to spend any time with them that wasn't initiated by them. This meant that for the most part, my time at the allotments was spent chatting to the parents and other adults and various siblings scattered across the site. Over time, as I became more familiar, Zac in particular began to initiate interaction with me, for the first time, in the hunt for dock leaves after he got a particularly distressing nettle sting:

> I'm pottering away weeding the seamlessly endless knots of weeds around the raspberries, chatting away to one of the mums about schools and classrooms and difficulties with friends in playgrounds. Zac is brought to my attention with a sharp scream before I catch sight of him in my periphery. He yelps, whoops and sobs, dragging me by the arm through the site to an area where he'd previously found the helpful leaf. I turn back to his mum to check she doesn't want to intervene. She looks a little shocked and mouths quietly, 'Let's see what happens. He always comes running to me. It's good that he's not'. I scramble for a leaf, with a vague panic that my choice wouldn't be a medicinal leaf but something poisonous and assist in the ritual rubbing of the nettle sting until his sobs subside. Subdued, red in the face and a little snotty, Zac leans in to me for a moment and then carries on his merry way.

On a different occasion, Max brought home the slippery task of truly informed consent and the difficulty in clearly articulating exactly what involvement in the project actually meant (Smith 2016a):

> When I asked Max to write a story with me, about whatever he wanted, something that told me about himself, he was at first reluctant, then nervous, and eventually refused. Once he felt comfortable enough to share his objections it was clear that his unwillingness to participate was a caution that I should heed. His understanding of a story was something made-up. If the story was going to be about him then it wasn't

made-up, because he was real, and ergo, whatever we did together wasn't a story. Perhaps, he suggested, what I was actually asking him to do was write an article, like in a newspaper. That told people real things about him. To Max, if he were to share with me his 'truth' then why dress it up as a 'story'?

Max's caution is a reminder of the need for clarity and an extended, negotiated process of consent. After all, mine and Max's versions of what constituted a story were of course different for a number of reasons, not least that I consider myself a storytelling researcher. I love writing and Max hates writing. It would be easiest to equate these crossed wires to a child/adult binary and to suggest that an adult would have understood what I had intended by the use of a singular word, 'story'. That somehow discredits Max's knowledge and overstates my explicitness. It has been helpful food for thought when considering the legitimacy of any process of consent as every being truly achieved within the procedure rather than a shared negotiated relationship between myself and the children and families. Joe, Max's older brother, challenged the legitimacy of ethics procedures, which are designed to protect and safeguard participants in research further in the following story.

Joe's Reminder of Risk

Coming towards the end of a visit to the Goodwins, I come down to the kitchen after a stint of serious den-building and am greeted by a chuckling Kate and Joe who eyes me with caution and humour. 'Joe has something he wants to ask you, Jill.' Kate smiles flitting her attention between me and Joe's grin. Joe returned his gaze to his computer screen seemingly presenting as nonchalant. 'He wanted to know if you were a paedophile. He asked me how I knew you weren't a paedophile and I realised couldn't say for sure, that I suppose I just assumed you weren't. I asked him why he thought you might be – why else would an adult want to play with children? He thinks it's weird. I told him you weren't a paedophile and that I trusted you. If I didn't, then I wouldn't let you spend all this time with my kids, would I? But then he asked if I'd be ok with you going up to my children's bedrooms and playing if you were a man and I realised that I wouldn't be – so my son's just pointed out that I'm sexist too!' All the while Joe gives half of his attention to the conversation and to mine and Kate's lighthearted dismissal of his lighthearted accusation. We all spend some time chatting through his astute recognition of such questionable consensual ethical agreements between myself and parents. Kate conceded that my university branding had given me de facto access to her children and de facto status as trustworthy and non-threatening. She had led her children to believe they were safe with me. She admitted that her willingness to take part in my project and to continually consent to my time spent with the children being somewhat reliant on my being a woman and a small, seemingly bubbly, young one at that. That if I'd been a man she'd have been suspicious – which she recognised as equally shaky but true nevertheless. Joe had recently been in trouble for having a 'voice chat' with someone he didn't know over the internet. He'd be chastised for talking to strangers which was explicitly against the clear and defined rules of his access to computers. He'd be trading something complicated (the understanding of which fails me) and the voice transaction had made it easier and quicker. Debates around safety, predatory adults, strangers, and paedophiles were a hot-topic between Joe and his mum at the moment and he'd spotted inconsistencies in his mum's line of argument by her agreement to let a relative stranger spend time alone with her children, something he considered far more risky than a virtual conversation.

As lightheartedly as Joe and his mum negotiated a serious, and within the family context, legitimate concern, it was a pertinent reminder of the powerful discursive foundations which are brandished, often unwittingly, through mine and the parents in this project's clandestine advocacy on the behalf of their children. It is a reminder that the will of the children in this project is always somewhat subjugated by that of their parent's willingness to invite me into their homes and the schools' willingness to open their classroom doors without question or hesitation. I am pleased that I am not asked if I'm a paedophile on a regular basis, that it is assumed that my intentions are legitimate rather than sinister, but I am also troubled by it. Without any sinister intent, it perhaps shouldn't be so readily assumed that my status as a university researcher makes me devoid of fault or the potential to harm (despite ethics procedures designed to formalise such a commitment). There is inherent risk in research with people and children that at some point or another, my presence or actions can cause distress or that in the writing of a project, a paper or a chapter, ethical integrity also becomes problematic. In storying the life of others, there is always the potential for violence, as McGuire (2010) cautions.

Advocating Otherwise

Here I draw on the overlap between the advocacy of parents consenting on behalf of their children, talking about their children within the storying of their lives, and the advocacy I rely on in my storytelling as a researcher. Many of the critiques of auto/ethnography as an ethical form of enquiry could equally be applied to the processes that happen when parents speak about their children, or *for* their children. Parents tread a line of 'auto' whenever they speak of their children as the storying of their lives as parents and the storying of their children's everyday lives are wholly intertwined. As Tolich (2010), speaking of auto/ethnography, reminds us, even when we think we are speaking of 'ourself', we are implicating others: 'the self is porous, leaking to the other' (p. 1608), which he fears is often without due ethical consideration of such blurring. Such leaking, Chang (2008) would argue, is fundamental to our lives as social beings, others are always visible and invisible in our storying of it, we do not live in a vacuum. Clandinin and Connelly (2000) then ask, if we tell a story, do we own it? I ask these questions of the stories I write in this chapter and the conversations I have with parents about their children. My negotiation of the ethical rub of storying others' lives is to consider Denzin's suggestion that 'telling does not subtract from other tellings; telling is not a zero-sum game' (Denzin 1996, p. 47). This is a reminder of the ever-multiple becoming of storying as always incomplete and contingent on the teller, listener, time, place and a whole host of other factors (Davies et al. 2004). What must be remembered here is that these stories, though pinned to the page of a book chapter, forever remain unfinished. These are stories shared in a moment, on a particular day and with a particular researcher. These stories have been told before in different ways and will become re-told and re-fashioned in other contexts on other days, informed and moulded by other experiences and the passage of time. In that sense, they forever remain complex, incoherent, changing and moving. I draw here on Pulsford's (2014) claim to story as rhizomatic—they will forever reach in multiple directions, morphing as they come into contact with other stories, creating, disrupting and blurring assemblages.

Stories Left Untold

It is worth a brief aside here to acknowledge another specific ethical mire of this project in relation to the sharing of stories, the conversations I had with parents that I felt could not (or should not) be written. The reasons for such hesitancy in writing up certain conversations into the storying of this chapter range from the blurring of the ethical integrity of telling others' stories (e.g. of children and families not part of the project) or a much debated issue of storying aspects of lives that the participants hadn't explicitly consented to being part of the project. Ellis (2007), a much revered auto/ethnographer, discusses the criticism that she has exploited consent as the people within her work had never given actual consent to be part of research. As much as I recognise that within an ethnographic process there are unexpected moments that could never be planned and prepared for, the only solace I could find within literature justifying either side of this coin was in Medford's (2006) call to only ever include material that you would be happy for participants to read. I don't expect that my participants will read my writing, in general, but have used such a tool as my yardstick for when to take fingers to keyboards and when to leave encounters unwritten. There were conversations that I had with parents that were no doubt influential to the storying of theirs and their children's everyday experiences that nevertheless felt too intimate for the page—stories of days spent with families in which I felt unable to write without drawing in aspects of their lives that I had never intended to be part of the project and they hadn't ever thought would be included. Such is everyday life and a project based around it. These stories, though never written, have nonetheless inevitably permeated my writing of the project as they permeated my ongoing relationships with the families; they coloured my knowing and understanding of them and framed what was possible to know and understand beyond it. It may seem somewhat of a teaser to speak of untold stories but it is an acknowledgement of the limitations of any project in its written form and any writing to always be bounded and to recognise that any story told is never the only story possible.

Conclusions

I am cautious and mindful to attend to the implicit discourses embedded in reductive or representational leaps of storying the experiences I shared with children and their families in this project. I cling tightly to a Critical Disability Studies imperative to expose and trouble ableism stalking the stories I told and the analyses I went on to make. McGuire's (2010) cautionary tales of the risk and violence of advocacy bled into the experience of storying and were related to the experience of narrating these children's and families' everyday lives. I used these tools along with critiques of auto/ethnography as yardsticks to evaluate the more slippery ethical dimensions of what should and shouldn't be written and how it should (or could) be analysed. The danger is always to slip into analytic practices that served no more of a productive purpose than the dominant discursive conceptualisations of children labelled with autism I seek to trouble. The potential and possibility of advocating otherwise (McGuire 2010) is to stay with the conception and deployment of ethical procedures always as situated, problematised and taking place *with* participants. The distinctness of disabled children's childhood studies ethics is to trouble conceptualisations and methods of participation, as I have shown in the development of consent processes, that challenge normative markers of agency that would exclude disabled children as less valuable contributors or unable to contribute (Curran and Runswick-Cole 2014). This is a dis/human turn to claim (active participation) and reject narrow definitions (normative modes of participation) of what it means to be a valuable and valued child in everyday life (Goodley and Runswick-Cole 2014).

References

Beresford, B., Tozer, R., Rabiee, P., & Sloper, P. (2004). Developing an Approach to Involving Children with ASD in a Social Care Research Project. *British Journal of Learning Disabilities, 32*(4), 180–185. doi:10.1111/j.1468-3156.2004.00318.x.

Billington, T. (2006). Autism: Speculation, Knowledge or Understanding? *Discourse: Studies in the Cultural Politics of Education, 27*(2), 275–285. doi:10.1080/01596300600676292.

Bulmer, M. (2008). The Ethics of Social Research. In N. Gilbert (Ed.), *Researching Social Life* (3rd ed., pp. 145–161). London: Sage.

Butler, J. (2004). *Precarious Life: The Powers of Mourning and Violence*. London: Verso.

Chang, H. (2008). *Autoethnography as Method* (Vol. 1). Walnut Creek: Left Coast Press Inc.

Christensen, P., & James, A. (2008). Introduction: Researching Children and Childhood Cultures of Communication. In P. Christensen & A. James (Eds.), *Research with Children: Perspectives and Practices* (2nd ed., pp. 1–10). London: Routledge.

Christensen, P., & O'Brien, M. (Eds.). (2003). *Children in the City: Home Neighbourhood and Community*. London: Routledge.

Clandinin, D. J., & Connelly, F. M. (2000). *Narrative Inquiry: Experience and Story in Qualitative Research*. San Francisco: Jossey-Bass.

Clark, A. (2005). Listening to and Involving Young Children: A Review of Research and Practice. *Early Child Development and Care, 175*(6), 489–505.

Curran, T. (2013). Disabled Children's Childhood Studies: Alternative Relations and Forms of Authority? In T. Curran & K. Runswick-Cole (Eds.), *Disabled Children's Childhood Studies: Critical Approaches in a Global Context* (pp. 121–135). New York: Palgrave Macmillan.

Curran, T., & Runswick-Cole, K. (2013). *Disabled Children's Childhood Studies Critical Approaches in a Global Context*. Basingstoke: Palgrave Macmillan.

Curran, T., & Runswick-Cole, K. (2014). Disabled Children's Childhood Studies: A Distinct Approach? *Disability & Society, 29*(10), 1617–1630. doi:10.1080/09687599.2014.966187.

Danby, S. J. (2002). The Communicative Competence of Young Children. *Australian Journal of Early Childhood, 27*(3), 25–30.

Davies, B., Browne, J., Gannon, S., Honan, E., Laws, C., Mueller-Rockstroh, B., & Petersen, E. B. (2004). The Ambivalent Practices of Reflexivity. *Qualitative Inquiry, 10*(3), 360–389. doi:10.1177/1077800403257638.

Davis, J. (2012). Conceptual Issues in Childhood and Disability: Integrating Theories from Childhood and Disability Studies. In N. Watson, A. Roulstone, & C. Thomas (Eds.), *Routledge Handbook of Disability Studies* (pp. 414–425). London: Routledge.

Davis, J., Watson, N., & Cunningham-Burley, S. (2008). Learning the Lives of Disabled Children: Developing a Reflexive Approach. In P. Christensen & A. James (Eds.), *Research with Children: Perspectives and Practices* (pp. 201–224). London: Routledge Flamer.

Denzin, N. K. (1996). *Interpretive Ethnography: Ethnographic Practices for the 21st Century*. Thousand Oaks: Sage.

Ellis, C. S. (2007). Telling Secrets, Revealing Lives Relational Ethics in Research with Intimate Others. *Qualitative Inquiry, 13*(1), 3–29. doi:10.1177/1077800406294947.

Goodley, D. (2014). *Dis/Ability Studies: Theorising Disablism and Ableism*. London: Routledge.

Goodley, D., & Runswick-Cole, K. (2014). Becoming Dishuman: Thinking About the Human Through Dis/ability. *Discourse: Studies in the Cultural Politics of Education, 37*, 1–15. doi:10.1080/01596306.2014.930021.

Goodley, D., Runswick-Cole, K., & Liddiard, K. (2016). The DisHuman Child. *Discourse: Studies in the Cultural Politics of Education, 37*(5), 770–784. doi:10.1080/01596306.2015.1075731.

Hackett, A. (2014). Zigging and Zooming All Over the Place: Young Children's Meaning Making and Movement in the Museum. *Journal of Early Childhood Literacy, 14*(1), 5–27. doi:10.1177/1468798412453730.

Hackett, A. (2015). Young Children as Wayfarers: Learning About Place by Moving Through It. *Children and Society*. doi:10.1111/chso.12130.

Homan, R. (1992). The Ethics of Open Methods. *British Journal of Sociology, 43*, 321–332.

James, A., & Prout, A. (1997). *Constructing and Reconstructing Childhood: Contemporary Issues in the Sociological Study of Childhood*. London: Falmer Press.

Mayall, B. (2008). Conversations with Children: Working with Generational Issues. In P. Christensen & A. James (Eds.), *Research with Children: Perspectives and Practices* (2nd ed., pp. 109–124). London: Routledge.

McGuire, A. (2010). Disability, Non-disability and the Politics of Mourning: Re-conceiving the 'We'. *Disability Studies Quarterly, 30*(3/4). Retrived from http://dsq-sds.org/.

Medford, K. (2006). Caught with a Fake ID Ethical Questions About Slippage in Autoethnography. *Qualitative Inquiry, 12*(5), 853–864. doi:10.1177/1077800406288618.

Morris, J. (1998). *Don't Leave Us Out: Involving Disabled Children and Young People with Communication Impairments.* York: Joseph Rowntree Foundation/York Publishing Services.

Morris, J. (2003). Including All Children: Finding Out About the Experiences of Children with Communication and/or Cognitive Impairments. *Children & Society, 17*(5), 337–348. doi:10.1002/CHI.754.

Pulsford, M. (2014, June 19–20). *Rupturing Narratives: Material-Discursive Entanglements and the Becoming-Other of Male Primary Teachers.* Paper Presented at Troubling Narratives: Identity Matters at Huddersfield University.

Rabiee, P., Sloper, P., & Beresford, B. (2005). Doing Research with Children and Young People Who Do Not Use Speech for Communication. *Children & Society, 19*(5), 385–396. doi:10.1002/chi.841.

Smith, J. C. (2016a). The Embodied Becoming of Autism and Childhood: A Storytelling Methodology. *Disability & Society, 31*(2), 180–191.

Smith, J. C. (2016b). *The Talking, Being, and Becoming of Autism, Childhood, and Dis/ability.* Unpublished PhD Thesis, The University of Sheffield.

Titchkosky, T. (2007). *Reading and Writing Disability Differently: The Textured Life of Embodiment.* Toronto: University of Toronto Press.

Tolich, M. (2010). A Critique of Current Practice: Ten Foundational Guidelines for Autoethnographers. *Qualitative Health Research, 20*(12), 1599–1610. doi:10.1177/1049732310376076.

Watson, N. (2012). Theorising the Lives of Disabled Children: How Can Disability Theory Help? *Children & Society, 26*(3), 192–202. doi:10.1111/j.1099-0860.2012.00432.x.

Jill Pluquailec is Course Leader of the MA Autism Spectrum at Sheffield Hallam University and teaches across undergraduate and postgraduate courses around disability, education and childhood. Her research involves working with disabled children and their families. She works in family homes, schools, playgrounds and allotments, to name a few, gathering and reflecting on stories of what everyday life looks like, and feels like, for children with a label of autism in the UK today. Jill works with methods of embodiment, sensory ethnography and narratives to develop stories with families about their everyday experiences. Her work sits within social justice, the social, cultural and political constructions of autism, and the development of more diverse ways we can move towards honouring difference in all aspects of life.

Part III

Research Involving Parents of Disabled Children, Young people and Adult Children

This section centres on the multiple ways of researching the lives of disabled children and their families and allies. Contributors discuss a range of empirical methodologies, methods, and epistemic and ontological approaches and concerns, for example, auto-ethnography, ethics, storytelling, multimedia and film, participation and co-production, and the necessary blurriness of researcher/researched identities. Specifically, Wendy, Joanne, Barbara, Katherine and Tania all write as parents of disabled children and as researchers. As 'insiders' they show how their identity positively contributes to framing research questions, engaging with participants' experiences and drawing out the significant changes needed for disabled children and their families to benefit. Their research careers come from continuing activism and their journeys take place in the context of blame and inequality of 'austerity parenting'.

In Chap. 16, **Katherine Runswick-Cole** and **Dan Goodley** critique 'austerity parenting' as a form of neoliberal-ableism that is so often justified by the partial use of 'brain based' child development science. 'Good parenting' is mobilised by the government as the primary route to mending the economy, but is viewed here as a strategy that blames mothers in particular and denies the wider context of social and structural inequality. In response to the neoliberal agenda, the authors invoke 'disability commons' as a coming together in small supportive circles and in far-reaching campaigns to demonstrate common humanity and the value of interdependence in the lives of families of disabled children.

In Chap. 17, **Joanne Heeney** shares her study of fathers of children with the label of autism and discusses the intersectionality of gender and disability. These, she explains, are not fixed identities but being a father and being a child with such a label are gendered and ableist experiences, and assumptions about masculinity and childhood are constantly contested. Out of this discussion comes a rich appreciation of diversity, fluidity and the importance of recognising intersectionality with further dimensions of diversity and its transformative potential for better-understood and better-enjoyed life.

In Chap. 18, **Tania Watson** discusses the experiences of parents of children with diagnosis of behavioural disability from her perspective both as a parent and as a researcher. She illustrates how teachers and others disregard the child's diagnosis by making the child and their family accountable for their behaviour. She challenges this practice as a form of discrimination and oppression endorsed in education policy by the neoliberal values underpinning improvement imperatives in UK policy. Tania raises the ethical issues of sharing experiences as a many-layered concern and drawing on disability studies and provides examples of practice that are supportive, simple and appreciated.

In Chap. 19, **Barbara Coles** discusses the role of a 'Suitable Person', the legal term in England for someone who agrees to take on the management of their adult child's Direct Payment (social care funding) and their personalised support arrangements to ensure that their adult child has *choice* and *control* over their lives. She draws on her auto ethnographic research (Coles 2013) which looked at the experiences of twelve parents of adult children who have a severe learning disability and other attached labels. The analysis shows why formalisation of parental care for adult children with learning disabilities and the dichotomy of private versus public policies must be challenged. Although these parents are a vital source in contributing to a cash-strapped economy, and they have a public image of being strong and articulate, the Suitable Person role has actually made them vulnerable people in their own right. In particular the actions and attitudes of professionals need to change if 'partnership' is to be meaningful and different to the highly difficult relationship experienced at present.

The 'Disability Commons': Re-thinking Mothering Through Disability

Katherine Runswick-Cole and Dan Goodley

Key Points

- In England, 'good parenting' has become a focus for government policy alongside the view that early intervention in children's lives is critical for their cognitive and emotional development;
- Despite the gender neutral policy discourse, mothers still bear the majority of the responsibility for care;
- In austere times, mothers are expected to labour and care to produce children who do not place a social or economic burden on the state—this is 'austerity parenting';
- 'Austerity parenting' makes mothers of disabled children precarious as they and their children are seen as making present and future demands on the resources of the state;
- In order to escape blame, mothers of disabled children must accept their child's difference and disorder;
- Mothers of disabled children find themselves having to claim that their disabled children are both 'same as' and 'different from' other children in order to claim their right to be included in wider society;
- We describe the temporal and geographical location of the seemingly 'natural' importance of the mother-child dyad within studies of childhood;
- We conclude by re-thinking mothering through disability to call for a coming together of the 'disability commons' to campaign for the rights of disabled children and young people.

K. Runswick-Cole (✉) • D. Goodley
The University of Sheffield, Sheffield, UK

© The Author(s) 2018

231

K. Runswick-Cole et al. (eds.), *The Palgrave Handbook of Disabled Children's Childhood Studies*, https://doi.org/10.1057/978-1-137-54446-9_16

Introduction

In 2008, one of us (Ryan and Runswick-Cole 2008a) grappled with questions about what it meant to mother a disabled child in England. One of the issues we struggled with in our discussion of mothering a disabled child was whether this was different from or same as mothering a non-disabled child. Here we return to that question as a starting point for further discussion of contemporary understandings of mothering disabled children. We locate our discussions writing from England in a time of economic downturn, cuts to welfare and austerity measures. We reflect on the emergence of the requirements of 'austerity parenting' as we explore the increasing expectations put upon *all* mothers in neoliberal-able times. Neoliberal-ableism might be defined as a narrowing of self-sustained citizenship demanded by governments as they seek to decrease public expenditure through rolling back the welfare state (Goodley 2014). This citizen is assumed to be ready, willing and able to take responsibility for their own individual welfare and that of their families. This isolated citizenship promotes forms of atomised individuals cocooned in their own contexts, independently and stubbornly cut off from connections with others. In contrast, through our work with families (and specifically mothers) of disabled children, we have witnessed more expansive forms of citizenship that we want to affirm in this chapter.

We need to acknowledge that we are critical of the persistent focus on the mother-child dyad as the site of surveillance and intervention in the lives of children who are deemed to develop atypically. Drawing on historical and geographical critiques of global North models of mothering, we resist the 'austerity parenting' narrative by affirming interdependence and community in children and families' lives and rejecting the individualising practices of the neoliberalisation of the family (Gillies 2007). Finally, we invoke 'the disability commons', as a collective and affirmative alternative approach, to individualising models of parenting that oppress both mothers and disabled children.

Austerity Parenting

So, if we want to have any hope of mending our broken society, family and parenting is where we've got to start. David Cameron, British Prime Minister, 15 August 2011a (cited in de Benedictus 2012: 1)

In the United Kingdom, 'good parenting' is a central plank of public policy discourse and popular culture; it is constructed as *the* primary route for securing good outcomes for children (Jensen 2012). More so, 'good parenting' has taken on a wider social significance as it has been represented by government as *the* route through which 'broken Britain' will be mended (Cameron 2011). The coalition government enthusiastically embraced the 'good parenting' mantra that emerged during the New Labour administration (1997–2010). In contemporary England, 'good parenting' is seen as a crucial means of increasing both social mobility and social inclusion (Jensen 2012). Increasingly, in neoliberal times, 'good parenting' is tied to discourses of 'cost effectiveness' with the view that 'early intervention' in children's lives will save the state money later on (Jensen 2012). Parenting pedagogy programmes have become the preferred mechanism for intervention; the government believes that it is crucial for all parents to learn to parent well (Department for Communities & Local Government 2012). A rise in what are described as brain-based understandings of child development has been used to shore up this policy shift (Lowe et al. 2015). Brain-based models take as their starting point the contestable assertion that the early years are *the* most important in a person's life because they play a crucial and irreversible role in the child's emotional and cognitive development; early intervention is, thus, not only justified but seen as vital for the development of the child and for the good of wider society (Lowe et al. 2015). As Skeggs reminds us, capitalism seeps into the everyday, and parenting has become a site where '[e]verybody is expected to display their selves as a source of worth' (Skeggs 2010: 41). The rise of a neurocultural discourse (Lowe et al. 2015) has been seized upon as providing a 'scientific basis' for capitalist demands for 'good parenting' in austere times. The elision of parenting and brain development classically psychologises policy narratives and associated interventions (Ecclestone and Hayes 2008). To psychologise is not simply to reify the psychological or psychical as the layer of humanity at which we seek to meddle; it also captures the ways in which practices such as parenting—which of course are historically, socially and culturally prescribed—are understood solely through the discourse of individualising psychology.

Above all, twenty-first-century parenting in England has been re-imagined as an individualised task. Gillies (2007) describes this as the 'neoliberalisation of the family' (Gillies 2007: 4 cited in de Benedictus 2012: 3). Through individualising parenting, families and children emerge as the site of the problem, intervention and blame. While the neoliberal language of the 'parent' masks the gendered aspects of parenting (Traustadottir 1995), it is still mothers, or maternal figures, who are expected to take on the major responsibility for care (de Benedictus 2012). Lone working-class mothers, in particular, are held to account for a host of societal ills from juvenile delinquency to societal collapse (Gillies 2005; Tyler 2008). Mothers are blamed for a series of 'wrong' choices for their children and for breaking the 'new sexual contract' (McRobbie 2009 cited in de Benedictus, 2012: 4) in which women are expected 'simultaneously' to 'labour/consume and mother/care' (de Benedictus 2012: 4). The neoliberalisation and psychologisation of the family demand individual self-governance and wilfully obscure the role that contemporary political and societal structures play in family life. When socioeconomic inequalities are sidelined, Jensen argues that 'good parenting' is confined to the realm of 'culture and aspiration' (Jensen 2012: 8) and, to this we might add, to the realms of the neurocultural (Lowe et al. 2015). Crucially, in the context of the economic downturn, the expectation is that 'good mothers' will engage in labour as well as take primary responsibility for care in order to ensure that their children too do not financially or socially burden the state (de Benedictus 2012).

Mothering Disabled Children in Austere Times

What do the requirements of 'austerity parenting' mean for mothers of disabled children, especially in a time of psychologisation and neoliberal-ableism? In austere times, as we have seen above, all mothers are made precarious in bearing the responsibility for labour and care (Puar 2012). Skeggs (2004, 2005), Tyler (2008), Jensen (2012) and de Benedictus (2012) rightly pay attention to the classed nature of 'good parenting' and the vilification of working-class, single mothers. Precarity is differentially, rather than equally, spread (Puar 2012), and lone or solitary working-class mothers are certainly made more precarious than other mothers in the 'good parenting' discourse as Tyler's (2008) discussion of *Chav Mum, Chav Scum* so startlingly illustrates. However, here, we argue that mothers of disabled children also emerge as differentially precarious, although we do so without wishing to deny the impact of the intersectional relationships between class, gender, race and disability in their lives. While not the primary focus of this chapter, it is important to remember that mothers of disabled children are sometimes disabled people too and that disabled motherhood, regardless of the disability status of the child, is inevitably seen as always-irresponsible/risky and more costly/burdensome to the state.

First, mothers of disabled children are made precarious because while austerity parenting requires mothers to produce children who are neither a social nor a financial burden on the state, mothers of disabled children are regarded as having produced children whose very embodiment represents both a present and a future drain on the resources of the state and on the 'healthy' function-ing of the family. The two-pronged policy rhetoric of 'prevention' and 'cure' leaves disabled children who fail to respond to 'early intervention' in the realm of deficit and lack and as a drain on finite resources now and in the future. Accounts of the disabled child-mother dyad are characterised through a narra-tive of negative reciprocity: 'bad' mothering threatens the child's development (Lowe et al. 2015) while the presence of the disabled child threatens the mother and wider family's well-being as the mother learns to adjust to the loss associ-ated with mothering a disabled child (Lazerus and Folkman 1984). The rise of psychological norms of childhood development in the last century (Nadesan 2005), accompanied by a shift as the site of intervention from the child to the mother (de Benedictus 2012), positions both disabled children and their mothers as a problem that must be subjected to constant monitoring and sur-veillance (Ryan and Runswick-Cole 2008a), justified further by the rise of the neurocultural narrative we described above (Lowe et al. 2015).

Second, 'austerity parenting' requires mothers to engage in paid labour as well as taking primary responsibility for care (care, which is now fundamen-tally under-resourced). And yet mothers of disabled children are 'so often confined throughout their working lives to the piecemeal and unsatisfactory employment patterns' (Ryan and Runswick-Cole 2008a: 206). A lack of affordable and accessible child care means that only 16% of mothers of dis-abled children are in paid work compared with 61% of mothers of non-disabled children (Contact-a-Family 2011). In a context of austerity, mothers and their disabled children are represented as a financial burden to the state and, conversely, mothers are expected to take on the dual roles of worker and carer (roles which are of course often under-paid and devalued).

While Jensen (2012) notes that 'austerity parenting' has led to a rise in the 'self-help movement' that supports all parents in raising happy, confident chil-dren, 'good mothers' of disabled children, in particular, must be seen to bow to the demands of the psy-professions and invest in the promise of therapeutic interventions that will move their children closer to the ever elusive 'norm' (Curran and Runswick-Cole 2014). 'Good mothers' of disabled children become both producers and consumers of psy-knowledges in their quest for the norm (Mallett and Runswick-Cole 2012). (e.g. see Jackson 2004; Moore 2012). Yet again, the roles of mothers of disabled children are expanded: they are to work, consume and care (as good citizens) and anticipate, utilise and enact a whole plethora of specialist early interventions (which are increasingly neurological and psychological in character).

The search for the norm is tied to the view that a disabled child is in need of intervention and cure. Acceptance of this view by mothers seems to promise a route out of the precarious position they find themselves in (Puar 2012). By adopting the traditional 'sick role' (Parsons 1951) for their child, and by seeking diagnostic labels and interventions, they hope to locate the 'problem' within the individual brains and bodies of the child and by implication outside of the mother-child relationship. Understandably, mothers of disabled children aspire to escape their designation as incapable parents or worse still, perhaps, as 'chav mums' (Tyler 2008). However, the promise of a less precarious life is nothing more than cruel optimism (Berlant 2006). In neoliberalable times, Berlant describes cruel optimism as the persistent attachment we have to the belief in the power of the market to liberate us (Runswick-Cole and Goodley 2015). Belief in the power of medicine and diagnostic labels also seems to offer a route to liberation from the categorisation of 'bad mother'. But to accept her child's 'disorder' also means accepting 'handicap, social stigma, dependence, isolation and economic disadvantage' (Stone 1984: 4) that this implies. It is only then that a 'state of exception' can be granted (Stone 1984: 4) and the mother and child can benefit from the re-distributive practices of the welfare state to the 'worthy' poor (Runswick-Cole 2014). The cruelty is that the price paid for escaping maternal blame is acceptance of psychological difference and pathological disorder and a devalued and stigmatised identity for the child. Worse still, the promise of absolution for the mother from blame for the child's difference is unfulfilled as mothers of disabled children are still held to account for their children's development and behaviour, no matter their impairment status (e.g. see Ryan 2005; Broomhead 2013). Mothers are, after all, the key agents of change for their kids in these times of austerity.

Difference and Sameness

Above, we described how the mother must accept her disabled child's stigmatised identity as different and disordered to be granted 'a state of exception'— or difference. In what follows, we further explore the complex relationship of mothers of disabled children and their children's experience in relation to notions of sameness and difference. We return to the question: is mothering a disabled child the *same as* or *different from* other mothering? For Gregory (1991: 121 cited in Ryan and Runswick-Cole 2008a: 204), mothering a disabled child is 'to be different':

> a mother because she undoubtedly has a child, yet somehow not a mother in terms of the conventional notions of motherhood that pervade our society.

Greenspan (1998: 57 cited in Ryan and Runswick-Cole 2008a: 204) describes mothering a disabled child as 'parenting without a developmental map' and that mothers of disabled children are offered often competing and conflicting advice on how 'properly' to parent their child (Ryan and Runswick-Cole 2008a: 204).

It is worth pausing for a moment to consider why the question of whether or not parenting a disabled child is the same as or different to parenting a non-disabled child has drawn discussion? The question matters because being seen as 'same as' or 'different from' other mothers and children has real consequences for families' lives. The question is also important because we could argue that all parents are under an increasing amount of pressure in a time of reduced and cut public services. Take, for example, the demands of austerity parenting; if mothering a disabled child is the same as mothering a non-disabled child then the requirement to raise children who neither socially nor economically burden the state is the same and mothers of disabled children must care and labour in the same way as mothers of non-disabled children (and vice versa). However, if mothers of disabled children assert their difference, by claiming their child's disorder through the practices of labelling and pathologisation, then they may hope that the neoliberal state will re-distribute resources to them as the 'worthy' poor (Runswick-Cole 2014). And yet, as we saw above, claiming difference is a risky strategy; it positions disabled children on the margins—'they' become 'the not quite as same' as non-disabled children (Goodley et al. 2015). Being 'same, but not quite' means that disabled children occupy a borderlands position (Goodley and Runswick-Cole 2014a) and are not offered or expected to have the experiences and opportunities as non-disabled children: indeed, their play is categorised as disordered (Goodley and Runswick-Cole 2010); they are excluded from leisure opportunities (Hodge and Runswick-Cole 2013); education (Runswick-Cole 2011) and denied employment support (Bates et al. 2017). At worst, they become so dehumanised that they experience neglect, violence and even death (Goodley and Runswick-Cole 2011b; Goodley et al. 2015).

There is a host of literature that documents the campaigns mothers of disabled children engage in to challenge these multiple exclusions and to advocate for support and services for their disabled children (McLaughlin et al. 2008; Read 2000; Runswick-Cole 2007; Ryan and Runswick-Cole 2008b). Crucially, these campaigns depend on the mothers' claims that their disabled children are both simultaneously *same as* and *different from* other children. For example, in England, a mother might argue that her child has a right to education because of her status as **child (same)** under, for example, the

United Nations Convention on the Rights of the Child (UNICEF 1989) and yet she might simultaneously claim that her child has the right to additional resources and adaptations in education precisely because she is a **disabled child (different)** (Goodley et al. 2015).

This position of claiming difference and sameness at the same time is one that we have discussed elsewhere as a DisHuman reality (Goodley and Runswick-Cole 2014b):

> one which, we contend, simultaneously acknowledges the possibilities offered by disability to trouble, re-shape and re-fashion traditional conceptions of the human (to 'dis' typical understandings of personhood) while simultaneously asserting disabled people's humanity (to assert normative, often traditional, understandings of personhood). (Goodley and Runswick-Cole 2014b)

While a DisHuman position allows us to reflect on the conflict inherent in claiming sameness and difference in disabled children's lives, we also see our exploration of the DisHuman as an opportunity to recognise and to celebrate the ways in which disabled children positively disrupt, reframe and expand what it means to be 'normal' (Goodley and Runswick-Cole 2014b; Goodley et al. 2015). As Braidotti (2013: 6) reminds us '[t]he human norm stands for normality, normalcy and normativity'. The same things could be said about the child as s/he is normatively understood and subjected to normalising processes of development. And yet, disabled children demand us to re-think the norm in the contexts of play, family, school and sexuality (Goodley and Runswick-Cole 2010; Goodley et al. 2015), and in doing so they demand us to re-think notions of what it is to be human (Goodley and Runswick-Cole 2014b).

Here we might add that a DisHuman position has the potential to disrupt normative notions of mothering. For instance, we have seen that disabled children demand DisMothering by paying attention to the ways in which the mother and the child can be both same as and different from 'the norm' at the same time by demanding sameness in their rights to education, health and leisure while demanding to be treated differently in their quest to be treated equally (Goodley and Runswick-Cole 2014b).

However, thus far, we have left the assumption that the mother-child dyad should be the focus of discussion and debate intact. Despite the rise of a 'corrective approach' (Ryan and Runswick-Cole 2008a) that emphasises the positive (or implicitly the negative) aspects of mothering disabled children (Read 2000; McLaughlin et al. 2008; Ryan and Runswick-Cole 2008a, b), there is a danger that even this positive focus on the mother and child merely reinforces the idea that mothering is 'naturally' the woman's role and responsibility (McLaughlin et al. 2008). We recognise the continued need for a radical reappraisal of the wider social contexts in which austerity parenting is currently taking place and the possibilities of exploring the positive ways in which disabled children disrupt normative notions of mothering. So, in the next section, we explore the possibilities for an approach to resistance offered by de-centring attention away from the mother-child dyad.

Re-thinking Mothering

A seemingly 'natural' preoccupation with the mother-child dyad in parenting practice and policy in England masks its emergence as both a temporally and a geographically located phenomenon. During the nineteenth century, state surveillance and control increased alongside the rise of the professions and the identification of 'deviancy' (Nadesan 2005). However, it was not until 1924 that Jean Piaget identified 'the "normal" stages of childhood cognition … thereby enabling the identification of "abnormal" or delayed cognitive development' (Nadesan 2005: 69). While not holding Piaget individually responsible, his influence on the rise of developmental psychology ensured that the role of the mother was emphasised as a primary factor in models of child development. Theorists, including Anna Freud and Melanie Klein, began to describe mothering as the key to a child's 'psychic development and personality' (Nadesan 2005: 70). At the same time, mother craft manuals were teaching mothers their roles and responsibilities in ensuring their child's typical development: '[e]very child is an individual and develops along individual lines', but 'it is well for the mother [...] to know the average so that they may recognize any large departure and be able to get proper advice' (Liddiard 1924: 102 cited in Cooper 2013: 144). The taken-for-granted importance of the mother-child relationship in child-rearing practices emerges as a peculiarly twentieth- and twenty-first-century phenomenon.

Indeed, such preoccupations are geographically as well as historically located. While contemporary austerity parenting narratives in the global North seek to individualise parenting, Chataika and McKenzie (2013: 158) remind us that many African cultures continue to value family and community 'more than individual differences or other human attributes'. They describe the notion of ubuntu:

Whatever happens to the individual happens to the whole group, and whatever happens to the whole group happens to the individual. The individual can only say: 'I am, because we are; and since we are, therefore I am' (Mbiti 1992, p. 109, cited in Chataika and McKenzie 2013: 158)

In sharp contrast to the focus on the mother-child dyad in the global North, in many global South cultures, it is the extended family that provides for a child, highlighting the deep significance of being part of a whole (Chataika and McKenzie 2013). For some children, we could argue, there are many (m)others.

The Maternal Commons

Being part of a whole is not, however, just a global South phenomenon. In *Revolting Subjects: Social Abjection and Resistance in Neoliberal Britain,* Tyler (2013) offers a harrowing account of the protests of a group of mothers at the Yarl's Wood Immigration Removal Centre in Bedfordshire. Yarl's Wood is a detention centre for immigrants to England who the government is seeking to deport. Tyler (2013) describes the protests that followed when a young Berundian mother was separated from her six-year-old son and placed in solitary confinement. The other mother detainees demanded to know what had happened to the mother and child (Tyler 2013). In the protest that followed, the mothers stripped bare, engaging in a naked protest 'in a deliberate impersonation of their dehumanisation' (Tyler 2013; Bates et al. 2017). Through their collective protest, the mothers were seeking to resist their constitution as 'wasted humans' (Tyler 2013: 123). The mothers faced huge challenges and yet they were able to engage in resistant acts and to demonstrate their agency (de Benedictus 2012). This coming together has been described, by Tyler (2013), as the 'maternal commons'.

While Tyler's (2013) discussion of the 'maternal commons' emerges from the lives of mothers seeking asylum in England, we also see moments where the 'maternal commons' emerges in the lives of mothers and their disabled children. On 4 July 2013, Connor Sparrowhawk died in the bath at a National Health Service Assessment and Treatment Unit, in Oxford, in England. Connor was a young man with a learning disability and epilepsy who had been left alone in the bath. A year later (yes, a year later), the *Independent investigation into the death of CS* (Hussain and Hyde-Bales 2014) was published; it documented a catalogue of errors in the care offered to Connor that resulted in his preventable death.

Connor's tragic and unnecessary death was the impetus for a campaign for justice to hold to account those responsible for Connor's death and to campaign for an informed debate about the status of learning disabled people as full citizens (http://justiceforlb.org). The campaign led to *#107 Days of Action* (http://107daysofaction.wordpress.com) in support of the campaign including blogs, academic presentations, sponsored events, a campaign quilt and fundraisers for the family's fees for legal representation at the inquest into Connor's death. Subsequently, other such campaigns, highlighting the deaths of young people with learning disabilities in the 'care' of the state in England, have also sprung up, including campaigns for Nico Reed (http://justicefornico.org) and Thomas Rawnsley (https://www.facebook.com/pages/IAmThomas/669649606478943), both of whom also died in state care. While the #JusticeforLB campaign, and others, demands us to think again about how we value and treat young people and how we understand our shared humanity whilst valuing human diversity and difference (Goodley et al. 2015), the campaign might also be seen as demanding us to think again about the pressures that global North cultures put on mothers as carers, labourers and campaigners for their disabled children. The campaigns offer an alternative response through the coming together of the 'commons'.

The Disability Commons

While many of the #justiceforLB campaigners are mothers of disabled children, the campaign has drawn support from a range of people: men, women, disabled people, parents, siblings, activists and those allied to disability politics. Elsewhere, we have described this form of campaigning as the 'disability commons' (Runswick-Cole and Goodley 2015). Such campaigns are formed through recognition of common humanity and interdependence. They fly in the face of the neoliberal-ableisation of the family, a lens through which such tragedies might only be constructed as individualised, private troubles for mothers of disabled children. Through the engagement of the disability commons, such private troubles have become public matters (Wright Mills 1959) with the #justiceforLB campaign demanding a change in the law so that disabled people have the right to live in their communities (http://lbbill.wordpress.com).

In a research, *Big Society? Disabled people with learning disabilities and civil society* (funded by the Economic and Social Research Council ES/K004883/1, June, 2013—September, 2015—https://bigsocietydis.wordpress.com), we have documented other moments when we see 'the disability commons' emerge, thankfully, in less tragic circumstances. Take Henry, for example:

> *Henry is an 18 year-old-young man with the label of learning disabilities. He is going through what is known as 'transition' in English education policy[1] as he moves from children's to adult services in education, health and social care. At this time, young people with learning disabilities and their families have to navigate complex service systems and negotiate new support packages (Goodley and Runswick-Cole 2011a). Working with a circle of support made up of Henry facilitator, friends and family members, including his mother and father, the circle has been meeting regularly to plan for Henry's future. The circle created a one-page profile to share with people working with him as well as developing a weekly plan including college and work experience. Having supported Henry in his transition beyond school, the next steps are for Henry to move into paid employment.*

The circle represents 'the disability commons' in Henry's life. Rather than the responsibility for care and for planning for the future for her son resting with his mother alone, it is now a shared responsibility. We do not wish to overstate the case here; Henry's mother plays a key role within the circle. She still takes the role of meeting practitioners, attending meetings and filling in forms—in 'austere parenting' times, she is still held to account for her son's development and behaviour by professionals. However, 'the disability commons' she is part of, formed around her son, allow her to experience some moments where it is possible to de-individualise parenting and to share responsibility.

Conclusion

In austere times, mothers of disabled children bear the responsibility more than ever for their children's care. The mother-child relationship continues to be the central site of surveillance of deviancy and for the practice of therapeutic intervention in the twenty-first century. A twenty-first-century appeal to neuroscience (Lowe et al. 2015) has confirmed the twentieth-century view that the quality of mother-child interactions is vital for early childhood development and for a 'healthy' state. Mothers are being held to account for the future development of 'good' citizens as the socioeconomic conditions in which parenting takes place are ignored. Mothers of disabled children find themselves differentially precarious as their children have come to represent both a present and a future danger to scarce state resources in a time of austerity. In order to benefit from the re-distributive policies of neoliberalism, mothers of disabled children must accept their children's stigmatised identities.

However, we suggest that it might be possible to resist and revise the dominant austerity parenting narrative, first, by exposing its historical and geographical location and, second, by appealing to more interdependent and collectivist models of child rearing that do not simply reinforce the oppressive individualising practices of austerity parenting and the psy-disciplines. Through recognition of our common humanity, whilst valuing human diversity and difference, when the disability commons emerge, it becomes possible to move beyond the oppressive limits of the focus on the mother-child dyad and to celebrate interdependence in all our lives.

Notes

1. Transition is the term used in policy in England to describe the period of time in which disabled young people enter adult services in health, education and social care.

References

Berlant, L. (2006). Cruel Optimism. *Journal of Feminist Cultural Studies, 17*(3), 20–36.

Braidotti, R. (2013). *The Posthuman*. Malden: Polity Press.

Broomhead, K. E. (2013). Blame, Guilt and the Need for 'Labels'; Insights from Parents of Children with Special Educational Needs (SEN) and Educational Practitioners. *British Journal of Special Education, 40*(1), 14–21.

Cameron, D. (2011). *Speech on the Big Society*. Available from: http://www.number10.gov.uk/news/speechon-the-big-society/. Accessed 20 Oct 2011.

Chataika, T., & McKenzie, J. (2013). Considerations for an African Childhood Disability Studies. In T. Curran & K. Runswick-Cole (Eds.), *Disabled Children's Childhood Studies: Critical Approaches in a Global Context*. Basingstoke: Palgrave Macmillan.

Contact-a-Family. (2011). *Forgotten Families: The Impact of Isolation on Families with Disabled Children Across the UK*. http://www.cafamily.org.uk/media/381636/forgotten_isolation_report.pdf. Accessed 7 Mar 2015.

Cooper, H. (2013). "The Spectre of the Norm": Historicising the Notion of the 'Normal Child'. In T. Curran & K. Runswick-Cole (Eds.), *Disabled Children's Childhood Studies: Critical Approaches in a Global Context*. Basingstoke: Palgrave Macmillan.

Curran, T., & Runswick-Cole, K. (2014). Disabled Children's Childhood Studies: An Emerging Domain of Inquiry? *Disability & Society, 29*(10), 1617–1630.

de Benedictis, S. (2012). 'Feral' Parents: Austerity Parenting Under Neoliberalism. *Studies in the Maternal, 4*(2), 1–21.

Department for Communities & Local Government. (2012). *Helping Troubled Families Turn Their Lives Around.* https://www.gov.uk/government/policies/ helping-troubled-families-turn-their-lives-around. Accessed 20 Feb 2015.

Ecclestone, K., & Hayes, D. (2008). *The Dangerous Rise of Therapeutic Education.* London: Routledge.

Gillies, V. (2005). Meeting Parents' Needs? Discourses of 'Support' and 'Inclusion' in Family Policy. *Critical Social Policy, 25*(1), 70–90.

Gillies, V. (2007). *Marginalised Mothers: Exploring Working-Class Experiences of Parenting.* Abingdon: Routledge.

Goodley, D. (2014). *Dis/ability Studies: Theorising Disablism and Ableism.* London: Routledge.

Goodley, D., & Runswick-Cole, K. (2010). Emancipating Play: Dis/abled Children, Development and Deconstruction. *Disability & Society, 25*(4), 499–512.

Goodley, D., & Runswick-Cole, K. (2011a). Problematising Policy: Conceptions of 'Child', 'Disabled' and 'Parents' in Social Policy in England. *International Journal of Inclusive Education, 15*(1), 71–85.

Goodley, D., & Runswick-Cole, K. (2011b). The Violence of Disablism. *Journal of Sociology of Health and Illness, 33*(4), 602–617.

Goodley, D., & Runswick-Cole, K. (2014a). Critical Psychologies of Disability: Boundaries, Borders and Bodies in the Lives of Disabled Children. *Emotional and Behavioural Difficulties.* http://dx.doi.org/10.1080/13632752.2014.947096. Accessed 7 Mar 2015.

Goodley, D., & Runswick-Cole, K. (2014b). Becoming Dis/human: Thinking About the Human Through Disability. *Discourse: Studies in the Cultural Politics of Education.* http://www.tandfonline.com/doi/abs/10.1080/01596306.2014.9300 21#preview. Accessed 7 Mar 2015.

Goodley, D., Runswick-Cole, K., & Liddiard, K. (2015). The DisHuman Child. *Discourse: The Cultural Politics of Education, 37*(1), 1–15.

Greenspan, M. (1998). 'Exceptional' Mothering in a 'Normal' World'. In K. Weingarten (Ed.), *Mothering Against the Odds: Diverse Voices of Contemporary Mothers.* London: Guildford Press.

Gregory, S. (1991). Mother's and Their Deaf Children. In Motherhood: Meanings, Practices and Ideologies. In E. Lloyd (Ed.), *Motherhood.* London: Sage.

Hodge, N., & Runswick-Cole, K. (2013). They Never Pass Me the Ball': Disabled Children's Experiences of Leisure. *Children's Geographies, II*(3), 311–325.

Hussain, T., & Hyde-Bales, K. (2014). *Independent Investigation into the Death of CS.* London: Verita.

Jackson, J. (2004). *Multicoloured Mayhem: Parenting the Many Shades of Adolescents and Children with Autism, Asperger Syndrome and AD/HD.* London: Jessica Kingsley Publications.

Jensen, T. (2012). Tough Love in Tough Times. *Studies in the Maternal, 4*(2), 1–26.

Lazarus, R. S., & Folkman, S. (1984). *Stress, Appraisal and Coping.* New York: Springer.

Lowe, P., Lee, E., & Macvarish, M. (2015). Biologising Parenting: Neuroscience Discourse, English Social and Public Health Policy and Understandings of the Child. *Sociology of Health & Illness, 37*(8), 198–211.

Mallett, R., & Runswick-Cole, K. (2012). Commodifying Autism: The Cultural Contexts of 'Disability' in the Academy. In D. Goodley, B. Hughes, & L. J. Davis (Eds.), *Disability and Social Theory* (pp. 33–51). Basingstoke: Palgrave Macmillan.

McLaughlin, J., Goodley, D., Clavering, E., & Fisher, P. (2008). *Families Raising Disabled Children: Enabling Care and Social Justice.* London: Palgrave.

McRobbie, A. (2009). *The Aftermath of Feminism : Gender, Culture and Social Change.* London: Sage.

Moore, C. (2012). *George and Sam.* London: Penguin Books.

Nadesan, M. H. (2005). *Constructing Autism: Unravelling the Truth and Constructing the Social.* London: Routledge.

Parsons, T. (1951). *The Social System.* London: Routledge.

Puar, J. K. (2012). Precarity Talk: A Virtual Roundtable with Lauren Berlant, Judith Butler, Bojana Cvejic, Isabell Lorey, Jasbir Puar, and Ana Vujanovic. *TDR: The Drama Review, 56*(4), 163–177.

Read, J. (2000). *Disability, the Family and Society: Listening to Mothers.* Buckingham: The Open University Press.

Runswick-Cole, K. (2007). The Tribunal Was the Most Stressful Thing: More Stressful than My Son's Diagnosis or Behaviour': The Experiences of Families Who Go to the Special Educational Needs and Disability Tribunal (SENDIST). *Disability and Society, 22*(3), 315–328.

Runswick-Cole, K. (2011). Time to End the Bias Towards Inclusive Education? *British Journal of Special Education, 38*(3), 112–120.

Runswick-Cole, K. (2014). "Us" and "Them"? The Limits and Possibilities of a Politics of Neurodiversity in Neoliberal Times. *Disability & Society, 29*(7), 1117–1129.

Runswick-Cole, K., & Goodley, D. (2015). Disability and Austerity: 'Cruel Optimism' in Big Society. *Canadian Journal of Disability Studies, 4*(2), 162–186.

Ryan, S. (2005). Busy Behaviour in the 'Land of the Golden M. *Journal of Applied Research in Intellectual Disabilities, 18*, 65–74.

Ryan, S., & Runswick-Cole, K. (2008a). Repositioning Mothers: Mothers, Disabled Children and Disability Studies. *Disability and Society, 23*(3), 199–210.

Ryan, S., & Runswick-Cole, K. (2008b). From Advocate to Activist? Mapping the Experiences of Mothers of Children on the Autism Spectrum. *Journal of Applied Research in Intellectual Disabilities, 22*(1), 43–53.

Skeggs, B. (2004). *Class, Self, Culture.* London: Routledge.

Skeggs, B. (2005). The Making of Class and Gender Through Visualizing Moral Subject Formation. *Sociology, 39*(5), 965–982.

Skeggs, B. (2010). The Value of Relationships: Affective Scenes and Emotional Performances. *Feminist Legal Studies, 18*(1), 29–51.

Stone, D. (1984). *The Disabled State*. Philadelphia: Temple University Press.

Traustadóttir, R. (1995). A Mother's Work Is Never Done: Constructing a "Normal" Family Life. In S. J. Taylor, R. Bogdan, & Z. M. Lutfiyya (Eds.), *The Variety of Community Experience: Qualitative Studies of Family and Community Life*. Baltimore: Paul H. Brookes.

Tyler, I. (2008). Chav Mum Chav Scum. *Feminist Media Studies, 8*(1), 17–34.

Tyler, I. (2013). *Revolting Subjects: The Politics of Abjection and Resistance in Neoliberal Britain*. London: Zed Books.

UNICEF. (1989). *United Nations Convention on the Rights of the Child*. Geneva: Office of the High Commissioner for Human Rights.

Wright Mills, C. (1959). *The Sociological Imagination*. Oxford: Oxford University Press.

Katherine Runswick-Cole is Chair in Education, The School of Education, The University of Sheffield, Sheffield, United Kingdom. Her research draws on critical disability studies approaches to explore the relationships between disability, childhood and families. Her research is informed by her experiences of mothering two young adult children, one of whom is disabled.

Intersectionality Theory in Research with the Fathers of Children with the Label of Autism

Joanne Heeney

Key Points

- Research with fathers of children with the label of autism has not reflected diversity amongst fathers, families and children, nor how societal changes have shaped fatherhood and fathering.
- Research with fathers of children with the label of autism can move beyond essentialism by considering the nature of power and oppression, and the contextual and individual factors which shape male parenting and the relationships between fathers and children.
- Intersectionality is a feminist theory which can help to recognise these complexities and their impact on social identities, values and practices in shifting times and locations.

Introduction

The main aim of this chapter is to acknowledge diversity amongst fathers, families and people with the label of autism and to recognise the ways in which gender and autism overlap with other identity markers, such as context and age, to shape fathers' involvement in children's lives.

J. Heeney (✉)
Centre for Women's Studies, University of York, York, UK

© The Author(s) 2018
K. Runswick-Cole et al. (eds.), *The Palgrave Handbook of Disabled Children's Childhood Studies*, https://doi.org/10.1057/978-1-137-54446-9_17

Using examples from my ongoing PhD research, an intersectional analysis of how fathers of children with the label of autism parent, and drawing on Connell's (1995) work on hegemonic and marginalised masculinities and intersectionality theory (Crenshaw 1989), simple binary understandings in relation to fathers in relation to children with the label of autism can be avoided by recognising that gender and disability are theoretically important, both mutually and in their own right, but are not the only factors at play (Goodley 2011).

Background

Although gender remains a useful frame through which to study disabled children's childhoods and family lives, it can be used in reductive ways. As Crompton and Lyonette (2005) suggest, offering reductionist biological explanations to gendered phenomenon fails to adequately account for the societal and cultural influences which shape inequalities in gender and so in parenting.

Research with fathers has often been influenced by reductionism; studies are often comparative, seeking to address the similarities or differences between male/female parenting, men's capacity to parent, and the long-term outcomes for children raised with (or without) fathers (Coles 2015). Some recent studies, for example, work by Hartley et al. (2014); Keller et al. (2014); and O'Halloran et al. (2013), adopt a different, more progressive position to reflect changes to how autism is conceptualised by fathers and changes in paternal values and practices to those expressed in previous literature.

However, Cabrera et al. (2014) suggest that a more comprehensive analysis of fatherhood needs to reflect the changing roles of fathers in society, and similarly, Roseneil and Budgeon suggest there persists a bias in research more generally with a continuing focus on relationships 'almost solely practised under the auspices of "family"'(2004, p. 136). The emergence of new configurations of fatherhood and the family, with corresponding shifts in family roles, caring and employment patterns for fathers and mothers, have often remained unaddressed. Furthermore, the ways in which the complex web of ideas about gender and disability are influenced by other variables to shape fathers identities, values and practices have not been fully explored. In summary, much research with fathers of children with the label of autism infers a problematic relationship between autism and masculinity (Shuttleworth et al. 2012) generally underpinned by traditional family relationships and reconfigurations of hegemonic masculinity (Demetriou 2001).

On the other hand, research conducted from a broadly feminist perspective seeks to challenge gender essentialism through a focus on how ideas about gender develop and create social inequalities. Although these approaches initially focused on oppression in the lives of women, masculinities research increasingly illuminates the ways in which gender also creates problems in the lives of men. Most notably, Connell's (1995) concepts of hegemonic and marginalised masculinities recognise the diversity amongst men and the different levels of social power that men hold. According to Connell, idealised, hegemonic masculinity is associated with particular traits, behaviours and physical attributes such as bodily strength, being in paid employment, and control of the self and of others. For example, an unemployed man may not fully meet with these norms and is therefore unable to draw on the power that a male gender identity provides. Thus, he may be considered, at times, marginalised. Connell's work is not without criticism. An analysis of men's power as an either/or (Coston and Kimmel 2012) leads to a theorising of masculinity which fails to reflect the contradictory ways in which fathers draw on gender as both a problem and as a source of domination and advantage (Matthews 2016).

Intersectionality theory, originating in the work of Crenshaw (1989), also draws on a feminist paradigm. When drawing on intersectionality alongside Connell's theories, subordination and domination may be recognised in the same man, and so complex and situational paternal identities and practices emerge which shape the relationship between fathers and children with the label of autism. An intersectional approach therefore questions how, when and why different forms of power and identity intersect and overlap, so that the 'natural order' of things can be questioned (Garland-Thomson 2002).

Intersectionality can also enrich studies with people with the label of autism. Hodge (2005) finds that the label of autism can result in an overshadowing of all other aspects of a child's identity as the child becomes defined by his or her diagnosis, and so the diversity amongst people with the label of autism, and the ways in which class, race, age, and so on shape people's lives can be overlooked. For example, Bumiller (2008) argues that there is a frequent association of autism with boys and men that leads to the support needs of girls and women with the label of autism remaining significantly overlooked.

The following stories from research demonstrate that fathers' relationships with autism and gender are rarely straightforward. They illustrate, in particular, some of the ways in which gender and autism overlap with other social categories, with real consequences for men's practices specifically as fathers to children with the label of autism. Thus by thinking outside of simple essentialist identity categories, we can understand how difference influences the lives of fathers of children with the label of autism, and how this shapes their relationships, and the roles that they play.

Research Sample and Justification

The three fathers, whose accounts are presented here, participated in a larger ongoing qualitative research project which sought to gather the experiences of fathers in relation to parenting children with the label of autism. Peter, Simon and Sam (fictitious names) provide primary or significant care to children with the label of autism, and identify as lone parents, divorced or separated, or as the main carer in their household. None are full-time employed. All live in working-class communities in a large city in England. Because of their personal and social circumstances, these men are less likely (by choice or through necessity) to rely on mothers to take up particular responsibilities, and so they experience opportunities and barriers in their parenting that other men may be denied. Therefore, they have some opportunity to shape their identities and paternal behaviours and accountabilities within a set of cultural standards which may, at times, differ from the hegemonic norm.

Ethical and Theoretical Considerations

It is important that I acknowledge at this point my specific focus on fathers of children with the label of autism and the tensions that come with this work. This research has a theoretical and ethical grounding in emancipatory principles of feminist and critical disability research which aims to produce politically accountable work that aims to address issues of social justice and inequality (Barnes 2008). Ongoing debates concerning gender inequalities in the global North with regard to the roles played by fathers and mothers as parents to children, with the label of autism in particular, cannot be addressed in any depth in this chapter.

However, whilst this chapter aims to problematise the essentialisation of the social categories 'father' and 'person with the label of autism', both separately and in relation to each other, it is important to acknowledge the ways in which ideologies of gender intersect with ideologies of disability, specifically in the lives of parents of disabled children, and in particular, the ongoing responsibility placed on mothers (Goodley and Runswick-Cole 2011). The ongoing discrimination experienced by people with the label of autism and gender inequalities also present in the lives of disabled people more broadly are a continuing concern. (See Featherstone 2010; Ryan and Runswick-Cole 2009; Scott 2015 for discussions).

Furthermore, the discriminatory values and beliefs of some parents have led to their occupying a difficult and contentious place in disability research (Shakespeare 2014). However, recent work has reflected changing attitudes to and perspectives on disability and a focus on the stressful aspects of parenting a disabled child (e.g. Gray 2003) has been followed with research which acknowledges the ways in which mothers have challenged the systems of oppression which disable their children (Derbyshire 2013). A powerful, active, challenging and confrontational range of conceptualisations of autism and corresponding maternal roles and identities is reflected in this work (Bagatell 2007; Ryan and Runswick-Cole 2009; Rocque 2010). Recent research reflects personal accounts of autism, and the neurodiversity movement, which recognises autism as a difference rather than a disorder, and challenges the discrimination faced by autistic people (e.g. Broderick and Ne'eman 2008; Bumiller 2008); however, the voices of fathers in this research remain a significant gap. Much of the small body of existing research conducted with fathers who have children with the label of autism is underpinned by biomedical understandings of autism, and a preconceived assumption that disability and masculinity are a problematic combination (Hornby 1992; Shuttleworth et al. 2012).

My intention to develop an inclusive research design which sought to incorporate the voices of children alongside those of fathers, by working with father–child dyads, raised a number of practical and ethical barriers including time, money, manageability and uptake which made the project untenable but a potentially fruitful future possibility. (See Beresford et al. 2004 for a fuller account of the difficulties that come with such a project.)

Nevertheless, the fathers' narratives I include here aim to offer some brief examples of the active, complex nature of the relationship between fathers and children with the label of autism, and also the tensions that emerge for these fathers in particular. It is important to address the limitations of this study; the small sample size and cultural composition limit the extent to which findings can be considered representative. The experiences of fathers of colour, for example, are not included here. Furthermore, there can be few fathers who are willing to explicitly discuss their lack of skills, concern or interest in their children, nor reveal any misogyny. Aspects of masculinity considered undesirable may be concealed, as may any discriminatory attitudes towards children and/ or autism. A further issue concerns the lack of voices of mothers and female partners. Although they played a different role in these families, they may perhaps provide very different accounts of the stories that fathers tell. The intention is to offer insight and generate further questions from this small study.

Themes

The following themes begin with the literature and then present the data analysis from individual fathers as a way of showing how the data supports or differs.

Theme 1: Autism, Fathers and Gender Identity

Lester and Paulus (2012) find that both autism and gender are complex concepts that parents interpret and understand in different ways at different times. For the fathers I discuss here, gender is a complex aspect of their own identities and the identities of others which can have both positive and negative implications (Robinson and Hockey 2011).

Relationships between fathers and children are active and dynamic; fathers and children shape each other's gender identities in mutual ways. For example, Raley and Bianchi (2006) find that a child's gender influences the way in which they are treated in families, whilst Daly et al. (2012) find that men's awareness of their values and practices, and the potential to experiment with a greater range of masculinities, is brought into focus through relationships with their children. Whilst this is a positive finding, gender can also function to limit the ways in which fathers engage with their children. It can be deployed by others to govern fathers and to dictate the boundaries of their relationships, practices and behaviours, the matricentral nature of child disability policy being just one example of this.

Furthermore, Peuravaara (2013) and Scott (2015) both discuss how gender is deployed at the intersection with disability. Gender can be used as a vehicle with which to deny or claim personhood, and this is evident in the ways in which some fathers used gender in relation to their children as a tool of normalisation, discussing and encouraging particularly normative gender-specific behaviours and traits whilst rejecting others.

These points are illustrated in the accounts which follow, which show how fathers in this study seemed to enjoy the opportunity to dismantle the restrictions imposed on typical father–child relationships and male stereotypes through discussing the value they placed on non-hegemonic masculine values of intimacy, gentleness, sensitivity and affection. Therefore whilst fathers expressed how a relationship with a child with the label of autism had allowed them to resist stereotypical expectations of how 'men' should behave, and allowed for positive and non stereotypical narratives of children with the label of autism to emerge, it is important to also reflect on how, in many ways, gender remained a constant. In particular, the gender identity of the child in question had repercussions not just for how the father in each case parented, but also how he framed each child in terms of male or female. For example, reflections in relation to sons were often complemented with a counternarrative about physical size and strength, or another characteristic associated with normative masculinity whilst discussions about bodies and care were more difficult for fathers to enter into if they had daughters.

Buzzanell and Turner (2003) suggest, men may fall back into traditional gendered patterns in situations where they feel uncertain about what is an appropriate role or response.

Peter's account illustrates these tensions well.

Peter is keen for me to understand his daughter as an individual young woman in her own right and discusses her love of, amongst other things, pop star Katy Perry, and shoes. His discussion of his daughter demonstrated an awareness of her difference, but showed a defiant rejection of aspects of normalisation and the shackles of traditional fatherhood and hegemonic masculine practices.

Peter shared his sensitivity to his daughter's anxieties and explained how his attentive understanding of her behaviours had become an everyday, acceptable and enjoyable aspect of his parenting repertoire. This allowed him to intensively nurture her development, and demonstrate his clearly progressive and non-discriminatory attitude towards disability and fathering. However, through Peter's description of his daughter's femininity, he also narrates a more acceptable, traditional gender identity for them both. Furthermore, Peter is able to craft a range of complementary and acceptable masculinities for himself around his interpretation of his daughter.

Peter's account therefore contains clashes and tensions between both normative and alternative understandings of gender and disability, and issues relating to Peter's participation in caring for his daughter's body and her adolescent development have been a learning curve for him, and for other fathers. He discusses his involvement in these tasks as a necessity rather than a choice, indicating his initial discomfort in this highly gendered and medicalised world which he associates very much with the female. He seems to draw acceptability from his daughter's lack of concern about his engagement with these intimate and embodied aspects of her life to enable him to manage his own uncertainty about his role. However, the role of fathers in intimate care requires a more critical analysis to reflect the complexity of the issues involved and their impact on the relationships between fathers and children.

Theme 2: Autism, Fathers and Gender in Context

The need to recognise how context influences interactions between fathers and children with the label of autism is particularly stark when men discuss their parenting experiences in locations clearly divided by gender, such as public changing rooms and toilets. Kupers (2005) suggests that the more harmful aspects of masculinity, such as aggression, become magnified in certain contexts, although this cannot be applied universally to all men. However, men's willingness to discuss their participation in intimate care has been highlighted in the literature as an area that seems to lead to concerns about appearing predatory and dangerous (Morgan 2005).

Research by Doucet (2006) and Gabb (2012) indicates that even the privacy of the family home seems to raise concerns about father's bodies and fathers' roles, competencies and motives in relation to providing care. These concerns appear to be intensified in positioning men's bodies alongside disabled and gendered bodies. The acceptability of men's presence alongside disabled children in some particularly sensitive contexts and roles can breach normative masculinity, attracting significant penalties for fathers, as the following examples illustrate.

For the fathers who participated in this study, considerable time and effort is spent in performing the acceptable face of fatherhood consistently associated with fun and play (Cabrera et al. 2014). This 'play' was enacted in ways which sought to accomodate the sensory and emotional pressures that some people with the label of autism can experience (Davidson 2007). Fathers recognised and built on this need, adapting home environments to support the sensory needs and interests of their children, encouraging and providing computers and technology, or accompanying children on walks among nature and the outside world. One father in particular spoke about his children's love of patterns in water and light, observing their enjoyment of and engagement with particular sensory encounters such as rain, and creating safe opportunities for them to do so, for example through playing with the garden hose or through watching the smoke from a bonfire in the garden.

Some fathers also identified specific public locations where they felt accepted with their children. One father, Simon, who has three children with the label of autism, identified the subculture of gaming, cosplay and anime as a diverse and accepting environment, where he and his children felt welcomed. Cosplay is a portmanteau of the words costume and play. Cosplayers dress as fictional characters, often from fantasy films or comics, or the Japanese manga or gaming scene (Rosenberg and Letamendi 2013).

Fein (2015) finds that the cosplay and role play world is a supportive environment for people with the label of autism, and Simon's points affirm this. The gaming/cosplay world also seems to present a place where gender is more fluid, and where the need for both he and his children to meet with norms of appearance and behaviour may be less rigid. This allows Simon and his children greater freedom in their behaviours, appearances and interactions with each other, and with other people. In particular, Simon places emphasis on the complex and creative strategies and collaborations his children engage in through gaming and cosplay, which stand in stark contrast to stereotypes of autistic people (Milton 2012).

On the other hand, some research has reflected the enduring nature of gender stereotypes and divisions in the coplay and gaming worlds. Gn (2011) is critical of an association of cosplay with a rejection of gender binaries; through the hyper-sexualisation of female characters, some elements of cosplay subculture appear misogynistic. Furthermore, King et al. (1991) and Kivikangas et al. (2014) find the competitive aspects of game playing remain more strongly associated with hegemonic masculinity and therefore males rather than females, and gaming culture reflects these ideas about gender.

These contradictions are evident in Simon's discussion. Simon explains that the presence of female cosplayers in revealing costumes allows him to teach his sons to behave respectfully towards women. In doing so, he reveals his own values regarding his role as a father, about gender and about appropriate masculine behaviour (Coston and Kimmel 2012). Although his intentions are laudable, indicating a sensitivity to the objectification of women, they are undergirded by clear biological and behavioural distinctions between male and female, and concerns about predatory masculinity. Nevertheless, for Simon and his children, the cosplay scene is a context in which gender and disability can be simultaneously fractured and affirmed.

However, concerns about displaying aspects of 'toxic masculinity' are particularly evident in the accounts of the three fathers who have daughters with the label of autism. These fears are strongly context related. Kupers (2005) defines toxic masculinity as 'the constellation of socially regressive male traits that serve to foster domination, the devaluation of women, homophobia and wanton violence' (p. 714). Kupers also finds that context can magnify the effects of toxic masculinity. Gabb's (2012) research on father–child intimacy and family attitudes towards nudity in the home demonstrates the ways in which toxic ideas about men and male bodies, particularly in juxtaposition to children's bodies, are interpreted as 'risky'. This interpretation of men's bodies sits uncomfortably alongside the portrayal of disabled female bodies as problematic, vulnerable and weak (Garland-Thomson 2002) to create tensions and concerns for fathers. We should remain especially vigilant to the ways in which these essentialist ideas about gender/disability shape relationships between fathers and female children with the label of autism, and Peter vividly illustrates this through recounting an occasion when he was stopped and questioned by the police following a trip to the park with his daughter. When she became distressed by the sound of a passing motorbike, Peter guided her away. A member of the public consequently reported that he was abducting a child.

Theme 3: Autism, Fathers, Gendered Bodies and Time

Marshall and Katz (2012) discuss the importance of a temporal approach to researching age, bodies and gender. Father's involvement in intimate caring practices is an under-researched area (Hobson and Noyes 2011), and it is perhaps through these most intimate of practices where ideologies of gender, age and sexuality intersect with ideologies of disability to shape and govern relationships between fathers and their children. Ideas about who is best placed to undertake caring practices, particularly intimate care, are strongly influenced by gender and these influences shape the relationship between fathers as givers of care, and children with the label of autism as recipients of care (Mc Kie et al. 2002; Dermott 2008; Bowlby 2012).

Through the examples here, we can understand the difficulties and taboos that involvement in these practices can raise for fathers. Concerns about the misinterpretation of their actions are evident throughout gaps in conversations and uneasy discussions of their involvement in these tasks. Researchers should be sensitive to some of the more predatory and harmful ideas about men, and the ways in which they shape fathers' attitudes (and those of others) towards participation in these tasks, as well as their willingness to discuss them in a research context (Morgan 2005; Dermott 2008; Gabb 2012).

Paternal participation in the intimate care of disabled teenagers and adults, such as bathing, toileting, and supporting adolescent development, and the acceptability of the involvement of men in these tasks stimulate highly complex, emotive and tense discussions and throws into focus a sharp gender divide. A father's involvement even in seemingly simple acts, such as using public toilets, may be considered inappropriate or even dangerous, particularly as a child moves into adolescence, and especially if the child is female (Bichard et al. 2005; Anthony and Dufresne 2007). Fathers are sensitive to this bias and the ways in which it shapes their parenting in both public and private contexts.

Raley and Bianchi (2006) suggest fathers may not be aware of the more subtle ways in which their parenting is shaped by their children's gender, and the contradictions in fathers' accounts become more visible when adolescent sexuality and sexual development is discussed. For example, Sam reports concerns raised by family that it was no longer appropriate that he bathe his daughter, despite his protests that he had undertaken this task since his children were babies. Thus, his parenting practices must change to meet with the social conventions of his gender and age, and the gender and age of each child, a demand he finds particularly difficult and offensive.

As research demonstrates that many people labelled with a disability are denied their right to a sexuality, the fathers in this study who expressed affirmative and open attitudes to their son's sexual development should be commended (see Van Schalkwyk et al. 2015). Nevertheless, as Coston and Kimmel (2012) find, through their interpretation of their son's emerging sexual behaviours, fathers reveal their own values about appropriate heterosexual masculinity and sexuality. Given that daughters were not generally discussed in the same depth, this illustrates not only the restrictions placed on female disabled bodies but also the contradictions, fears and dichotomies that come with discussing such sensitive issues for fathers in particular. As Buzzanell and Turner (2003) suggest, it is therefore unsurprising that men may fall back into more traditional masculine responses when what is acceptable in a given context is unclear.

Discussion

The men who participated in this research expressed a desire and a requirement to do fatherhood in relation to children with the label of autism differently. Their unique personal situations enabled (or necessitated) engagement in some practices which may have been denied to other fathers. On the other hand, other, more intimate practices considered inappropriate for fathers makes clear the gendered and contextual nature of care and caring specifically in relation to children with the label of autism, and shows how often unconscious ideas about inappropriate and predatory masculinities, require fathers to avoid or negotiate some tasks and contexts in their everyday lives in favour of more socially acceptable masculine practices (Dermott 2008). However, men found no joy or benefit in this restriction (Hill Collins 1991) and restricting father's participation in certain aspects of their children's lives does nothing to improve the lives of the children themselves. Thus these fathers in particular must, at times, negotiate inclusion for their children and themselves, which has a disabling effect on children and a harmful effect on father–child relationships in limiting the scope of their daily lives, influencing children's attitude to gender and the activities they are able to engage in with their fathers. Furthermore, as the roles that mothers and women play in relation to children with the label of autism is affirmed as natural, so gender inequalities remain (Goodley and Runswick-Cole 2011).

Concluding Remarks

An intersectional focus on fatherhood and autism can potentially mutually enhance both masculinity and disability theory through illuminating the complexity of fatherhood and fathering, specifically in relation to autism.

Through avoiding the use of gender and disability as sole theoretical drivers, we develop a fuller understanding of men's complex, contextual relationships and fluctuating compliance with care, gender normativity and 'compulsory ableism' (Goodley et al. 2014). Instead of relying on harmful, essentialised explanations, we can recognise some of the ways in which men are regulated, negotiate and, at times, excuse their responsibilities as parents to children with the label of autism in particular.

There are also, of course, implications for children with the label of autism. Disabled children are routinely denied their rights. As their competency, autonomy and control over their lives is questioned (Fawcett 2016), so therefore the choices disabled children make about who, how and why people should become involved in the most personal areas of their lives are undermined. As Beresford (2008) discusses, intimate, respectful relationships based on love and support may be replaced with commodified and impersonal systems of care.

Children with the label of autism are engaged social actors, continually learning, developing and interacting with others across a lifetime. Therefore, the views and aspirations they develop about themselves, their future adult lives, relationships and as potential future parents themselves are shaped by the social situations they experience. Thus, whilst I hope I have explained the need for a reconsideration of the roles played specifically by fathers of children with the label of autism, I also believe that such a reconsideration will benefit children themselves.

References

Anthony, K. H., & Dufresne, M. (2007). Potty Parity in Perspective: Gender and Family Issues in Planning and Designing Public Restrooms. *Journal of Planning Literature, 21*(3), 267–294.

Bagatell, N. (2007). Orchestrating Voices: Autism, Identity and the Power of Discourse. *Disability and Society, 22*(4), 413–426.

Barnes, C. (2008). An Ethical Agenda in Disability Research: Rhetoric or Reality. In D. M. Martens & P. E. Ginsberg (Eds.), *The Handbook of Social Research Ethics* (pp. 458–473). London: Sage.

Beresford, P. (2008). *What Future for Care?* (pp. 1–16). York: Viewpoint Joseph Rowntree Foundation.

Beresford, B., Tozer, R., Raibee, P., & Sloper, P. (2004). Developing an Approach to Involving Children with Autism Spectrum Disorders in a Social Care Research Project. *British Journal of Learning Disabilities, 23*, 180–185.

Bichard, J., Hanson, J., & Greed, C. (2005). *Cognitive Aspects of Public Toilet Design.* Proceedings of the Eleventh International Conference on Human—Computer Interaction (HCI) International, Las Vegas, Nevada, USA.

Bowlby, S. (2012). Recognising the Time- Space Dimensions of Care: Caringscapes and Carescapes. *Environment and Planning, 44*, 2101–2118.

Broderick, A. A., & Ne'eman, A. (2008). Autism as Metaphor: Narrative and Counter-Narrative. *International Journal of Inclusive Education, 12*(5–6), 459–476.

Bumiller, K. (2008). Quirky Citizens: Autism, Gender and Reimagining Disability. *Signs, 33*(4), 976–991.

Buzzanell, P. M., & Turner, L. H. (2003). Emotion Work Revealed by Job Loss Discourse: Backgrounding- Foregrounding of Feelings, Construction of Normalcy and (Re) instituting of Traditional Masculinities. *Journal of Applied Communication Research, 31*(1), 27–57.

Cabrera, N. J., Fitzgerald, H. E., Bradley, R. H., & Roggman, R. (2014). An Ecology of Father—Child Relationships: An Expanded Model. *Journal of Family Theory and Review, 6*, 336–354.

Coles, R. L. (2015). Single—Father Families: A Review of the Literature. *Journal of Family Theory and Review, 7*, 144–166.

Connell, R. W. (1995). *Masculinities.* Cambridge: Polity Press.

Coston, B. M., & Kimmel, M. (2012). Seeing Privilege Where It Isn't: Marginalised Masculinities and the Intersectionality of Privilege. *Journal of Social Issues, 68*(1), 97–111.

Crenshaw, K. W. (1989). Demarginalizing the Intersection of Race and Sex: A Black Feminist Critique of Antidiscrimination Doctrine, Feminist Theory and Antiracist Politics. *University of Chicago Legal Forum, 1*(8), 139–167.

Crompton, R., & Lyonette, C. (2005). The New Gender Essentialism Domestic and Family 'Choices' and Their Relation to Attitudes. *British Journal of Sociology, 56*(4), 601–620.

Daly, K. J., Ashbourne, L., & Brown, J. L. (2012). A Reorientation of Worldview: Children's Influence on Fathers. *Journal of Family Issues, 34*(10), 1401–1424.

Davidson, J. (2007). "In a World of Her Own…" Re-presenting Alienation and Emotion in the Lives and Writings of Women with Autism. *Gender Place and Culture, 14*(6), 659–677.

Demetriou, D. M. (2001). Connell's Concept of Hegemonic Masculinity: A Critique. *Theory and Society, 30*, 337–361.

Derbyshire, L. (2013). A Mug or a Teacup and Saucer? In T. Curran & K. Runswick-Cole (Eds.), *Disabled Children's Childhood Studies Critical Practice in a Global Context* (pp. 30–35). Hamps: Palgrave Macmillan.

Dermott, E. (2008). *Intimate Fatherhood a Sociological Analysis.* London: Routledge.

Doucet, A. (2006). 'Estrogen –Filled Worlds': Fathers as Primary Caregivers and Embodiment. *The Sociological Review, 54*(4), 696–716.

Fawcett, B. (2016). Children and Disability: Constructions, Implications and Change. *International Social Work, 59*(2), 224–234.

Featherstone, B. (2010). Writing Fathers in but Mothers Out!!! *Critical Social Policy,* *30*(2), 208–224.

Fein, E. (2015). Making Meaningful Worlds: Role—Playing Subcultures and the Autism Spectrum. *Culture, Medicine and Psychiatry, 39*, 299–321.

Gabb, J. (2012). Embodying Risk: Managing Father-Child Intimacy and the Display of Nudity in Families. *Sociology, 47*(4), 639–654.

Garland-Thomson, R. (2002). Feminist Disability Studies. *Signs: Journal of Women in Culture and Society, 30*(2), 1557–1587.

Gn, J. (2011). Queer Simulation: The Practice, Performance and Pleasure of Cosplay. *Continuum Journal of Media and Cultural Studies, 25*(4), 583–593.

Goodley, D. (2011). *Disability Studies an Interdisciplinary Introduction.* London: Sage.

Goodley, D., & Runswick-Cole, K. (2011). Problematizing Policy: Conceptions of 'Child', 'Disabled' and 'Parents' in Social Policy in England. *International Journal of Inclusive Education, 15*(1), 71–85.

Goodley, D., Lawthom, R., & Runswick-Cole, K. (2014). Dis/ability and Austerity: Beyond Work and Slow Death. *Disability and Society, 29*(6), 980–984.

Gray, D. E. (2003). Gender and Coping: The Parents of Children with High Functioning Autism. *Social Science and Medicine, 56*, 631–642.

Hartley, S. L., Mihalia, I., Otalora-Fadner, H. S., & Bussanich, P. M. (2014). Division of Labor in Families of Children and Adolescents with Autism Spectrum Disorder. *Family Relations: Interdisciplinary Journal of Applied Family Studies, 63*, 627–638.

Hill Collins, P. (1991). *Black Feminist Thought Knowledge, Consciousness and the Politics of Empowerment.* London: Routledge.

Hobson, L., & Noyes, J. (2011). Fatherhood and Children with Complex Healthcare Needs: Qualitative Study of Fathering, Caring and Parenting. *BMC Nursing,* *10*(5), 1–13.

Hodge, N. (2005). Reflections on Diagnosing Autism Spectrum Conditions. *Disability and Society, 20*(3), 345–349.

Hornby, G. (1992). A Review of Fathers' Accounts of Their Experiences of Parenting Children with Disabilities. *Disability Handicap and Society, 7*(4), 363–374.

Keller, T., Ramsich, J., & Carolan, M. (2014). Relationships of Children with Autism Spectrum Disorders and Their Fathers. *The Qualitative Report, 9*(66), 1–15.

King, W. C., Jr., Miles, E. W., & Kniska, J. (1991). Boys Will Be Boys (and Girls Will Be Girls): The Attribution of Gender Role Stereotypes in a Gaming Situation. *Sex Roles, 25*(11/12), 607–621.

Kivikangas, J. M., Kätsyri, J., Järvelä, S., & Ravaja, N. (2014). Gender Differences in Emotional Responses to Cooperative and Competitive Game Play. http://journals.plos.org/plosone/article/authors?id=10.1371%2Fjournal.pone.0100318. Accessed 22 July 2016.

Kupers, T. A. (2005). Toxic Masculinity as a Barrier to Mental Health Treatment in Prison. *Journal of Clinical Psychology, 61*(6), 713–724.

Lester, J. N., & Paulus, T. M. (2012). 'That Teacher Takes Everything Badly': Discursively Reframing Non–normative Behaviors in Therapy Sessions. *International Journal of Qualitative Studies in Education, 27*(5), 641–666.

Marshall, B. L., & Katz, S. (2012). The Embodied Life- Course: Post-ageism or the Renaturalization of Gender? *Societies, 2,* 222–234.

Matthews, C. R. (2016). The Appropriation of Hegemonic Masculinity Within Selected Research on Men's Health. *NORMA International Journal for Masculinity Studies, 11*(1), 3–18.

Mc Kie, L., Gregory, S. G., & Bowlby, S. (2002). Shadow Times: The Temporal and Spatial Frameworks and Experiences of Caring and Working. *Sociology, 3*(6), 897–924.

Milton, D. E. M. (2012). On the Ontological Status of Autism: The 'Double Empathy Problem'. *Disability and Society, 27*(6), 883–887.

Morgan, D. (2005). Class and Masculinity. In M. S. Kimmel, J. Hearn, & R. W. Connell (Eds.), *Handbook of Studies on Men and Masculinities.* London: Sage.

O'Halloran, M., Sweeney, J., & Doody, O. (2013). Exploring Fathers' Perceptions of Parenting a Child with Asperger Syndrome. *Journal of Intellectual Disabilities, 17*(3), 198–213.

Peuravaara, K. (2013). Theorizing the Body: Conceptions of Disability, Gender and Normality. *Disability and Society, 28*(3), 408–417.

Raley, S., & Bianchi, S. (2006). Sons, Daughters and Family Processes: Does Gender of Children Matter? *Annual Review of Sociology, 32,* 401–421.

Robinson, V., & Hockey, J. (2011). *Masculinities in Transition.* Hamps: Palgrave Macmillan.

Rocque, B. (2010). Mediating Self-Hood: Exploring the Construction and Maintenance of Identity by Mothers of Children Labeled with Autism Spectrum Disorder. *Disability and Society, 25*(4), 485–497.

Rosenberg, R. S., & Letamendi, A. M. (2013). Expressions of Fandom: Findings from a Psychological Survey of Cosplay and Costume Wear. *Intensities: Journal of Cult Media, 5,* 9–18.

Roseneil, S., & Budgeon, S. (2004). Cultures of Intimacy and Care Beyond 'The Family': Personal Life and Social Change in the Early 21st Century. *Current Sociology, 52*(2), 135–159.

Ryan, S., & Runswick-Cole, K. (2009). From Advocate to Activist? Mapping the Experiences of Mothers of Children on the Autism Spectrum. *Journal of Applied Research in Intellectual Disabilities, 22,* 43–53.

Scott, J. A. (2015). Almost Passing: A Performance Analysis of Personal Narratives of Physically Disabled Femininity. *Women's Studies in Communication, 38*(2), 227–249.

Shakespeare, T. (2014). *Disability Rights and Wrongs Revisited* (2nd ed.). Oxon: Routledge.

Shuttleworth, R., Wedgwood, N., & Wilson, N. J. (2012). The Dilemma of Disabled Masculinity. *Men and Masculinity, 15*(2), 174–194.

Van Schalkwyk, G. I., Klingensmith, K., & Volkmar, F. R. (2015). Gender Identity and Autism Spectrum Disorder. *The Yale Journal of Biology and Medicine, 88*(1), 81–83. (e collection accessed 22 July 2016).

Joanne Heeney is a PhD candidate at the University of York Centre for Women's Studies. Her research interests are working-class life, masculinities/ fathering, gender and visual methodologies. She currently works at the Department of Social Work, Care and Justice at the Liverpool Hope University.

The Construction of Life Trajectories: Reflections, Research and Resolutions for Young People with Behavioural Disabilities

Tania Watson

Key Points

- This chapter draws upon my maternal experience of parenting children with behavioural disability and the experience of other families who engaged with me as part of my doctoral research.
- Despite the development of neurological explanations for many psychological and behavioural differences, for children diagnosed with disabilities which impact on behaviour and their families, blame rather than understanding persists.
- Societal discourses are shown to be disavowing of personal and familial dignity and productive of deficit life pathways, tendencies which have intensified within the contemporary culture of neo-liberal individualism.
- This chapter challenges the practice of holding children and young people accountable for the behavioural effects of a disability and claims such practices amount to acts of discrimination.

Introduction

This chapter seeks to raise awareness of the injustices faced by children and young people identified with neurodevelopmental disabilities both in the school context and in the wider community. I refer to behavioural disability

T. Watson (✉)
The University of Newcastle upon Tyne, Newcastle, UK

© The Author(s) 2018
K. Runswick-Cole et al. (eds.), *The Palgrave Handbook of Disabled Children's Childhood Studies*, https://doi.org/10.1057/978-1-137-54446-9_18

to describe disorders that affect behaviour. Neurodevelopmental disorders 'are a group of conditions with onset in the developmental phase' (APA 2013, p. 31) and include the common childhood diagnoses such as autistic spectrum disorders and attention deficit hyperactivity disorder (ADHD). Neurodevelopmental disorders also extend to lesser diagnosed conditions, for example, Tourette's syndrome, as well as generic delays in intellectual and/or physical functioning. Neurodevelopmental disorders impact on behaviour and can occur irrespective of intellectual ability (Baker and Blacher 2015). Problematically average intellectual functioning can impede recognition of disability, particularly in schools (Curtis 2002). A notable example of a neurodevelopmental disorder frequently accompanied by normal intellectual functioning is Pathological Demand Avoidance Syndrome (PDA). PDA, which although now accepted as part of the autistic spectrum, manifests with perplexing presentations, which may also generate alternative interpretation as bad behaviour (Christie et al. 2012). This variation of presentation and ability can result in children and their families being held accountable for behavioural symptoms in a way other disabled peers are not.

I refer to 'challenging childhoods' as the long-term experience of behavioural disability, where a child's childhood becomes overwhelming for the child and for schools and parents' ability to manage and support the child. I also discuss the ways in which accountability for behaviour occurs around children with behavioural disabilities. Accountability is considered different to blame, which is interpreted as pertaining more to single instances enacted by individuals. It is also a term used here to explain how children with behaviour disability are not being understood as disabled and are thus subject to discrimination.

In the neo-liberal UK context, Slee (2013) states, 'students are viewed as the bearers of results and ultimately schools exercise educational triage' (p. 896). Looking at the concept of triage in regard to pupils exhibiting challenging behaviours, I suggest that this is effected through the mechanisms schools employ to exclude or separate 'difficult' pupils from the main pupil body. The employment of medical labels is viewed as central to these mechanisms, serving to not only formalise difference but to effect a permanence to its guise. It is therefore pertinent to question whether pupils with a behavioural disability can ever be a marketable commodity. Kurtz (2016) asserts that schools remain prime sites of inequality, where family status and resources are prime predictors of academic success. Kurtz finds also that schools reward pupils who at earlier stages of their schooling have demonstrated their worth, emphasising a continuity of profile across school sectors.

Parents of children with disabilities are vulnerable to disadvantage, both socially and economically (Kingston 2007; McLaughlin et al. 2008a; Rogers

2007b; Papworth Trust 2016). Such vulnerability is heightened when behaviour is an issue, not least because schools often resort to exclusionary strategies to manage challenges posed. These strategies involve formal and illegal exclusions (OCC 2013; AA 2014; DfE 2016a) and compound child and parental disadvantage, strain which is often inexpertly conveyed by parents resulting in positions of defence between school and home. Resulting communication patterns can present as confrontational, thus serving to reinforce negative perceptions (Rogers 2011).

The neo-liberal policy context stresses individual performance, particularly in education. In particular the White Paper Educational Excellence Everywhere (DfE 2016b), provides indication of the frenetic pace and ongoing governmental pressure on schools to evidence improvement:

'Five years on, our schools system still has further to go. We need to extend and embed the last Parliament's reforms so that pupils and families across the country benefit; and we must raise our game again to reflect higher expectations from employers and universities, and to keep up with other leading countries around the world. Other education systems – from Shanghai and Singapore to Poland and Germany – are improving even faster than we are'.

Paradoxically, this publication continues to state:

'Most importantly of all, these problems are particularly acute in some areas – too many children still suffer a poor education because of where they live'.

There is nevertheless little acknowledgement of the social exigencies that might contribute to disadvantage, nor the government's role in its perpetuation. It does however intimate that social barriers can be overcome, if teaching standards are elevated and a pupil is sufficiently motivated to succeed. Inevitably and unfairly, for some young people, the demands for continued and sustained improvement are unrealistic through no fault of their own, yet attract accountability and sanction nevertheless (DfES 2005; Rogers 2007a, b; OFSTED 2012, 2014a).

This chapter argues that to blame and punish a child, or their family for behaviour which stems from a disability, contradicts the obligations laid down by The Equality Act 2010, (Parliament 2010). The Equality Act 2010 replaced the former separate equality legislation and co-ordinated protection, forming one umbrella act. Despite this Act embodying nine 'protected characteristics', of which one is disability (Chap.1, point 4, p. 4), the triaging tendencies noted by Slee (2013) and the inequalities Kurtz (2016) found to persist, are considered to disavow behavioural disability as a protected characteristic. Blame in the school context also contravenes the obligations stated in the Equality Act to make 'reasonable adjustments' and to act in an anticipatory manner (Part six, Chap. one, p. 55). Similarly, familial blame may be seen as 'discrimination by association', conduct also prohibited under the Equality Act (Section 19, p 10).

Accountability and specific instances of blame are thus regarded here as acts of discrimination, although they are rarely viewed as such in the school context or the criminal justice system. As O'Connell (2016) notes, behaviour that occurs as a result of disability 'confounds the vulnerability/aggression divide that separates discrimination law and criminal law, showing each to be uncomfortably intertwined' (O'Connell 2016, p. 22). Schools as a microcosm of society mirror this tension, leading to an individualisation of accountability (Parsons 2005; Jull 2008).

Underachievement is arguably the outcome of discrimination. Mordre et al.'s (2012) longitudinal study in Norway found that persons diagnosed with 'milder' autism and pervasive developmental disorders—non-specified, who exhibited 'normal' intellectual functioning—faired similarly or worse than their 'less intellectually able' peers in core areas such as employment and relationships across the life span. Indeed, the disadvantages endured by persons with average or above-average intellect are recognised as an international concern (Esbenser et al. 2010; Taylor 2011; Mordre et al. 2012). In the UK, there is underachievement of children and young people with behavioural challenges, as well as an overrepresentation of young people with neurodevelopmental disorders in the criminal justice system (Bishop 2008; NACRO 2011; Hughes et al. 2012). Problematically, these are vulnerabilities also associated with school disaffection (McCrystal et al. 2007; Bacon 2015).

Methodology

My doctoral research, carried out between 2012 and 2015 in the North East of England, explored the experience and opinions of parents and teachers towards childhood behavioural and learning disability. The overall aim was to understand both the nature of, and justification for, holding children and their families accountable for the manifestations of behavioural disabilities. Elsewhere (Watson thesis forthcoming 2017), I explore whether teachers considered all disability labels as being equally valid, given my own experience where the validity of a psychologist's diagnosis was dismissed in school and accountability placed upon my child and his family. This chapter is based on the parents' views, and represents both the experience of parents who participated in my research and my own experiences as a mother. Personal account and narrative research is shared to offer a means of exposing the most personal and detailed aspects of social phenomenon (Czarniawska 2004; Webster and Mertova 2007). As Vryan (2006) suggests, personal account can offer a unique insight that may not be easily accessible by conventional research means. As both a researcher and a mother of children who display and endure behavioural challenges, I saw sharing such experience a duty, not least to expose the injustices personally faced, but also to highlight those continuing to be levelled against other families.

It was considered equally important to invite the reader to consider what being a challenging child is like for that child. Drawing upon my data, I suggest that children enduring behavioural disabilities are caught in a double bind of disability effect and social expectation. Being unable to comply with social and school expectations for reasons that are poorly understood, many children find themselves subject to intrusive psychological assessments and multiple-agency input. Their childhood one of heightened visibility and judgement. Additionally the professional supports designed to support, in working practice too frequently evaluate and regulate, robbing both the child and family of dignity. Not least of the right to make and rectify mistakes with a privacy other non-disabled children and their families assume as right. Challenging childhoods rescind such privacy once additional 'support' mechanisms are triggered, and it was this which was found personally to be productive of an enduring negative identity.

Twelve families agreed to be interviewed initially and post-interview were invited to a follow on interview a year later. Seven families agreed, although only six successful follow-on interviews were possible, as the seventh family faced an unanticipated crisis. There was a notable gender disparity; as of the twelve participating families, only three interviews were conducted with both parents present. The remaining nine families were represented solely by their mother. This gender difference supports a widely held view that mothers adopt the primary role when their child has a disability (Kingston 2007; Rogers 2007a, b, c; McLaughlin et al. 2008b; Gill and Liamputtong 2011). It also emerged during re-interviews that two of the mothers had recently experienced relationship breakdowns, whilst a further three spoke of ongoing marital strain.

Ethical Implications

There are complications to talking publicly about behaviours that are socially reprehensible and at times illegal, not least because there is risk of public humiliation and longer-term stigma for the parties concerned. This section considers the ethics of insider research and life writing, with the children and family's privacy a core concern. How to 'see' the child was a primary ethical concern. As a mother, my 'knowing' of my children extends across many private and public levels; for example, I know that how my children are at home when feeling relaxed and safe, is often very different to the personas they present in public situations. This type of 'knowing' typically exceeds the bounds of a child's identified disability, but is not easily achieved by persons outside the family, particularly in social contexts, whereupon the effects of a disability (behaviour) have negative implications for others.

This is a persistent dilemma; indeed, 'see the person not the disability' is a slogan that has been employed countless times by disability advocates in poster campaigns (e.g. see http://www.campaignbrief.com/2010/12/scope-see-the-person-not-the-d-1.html). Notably, some disabled activists reject this separation of self and disability, considering their disabilities to be an inextricable part of who they are. Sinclair (1993) for example appeals to parents of autistic children to accept their child for who he/she is, rather than try to change or remediate them. At times of behavioural crisis, however, it is hard for parents and others to focus on the whole child, as the research below shows, much less to accept he/she as presenting in the moment. How therefore can one 'see' a child with a health condition or impairment that impacts on their behaviour as logically, it is as discriminatory to see a child with a behavioural disability as the sum of behavioural symptoms, as it is to dismiss a child in a wheelchair as physically less than others. Many authors state that disabled children should first and foremost be viewed as children (e.g. Shakespeare, most recently in Traustadóttir 2015, p. 13). However, such a view raises the question as to why disabled children would not be viewed, first and foremost, as children and why we need to make it an ambition.

A second ethical concern surrounded my role as a doctoral researcher using 'insider' personal experience in terms of the research relationships engendered. For Rogers (2003) and Cooper and Rogers (2015), the main strengths of insider research are the pre-existing detailed understanding of the area being studied, alongside ease of access to the research field. Nevertheless, Cooper and Rogers (2015) warn that 'insider' familiarity may also foster complacency, making the researcher vulnerable to unstated assumptions. Equally problematic is how the researcher/insider role is established, most specifically how to reconcile the relationship boundaries that stem from being a researcher, with the expectations of intimacy which accrue from being an 'insider'. Ethical guidelines are unhelpful in these respects as they pertain chiefly to the validity of the research project and the well-being of the research participants. Although overseen via processes of governance and supervision through universities and other research funders, Bahn and Wetherill (2012), likewise Emerald and Carpenter (2015), have become increasingly aware of the impact of the research process on the researcher, especially where 'insider' projects broach sensitive subjects and merge the personal with the professional.

The third ethical concern was centred around consent. For an ethical informed consent process, I sought parents' permissions (Miller and Boulton 2007) and considered capacity to consent (O'Neill 2003; Parsons et al. 2015). I also decided not to include direct instances (data) from my family, as they were vulnerable to being identified in the public domain, and even if they did consent in the moment, they may later want to retract these permissions and it would not then be possible. Nevertheless reflecting on my personal life helped me to think about these concerns in relation to my participant's children, particularly as they had no personal involvement in the research or opportunity to reply. These concerns were balanced against awareness that there is a lack of research data in this area, as well as both silence and invisibility, shrouding the lived realities of families managing children's behavioural disabilities (Carpenter and Austin 2007; Carpenter and Emerald 2009; Emerald and Carpenter 2015). This generated a tension between the roles of the mother and researcher. On reflection, I determined in this context that they were indivisible and constructive of a hybrid role, and hence both roles' priorities required resolution to the best of my ability. In resolution, parents' narratives are shared below as narrated to me, but presented in a blended format to prevent identification of any single family's history. I also draw on relevant literature as well as personal insight in my analysis of their accounts.

The fourth ethical concern was around child protection. In the information sheet, I stated that any incidences of safeguarding would need to be reported; however, as shown below, being at risk and being safe are contested terms and for some irreconcilable. For example, some parents had lodged challenges in respect of the treatment of their children by police and statutory services, only to have them dismissed by the complaints authorities; I therefore aim as a researcher to generate debate about what counts as reasonable response/force and or treatment.

Research Analysis: Constructions of Life Trajectories

There were a number of points shared by all the parents. Parents gave accounts of 'typical' childhood issues around friendships and parental boundaries. They also spoke of the difficulties they had faced getting medical recognition for their children's difficulties, and of the need for such recognition to enable them to find both appropriate school provision and ancillary support. All of the parents emphasised their children had vulnerabilities, irrespective of the seriousness of the behaviours they engaged in. Parents also highlighted the value of a sense of humour, likewise maintaining a sense of perspective and seeking to see the positives within their children.

The extreme situations described varied, and included violence, drug abuse and responses such as school exclusion and court summonses. Parents also described not being able to leave the family home for work or leisure purposes and of feeling misunderstood. At this point, Roger's (2013) distinction between 'caring for' and 'caring about' resonated when, for some respondents, the depth of 'caring about' at times of crisis, outweighed their ability to 'care for' their child. Although in some accounts even 'caring about' was stretched to its limits at times.

Parents attributed these strains not to their child per se, but to their disabilities and a lack of wider support. Problematically, in periods of crisis, it was often the police who attended the family home, as there was no clear protocol for medical services to attend a behavioural crisis. The risks posed during these episodes included self-harm, drug and alcohol abuse, promiscuous behaviour, stealing and threats of violence to wider family members. Even those parents whose children had a dedicated psychologist had no access to immediate medical response in times of crisis, yet support was clearly needed to protect themselves and their children from immediate harm, so the police were the only available option.

Parents felt that reliance on the police was inappropriate and spoke of police 'assaults', including aggressive restraint practices, such as the use of pepper spray and handcuffs. These reports raised safeguarding issues. Yet, when probed by me as to how parents dealt with this issue, parents told of how some instances had been formally reported, yet upon a police hearing, they were explained by the police complaints department as a reasonable force in the execution of official duty. I found this deeply upsetting as it appeared to increase the young person's vulnerabilities, yet, as a parent, you are forced by circumstance to rely on professional help and assistance in times of crisis. At this juncture, it appeared that disability rights were usurped by common and criminal law. The conceding of disability protections to criminal law is a practice which has also been noted by O'Connell (2016), who further found that where disability was accepted as mitigation, it could result in increased restrictions for the individual, not least a vulnerability to incarceration, founded upon a deterministic belief of the risks posed to self and others.

There were notable differences in experience. Two families said that a statutory response was a necessary safeguard for their child, and that a certain degree of empathy was shown to them and their child because of the child's disability. However, this was not routine protocol and occurred only after several professionals had intervened and managed to have the information logged onto the police database. Mostly, parents described professionals as being indifferent to the vulnerability of their children, more so regarding boys than girls. These children were seen to pose a risk rather than to be at risk and parents suggested that interventions were rarely offered until someone other than their child or themselves was perceived to be at risk.

Parents explained how their children struggled to see behavioural and social boundaries, and did not understand fully the consequences of ignoring them. Behavioural difficulties were also considered rarely understood by others to indicate vulnerability. Parents also spoke of the disparaging tone adopted in official records of meetings, including the diminishing use of the term 'mum' as an address when all the other adults in the room were referred to by their names and professional titles. These details were seen as generative of an 'us and them' divide, erecting both a barrier to working collaboratively and to keeping the focus on the best interests of the child.

In meetings, parents said they were regularly called upon to articulate the support needed, yet also stated that they were held accountable for both the actions of their children, and for not knowing what was needed to modify their actions. Notably, none of the parents in my study had been offered advanced medical or behavioural training, although two of the families told me they had been recommended for parenting classes. Such recommendation was resisted and viewed as an insult to both the seriousness of the challenges posed by their children and the ongoing efforts they were making. Carpenter and Emerald (2009) have described the position of mothers of children with neurodisability as being on the margins, absent from the scripts of normal or successful mothering, rendering their experiences silent. Parents repeatedly stressed that when things were going badly at school—not only did this have a worsening effect on the challenges their children posed at home, it also had a negative effect on their child's confidence and overall emotional well-being.

Despite indications of despair, parents expressed motivation to support their children and reduce both the risks they posed and those posed towards them. Parents also indicated concern towards the childhoods their children were living, and spoke of sadness that the struggles their children faced were being obscured by professionals' limited focus on the challenges they were seen to pose. Notably, parental accounts of successes also revealed forms and degrees of exclusion. A mother shared her unexpected pleasure when during a school parents' evening to discuss post-14 course choices, one teacher said he hoped her son would join his class. Her joy was disproportionate, she said, '*I really thought no one would want him. I felt so stupid crying in the school hall, but I was just so happy.*' Another parent spoke of feeling overwhelmed when, following a move from mainstream into a special school, her child told of how she and her classmates had decided that they (as a group) were normal and it was everyone else (other children) that were weird. This parent also intimated that this was the first occasion her daughter had indicated having friends.

Both myself and parents in my study affirmed that we considered our children to be more than the sum of their difficulties. In contrast, parents said they felt that teachers and aligned professionals focused exclusively on their children's difficulties, rendering their 'knowing' partial. Diagnosis brought relief to some parents in my study, offering children an alternative identity and parents the means to understand the difficulties faced. Nevertheless, the diagnostic process is slow, leaving the children vulnerable to interim blame for the difficulties they displayed. Diagnostic outcomes can also result in many labels, generating conflicting diagnostic identities. One mother told of how her son was given several labels, Atypical Autism then ADHD and finally Oppositional Defiance Disorder. Others parents alluded similarly, outlining the various conditions that are known to co-occur—these included Tourette's syndrome, Fragile X, Foetal Alcohol Syndrome and Attachment Disorder. Parents also impressed upon me that the multiple experience of being told about the child's diagnosis or having to tell it to others was not only intrusive, but also frustrating and exhausting.

Schooling in the UK is divided between two stages, primary school (ages from four to eleven years) and secondary school (ages from eleven to eighteen years). Families indicated that failings (social, behavioural and academic) at primary level heightened vulnerabilities at secondary level. Parents also spoke of difficulties across and beyond these educational stages including negative social reaction at community level. These 'difficulties' manifested as threats of violence at their home for one family from other mothers in her child's school, whilst for another family, repeated complaints by neighbours to the local council nearly resulted in their eviction. Parents strongly expressed not only their sense of powerlessness to effect change in their child, but also the additional stress that external blame caused, in and out of school.

Effective parent advocacy to deflect blame and accountability was found to require complex parental skills and depended on the resources parents held. Common examples included seeking secondary roles such as parent governor or membership of the school fundraising committee. Both were seen as a means of 'getting in to school' and of generating a positive profile. Other parents indicated reliance on disability-specific lobby groups for advocacy support. The National Autistic Society offers an example of an organisation which provides individual parent support in formal meetings, as well as offering whole-school dedicated training packages. One parent participant exceeded these typical routes of influence and was herself providing a Tourette's training course for schools; in so doing, she ensured informed support for her child, alongside respect from school. I alternatively resorted to an academic career and became well versed in education law. We were the fortunate parents; others had fewer resources and indicated feeling doubly powerless.

Parents' greatest commonality was sadness at the impact their children's difficulties had on their emergent identities, as well as the childhoods these engendered and the perceived limitations of life chances beyond school. Parents also indicated awareness of the interconnectedness of their child's current identity to that which was likely to develop in the future. Parents spoke of feeling undermined and unheard, holding suspicion that professionals met in private to discuss their children and then had a further meeting with parents present. These worries were a major impetus for parents to fight for special school placements, which were considered 'protective', offering supportive educational opportunities and the potential for positive relationships. Similarly, special schools were viewed as being able to manage the effects of behaviour in the immediate and longer term without judgement or blame.

Bearing in mind that children in primary school are aged eleven years or less, it was notable that parents spoke of acts of injustice and instances of social segregation and social humiliation in this sector. One family eventually became aware that their child had been forced to eat in isolation for over a year in a computer suite separate from other children. Another parent spoke of the visibility generated by their child (aged nine), being forced to start and end school at a different time to their peers through a different entrance and exit. Visibility was a common theme. Parents shared how other parents were privy to their child's difficulties and spoke openly about them in the schoolyard, leading to feelings of shame and stigma. One father told of how his son (a young boy of eight) was given a designated carpet square to sit on during circle time and indeed any other time his conduct was considered unacceptable, whilst other children were instructed to keep a stated distance from him. Another mother described how she accidently discovered that her son, aged six, had been left to wander the school corridors because staff 'could not keep him' in his classroom. Parents collectively described how they and their children were held accountable for the difficulties their children posed, yet also indicated that school responses rarely acknowledged their vulnerabilities, or appeared to unequivocally accept a diagnosis.

Parents of older children emphasised how the challenges their children had shown in the primary sector magnified with the onset of adolescence and their secondary school careers. Notably, none of the families of secondary school-age children had successfully completed their education in the mainstream. Some pupils had changed schools, or been excluded, whilst others had endured escalating support and supervision in the mainstream which had become untenable, forcing them to seek alternative provision in the special sector. For two families, school provision was provided via an outreach programme of only six contact hours a week; another family relied on local authority-provided home tutoring (one hour, three times a week). Parents spoke candidly about their children's risks, discussing criminal activity; drug use; promiscuity and absconding. A few respondents indicated that their child needed the safety of secure accommodation as stated behaviours included violence in the family home. This prompted disclosures of fears about the future, and parents alluded to necessary adjustments, the hiding of valuables and kitchen knives and also the locking of rooms and medicine cabinets, responses which do not sit easily with the notion of feckless or complicit parenting.

Parents' dread of the knock on the door or phone call from either school or police restricted their freedom to work or socialise. Indeed, some parents were uncomfortable socialising with parents whose children were 'successful'. Many of these parents told of being refused support in early childhood, justified by a 'wait-and-see' professional response. Yet, at the same time, they also spoke of being given formal warnings of their obligation to manage their child's behaviour. Overall, parents described their children's secondary school years as defining of theirs and their child's identities, and spoke of longer-term concerns for their adulthood.

The effects on parents were evident and included partnership breakdowns and employment difficulties, factors found to have a deleterious effect on the physical and mental well-being of mothers (Dobson et al. 2001; Eisenhower 2005; Greene 2007; McConkey et al. 2008; Griffith et al. 2010). One mother in particular revealed serious depression, brought about by years of maternal proactivity and denial of her own needs. Others spoke more generally of lost careers, friendships and even the support of wider family. Yet although the life experiences shared emitted mixed emotions, parents also signalled a unanimous acceptance of their children. Notably, none of the parents spoke of burden or grief, echoing the sentiment Green (2007) encapsulates in the title of her article, 'we are not sad we are tired'.

The strongest fear expressed by parents and indeed by myself was fear of harm to our children, both self-harm and harm done by others. Morale amongst parents in the study varied and contrasted sharply with what might be termed the 'typical ambitions' of parents in regard to childhood achievements. Parental success and ambition is typically measured through indicators such as a child's physical and psychological well-being, social popularity, compliance in school and academic success. These markers of success reflect what Carpenter and Emerald (2009) describe as the dominant discourse of mothering. Nevertheless, they also serve to silence and devalue mothering experiences which do not, or cannot, mirror such markers.

It is notable that parents of primary children in my study expressed an ambition to obtain a 'statement'—the legal term used at that time to specify educational support needs. For parents of children leaving education, the general indicators of success or ambition for their child's future (e.g. work, university or independence) were unstated. There were nevertheless regrets and questions of what could or should have been done differently. Interestingly, these parents seemed to be looking back rather than forward. This was considered illustrative of both lack of hope and a sense of realism. For all the parents, mainstream schooling had been at times alienating and productive of a negative identity for their child. Parents appeared to find this hard to resist and within my study and indeed my own personal experience, the ability to resist was inextricably bound up with the resources parents could muster. Parents clung to the child they knew and said this was central to the resisting of external definitions. Parents also found that adulthood brought fewer rights to parental involvement, despite the ongoing support needs of their children, alongside even greater personal accountability.

Discrimination, But Why?

Overall, the experiences shared by parents were troubling, not only in content but in the manner in which they were justified. Equally troubling was the absence of our children's experience in the literature or due academic concern towards the concerns raised, despite a global expansion of neurodevelopmental disabilities (Conrad 2007; Conrad and Bergey 2014; Leonard et al. 2010). Carpenter and Emerald (2009) note that little is written to elucidate the childhoods of children with behavioural disability, particularly those children who have average or above-intellectual functioning, but poor behaviour and social adaptions. Thusforth whilst the support voids that parents in my study illustrated would be unthinkable and indefensible if levelled against someone with a physical condition, they remain unacknowledged when behaviour is the issue.

Parent's confided experience of unfavourable treatments, directly linked to the effects of their children's identified disabilities. These children needed and warranted protection and support as laid down by equality legislation, but in practice attracted less support and were also deemed blameworthy. They were thus subject to disadvantage which was sanctioned by official discourses founded upon behavioural control and accountability. This research suggests that such response is discriminatory and invites wider address as to why it remains unacknowledged.

Proffering an explanation, I am minded of Giroux's (2009, 2011) assertion that there is an expansion of abandoned youth in American society, a surplus population (Bauman 2004), predicated upon an increasing distrust of youth generally. This resonates with the experiences parents described, leading me to question their children's value in society. Indeed, it would appear that these children are caught in between the tensions generated by inclusion and competitive education discourses (Tomlinson 2005, 2008; Youdell 2011). Also that contrary to expectation, the expansion of neurodevelopmental disabilities has interceded with these discourses, giving rise to a more punitive response through systems which are unaccountable under equality law. Such disadvantage in school is evidenced through pupils with behavioural challenges' disproportionate vulnerability to formal and internal exclusion (Lamb 2009; AA 2014; OCC 2013; DfE 2013, 2014). Notably exclusionary sanctions are frequently substantiated on the basis of behaviour, described in ambiguous terms such as persistent disruptive behaviour (OfSTED 2014b), which Sellgren (2014) found are also behavioural dispositions associated with many common neurodevelopmental conditions.

Conclusions

This chapter has sought to illuminate how life trajectories accrue from others responses to behavioural disabilities. These trajectories stem from a systemic failure to identify and establish effective supports in earlier childhood, able to pre-empt the heightened needs and additional strains found common to adolescence. Indeed, parents told how effective responses were triggered only when external risks were posed, transforming the young person from a profile of vulnerability to that of perpetrator. It is my contention that the silence surrounding 'challenging childhood' needs to be broken as a first step towards change. This necessitates the deconstruction of barriers which inhibits families sharing the realities of 'challenging' childhood. There is also a need for a pooling of resources between the family and school, to enable a fair and proportionate response to behavioural challenges. Problematically this distance cannot be bridged without parental willingness to share the realities of their children's childhoods, yet continued stigma operates as a disincentive, acting to reinforce discriminatory practices. Future research needs to probe more deeply familial experiences, it also needs to ask the young people first hand about their childhoods, in order to work through the ethical and inequality issues such elucidation of their experience and perspective warrants. Particularly as studies of such childrens problems, or of their being problems in the eyes of others, do not constitute studies of their lived childhoods.

References

AA (Ambitious about Autism). (2014). *Ruled Out. Are Children with Autism Missing Out on Education?* (Campaign Report 2014). London: Ambitious about Autism.

APA (American Psychiatric Association). (2013). *Diagnostic and Statistical Manual of Mental Disorders—5*. Arlington: American Psychiatric Association.

Bacon, A. (2015). *Gove Admits Link Between Exclusion and Criminality*. School Exclusion Project accessed at https://schoolexclusionproject.com/gove-admits-link-between-exclusion-and-criminality/

Bahn, S., & Weatherill, P. (2012). Qualitative Social Research: A Risky Business When It Comes to Collecting 'Sensitive' Data. *Qualitative Research, 13*, 19–35.

Baker, B. L., & Blacher, J. (2015). Disruptive Behaviour Disorders in Adolescents with ASD: Comparisons to Youth with Intellectual Disability or Typical Cognitive Development. *Journal of Mental Health Research in Intellectual Disabilities, 8*(2), 98–116.

Bauman, Z. (2004). *Wasted Lives*. Cambridge: Polity Press.

Bishop, D. (2008). An Examination of the Links Between Autistic Spectrum Disorders and Offending Behaviour in Young People. *Internet Journal of Criminology*, 1–32.

Carpenter, L., & Austin, H. (2007). Silenced, Silence, Silent: Motherhood in the Margins. *Qualitative Inquiry, 13*, 660–674.

Carpenter, L., & Emerald, E. (2009). *Stories from the Margin: Mothering a Child with ADHD or ASD*. http://www.postpressed.com.au/book/stories-from-the-margin/

Christie, P., Duncan, R. F., & Healy, Z. (2012). *Understanding Pathological Demand Avoidance in Children*. London: Jessica Kingsley Publishers.

Conrad, P. (2007). *The Medicalisation of Society*. Maryland: The John Hopkins University Press.

Conrad, P., & Bergey, M. R. (2014). The Impending Globalization of ADHD: Notes on the Expansion and Growth of a Medicalized Disorder. *Social Science & Medicine, 122*, 31–43.

Cooper, L., & Rogers, C. (2015). Mothering and 'Insider' Dilemmas: Feminist Sociologists in the Research Process. *Sociological Research Online, 20*(2), 5.

Curtis, J. (2002). *Has Your Child Got a Hidden Disability?* London: Hodder & Stoughton.

Czarniawska, B. (2004). *Narratives in Social Research*. London: Sage.

DfE. (2013). *Permanent and Fixed Period Exclusions from Schools and Exclusion Appeals in England, 2011/12*. Statistical First Release. London: DfE.

DfE. (2014). *Special Educational Needs in England: 2014*. Statistics First Release. London: DfE.

DfE. (2016a). *Special Educational Needs: An Analysis and Summary of Data Sources*. London: DfE.

DfE. (2016b). *Educational Excellence Everywhere*. London: DfE.

DfES. (2005). *Higher Standards: Better Schools for All*. London: DfES.

Dobson, B., Middleton, S., & Beardsworth, A. (2001). *The Impact of Childhood Disability on Family Life*. York: Joseph Rowntree Foundation.

Eisenhower, A. S. (2005). Pre-school Children with Intellectual Disability: Syndrome Specificity, Behavioural Problems and Maternal Well Being. *Journal of Intellectual Disability Research, 49*(9), 657–671.

Emerald, E., & Carpenter, L. (2010). ADHD, Mothers, and the Politics of School Recognition. In L. J. Graham (Ed.), *(De)constructing ADHD: Critical Guidance for Teachers and Teacher Educators* (pp. 99–118). New York: Peter Lang.

Emerald, E., & Carpenter, L. (2015). Vulnerability and Emotions in Research Risks, Dilemmas, and Doubts. *Qualitative Inquiry, 21*(8), 741–750.

Esbenser, A. J., Bishop, S., Seltzer, M. M., Greenburg, J. S., & Taylor, J. L. (2010). Comparisons Between Individuals with Autistic Spectrum Disorders and Individuals with Down's Syndrome in Adulthood. *American Association on Intellectual and Developmental Disabilities, 115*(4), 277–290.

Gill, J., & Liamputtong, P. (2011). Walk a Mile in My Shoes: Life as a Mother of a Child with Asperger's Syndrome. *Qualitative Social Work, 12*(1), 41–56.

Giroux, H. A. (2009). *Youth in a Suspect Society*. New York: Palgrave Macmillan.

Giroux, H. A. (2011). Shattered Bonds: Youth in the Suspect Society and the Politics of Disposability. *Power Play: A Journal of Educational Justice, 3*(1), 6.

Green, S. E. (2007). "We're Tired, Not Sad": Benefits and Burdens of Mothering a Child with a Disability. *Social Science & Medicine, 64*(1), 150–163.

Griffith, G. M., Hastings, R. P., Nash, S., & Hill, C. (2010). Using Matched Groups to Explore Child Behavior Problems and Maternal Well-Being in Children with Down's Syndrome and Autism. *Journal of Autism and Developmental Disorders, 40*, 610–619.

Hughes, N., Williams, H., Chitsabesan, P., Davies, R., & Mounce, L. (2012). *Nobody Made the Connection: The Prevalence of Neurodisability in Young People Who Offend*. London: The Office of the Children's Commissioner.

Jull, S. K. (2008). Emotional and Behaviour Difficulties (EBD): The Special Educational Need Justifying Exclusion. *Journal of Research in Special Educational Needs, 8*(1), 13–18.

Kingston, A. K. (2007). *Mothering Special Needs: A Different Maternal Journey*. London: Jessica Kingsley Publications.

Kurtz, R. (2016). Why Have Attempts to Promote Equality of Opportunity in Schools in the UK and/or Other Countries Failed? *The STEP Journal, 3*(1), 4–10.

Lamb, B. (2009). *The Lamb Inquiry. Special Educational Needs and Parental Confidence*. Nottingham: DCSF.

Leonard, H., Dixon, G., Whitehouse, A. J., Bourke, J., Aiberti, K., Nassar, N., Bower, C., & Glasson, E. J. (2010). Unpacking the Complex Nature of the Autism Epidemic. *Research in Autism Spectrum Disorders, 4*(4), 548–554.

McConkey, R., Truesdale-Kennedy, M., Chang, M. Y., Jarrah, S., & Shukri, R. (2008). The Impact on Mothers of Bringing Up a Child with Intellectual Disabilities: A Cross Cultural Study. *International Journal of Nursing Studies, 45*(1), 65–74.

McCrystal, P., Percy, A., & Higgins, K. (2007). Exclusion and Marginalization in Adolescence: The Experience of School Exclusion on Drug Use and Antisocial Behaviour. *Journal of Youth Studies, 10*(1), 35–54.

McLaughlin, J., Goodley, D., Clavering, E., & Fisher, P. (2008a). *Families Raising Disabled Children Enabling Care and Social Justice*. Hampshire: Palgrave Macmillan.

McLaughlin, J., Goodley, D., Clavering, E & Fisher, P. (2008b). *Families Raising Disabled Children Enabling Care and Social Justice*. Hampshire: Palgrave Macmillan.

Miller, T., & Boulton, M. (2007). Changing Constructions of Informed Consent: Qualitative Research and Complex Social Worlds. *Social Science & Medicine, 65*(11), 2199–2211.

Mordre, M., Groholt, B., Knudsen, A., Sponheim, E., Mykletun, A., & Myre, A. M. (2012). Is Long Term Prognosis for Pervasive Developmental Disorder Otherwise Non Specified Different From Prognosis for Autistic Spectrum Disorder? Findings from a 30 Year Follow Up Study. *Journal of Autism and Developmental Disorders, 42*, 920–928.

NACRO. (2011). *Speech, Language and Communication Difficulties; Young People in Trouble with the Law*. London: NACRO.

O'Connell, K. (2016). Unequal Brains: Disability Discrimination Laws and Children with Challenging Behaviour. *Medical Law Review, 24*(1), 76–98.

O'Neill, O. (2003). Some Limits of Informed Consent. *Journal of Medical Ethics, 29*(1), 4–7.

OCC (Office of the Children's' Commissioner). (2013). *"Always Someone Else's Problem": Office of the Children's Commissioners Report on Illegal Exclusions*. London: OCC.

OFSTED. (2012). *Pupil Behaviour in Schools in England*. London: OFSTED.

OFSTED. (2014a). *"Raising Standards, Improving Lives". The Office for Standards in Education. Children's Services and Skills (OFSTED) Strategic Plan 2014–2016*. London: HMSO.

OFSTED. (2014b). *Below the Radar: Low-Level Disruption in the Country's Classrooms*. London: OFSTED.

Parliament, U. K. (2010). *The Equality Act*. London: HMSO.

Parsons, C. (2005). School Exclusion: The Will to Punish. *British Journal of Educational Studies, 53*(2), 187–211.

Parsons, S., Abbott, C., McKnight, L., & Davies, C. (2015). High Risk Yet Invisible: Conflicting Narratives on Social Research Involving Children and Young People, and the Role of Research Ethics Committees. *British Educational Research Journal, 41*(4), 709–729.

PT (Papworth Trust). (2016). *Disability in the United Kingdom 2014: Facts and Figures*. Cambridge. Retrieved August 2, 2016, from http://www.papworthtrust.org.uk/sites/default/files/Disability%20Facts%20and%20Figures%202016.pdf

Rogers, C. (2003). The Mother/Researcher in Blurred Boundaries of a Reflexive Research Process. *Auto/Biography, 11*(1&2), 47–54.

Rogers, C. (2007a). *Monitoring Parents': Apportioning Blame for "Deviant" Behaviour Prior to Diagnosis of a "Special Educational Need"* [Spoken Paper]. Monitoring Parents': Childrearing in the Age of 'Intensive Parenting'. University of Kent.

Rogers, C. (2007b). Disabling a Family? Emotional Dilemmas Experienced in Becoming a Parent of a Learning Disabled Child. *British Journal of Special Education, 34*(3), 136–143.

Rogers, C. (2007c). *Parenting and Inclusive Education: Discovering Difference, Experiencing Difficulty.* Houndmills: Palgrave Macmillan.

Rogers, C. (2011). Mothering and Intellectual Disability, Partnership Rhetoric. *British Journal of Sociology of Education, 32*(4), 563–581.

Rogers, C. (Ed.). (2013). *Critical Approaches to Care: Understanding Caring Relations, Identities and Cultures.* London: Routledge.

Sellgren, K. (2014). Children with Autism Face 'Illegal Exclusions'. *BBC News.* London: British Broadcasting Corporation.

Sinclair, J. (1993). Don't Mourn for Us. *Our Voice, 1*(3), 3–6.

Slee, R. (2013). How Do We Make Inclusive Education Happen When Exclusion Is a Political Predisposition. *International Journal of Inclusive Education, 17*(8), 895–907.

Taylor, J. L. (2011). Employment and Post-secondary Educational Activities for Young Adults with Autistic Spectrum Disorders During Transition to Adulthood. *Journal of Autism and Developmental Disorders, 41*(5), 566–574.

Tomlinson, S. (2005). *Education in a Post Welfare Society.* London: Open University Press.

Tomlinson, S. (2008). Gifted, Talent and High Ability: Selection for Education in a One- Dimensional World. *Oxford Review of Education, 34*(1), 59–74.

Traustadóttir, R., Ytterhus, B., Egilson, S. T., & Berg, B. (Eds.). (2015). *Childhood and Disability in the Nordic Countries: Being, Becoming, Belonging.* Basingstoke: Palgrave Macmillan.

Vryan, K. D. (2006). Expanding Analytic Autoethnography and Enhancing Its Potential. *Journal of Contemporary Ethnography., 35*(4), 405–409.

Watson, T. (2017). *Disability and Challenging Behaviour in Schools: The Necessity for a Culpability Model of Disability* (Unpublished thesis). Newcastle University.

Webster, L., & Mertova, P. (2007). *Using Narrative Inquiry as a Research Method: An Introduction to Using Critical Event Narrative Analysis in Research on Learning and Teaching.* Abingdon: Routledge.

Youdell, D. (2011). *School Trouble: Identity, Power and Politics in Education.* Oxon: Routledge.

Tania Watson has recently completed a doctorate at Newcastle University and puts forward a Culpability Model of Disability to explain the on-going accountability levelled toward children and families for the manifestations of behavioural disability. Tania's research interests are disability accountability and its incongruence with the tenets of anti-discrimination legislation. Tania is mother to eleven children and has extensive maternal experience of Autistic Spectrum Disorders. She is currently seeking to expand her doctoral research by exploring further the familial impact of behavioural disability and disability accountability.

Personalisation Policy and Parents: The Formalisation of Family Care for Adult Children with Learning Disabilities in England

Barbara Coles

Key Points

This chapter discusses the experience of parenting disabled men and women who have been labelled as having a severe learning disability.

It draws on (auto) ethnographic research into the role of Suitable Person in England.

It explains the role of Suitable Person in assisting with, and taking responsibility for, all decision-making before exploring a key theme arising from the data: 'power within partnership working between parents and professionals'.

The chapter highlights the risks of parents becoming vulnerable in the role of Suitable Person, and suggests urgent action to change this serious situation in order to ensure disabledadults have choice and control over their life.

Introduction

In England, there is a difference in the status of parental decision-making for children under, and over, the age of eighteen. For children under the age of eighteen, parents are legally responsible for their child's wellbeing, such as feeding and clothing them, making decisions about schooling, deciding whether to consent to medical treatment, presenting them in legal proceedings

B. Coles (✉)
Family Carer Researcher, Bristol, UK

© The Author(s) 2018   **281**
K. Runswick-Cole et al. (eds.), *The Palgrave Handbook of Disabled Children's Childhood Studies*, https://doi.org/10.1057/978-1-137-54446-9_19

and making decisions about where they live and about their upbringing. Parents do not have these legal responsibilities once their child reaches the age of eighteen. However, if an adult has limited capacity to make decisions as defined by The Mental Capacity Act (DoH 2005, 3–1), parents may continue to hold responsibilities and take on formal roles, like managing their adult child's Direct Payment (DP) and support arrangements. DPs are cash payments made by Local Authorities (LAs) to individuals who have been assessed as eligible for community care services (DoH 1996, 2003, 2009). DPs are generally used to purchase the services of personal assistants who will provide the help the recipient needs in relation to their personal care and daily living activities, and pay for other LA-agreed expenses, so that they can live independently in their own homes. Thus, the parental role and its status is shifting in England.

Recent research into this area reveals the level of scrutiny disabled families are subjected to, with the theme of 'fighting' and battles running through much of it. For example, parents often find themselves in precarious situations because of having to fight for services and for the rights of their disabled child, whilst simultaneously providing direct care and support (Glendinning et al. 2009; Mitchel, et al. 2014; Williams et al. 2013). But DPs do not only have an impact on the 'care' role of family carers, they also have an impact on their role as managers of services. Worries about funding being inadequate to meet the assessed needs of their son or daughter have also been a constant thread through this literature. Research has highlighted a shortfall in the DP to cover staff supervision and training and other necessary expenses in running a DP, and reported on how respondents have felt the need to fill this funding gap out of their own pocket ('Anonymous Family Carer' 2008; Carers UK 2008; Coles 2015; Moran et al. 2011). There is also the issue of DPs (and individual budgets—another form of personal budget) being less than the value of commissioned services (Glendinning et al. 2008, 2009; Williams et al. 2013).

Caring responsibilities are associated with the ill health of carers, which are often stress related, yet Williams and Robinson (2000) show how family carers played down their own needs. A negative impact on carers' personal relationships was also reported due to the fact that their social lives were taken over by their caring role (Williams and Robinson 2001; Williams et al. 2003; Glendinning et al. 2009). Arksey and Baxter (2012) reported that a lack of support from LAs resulted in people ceasing to use DPs after a relatively short period of time. All these factors would thus seem to be compounded by the additional responsibilities some parents are now taking on in managing DPs in a time when budgets are under threat. Yet research has established that people with learning disabilities who have complex support needs require *personalised* solutions, which are often found within the context of their own families, rather than outside of them (Emmerson and Hatton 2008; Williams, 2010; Williams and Robinson 2000). Support services that are offered to family carers in this position certainly need to be better examined because the small amount of research there is in the UK seems to point to the fact that family carers managing DPs are left alone to fight their own corner under increasingly difficult circumstances.

The body of research discussed above, however, did not involve in-depth qualitative analysis from the point of view of family carers themselves. There is anecdotal 'insider accounts' of the role being carried out by parents; there are research accounts that appear to gloss over the experience of parents/Suitable Person (SP) to some extent too, but this chapter draws on my doctoral research, which represents an important attempt to combine the insider view with a thorough ethnographic analysis of parents' experiences of managing DPs and support arrangements for adults with complex needs (Coles 2013).

As a way of understanding the care and support these parents are providing to their adult child, an overview of the personalisation agenda in the UK is given. This is followed by an outline of the methodological approach used, which demonstrates the importance of 'insider' research. The chapter then gives an insight into the parents' role tasks before discussing one key theme arising from the data: 'power within partnership working between parents and professionals'.

Personalisation Policy in the UK

The emergence of the personalisation agenda came out of the policy document, 'Our Health, Our Care, Our Say' (DoH 2006), which confirmed that people wanted timely support delivered in a way that fits into their lives with a greater focus on preventative approaches to promote their independence and wellbeing. The government implemented what it called its 'personalisation programme' to make this approach a reality for people and stated that 'every person who receives support, whether provided by statutory series, or funded by themselves, will be empowered to shape their own lives and the services they receive in all care settings' (DoH 2008). To make this a reality for adults with learning disabilities, under the Mental Capacity Act 2005 and the subsequent Health and Social Care Act 2008, some parent carers have taken up the position of a Suitable Person (SP), which is a parent (or other close relative) who agrees to take on the management of a DP and act in the individuals 'best interests' at all times. It is this that has led to the formalising of family care arrangements, although the role is not viewed as formal or professional.

The Research Study

The research presented here looked at the experiences of twelve parents in the role of SP for an adult child living in their own home (not the parental home) who have had labels such as severe learning disabilities, autism, and challenging behaviour attached to them, and who have complex support needs. Their parents were managing their adult child's DP/support arrangements long before the launch of the personalisation agenda. All reported having positive expectations about their adult child's lives, and were innovators of more personalised support. Indeed, they played a major part in redefining the lives of adults with learning disabilities so that they can live valued lives. I act as SP on behalf of my adult child and I wanted to include my experiences of carrying out this role in the data so as an 'insider' there were a number of ethical and methodological decisions to make that are discussed next.

'Insider Research': An (Auto) Ethnographical Approach

My aim was to explore an unknown territory in order to gain an understanding of parents' experiences, including my own, of managing DPs and personalised support arrangements for an adult child who has severe learning disabilities and complex support needs. The research was therefore generated from the 'bottom up', in this instance by parents—me, rather than the traditional 'top-down' approach, whereby the research is commissioned and funded by a third party in accordance with their own policy priorities. Even though it is 'policy relevant research', in its approach it is openly partisan.

My enquiry was based on the research literature and my own experiences. The research questions were as follows:

1. What factors did the parents consider when making their decision to take on this role?
2. What was the nature and extent of their role?
3. How do parents measure 'outcomes' for (a) their adult children, (b) themselves, as a result of providing this service?
4. What (if any) support systems do parents have in place to help them carry out this role?
5. Do parents feel that they are treated as 'expert care partners'?
6. Do parents have any issues or concerns regarding the development of this role?

The research sample was spread across seven counties in England and was made up of twelve participants, eight mothers and four fathers, four of whom were couples, including my husband and me. The data from this size sample does not tell us that these families are typical, but it does tell us what the experience can be like for some parents who are managing DPs on behalf of their adult child. Table 1 offers a reference table providing details of the participants.

Data Generation

An ethnographic multi-method approach of data gathering was adopted beginning with a semi-structured interview with each parent based on the research questions. The amount of time I spent with the parents thereafter depended upon their particular circumstances at any given time, and my own. These situations evolved, and I was then able to undertake participant observation as they carried out various role tasks (see below). I also engaged with them via telephone conversations.

Many of our conversations were audio-recorded and transcribed; otherwise I relied on writing field notes. These consisted of descriptive accounts of contextual information (dates and times, settings, participants, body language and 'talk'). These notes show too how I drew out the emerging sensitivities of the parents (e.g. their own health and wellbeing) as well as my deep local knowledge (e.g. issues concerning safeguarding and the professionalisation of the family home). They also show how I was comparing and contrasting the parents' experiences with my own. My reflections were used as data themselves.

Ethnography can incorporate elements of narrative analysis (Hammersley and Atkinson 2009), but because of my aim to adopt an 'insider' critical

Table 1 Participant details

Parent's names (Pseudonyms)	DP recipient	Time managing DP
Brenda	Son aged 25	7 years
Elizabeth	Son aged 39	11 years
Helen & James	Daughter aged 30	6 years
Joanna	Son aged 26	8 years
Kevin & Lesley	Son aged 25	6 years
Ruth & John	Son aged 40	8 years
Sally	Daughter aged 26	8 years
Barbara & Chris	Son aged 31	12 years

approach, I went beyond ethnography to 'auto ethnography' (Spry 2001) and using Geertz's (1989) framework of 'Being Here' and 'Being There' as a way of communicating the two distinct positions I held. When I wrote as a researcher, offering my reflective voice, I wrote under the heading of 'Being Here'. 'Being Here' led me to undertake the research as, although other research has critiqued aspects of personalisation incorporating the support given to families, I wanted a greater understanding of what was going on in my life, and that of my peers, as a consequence of taking on the role of a SP, and it was this that led me to pursue academic research.

When I wrote as a member of the research population, I wrote under the heading of 'Being There'. In my thesis (Coles 2013), I discussed how I have made a significant difference to my son's life through learning about him, listening to what he is saying and showing him that I have listened by changing the things that are not working well for him.

'Being here' and 'being there' are dual roles. As a demonstration of how deeply linked these two roles are, the following is an extract from my reflexive log:

> "How can these parental skills be transferred and learnt by practitioners, and why is it that many professionals and social care practitioners do not appear to be able to work in this way?" I think that this is because whilst parents and social/health care practitioners 'say' they share the same aim, the critical difference is that whilst I have taken on what *I* consider to be a 'formal' role of a SP by managing my son's DP and support arrangements, I never ever take off my 'informal' *parent hat* even though in law, as my child is over the age of eighteen, I am no longer responsible for him. That *parent hat* is deeply entrenched in my culture and for the vast majority of parents in this study the love of a parent surpasses any legislative desire, professional rhetoric or budgeting constraint. I believed that professionals and practitioners in the social care sector do not carry the love and affection that drives a parent to do the utmost for their offspring, whatever it takes. This is why I feel that I have generally been going against the general wisdom of professional practice. That said, I have tried to value and work together with a long list of social/health care professionals that have come into my son's life, so in a wider sense, I have always practiced the concept of 'partnership working'. My story seems to me however, to raise questions about whose wisdom actually counts! (Coles 2013, p. 211)

After analysing the data using thematic analysis (Taylor and Bogdan 1989) and building a valid argument for the chosen themes, I was ready to formulate theme statements to develop my storyline which begins with the role tasks of the parents/SP.

Role Tasks of the Parents/SP

The parents/SP in this study are implementing personalised tailored solutions for their adult child's care and support by giving them more *choice* and *control* over their lives, which is exactly what DPs were intended to do. But the formal support they were delivering to their adult child was quite extraordinary as they were providing additional and substantial layers of support over and above that what would generally be given by parents to children of a similar age who did not have such complex support needs. Their work entailed ensuring that their adult children were appropriately supported to engage in activities that were important to them at a time of their choosing. This meant that parents had to recruit, train and manage a team of personal assistants who could implement person-centred risk assessments in order to keep their son or daughter, themselves, and others, safe at all times. The parents were also providing a 24-hour on-call service, and for most parents this part of their role also involved being ready to cover gaps in staff teams due to staff absence, holidays and sickness. Parents' role included monitoring their adult child's health and seeking medical assistance when required, managing their adult child's home, which included overseeing household tasks in a way that was acceptable to their son or daughter, as well as working in partnership with housing providers to coordinate maintenance repairs. It involved managing social care funding and private finances, and running separate bank accounts accordingly. The parents were playing a major role on behalf of their son or daughter in community care reviews too, which involved attending meetings, analysing reports and of course advocating for their adult sons and daughters. In order to perform this part of their role well, it meant keeping abreast of relevant laws and government policy and guidance. Alongside all of this, these parents were doing the usual things parents do for much younger children, like seeing that their adult children would not be compromised by their behaviour or appearance. A key theme which is discussed next, however, demonstrates that the climate in which the parents/SP performed their tasks is an unforgiving one.

Power Within Partnership Working Between Parents and Professionals

Partnership working is generally defined as bringing together people who may have different roles, but who share the same goals (Williams 2013, pp. 74–75). However, it was clear in my research that the goals the participants were pursuing were not always the same goals that social care professionals wished to pursue. Parents said professionals overrode their goals even though, at the micro-level of individual families, policy rhetoric asserts that family carers should be respected as 'expert care partners' (DOH 2008). Also, although 'power' has been devolved to the parents in the role of SP, LAs effectively maintain the right to counter their initial decision to delegate to the SP, and parents spoke of confrontations and conflicts between themselves and practitioners, arising due to this unequal power relation. Many of the stories told by the parents were about individual incidents with particular practitioners. However, as a researcher I was more interested in understanding in how the system responded to the parents, given that there was a move towards including family members as 'care partners' alongside service users in both determining and providing aspects of social care as far back as the 1980s and 1990s. (Beresford 2001)

Personally, rather than working in partnership with professionals, sometimes it feels like working in opposition, as when I am 'Being There' I have experienced professional power as:

> I [the professional] can ask for information from you and you must provide it; I can tell you what I will be doing, when and where I will do it; and because of my position I can give you a decision, and I can change that decision, even though publicly it appears that you might be able to override it, (i.e. through the complaints procedure, the ombudsman, mediation, the law). (Author)

Indeed for all the parents in this research, their private lives were being turned over to the public domain no matter how much they strived to keep this to themselves. They were expected to accept professionals coming into the family home (it was not always possible to meet in their adult child's home) and expected to answer personal questions relating to their own relationships, health and finances. If they did not make accommodations, they were in danger of being labelled as difficult or obstructive. Parents reported as being treated as non-persons. One parent said:

> … *they [social care professionals] think they have 'access all areas'. What and who gave them the right to behave like this? You are a non-person in their eyes, something they have trodden in.* (Lesley in Coles 2013)

Another parent said:

> *Life experience makes you what you are and now I am bitter and angry and fuming and the Local Authority are responsible for this. Running the DP is a lot of bother*

now. It's just everyday unnecessary stress that we have to deal with and it is coming right into our home. They have walked all over me and there is nothing I can do about it because if I throw the towel in X [son] will be the loser. They have got me over a barrel and they know it. (Joanna in Coles 2013, p. 202)

Thus the power imbalance within these relationships needs serious consideration. Power, according to Foucault, 'makes individuals subject to someone else's control and dependence ...' (Foucault 1982, p. 212) and in my view, because the system is opaque, not transparent, and because of the mystifying expressions of power in practice, it has the opposite effect of what the policy rhetoric claims to achieve in respect of partnership working at the level of these individual families. However, resistance, according to Foucault, begins with the recognition of such power relations and forms of power that apply to everyday life, and although the parents struggle with power at certain times, they are not completely helpless. This is demonstrated by the ways in which they have exerted power in getting the services up and running, and in their efforts to keep things moving forward for our adult sons and daughters. The role of the SP has on the one hand therefore power to pursue support resources, but on the other hand it is entirely dependent on a LA decision to drop a parent's role as SP. I call this latter form of power relation 'airbrushing' power, as some of the parents expressed fears that they could be replaced at a moment's notice; they spoke about being 'airbrushed out' of their adult children's lives, which left them with a high sense of insecurity:

come hell or high water lead council employees wanted to sweep us out of the way. (Kevin, in Coles 2013, p. 198)

It's quite frightening how they are trying to remove me from my son's life. (Joanna, in Coles 2013, p. 198)

The factors that contribute to this power imbalance need careful consideration. Firstly, it is the paid/unpaid nature of the different partners and the fact that parents are, in some respects, recipients of public funds. Consideration must also be given to the multiple roles parents are expected to perform within these partnerships, like being a parent but also being a provider of 'formal' social care services. These tensions cause some of the problems, for whilst they are carrying their extraordinary parental role, they are at the same time being a 'partner' in managing services for their adult child, which meant that they have taken on considerable 'professional' and business roles in managing DP funds and a staff team.

The Business of Running a Direct Payment

The research showed the unequal footing on which the parents have to conduct the business of running a DP too. My observations of parents as business managers running a business from their private home made me reflect on the differences between the business role of the SP and commercial business. In a commercial business expenses can be claimed at the very least for the costs of one's heating, lighting and telephone for tax purposes, yet the parents were not in a position to make such claims because it is not deemed to be a 'commercial business'. Parents also missed out on any welfare criteria based on 'risk' and 'needs': reasonable cost for the recruitment and retention of staff, to cover the cost of room hire for conducting interviews, supervisions, training and team meetings for instance had not been budgeted into the DPs. Likewise, mobile phones, which appeared to be the most vital piece of equipment (one for the staff on duty, and one for the parent who was on call 24 hours a day), were not funded through the DP, yet it was clear in all cases that not having this communication system in place would put the individual, his/her staff and possibly members of the general public at risk. A mobile phone acts as a back-up system that enabled their adult children to live as they are—staff and parents alike appreciated being able to have this level of contact. Parents clearly felt that one set of mobile phones met a safeguarding and social care need and therefore represented a reasonable expense of a DP. Where a 'need' like this went unrecognised, it had to be funded at the expense of the parents themselves. The parents equated this to not being recognised as valued and equal 'partners in care'. This power imbalance appeared to threaten the chances of building good working partnerships. None of the LAs discussed by the parent/SP appeared to recognise that running a DP equates to running a business, yet setting up businesses that have little financial support is fraught with danger, as was the 'power of veto' professionals held over the elements that underpinned their adult child's DP. Having to make a business case or a welfare case around 'risk' and 'need' takes us a long way from the notion of 'rights' (and rights are discussed further below).

The Power of Veto

This imbalance of power also plays itself out in the fact that social workers and commissioners hold 'veto' over their adult child's assessment processes and care plans as well as the amount of DP funding that is allotted to them, and also how this can be spent. So although DPs constituted a significant cultural shift in the delivery of social care when they were first introduced, there are significant limits to the extent that power has transferred to the individual in receipt of the DP or their family carers as managers of these services. This again raises questions about partnership working. Parents in this study had clearly experienced a shift in power, with the trust, support and activism of the early days of managing DPs gradually fading. Partnerships which were built on the basis of equality, now appeared to be lacking:

> ...our LA had pretended to give her [daughter] and us power, some involvement, but then gave all sorts of reasons to reel this power back in again... (Sally in Coles 2013, p. 194)

> ... who would go into partnership with a party who lays the law down and says that is what you will do? They don't talk about working in partnership because they don't want to do it, they have control and in partnership that is usually negotiated... (Kevin in Coles 2013, p. 194)

Emotional Caregiving and the Exploitation of Parents: Suitable People at Risk

Caregiving, whether paid or unpaid, can be very emotionally demanding work, yet there is an added real tension for these parents as they described themselves as being morally bound to take on this role due to their close and intimate parental relationships with their adult children together with a distinct lack of alternative person-centred and safe support arrangements. This situation made them particularly vulnerable people in their own right as evidenced by talk about their own deteriorating wellbeing. This was attributed directly to the relentless negative actions of social care professionals. The toll this was taking on them appeared to be significant. One parent vividly expressed the topic of suicide:

> People commit suicide or go over the bridge and take their child with them. Who is counting these people? We family carers are...but families don't dare say this out loud, only to other trusted families. I hope desperately that my son goes before me. This is not the order it should be. Am I bad for thinking like this? I can trust you can't I Barbara? I can trust you because you know how I feel don't you? I'm not saying that this is the way I am going out or that I am going to take him with me when I go but I bet those other families that you have spoken to would say the same. If they were pushed just that little bit too far than they are being well who knows... (Anonymous, in Coles 2013, p. 199)

Another parent expressed anxieties about not being around to support her adult child in a slightly different way, saying that if she knew that she was going to die then without hesitation she would take her son with her because:

> Social care has become a big business and it has created a lot of jobs, but it's created an industry without a heart. (Anonymous, in Coles 2013, p. 220)

Due to the nature of the topic there was always a chance that the parents would express signs of anxiety and stress when sharing their experiences with me. In these two instances, the parents were signposted to support network/health professionals to speak about these feelings. However, people do think about death and dying, but here the parents seemed to be saying the unthinkable. Can we take from these accounts the literal view, expressed by the parents, namely that social care practice is dangerous to vulnerable adults, and that is why the parents said they have to think about exit strategies in order to keep their adult sons and daughters free from living suffering lives when they were no longer around to watch over them? This issue was discussed in supervision. We felt that there is undeniably an element of both but that it would not be justified to suggest that these parents are a danger to their adult children, indeed the whole research argues otherwise, based on an analysis of the parents' own experiences and narratives. It is clear though that these parents' lived realities bare no relation to policy rhetoric which states that 'carers will be supported to stay mentally and physically well' (DoH 2008, pp. 9–10) and that their efforts will be 'recognised', 'valued' and 'supported' (DoH 2010a, b).

Conclusion

It must be noted that this research was conducted under legislation that has since been superseded by the Care Act 2014. This latest Act has a strong emphasis on promoting the eligible person's *wellbeing* alongside meeting their needs and deciding if he or she is being deprived of his or her liberty. 'Wellbeing' is not a new concept in policy (DoH 2006); however, it is a broad concept with no hierarchy. The parents in this research offered a holistic understanding of their adult sons and daughters and therefore had, and will continue to have, a crucial part to play in identifying their 'wellbeing' in all aspects of their lives.

Although this chapter echoes a multitude of political, ethical and moral questions relating to the formalisation of parental care in respect of adult children with learning disabilities found in the literature reviewed, it demonstrates further that the current formalisation of parental support requires more transparency in order to bring successful outcomes for disabled adults—sons and daughters and their parents/SP. It has also shown how partnership and power are intimately linked; how the parents have expressed power in setting up and running their adult child's support services, whilst at the same time have experienced 'professional' power being applied to their everyday life. It has reiterated too that there is a real tension for these parents as they felt morally bound to take on this role due to their close intimate loving parental relationships, yet also felt forced into the role due to a distinct lack of alternative safe support arrangements, demonstrating therefore that partnership can never work where there is an unequal power balance. This chapter then allows us to understand how the clash between lived reality and policy rhetoric affects the lives of these parents and their adult children. Urgent action is required to influence and to address the seriousness of the situation for parents acting as SP:

Firstly, these parents have valuable skills in (a) understanding person-centred approaches; (b) managing and training frontline staff; (c) implementing positive ways of responding to and averting challenging behaviour; and (d) appropriately managing social care funding yet these skills are unrecognised and this needs addressing.

Secondly, the practice of care must consider and measure the *wellbeing* and *outcomes* of 'SP' alongside the DP recipient. Social care practitioners consider that they are safeguarding people from abuse, whether it is personal, physical or financial abuse, but the term 'abuse' is a contentious concept and the research raised awareness of another kind of abuse—systems abuse, abusive professional practice such as invasion of privacy; a lack of knowledge or failure to adhere to person-centred ways of working with the DP recipient and coercing the 'SP' into continuing with the role without the input of adequate funding.

Thirdly, it is imperative that parents/SP become legally literate (if they are not already) with regard to the DP framework under the Care Act 2014 and also the SP regulation under the Mental Capacity Act 2005 before it gets even harder for them to carry out their safeguarding role by preserving what is most important *to* and *for* their adult sons and daughters. Gaining this knowledge alongside professionals in the field would demonstrate good partnership working in practice; it may even provide space for joint understanding in the hope that some of the barriers parents/SP face can be ironed out before their adult child's individual care assessments, planning processes and financial decision-making begins. Finally, this auto ethnographic research, which entailed a great effort (from both the researcher and the participants) makes the lived experiences of parents/SP and their adult children visible. It calls for a 'reimagining' of disabled children's adulthoods, and that of their parents as SP. This requires a considerable change, both in culture and in public understanding, of their everyday lives.

References

Anonymous Family Carer. (2008). In Control? Making Sure We Are Not Out of Control! Some Issues for People Considering a Direct Payment or Individualized Budget. *The Journal of Adult Protection, 10*(3), 14–22.

Arksey, H., & Baxter, K. (2012). Exploring the Temporal Aspects of Direct Payments. *British Journal of Social Work, 42*(1), 147–164.

Beresford, P. (2001). Service Users, Social Policy and the Future of Welfare *Critical Social Policy, 21*(4), 494–512.

Carers UK. (2008). *Choice or Chore? Carers Experience of Direct Payments*. London: Carers UK.

Coles, B. A. (2013). *'Suitable People': An (Auto) Ethnographic Study of Parents' Experiences of Managing Direct Payments for Their Adult Children Who Have Severe Learning Disabilities and Complex Support Needs*. Unpublished, Norah Fry Research Centre, University of Bristol.

Coles, B. (2015). A 'Suitable Person': An 'Insider' Perspective. *British Journal of Learning Disabilities* (John Wiley & Sons Ltd.), *43*, 135–141.

Department of Health. (1996). *Disabled Persons (Services, Consultation and Representation) Act*. London: HMSO.

Department of Health. (2003). *Direct Payment Guidance: Community Care Services for Carers and Children's Services (Direct Payment Guidance)*. London: HMSO.

Department of Health. (2005). *Mental Capacity Act (England and Wales)*. London: HMSO.

Department of Health. (2006). *Our Health, Our Care, Our Say*. London: HMSO.

Department of Health. (2008). *An Introduction to Personalisation*. London: HMSO.

Department of Health. (2009). *Guidance on Direct Payments for Community Care, Services for Carers and Children's Services: England 2009*. London: HMSO.

Department of Health. (2010a). *Carers and Personalisation: Improving Outcomes*. London: HMSO.

Department of Health. (2010b). *Recognised, Valued and Supported: Next Steps for the Carers Strategy*. London: HMSO.

Emerson, E., & Hatton, C. (2008). *People with Learning Disabilities in England* (pp. 26–27). Lancaster: Centre for Disability Research. Lancaster University.

Foucault, M. (1982). The Subject and Power (Afterword). In H. L. Drefus & P. Rabinow (Eds.), *Michel Foucault: Beyond Structuralism and Hermeneutics*. Brighton: Harvester.

Geertz, C. (1989). Works and Lives: The Anthropologist as Author. In Spry, T. (2001). Performing Autoethnography: An Embodied Methodological Praxis. *Qualitative Enquiry, 7*(6).

Glendinning, C., Moran, N., & Rabiee, P. (2008). *Evaluation of the Individual Budget Initiative (IBSEN)*. York: Social Policy Research Unit, University of York. http://php.york.ac.uk/inst/spru/research/summs/ibsen.php

Glendinning, C., Tjadens, F., Arksey, H., Moree, M., Moran, N., & Nies, H. (2009). *Care Provision Within Families and Its Socio-Economic Impact on Care Providers*. York: Social Policy Research Unit, University of York.

Hammersley, M., & Atkinson, P. (2009). *Ethnography: Principles and Practice* (3rd ed.). London/New York: Routledge.

Held, V. (2006). The Ethics of Care: Personal, Political and Global. In Lloyd, L. (2012). *Health and Care in Ageing Societies: A New International Approach* (p. 4). The Policy Press.

Mitchell, W., Glendinning, C., & Brooks, J. (2014). Carers' Roles in Personal Budgets: Tensions and Dilemmas in Front Line Practice. *British Journal of Social Work*. doi:10.1093/bjsw/bcu018.

Moran, N., Glendinning, C., Stevens, M., Manthorpe, J., Jacobs, S., Wilberforce, M., Knapp, M., Challis, D., Fernandez, J. L., Jones, K., & Netten, A. (2011). Joining Up Government by Integrating Funding Streams? The Experiences of the Individual Budget Pilot Projects for Older and Disabled People in England. *International Journal of Public Administration, 34*(4), 232–233.

Spry, T. (2001). Performing Autoethnography: An Embodied Methodological Praxis. *Qualitative Inquiry, 7*, 706–723.

Taylor, S., & Bogdan, R. (1989). Introduction to Qualitative Research. In Aronson, J. (1994). A Pragmatic View of Thematic Analysis. *The Qualitative Report, 2*(1, Spring).

Williams, F. (2010). Claiming and Framing in the Making of Our Policies: The Recognition and Redistribution of Care. In Lloyd, L. (2012). *Health and Care in Ageing Societies: A New International Approach*. The Policy Press.

Williams, V. (2013). *Learning Disability Policy and Practice: Changing Lives?* London: Palgrave Macmillan.

Williams, V., & Robinson, C. (2000). *In Their Own Right: The Carers Act and Carers of People with Learning Disabilities*. Bristol: The Policy Press.

Williams, V., & Robinson, C. (2001). More Than One Wavelength: Identifying, Understanding and Resolving Conflicts of Interest Between People with Intellectual Disabilities and the Family Carers. *Journal of Applied Research in Intellectual Disabilities, 14*, 30–46.

Williams, V., Robinson, C., Simons, K., Gramlich, S., McBride, G., Snelham, N., & Myres, B. (2003). Paying the Piper and Calling the Tune? The Relationship Between Parents and Direct Payments for People with Learning Disabilities. *Journal of Applied Research in Intellectual Disabilities, 16*, 219–228.

Williams, V., Porter, S., & Strong, S. (2013). The Shifting Sands of Support Planning. *Journal of Integrated Care, 21*(3), 139–147.

Barbara Coles is a parent of an adult child with severe learning disabilities. Her work with other parents in this position pushes the boundaries of professional thinking by challenging the common assumption that families stifle their family member by placing an emphasis on care and protection rather than encouraging autonomy.

Part IV

Ethics and Values

Ethics and values are a central focus for all the authors in the Handbook as disabled children's childhoods are re-imagined. The chapters in this section provide substantial work on the identification of assumptions commonly made that construct disabled children as 'them'. The authors offer ethical principles for critique, research and practical change. They engage with issues of identity, inter-sectionality and context to illustrate the impact of decisions made for disabled children and their families.

In the chapter "Anonymity, Confidentiality and Informed Consent: Exploring Ethical Quandaries and Dilemmas in Research with and About Disabled Children's Childhoods", **Liz Thackray** discusses the ethical issues of writing about her experiences as a parent of a disabled child. While Liz and her child's experiences are closely linked, they are different. And while Liz has the right to share her story, she grapples here with the ethical issues this raises in talking about her child. The ethical codes used in the context of research in the United Kingdom require formal approval of research proposals and advance confidentiality and informed consent, but with insider, ethnographic research, ethical issues regarding anonymity and consent are multi-layered and complex. Identification can occur through the networks used for sampling, data security and in the details of the stories. Liz grapples with the tension between the benefit to developing knowledge and practice telling stories and the risks to disabled children and their families. Liz concludes that it is crucial for children and families to have their stories heard, and she offers a number of strategies to ensure children's voices are strengthened and that the ever-changing nature of personal accounts is appreciated.

In the chapter "Supporting Families in Raising Disabled Children to Enhance African Child Development", **Judy McKenzie** and **Tsitsi Chataika** introduce the context in Africa as part of the Global South, the African under-standing of child development towards cultural life and Ubuntu, the com-mitment to whole village support. Identity comes through participation in cultural life. They explain that identity is not an individualised matter, as it is usually constructed in the Global North; self and identity come about through other people. Providing kindness and care, for other children for example, is an early skill children learn. Able-bodied children and disabled children participate by assuming and undertaking productive roles as well as being cared for. Stigma and exclusion do occur with significant impact, as in the Global North, and early intervention is promoted to support the net-works and various philosophies of community.

In the chapter "Normalcy, Intersectionality and Ableism: Teaching About and Around 'Inclusion' to Future Educators", **Jenny Slater** and **Liz Chapman** discuss teaching about and around 'inclusion' to students on education courses in university. They draw on the ideas of normalcy, intersectionality and able-ism to show why a focus on disabled children's childhoods is not enough to counter the disablism within their lives and, worse still, this focus can be counter-productive when it repeats individualised definitions of difference. The authors locate their identities illustrating the significance of intersection-ality regarding privilege and marginalisation. Rather than highlighting the outcomes of oppression in individualised terms, they turn to the processes and context that generate ableism and the *structural* violence experienced by oppressed individuals and groups in education. The authors share methods used for students to critique norms, analyse exclusion, identify erasure and marginalisation of identity, and explore intersectionality and deep concerns around othering practices.

In the chapter "Just Sumaira: Not Her, Them or It", **Sumaira Naseem** details and illustrates ethical and unethical encounters with practitioners. Sumaira shares her experiences of a childhood where disability became objec-tified and was (and sometimes still is) a life where other people feel the need to create an 'us and them' rather than focusing on her and referring to her by her name, Sumaira. Alternatives to the medical gaze are discussed and from those examples she invites the reader to un-imagine and then to re-image ethical research with children for themselves in their own local contexts.

Anonymity, Confidentiality and Informed Consent: Exploring Ethical Quandaries and Dilemmas in Research with and About Disabled Children's Childhoods

Liz Thackray

Points of Interest

- The underlying premise on which this chapter is based is the right of all children to have their voices heard, regardless of any impairment. From this perspective, the ethics of research with disabled children apply to all children, but research with some more vulnerable children may need additional thought on the part of the researcher. The chapter does not pretend to offer conclusive answers, but rather encourages researchers and others to consider the current and ongoing implications of research undertaken with children and young people.
- What does informed consent mean in research with disabled children? Does this differ from assent? How can we avoid excluding children from research on the grounds of lack of competency?
- What do parent or other significant adult researchers need to consider when reporting their own and their disabled children's experiences?
- How might a young person or an adult view what was written about them in a research account about their childhood experiences written when they were a child?

L. Thackray (✉)
Open University, Milton Keynes, UK

© The Author(s) 2018
K. Runswick-Cole et al. (eds.), *The Palgrave Handbook of Disabled Children's Childhood Studies*, https://doi.org/10.1057/978-1-137-54446-9_20

Introduction

Research focusing on disabled children's childhoods often involves using qualitative research approaches and this may include the collection of narratives (or stories) of personal experiences from children, their parents and other allies. Research participants may be willing—and even eager—to share these accounts, regarding their stories as important in understanding the lives of disabled children and their families, or hoping that sharing such narratives will assist the researcher in identifying aspects of public policy that need to be further explored or challenged. Some may choose to share a story with a researcher in preference to making their story public in other ways viewing this as a way of protecting the identity of their child(ren) and family, knowing researchers are bound by ethical codes that may not be respected by journalists, pressure groups, or others sharing similar concerns. Although the account is shared willingly, this does not mean researchers can also freely share these accounts, but rather that careful thought has to be given to the possible consequences for the child (and others) in determining how and where to use this data. In this chapter, I discuss some fundamental principles of research ethics, namely anonymity, confidentiality and informed consent, and consider how these principles apply in research with and about disabled children and young people and their families. This discussion becomes more pertinent in a world of social media where much of life is lived on the screen with scant regard to personal privacy and the potential consequences of sharing sensitive information with others. I draw attention to a number of problematic areas, suggesting possible strategies for addressing some dilemmas, but I also recognise some ethical dilemmas have no easy solutions—and some may be insoluble.

Underpinning this discussion are some of the dilemmas I faced during my postgraduate research studies. My research focused on why parents and others so often used words like 'fight' and 'struggle' in discussing their experience of parenting their disabled children and in accessing appropriate support. My interest in this area stemmed from my involvement with parent support groups in both physical and virtual (online) settings and my own journey of trying to understand and get support for my son. In recruiting participants for my research study I set clear boundaries, excluding people I knew through the parent support group I facilitated, even though I knew many of them had stories to tell that were pertinent to the research. I was aware that trying to be both a researcher and member of the group would be confusing for me and for others and group members might feel under some obligation to participate in the study if asked to do so. In addition, my existing relationship with group members meant that I already knew a great deal about their stories, the challenges they faced and other personal information. No matter how careful I was, there was a danger of blurring the boundary between what they chose to share in the context of a research interview and what I already knew—and a risk that I might ask questions in order to elicit the information I wanted to hear, rather than what they chose to share. A further issue was that all members of the group knew a lot about each other and no matter how hard I might try to disguise people's identities, they would still be recognisable to other group members. I, therefore, recruited research participants who were previously unknown to me but that did not mean the risk of participants being identifiable was totally removed as I will discuss later in this chapter.

In considering my research methodology, I was influenced by what I read about auto/ethnography and the power of personal accounts (Ellis and Bochner 2000). As I heard other parents talk about their experiences with their children, I was very aware that I also had a story to tell and that some of my experiences were relevant to my research. I began to give thought to how I might include elements of my story and recognised that my story was not only my story, but also my son's story, the two being intertwined. To tell my story would involve identifying my son and possibly sharing information that he might not want sharing. As I puzzled over whether or not to include our story, I found other parent-researchers had faced similar dilemmas (Murray 2010; Rogers 2003) and struggled with how they might include personal data in their research in an ethical way.

This chapter discusses the guidance available from the various codes of practice and ethical guidelines that underpin research practice and what other writers have written about issues of anonymity, confidentiality and informed consent in regard to disabled children and their families and others who might be considered vulnerable. I consider the changing positioning of children within research studies and the role of stories in enabling us all to better understand the lived experience of disabled children's childhoods and family life. I conclude with some questions to consider when undertaking research with disabled children, their families and allies.

Codes of Practice and Guidelines for Research

Ethical codes of practice can be traced to at least the fifth century BCE and the formulation of the Hippocratic Oath (Alderson 2014). The atrocities, purporting to be medical research, of the 1939–45 war led to a new interest in research ethics involving human subjects. Whereas previously some people were viewed as research subjects that could be experimented on in order to further scientific understanding, people began to be recognised as research participants and co-researchers with the right to be fully informed about the nature of the proposed research and the right to decide whether or not they wished to participate in research studies. Over time some researchers moved from laboratories to working with people in their everyday settings. Professionals who worked with people in health, education and care settings began to explore the possibilities of combining research within their existing roles. People began to recognise the importance of personal experiences and stories and different types of research studies began to be undertaken. Although researchers may argue among themselves about the relative worth of different research methodologies, what they agree about are fundamental ethical principles of doing no harm, respecting research participants and protecting their identities, maintaining confidentiality and ensuring that research participants understand their right not to participate in research and to withdraw from research at any time without giving a reason for their decision. These principles are embedded in the ethical principles and guidelines produced by professional and research bodies, such as the British Educational Research Association, the British Sociological Association, the British Psychological Society, the Nursing and Midwifery Council, the Social Research Association, and the Economic and Social Research Council. Although the wording and detail of different codes may vary, the underlying principles remain the same. In addition, research funders both in the United Kingdom and elsewhere require information about the ethical considerations underpinning research proposals and research carried out in academic and other institutions is subject to approval by ethics committees.

Although ethical guidelines are helpful, they remain guidelines. The task of the researcher is to use those guidelines as an aid to engaging in ethical practices. This is the case whether the researcher is employed by an academic or other research institution or is a parent or practitioner wanting to understand more about an issue they have observed in their everyday life or practice. It is in the application of ethical guidelines in practice that problems can arise. The codes of practice and guidelines focus on principles rather than on providing solutions. In the remainder of this chapter, I consider some of the problems that may arise when researching disabled children's childhoods and discuss various solutions that have been suggested by different authors and make some suggestions about possible ways forward, focusing on the imperative to value the voices of disabled children and young people and their families and allies.

Anonymity and Confidentiality and Informed Consent, Assent and Competence

Ethical guidelines lay emphasis on anonymity and confidentiality:

> The confidential and anonymous treatment of participants' data is considered the norm for the conduct of research. Researchers must recognize the participants' entitlement to privacy and must accord them their rights to confidentiality and anonymity… (BERA 2011, S.25, p. 7)

There can be a tendency to conflate anonymity and confidentiality, but as Saunders et al. (2015) discuss in their study involving "interviews with family members of people in 'vegetative' and minimally conscious states" (p. 616), anonymity is not synonymous with confidentiality. They argue that anonymity "is one form of confidentiality – that of keeping participants' identities a secret" (p. 617) and they go on to suggest that it is impossible to promise confidentiality without also being prepared to omit much data from a research study. Saunders et al. (2015, citing Van den Hoonaard 2003) further suggest that "guaranteeing complete anonymity to participants can be an unachievable goal in qualitative research" (p. 617), as the identity of participants is known to the researcher if not to others. They go on to propose that anonymity is better viewed as a continuum from fully anonymous to nearly identifiable, where "researchers balance two competing priorities: maximising protection of participants' identities and maintaining the value and integrity of the data" (p. 617).

Similar arguments are presented by Merrill and West (2009), Gabb (2010), Murray et al. (2011) and Page (2013), all of whom discuss whether it is possible to conceal an individual's identity from those who know them well. Some authors limit the amount of case study material used in presenting research findings (Gabb 2009, 2010) but others argue this is not a realistic option (Ellis 2007; Ellis and Bochner 2000; Hollway 2009; Hollway and Jefferson 2000, 2013; Murray 2010; Murray et al. 2011), especially when the researcher is also the researched. Some researchers, who have chosen to include accounts of their experiences with their own disabled children, recognise that their child will be identifiable simply because of the family relationship and possibly a shared family name (Rogers 2003, 2007; Thackray 2013). Other researchers who are also parents limit their discussion of anonymity (Truss 2008). It is perhaps worth noting that the quotation from the British Educational Research Association cited earlier goes on to say:

> ...unless they or their guardians or responsible others, specifically and willingly waive that right. In such circumstances it is in the researchers' interests to have such a waiver in writing. Conversely, researchers must also recognize participants' rights to be identified with any publication of their original works or other inputs, if they so wish. In some contexts it will be the expectation of participants to be so identified. (BERA 2011, S.25, p. 7)

Perhaps the main point researchers need to be aware of is that while we have a duty to protect the identity of participants, participants need to be made aware that absolute anonymity cannot be promised or guaranteed and that they may need to consider this when deciding whether or not to participate in a research study.

A further consideration for researchers to take into account is that some sampling methods can exacerbate the potential risk of lack of anonymity. Recruiting research participants using a 'snowball' approach, where existing research participants are invited to identify or invite other potential participants, is particularly vulnerable to the risk of participants identifying themselves and others in any published research findings, as is recruitment of participants within a limited geographic area or amongst a limited population.

Saunders et al. (2015) went to considerable lengths to hide the identities of their participants, including not only the use of pseudonyms for names and places, but sometimes using a second pseudonym in order that a participant who might be recognisable from one contribution might be hidden in another. Facts about participants were also hidden by limiting identifiers of religious and cultural background, describing occupations generically and disguising the nature of some family relationships where the sexuality of parents or the status of a child as a stepchild or adopted might enable identification. However, despite their best efforts, the researchers found some research participants resisted attempts to anonymise them, viewing the published research findings as a lasting memorial to their family member.

Whereas anonymity is to do with hiding or disguising the identities of research participants, confidentiality is concerned with how data is protected. Not only should researchers "ensure that data is kept securely and that the form of any publication, including publication on the Internet, does not directly or indirectly lead to a breach of agreed confidentiality and anonymity" (BERA 2011, S.28, p. 8), but they should comply with the requirements of data protection legislation and also with any institutional and funding body requirements. Research participants have a right to know what data is being held about them, how it is being stored and how it might be used. If research includes the gathering of people's personal stories, it is likely that researchers will have to decide what to do with information shared by participants about others; "depending on aspects of the life told, the person's identity (or that of members of their family, or others connected in their lives) could be revealed, albeit inadvertently" (Page 2013, p. 858).

Research with and about disabled children and young people can frequently include collecting stories and personal accounts of different experiences. Sometimes the child or young person may be relating their experience and sometimes parents or allies may be giving an account, but whoever is telling the story, there are almost certainly going to be some identifying features in the story that is told. Although these identifiers may mean little to many who hear the stories (perhaps in a conference or other presentation) or who read the published research findings, others may be able to identify the story teller, whether or not they have been given a pseudonym, and may be able to identify other people and places involved in the story. Research participants need to be made aware of this and to know that they have the right to withdraw from a research study if this is a concern for them, even though such a withdrawal may be frustrating for the researcher.

In some disciplines, medicine being the most notable, it has been common practice to publish 'interesting' case studies using pseudonyms for patients, without necessarily obtaining the consent of the patient for the publication. Similarly, the legal profession publishes accounts of trial proceedings and judges decisions, without hiding identities. These practices appear to be based on the premise that such publication develops and extends the professional knowledge base and, in the case of the legal profession, makes the court transcripts more accessible. However, underlying this practice is the assumption that the 'subjects' of such case studies are unlikely to encounter the published work. This appears to elevate the advancement of medical or legal knowledge, above the rights of the individual. As demonstrated in a recent presentation by Professor Tom Couser at Liverpool Hope University, there are problems with the argument that 'patient subjects' are unlikely to read what has been written about themselves. Given the ubiquity of the Internet and the tendency we all have to use search engines to discover more about things that concern us, it is perhaps probable rather than possible that a person with a rare condition might 'google' that condition and find material about themselves expressed in ways they would not wish to share. Such an individual, finding their story in print, may feel affronted and/or distressed when they discover elements of their life story are in the public domain, even when they have been given a pseudonym and personal information has been minimised.

Research guidelines also emphasise the requirement for research participants to consent to being involved in a research study—and that consent should include the participant knowing and understanding what they are consenting to and what that means for them. The BERA (2011) guidelines deal specifically with informed consent in respect to vulnerable participants:

> In the case of participants whose age, intellectual capability or other vulnerable circumstance may limit the extent to which they can be expected to understand or agree voluntarily to undertake their role, researchers must fully explore alternative ways in which they can be enabled to make authentic responses. In such circumstances, researchers must also seek the collaboration and approval of those who act in guardianship (e.g. parents) or as 'responsible others' (i.e. those who have responsibility for the welfare and well-being of the participants e.g. social workers). (S.18, pp. 6–7)

Such informed consent requires a child or young person to exhibit a level of competence, based on their understanding, intelligence and maturity (Cocks 2006), but focusing on competence can result in some children being excluded from childhood studies, or consent being sought from parents or other carers without the child being informed of the nature of the research or told of their right not to participate. Cocks (2006) goes on to describe assent:

> (which) is represented within the relationship between the researched and the researcher, by the trust within that relationship and acceptance of the researcher's presence. (p. 257)

Such assent requires the researcher to be constantly aware of the child's responses and be responsive to them. As with informed consent, assent is not given just at the beginning of a research study, but should be considered an ongoing process. If a research study involves multiple engagements with a child, or family, it is appropriate to clarify on each encounter that the child is still happy to continue with the research—and to be prepared to accept that sometimes a child will choose to withdraw their consent (Connors and Stalker 2007).

The question also arises as to whether consent may change over time—and even after a study is complete and findings are published. This may be a particular issue for parents who are also researchers. Like many parents,

I struggled to obtain appropriate educational and other support for my son. There were elements of that struggle that I consider of wider relevance as they concern public policy issues, some of which remain unresolved. Although my son was willing for me to include reference to this content in my PhD thesis, we have agreed that it is better for me not to use it in any other context. On a personal level, I find this difficult as I still consider there are questions of social justice to be addressed, but I also recognise my son's right to refuse permission for me to share his story further. Though this creates a tension as his story and experiences are intrinsically connected with my story and experiences. In recognising my son's rights, I also accept, there are parts of my own story and experience I am not free to share.

Perhaps one of the insoluble dilemmas we face as researchers is the need to think not only about the way our research may reflect on our research participants in the present, but also of how they may view our published work in the future. This is perhaps all the more relevant in a digital age when research is not only disseminated in journals and books, but also in various forms on the Internet. There is perhaps a particular burden on parent-researchers whose children may willingly participate in studies at some stages in their development, but may want their privacy protected at other times.

Children as Research Participants

The Nuremberg Code (1947) considered children "to be too immature to be able to consent…[and banned them]…from taking part in research projects" (Alderson 2014, p. 86). This did not prevent children from being the focus of research studies, but it was only as views of children and childhood have changed, influenced by the United Nations Convention on the Rights of the Child (UNCRC 1989), that it was recognised that children have a contribution to make not only as the subjects of research, but also as research participants and as co-researchers (Lundy et al. 2011; Pahl and Pool 2011). Current research guidelines, while stressing the underpinning principles of doing no harm and of doing good, discuss in particular the care that needs to be taken when including vulnerable people in research. Children are regarded as vulnerable both because of their relative physical weakness and because of lack of knowledge and experience when compared to adults and by their position in society which means they lack economic and political power (Lauwers and Van Hove 2010). Although the UNCRC has led to more regard being given to the voice of children, disabled children and young people are regarded as vulnerable not only because of their youth and social position but also because of their disability, disabled people being regarded as more vulnerable than others. This can result in disabled children and young people being given even less of a voice than other children and young people. This presents a particular challenge for those engaged in researching disabled children's childhoods. It is essential that the right of children to protection is not allowed to supersede their right to express themselves and their views. Unfortunately, the deficit view that all too often underpins decision-making about disabled children can result in an overemphasis on welfare and protection rather than a recognition of children's right to express their own views.

Like any other research participant, children require sufficient information about the proposed research, presented in a way they can understand, in order to decide whether or not to participate in a study (Lauwers and Van Hove 2010; McNeilly et al. 2015). This includes clarity about the right not to participate in a study and the right to withdraw from the research without explaining why. It is normal for parents to be asked to sign a consent form to permit their children to participate in research, but this lays a responsibility on the researcher to ensure that a child also gives their consent, not in order to comply with parental wishes, but freely by the child. Parental consent on its own does not indicate or imply a child has understood what is being asked of them, or that they have consented to participate in the study. In discussing assent, Cocks (2006) lays emphasis on the reflexivity of the researcher in being aware of how a child is responding to their presence and behaving in such a way that the child determines the nature of the relationship.

The question can arise as to when a child can give consent on their own behalf, rather than the parent consenting for them. This may be an issue if a child wishes to take part in a study, perhaps school based, which their parent does not consent to out of a desire to protect the child. Similarly some young people may feel it is inappropriate to have to ask for parental permission when this is unnecessary in other aspects of their life. At the same time, it should be recognised that chronological age may have little to do with a child or young person's competence or capacity to consent. Some young people choose to use their parents, or other allies, to speak on their behalf into their late teens and 20s and beyond, knowing that they are being accurately represented, while other young people are well able to represent themselves at a much earlier age.

While giving paramount importance to hearing the voice of the child, parental voices may be important in some studies. A parent may be able to provide valuable background and contextual information, some of which a child may not be aware of. In addition, providing a parent with an opportunity to relate to the researcher may increase their confidence in providing access to their child and can provide an opportunity to discuss any additional support the child might need as a result of participation in the study, especially if it has in some way proved distressing for the child. However, researchers need to be aware that parents who have become familiar with acting as advocate and representative for their children may also act as an obstacle to their child being permitted to express themself freely.

Telling Stories

When I tell my/my son's story, it is not fixed but fluid, changing according to the time and place and the elements most important to me at the time. The same story recounted by my son differs from my account as he too applies filters. The same is true of the accounts given by other children and young people and by their parents and allies when they engage with researchers. Although all life stories are filtered and partial accounts of a life lived (Page 2013; Riessman 2008; Stanley 1992), this does not mean such accounts are inaccurate or untrue (Sikes 2000; Sykes 1965), but simply that our personal stories are constantly reinvented and reviewed as our perspective and understanding changes (Meerwald 2013). Inevitably the account of a child or young person will differ from that of the parent as their perspective and understanding is different.

Researchers need to be aware that their own research focus and the questions they ask and how they ask them may also lead to the story being presented in a specific way. In her study of mothers returning to work, Page (2013) provided participants with copies of summaries of their interviews, including her own comments and interpretation of what had been said. One participant responded critically to this document, saying the summary "concentrated on negatives... [it does not give] a realistic view of my life...not an honest story of my life...I live well" (Page 2013, p. 863). In this case the participant was offered the opportunity to amend the summary, but chose not to do so as she understood why her story had been interpreted as it was and that it did reflect a point in time, while not telling the whole story. However, the point is well made that as researchers we need to be aware that we may tell the story we want told, rather than accurately representing our participants.

Depending on the research focus, hearing the different voices of parent and child may not only be desirable but essential, but not all parents find it easy to permit their children's voices to be heard. The parent may struggle with relinquishing their role as the child's interpreter and representative or may want to protect their child out of concern that the child or young person may "not have sufficient understanding or communication to take part, or they would be too anxious to interact with a researcher" (McNeilly et al. 2015, p. 270). For some professionals, including researchers, this can offer a convenient way of avoiding interaction with the disabled child or young person if the professional is concerned that they lack appropriate communication skills for the task in hand. But to exclude the child, or to only hear the child's voice through the parent as interpreter can effectively mean liminal voices remain unheard (McNeilly et al. 2015; Meerwald 2013).

Researchers may be concerned about listening to children's accounts where the child's views may be different from those of the adult proxy. In my research, exploring the concept of 'struggle' in the experience of parents and practitioners, I was conscious that children might have a different perspective on events from the adults I interviewed, but justified my decision not to interview children on the basis that "inviting their participation in a study such as this could in some cases exacerbate an already difficult family relationship or result in other problems" (Thackray 2013, p. 85). I have since questioned this decision, recognising that I gave more priority to family relationships than to "the imperative to listen to disabled children" (Curran and Runswick-Cole 2014, p. 1625). Sometimes there may be no easy answer to such dilemmas, but researchers do need to make their decisions explicit, including recognising how such decisions may limit the scope of their research.

Implications for Practice

In their discussion of the emergence of disabled children's childhood studies as a distinct discipline, Curran and Runswick-Cole (2014) lay particular emphasis on taking the voices of disabled children and young people very seriously. They do not underestimate the challenges inherent in this approach, but challenge the tendency to sideline disabled children and young people because of assumptions that the vulnerable disabled child requires protection and safeguarding. In my discussion of anonymity, confidentiality and informed consent, most of (if not all) the points I have made apply just as much to typically developing children and young people and adults as they do to disabled children and young people. In considering how these issues translate into practice, it is not that we do one thing when researching disabled children's childhoods and another with a different group of participants, but that we need to be cognisant of how the different elements of our practice and the decisions we make may impact on our research participants whoever they are. In particular, there is a need to be cognisant of the risk of viewing disabled children as cases, as in the medical 'case' approach discussed earlier in this chapter, or to view them from a deficit perspective as 'children in need' or 'vulnerable' rather than as children with voices and experiences that should be heard.

As already discussed, various strategies have been proposed for protecting the identities of research participants, especially when working with life stories and intimate personal experiences. These strategies all involve hiding elements of the stories we explore. Thus research may make use of fictionalisation, changing the way people or places are represented. Pseudonyms may not only be used for research participants and places included in the study, but for other people and places mentioned. Sometimes a participant might be given more than one pseudonym so as to make it more difficult to identify the source of what has been said. In some cases, the suggestion is made that not only should research participants be anonymised, but also researchers should use pseudonyms to hide their own identity in their work, even to the extent of perhaps of using a pseudonym when authoring published work (Murray et al. 2011). Though all these approaches may protect the identity of the participant, it is also possible that whatever precautions are taken, people close to the participant may recognise them and their story in what is written. Perhaps more to the point, research participants may have fewer concerns about their identity being hidden than researchers, especially when they have something to say that they view as important and worth sharing in order to encourage, inform or bring about change. It may be that participating in a research project is the only way some people can have their voice heard!

For me a more challenging question is what happens if a research participant changes their mind about sharing their stories and experiences, or finds their experiences have been shared without their knowledge by a parent or other ally? As I write this, I think of videos I have seen of young children engaging with assistive technologies and wonder how those children view those videos several years on. I think of some of the accounts in my thesis of the behaviours of children on the autistic spectrum and wonder how those children would read those accounts as teenagers or young adults. I think of my son who was prepared to share some parts of his story in some contexts, but not in others. While I would argue these stories assist us all in understanding the lives of disabled children and young people, I also wonder whether it should continue to be possible in some way to withdraw from a research study even after the research has been published. This means that it is not only essential to act ethically in the here and now, but also to consider the implications of what we write and present for our research participants in the future.

References

Alderson, P. (2014). Ethics. In A. Clark, R. Flewitt, M. Hammersley, & M. Robb (Eds.), *Understanding Research with Children and Young People*. London: Sage.

BERA. (2011). *Ethical Guidelines for Educational Research*. London: British Educational Research Association.

Cocks, A. J. (2006). The Ethical Maze: Finding an Inclusive Path Towards Gaining Children's Agreement to Research Participation. *Childhood, 13*(2), 247–266.

Connors, C., & Stalker, K. (2007). Children's Experiences of Disability: Pointers to a Social Model of Childhood Disability. *Disability & Society, 22*(1), 19–33.

Curran, T., & Runswick-Cole, K. (2014). Disabled Children's Childhood Studies: A Distinct Approach? *Disability & Society, 29*(10), 1617–1630.

Ellis, C. (2007). Telling Secrets, Revealing Lives: Relational Ethics in Research with Intimate Others. *Qualitative Inquiry, 13*(1), 3–29.

Ellis, C., & Bochner, A. P. (2000). Autoethnography, Personal Narrative, Reflexivity: Researcher as Subject. In N. K. Denzin & Y. S. Lincoln (Eds.), *Handbook of Qualitative Research* (2nd ed., pp. 733–768). Thousand Oaks: Sage.

Gabb, J. (2009). Researching Family Relationships: A Qualitative Mixed Methods Approach. *Methodological Innovations Online, 4*(2), 37–52.

Gabb, J. (2010). Home Truths: Ethical Issues in Family Research. *Qualitative Research, 10*(4), 461–478.

Hollway, W. (2009). Applying the 'Experience-near' Principle to Research: Psychoanalytically Informed Methods. *Journal of Social Work Practice, 23*(4), 461–474.

Hollway, W., & Jefferson, T. (2000). Biography, Anxiety and the Experience of Locality. In P. Chamberlayne, J. Bornat, & T. Wengraf (Eds.), *The Turn to Biographical Methods in Social Science* (pp. 167–180). London: Routledge.

Hollway, W., & Jefferson, T. (2013). *Doing Qualitative Research Differently: A Psychosocial Approach* (2nd ed.). London: Sage.

Lauwers, H., & Van Hove, G. (2010). Supporting the Participation Rights of Children in a Sensitive Research Project: The Case of Young Road Traffic Victims. *The International Journal of Children's Rights, 18*(3), 335–354.

Lundy, L., McEvoy, L., & Byrne, B. (2011). Working with Young Children as Co-Researchers: An Approach Informed by the United Nations Convention on the Rights of the Child. *Early Education and Development, 22*(5), 714–736.

McNeilly, P., Macdonald, G., & Kelly, B. (2015). The Participation of Disabled Children and Young People: A Social Justice Perspective. *Child Care in Practice, 21*(3), 266–286.

Meerwald, A. M. L. (2013). Researcher | Researched: Repositioning Research Paradigms. *Higher Education Research and Development, 32*(1), 43–55.

Merrill, B., & West, L. (2009). *Using Biographical Methods in Social Research*. London: Sage.

Murray, B. L. (2010). *Secrets of Mothering.* PhD unpublished, University of Saskatchewan, Saskatoon.

Murray, L., Pushor, D., & Renihan, P. (2011). Reflections on the Ethics-Approval Process. *Qualitative Inquiry, 18*(1), 43–54.

Nuremberg Code. (1947). Directives for Human Experimentation. http://ori.hhs.gov/ori-introduction-responsible-conduct-research. Accessed 31 Aug 2015.

Page, J. M. (2013). Childcare Choices and Voices: Using Interpreted Narratives and Thematic Meaning-Making to Analyse Mothers' Life Histories. *International Journal of Qualitative Studies in Education, 27*(7), 850–876.

Pahl, K., & Pool, S. (2011). Living Your Life Because it's the Only Life You've Got. *Qualitative Research Journal, 11*(2), 17–37.

Riessman, C. K. (2008). *Narrative Methods for the Human Sciences.* London: Sage.

Rogers, C. (2003). The Mother/Researcher in Blurred Boundaries of a Reflexive Research Process. *Auto/Biography, 11*(1&2), 47–54.

Rogers, C. (2007). Experiencing an "Inclusive" Education: Parents and Their Children with "Special Educational Needs". *British Journal of Sociology of Education, 28*(1), 55–68.

Saunders, B., Kitzinger, J., & Kitzinger, C. (2015). Anonymising Interview Data: Challenges and Compromise in Practice. *Qualitative Research, 15*(5), 616–632.

Sikes, P. (2000). Truth and Lies Revisited. *British Educational Research Journal, 26*(2), 257–270.

Stanley, L. (1992). *The Auto/Biographical I.* Manchester: Manchester University Press.

Sykes, A. J. M. (1965). Myth and Attitude Change. *Human Relations, 18*(4), 323–337.

Thackray, L. (2013). *The Meanings of the 'Struggle/Fight Metaphor' in the Special Needs Domain: The Experiences of Practitioners and Parents of Children with High Functioning Autism Spectrum Conditions,* PhD unpublished, University of Sussex. Retrieved from http://sro.sussex.ac.uk/47168/

Truss, C. (2008). Peter's Story: Reconceptualising the UK SEN System. *European Journal of Special Needs Education, 23*(4), 365–377.

UNCRC. (1989). The United Nations Convention on the Rights of the Child. http://www.unicef.org.uk/UNICEFs-Work/UN-Convention/. Accessed 31 Aug 2015.

Liz Thackray is the mother of a young man with Asperger's Syndrome and Specific Learning Difficulties. As an Open University Associate Lecturer, she supports students studying modules focusing on issues of equality, participation and inclusion and research issues with children and young people. Her postgraduate research focused on the struggle/fight metaphor as used by parents of children with high-functioning autism.

Supporting Families in Raising Disabled Children to Enhance African Child Development

Judith McKenzie and Tsitsi Chataika

Key Points

- Most African families with disabled children in Africa lack support in raising their disabled children.
- An unsupportive environment makes it very difficult for families to foster the development of their disabled family member.
- African child development systems have the potential of supporting disabled children and their families.
- Such systems are based on the philosophy that it takes the whole village to raise a child.
- There is need for the support of disability organisations as well as inclusion in community groups and self-advocacy of disabled children.

Introduction

Africa is home to a large population of disabled children resulting from poverty, lack of adequate healthcare services and uncleared landmines over and above other causes of impairments evident in the global North. However,

J. McKenzie (✉)
University of Cape Town, Cape Town, South Africa

T. Chataika
University of Zimbabwe, Harare, Zimbabwe

© The Author(s) 2018
K. Runswick-Cole et al. (eds.), *The Palgrave Handbook of Disabled Children's Childhood Studies*, https://doi.org/10.1057/978-1-137-54446-9_21

establishing accurate statistical estimates on the prevalence of these impairments in Africa remains a huge challenge (ACPF 2014; WHO and World
Bank 2011). Furthermore, data and statistics on disabled children in Africa
are not credible and are inappropriately disaggregated, such that they inac-
curately capture the number of disabled children and their needs (ACPF
2014). The majority of these children and their families face massive social,
economic, educational and political barriers that have adverse impacts on
their physical, social, emotional and intellectual development and well-being
(WHO and World Bank 2011). Consequently, the strengths and abilities of
disabled children are invisible, their potential is consistently underestimated
and inadequate resources are allocated to social services for meaningful inclusion of disabled children.

In an exploration of an African childhood disability studies, Chataika
and McKenzie (2013) reflected on possible dis/connections with the
Northern context of childhood disability studies. A major feature of the
Southern context is the lack of support to families in raising their disabled
children, a lack that is exacerbated in times of forced migration or poverty.
In such circumstances, disability becomes almost exclusively a family
responsibility which is lived as a family (Grech 2013). This gives rise then
to the notion of a 'disability family', that is, a family in which disability is
an influence on the configuration and relationships within the family and
between the family and the community. We view the family as a set of relationships and contrast this with a perspective of competing rights of the
child and family, which is more closely akin to a human rights understanding of disability.

The disconnect with the global North, we believe, has its roots in a particular
understanding of the nature of disability which is only recently being critiqued
by scholars from the global South (Kalyanpur 2014; Meekosha 2008). The
discipline of Disability Studies has been highly influenced by the early historical
materialist approaches of activists such as Oliver (1996) and Abberley (1987),
who rejected the notion of disability as an issue of individual tragedy and fig-
ured it as one of oppression. The social model of disability, where barriers are
identified in the environment rather than within the person with impairment,
became a tool for liberation. Subsequently, the social model has become inextricably linked with a human rights based approach (HRBA) as enshrined in the
United Nations Convention on the Rights of Persons with Disabilities (WHO
and World Bank 2011). The HRBA brings with it strong advocacy for increased
autonomy and agency of disabled people and constructs the individual with the
disability as one who has the power to function independently if provided with

the appropriate supports. These supports may be human resources, assistive devices or environmental modifications amongst others (Barnes 1990).

The reality is that disability is disproportionately related to poverty, and supports are woefully lacking in poorly resourced settings (Palmer 2011). Consequently, it falls to the family and all its extended and different cultural structures to meet the needs of their disabled family members. Whilst family responsibility for care has been encouraged by neoliberal policy makers as a desirable alternative to welfare, the disability rights movement of the global North has criticised family support as yet another instance of paternalism (Mladenov 2015). Thus, the family structures that provide care find themselves unsupported by the state, critiqued by the disability rights movement and yet, holding all the responsibility for care. This is especially true for families who have family members with intellectual impairment, which is by definition an impairment that entails lifelong 'inevitable dependency' (Kittay et al. 2005:445), albeit of differing degrees, relative to the severity of the impairment and the availability of appropriate services. Casale (2015) in a study on community support for HIV/AIDS notes that:

> We have not paid near enough attention to the value of informal family and community networks for health, both in terms of their current role in promoting and protecting (mental and physical) health in resource-scarce contexts and in terms of their potential role in facilitating health service access and uptake (p. 22).

While often families show great resilience and ingenuity in dealing with issues of care and participation, it is also true that there are many cases where they are overburdened by care responsibilities, resulting in a situation where neither the family caregivers nor the disabled family members are able to flourish (McKenzie and McConkey 2016). This chapter aims to explore the parameters of successful care and participation of disabled children through theorising within a feminist ethics of care framework in an African child development context.

Disability Families in the African Context

As noted above, the family is of critical importance for understanding disability in an African context. The strength of the family bond extends beyond the parents and siblings and includes a complex set of relationships with the extended family and into the community in the form of informal organisations and associations (Casale 2015). In the face of often difficult circumstances, families support one another and share resources in such a way as to preserve the members of the family unit.

The close-knit family described above is changing, however, as urbanisation and Western education become more prevalent. In the South African context, for instance, traditional notions of the nuclear family are becoming less and less relevant. This is partly a result of urban men and women being less inclined to marry, thereby restricting the bonds between families that are associated with traditional forms of marriage and asserting a more individualistic and independent stance (Moore and Govender 2013). Grinding poverty experienced in current Zimbabwe has instituted massive migrations, which entirely disrupt family life (Tarusarira 2016). Also, conflict across the continent has forced families to migrate or to make other changes in order to survive. It is also true that climate change across the continent continues to reduce the possibility for agrarian activity and to drive a process of urbanisation (Barrios et al. 2006).

Chataika (2013) argues that, despite the emergence of the social model of disability and the right-based approach to disability, culture and religion still occupy a place in understanding disability in Africa. We recognise that it would not be helpful to homogenise the experiences of families with a disabled child in an African context. This could pose the danger of stereotyping and preserving colonial tropes of primitive beliefs about disability and disease. On the other hand, however, there is a danger in not interrogating African themes as they preserve the hold of the global North on discourse around disability. We therefore consider some cultural beliefs that maintain a strong hold in certain communities that may impact upon the successful participation of disabled children and therefore deserve consideration within disabled children's childhood studies.

Misconceptions about the causes of various forms of impairments are rooted in religious and cultural beliefs and traditions. The most frequently stated causes of having a disabled child in Africa include witchcraft, a curse or punishment from God, anger of ancestral spirits, bad omens, reincarnation, heredity, incestuous relationships and the misdemeanours of the mother (ACPF 2014; Chataika 2013). Apart from stigma, these misperceptions result in the demonisation of disabled children. As a result, children may be lashed in attempts to drive out 'evil spirits' causing the disability or may be neglected or even killed. Negative attitudes about disabled children within communities are reinforced at the household level and parents themselves often contribute to these children becoming invisible, virtually hidden from society (ACPF 2014). In some East African countries, many disabled children are abandoned by their parents, are not entitled to a clan name or are not allowed to inherit land (Terre des Hommes Nederland 2007). The continued adherence to traditional beliefs that apportion blame for disability seeks to appease the wrong done in the hope of cure.

On the other hand, the firm entrenchment of Christian values and increasing modernisation that is evident in many African cultures underpin a move towards a different understanding of causes and cures for disability, housed more within charitable and medical understandings of disability (Chataika 2013). In most African countries, addressing disability is often viewed as a matter of charity, with religious institutions or other organisations deemed appropriate to provide food or clothes for disabled children.

Nonetheless, there are also a number of positive cultural values and practices that enable disabled children to be included within their communities and cared for and protected from ostracism in Africa. These practices represent potential opportunities for policies and programmes, which can reinforce them to promote family-based and community-based protection of disabled children (ACPF 2014). For example, Greeff and Loubser (2008) reported that in the Xhosa-speaking families in the Western Cape in South Africa, family and family love are seen as gifts from God. Thus, parents and caregivers often express the importance of 'love' to their children, including those with disabilities. In the Tonga community of Zimbabwe, parents have no problem accepting a child with a disability and there is no evidence of Tonga families hiding their disabled children (Muderedzi and Ingstad 2011). The Zulu Ubuntu concept emphasises that *Umuntu ngumuntu ngabantu*, which literally means that 'a person is a person through other people'. Thus, Ubuntu is a concept that upholds common humanity and oneness, hence places an obligation on individuals to acknowledge the essential humanness of others (Louw 2006), including those with disabilities. The Ga tribes of the Accra region in Ghana treat people with intellectual impairment with respect because they believe that they are the reincarnation of a deity. Hence, they are always treated with great kindness, gentleness and patience (ACPF 2014).

Drawing from literature from the global North, it is apparent that in the context of raising a child with a disability, some studies established that parents with greater social support show more positive parenting behaviours (Ceballo and McLoyd 2002) and lower levels of parenting stress (Smith et al. 2001). One study showed that the presence of close social relationships helps parents cope with the stress of raising a disabled child (Knussen and Sloper 1992). Rauktis et al. (1995) examined the moderating effects of both positive and negative social interactions among caregivers of mentally ill family members. They found that negative interactions had a significant impact on caregivers' distress and depression and that the relationship between caregiving demand and stress was exacerbated when the caregiver had greater negative interactions. However, they did not find a significant buffering effect of positive interactions.

We build on prior literature by examining the context of African child development and applying this to the disabled child growing up in an African context. We believe that this chapter may assist both the affected individuals and professionals who work with parents to better understand the experiences of parenting a child with a disability from an African perspective.

African Child Development

We agree with Nsamenang (2006) that views on child development usually mirror mainstream Euro-American ethnocentrism and are presented as homogeneous or, rather, applicable to all of human diversity. Similarly, Burman (2008) argues that child development theories and practices do not often address the position of particular children in specific cultural and historical contexts as they are usually informed by Northern models and agendas. In contrast, an African worldview places social maturation at the centre stage of development, where children are assigned stage-appropriate developmental tasks (Nsamenang 2006). Thus, knowledge is not separated into discrete disciplines but is intertwined into a common embroidery, which is learnt by children at different developmental stages through the participation in the cultural and economic life of the family and society. Consequently, children are socialised into diverse ethno-cultural realities as co-participants in social and cultural life. Thus, child development is partly determined by the social ecology in which the development occurs and by how the child learns and develops.

We interpret African child development as the acquisition and growth of the physical, cognitive, social and emotional competencies required to engage fully in family and society (Nsamenang 2005). Thus, this type of development is transformation in the individual brought about by participation in cultural activities—implying a process of gradual and systematic social integration (Rogoff 2003). This conceptualisation of human growth 'differs in theoretical focus from the more individualistic accounts proposed by Freud, Erikson and Piaget' (Serpell 1994:18). As children are initiated into and actively engage in cultural life, they progressively and systematically assume particular levels of personhood, identity and being. This is where an individual comes to a sense of self and personal identity in search of individuality. However, within the African worldview, the sense of self cannot be achieved without reference to the community of others in terms of being interconnected and enacting one's social roles (Nsamenang 2005). Thus, the social maturation paradigm has its foundation in the concept of interdependence. Here, the concept of Ubuntu comes into play—thus, an individual is what he/she is because of other people (Louw 2006).

As African children grow, they are gradually assigned different roles according to the perception of their social maturity or competence. For African parents, social cognition translates into responsible intelligence, not in abstraction but primarily as it enhances the attainment of social ends (Nsamenang 2003). Consequently, in African family traditions:

> Socialization is not organized to train children for academic pursuits or to become individuals outside the ancestral culture. Rather, it is organized to teach social competence and shared responsibility within the family system and the ethnic community (Nsamenang and Lamb 1994:137).

Newborns in Central, East, Southern and West Africa are treated as 'precious treasures', nurtured and enjoyed by the whole family (Chataika 2007; Harkness and Super 1992). Although Westernisation seems to be eroding these child-rearing patterns, African attitudes to shared childcare, even under extreme poverty, remain positive (Pence and Nsamenang 2008). It is from the caring and generative role of the family that children begin to learn about moral life, participative skills, social values and ways of the world. The sense of community and spirit of mutuality make childcare a social enterprise in which caregiving functions are shared with others, including parents, relations, friends, neighbours and older siblings (Nsamenang 2004). Even in present-day Zimbabwe and South Africa, we have experienced older siblings, relatives or neighbours providing care to infants and pre-school children when their mothers are busy with house chores, working in the fields or have travelled elsewhere or have gone to undertake paid work.

It is also important to note that the concept of 'child labour' has little latitude in Africa as children are introduced to various household chores early as part of social maturation and not as a form of abuse. To train responsibility, parents and caregivers allocate chores to children or send them on neighbourhood errands (Ogunaike and Houser 2002). The 'work' children do socialises cognition, values and productive skills. It also generates knowledge and eases social integration. Some parents use evidence that a child has ability to give and receive social support and attend to the needs of others, as markers of mental and general developmental level (Weisner 1987).

In Zimbabwe, for instance, adults keep some mental tally of the proportion of errands that a given child performs adequately, and this serves as an index of at what level of *kutumika* [the child's ability to obey when sent to do some errands] the child is. This attribute is used to choose which child to send on another such errand (Serpell 1993). Episodes of a child's accurate enactment of roles feed into a history of that child's social competence and their responsible intelligence. In traditional Africa, the peer group plays a pivotal role in the development of this genre of cognition because, from toddlerhood, the child comes more under the purview of the peer culture than of the adult world. Thus, understanding the social cognition and intelligent behaviour of African children lies in capturing shared routines and participatory learning (social responsibility) rather than in completing school-based instruments. Thus, the evaluative criterion with which typical African parents determine child development and/or intelligent behaviour is social responsibility (Pence and Nsamenang 2008; Nsamenang 2004). It is against this background of African childhood development that we discuss disability families.

Disability Family Responsibilities

Kittay (1999), following the work of Sarah Ruddick, describes the responsibility of mothering as having three components: (a) child development, which concerns the need to ensure that the child learns the skills that are needed to succeed in their society, (b) child preservation, which relates to the role of mothers in providing healthcare, safety and nutrition, and (c) child acceptance, which is particularly relevant to disabled children since stigma often militates against a full acceptance of the disabled child in their community. Although these are referred to as mothering responsibilities, within a feminist ethics of care, these tasks do not have to be seen as gendered but rather the provision of all these forms of care needs to be agreed upon such that the individual receives the appropriate care package he or she requires. The carer's needs also have to be addressed so that he or she takes up the caring role without undue burden (Kittay et al. 2005). If we apply these notions within an African context, it might help us to understand what the experiences of a disabled child might be.

The first consideration in translation to the African context would be to acknowledge the role of an extended childcare system where the biological mother may experience greater degrees of shared childcare. It is apparent that where the child has an impairment, shared childcare becomes less available and the role of the mother changes to more individualised caregiving (De Sas Kropiwnicki et al. 2014). It is also worth noting the frequency with which fathers abdicate responsibility for their disabled child based on notions of punishment and shame related to the mother's behaviour (Gara 2007).

The component of development would relate to the extent to which the child is able and permitted to participate socially and gain in social responsibility. As we have noted above, it is by this measure that development is judged appropriate. In an African context, the preservative role is shared in a wider community, but poverty, migration and other environmental threats put a strain on the ability of communities to exercise this preservative function. The consequences of stigma in Africa, as in the global North, militate against acceptance. A lack of acceptance is potentially even more dire in an African context when development itself is contingent upon the disabled child being able to participate in order to acquire the social maturation necessary for success within the community.

One of the most difficult things for families of disabled children is dealing with the stigma that is attached as indicated by a West African disability activist who was quoted in *Times Live* on 2 December 2015:

> Children with disabilities in West Africa are often hidden at home or sent to beg in the streets by parents who deem them cursed, worthless and incapable of succeeding at school. This exclusion leaves disabled children at even greater risk of abuse and violence – some are raped, killed by their parents or even ritually sacrificed by secret societies.

A hostile environment makes it very difficult for families to foster the development of their disabled family member. The large majority of caregivers in South Africa and globally are women (Casale 2015). This role is increased in the context of disability where the issue of stigma often results in men leaving the mother of their disabled child to raise him or her as a single parent. Abandoned by the father of her child and isolated by stigma, this relationship between mother and the disabled child can become intensely close and protective, aimed at preservation rather than focusing on child development (McKenzie 2016). The closeness of this relationship is expressed in terms of the child being a 'gift from God'. This is informed by some Christian beliefs that God loves some people such that He finds it befitting to give them 'a special task to fulfil' (Chataika 2013:123). The focus of care here is on nutrition, healthcare and protection.

In facilitating acceptance for their disabled family member, families are called upon to make the world out there a better place for their child. This is a strategy adopted by many families as they strive to make sense of disability in their family. The development of support groups has been widely documented in the African setting as parents (once again, mainly mothers) draw strength from each other, given the isolation they may experience from the community (Aldersey 2012; Hartley et al. 2005). Parents may use such support groups to develop an activist stance that promotes the rights of their disabled child (Watermeyer and McKenzie 2014). However, we argue that in order to fulfil the three aspects of nurturing care of the disabled child, parents and families need to have their own support and care needs met. One element of this is to provide early intervention that supports families. Here, we argue that the family is the primary influence on the growth and development of a young child. Early childhood intervention recognises the centrality of the family and supports the child's relationships with parents and other primary caregivers, which include grandmothers, aunties, siblings and others.

Early Intervention Support for Families of Disabled Children

Every child, regardless of their needs, has the right to participate fully in their community and to have the same choices, opportunities and experiences as other children. Additional supports may be provided to disabled children and their families to help them participate in an inclusive society that enables them to fulfil their potential.

Research evidence shows that providing support early is linked with improved child development for disabled children, particularly when support is provided in the child's natural environment in order to promote social maturation (UNICEF 2013). Parents can be supported to enable their children's development through rehabilitation and educational services, and early intervention is needed to ensure that children do not lag behind in social maturation. Thus, families need to understand what the impairment entails and the skills that a child needs to learn to promote their personal development as well as enabling them to contribute to the family. Community-based early intervention offered by community-based workers can be very helpful here.

Equipped with limited or no knowledge of bringing up a disabled child, it becomes very difficult to nurture the health and safety of their disabled child, more so when families are living in poverty. It is here that the opposition of

the needs and rights of the child from those of the family can be really problematic. For example, in South Africa, families may receive a care dependency
grant for their disabled child. However, this money cannot only be spent on
the disabled child but must also support other family members (Chataika and
Mckenzie 2013). This sharing amongst the family is a practice that is often
frowned upon by disability professionals who feel that the child is not getting
what is his or her due.

Early intervention becomes necessary to ensure that parents of disabled
children get the relevant support to enhance child development, instead of
them spending much time asking themselves about the question 'why me?' as
well as looking only for support of 'getting rid of the impairment'. To support
such families in advocacy, they need to empower themselves to speak on
behalf of their disabled children. This requires the support of disability organisations as well as inclusion in community groups. Furthermore, there needs
to be self-advocacy by disabled children themselves as well.

The narrow focus on parents as mother and father sharing joint care responsibilities also becomes inappropriate. As pointed out earlier, it is usually mothers that are responsible for the care and most families do not live in a nuclear
family unit. Grandmothers are a significant part of care and yet their role is
often not properly understood. Siblings and cousins are a huge resource for
social inclusion. In a study where disabled adults recalled their childhood in a
rural area of South Africa, several of them referred to the importance of an
aunt or a sibling in promoting their independence and exerting some tough
love in contrast to the protectiveness of their mothers (McKenzie 2013).

It becomes crucial to engage other family members in positive interactions
with parents of disabled children. Ha et al. (2010) reported that providing
information to the family members about the children's impairment and the
needs of the parents who are caring for these children can enrich the family
functioning and facilitate the exchange of support. Their argument was that if
there are positive social interactions within nuclear and extended family members, the stress of having a child with a disability is significantly reduced.

The above findings tally with the Ubuntu philosophy, which we have discussed earlier. It is evident that communities and social connectedness are
important in Africa. This is illustrated by the widespread presence of informal
organisations and associations (such as savings clubs, religious associations
and community support groups) among many poor and displaced Southern
African populations, embodied in the 'notions of universal human interdependence, solidarity and communalism', which 'underlie virtually every
indigenous African culture' (Casale 2015:22).

Women who are raising children on their own may become isolated due to the time that it takes and not being able to get out of the house. They are also likely to be poorer than others. The connection between women in friendship can be a great source of support for families with disabled children. Where these women share the need to care for a disabled child, such contacts can develop into a support group, either formally or informally. In the Southern African settings, for instance, religious groups are ever present and an important source of support and hope. Many family carers are convinced that it is their belief in God, where their greatest support lies (McKenzie and McConkey 2016). Faith-based communities have a role to play in supporting families, not only with charitable support but also in providing inclusive spaces where positive attitudes to disability can be modelled and stigma overcome.

State services also have to act as a support to families. A narrow focus in rehabilitation of the child within health services needs to be reconstructed so that the well-being of the child is seen to be intimately related to the well-being of the carers. Social services can provide support to families such that it keeps them together and united with their disabled child. Perhaps, most important for disabled children is access to education. The number of Disabled children who attend school in Southern Africa are extremely low (less than 10%), and this inhibits both their social inclusion and opportunities for economic inclusion (ACPF 2014). The implication is that people with disabilities are less likely than their nondisabled peers to be literate and often have very little or no education. Regrettably, many parents, teachers, school administrators and policymakers have the false perception that disabled children cannot be educated.

Given the daunting task that families face in developing, nurturing and advocating for their disabled family member, what happens to the voice of the disabled child as a distinct and unique individual? This is a recurrent concern of childhood studies (James 2010). Somehow, these caring practices of families enhance the life of disabled children in themselves, but at what point do children's own choices and contributions become significant? We would like to suggest that role models of successful disabled adults can be a force for empowerment. Where disabled children do not see or meet anyone like themselves, their dreams and hopes might be restricted. Therefore, the issue at stake here is that while parents and their families need to be empowered, disabled children should also be in a position to define their destiny, hence the need for their participation in order to realise meaningful child development.

Key issues arising in attempting to support families of disabled children are the adoption of three concepts, namely family-centred care, family support services and family empowerment (California Department of Developmental Services [CDDS] 2012). Here, family-centred care, according to CDDS (2012), implies a philosophy and approach to service delivery where services are targeted at the family. Family support services mean specific services for families that enhance their child's development. Family empowerment is the concept that families are supported and given the opportunity to participate as full partners. Thus, a family-centred approach builds family confidence and the capacity to participate in all stages of their child's care, from evaluation and implementation to transition to other service systems. Ensuring a family has access to resources and leadership-building activities means the family has the tools they need for success in supporting the development of a child with a disability. Informing families of their rights, facilitating their participation in the decision-making process and supporting active participation in the delivery of early intervention services empower families to be active in enhancing their child's development (CDDS 2012).

We are convinced that these three concepts are critical to understanding how best to serve young children and their families, and if operationalised in daily practice, they are most likely to provide more effective early intervention services to disabled children and their families. We believe that if applied properly and consistently, these can create effective change in the way society conceptualises disability, as well as improving in services provided in various African countries and beyond, resulting in more positive outcomes for disabled children and their families.

We appraise that when parents are approached as the primary agent of change in their child's life, the dynamic is changed from the professional 'fixing' of the child to the parents' capacity to anticipate and meet the needs of their child. This change strengthens both self-esteem and resilience. Our argument is that, while we are profiling aspects that empower families, it is also important to ensure that professionals be oriented to ways that view families as equal partners, who also have a stake in the lives of their children.

While dealing with parents, one has to acknowledge one's cultural and religious beliefs, rituals, customs and practices (Chataika 2013). The reason is that culture is a social practice that is a mirror through which one views the world and makes sense of it, eventually influencing actions and relationships. Similarly, religion also shapes one's belief systems and practices (Kisanji 1995). Therefore, it is imperative to establish those cultural and religious elements that embrace diversity, with the view of capitalising on them when bringing up a disabled child.

Conclusion

We have argued in this chapter that disabled children cannot be seen as distinct from their families, especially in situations of poverty. Indeed, we have gone so far as to say that it is a disservice to these children and their families to separate their needs. Thus, we have discussed at some length how we understand African child development and the roles that families with disabled children must take on, as well as the supports they need to fulfil these roles. It is our belief that to continue making families invisible will be detrimental to the growth and development of disabled children within these families, especially if African child development values are to be fostered.

References

Abberley, P. (1987). The Concept of Oppression and The Development of Social Theory of Disability. *Disability, Handicap and Society, 2*, 5–19.

ACPF. (2014). *The African Report on Children with Disabilities: Promising Starts and Persisting Challenges*. Addis Ababa. The African Child Policy Forum (ACPF).

Aldersey, H. M. (2012). Family Perceptions of Intellectual Disability: Understanding and Support in Dar es Salaam. *African Journal of Disability, 1*(1). doi:10.4102/ajod.v1i1.32.

Barnes, C. (1990). *"Cabbage Syndrome": The Social Construction of Dependence*. London: Falmer Press.

Barrios, S., Bertinelli, L., & Strobl, E. (2006). Climatic Change and Rural–Urban Migration: The Case of Sub-Saharan Africa. *Journal of Urban Economics, 60*(3), 357–371.

Burman, E. (2008). *Developments: Child, Image, Nation*. New York: Routledge.

California Department of Developmental Services. (2012). Effective Practice in Providing Family Support: Making It Real for Families of Infants and Toddlers with Disabilities. Retrieved from: http://www.dds.ca.gov/EarlyStart/docs/17739_EffectivePractice_FamilySupport_final100212.pdf. Accessed 17 Dec 2015.

Casale, M. (2015). The Importance of Family and Community Support for the Health of HIV-Affected Populations in Southern Africa: What Do We Know and Where to From Here? *British Journal of Health Psychology, 20*(1), 21–35. doi:10.1111/bjhp.12127.

Ceballo, R., & McLoyd, V. C. (2002). Social Support and Parenting in Poor, Dangerous Neighborhoods. *Child Development, 73*(4), 1310–1321.

Chataika, T. (2007). *Inclusion of Disabled Students in Higher Education in Zimbabwe: From Idealism to Reality-a Social Ecosystem Perspective* (Doctoral Dissertation, University of Sheffield).

Chataika, T. (2013). Cultural and Religious Explanations of Disability and Promoting Inclusive Communities. In J. M. Claassen, L. Swartz, & L. Hansen (Eds.), *Search for Dignity: Conversations on Human Dignity, Theology and Disability* (pp. 117–128). Cape Town: African Sun Media (Stellenbosch University). ISBN 978-1-919985-47-3.

Chataika, T., & McKenzie, J. (2013). Considerations of an African Childhood Disability Studies. In K. Runswick-Cole & T. Curran (Eds.), *Disabled Children's Childhood Studies: Critical Approaches in a Global Context* (pp. 152–163). New York: Palgrave Macmillan.

De Sas Kropiwnicki, Z. O., Elphick, J., & Elphick, R. (2014). Standing by Themselves: Caregivers' Strategies to Ensure the Right to Education for Children with Disabilities in Orange Farm, South Africa. *Childhood, 21*(3), 354–368. doi:10.1177/0907568214526263.

Gara, N. (2007). Effects of Caring on Mothers of Intellectually Disabled Children in Alice, Eastern Cape, South Africa. (M Phil, School of Health and Rehabilitation Sciences, Faculty of Health).

Grech, S. (2013). Disability, Childhood and Poverty: Critical Perspectives on Guatemala. In K. Runswick-Cole & T. Curran (Eds.), *Disabled Children's Childhood Studies: Critical Approaches in a Global Context* (pp. 89–104). Basingstoke: Palgrave Macmillan.

Greeff, A. P., & Loubser, K. (2008). Spirituality as a Resiliency Quality in Xhosa-Speaking Families in South Africa. *Journal of Religion and Health, 47*(3), 288–301.

Ha, J., Greenberg, J. S., & Seltzer, M. M. (2010). Parenting a Child with a Disability: The Role of Social Support for African American Parents. *Families in Society, 92*(4), 405–411.

Harkness, S., & Super, C. M. (1992). Parental Ethnotheories in Action. In I. Sigel, A. V. McGillicuddy-DeLisi, & J. Goodnow (Eds.), *Parental Belief Systems: The Psychological Consequences for Children* (2nd ed., pp. 373–392). Hillsdale: Erlbaum.

Hartley, S., Ojwang, P., Baguwemu, A., Ddamulira, M., & Chavuta, A. (2005). How Do Carers of Disabled Children Cope? The Ugandan Perspective. *Child: Care, Health and Development, 31*(2), 167–180. doi:10.1111/j.1365-2214.2004.00464.x.

James, A. L. (2010). Competition or Integration? The Next Step in Childhood Studies? *Childhood, 17*(4), 485–499. doi:10.1177/0907568209350783.

Kalyanpur, M. (2014). Distortions and Dichotomies in Inclusive Education for Children with Disabilities in Cambodia in the Context of Globalisation and International Development. *International Journal of Disability, Development & Education, 61*(1), 80–94. doi:10.1080/1034912X.2014.878546.

Kisanji, J. (1995). Growing Up Disabled. In P. Zinkin & H. McConachie (Eds.), *Disabled Children and Developing Countries* (pp. 183–199). London: MacKeith.

Kittay, E. (1999). *Love's Labour: Essays on Women, Equality and Dependency*. New York: Routledge.

Kittay, E., Jennings, B., & Wasunna, A. A. (2005). Dependency, Difference and the Global Ethic of Longterm Care. *Journal of Political Philosophy, 13*(4), 443–469. Retrieved from doi:10.1111/j.1467-9760.2005.00232.

Knussen, C., & Sloper, P. (1992). Stress in Families of Children with Disability: A Review of Risk and Resistance Factors. *Journal of Mental Health, 1*(3), 241–256.

Louw, D. J. (2006). The African Concept of Ubuntu. In D. Sullivan & L. Tifft (Eds.), *Handbook of Restorative Justice: A Global Perspective* (pp. 161–174). New York: Routledge.

McKenzie, J. (2013). Disabled People in Rural South Africa Talk About Sexuality. *Culture, Health & Sexuality, 15*(3), 372–386. doi:10.1080/13691058.2012.748936.

McKenzie, J. A. (2016). An Exploration of an Ethics of Care in Relation to People with Intellectual Disability and Their Family Caregivers in the Cape Town Metropole in South Africa. *ALTER-European Journal of Disability Research/Revue Européenne de Recherche sur le Handicap, 10*(1), 67–78.

McKenzie, J., & McConkey, R. (2016). Caring for Adults with Intellectual Disability: The Perspectives of Family Carers in South Africa. *Journal of Applied Research in Intellectual Disabilities, 29*(6), 531–541.

Meekosha, H. (2008). Contextualizing Disability: Developing Southern/Global Theory. Powerpoint Presentation. 4th Biennial Disability …(September). Retrieved from http://wwda.org.au/meekosha2008.pdf. Accessed 10 Feb 2016.

Mladenov, T. (2015). Neoliberalism, Postsocialism, Disability. *Disability & Society, 30*(3), 445–459.

Moore, E., & Govender, R. (2013). Marriage and Cohabitation in South Africa: An Enriching Explanation? *Journal of Comparative Family Studies, 44*(5), 623–639.

Muderedzi, J., & Ingstad, B. (2011). Disability and Social Suffering in Zimbabwe. In A. E. Eide & B. Ingstad (Eds.), *Disability and Poverty, A Global Challenge*. Bristol: Policy.

Nsamenang, A. B. (2003). Conceptualizing Human Development and Education in Sub-Saharan Africa at the Interface of Indigenous and Exogenous Influences. In T. S. Saraswathi (Ed.), *Cross-Cultural Perspectives in Human Development: Theory, Research, and Applications* (pp. 213–235). New Delhi: Sage.

Nsamenang, A. B. (2004). *Cultures of human development and education: Challenge to growing up African*. New York, NY: Nova Science Publishers.

Nsamenang, A. B. (2005). The Intersection of Traditional African Education with School Learning. In L. Swartz, C. de la Rey, & N. Duncan (Eds.), *Psychology*. Oxford: Oxford University Press.

Nsamenang, B. (2006). Human Ontogenesis: An Indigenous African View on Development and Intelligence. *International Journal of Psychology, 41*(4), 293–297.

Nsamenang, A. B., & Lamb, M. E. (1994). Socialization of Nso Children in the Bamenda Grassfields of Northwest Cameroon. In P. M. Greenmailed & R. R. Cocking (Eds.), *Cross-Cultural Roots of Minority Child Development* (pp. 133–146). Hillsdale: Lawrence Erlbaum Associates, Inc.

Ogunaike, O. A., & Houser, R. F., Jr. (2002). Yoruba Toddler's Engagement in Errands and Cognitive Performance on the Yoruba Mental Subscale. *International Journal of Behavioral Development, 26*, 145–153.

Oliver, M. (1996). *Understanding Disability: From Theory to Practice*. New York: St. Martin's Press.

Palmer, M. (2011). Disability and Poverty: A Conceptual Review. *Journal of Disability Policy Studies, 21*(4), 210–218.

Pence, A., & Nsamenang, B. (2008). *A Case for Early Childhood Development in Sub-Saharan Africa* (Working Paper No. 51). The Hague, The Netherlands: Bernard van Leer Foundation.

Rauktis, M. E., Koeske, G. F., & Tereshko, O. (1995). Negative Social Interactions, Distress, and Depression Among Those Caring for a Seriously and Persistently Mentally Ill Relative. *American Journal of Community Psychology, 23*(2), 279–299.

Rogoff, B. (2003). *The Cultural Nature of Human Development*. New York: Oxford University Press.

Serpell, R. (1994). An African Social Selfhood: Review of A. Bame Nsamenang (1992): Human Development in Cultural Context. *Cross-Cultural Psychology Bulletin, 28*, 17–21.

Serpell, R., Mariga, L., & Harvey, K. (1993). Mental retardation in African countries: Conceptualization, services, and research. *International review of research in mental retardation, 19*, 1–39.

Smith, T. B., Oliver, M. N., & Innocenti, M. S. (2001). Parenting Stress in Families of Children with Disabilities. *American Journal of Orthopsychiatry, 71*(2), 257.

Tarusarira, W. (2016). *The Family-Support Needs of Zimbabwean Asylum-Seeking Families Living with Their Disabled Children in the Western Cape Province of South Africa*. Master's in Philosophy (MPhil) in Disability Studies. Faculty of Health Sciences. University of Cape Town.

Terre des Hommes Nederland. (2007). *Hidden Shame: Violence Against Children with Disabilities in East Africa*. Retrieved from: http://www.ohchr.org/Documents/Issues/Women/WRGS/GirlsAndDisability/OtherEntities/TerreDesHommes.pdf. Accessed 16 Dec 2015.

The African Child Policy Forum. (2014). The African Report on Children with Disabilities: Promising Starts and Persisting Challenges. Addis Ababa: The African Child Policy Forum (ACPF).

Times Live. (2015). *West* Africa Schools Tackle Stigma of Disability. Retrieved from: http://www.timeslive.co.za/africa/2015/12/02/West-Africa-schools-tackle-stigma-of-disability. RETUERS. Accessed 17 Dec 2015.

UNICEF. (2013). *The State of the World's Children 2013: Children with Disabilities*. New York: UNICEF.

Watermeyer, B., & McKenzie, J. (2014). Mothers of Disabled Children: In Mourning or on the March? *Journal of Social Work Practice, 28*(4), 405–416.

Weisner, T. S. (1987). Socialization for Parenthood in Sibling Caretaking Societies. In J. B. Lancaster, J. Altman, A. S. Rossi, & L. R. Sherrod (Eds.), *Parenting Across the Lifespan: Biosocial Dimensions* (pp. 237–270). Hawthorne: Aldine de Gruyter.

World Health Organisation & World Bank. (2011). *World Report on Disability*. New York: WHO & World Bank.

Judith McKenzie is head of the Disability Studies Division in the Department of Health and Rehabilitation Sciences at the University of Cape Town (UCT), South Africa, where she convenes a postgraduate diploma in disability studies. Her research interests relate to inclusive education with a particular focus on intellectual disability and family support needs within low-income contexts.

Tsitsi Chataika is a senior lecturer in inclusive education, Department of Educational Foundations (University of Zimbabwe). Her research interest is in how disability intersects with education, development, policy, childhood studies, gender, religion and postcolonial theory. Chataika has a passion for promoting inclusive sustainable development through influencing policy and practice within an African context.

Normalcy, Intersectionality and Ableism: Teaching About and Around 'Inclusion' to Future Educators

Jen Slater and Elizabeth L. Chapman (Liz)

> *whilst claiming 'inclusion', ableism simultaneously always restates and enshrines itself. On the one hand, discourses of equality promote 'inclusion' by way of promoting positive attitudes (some legislated in mission statements, marketing campaigns, equal opportunities protections) and yet on the other hand, ableist discourses proclaim quite emphatically that disability is inherently negative, ontologically intolerable and in the end, a dispensable remnant.*
> *(Campbell 2009, 12)*

Key Points

- *We talk about teaching university students about inclusion in schools and universities.*
- *We began by focusing our teaching on disabled children and other 'groups' such as children of colour.*
- *However, this did not work very well. Our students wrote essays that focused on the differences between disabled and non-disabled people.*
- *We changed our teaching to focus on the problems caused by an unfair society. This has worked better.*
- *We also include disabled people's personal stories in our teaching.*

J. Slater (✉) • E. L. Chapman (Liz)
Sheffield Hallam University, Sheffield, UK

© The Author(s) 2018
K. Runswick-Cole et al. (eds.), *The Palgrave Handbook of Disabled Children's Childhood Studies*, https://doi.org/10.1057/978-1-137-54446-9_22

Introduction

This chapter reflects on our experiences of teaching about and around 'inclusion' to undergraduate students on an Education Studies Programme, in a post-1992 (new) university in the north of England. The focus on 'inclusion' has emerged through a number of modules. In all these modules (and, indeed, in this chapter), we have kept disabled children and young people in the forefront of our minds. We argue here, however, that despite good Disability Studies, de-individualising intentions, approaching 'inclusion' with a focus solely on disabled children in education can be detrimental. Despite what message a teacher (us!) thinks is being *taught*, the strong dominance of individualising discourses of disability means that the *differences* between disabled children and their non-disabled peers are what students often *learn*.

To give this some context, our teaching is around the academic study of education. Although none of the courses that we teach qualify the students to teach, many students do go into work as educators (often through further teacher training).

We felt it important to reflect on our own positionalities as they relate to both teaching (discussed later) and writing this chapter. One of us (Jen) has been teaching the Education Studies Programme discussed for five years. They have a background in Disability Studies (particularly in relation to youth and young people, see Slater 2015). The Education Studies Programme encompasses a range of courses and when they began teaching, Jen was largely teaching a course in Education and Disability Studies. Now, they teach more broadly around social justice issues in/of education. The other one of us (Liz) comes from a background in Library and Information Studies, where her work is focused on inclusive provision, particularly LGBTQ* inclusion in libraries and representation in young people's literature (Chapman 2013, 2015). Liz joined the Education Studies Programme in January 2014 and also teaches on social justice issues.

We both identify ourselves as queer, white and non-disabled. Jen also identifies as a non-binary person and Liz as cisgender woman. As we will go on to discuss, these various intersecting areas of privilege and marginalisation come into play in our teaching.

Jen's first semester of teaching gave them two modules relevant to this chapter: *Disability and the Family* (key text: Curran and Runswick-Cole 2013) and *Inclusion in Educational Contexts*. These modules had been taught for several years and were popular with students. So, with only a few weeks to settle in to her new job and get prepared, Jen initially taught them largely as they were previously set out.

Disability and the Family was organised so that each week the class discussed and theorised a particular family role. Jen attempted to discuss these 'family roles' as relational. For example, the class looked at 'disabled children and their parents' one week and 'disabled parents' the next. The students' assignment was to use secondary sources (e.g. families already in the media or fictional accounts) to provide a 'case study of a family where one or more person is labelled with an impairment'.

In some ways, *Inclusion in Educational Contexts* functioned similarly. The taught sessions were separated out to look at particular 'groups': one week was spent on 'gender', one on 'race', one on 'disability' and so on. The students' task was to 'explore the main barriers to inclusion for two excluded groups'. For example, a student may concentrate on 'disability' and 'race', looking at the barriers for disabled children and children of colour[1] in education.

As Jen continued through the first semester, however, they felt troubled. There was a disjuncture here between what (Jen thought) they were teaching and what the students were learning (Kelly 2009). The work students were handing in was overwhelmingly individualising and far from the largely disability studies teachings that Jen thought had been delivered. Writing this with hindsight, we can both see how and why student accounts became individualised. Both modules made it too easy for the focus to be on the individual student and/or family/family member, rather than exclusionary and oppressive systems. Although far from the intention of teaching sessions, the message which was fed back through student assignments was largely that the 'problem' was within the individual (or, at the least, the particular 'group').

Disability and disabled children still remain paramount in our teaching. Reflecting on our own teaching, however, we will argue through this chapter that *starting* with disabled children's experiences when teaching around issues of inclusion can be detrimental. Whilst important to share, disabled children's experiences need to be strongly foregrounded and contextualised within a focus on the systemic and violent dis/ableism of educational systems which sustain a narrative of disability as devalued difference (Goodley and Runswick-Cole 2011). Whilst writing about the experiences of Black Muslim women in Britain, Johnson (2014, 8) asks us to consider what would happen if 'instead of focusing solely on the product of [...] differences (which is an endless task) we [...] focus on the processes that precede these differences'? In this chapter, we argue similarly: what happens if, instead of concentrating endlessly on the (often harmful) product of disabled children's perceived differences in the education system, we concentrate on how these differences are produced in the first place?

To make such an argument, this chapter is structured as follows. We first introduce three concepts which have been crucial to our own teaching around 'inclusion': 'ableism' (Campbell 2009), 'intersectionality' (Crenshaw 1989) and 'normalcy' (Davis 2010). We then move on to reflect upon our own teaching, outlining how a shift to utilise these concepts has led to a shift in gaze—from one on disabled children and young people to one on oppressive systems and structures. Before we begin, however, it is important to stress that the concepts outlined in this chapter are, through necessity of space, somewhat simplified. Furthermore, there are debates as to the co-option of intersectionality by white people, when it was originally a term used to theorise the lives of women of colour (Johnson 2014), and similar debates within and around Disability Studies about the use (and possible appropriation) of queer theory (Sherry 2004, 2013), postcolonial theory (Sherry 2007) and so on. We are always learning (from students, from each other and from external sources) and from this reflecting on and revising our teaching. We have surely not got everything quite 'right' and would welcome further discussion. However, we remain mindful of our own positionalities within teaching around these complex issues, whilst also considering the positionalities of our students for whom these theories may be a way to navigate the world.

For the sake of space and purpose in this chapter, therefore, we have given an account that is 'a way in'. We have also pointed to where more in-depth accounts of each concept can be found. All the texts we refer to below are texts that have been used and discussions that have been had (and proven productive) with students.

Three Key Concepts: Ableism, Intersectionality and Normalcy

Concept 1: Ableism

According to Campbell (2001, 44), ableism is a 'network of beliefs, processes and practices that produces a particular kind of self and body (the corporeal standard) that is projected as the perfect, species-typical and therefore essential and fully human'. Disablism, on the other hand, is the resultant 'attitudes and barriers that contribute to the subordination of people with disabilities' (Campbell 2009, 4). She argues that instead of focusing all our attention on disabled people[2] (and indeed disablism), we should instead think about how dominant ideas of the 'able body' (which she maintains is a social construct) are *produced* in the first place.

Let's take an educational example. In the run-up to the UK general elections 2015, there was an announcement from the Conservative Education Secretary, Nicky Morgan, that all children should know their 12 times table by age 11 (BBC News 2015). Such a declaration is an example of ableism. It projects an image of 'a particular kind of [11-year-old] self and body' (Campbell 2009, 44) that can, along with other things, perform their 12 times tables. Any 11-year-old unable to perform their 12 times tables is made the Other to this standard set out. Disabled children are one group that can become Othered through this announcement (and other recent UK announcements around a shift back to 'rote-based' learning) (Contact A Family 2013a). This particular *ableist* statement (that projects an 11-year-old doing their 12 times table as the expected norm) leads to *disablism*. There are a number of disablist practices that could result from this. For example, disabled children could be met with paternalism. There may be an assumption that disabled children cannot perform these tasks and an assurance that the announcement was not aimed at them, that they will have alternative provision. This, however, could lead to segregation, especially in a climate where school leagues tables are key, so disabled children could be considered to be compromising that school (ALLFIE 2011). It could also lead to expulsion. In 2013, Contact A Family reported that disabled children are routinely illegally excluded from school (Contact A Family 2013b).

We see then that ableism (the expectation of an 'able' body and mind) leads to disablism (the marginalisation and oppression of disabled people). Campbell points out, however, that much scholarship and practice in the field of Disability Studies has concentrated on the experiences of disablism, 'essentially relat[ing] to reforming those negative attitudes, assimilating people with disabilities into normative civil society and providing compensatory initiatives and safety nets in cases of enduring vulnerability' (Campbell 2009, 4). Of course, attending to experiences of disablism is important. Yet, reflections on our own teaching (which follow) tend to support Campbell's argument. When we concentrate only on looking at the disablism faced by disabled children and young people, '[d]isability, often quite unconsciously, continues to be examined and taught from the perspective of the Other (Marks 1996; Solis 2006)'. For Campbell, then, the challenge 'is to reverse, to invert this traditional approach, to shift our gaze and concentrate on what the study of disability tells us about the production, operation and maintenance of ableism' (Campbell 2009, 4).

As we move on to outline some of our own teaching experiences, we show how by focusing only on experiences of disablism, without foregrounding with an understanding of ableism, disabled children remain a 'special case', requiring 'special provision', they remain the Other. The disabled body continues to 'secure the performative enactment of the normal' (Campbell 2009, 12). Also key to Campbell's definition of ableism is that this projected (and expected) 'able body' isn't only reliant on the category of dis/ability; rather, it has 'specific cultural alignments with other factors such as race, gender, sexuality and coloniality' (Campbell 2012, 214). Mingus (2011) therefore argues that 'ableism' is not just about disability or disabled people but an important way to understand all experiences of systemic oppression or marginalisation:

> Ableism cuts across all of our movements because ableism dictates how bodies should function against a mythical norm—an able-bodied standard of white supremacy, heterosexism, sexism, economic exploitation, moral/religious beliefs, age and ability. Ableism set the stage for queer and trans people to be institutionalized as mentally disabled; for communities of color to be understood as less capable, smart and intelligent, therefore 'naturally' fit for slave labor; for women's bodies to be used to produce children, when, where and how men needed them; for people with disabilities to be seen as 'disposable' in a capitalist and exploitative culture because we are not seen as 'productive;' for immigrants to be thought of as a 'disease' that we must 'cure' because it is 'weakening' our country; for violence, cycles of poverty, lack of resources and war to be used as systematic tools to construct disability in communities and entire countries.

Mingus' analysis of ableism allows us to see how disability as a difference (Erevelles 2011) is produced in relation to axes of race, sexuality, gender, class/poverty, faith, global location and age. To return to the example offered above, we could also think of the ableist expectation of all 11-year-olds knowing their 12 times table along some of these other 'axes of difference'. For example, we could see this pronouncement as classed, in that 'attainment' is consistently lower in those with a low socio-economic status (Department for Education 2014a; Goodman and Gregg 2010) and that 'rote learning' sustains the already 'middle-class' field of education. We can see it as raced (and colonial), as it comes as part of a package in a Conservative vision of an education system aiming to 'promote British values' (Department for Education 2014b). We can see it as gendered as it emerges as part of a wider shift back to more 'traditional' subjects in response to the so-called 'feminisation' of the curriculum purportedly favouring girls (Department for Children, Schools and Families 2009), the assumption of which also works through cultures of cissexism and heteronormativity (see, Payne and Smith 2012; Snyder and Broadway 2004; Sumara and Davis 1999). This brings us to our second concept, *intersectionality*.

Concept 2: Intersectionality

Kimberlé Crenshaw (1989) is widely credited as the originator of the term 'intersectionality'. She used it to describe how structures and processes relating to race, class and gender worked to oppress women of colour (in ways that were different to those experienced by men of colour, or white women, or other poor people). In order to describe this, in 1989, Crenshaw (1245–1246) wrote:

> Many women of color, for example, are burdened by poverty, child care responsibilities, and the lack of job skills. These burdens, largely the consequence of gender and class oppression, are then compounded by the racially discriminatory employment and housing practices women of colour often face, as well as by the disproportionately high unemployment among people of color that makes battered women of color less able to depend on the support of friends and relatives for temporary shelter.

For Crenshaw, however, these different 'axes of difference' are not merely additive or descriptive but are co-constituted through and by one another. Intersectionality, then, can help us to understand that processes of categorisation (through class, gender, sexuality, dis/ability, age and so on) are not just *descriptive* markers which produce different experiences but are in fact co-constituting of one another (Erevelles 2011).

The work of disability and critical race education scholar, Nirmala Erevelles, is particularly useful here. In a paper with Ivan Watts, for example, Watts and Erevelles (2004) explore 'violence' in/of schools. Although this paper has a US focus, it is pertinent to us in the UK (similar processes are explored in a UK context in Slater 2016). Watts and Erevelles highlight that 'violent' is a label often given to young men of colour. They argue, however, that by individualising 'violence' (considering it as a problem belonging to a particular racialised person/population), we ignore the *structural* violence of school systems:

> the real violence in schools is a result of the structural violence of oppressive social conditions that force students, especially low-income African American and Latino male students, to feel vulnerable, angry, and resistant to the normative expectations of prison-like school environments. (Watts and Erevelles 2004, 274)

Watts and Erevelles explain how many poor young men of colour, considered 'violent', are then excluded from the school system. This often means they end up in more violent systems (streets, prisons and so on) (Davis 2003; Zahm 1997). However, when 'school administrators have refrained from using expulsion and suspension to remove "violent" students from schools, they have often labelled those students as mildly mentally retarded, behaviourally disordered, or emotionally conflicted, and have banished them to segregated special education classrooms (Noguera 1995; Artiles 2003)' (Watts and Erevelles 2004, 288). We begin to see then how processes of racialisation and labels of 'special educational needs' may not merely be productive of similar or different experiences but processes that co-constitute one another.

Concept 3: Normalcy

In short, normality and normalcy is achieved through an unsaying: an absence of descriptions of what is to be normal (Goodley 2009, x)

The final concept we introduce here is that of 'normalcy' (Davis 2010). This is the concept we have found students to grasp most readily and it is useful in order to grapple with both ableism and intersectionality. As Mallett and Runswick-Cole (2014, 23–24) explain:

Davis contends that in order to understand 'disability', we must begin by examining the idea of 'normal'. Indeed, he draws our attention to what he describes as the hegemony, or dominant, of the 'world of norms' (1995: 23). The world of norms is one in which intelligence, height, weight and many other aspects of the body are measured in comparison to the 'normal'. In some disciplines, such as psychology and medicine, the 'normal' range is often depicted on a bell-shaped graph that offers a visual representation and statistical description of the limits of normal

In the same way that ableism helps us to understand the social construction of the 'able' body, normalcy helps us to turn our attention onto the social construction of 'norms'. Davis points out that '[o]ur children are ranked in school and tested to determine where they fit into a normal curve of learning, of intelligence' (Davis 2002, 3). Let us again return to the expectation on 11-year-olds to know their 12 times tables. We can begin to deconstruct this around the norms it is based upon. Developmental psychology, and the associated 'learning theories' (Piaget, Vygotsky and so on), is a good place to begin here (Burman 2008). From developmental psychology, there is an expectation that by a certain *age*, one should have met a certain *stage*. Yet, although human 'development' is often presented to us as a 'biological reality' (Slater 2015, 40), according to Burman (2008, 5), studies of child development have always been 'instrumental in terms of the fashioning of future citizens – including the generation of appropriate workers and consumers'. Our interrogation then becomes broader: we begin to hunt for developmental assumptions within the education system; we simultaneously ask what the purpose of education is (especially in relation to capitalist relations and producers/consumers) and we think of disabled people's place, not only in education but also in society more broadly.

Utilising 'Ableism', 'Intersectionality' and 'Normalcy' in Teaching

Reflecting on our own teaching, we have changed, and continue to change, our approach to teaching. We are going to concentrate for the majority of this chapter on *Inclusion in Education Contexts* (partially because *Disability and the Family* no longer runs in the institution, partially because modules on 'inclusion' are more commonly taught than those focusing explicitly on disability and the family, and partially because this is the module on which both authors have taught). However, we want to give a 'nod' to how, for the second and final time Jen taught it, *Disability and the Family* was revamped (resulting in assignments much more focused on structural, systemic and societal problems, rather than those perceived to 'belong' to individuals).

Rather than focus on individual family members, Jen set out by talking about normative assumptions around 'families'. The approach became rooted in critical disability studies. As Goodley (2011, 157) puts it, 'while critical disability studies may start with disability, they never end with it'. We worked with other critical theory. Rather than thinking about 'disabled children', for example, we used critical psychology to examine how expectations of children work upon normative developmental assumptions (Burman 2008) and asked how that positions disabled children as 'abnormal'. We drew on queer theory throughout to deconstruct normative notions of 'the family' and applied this to think about the implications of normative ideas of the family for disabled people. Rather than consider 'disabled parents' or 'disabled young people', we thought about the discursively oppositional positioning of disability and sexuality (Liddiard 2012; Liddiard and Slater 2017; Slater 2012, 2015) and how this might lead to certain perceptions about disabled people's family roles. The final session drew on Allison Kafer's (2011) analysis of Sharon Duchesneau and Candy McCullough's fight, as a d/Deaf lesbian couple, to use the sperm of a deaf donor, in the hope of conceiving a d/Deaf baby. The discussions in class centred around the bureaucratic hoops that a same-sex couple may have to jump through in order to conceive/adopt (and how these may also be classed, raced, gendered, dis/ableist and so on), alongside dis/ableist assumptions 'that life as a Deaf person is inferior to life as a hearing person' (Kafer 2011, 228). The session therefore helped students to think about ableist assumptions around families, alongside structures of heteronormativity.

Rather than say any more about *Disability and the Family*, however, we want to concentrate for the remainder of this chapter on teaching about and around 'inclusion'. Our approach is similar to the one outlined in *Disability and the Family*. We start with the education system, and from there we think about how it functions to oppress individual lives, framing with the three key concepts outlined earlier: ableism (Campbell 2009), normalcy (Davis 2010) and intersectionality (Crenshaw 1989). We feel that it is also important to note here that we introduce these three concepts early in the module—partly to give students a chance to understand the concepts and partly so that they can apply them throughout the sessions.

As discussed in the introduction, the module as originally devised focused on one 'marginalised group' each week. The first move we made was to move away from this structure, as it inadvertently gave the impression that such groups were discrete and existed in isolation to one another; instead, we encouraged students to think intersectionally throughout the module. We also chose to move away from this structure as it encouraged a tick-box approach: that when you have had the session on 'race', for example, you know everything there is to know about race and education and when you have finished the module you have covered all the 'marginalised groups'. We wanted students to understand 'inclusion' as complex, often contradictory and ongoing (not something that can be 'achieved'): as Naylor (2005) puts it, 'always a journey, never a destination'. Finally, in purely practical terms, a structure that focuses on each group in turn leads to low student attendance at later sessions once they have decided which 'groups' they are focusing on in their assignment.

Students begin by reading Michalko's (2001) '*Blindness Enters the Classroom*'. The assumption that many students enter with is that the module will be around 'how to teach disabled students'. Michalko's piece straight away 'disorientates' them, by getting them to think about disabled educators.

Michalko's account of lecturing as a blind man beautifully captures the ableist assumption of teacher = non-disabled. In a subsequent lecture which brings in critiques of developmental psychology (Burman 2008), we ask students to read Baglieri et al.'s (2011) *"Inclusive Education" Toward Cohesion in Educational Reform: Disability Studies Unravels the Myth of the Normal Child'*. As part of this preparatory work, students are also asked to think about ideas of normalcy (Davis 2010) by making a list of what we expect from the 'normal' student at school, which we then discuss in class. Through these lectures, we interrogate who the 'expected participant' (Titchkosky 2011) is within our education systems. This serves a threefold purpose of critiquing ableist structures which posit an expected 'normal' student, helping us to remain mindful about the complex intersecting identities of our students and encouraging the students to not make assumptions about who is in the classroom as either 'student' or 'teacher'.

Both of us are (continuously) 'coming out' to our students as openly queer and discuss this in the context of the module. This is, of course, a personal decision but also one that is for us political. It was a decision that began to feel more possible after some years of experience of teaching and in the context of a particular set of circumstances, including relatively privileged positions and a particular working environment. Turner (2010, 287) discusses (in an American context) how, for many academics, especially those not on permanent contracts, 'the decision to be "out" in the classroom is perhaps joyous, unadvisable, potentially dangerous and often difficult'. This resonates—there have been both positive and negative aspects of this process for us. Positives include a potentially safer space for discussion of some complex issues and opportunities for queer (and potentially other marginalised) students to share their experiences. Negatives include a potential for negative student feedback or reaction and being viewed as 'the face of an agenda' (Turner 2010, 297). The issue of student self-censorship falls somewhere between 'positive' and 'negative': positive in that it perhaps offers some protection to other students holding that particular identity within the classroom but negative as it may dissuade students from expressing and unpicking views on important issues in both the classroom situation and their written work.

We also encourage attention to the privileged aspects of our and student identities; by doing this, we hope to model a process of critical reflexivity to potential future educators. Like Campbell (2009), we try to notice the supposedly 'unmarked' identities of 'ablebodiedness', 'Whiteness', 'heterosexuality' and so on (Dyer 1997). This draws attention to the fact that 'identity' is not the sole preserve of people marked as the Other. We all have identities and thus intersecting areas of privilege and marginalisation (Crenshaw 1989). As Dyer (1997, 1) notes, 'As long as race is something only applied to non-white peoples, as long as white people are not racially seen and named, they/we function as a human norm. Other people are raced, we are just people.'

Moreover, this encourages students to think critically about how privileged aspects of their identities might give them the luxury of overlooking some aspects of exclusion in education. For example, many students begin the module with the assumption that education is 'fair'. In one session, we challenge this assumption by showing students statistics around school exclusions in the UK (Department of Education 2014). These statistics show disproportionately high levels of school exclusion amongst Black Caribbean and dual-heritage young men. We ask the students to work in groups to identify potential societal explanations for the figures, considering the ways in which raced and gendered stereotypes position young Black men as violent (Watts and Erevelles 2004) and the ways in which 'challenging behaviour' is read as pathological (Timimi 2005). (The students have been asked to read the two previously referenced articles in preparation for the session.) To make the task concrete (and to open the chance for class discussion), part of their task is to finish the sentence: 'Statistics on school exclusions show us the importance of taking an intersectional approach to think about "inclusion" because...' As with the *Disability and the Family* module, this shifts the focus from the 'problematic' individual to societal structures of oppression.

Before we conclude, we want to make clear that although we have focused upon the structural in the examples given above, this is not to say that the use of personal stories isn't relevant or necessary. Indeed, personal narrative is something that we utilise throughout the module alongside other forms of 'evidence'. For example, in one session, we give the students 'packs' containing different sources of information. These include statistics about attainment, progression into further and higher education and the representation of staff with different social positionings. Alongside these, we use personal narratives (including accounts of disabled childhoods), whether published in academic books (Haraldsdóttir 2013), newspaper articles (Sennello 2013) or blogs (Sheffield University BME Students' Committee 2015). We encourage students to think about how these different forms of 'evidence' are valued, which dominate in the media, and the different perspectives they provide on educational and societal in/exclusion. We see the use of personal stories as really important, so long as they are contextualised within wider systems and structures (Curran and Runswick-Cole 2013).

Conclusion

In this chapter, we have by necessity only given a few (somewhat simplified) examples of teaching tools, methods and concepts. Of course, the relational nature of pedagogy means that each time we teach this module, it is different. There are always moments where a student challenges the teacher or another student, where we redirect or broaden thinking ('how about if you think about this?') or where we recognise – or a student draws attention to – areas for improvement in our own teaching. We do not seek here to give definitive answers but rather would welcome further discussion with educators, students and others with an interest in the topics discussed. Indeed, in writing this chapter, we have already noticed changes that we'd make. For instance, our example of engaging with the concept of intersectionality inadvertently refocused attention on experiences of Black men, which is somewhat troubling in light of the theory's original aim of creating a space to discuss the experiences specific to Black women. In future, further attention needs to be paid to social structures that exclude Black women in educational contexts (Alexander and Arday 2015).

We are also aware that the focus in this chapter hasn't solely (or even predominantly) been on disabled children and young people, as audiences of this book may expect. However, as outlined in the introduction, in previous teachings, a focus on specific 'groups' has led to individualising perspectives, whereas a focus shifted to structures, as outlined in this chapter, has resulted in less Othering approaches. We hope that students come away from the module with less of an idea of inclusion as something which they, as potential future educators, will (or will not) attempt to do 'to' particular groups. Instead, exclusionary structures affect us all to differing extents depending upon our intersecting social positions of privilege and oppression.

Notes

1. We here use the term 'children of colour' which is a preferred term in the North American context. We prefer this to the common UK term 'black and minority ethnic' as the word 'minority' can be taken to imply a subordinate position; moreover, students of colour are not necessarily in the minority in our university classrooms or in schools. We have also avoided the term 'non-white' as this defines all people of colour with reference to the 'unmarked' white majority. 'People of colour' allows for solidarity on the basis of shared oppression, without assuming a biological commonality (Vidal-Ortiz 2008).

2. We use the term 'disabled people/children/young people' in this chapter following the social model of distinction between 'impairment' (meaning the problematically perceived difference in body/mind) and 'disability' (meaning the subsequent societal oppression faced by people with impairments) (Oliver 1990). Where terminology alters, that is due to its use in another context. For more on language, see Mallett and Slater (2014).

References

Alexander, C., & Arday, J. (Eds.). (2015). *Aiming Higher: Race, Inequality and Diversity in the Academy*. London: Runnymede. http://www.runnymedetrust.org/uploads/Aiming%20Higher.pdf. Date Accessed 11 Mar 2016.

ALLFIE. (2011). *Response to the Government 'Support and Aspiration: A New Approach to Special Educational Needs and Disability' Green Paper*. London: ALLFIE.

Cagliari, S., Beloin, L. M., Broderick, A. A., Connor, D. J., & Valle, J. (2011). [Re]Claiming "Inclusive Education". Toward Cohesion in Educational Reform: Disability Studies Unravels the Myth of the Normal Child. *Teachers College Record, 113*(10), 2122–2154.

BBC News. (2015, February 1). Nicky Morgan Announces 'War on Illiteracy and Innumeracy'. *BBC News*. http://www.bbc.co.uk/news/uk-31079515. Date Accessed 11 Mar 2016.

Burman, E. (2008). *Deconstructing Developmental Psychology*. Hove: Routledge.

Campbell, F. K. (2001). Inciting Legal Fictions – Disability's Date with Ontology and the Ableist Body of the Law. *Griffith Law Review, 10*(1), 42–62.

Campbell, F. K. (2009). *Contours of Ableism: The Production of Disability and Abledness*. Basingstoke: Palgrave Macmillan.

Campbell, F. K. (2012). Stalking Ableism: Using Disability to Expose "Abled" Narcissism. In D. Goodley, B. Hughes, & L. Davis (Eds.), *Disability and Social Theory: New Approaches and Directions* (pp. 212–230). Basingstoke: Palgrave Macmillan.

Chapman, E. L. (2013). No More Controversial than a Gardening Display? Provision of LGBT-Related Fiction to Children and Young People in U.K. Public Libraries. *Library Trends, 61*(3), 542–568.

Chapman, E. L. (2015). *Provision of LGBT-Related Fiction to Children and Young People in English Public Libraries: A Mixed-Methods Study*. PhD, University of Sheffield, Sheffield. http://etheses.whiterose.ac.uk/11802/. Date Accessed 11 Mar 2016.

Contact A Family. (2013a). *Changes to National Curriculum Could Disadvantage Disabled Children*. http://www.cafamily.org.uk/news-and-media/changes-to-the-national-curriculum-could-disadvantage-disabled-children/. Date Accessed 11 Mar 2016.

Contact A Family. (2013b). *Disabled Children Illegally Excluded from School Every Week.* http://www.cafamily.org.uk/news-and-media/disabled-children-illegally-excluded-from-school-every-week/. Date Accessed 11 Mar 2016.

Crenshaw, K. (1989). Demarginalizing the Intersection of Race and Sex: A Black Feminist Critique of Antidiscrimination Doctrine, Feminist Theory and Antiracist Politics. *The University of Chicago Legal Forum, 140,* 139–167.

Curran, T., & Runswick-Cole, K. (Eds.). (2013). *Disabled Children's Childhood Studies: Critical Approaches in a Global Context.* Basingstoke: Palgrave Macmillan.

Davis, L. J. (2002). *Bending Over Backwards: Disability, Dismodernism, and Other Difficult Positions.* (New York/London: New York University Press.

Davis, A. Y. (2003). *Are Prisons Obsolete?* New York: Seven Stories Press.

Davis, L. J. (2010). Constructing Normalcy. In L. J. Davis (Ed.), *The Disability Studies Reader* (3rd ed., pp. 3–19). New York/London: Routledge.

Department for Education. (2014a, March 27). *GCSE and Equivalent Attainment by Pupil Characteristics: 2013.* http://www.gov.uk/government/statistics/gcse-and-equivalent-attainment-by-pupil-characteristics-2012-to-2013. Date Accessed 11 Mar 2016.

Department for Education. (2014b). *Promoting Fundamental British Values as Part of SMSC in Schools: Departmental Advice for Maintained Schools.* London: HMSO. https://www.gov.uk/government/uploads/system/uploads/attachment_data/file/380595/SMSC_Guidance_Maintained_Schools.pdf. Date Accessed 11 Mar 2016.

Department of Children School and Families. (2009). *Gender and Education – Mythbusters Addressing Gender and Achievement: Myths and Realities.* London: HMSO. http://webarchive.nationalarchives.gov.uk/20130401151715/http://www.education.gov.uk/publications/eOrderingDownload/00599-2009BKT-EN.pdf. Date Accessed 11 Mar 2016.

Department of Education. (2014). *Statistics: Exclusions.* https://www.gov.uk/government/collections/statistics-exclusions. Date Accessed 11 Mar 2016.

Dyer, R. (1997). *White.* London: Routledge.

Erevelles, N. (2011). *Disability and Difference in Global Contexts.* New York: Palgrave Macmillan.

Goodley, D. (2009). Foreword. In F. K. Campbell (Ed.), *Contours of Ableism: The Production of Disability and Abledness* (pp. ix–xiv). Basingstoke: Palgrave Macmillan.

Goodley, D. (2011). *Disability Studies: An Interdisciplinary Introduction.* London: Sage.

Goodley, D., & Runswick-Cole, K. (2011). The Violence of Disablism. *Sociology of Health & Illness, 33*(4), 602–617.

Goodman, A., & Gregg, P. (2010). *Poorer Children's Educational Attainment: How Important Are Attitudes and Behaviour?* York: Joseph Rowntree Foundation.

Haraldsdóttir, F. (2013). Simply Children. In T. Curran & K. Runswick-Cole (Eds.), *Disabled Children's Childhood Studies: Critical Approaches in a Global Context* (pp. 13–21). Basingstoke: Palgrave Macmillan.

Johnson, A. (2014). *Questioning "Intersectional" Identities Through Clothing Practices: The Experiences of Black Muslim Women in Britain.* Paper Presented at the Postgraduate Gender Research Network Seminar, University of Sheffield.

Kafer, A. (2011). Debating Feminist Futures: Slippery Slopes, Cultural Anxiety, and the Case of the Deaf Lesbians. In K. Hall (Ed.), *Feminist Disability Studies* (pp. 218–242). Bloomington: Indiana University Press.

Kelly, A. (2009). *The Curriculum: Theory and Practice* (6th ed.). London: Sage.

Liddiard, K. (2012). *(S)exploring Disability: Intimacies, Sexualities and Disabilities.* PhD, University of Warwick.

Liddiard, K., & Slater, J. (2017). "Like, Pissing Yourself Is Not a Particularly Attractive Quality, Let's Be Honest": Learning to Contain Through Youth, Adulthood, Disability and Sexuality. *Sexualities Special Issue: Disability and Sexual Corporeality: Possibilities for Pleasure.*

Mallett, R., & Runswick-Cole, K. (2014). *Approaching Disability: Critical Issues and Perspectives.* London: Routledge.

Mallett, R., & Slater, J. (2014). Language. In C. Cameron (Ed.), *Disability Studies: A Student's Guide* (pp. 91–94). London: Sage.

Michalko, R. (2001). Blindness Enters the Classroom. *Disability & Society, 16*(3), 349–359.

Mingus, M. (2011, August 22). *Moving Toward the Ugly: A Politic Beyond Desirability.* http://leavingevidence.wordpress.com/2011/08/22/moving-toward-the-ugly-a-politic-beyond-desirability/. Date Accessed 11 Mar 2016.

Naylor, C. (2005). *Inclusion in British Columbia's Public Schools: Always a Journey, Never a Destination?* Paper Presented at Building Inclusive Schools: A Search for Solutions, Ottawa. http://bctf.ca/diversity/reports/inclusionjourney/report.pdf. Date Accessed 11 Mar 2016.

Oliver, M. (1990). *The Politics of Disablement.* Basingstoke: Macmillan.

Payne, E., & Smith, M. (2012). Rethinking Safe Schools Approaches for LGBTQ Students: Changing the Questions We Ask. *Multicultural Perspectives, 14*(4), 187–193.

Sennello, A. (2013, April 11). My Story: I've Been an Outcast at School Because I'm Transgender. *The Guardian* http://www.theguardian.com/commentisfree/2013/apr/11/transgender-discrimination-in-schools-my-story. Date Accessed 11 Mar 2016.

Sheffield University BME Students' Committee. (2015). *I, Too, Am Sheffield.* http://itooamsheffield.tumblr.com/. Date Accessed 11 Mar 2016.

Sherry, M. (2004). Overlaps and Contradictions Between Queer Theory and Disability Studies. *Disability & Society, 19*(7), 769–783.

Sherry, M. (2007). (Post)colonising Disability. *Wagadu, 4,* 10–22.

Sherry, M. (2013). Crip Politics? Just … No. *The Feminist Wire.* http://thefeminist-wire.com/2013/11/crip-politics-just-no/. Date Accessed 11 Mar 2016.

Slater, J. (2012). Youth for Sale: Using Critical Disability Perspectives to Examine the Embodiment of "Youth". *Societies, 2*(3), 195–209.

Slater, J. (2015). *Youth and Dis/ability: A Challenge to Mr Reasonable*. Farnham: Ashgate.

Slater, J. (2016). The (Normal) Non-Normativity of Youth. In R. Mallett, C. A. Ogden, & J. Slater (Eds.), *Theorising Normalcy and The Mundane: Precarious Positions* (pp. 14–44). Chester: Chester University Press.

Snyder, V. L., & Broadway, F. S. (2004). Queering High School Biology Textbooks. *Journal of Research in Science Teaching, 41*(6), 617–636.

Sumara, D., & Davis, B. (1999). Interrupting Heteronormativity: Toward a Queer Curriculum Theory. *Curriculum Inquiry, 29*(2), 191–208.

Timimi, S. (2005). *Naughty Boys: Anti-Social Behaviour, ADHD and the Role of Culture*. Basingstoke: Palgrave Macmillan.

Titchkosky, T. (2011). *The Question of Access: Disability, Space, Meaning*. (Toronto/London: University of Toronto Press.

Turner, S. L. (2010). Undressing as Normal: The Impact of Coming Out in Class. *The Teacher Educator, 45*(4), 287–300.

Vidal-Ortiz, S. (2008). People of Color. In R. T. Schaefer (Ed.), *Encyclopedia of Race, Ethnicity, and Society* (pp. 1037–1039). London: Sage.

Watts, I. E., & Erevelles, N. (2004). These Deadly Times: Reconceptualizing School Violence By Using Critical Race Theory and Disability Studies. *American Educational Research Journal, 41*(2), 271–299.

Zahm, B. (1997). The Last Graduation: The Rise and Fall of College Programs in Prison. *Lock Down USA*. TV series. Washington, DC: Citizens for Independent Public Broadcasting.

Jen Slater is a Reader in Disability Studies and Education at Sheffield Hallam University. Their research draws on critical disability studies, queer theories and feminisms to explore how relationships between disability, gender, sexuality, race and youth/development function under (neo)liberal agendas of transnational capitalism. This work is currently being done through a collaborative exploration of toilets as socio-cultural spaces (aroundthetoilet.wordpress.com).

Elizabeth L. Chapman (Liz) is an Associate Lecturer in Education and Disability Studies at Sheffield Hallam University. She recently completed her PhD on provision of LGBTQ* fiction to children and young people in English public libraries, and now divides her time between working for Sheffield Libraries and lecturing at Sheffield Hallam University. She is Section Editor for Equality and Diversity for the *Journal of Radical Librarianship*.

"Just Sumaira: Not Her, Them or It"

Key Points

- I think everyone should be able to share their own story about their life but only if they want to do this.
- If you talk, write or use someone else's picture without asking them in research or in practice, then it can hurt them if they find out. Don't think they won't or can't find out that the picture has been used.
- In this chapter I talk about what it is like when someone tells your story without permission and thinks it is okay to do this because a child has a disability or long-term medical condition.
- It is not okay for someone to tell a story without the person concerned being involved in the storytelling. I will never forget the horrible feeling of finding my photograph on the internet where anyone can find it. That picture haunts me.
- If you talk or write about someone, then make sure they know when and where the story and pictures will be heard or seen.

*   *   *

This chapter offers a glimpse of my experiences of a childhood where the disability became the focus in order to see me as different and other. My life (like

S.K. Naseem (✉)
Manchester Metropolitann University, Manchester, UK

© The Author(s) 2018
K. Runswick-Cole et al. (eds.), *The Palgrave Handbook of Disabled Children's Childhood Studies*, https://doi.org/10.1057/978-1-137-54446-9_23

that of many children with disabilities and long-term medical conditions) was (and sometimes still is) a life where other people feel the need to create an "us and them". I am always "them", "she" or "it". I move on to a description of what I see as immoral exploitation of disability especially in childhood. I focus on my personal experience of living with a long-term medical condition.

I begin by explaining my choice of title: her, them or it. These labels are all examples of the ways in which I was objectified through disability both as a child and an adult rather than focusing on me or referring to me by my name, Sumaira. These examples of objectification are general, but for this chapter, I want to focus on specific examples in medical contexts, particularly research, though such treatment is not limited to medicine. These are my own experiences but the issues apply to any disability relating to a medical condition.

Michel Foucault's concept of the "clinical gaze" is useful here and Kenneth Allan describes this as:

> The patient can't get in the way of the symptoms; the symptoms and the disease are the same and exist within the body. This ... created the clinical gaze. (p. 213) (Allan 2012, p. 213)

> a gaze that makes the body an object ... [and] see the person as an object. (p. 214) (Allan 2012, p. 214)

* * *

Immoral Exploitation

In my earlier work, I have described such objectification in research as immoral exploitation (Naseem 2013, 2015). My definition of immoral exploitation is partially based on a quote from a poet called Jean "Binta" Breeze who was speaking on a radio programme:

> One of the things I've always said is that if as a poet, I'm looking on the river bed and I see a woman washing her clothes in the river, who has never read a poem or read a book and that inspires me to write a poem, about the woman washing her clothes on the river, then that poem should be accessible to that woman because she inspired it. And if it's not - if you then, choose to write it in a language, or not speak it in a way that's available to her, it's exploitation. (Breeze 2013)

This is the principle that I am suggesting we follow in research.

Previously I have spoken about the haunting memories of finding photographs of my body published in medical journal articles which are freely available for anyone to find through a simple online image search (Naseem 2013, 2015). I describe this treatment of my life (where I am often just a set of symptoms) as the immoral exploitation of disability in childhood because of the unethical approach used to document my life as a set of symptoms and in a way that I am identifiable. Ethics is defined as a set of moral principles (Oxford English Dictionary 2016) or values (thesaurus.com 2016). However, this process is turned into a mandatory exercise in which researchers must fill in forms or go through a checklist. Somewhere between the desire to get ethical approval and a fear of being liable for causing harm to participants as well as ensuring adequate insurance provision, the *actual* harm to the people "being researched" gets lost and fully informed consent is absent. Although I draw on my personal experience of medicine, such unethical approaches to research and story telling are not exclusive to medicine, academia or publications. In these situations, ethics are no longer a set of moral values or principles because they have become no more than a checklist or a series of inconvenient hurdles to jump. So the telling of stories in this research becomes immoral exploitation because childhoods and lives like mine are documented and described without consent or understanding and it often seems with a lack of consideration of the impact that it may have on children and young people if they found them. Researchers wrongly assume that children and young people will not have access to the stories they tell about them because of a perception about the effects of their impairments and their access to professional/academic knowledge. I understand the important role of such medical research and publications but believe that such activity can be carried out differently where people with the long-term medical conditions are involved in telling their holistic and ethical stories (Naseem and Burke 2015).

* * *

Genetic Study

Image 1 is drawn and coloured in black, grey and white. There are two rows of oval shapes. There are six ovals in total. The first row has two pairs of ovals. In each pair, one oval is a black outline and is white inside. The other oval is shaded in grey. The two pairs of ovals are linked together with a black line drawn in pen. The third pair of ovals is under these pairs and is in the centre. Both the ovals are coloured in black. A line, also drawn in black pen, links this pair together like the other pairs. The line connects back to the two pairs of ovals above it. The shading and colouring of the ovals has been done using computer software.

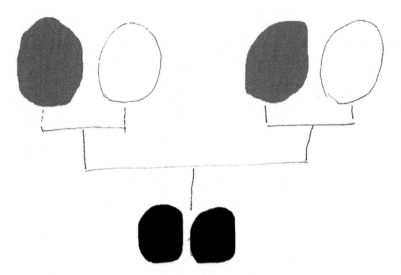

Image 1 Genetic study

I have recreated a diagram that a geneticist drew to explain why I had my medical condition. It showed two genes in oval shapes for each of my parents and myself. One gene for each parent is coloured in black to show what the geneticist called a "bad" gene. Both of my genes are coloured in black, although I couldn't see her drawing the picture, I could hear the sound of the pen, going over and over, colouring the black genes. The geneticist did not involve me in the conversation and this diagram, particularly the way in which the genes were coloured, made me feel like a bad apple. When I reproduced the image, I made my genes black and my parents' genes grey because this was the way she made me feel. This illustrates how I feel about this experience. To paraphrase Janice McLaughlin, such diagrams offer one description of one aspect of who someone is and their embodiment (McLaughlin 2013, p. 11).

Image 2 is a black and white drawing made using computer software. The first drawing shows an adult photographing a child. There is a black arrow pointing towards a child sitting on a bed or table with wheels or legs whilst the adult stands next to the child holding a camera close to the child's head. A black arrow points to them from the phrase "Taking and sharing photographs". They are being observed by a group of four or five people who are stood huddled together in the bottom right of the drawing. Another black arrow points towards them from the word "Observation". Everything except the white background is drawn or written in thick black ink.

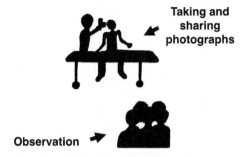

Image 2 Taking and sharing photographs of the comic strip

This drawing shows two examples of immoral exploitation that of observation, taking (and later sharing) photographs. I am the child being photographed by a medical professional and we are being observed by medical students and other medical professionals. I now briefly explain why these are examples of immoral exploitation and the ethical issues that arise as well as relating the impact of such practices.

1. Observation
   Here, the issue is that I have not given consent for the observers to be present. They might already be present in the room or my parents might be under the impression that they need to be present to help with current or future treatment. When there were observers present, they were rarely introduced or drawn to my attention. Sometimes, I would realise that there were people watching me when someone apart from the medical professional or my parents spoke or made a sound. This made me really uncomfortable and I only started asking people to leave the room well into adulthood.

2. Taking and sharing photographs
   The second example of immoral exploitation in this drawing is medical professionals taking (and later sharing) photographs. These photographs would have been taken with my parents' permission although this is not necessarily fully informed consent. They were often left with the impression that these photographs may lead to a cure for my condition. The ways in which these photographs would be repeatedly shared were hardly ever fully or clearly explained.

My Experience

Image 3 is a one-page comic strip drawn in pencil (Image 3). This short comic shows my experience of this process of the taking and sharing photographs of me by medical professionals and how I came to find them without knowing that they were freely available. There are six boxes or panels. Here is a description of the image:

Image 3   Immoral exploitation

- The first panel shows someone sitting on a bed. Another person holding a camera asks if they can take a photo.
- The second panel shows a person pointing to a projector showing an eye to other people sitting in a row.
- The third panel shows a laptop computer with the picture of an eye on the screen with the words "time to publish" in a speech bubble.
- The fourth panel shows a rectangle which could be a piece of paper with the letters BMJ at the top and the same eye picture.
- The fifth panel shows someone looking at a book or magazine with the eye picture on the front cover. They ask, "Is this me?"
- The sixth and final panel shows someone looking at the eye picture on a screen with the eye picture. They have an exclamation mark above their head asking, "When did they take this and why?"

The issues raised here include that I was not informed, even as an adult, that these photographs would be available online. Furthermore, the ways in which these photographs are used in journal articles and at conferences are not accessible to me because of the use of medical language as well as the poor attention to consent and lack of information. When I find that I am one of the patients in a journal article or conference presentation, I realise that I wasn't told that this would take place. In research, such a life has been documented in a way where the medical condition and disability is being objectified because the photographs lose sight of the patient as a person but instead they are reduced to a set of symptoms as Foucault's concept of the clinical gaze describes. Therefore, this is immoral exploitation because the taking and sharing of photographs of my body did not consider full informed consent but rather reduced my life to an object by documenting a set of symptoms.

Conclusion

This chapter has explored the impact of documenting the lives of children living with disability and long-term medical conditions, particularly through photographs and images. I have argued that disabled people and people with long-term medical conditions, like everyone else, should consent and control the way in which their lives are documented. I drew on my experiences of being photographed and researched in medical research without a full understanding of who could access such information and what they would make of it. I believe that this practice (regardless of the discipline) is unethical and that everyone should be able to tell (or choose not to tell) their story. No story is worth telling or writing if it harms the people it affects even if it is documented for some perceived greater good and might help someone else, although this is often the way that medical or social research in particularly (but not exclusively) is justified.

I want to conclude this chapter by inviting you to consider the following questions:

- Can we "un-imagine" (Wenzel 2013) immoral exploitation of disability and reimagine a realistic but positive and accessible way for children to communicate their childhood in their preferred language?
- Is it worth telling or writing a story if it harms the people it affects, even if the story is collected for some perceived greater good and might help someone else?
- How can we hold on to small examples of good practice with a view to make long-term change?

Acknowledgements I thank all of those people who took part. I appreciate the support of the organisers Tillie, Katherine and Kirsty in this work and particularly I am thankful to family members who offered an immense amount of support which enabled me to do this work: my brother Nadeem who enabled me to create the images for this book chapter.

References

Allan, K. (2012). *Contemporary Social & Sociological Theory: Visualising Social-Worlds.* London: Sage.

Breeze, Jean 'Brinta' (2013). The Forum. *BBC World Service,* First Broadcast on 16th March 2013 at 13.05.

.... "Ethics" Definition. *Oxford English Dictionary Online.* http://www.oed.com.ezproxy.mmu.ac.uk/view/Entry/355823?redirectedFrom=ethics#eid. Accessed on 28 Sep 2016a at 17.35 BST.

McLaughlin, J. (2013). *Digital Imagery and Child Embodiment in Paediatric Genetics: Sources and Relationships of Meaning.* http://soc.sagepub.com/content/48/2/216. Accessed 28 Jun 2016.

Naseem, S. K. (2013, June 18–19). *Ending the Immoral Exploitation of Disability in Childhood.* Paper Presented at Child, Youth, Family and Disability Conference, Manchester Metropolitan University.

Naseem, S. K. (2015, June 7–8). *Not Her, Them or It.* Workshop Facilitated at Child, Youth, Family and Disability Conference, The University of the West of England, Bristol.

Naseem, S. K., & Burke, L. (2015, December 16). *Writing an Ethical and Holistic Story of a Long Term Medical Condition Using a Multisensory Transdisciplinary Lens: The Case of Epidermolysis Bullosa.* Paper Presented at the Symposium of Literary and Cultural Disability Studies at Liverpool Hope University, Liverpool.

…. Values as Related to Ethics and Principles. *thesaurus.com.* http://www.thesaurus. com/browse/principles. Accessed on 28 Sep 2016b at 17.50 BST

Wenzel, J. (2013, April 29). *Reading for the Planet: World Literature and Environment Crisis.* Public Lecture Given as Part of the Humanities in Public Series, Manchester Metropolitan University, Manchester.

Sumaira Khalid Naseem is a postgraduate research student in a transdisciplinary project. Her work explores a long-term medical condition with which she lives, works and researches. She is interested in engaging with experiences of visual difference and multi-sensorial ways of knowing. She is involved in volunteering and activism relating to issues of inclusion and difference.

Part V

Theory and Critical Ways of Thinking

In this section, the authors ask some critical questions of disabled children's childhood studies as a theoretical movement in the lives of disabled children and their families. Each chapter draws upon the multiple intimacies in the life of the Othered child, exploring how affect, emotion, love, care, family, community, belonging, participation, advocacy and a range of relationships are contoured and mitigated through the *everyday* of disability and dis/ableism. In exploring and exposing intimacies and their disruptions, contributors offer alternative theorisations of disabled childhoods.

In the chapter "What's Wrong with 'Special'? Thinking Differently in New Zealand Teacher Education About Disabled Children and Their Lives", **Gill Rutherford and Jude McArthur** describe approaches to teacher education in New Zealand that seek to disrupt student teachers' understandings of disability, education and rights, and to move away from models of education based on deep-seated negative assumptions about 'difference' in childhood towards more respectful understandings of all children's rights and capabilities. They explore the ways in which they work with student teachers to make schools better places for disabled children and young people.

In the chapter "A Diversity of Childhoods: Considering the Looked After Childhood", **Luke Jones** and **Kirsty Liddiard** explore the possibilities of disabled children's childhood studies, asking to what extent might it be a useful political, methodological, and theoretical framework to think through the forms of (non-normative) childhood. Centring the lives of Looked After Children (LAC) – those who come to be looked after by the State – the authors draw upon their own lived and affective experiences of being family foster carers. In doing so, their reflexive analysis examines the overlaps in the lived experiences of disabled and LAC. These include professional surveillance, incessant measurement against the 'standard child' (and subsequent pathologisation and psychologisation) and disruptions to familial intimacies. The chapter ends by re-examining the role of vulnerability in the futures of disabled and LAC and young people.

In the chapter "A Relational Understanding of Language Impairment: Children's Experiences in the Context of Their Social Worlds", **Helen Hambly** explores the experiences of children with a diagnosis of language impairment (LI), alongside the experiences of family, friends and the professionals that support them. The label of LI is given to children deemed to have difficulties with various aspects of speech, language and memory. Highlighting the need for ethical research that listens to children and families, the author stresses the need to move away from cognitive, linguistic, neurological and biological explanations for atypical communication to instead explore LI as a psychosocial experience: one that acknowledges the child not as deficit but as a relational subject.

In the chapter "Resilience in the Lives of Disabled Children: A Many Splendoured Thing", through a critical focus on resilience and disabled childhoods, **Katherine Runswick-Cole**, **Dan Goodley and Rebecca Lawthom** contest normative and individualist modes of what it means to be a 'resilient child'. Centring the lives of disabled children and young people, they reframe resilience not as a humanly possession – something we hold as individuals – but as a dynamic interplay of the human and a host of resources around them. Resources such as community participation and acceptance are keys to the promotion of positive identities. Importantly, the authors locate this analysis in the context of the global economic crises and subsequent austerity policy in the UK. In doing so, they highlight the precarity of resilience in the lives of disabled children at a time where resources that support advocacy and care are routinely under threat.

In the chapter "Growing Up Disabled: Impairment, Familial Relationships and Identity", **Brian Watermeyer** offers an important reflexive analysis of the relationships between family, disability and self. In doing so, he centres his own family story and lived experience of an inherited visual impairment to explore the divide between family-centred, politically-aligned analyses of 'disability families' and psychological approaches curious about intra-psychic and relational implications of impairment. The author concludes by considering the impact of the 'disability curriculum' that emanates from within the family upon subsequent relationships, self-formation and growth, and emotional selfhood.

In the chapter "Autistic Development, Trauma and Personhood: Beyond the Frame of the Neoliberal Individual", **Damian Milton** unpacks Western neoliberal notions of child development and personhood, situating autistic development not as a disorder but as an affront to pervasive ideas of productivity and functionality and autonomous notions of selfhood. Through autethnography, which centres autistic subjectivity, the author explores a series of small photographic projects carried out with his immediate family. Focusing on family trauma, with his mother he creates an alternative family album which centres upon emotional impact. This enabled connections to grow between himself and his mother, a retracing of intimate family relationships and traumas, and a new aut sense of self within histories of fragmentation and fracture.

What's Wrong with 'Special'? Thinking Differently in New Zealand Teacher Education About Disabled Children and Their Lives

Gill Rutherford and Jude MacArthur

Key Points

1. The ideology and discourse of 'special education' can still be found in thinking, policy and practice in education despite almost 50 years of critique in relation to the arbitrary nature of the term and its negative impact on disabled children and young people.
2. Neoliberal ideologies and the rationalization of some teacher education programmes mean that disability can be left out of discussions in teacher education about social justice.
3. Initial teacher education (ITE) and postgraduate (PG) teacher education programmes can be designed and taught in ways that interrupt students' received truths, and trouble normative thinking and deficit ideologies inherent in 'special' education.
4. Teacher education programmes that work at the nexus of disability studies and childhood studies can support students to challenge ideas about 'special' and uphold children's agency, competence and rights as a foundation for teaching and learning.

G. Rutherford (✉)
University of Otago, Dunedin, New Zealand

J. MacArthur
Massey University, Palmerston North, New Zealand

© The Author(s) 2018
K. Runswick-Cole et al. (eds.), *The Palgrave Handbook of Disabled Children's Childhood Studies*, https://doi.org/10.1057/978-1-137-54446-9_24

5. Inclusive pedagogies and approaches such as Learning Without Limits (LWL) and Universal Design for Learning (UDL) turn teachers' attention to the use of teaching approaches that are designed for all students.

[Mack observed that he] "does stuff with a boy just like me." He explained that although this boy did not wear glasses and had different coloured hair, he did have "special needs--he's got a teacher aide and I have a teacher aide." When asked what "special needs" meant, he replied, "[I] actually don't know what special needs is--you're special and need help?" (11-year-old student, cited in Rutherford 2008, p. 125)

We begin this chapter with Mack's comments for two reasons. Firstly, we believe that children and young people serve as powerful teachers, positioned as they are on the receiving end of teachers' and policy makers' decisions and practices. Failure to attend and respond to their perspectives and experiences of education diminishes the act of teaching and learning by silencing those who are to be educated, which in turn denies students their right to have a say in matters that affect them (United Nations Convention on the Rights of the Child [UNCRC] 1989; United Nations Convention on the Rights of Persons with Disabilities [UNCRPD] 2006). Beginning with Mack's comments is consistent with the tenets of disabled children's childhood studies, in which children and young people constitute the starting place and heart of education and inquiry (Curran and Runswick-Cole 2014). Secondly, the substance of Mack's remarks reveals the entrenched tenacity of 'special' and its impact on those who are so labelled. At a relatively young age, he has internalized the unquestioned 'truth' that certain students are different from others and 'need' help—in this case from a teacher aide, who acts as a marker of his 'special needs' identity.

This chapter explores, from our perspectives as teacher educators, what is wrong with 'special' and why we need to think differently about disabled children and their lives. As a means of contextualizing our discussion, we provide an overview of the New Zealand educational policy and teacher education contexts, in which conflicting ideologies create significant disparities in policy and practice that determine the differential nature and quality of students' educational opportunities and achievements. The focus then shifts to our work in teacher education contexts, including both ITE with student teachers and PGs with experienced registered teachers. While employed by different universities, our teaching is underpinned by similar values and beliefs and positioned within the juncture of the theoretical frameworks of disability studies and childhood studies, which is very much aligned with the new field of disabled children's childhood studies (Curran and Runswick-Cole 2014).

We offer examples of our attempts to support teacher education students to question and abandon 'special needs' and other deficit ideologies in favour of more respectful understandings of human difference that focus on *all* students' strengths, capacities and rights. Our commitment to respecting students' perspectives is demonstrated in the final part of the chapter, in which samples of our students' work are shared. In our closing remarks, we acknowledge that our efforts in teacher education are always very much a work in progress, in an endeavour to bridge the distance between 'what is' and 'what could be' in terms of educational equity and excellence for all students.

What's Wrong with 'Special'?

In 1968, Lloyd Dunn wrote a provocative article entitled 'Special Education for the Mildly Retarded: Is Much of It Justifiable?' In 2015, 47 years later, the same question—and much of Dunn's article—remains valid. Despite a plethora of international evidence regarding the stigmatizing effects of branding students as 'special' (e.g., Brantlinger 2006; Florian 2010; Slee 2011), the ubiquitous ideology and discourse of 'special education' retain its potent hold over educators' thinking, policy and practice (Florian 2010; Runswick-Cole and Hodge 2009; Slee 2011). As Slee (2011, p. 156) cautions, words act as 'instruments of power'—'language not only describes the world, it orders and recreates it'. The label of 'special needs' is underpinned by and perpetuates flawed determinist assumptions that attribute 'problems' in learning to faulty functioning of students' brains and/or bodies (Lalvani and Broderick 2015; Runswick-Cole and Hodge 2009). It can detract from contextual and relational factors that are central to teaching and learning, and also from students' rights to experience childhood in their local community schools.

The folly of 'special' is exacerbated by the arbitrary nature of education systems' sorting processes, a point emphasized a decade ago by Powell (2006). More recently, Slee (2011) has referred to the same processes that effectively separate and sort students 'into their allotted tracks, into the streams that assign them to unequal destinations' (p. 151). A range of factors are involved, including how teachers and policy makers think about students, their capacities and right to learn; the purposes of labelling practices (e.g., to access resourcing and to separate students assumed to have 'limited ability' from those perceived to have 'greater ability'); as well as political and sociocultural values and priorities at any given time (Powell 2006; Slee 2011). Thus, the same student could be categorized as 'special needs' in a particular class/school, yet be unfettered by this status in a different class/school. Powell's

(2006, p. 577) cross-national comparison of special education, tellingly entitled 'Special Education and the Risk of Becoming Less Educated,' reveals that:

> ... which students bear the greatest risk of becoming less educated depends principally on the institutionalization of special education systems and on definitions of 'special educational needs'.

So what happens in the New Zealand education system? To what extent is 'special education' embedded in policy and practice, with the attendant risk that certain students become 'less educated'?

New Zealand Educational Policy Context

Given the inherently political nature of education, this section begins with a critical review of the political forces that have shaped New Zealand educational policy and practice in the last 25 years, followed by an overview of the current system. In 1989, a series of political reforms were implemented, driven by a neoliberal ideology that privileged a market-based economy, competitive individualism, parental choice and devolution of government control to local self-managing schools (Alcorn 2014; Kearney and Kane 2006). In such meritocratic education systems, 'special' education practices play an important role in legitimizing the identification, separation and control of students who may disrupt the learning and achievement of 'capable' students (Kearney and Kane 2006; Runswick-Cole 2011). Concurrently, in 1989, an amendment to the Education Act granted disabled students the right to attend local state schools, thereby requiring all schools to assume responsibility for the education of all students (Carrington et al. 2012). The juxtapositioning of the 1989 legislative change alongside the neoliberal reforms reflects antithetical values and beliefs about education.

Since 1989, New Zealand educational policy has been described as 'higgledy-piggledy' (Higgins et al. 2006) and oxymoronic (Kearney and Kane 2006), the latter referring to the flawed alignment of 'special' and inclusive education. Since 1996, however, some promising policies have emerged, such as *Special Education 2000* (Ministry of Education 1996) and *Success for All— Every School, Every Child* (Ministry of Education n.d.), reflecting a gradual, albeit tenuous shift towards inclusive education, with contemporary understandings evident on the Ministry's website:

> Inclusive education is where all children and young people are engaged and achieve through being present, participating, learning and belonging. (Ministry of Education 2015a)

The online knowledge centre, *Inclusive Education: Guides for Schools* (Te Kete Ipurangi 2015), and other initiatives also reflect a desire to enhance culturally responsive, evidence-based teaching practice. Nonetheless, we use the word 'tenuous' because the legacy of 'special' still casts long shadows over the education system. Although the goal of *Success for All* is for all schools to be 'demonstrating inclusive practices by 2014' (Ministry of Education 2015a), a categorical and service-oriented approach remains whereby students whose bodies, minds, senses and/or behaviours are considered to fall beyond the boundaries of 'normal' must prove their *needs* for *additional* supports. Defined as 'special' students, they 'will require *extra* assistance, *adapted* programmes or learning environments, *specialised* equipment or materials to support them in *special or regular* education settings (Ministry of Education 1998/2015, italics added). In addition, there are still 38 state funded segregated special schools (Education Counts 2015) as 'part of the schooling network in New Zealand [which] offer specialist teaching to students who have a high level of need' (Ministry of Education 2015b).

Segregated education stands in contrast to the rights-based and disability equality perspective advanced by self/advocacy organizations and others that quality education in the local school is needed if we are to enhance the learning of all children and young people and eliminate prejudice and discrimination. However, while the 1993 Human Rights Act, the New Zealand Disability Strategy (Minister for Disability Issues 2016) and the UNCRPD (United Nations 2006) all provide important mechanisms for responding to discrimination and contesting the legitimacy and efficacy of 'special' education, we suggest that the hegemony of neoliberalism remains largely intact.

Macro-level educational policy, whatever its ideological underpinning, is made real through its enactment at the micro-level of schools, by principals, teachers and support staff. How educators think about students, learning and rights is evident in their language and daily teaching practice. We turn now to the question of what happens within teacher education to inform the latter's thinking and actions.

New Zealand Teacher Education Context

Teacher education is positioned within and shaped by the policy contexts described above. Neoliberal ideology has made its meritocratic mark on tertiary education in general, and teacher education in particular (Alcorn 2014), as evident in the turn to managerialism and performativity, in which research outputs are the currency by which academic staff are categorized, measured and valued (Ball 2003). This is compounded by the cutting/'rationalization'

(O'Neill 2012) of some teacher education programmes, courses, contact time and the concomitant increase in class sizes and mass lecture delivery (the irony of which is not lost on student teachers).

Given the increasingly diverse nature of students in today's schools, we might also consider whether students in teacher education represent this same diversity and/or understand diversity in terms of 'other' ways of being and living (Gonsalves 2007; Mills 2008). Furthermore, Bartolomé (2007) reminds us that student teachers may privilege classroom practice over theory and a critical examination of the impact of their values, beliefs and life experiences on their work as teachers. This is evident in some student teachers' dismissal of theoretical and ideological understandings, and a 'just tell me what to do with special needs' kids' mind-set. How we attempt to address such concerns in our work with teacher education students is the focus of the following section.

Teacher Education for Equity and Excellence

In working within and beyond the boundaries of current educational prac-tices, we aim to facilitate the development of teachers who will be committed to socially just education for *all* students. This can be conceptualized as a pro-cess of transformation for ITE students and teachers undertaking PG study, which involves making the familiar unfamiliar, interrupting and unlearning received truths (Ainscow 2005; Bartolomé 2007; Slee 2004). Central to this process is providing student teachers with opportunities to make explicit and critically examine their assumptions, beliefs and values (Bartolomé 2007; Gonsalves 2007) and to consider alternative ways of being and knowing, which enable them to notice, question and contest the injustices they witness in school life. For some students whose experiences have already alerted them to the latter, this educational process may clarify and confirm their sense of social justice and agency as teachers to make a difference.

The framework that we use to conceptualize students' shift in thinking throughout the process of teacher education is positioned within the nexus of childhood studies and disability studies (see Fig. 1). Very much a work in progress, this graphic represents some of the hegemonic ideologies that are discriminatory and harmful to the educational opportunities and life chances of disabled and other minoritized students. In particular, the lingering legacy of the bell curve (Florian 2010) and its associated deficit ideologies, including 'normalcy/ableism', 'intelligence', 'fixed ability' and 'special' education, are made visible and critiqued. Counter-hegemonic narratives and research that

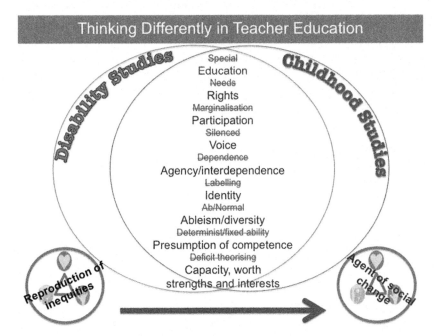

Fig. 1 Thinking differently in teacher education

privilege students' experiences and promote more democratic, respectful and hopeful understandings of the rights, worth and capability of each and every student constitute the focus of inquiry. We endorse Runswick-Cole and Hodge's (2009, p.198) advocacy 'for the abandonment of the phrase "special educational needs" and for the adoption of the phrase "educational rights"' and hope that these different ways of thinking imbue future teachers with a sense of possibility of what can be learnt with and from each student they have the privilege of teaching.

Putting It into Practice in ITE and PG Teacher Education

As ITE calls for different approaches to those utilized with experienced teachers, the following section provides separate overviews of our respective work and is accompanied by examples of students' perspectives and work in each context.

Initial Teacher Education (Gill)

Mention has already been made of a tendency for student teachers to focus on the practical—the 'doing' component of teaching. While this is understandable, simply acquiring the skills and curriculum knowledge is insufficient, as elucidated by Ainscow (2005, p. 117):

> Even the most pedagogically advanced methods are likely to be ineffective in the hands of those who implicitly or explicitly subscribe to a belief system that regards some students, at best, as disadvantaged and in need of fixing, or, worse, as deficient and, therefore, beyond fixing.

Working within the theoretical framework presented in Fig. 1, I have found Shulman's (2004) conceptualization of professional learning helpful in conveying to students that teacher education cannot be reduced to solely 'doing' (see also Rouse 2008, who presents a similar framework for teacher education). Shulman proposes that the education of individuals who are aspiring professionals involves the interaction of three apprenticeships, relating to the heart, the head and the hand. The apprenticeship of the head focuses on the specific knowledge that forms the theoretical basis of a profession, including national curriculum and pedagogy. The apprenticeship of the hand refers to practical and technical skills required in teaching practice. Underpinning both is the apprenticeship of the heart, involving professional and personal values, beliefs, ethical and moral dimensions that are central to teaching. While knowledge and skills are critical, what we know and do is determined by and reflects what we value and feel.

Mindful that it takes time to reflect upon one's implicit beliefs and values, initial engagement with student teachers at the start of their programme involves inviting them to consider what they already know about disability, how they came to know this, and how accurate it may be as a source of knowledge. I draw from Slee's (2004) thought-provoking account of his earliest encounters with disability, as a 'way in' to explore, in a non-threatening manner, the received truths, stereotypes, associated ideologies and implications for individuals upon whom a master status of 'disability' is imposed. I encourage students to be open to questioning hegemonic truths about 'special needs' students, to trouble such reified knowledge and to imagine otherwise about people, in terms of respecting individuals' capacities, rights and complexities. Offering a range of individuals' narratives and self-advocacy media that are aligned with the tenets of disability studies and childhood studies is an essential and powerful means of engaging students in the process of (re)learning.

Subsequent work with students focuses on offering as many opportunities as possible to explicitly think about their own values and assumptions and how these determine their teacher identity and practice. Students are encouraged to pay critical attention to language matters and other indicators of discriminatory, normative and ableist practices in schools and wider society, and to develop inclusive pedagogical practices that are responsive to and respectful of students' diversity, rather than 'special' and 'in addition to' what is ordinarily available (Florian 2010; Spratt and Florian 2015). The theoretical and practical components of *Learning Without Limits* (LWL) (Hart and Drummond 2014) and *Universal Design for Learning* (UDL) (Rose et al. 2014) are valuable in informing both my own teaching practice and the content shared with student teachers.

LWL provokes questioning of determinist policy, structures and practices that continue to place limits on many students' learning and can spark student teachers' thinking otherwise about children's capability. The use of LWL concepts has been well documented in teacher education (e.g., Florian and Rouse 2009; Spratt and Florian 2015). One of UDL's key characteristics is its recognition of the potentially disabling nature of many aspects of teaching and learning for students who do not represent the 'norm'; utilizing UDL shifts the focus of barriers to learning from the individual student's 'needs' to the curriculum and other external factors that are within teachers' power to change (Rose et al. 2014). UDL is increasingly recognized internationally as a powerful research-based framework that supports the right and capacity of *all* students to learn. In its emphasis on assuming diversity as *the starting place* for all aspects of the teaching and learning process, it has the potential to help dismantle the special-normal student binary that constrains many Western education systems.

Teaching and learning about human difference, inclusive education and rights is not easy, as it can evoke uncertainty and discomfort about what is known and how and, in some instances, a re-thinking of what it means to be human. Changing our minds, our personal beliefs and values is challenging, particularly over the relatively short timeframes allocated to matters of disability within teacher education programmes. As noted by Gonsalves (2007) in relation to multicultural education, 'the complex process of challenging prior socialization illustrates why a one-semester course is not sufficient to have a long-term impact on beliefs and values' (p. 22). For many student teachers, the power of practicum typically trumps university learning and can act to re-inforce 'special' thinking and practice or confirm a commitment to inclusive education.

Lily sits with me while I have lunch. It
makes me so mad. I want to have lunch with
the other kids. Does she think I'm too dumb
for that too?

I find maths and reading hard. Not lunch.

Fig. 2 Sample of student's work in ITE

On a hopeful note, the thoughtfulness of many student teachers is evident in their studies. Utilizing the principles of UDL, in which students have choice in assignment topics, resources and presentation, the following example is offered as an evidence of a second-year student teacher's learning. The assignments involved investigation of a topic relating to inclusive education; this student was particularly interested in disabled students' experiences of school and created a picture book and a teacher's handbook, with accompanying reflection of learning, to demonstrate her critical understanding of the importance of education for all (see Fig. 2).

Students' Perspectives of School

Lucy Collins-McKenzie, 2014

Reflection of learning

This assignment was incredibly enriching and thought provoking. Looking at schooling through the eyes of students with disability gave an insight on how education can be changed to benefit these students.

Many of the studies portrayed schools as a hegemonic society. Disabled students were often subjected to bullying, low expectations and isolation. Difference was often seen negatively despite the students' efforts to recognize the sameness between themselves and their peers. Students saw themselves in terms of their appearance, personality and the things they were good at. This is an important lesson to teachers. We need to see the child and what they can do in order to deliver high-quality education to all. Making assumptions based on labels benefits no one.

Through the readings, I developed a visceral response. Many students were made to feel unsafe, undervalued and as second-class citizens within their school. Despite the circumstances, students were often resilient, forgiving and adopted a pragmatic approach to their situation. In saying this, students would still become hurt or embarrassed from the negative treatment they received. The stories they shared were often heart breaking and made me really consider the qualities I needed to be an inclusive teacher.

The subject of teacher aides was one that interested me. They were seen as a valued member of the class, but students often felt torn between the fact that they help to enhance educational opportunities but can hinder socializing with their peers. Teacher aides often highlighted this difference. However, when teacher aides were used effectively in inclusive classes, then they didn't so much belong to the child as they did to the class.

Studies showed that students understood how their education could be changed to benefit them. Interestingly, the studies presented mostly the same ideas. Students wanted to be present inside the classroom, to have space, to be challenged and to be valued. These are not big asks, but they are rights and should be available to all. This point, in my opinion, is the most important. If we fail to listen to our students, then we cannot implement any of the points raised from the slide effectively.

Creating this teacher handbook has been an effective method in identifying the kind of teacher I want to be. Students' perspectives have not always been researched nor taken into account. However, when we ask and are prepared to listen, we discover that they have ideas about how their education can be improved and what we can do to help. My learning from this assignment has been invaluable and something that I will always hold with me through my career as a teacher.

Postgraduate Teacher Education (Jude)

The *Postgraduate Diploma in Specialist Teaching* is a programme for experienced teachers who work primarily in support roles in schools. The two-year course adopts an inquiry-based, interprofessional education approach using blended learning options for students, regardless of location around New Zealand, and has seven endorsement areas. While titled 'specialist', an interprofessional learning and practice focus ensures students work together across endorsement areas, building their knowledge and capability to work interprofessionally by learning with, from and about each other within a community of practice (Mentis et al. 2012). Consistent with Māori concepts of *whanaungatanga* (relationships, collaboration), and *manaakitanga* (kindness, support), sharing and respecting the skills and knowledge of others is a foundation principle, an idea that is expressed in the Māori whakatauki:

>Nau Te Rourou   With your food basket
>Naku Te Rourou   And my food basket
>Ka ora te iwi   There will be ample

Within this programme, I work with a colleague in the area of inclusive education for children and young people deemed to have 'complex educational needs' ('high/very high needs' for the purposes of school resourcing). Teachers complete the course while still teaching, providing opportunities to explore new ideas through their day-to-day teaching practice. An 'evidence-based practice' model is used to situate teachers' ethical and reflective teaching practice at the centre of three interconnecting areas of knowledge (Bourke et al. 2005) (see Fig. 3):

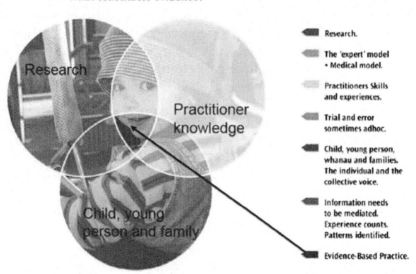

Fig. 3 An evidence-based model of practice developed in the Ministry of Education (Bourke et al. 2005)

1. Evidence from the child/young person and their family/whānau regarding their perspectives, experiences, circumstances and contexts (whānau is a Māori concept referring to kinship group, it is more than 'family' and denotes an economic, political and sociocultural bond with and within tribes and sub-tribes of hapu and iwi),
2. Evidence from teaching and professional backgrounds and experience and
3. Evidence from research that informs assessment, teaching and learning, problem solving and decision-making about teaching practice.

Teaching practice is considered evidence based only when it integrates all three types of evidence.

To the 'research' circle, we have added knowledge from human rights conventions, policy and legislation as powerful reminders of children's human and legal rights to an inclusive education in their local school.

Based on the principle that theory always sits behind teaching practice, we conceptualize the evidence-based practice model as having an overarching disability studies and childhood studies framework, supporting teachers to critique the ideas that form their own theories of practice. Ballard (2012) sees this process as vital in advancing inclusion and social justice in education because inclusion is 'about ourselves and our relationships with others ... we need to change ourselves as part of engendering change in schools and communities' (p. 68):

> For example, if we believe in special education then we are operating with ideas from a medical model of disability. If we do not understand how this model shapes teaching practice, we will continue to work in ways that disability groups identify as oppressive. (p. 67)

Childhood studies, in conjunction with children's rights and sociocultural theory, provide a conceptual framework for understanding children and childhood that is particularly useful in our course. As Smith (2013, p. 14) points out:

> together these theories suggest that children are entitled to social justice, that ideas and expectations of children and childhood differ, and that shared social experiences interacting with sensitive and responsive partners help children to become social actors and contributors to society.

Childhood studies positions children as participating subjects, knowers and social actors and therefore as competent, rational, experienced and as having agency (James and Prout 1997). Participation rights under the UN Convention on the Rights of the Child (United Nations 1989) assert that children should be viewed and treated as citizens who are an important part of the society. Teachers in our course engage with participation rights, particularly in relation to children's rights to receive and give information and to take part in decisions in matters that affect them. Children with complex needs, particularly children who do not speak, are at risk in this area since they often rely on the capacity of others to *recognize* that they *are* children with rights, that they have ordinary childhoods and that they have agency, are competent and must participate if they are to learn, have friends and have a good life in their family and community. Teachers therefore explore the many ways (pedagogical, social, technological and structural) that children can fully participate at school. This is framed not simply as a technical challenge but rather as a complex, professional challenge driven by a rights agenda.

Keeping in mind Rouse's (2008) conceptualization of teachers as playing a central role in promoting inclusion and reducing underachievement, the shift in Fig. 1 to being an agent of social change takes on some importance for teachers in our course. Florian and Graham (2014) describe the kind of 'postcode lottery' that occurs when a child or young person is identified as having 'special educational needs' in one school but not in another. While the child is constant, the difference is in how teachers conceptualize and organize support, exemplifying the powerful nature of ideas and language in shaping practice. Equipping teachers with the knowledge, skills, theories, values and confidence to interrogate their own and others' theories and practice is central to our work. Through engagement with course content, online discussion forums and the development of ideas and resources in an e-portfolio, we encourage teachers to resist and shift hegemonic thinking away from 'special' (where disability is located within the child) to a more respectful understanding of learning for all, where children's and young people's rights, capabilities, strengths, interests and agency are recognized in the schools and early childhood services teachers work in (Runswick-Cole and Hodge 2009).

At the level of practitioner knowledge, we use Florian and Black-Hawkins' (2011) work to turn attention to the relational spaces in which teachers work with students and other professionals and where variations in teaching practice might be found and explained. Drawing on sociocultural interpretations of learning as a shared activity in social contexts, teachers critique the notion of doing things differently on the basis of perceived additional 'special needs'. They are encouraged to appreciate teachers' professional craft knowledge (Cooper and McIntyre 2006); to adopt an inclusive pedagogical approach based on sensitive professional judgements that support the learning of every student; and to think about all children and adults in the classroom and how they can work together. Florian and Graham (2014) describe this as 'a deliberate decision-making process that actively avoids practices that may mark some students as different or less able' (p. 468). Children and young people with complex needs have a long history of segregation in education, so the idea that experienced teachers can bring valued knowledge and experience to the task of teaching these students is affirming and confidence building for teachers working in support roles and for the teachers and other professionals they work with.

Roger Slee's work on the link between the formation of knowledge (how we come to 'know' something) and the social exclusion of some people in society, including people with disabilities, has been helpful at the outset of the course to challenge what teachers know and make them think about whose voice carries weight and whose voice never gets heard (Slee 2000). Working at the centre of the three circles of evidence, students engage directly and through media and research with the experiences and perspectives of disabled adults, young people, children and their families to critically reflect on their own assumptions. Historical accounts of breaches of human rights that occurred through the institutionalization of Māori and Pakeha (non-Māori New Zealanders) children and adults with disabilities up until the early 2000s allow students to consider the social policies that saw the widespread removal of children with disabilities from their families and communities and the damaging effects on people's lives. Through a consideration of how disability was understood in this context; how the institutionalization of disabled people was justified by society; and how institutional thinking can linger insidiously to impact on disabled children, young people and their families in contemporary society, teachers are encouraged to re-imagine disability from a more nuanced, broadly informed perspective (Shakespeare 2009).

Through an appreciation of how people come to think the way they do; why such thinking is sustained at professional levels; who has the power and who lacks it; and the power imbalances that result in schooling being designed for 'some' rather than 'all', we trust that teachers are better placed to understand and enact through their practice the changes that are needed for schools to develop as inclusive communities (Ballard 2012; Florian et al. 2010). The following examples from teachers' e-portfolios illustrate their learning and practice as they endeavour to support good lives for disabled children and young people and their families.

Primary teacher, Maggie, used the analogy of a puzzle to explain how her learning in the first domain of the course (the Historical and Conceptual

Context) had contributed to her developing professional identity as a change agent:

> *Learning about the historical aspects of policy, practice and service provision evolving to what they are now, including how we aspire for inclusiveness for all, much challenged my own thinking about how I have come to understand disability and firmly grounded the first piece of the learning puzzle. I pieced together aspects such as cultural considerations; friendships and relationships; access (physical and learning); and health needs (as highlighted by Jill Bevan Brown, Massey University, 2013). Reflecting on what is a 'good life', contributed to informing responsive approaches; to enable, rather than disable families, in order to support our students to have a good life and be all that they want to be. My challenge now is to challenge the way some of my colleagues might understand disability, to promote inclusive thinking and practice.*

Applying new learning to her practice, Maggie 'explored some of the issues and barriers faced by families of children with complex educational and high health needs' and constructed a diagram to represent some of the responsive approaches that can be taken by schools to support those families to enable their children to live a well-supported 'good life' (see Fig. 4).

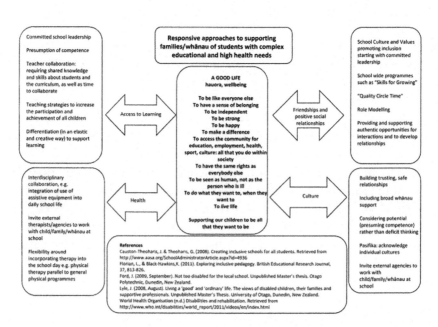

Fig. 4 Responsive approaches to supporting families/whānau of students with complex educational and high health needs

Working in an early childhood context, and reflecting on her learning in her first year, Kate said:

> *Central to my practice and understanding was immersing myself in the history and the dominant discourse surrounding inclusion and the models of disability associated to this. This allowed me to shift my thinking towards change through understanding where we do not want to go. Armed with this knowledge I feel I am now able to make a shift to what we can do to take action and make changes that benefit all children. I feel that through having a strong historical and conceptual background I am also now ready to influence and educate others to benefit our families and children. Creating an inclusive environment through "identifying and removing barriers that get in the way of a child's full acceptance, participation, and learning, so that all children receive high-quality, inclusive early educational experiences" (Purdue, 2006) is extremely important to me because, inclusion is providing for all not just for not of some.*

She acknowledged that 'My views and thoughts on inclusive education have shifted since the beginning of the course. I now have a deeper understanding on how our practices can included or exclude children within our environment.' To consolidate her thinking around the foundations for inclusion, she began by creating a model that helped her to appreciate how inclusion differed from special education (see Fig. 5).

Kate emphasized that:

> *The removal of barriers, whether policy, attitudinal, values or practice, is something that I strongly take away from this. From my learning, I wanted to develop a tool that I could use in my practice as well as in other settings to identify whether as a team or individual our practices were inclusive.*

She developed her model further to create a poster for teachers in her early childhood centre that drew attention to children's rights and teaching practices that either include or exclude (see Fig. 6). *Manaakitanga* is a Māori concept referring to an ethos of care; tuakana teina refers to a process of cross-age mentorship, a cultural role where the older is responsible for the younger.

Secondary teacher, Ella, became interested in students' capability in the area of communication. Figure 7 is part of a larger critical reflection on her learning in the practicum. She draws on ideas from childhood studies about young people's agency and rights to consider how her own strengths can be used to uphold students' participation rights:

Children's strengths, capability and rights took pride of place in her final professional philosophy where she used the analogy of standing on the back

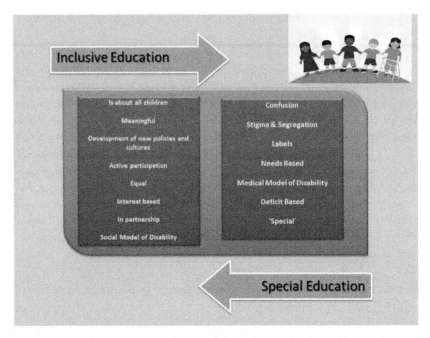

Fig. 5 How inclusion differs from special education

of a boat to acknowledge the competencies that she hoped would sustain her as a change agent in her future practice:

> It is my belief that all children can learn and "develop the knowledge, values and competencies that will enable them to live full and satisfying lives" and become "confident, connected active lifelong learners" (Ministry of Education, 2007, p. 7). This is best achieved when children attend their local schools – schools where an inclusive culture ensures diversity is valued and nurtured; where there is an ongoing commitment to identifying and breaking down barriers to presence, participation and achievement; and where teaching and learning are firmly situated within the New Zealand curriculum … Drawing on the te ao Māori notion of Hokinga Maumahara – drawing from the past enlightening the future – I need to ensure that as I move forward into unchartered waters and new experiences I continue to stand on the deck at the back of my ship and look back along the wake that I have left. It is in the patterns of that wake, in the what has been as well as the what is now, that I will learn what to carry with me, what to leave behind and what I need to add to my kete (flax basket) to sustain me and ensure I continue to make progress on my journey to be coming a more effective specialist teacher.

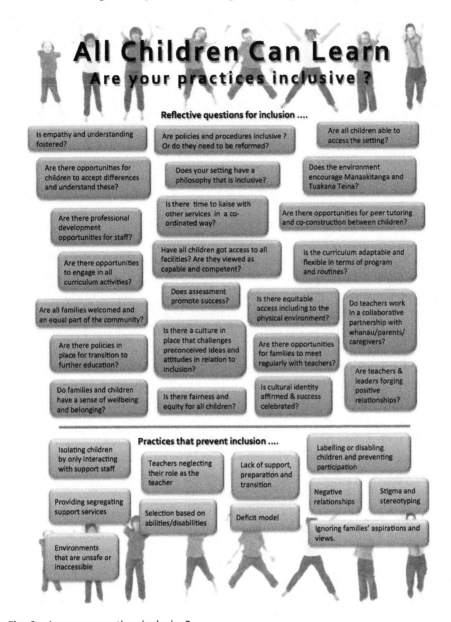

Fig. 6   Are your practices inclusive?

Looking Ahead

Space precludes describing our courses in depth, and we have provided just a glimpse into some of the ways in which we work with students at the nexus of

During my practicum I have continued to build my experience working with students with complex communication needs and this has cemented two areas of particular strength and interest for me. Interestingly, these areas link directly back to my origins as a language teacher.

Firstly, I am passionate about ensuring that students have a voice in every sense of the word. They must be supported to develop self-determination to the highest possible degree, and for those with communication needs, it is vital that action be taken to provide a suitable system of communication so that they can truly be heard and be active participants in the planning of their future.

Fig. 7 Ella's reflection on her practicum

disability studies and childhood studies in ITE and PG programmes. While we work with different cohorts, we share a commitment to foreground approaches to teaching and learning that enhance the lives of disabled children and young people and their families/whānau in New Zealand. Our goal is unashamedly to shift students from a position where they reproduce social inequalities to one where they have the dispositions, confidence and support to be an agent of change, contributing to the development of inclusive school communities.

Looking ahead, we will have more conversations about what it might mean to truly work at the centre of disabled children's childhood studies. Recent work by Curran and Runswick-Cole (2014) challenges us to recognize and celebrate 'non-normative lives', and to be mindful of the relational nature of childhoods and the power relations with adults that impact on children's rights and participation at school. As researchers, our pedagogical knowledge will be advanced when we undertake methodologically and ethically responsive research with disabled children and young people. For now, we are sustained by the thoughtful work and contributions of our students as they make schools better places for all children and young people. At the same time, we believe there is still work to be done to ensure that students leaving our programmes are also sustained in their efforts to advance a more inclusive school system where 'special' is replaced with rights-based, inclusive pedagogies and learning for all.

Acknowledgements Gill and Jude: We wish to acknowledge the thoughtful work of our students. We value your contributions, and we celebrate the good work you are doing in school communities. Thank you for your contribution to this chapter. We learn from you.

Jude: I wish to acknowledge the hard work and support of the staff at Massey University and the University of Canterbury who have developed and/or teach on the Postgraduate Diploma in Specialist Teaching. In particular, Associate Professors

Mandia Mentis and Alison Kearney, Wendy. Holley-Boen and Dr Laurie McLay who have developed content in the area of 'complex educational needs' with me. You all sit behind part of this work.

References

Ainscow, M. (2005). Developing Inclusive Education Systems: What Are the Levers for Change? *Journal of Educational Change, 6*(2), 109–124.

Alcorn, N. (2014). Teacher Education in New Zealand 1974–2014. *Journal of Education for Teaching: International Research and Pedagogy, 40*(5), 447–460.

Ball, S. J. (2003). The Teacher's Soul and the Terrors of Performativity. *Journal of Education Policy, 18*(2), 215–228.

Ballard, K. (2012). Inclusion and Social Justice: Teachers as Agents of Change. In S. Carrington & J. MacArthur (Eds.), *Teaching in Inclusive School Communities* (pp. 65–87). Milton: John Wiley Publishers.

Bartolomé, L. I. (2007). Introduction: Beyond the Fog of Ideology. In L. I. Bartolomé (Ed.), *Ideologies in Education: Unmasking the Trap of Teacher Neutrality* (pp. ix–xxi). New York: Peter Lang Publishing, Inc.

Bourke, R., Holden, B., & Curzon, J. (2005). *Using Evidence to Challenge Practice: A Discussion Paper*. Wellington: Ministry of Education.

Brantlinger, E. A. (2006). Conclusion: Whose Labels? Whose Norms? Whose Needs? Whose Benefits? In E. A. Brantlinger (Ed.), *Who Benefits from Special Education? Remediating (Fixing) Other People's Children* (pp. 430–458). Mahwah: Lawrence Erlbaum Associates, Inc..

Carrington, S., MacArthur, J., Kearney, A., Kimber, M., Mercer, L., Morton, M., & Rutherford, G. (2012). Towards an Inclusive Education for All. In S. Carrington & J. MacArthur (Eds.), *Teaching in Inclusive School Communities* (pp. 3–38). Milton: John Wiley and Sons Australia.

Cooper, P., & McIntyre, D. (2006). The Crafts of the Classroom: Teachers' and Students' Accounts of the Knowledge Underpinning Effective Teaching and Learning in Classrooms. *Research Papers in Education, 10*(2), 181–216.

Curran, T., & Runswick-Cole, K. (2014). Disabled Children's Childhood Studies: A Distinct Approach? *Disability & Society, 29*(10), 1617–1630.

Dunn, L. M. (1968). Special Education for the Mildly Retarded: Is Much of it Justifiable? *Exceptional Children, 35*, 5–22.

Education Counts. (2015). *Number of Schools*. Available at: https://www.education-counts.govt.nz/statistics/schooling/number-of-schools. Date Accessed 24 Aug 2015.

Florian, L. (2010). Special Education in an Era of Inclusion: The End of Special Education or a New Beginning? *The Psychology of Education Review, 34*(2), 22–29.

Florian, L., & Black-Hawkins, K. (2011). Exploring Inclusive Pedagogy. *British Educational Research Journal, 37*(5), 813–828.

Florian, L., & Graham, A. (2014). Can an Expanded Interpretation of Phronesis Support Teacher Professional Development for Inclusion? *Cambridge Journal of Education, 44*(4), 465–478.

Florian, L., & Rouse, M. (2009). The Inclusive Practice Project in Scotland: Teacher Education for Inclusive Education. *Teaching and Teacher Education, 25*, 594–601.

Florian, L., Young, K., & Rouse, M. (2010). Preparing Teachers for Inclusive and Diverse Educational Environments: Studying Curricular Reform in an Initial Teacher Education Course. *International Journal of Inclusive Education, 14*(7), 709–722.

Gonsalves, R. E. (2007). Hysterical Blindness and the Ideology of Denial: Preservice Teachers' Resistance to Multicultural Education. In L. I. Bartolome (Ed.), *Ideologies in Education: Unmasking the Trap of Teacher Neutrality* (pp. 3–28). New York: Peter Lang Publishing, Inc.

Hart, S., & Drummond, M. J. (2014). Learning Without Limits: Constructing a Pedagogy Free from Determinist Beliefs About Ability. In L. Florian (Ed.), *The Sage Handbook of Special Education* (pp. 439–458). London: Sage Publications.

Higgins, N., MacArthur, J. & Reitveld, C. (2006) 'Higgledy-Piggledy Policy: Confusion About Inclusion',*Childrenz Issues*, 10, 1, 30–36.

James, A., & Prout, A. (Eds.). (1997). *Constructing and Reconstructing Childhood: Contemporary Issues in the Sociological Study of Childhood* (2nd ed.). London: Routledge Falmer.

Kearney, A., & Kane, R. (2006). Inclusive Education Policy in New Zealand: Reality or Ruse? *International Journal of Inclusive Education, 10*(2–3), 201–219.

Lalvani, P., & Broderick, A. A. (2015). Teacher Education, InExclusion, and the Implicit Ideology of *Separate but Equal*: An Invitation to a Dialogue. *Education, Citizenship and Social Justice, 10*(2), 168–183.

Mentis, M., Kearney, A., & Bevan-Brown, J. (2012). Interprofessional Learning and Its Contribution to Inclusive Education. In S. Carrington & J. MacArthur (Eds.), *Teaching in Inclusive School Communities* (pp. 296–312). Milton: John Wiley & Sons Publishers.

Mills, C. (2008). Making a Difference: Moving Beyond the Superficial Treatment of Diversity. *Asia-Pacific Journal of Teacher Education, 36*(4), 261–275.

Minister for Disability Issues. (2016). *New Zealand Disability Strategy*. Available at: http://www.odi.govt.nz/nzds/. Date Accessed 24 Aug 2015.

Ministry of Education. (n.d.). *Success for All – Every School, Every Child*. Available at: http://www.education.govt.nz/assets/Documents/School/Inclusive-education/SuccessForAllEnglish.pdf. Date Accessed 18 Dec 2015.

Ministry of Education. (1996). *Special Education 2000 Policy*. Wellington: Ministry of Education.

Ministry of Education. (2007). *The New Zealand Curriculum*. Wellington: Author.

Ministry of Education. (1998/2015). *Managing the Special Education Grant: A Handbook for Schools*. Available at: http://www.education.govt.nz/school/student-support/special-education/managing-the-special-education-grant-a-handbook-for-schools/. Date Accessed 24 Aug 2015.

Ministry of Education. (2015a). *Inclusive Education*. Available at: http://www.education.govt.nz/school/running-a-school/inclusive-education/. Date Accessed 24 Aug 2015.

Ministry of Education. (2015b). *Day Special Schools for Students with High Needs*. Available at: http://www.education.govt.nz/school/student-support/special-education/day-special-schools-for-students-with-high-needs/. Date Accessed 24 Aug 2015.

O'Neill, J. (2012). Rationality and Rationalisation in Teacher Education Policy Discourse in New Zealand. *Educational Research, 52*(2), 225–237.

Powell, J. J. W. (2006). Special Education and the Risk of Becoming Less Educated. *European Societies, 8*(4), 577–599.

Purdue, K. (2006). Children and Disability in Early Childhood Education: 'Special' or Inclusive Education? *Early Childhood Folio, 10*, 12–15.

Rose, D. H., Gravel, J. W., & Gordon, D. T. (2014). Universal Design for Learning. In L. Florian (Ed.), *The Sage Handbook of Special Education* (pp. 475–489). London: Sage Publications.

Rouse, M. (2008). Developing Inclusive Practice: A Role for Teachers and Teacher Education. *Education in the North*, *16*(1), 6–13. Available at: http://www.abdn.ac.uk/eitn/uploads/files/issue16/EITN-1-Rouse.pdf. Date Accessed 24 Aug 2015.

Runswick-Cole, K. (2011). Time to End the Bias Towards Inclusive Education? *British Journal of Special Education, 38*(3), 112–119.

Runswick-Cole, K., & Hodge, N. (2009). Needs or Rights? A Challenge to the Discourse of Special Education. *British Journal of Special Education, 36*(4), 198–203.

Rutherford, G. (2008). *Different Ways of Knowing? Understanding Disabled Students' and Teacher Aides' School Experiences Within a Context of Relational Social Justice*. Dunedin: University of Otago. Available at: http://hdl.handle.net/10523/357. Date Accessed 24 Aug 2015.

Shakespeare, T. (2009). *Re-Imagining Disability*. Available at: https://vimeo.com/5161684. Date Accessed 24 Aug 2015.

Shulman, L. S. (2004). *The Wisdom of Practice: Essays on Teaching, Learning, and Learning to Teach*. San Francisco: Jossey-Bass.

Slee, R. (2000). Reflection. In P. Clough & J. Corbett (Eds.), *Theories of Inclusive Education: A Students' Guide* (pp. 125–128). London: Sage Publications.

Slee, R. (2004). Meaning in the Service of Power. In L. Ware (Ed.), *Ideology and the Politics of (in)Exclusion* (pp. 46–60). New York: Peter Lang.

Slee, R. (2011). *The Irregular School: Exclusion, Schooling and Inclusive Education*. London: Routledge.

Smith, A. B. (2013). *Understanding Children and Childhood* (5th ed.). Wellington: Bridget Williams Books Ltd.

Spratt, J., & Florian, L. (2015). Inclusive Pedagogy: From Learning to Action. Supporting Each Individual in the Context of "Everybody". *Teaching and Teacher Education, 49*, 89–96.

Te Kete Ipurangi. (2015). *Inclusive Education: Guides for Schools.* Available at: http://inclusive.tki.org.nz/. Date Accessed 24 Aug 2015.

United Nations. (1989). *United Nations Convention on the Rights of the Child.* Available at: https://treaties.un.org/pages/viewdetails.aspx?src=treaty&mtdsg_no=iv-11&chapter=4&lang=en-title=UNTC-publisher. Date Accessed 24 Aug 2015.

United Nations. (2006). *United Nations Convention on the Rights of Persons with Disability.* Available at: http://www.un.org/disabilities/convention/convention-full.shtml. Date Accessed 24 Aug 2015.

Gill Rutherford is Senior Lecturer in Education and Disability Studies at the University of Otago. Rutherford's teaching and research include a focus on preservice and qualified teachers' thinking about disability; the importance of being responsive to students' perspectives and rights; the role of teacher aides; and Universal Design for Learning (UDL)/inclusive pedagogies.

Jude MacArthur is a senior lecturer in the Institute of Education, Massey University, New Zealand. Her teaching and research centre around the development of democratic, inclusive school communities, with a particular focus on the rights and experiences of children and young people who are vulnerable to exclusion at school because of disability.

A Diversity of Childhoods: Considering the Looked After Childhood

Luke Jones and Kirsty Liddiard

Key Points

- This chapter centres on the lives of disabled children and 'Looked After Children', many of whom are disabled.
- We ask: Can disabled children's childhood studies (DCCS) be useful towards thinking about other forms of non-normative childhood?
- We focus on three areas: (i) surveillance and intimacy; (ii) pathology and psychologisation; and (iii) vulnerability and future.
- We conclude that DCCS offers new perspectives on the lives of Looked After Children and that it is a framework that can be used to think through other 'non-normative' childhoods.

Introduction

We have written this chapter over many bottles of wine and just as many bonfires in the garden. In order to write, we have sat, under evening skies, reflecting, debating, and contesting. As co-authors (and, we should disclose,

L. Jones (✉)
Cygnet Health Care, Bradford, UK

K. Liddiard
The University of Sheffield, Sheffield, UK

© The Author(s) 2018
K. Runswick-Cole et al. (eds.), *The Palgrave Handbook of Disabled Children's Childhood Studies*, https://doi.org/10.1057/978-1-137-54446-9_25

life partners), we have disagreed more than we thought we might. This is because professionally, and sometimes politically, we inhabit quite different worlds where disability, childhood, and mental health are concerned. One of us (Kirsty) is a disabled feminist academic and researcher whose activist scholarship focuses on the lives of disabled people, while the other (Luke), is a mental health social work practitioner. Thus, we work in markedly different contexts (with differing constraints) that often shape our views significantly. We have found that, in writing together for the first time, our respective views are further determined by class, gender, and disability. However, in this chapter, we come together to offer a reflection on our own lived experiences of disability, fostering, and childhood as long-term family foster carers to a Looked After Child. In the UK, from where we write this chapter, a Looked After Child is a child who is looked after by the State.

We should say, at this juncture, that this chapter has been very difficult to write: practically, emotionally, and ethically. Practically, because living together and loving and knowing each other deeply didn't miraculously transcend to an effective co-authoring relationship. Writing has been tough; we have disagreed. Layered on top of this, our chapter has been emotionally complicated to write because our lives are its contents, and not merely theory and practice. While we both employ reflexive practices as standard in our respective work, the experiences we detail in this chapter are relatively new (and have been painful) for us. But rather than writing this emotion out, we centre it. In doing so, we follow Burkitt (2012: 458), conceptualising emotion and feeling not as barriers 'to clear reflexive thought' but as necessary forms of affective labour for reflexivity itself.

It is, however, the ethical quagmire of writing about our caring experiences—which cannot explicitly be divorced from those for whom we care—which has shored up multiple rewrites and endless worry. We want to make it clear that this chapter isn't about the Looked After Child in our care, but about our own lived, material, and affective experiences as foster carers. We note that the fact that we share our own experiences as carers in a book *about* children and childhood produces a tension that impacts upon children and young people. Our own experiences are unavoidably layered throughout our analysis—largely because much of our knowledge does not come from literature and research (typically situated as forms of 'evidence' in academic work) but through oft-difficult moments, meetings, and memories. However, we think it's crucial to acknowledge that in such an embodied analysis, we implicitly story others (e.g. workers, other carers, and wider family) and, most importantly, the person with whom we are tasked to protect, advocate, and care: the child. Further, we do so in a context where, because of the systemic circumstances in the life of a Looked After Child, as a family we are already subject to surveillance and intervention. Therefore, our lives (and perspectives) are essentially entangled and cannot be separated in ways that feel ethically *comfortable*. Instead, we have worked to develop the beginnings of a set of ethical practices that have enabled us to write (and publish) this chapter. Further, we feel these embody some of the political aims of DCCS:

1. We have discussed the contents of this chapter with the child in our care and have sought their consent.
2. We have made efforts to anonymise people, workers, and moments in our lives.
3. We have talked endlessly, both together and with trusted others, with regard to writing about this aspect of our lives. We have sought the views of trusted colleagues: scholars, researchers, and practitioners.
4. We have been very selective about what is included. For example, there are many things that we *don't* share in this chapter, even though we would like to. Markedly, even at times where lived anecdotes can serve as accessible, available tools for explaining the complexities of systemic oppression. We don't detail these moments, because, as carers (and, by extension, allies and advocates), we work hard to protect the privacy of the Looked After Child in our care, to subvert oppressions they face where we encounter them, and advocate for our rights as a family.

These points are in constant development and are by no means a finished project. They merely stand as 'entry points' for us to even begin writing. It is important to note here, as we do throughout the chapter, that DCCS is unique because it makes space for personal engagement where other forms of analysis do not; it positions lived experience, authenticity, and the 'care taken around ethics' (Curran and Runswick-Cole 2014: 1618) as imperative to understanding the lives of children and young people, and their families.

As a new field of study, then, DCCS offers a distinct engagement with (disabled) childhoods. As Curran and Runswick-Cole state (2014: 1618), this emerging area of study has three distinct premises:

First, disabled children's childhood studies offers a different starting point for discussion that shifts the focus away from discussion 'about' disabled children, which is so often conflated with talk of impairment, inequality and abuse; the second is an approach to ethics and research design that positions the voice and experiences of disabled children at the centre of inquiry and; the third is a contextualised agenda for change that seeks to trouble the hegemony of the 'norm'

(Davis 1995). The aim of disabled children's childhood studies is to enable disabled children to step outside the 'normative shadows' that so often cloud discussions of their lives (Overboe 2004). This also entails re-thinking children's relationships with parents/carers, with family members and with communities. The studies do not originate from policy directives, service outcomes or professional practice debates, although the links and impact of those are salient in disabled children's childhood studies. This is the case not only at the level of direct intervention, but in generating, sustaining and changing wider cultural practices.

Thus, there is recognition within DCCS that disabled children and young people are experts in their own lives, over and above the often-individualising focus on the conditions and subsequent diagnoses which proliferate in the professional discourse within the 'team around the child'. As such 'disabled children's childhood studies are written by disabled children and young people, disabled scholars and activists reflecting on their childhoods, as well as parents/carers of disabled children, allies and academics listening directly to disabled children and young people's voices' (Curran and Runswick-Cole 2014: 1618). This brings alternative analyses to those found in what Mallet and Runswick-Cole (2014: 39) call 'new sociologies of childhood' which, they argue, is a 'product of white, middle class Western academics'. In DCCS, then, disabled childhoods are viewed as very important and worthy of inquiry, in ways that substitute their absence from mainstream sociologies of childhood and other disciplines (Mallet and Runswick-Cole 2014).

In this chapter, we explore the Looked After Childhood through the lens of DCCS (Curran and Runswick-Cole 2014). While this chapter isn't about disabled children per se (although many Looked After Children are also disabled children; see Kelly and Dowling's insightful chapter 'Disabled Children in Out-of-Home Care: Issues and Challenges for Practice', in this volume), we draw together some disparate threads, asking what DCCS as an emerging area of study offers our understanding of the lives of other Othered children living 'non-normative', diverse childhoods. As Curran and Runswick-Cole (2014: 1619) state, 'disabled children's childhood studies starts with childhood and disability but never ends there'. Our analysis speaks, in some way, to the commonalities in experiences of Looked After and Disabled Children. Through the chapter, we reflect upon our impetus for this analysis, our lived experiences, and (some) existing policy and practice which dominates disabled and Looked After Childhoods. We critically question the extent to which DCCS offers both a theoretical and empirical framework with which to theorise Looked After Childhoods, and whether DCCS enables the category of disability to be expanded to this end. We conclude by arguing that DCCS has much to offer both rethinking and researching Looked After Childhoods and offers new ways of conceptualising the Looked After Childhood in positive and productive ways.

Looked After Childhoods: Rising Numbers

A 'Looked After Child' in UK Law (Children's Act 1989) is a child who is being cared for by the local authority. More commonly known as a 'child in care', children come to be looked after by their local authority for a wide variety of reasons. These reasons stem from issues such as family breakdown to child protection concerns around care, abuse, and violence. A Looked After Child can reside at home with parents under the supervision of Social Services but will more commonly be removed from the family home to reside in temporary and/or permanent forms of local authority-controlled care. These include foster care, children's homes, and other types of residential facility (e.g. a secure unit for young offenders and/or a secure mental health unit). At the beginning of 2014, there were 68,840 Looked After Children in England (DoE 2015; see also DfE 2013). When a Care Order—an order given by a court that 'allows a council to take a child into care' (https://www.gov.uk/if-your-child-is-taken-into-care/overview)—is granted, it becomes the responsibility of local authority elected members and officers to 'provide a standard of care that would be good enough for their own children' (NCB 2015). The terminology applied to local authority elected members and officers—an oxymoron if ever there was one—is 'Corporate Parent'. As such, the State, via the local authority, becomes the Corporate Parent of the Looked After Child. While the language of 'Corporate Parent' is somewhat jarring, we could ask how families, parenting, and intimacy, in general, are marked by neoliberalism; by this we mean, is it possible to be anything other than a Corporate Parent, for anyone, where the primary expectation of all parents in neoliberal cultures is that they invest fully in their children's futures?

Numbers of Looked After Children are rising for a variety of reasons. Most recently, the criminalisation of emotional abuse known as the 'Cinderella Law' have re-categorised emotional cruelty and neglect as abuses which warrant greater Child Protection intervention. Following a three-year campaign by the children's charity Action for Children, in her speech on 4 June 2014, the Queen announced that the Government would bring forward a Serious Crime Bill to tackle child neglect. While it is too early to grasp the full effects of this legislation change, it has been argued that it dramatically changes key criteria around child protection intervention and safeguarding practice

(Cabezas 2016). Such a focus on emotional harm is rooted in concerns for children's futures—that emotional abuse and neglect are key risk factors in longer-term mental illness, distress and disorder, unemployment, disenfranchisement, criminalisation, poverty, and substance misuse (see Cabezas 2016).

Others have cited rising poverty as the key determinant in the increase of Looked After Children. Ridge (2013: 414) cites the impact of austerity and welfare retrenchment upon the family. He argues:

> Child poverty is being privatised as children's needs are repositioned back into the family; a family setting that is under siege, bearing the heaviest burden in relation to welfare cuts and financial insecurity and systematically undermined through political rhetoric and media hyperbole.

Rather than passive subjects, Ridge (2013: 414) argues that within the family, it is children who 'mediate and manage some of the worst effects of austerity'. In July 2015, all four UK Children's Commissioners called upon the UK Conservative Government to stop making cuts to benefits and amend its welfare reforms in order to protect children from the harshness of austerity. Underpinning this request are rates of child poverty that are unacceptably high and rapidly increasing (Family Law 2015). Under current UK Conservative Government policies, child poverty figures are expected to continue to rise, with 4.7 million children projected to be living in poverty by 2020 (Family Law 2015). Importantly, this pattern is not the preserve of the UK alone, but a reality across the EU, with over half of member states experiencing increases in poverty and social exclusion through austerity measures (Frazer and Marlier 2011).

Shifts within social work practice have also been cited to explain the increasing numbers of Looked After Children (Macleod et al. 2010). Recent years have seen a number of high-profile cases where children have died from abuse and neglect at the hands of parents, carers, and other family members, and where the appropriate services (health, education, and social care) have failed to protect them (Macleod et al. 2010). Many of these tragic deaths have been taken up in the media in ways that vilify local authority child protection services, and those who work for them. Such vilification impacts practice, as social workers become more risk averse. For example, Macleod et al. (2010: iv) found clear evidence to indicate that 'the levels of Section 31 applications [an application made by a social worker to a court for a Care Order to remove a child from the family home] made by English local authorities rose in the wake of the publicising of the case of Baby Peter (in November 2008), and, in the period that followed, has continued to rise to a level higher than any experienced since April 2007'. This has become known widely as the 'Baby P effect'.

Such significant rise in the numbers of Looked After Children is worthy of an analysis that centres ethics and children's own lifeworlds. Often—though perhaps not surprisingly—the voices of Looked After Children are absent from the policy consultations that determine their lives in the present and their life chances for the future (Munro 2001). This is despite the fact that the United Nations Convention on the Rights of the Child (UNCRC) states that children and young people must be consulted about all decisions that affect their lives (see Beresford et al. 2007). Further, research into the lives of Looked After Children emanates primarily from the disciplines of Social Work, Sociology (specifically sociologies of childhood and youth), Psychiatry, and Education. Our aim in this chapter, then, is to extend these analyses in ways that do not reproduce children and young people through deficit discourses, but offer a more affirmative analysis of the lives of Looked After Children.

Surveillance and Intimate Spaces: Relational Moments

Disabled lives and selves are subject to extensive surveillance and containment through dis/ableism (see Liddiard and Slater 2017). For clarity, we define ableism as 'particular kind of self and body (the corporeal standard)

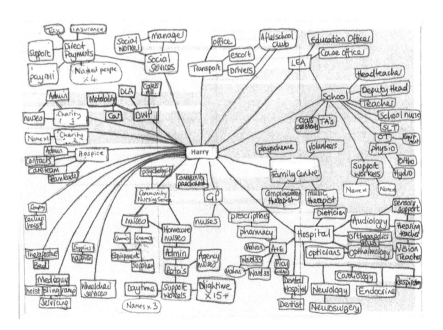

Fig. 1 Mind map (Image courtesy of Debby Watson 2014)

that is projected as the perfect, species-typical and therefore essential and fully human' (Campbell 2009: 44). Disablism, on the other hand, is the resultant oppressive treatment of disabled people. By dis/ableism, then, we mean the iterative processes of ableism and disablism. In the context of disability, categorisation, diagnosis, institutionalisation, and segregation materialise as acute forms of surveillance and management. The image above was produced by a mother of a disabled child that one of us met at a conference (see Debby Watson's chapter "Expressive Eyebrows and Beautiful Bubbles: Playfulness and Children with Profound Impairments", in this volume); it depicts her mapping of the extent to which her son is deeply entangled in an expansive network of professionals. The image speaks to the ways in which her child, and, by extension, herself and her family are unavoidably rooted in multiple forms of observation, assessment, and monitoring. This is not surprising, given the extent to which disability ensures family life can come to be dominated by professional knowledges.

In much the same way, myriad professionals and services are situated around the Looked After Child: multiple social workers (across multiple teams); Child and Adolescent Mental Health practitioners; educational psychologists; contact supervisors; youth workers; an Independent Reviewing Officer; and duty staff (where needed). Despite the fact that we are family foster carers, recent legislation means we are at the same time required to be paid employees of the local authority as Approved Foster Carers if we are to receive funding. Thus, we are woven into the professional web that surrounds the child. Moreover, this labour is extensive: advocacy; forms; monitoring; training; meetings; and being a liaison and coordinator between and across the multiple practitioners involved in the life of the Looked After Child. As 'paid for' allies, we are allied with professionals in ways that we feel compromise familial intimacies. Ryan and Runswick-Cole (2008: 202) have noted how difficult and complex it can be to be rendered an ally for a child whom you love, and that 'parents' intimate, enduring and loving relationships with their children are in stark contrast to the professional's payment for limited hours of contact and emotional attachment'. They suggest that mothers of disabled children are more than just allies, namely because 'they experience directly and by proxy many of the discriminatory practices and attitudes their disabled children face' (Ryan and Runswick-Cole 2008: 202). Thus, in the context of child welfare, namely fostering and adoption, caring is professionalised and institutionalised in ways that could be argued to be particularly disabling for Looked After Children.

Like mothers of disabled children, then, as carers, our own intimate and personal lives cannot exist outside of professional surveillance. Due to the fact that this allied role is located within 'family life', it routinely reaches into the intimate spaces of our lives: ourselves, our home, and our ways of living. Thus, having noted already the professionalisation of our family labour, the segment from Kirsty's fostering diary below shows how we are at once the object and the subject of professional gaze; it could be argued that this dual professionalisation makes us ambivalent kin and allies to the child in our care:

> I answered the door in my crap old denim hot pants – the ones I slob around the house in, an old Beatles t-shirt, greasy hair scraped on top of my head, having not yet showered. OK, it was 1pm, but [Looked After Child] and The Boy [Luke] were off to [hometown], leaving me with a crafty day at home on my own. Sad to say I used it to work, but anyway, I was at least enjoying some peace. As I opened the door (thinking it was the postman) the woman at the door said she was from the local authority and was here to do our "unannounced visit". This does what it says on the tin – a social worker turns up – unannounced – to take a look around the home, and "see" the Looked After Child in their home environment. In that moment I felt the blood drain from my face. The house was a *tip*. Saturday mornings are marked for weekly cleaning, and we normally all do it before going out on Saturday afternoons. This wasn't a normal weekend, because [Looked After Child] and The Boy [Luke] weren't here, so the house was in its typical end-of-the-week-untidy state – a state I'm sure most homes across Britain are in on a Saturday morning. It dawned to me then, there, that we are not most homes, and won't ever be. Every inch of our lives, loves, and spaces are reachable, assessed, surveyed. As the social worker sat at my kitchen table and filled out her form, she said awkwardly, "I'll just put it's [the home] a little untidy…Mine's the same, don't worry". If yours is the same, why are you writing it down? I wondered, in that moment, what norms and standards we were being measured against. I don't think I'd ever felt embarrassment like that in my entire life – shame, fear (that we weren't "proper" adults), and that our mess was detriment to the well-being of [Looked After Child] – something we work tirelessly to maintain and protect. (Fostering Diary 2015)

The 'unannounced visit' included checking our bedrooms, looking at our toilet, and into our sinks. We had clearly not 'passed' on this occasion, or at least this was how it was interpreted. Recording this failure inevitably invokes the use of categorisation: the reification of institutional norms for what a fostering household should look like, and the fact that we had not met them on this occasion. Such norms are used to guide our practice as foster carers, notably, towards a standard of care to which most other families are not measured. This lack of privacy makes us vulnerable as carers, as we are assessed against arbitrary targets; targets that we are expected to not only meet but also exceed.

It is a similar situation for parents of disabled children, whose care and caring comes into contact with multiple services and professionals, opening them up to critique and intervention at any time. As Ryan and Runswick-Cole suggest 'the competence of mothers [of disabled children] is constantly under surveillance and, in some cases, challenged because of their close involvement with a range of statutory bodies and professionals'. Once again, the family shifts from a space of intimacy to a professionalised and institutionalised zone where intervention—often experienced (certainly by us) as a disruption to intimacy—can come at any time.

Aside from intensive and extensive professional surveillance, there are further relational problematics of being a non-normative family that overlap somewhat with the disability experience. Mallet and Runswick-Cole (forthcoming) draw attention to the relational work that comes into being with others' 'urge to know' an impairment label or impairment type upon meeting or seeing a disabled person. Desiring to know 'what's wrong' with the disabled person reveals the impairment label to have great social and cultural meaning (Mallet and Runswick-Cole forthcoming). It is a means through which to come to understand and *know* the person with whom you're speaking—a way to classify. In our case, people routinely ask how our family's caring situation came to be. The true answer is long and complex, and not easily explained in brief interactions. In this scenario, we are often thrown into a (moral) quandary as to 'how much' to reveal, forever mindful of the implications of what and whom we tell. Regardless of our responses (we have formed many over the past two years), what's curious is the *urge* to know (Mallet and Runswick-Cole forthcoming), as it emerges as a relational desire to account for and explain difference.

For disabled people, this *urge* can equate to a form of psycho-emotional disablism (Mallet and Runswick-Cole (forthcoming) defined by Thomas (1999: 60) as 'the socially engendered undermining of emotional well-being'. Psycho-emotional disablism is an inherently relational form of disablism: it further inculcates from experiences of exclusion; through routine objectification and voyeurism perpetrated by (but not exclusive to) non-disabled others; and via internalised oppression—the internalisation of feeling Other (Reeve 2004). Further embodied through 'hostility or pitying stares, dismissive rejection, infantilisation, patronising attitudes, altruism, and help and care on the part of non-disabled people' (Goodley 2010: 96), psycho-emotional disablism 'frequently results in disabled people being made to feel worthless, useless, of lesser value, unattractive, a burden' (Thomas 2006: 182).

While disability is not the object in our case, 'telling' can be an exhaustive emotional labour as a family foster carer. 'Telling too much' feels deeply problematic, as we give away a history which, to a large extent, is not our own. Yet, at the same time prevails a need to satiate the desire of the other: to relent to the (intrusive but innocent) curiosity of the person asking. Where disability is concerned, these kinds of intrusive encounters have been highlighted as forms of complex emotional work and 'emotional labour' (Liddiard 2014; see also Hochchild 1983). This intricate management of feeling and performance takes place for the benefit of the person who has the urge to know, not for the performing subject (see Exley and Letherby 2001). It is also largely an invisible labour.

Our reason for sharing these intimate experiences of relational oppression in the context of care, then, is to highlight the way in which DCCS positions such analyses as important within the lives of disabled children and young people, and those who care for them. Rather than write out the affective, emotional, and intimate, as many studies of disability have done since the birth of disability studies (Shakespeare et al. 1996; Reeve 2002), DCCS makes space for the close encounters, the in-between and liminal spaces of disabled lives, and the affective politics of disability *life*. Thus, 'disability' is considered to have 'political, material, economic, structural, emotional, intimate, and personal dimensions' (Liddiard 2014: 116). Redefining disability (and difference) in this way acknowledges that 'the oppression disabled people can experience operates on the "inside" as well as on the "outside"' (Thomas 2004: 40). Or, as Reeve (2004: 84; original emphasis) articulates, 'operates at both the public and personal levels, affecting what people can do, as well as what they can be'. In the context of the Looked After Child, for whom a lack of privacy, significant trauma, and harm and abuse happens within the intimate and emotional spaces of life, self, and family, such analyses are necessary towards acknowledging the lived and affective lifeworlds of these Othered children (and those who care for them). Importantly, such analyses are rooted *in* disability studies rather than psychology and/or psychiatry, and other health disciplines, which further avoids reproducing the Looked After Child as a psychologised and psychiatrised subject, which is where we now turn.

Pathologised Childhoods

Looked After and disabled childhoods are dominated by deficit discourses that render children as tragic and their lives lacking vitality, vibrancy, and future. In the case of the Looked After Child, psychological theories of attachment routinely lurk as weapons in ways that reduce the child as an inevitably vulnerable subject: a lonely passenger on the journey towards an unknown and uncertain future. The same can be said for disabled children, whose futures are always in question (Kafer 2013). We know too that Looked After Children who cannot be contained through psy knowledges are readily criminalised: in the UK, 30% of the male prison population and 44% of the female prison population are care leavers (Nicolas 2014). Thus, containment through criminalisation subsists as another way to manage the Other.

The Looked After Child is routinely pathologised—considered abnormal—and psychologised; that is understood in psychological terms and through psy knowledges (see Levinson and McKinney 2013). For example, the first national survey of the mental health of young people looked after by local authorities in England found that of 'nearly three quarters of the children in residential care, 72%, were clinically rated as having a mental disorder: 60% had conduct disorders, 18% were assessed as having emotional disorders, 8% hyperkinetic disorders, and 13% less common disorders' (Meltzer et al. 2003: 26). As with disabled children, the ferocity to label ab/normality in Looked After Children is significant. This is despite the fact that, rather than disordered, Looked After Children are commonly in significant *distress*, and that this is a natural response to the common traumas of abuse, violence, removal from the family home, living away from siblings, and existing through the State care system (Nicolas 2014). Like disabled children, Looked After Children are monitored and measured routinely against emotional, behavioural, and psychological developmental norms. The 'Cinderella Law' we cited earlier rests upon harm to a child's 'physical, intellectual, emotional, social or behavioural development' (Phillips 2014) and asserts that the 'child's health or development shall be compared with that which could reasonably be expected of a similar child'.Such an invoking of the 'standard child' (Curran and Runswick-Cole 2014: 1617) and normative childhood, then, firmly defines the Looked After Child as Other: an abnormal, monstrous child in need of containment (see Goodley et al. 2015).

DCCS' rejection of deficit discourses of childhood and its disruption of the tyranny of hegemonic norms where children's lives are concerned (Curran and Runswick-Cole 2014) offer new ways of understanding the Looked After Childhood. As Goodley et al. (2015: 6) suggest, 'disabled children and young people are routinely subjected to the de-humanising practices of the psy-professions that render them less than fully human[...] Disabled children have been marginalized by or excluded from the expectations, opportunities and aspirations afforded to so-called "typically developing children"' (see also Goodley and Runswick-Cole 2010, 2011, 2012).

Liddiard and Slater (2017) remind us that 'development' is not a natural state, but a socio-cultural and political tool, 'used to serve a function of a particular time and place'.

If we turn our attention to those that manage this pathologisation, as a social worker, one of us (Luke) argues that critically engaged and radical forms of social work theory and practice can serve to depathologise Looked After Childhoods. Yet, Taylor (2004) argues that social work practice has lacked a critical and reflexive engagement with child development literature. Goodyer (2013: 396) argues that psychosocial understandings are endemic to child and family social work, which explains the 'ecological approach that underpins framework assessments'. One of us has practiced as a child protection social worker, albeit only within the context of a student degree placement. Thus, we feel it important to highlight the difficult contexts in which social workers practice, and how these serve to close down possibilities for radical practice in ways that can benefit Looked After Children. In child and family services, for example, radical practice requires critical knowledges, time, greater resources, effective supervision, and, for newly qualified workers, protected space and time to develop alternative practice-based knowledges. Austerity bites (again) here, in multiple ways. The slashing of local authority budgets combined with increasing poverty and precarity in children's lives generally means significantly higher caseloads for Social Workers, many of who are already overworked and vulnerable to burnout (Smullens 2015). Thus, austerity slowly eats away at the fundamentals for radical practice.

At the same time, social work professionals are bound to legislative and protective frameworks that can restrict their autonomy as practitioners and further inhibit opportunities for new kinds of practice. These factors are rooted in a historic strained relationship with the State, where successive governments in the UK have not valued public services, particularly Social Work. Social Work, as a discipline and practice, has been subject to extensive change over the last 20 years, with rapid professionalisation (development from diploma-level to degree-level qualification, professional regulation, protection of title). Since then, it has been subject to increasing de-professionalisation through (i) a New Labour Government modernisation; (ii) the Coalition Government's 'Big Society'—a means to devolve State power and hand to communities (Runswick-Cole and Goodley 2015); and now, (iii) the Conservative Government's increasing privatisation of (public) services. Ultimately, de-professionalisation is a process that reduces workers' professional discretion and autonomy, and thus their capacity to act in the best interests of the children, young people, and families they support.

Possible Futures: The Place of Vulnerability

We end by thinking about vulnerability and future. Initially, we want to draw upon transition—the move from children and young people's services to adult services (if required) and an independent, adult life and future (if desired), before (re)thinking vulnerability in affirmative ways. We do so because transition can be complex, traumatic, and distressing time for both disabled young people and Looked After young people, making uncertain futures a common experience. Speaking about disability, Parker et al. (2013: 3) define transition as a 'move from services and supports that focus on children and families to those addressing the needs of adults'. Looked After young people come to be categorised as 'care leavers', with little scope for continued support. In line with the increase in the number of children becoming 'looked after' across England and Wales (DfE 2013), as we stated at the outset, it follows that the number of young people ageing out of care is also increasing (Buchanan 2014). This is emphasised by recent changes to The Leaving Care Act 2000, (amended from previous provisions for care leavers in The Children Act 1989), which changed the age at which young people leave foster or local authority care from 16/18[1] to 21 years (up to 24 years if they remain in education). This change emerged through concerns that those who leave the care system are deeply under-supported in early adult life. Further, in May 2014, the Children and Families Act 2014 introduced a new duty for local authorities in England to support a 'staying put' arrangement when a fostered young person reaches the age of 18, so that they can remain with their foster carer up to the age of 21 years. Looked After young people now have access to 'personal advisor' (or social worker) who can offer support in transition to adult life. There is also some financial support available to help pay for college and/or university and setting up a home. The Fostering Network (2015) has argued that *Staying Put* 'represents the biggest change to foster care for a generation; it will make real change for young people in foster care, who have previously faced the prospect of living alone too soon'.

Despite such policy change, research shows that transition for both Looked After and disabled young people is woefully lacking (Abbott and Carpenter 2014; Hiles et al. 2014). As Buchanan (2014: 5; see also Holland and Crowley 2013) aptly states 'as the number of children and young people in and leaving care continues to rise, so too does the need for research in order to understand how this population can be offered appropriate and timely support both throughout their time in care and during the transition into independent, adult life'. Importantly, Looked After young people have seldom been asked about their expectations or desired plans for their futures (Sulimani-Aidan and Benbenishty 2011), despite the fact that research has shown that young care leavers often have high expectations for their future (see Sulimani-Aidan 2015).

Ultimately, transition as currently constructed is about future; as a concept, it is rooted in normative temporalities of the life course and the development stages of the *ideal* adult citizen, who is always normatively gendered, heterosexual, white, and able (Slater 2015). The ways in which DCCS makes space to explore alternative temporalities of disability *life* and disrupt humanist theories of normative development, time and future shows its usefulness towards thinking about Looked After lives, which often deviate from the ideal (Braidotti 2013; Kafer 2013). In a similar vein, we think that the lives of young care leavers remind us that all humans need support—not only in times of transition but throughout our lives and across the life course. As we rely on multiple supports, systems, people, and communities to survive, we are all only ever interdependent subjects (Goodley et al. 2015). Like disability, which Goodley and Runswick-Cole (2014: 3) suggest, has 'the radical potential to trouble the normative, rational, independent, autonomous, subject that is so often imagined when the human is evoked', Looked After lives bring into view a new politics of vulnerability.

Fittingly, a DCCS analysis affirms that vulnerability is only ever imposed, and we suggest that in vulnerability there is value. There are many aspects of advanced capitalism that make all people vulnerable: the increasing psychologisation of life and self; the intensification and extensification of work and labour; increasing militarism; global terrorism; and global economic instability. And let's not forget the unequal systems of power that these produce: racism, neocolonialism, sexism, misogyny and heterosexism, ableism and disablism, and ageism and transphobia. We could argue, then, that these are some very vulnerable times. But what happens to culture, community, and humanity when we understand vulnerability as a 'universal, inevitable, enduring aspect of the human condition' (Fineman 2008: 8)? That which is 'necessary for human being and human understanding, fundamental to relationships and to social life' (Rice et al. 2015: 520)? Rather than vulnerability equating only to victimhood, to sapped resilience, and dependence on external support, DCCS makes space to think about how our shared vulnerable selves could be a starting point to build a more equal and just society, where 'vulnerability is the ground for human exchange, empowerment, and growth; necessary for human being and human understanding' (Rice et al. 2015: 520); a springboard for resistance, justice, and change (Ecclestone and Goodley 2014). Applying these understandings *proffers* new forms of futurity and future (Kafer 2013) and at the same time as countering dis/ableist imperatives that deny Othered futures, or at best, render them spaces of failure.

Drawing Some Conclusions

In this chapter, we have only really scratched the surface of the usefulness and applicability of DCCS to other types of non-normative childhood. We agree with Curran and Runswick-Cole (2014: 1627) who suggest that 'through a programme of research, creative activities and gatherings, disabled children's childhood studies can be helpful in thinking about all children's lives (disabled and non-disabled) in positive and productive ways'. As we have demarcated in our contribution to this impressive volume, DCCS enables a way of viewing Looked After Childhoods in new ways; away from tragedy models and deficit discourses which reproduce the child as lacking vitality and future. In de-individualising our own lived experience, and using DCCS to theorise and politicise the relational, political, and affective aspects of caring for a Looked After Child, it has again shown its poignancy, power, and worthiness.

Notes

1. Legislation differs between England, Scotland, and Wales.

References

Abbott, D. W. F., & Carpenter, J. S. W. (2014). 'Wasting Precious Time': Young Men with Duchenne Muscular Dystrophy Negotiate the Transition to Adulthood. *Disability & Society, 29*(1), 1192–1205.
Beresford, B., Rabiee, P., & Sloper, P. (2007). *Outcomes for Parents with Disabled Children, Research Works, 2007–03*. York: Social Policy Research Unit, University of York.
Braidotti, R. (2013). *The Posthuman*. London: Polity Press.
Buchanan, A. (2014). *The Experience of Life Story Work: Reflections of Young People Leaving Care* (Unpublished D.Clin. Psy. Thesis). Cardiff University.
Burkitt, I. (2012). Emotional Reflexivity: Feeling, Emotion and Imagination in Reflexive Dialogues. *Sociology, 46*(3), 458–472.
Cabezas, M. (2016). 'Child Psychological Abuse, Public Health and Social Justice: The Cinderella Law Debate', In J. Drerup, G. Graf, C. Schickhardt, G. Schweiger (Eds.) *Justice, Education and the Politics of Childhood: Challenges and Perspectives*. Switzerland: Springer International Publishing. pg. 137-153

Campbell, F. K. (2009). *Contours of Ableism: Territories, Objects, Disability and Desire.* London: Palgrave Macmillan.

Children Act. (1989). London: HMSO.

Curran, T., & Runswick-Cole, K. (2014). Disabled Children's Childhood Studies: A Distinct Approach? *Disability & Society, 29*(10), 1617–1630.

Davis, L. J. (1995). *Enforcing Normalcy: Disability, Deafness, and the Body.* New York: Verso.

Department for Education. (2013). *Children Looked After by Local Authorities in England (Including Adoption and Care Leavers) – Year Ending 31 March 2013.* London: Department for Education.

Department for Education. (2015). *Children Looked After in England (Including Adoption and Care Leavers) Year Ending 31 March 2014.* London: Department for Education.

Ecclestone, K., & Goodley, D. (2014). Political and Educational Springboard or Straitjacket?: Theorising Post/Humanist Subjects in an Age of Vulnerability. *Discourse: Studies in the Cultural Politics of Education.* doi:10.1080/01596306.2014.927112.

Exley, C., & Letherby, G. (2001). Managing a Disrupted Life Course: Issues of Identity and Emotion Work. *Health, 5*(1), 112–132.

Family Law. (2015). *UK Children's Commissioners Urge UK Government to Protect Children from Austerity Measures.* Online. Available from: http://www.familylaw.co.uk/news_and_comment/uk-children-s-commissioners-urge-uk-government-to-protect-children-from-austerity-measures#.VztM8avfDFI. Accessed 3 May 2016.

Fineman, M. (2008). The Vulnerable Subject and the Responsive State. *Yale Journal of Law and Feminism, 20*(1), 1–22.

Frazer, H., & Marlier, E. (2011). *Assessment of Social Inclusion Policy Developments in the EU: Main Findings and Suggestions on the Way Forward.* Brussels: European Commission.

Goodley, D. (2010). *Disability Studies: An Interdisciplinary.* London/New Delhi/Singapore: Sage Publications Ltd.

Goodley, D., & Runswick-Cole, K. (2010). Emancipating Play: Dis/abled Children, Development and Deconstruction. *Disability and Society, 25*(4), 499–512.

Goodley, D., & Runswick-Cole, K. (2011). The Violence of Disablism. *Sociology of Health and Illness, 33*(4), 602–617.

Goodley, D., & Runswick-Cole, K. (2012). Reading Rosie: The Postmodern Dis/abled Child. *Educational and Child Psychology, 29*(2), 53–66.

Goodley, D., & Runswick-Cole, K. (2014). Becoming Dishuman: Thinking About the Human Through Dis/ Ability. *Discourse: Cultural Politics of Education, 37*(5). doi:10.1080/01596306.2014.930021.

Goodley, D., Runswick-Cole, K., & Liddiard, K. (2015). The DisHuman Child. *Discourse: Studies in the Cultural Politics of Education: Special Issue: Fabulous*

Monsters: Alternative Discourses of Childhood in Education, 37, 5. doi:10.1080/0 1596306.2015.1075731.

Goodyer, A. (2013). Understanding Looked-After Childhoods. *Child & Family Social Work, 18*(4), 394–402.

Hiles, D., et al. (2014). "So What Am I?" – Multiple Perspectives on Young People's Experience of Leaving Care. *Children and Youth Services Review, 41,* 1–15.

Hochschild, A. R. (1983). *The Managed Heart: Commercialization of Human Feeling.* Berkeley/Los Angeles/London: University of California Press.

Holland, S., & Crowley, A. (2013). Looked-After Children and Their Birth Families: Using Sociology to Explore Changing Relationships, Hidden Histories and Nomadic Childhoods. *Child & Family Social Work, 18,* 57–66.

Kafer, A. (2013). *Feminist, Queer, Crip.* Indiana: University of Indiana Press.

Levinson, J., & McKinney, K. A. (2013). Consuming an Edge: ADHD, Stimulant Use, and Psy Culture at the Corporate University. *Transcultural Psychiatry, 50*(3), 371–396.

Liddiard, K. (2014). The Work of Disabled Identities in Intimate Relationships. *Disability and Society, 29*(1), 115–128. doi:10.1080/09687599.2013.776486.

Liddiard, K. (2015) Fostering Diary. Personal Account.

Liddiard, K., & Slater, J. (2017). "Like, Pissing Yourself Is Not a Particularly Attractive Quality, Let's Be Honest": Learning to Contain Through Youth, Adulthood, Disability and Sexuality. *Sexualities.* Special Issue: Disability and Sexual Corporeality. Online First.

Macleod, S., Hart, R., Jeffes, J., & Wilkin, A. (2010). *The Impact of the Baby Peter Case on Applications for Care Orders, LGA Research Report.* Slough: NFER.

Mallet, R., & Runswick-Cole, K. (2014). *Approaching Disability: Critical Issues and Perspectives.* New York: Routledge.

Mallet, R., & Runswick-Cole, K. (forthcoming). The 'Urge to Know' Normal: Theorising How Impairment Labels Function. In R. Mallett, C. Ogden, & J. Slater (Eds.), *Precarious Positions: Theorising Normalcy and the Mundane.* Chester: University of Chester Press.

Meltzer, H., Gatward, R., Corbin, T., Goodman, R., & Ford, T. (2003). *The Mental Health of Young People Looked After by Local Authorities in England.* London: HMSO.

Munro, E. (2001). *Empowering Looked After Children.* London: LSE Research Articles Online. Available at: http://eprints.lse.ac.uk/archive/00000357/. Accessed 5 May 2016.

National Children's Bureau (NCB). (2015). *Corporate Parenting Toolkit.* Online. Available from: http://www.ncb.org.uk/corporate-parenting/resources/corporate-parenting-tool-kit. Accessed 3 May 2016.

Nicolas, J. (2014). Is new 'Cinderella's Law' on Emotional Neglect 'Draconian and Unhelpful'? *Community Care.* Online. Available from: http://www.communitycare.co.uk/2014/04/10/new-cinderellas-law-emotional-neglect-draconian-unhelpful/. Accessed 25 April 2016.

Overboe, J. (2004). *Articulating a Sociology of Desire Exceeding the Normative Shadows* (Unpublished PhD Thesis). The University of British Columbia, Vancouver.

Parker, C., Honigmann, J., & Clements, L. (2013). *Transition to Adulthood a Guide for Practitioners Working with Disabled Young People and Their Families*. Carmarthen: Cerebra.

Phillips, N. (2014). Researching Reform: Cinderella Law – How Might the New Criminal Measures Affect Already Existing Family Legislation? *Family Law*. Online. Available from: http://www.familylaw.co.uk/news_and_comment/researching-reform-cinderella-law-how-might-the-new-criminal-measures-affect-already-existing-family-legislation#.VztJNqvfDFI. Accessed 2 May 2016.

Reeve, D. (2002). Negotiating Psycho-emotional Dimensions of Disability and Their Influence on Identity Constructions. *Disability and Society, 17*(5), 493–508.

Reeve, D. (2004). Psycho-Emotional Dimensions of Disability and the Social Model. In C. Barnes & G. Mercer (Eds.), *Implementing the Social Model of Disability: Theory and Research*. Leeds: The Disability Press.

Rice, C., Chandler, E., Harrison, E., Liddiard, K., & Ferrari, M. (2015). Project Re•Vision: Disability at the Edges of Representation. *Disability and Society, 30*(4), 513–527. OPEN ACCESS.

Ridge, T. (2013). 'We Are All in This Together'? The Hidden Costs of Poverty, Recession and Austerity Policies on Britain's Poorest Children. *Children & Society, 27*, 406–417.

Runswick-Cole, K., & Goodley, D. (2015). DisPovertyPorn: Benefits Street and the Dis/Ability Paradox. *Disability and Society, 30*(4), 645–649.

Ryan, S., & Runswick-Cole, K. (2008). Repositioning Mothers: Mothers, Disabled Children and Disability Studies. *Disability & Society, 23*(3), 199–210. doi:10.1080/09687590801953937.

Shakespeare, T., Gillespie-Sells, K., & Davies, D. (1996). *Untold Desires: The Sexual Politics of Disability*. London/New York: Cassell.

Slater, J. (2015). *Youth and Disability: A Challenge to Mr Reasonable*. Oxon: Ashgate Publishing Plc.

Smullens, S. (2015). *Burnout and Self-Care in Social Work: A Guidebook for Students and Those in Mental Health and Related Professions*. Washington, DC: NASW Press.

Sulimani-Aidan, Y. (2015). Do They Get What They Expect? The Connection Between Young Adults' Future Expectations Before Leaving Care and Outcomes After Leaving Care. *Children and Youth Services Review, 55*, 193–200.

Sulimani-Aidan, Y., & Benbenishty, R. (2011). Future Expectations of Adolescents in Residential Care in Israel. *Children and Youth Services Review, 33*, 1134–1141. doi:10.1016/j.chilyouth.2011.02.006.

Taylor, C. (2004). Underpinning Knowledge for Childcare Practice: Reconsidering Child Development Theory. *Child & Family Social Work, 9*(3), 225–235.

The Fostering Network. (2015). *Staying Put*. Online. Available from: https://www.thefosteringnetwork.org.uk/policy-practice/practice-information/staying-put. Accessed 2 May 2016.

Thomas, C. (1999). *Female Forms: Experiencing and Understanding Disability*. Buckingham: Open University Press.

Thomas, C. (2004). The UK Social Model of Disability: Rescuing.

Thomas, C. (2006). Disability and Gender: Reflections on Theory and Research. *Scandinavian Journal of Disability Research, 8*(2-3), 177–185.

Watson, D. (2014) *Encouraging Playfulness to Thrive in Children with Profound Impairments: Views from Three Perspectives and a Demonstration of Art Work Produced Using Eye Gaze Technology*. Paper presented at 'There is No Them!' The 8th Child, Youth, Family & Disability Conference, University of the West of England, 7 and 8 July.

Luke Jones is a forensic mental health social worker. He is a social work lead at Cygnet Hospital Bierley, a secure mental health unit in Bradford in the north of England. Prior to this, he worked for the Canadian Mental Health Association in Ontario, Canada. He is pursuing an MA in Safeguarding at the University of Huddersfield.

Kirsty Liddiard is a research fellow in the School of Education at the University of Sheffield. Her research spans disability, gender, sexuality and intimacy, and youth, with a particular interest in how disablism and ableism both inform and shape these experiences in the everyday lives of disabled people. She tweets at @kirstyliddiard1. To read more about Kirsty's work, please visit kirstyliddiard.wordpress.com

A Relational Understanding of Language Impairment: Children's Experiences in the Context of Their Social Worlds

Helen Hambly

Key Points

- Children's experiences of language impairment (LI) were predominantly relational—they varied depending on the social situation and the attitudes and behaviours of others towards them.
- Other people's understandings and interpretations of children's language behaviours varied widely.
- Children's experiences of agency were closely associated with emotional experience and participation in or withdrawal from situations.
- Professional support for children with LI may be improved by targeting relationships between children and others rather than predominantly focusing on individuals' impairments.

This chapter explores the experiences of four children with LI, alongside the experiences of their family, friends and the professionals that support them. LI is a diagnosis given to children who have difficulties with various aspects of speech, language and memory in the absence of other physical and neurological impairments. Many children with a diagnosis of LI experience challenges beyond their speech and language in areas of their social and emotional lives. The vast majority of studies investigating LI within academic research have tended to focus attention on cognitive, linguistic, neurological and biological

H. Hambly (✉)
Peninsula Cerebra Research Unit (PenCRU), University of Exeter Medical School, Exeter, UK

© The Author(s) 2018
K. Runswick-Cole et al. (eds.), *The Palgrave Handbook of Disabled Children's Childhood Studies*, https://doi.org/10.1057/978-1-137-54446-9_26

explanations for children's atypical communication behaviours. This chapter describes findings from my doctoral study (Hambly 2014), which used alternative methods to those that dominate our current understanding of LI. My interest was in listening to and analysing the experience of children with LI, alongside their family, peers and professionals in order to explore the psychosocial experience. Children's and families' descriptions of their experiences of LI emphasise that for these individuals, LI does not solely exist 'within' the child as deficiencies in language and memory. Instead, LI is a relational phenomenon, and as such, difficulties are primarily experienced within social relationships and situations. The chapter concludes with my reflections on the ethics of this research.

Listening to Children and the Voices of Others in Their Social Worlds

In the UK, research, policy and practice in speech and language therapy (SLT) are still heavily influenced by medical models of disability. Objective assessments are used to diagnose children with specific 'disorders', despite continuing arguments about diagnostic criteria and co-morbidity with a number of different developmental disorders (Bishop 2014; Reilly et al. 2014). Education practice takes a different approach in the UK, classifying children according to their special educational needs (SEN) in broad areas, such as communication and interaction and social, emotional and mental health difficulties, in order to manage children's additional needs within the education system.

Ideas from childhood studies challenge the prevalent discourses and policy in relation to children with LI in terms of medical diagnoses of developmental disorders of childhood. They highlight the need to consider children as individuals rather than a collective group, with rights in the present and voices that should be listened with respect and response, and as agents influencing their own and others' lives and societies. In the last two decades, there has been an encouraging shift towards listening to children in both health and social care practice. The introduction of education, health and care (EHC) plans in England (Department for Education 2011, 2012) places the child's voice as central to care planning, but there is still emphasis in SLT on the investigation of symptoms of abnormal communication behaviours and diagnosing these as 'disorders' within the child.

Dan Goodley (e.g. Goodley and Roets 2008) has been at the fore of a movement to bring psychology to disability studies. Acknowledging the complex relationship between individual and social worlds, the authors argue for the need to explore the space between the binary of medical and social models of disability. They draw upon social and community psychologies to explore how individuals construct narratives, attitudes and identities, and how these shift and change and interact with their social and cultural environments and discourse. More recently, psychology, sociology and disability studies have been brought together to explore children's experiences and consider disabled children's childhoods (Curran and Runswick-Cole 2013; Hodge and Runswick-Cole 2013). The multi-perspective study described below placed individuals' voices, and their experiences of LI, as a central focus for examining psychosocial processes at play and informing support for children with LI.

Research Methods

The study design was informed by interpretive phenomenological analysis (Smith et al. 2009), a method that is committed to understanding 'lived experience' through interpreting individuals' reports and descriptions of their experiences in the context of social discourse. Four children aged eight to ten years who were receiving SLT for a diagnosis of LI took part in the study, alongside 18 of their parents, siblings, friends, teachers, learning support assistants (LSAs) and speech and language therapists.

Arts-based interview methods were used to engage children and listen to their views (Clark and Moss 2001; Coad 2007). Activities were developed around four key questions: what's your day-to-day life like for you? What's difficult for you at home and at school? Who and what is helpful? What are your hopes and fears for the future? Underlying these questions was a desire to explore children's understandings of their LI and the professional support they received. Activities aimed to build on each other, so answers and artwork in one activity could be used as prompts in subsequent activities. A variety of stickers and arts materials that the children could cut up, draw on and stick with were provided to offer choice in how children engaged with each activity. Scrapbooks were given to the children to complete several weeks prior to the interview to encourage children to express themselves freely. It was also hoped that the use of the scrapbook would balance the power relationship between me and the child by giving the child time to think about their experience and have more control over the direction of the interview. Talking Mats (Murphy et al. 2005) was used to elicit the children's experience of ease or difficulty over different aspects of their lives. Talking Mats is a pictorial communication tool that is developed around one open question with a 3-point response scale with picture symbols used to prompt for areas or activities in a person's life.

Interviews with families, friends and professionals also involved the Talking Mats activity and explored their experiences of being with the child and their views and understandings of the child's day-to-day experiences. All interviews were transcribed and analysed in three phases: the first phase focused on each child and those individuals associated with that child, the second phase of analysis moved across the different children and the third phase involved analysing and discussing identified themes in relation to other literature.

The study methods and materials were approved by local National Health Service and university research ethics committees. Individuals' names have been changed to protect their identities.

Looking Through Small Windows

It is important to emphasise that one of the broader aims of the research was to inform professional support for children with LI, and as such, the focus of analysis was somewhat skewed towards those experiences that were difficult for children. The interviews were set up to allow children to talk about their daily experiences and engage in free play before moving to my research agenda and specific questions about their experiences of daily activities through Talking Mats. Like other studies of children and young people with speech, language and communication needs (Roulstone et al. 2012; McLeod et al. 2013) and studies of adults and children with other conditions (Watson 2002; Wickenden 2010), within the interviews, the children spontaneously described their lives in a positive light, and talked enthusiastically about their families and interests. Children talked about experiences that were difficult for them also but only when they were prompted to as part of my research agenda that focused on professional support of children. It is difficult to know the extent to which negative emotions and difficult experiences pervade these children's lives, and though the approach did not assume a deficit or negative experience, it was important to give children the opportunity to have the problems they might face recognised. As we shall see below, the impact of LI on children's experiences is very situational and so is likely to vary depending on the social contexts of children's lives. The lack of spontaneity in children's description of their negative experiences may indicate that in the main, children do not focus and reflect on negative experiences. It may also be indicative of a learned social expectation to talk about positive aspects of their lives, or children may be protective of their personal experiences. Thus, the findings described below are largely through prompting interviewees about children's difficult experiences rather than their spontaneous talk in play about their families, friends and imaginary activities, and, as such, should not be seen as children's overarching experiences.

Three key themes were identified in the analyses of individuals' interviews: 'agency', 'understandings and misunderstandings' and 'making sense of difference' (Hambly 2014). This chapter draws upon the latter two of these themes to emphasise and discuss the social, relational nature of experience with LI.

Language Impairment: Whose Problem Is It?

Within mainstream SLT and psychological literature and practice, the focus of professional intervention is on the child with a diagnosis of LI. This medical discourse focuses predominantly on a child's impairments rather than listening to a child's perspective and how they experience life. In contrast, within this study, children's and families' experiences of LI suggest that the focus of understanding, support and responsibility for change should be wider than the individual child, and they should take into account children's relationships with others and their social worlds.

Children were open about activities and social situations they found difficult and tended to describe their experiences in terms of other people's behaviours and classroom situations, rather than their own language or memory. For example, Pete told me that he does not like school and often finds work hard. He described his frustration when he feels unable to keep up with his peers and complete his assignment in class. He does not focus on the experience of finding writing hard, but is upset that he is not able to complete his work. His ambitions to complete his work are halted by other children's speed of working within the classroom.

H: *What would be a bad day at school?*
PETE: *if I do some hard work*
H: *yeah? What work is hard. There's particular things at school that's hard?*
PETE: *um [pause] doing my news*
H: *your news?*
PETE: *yeah*
H: *what's your news*
PETE: *doing all hard work and everybody takes too long to do my writing and then then I*
        don't get to do my my work

On occasions children's older siblings and parents also echoed children's placement of responsibility for difficulties in relationships with other people rather than with 'impaired' behaviours of children themselves. For example, Sarah's older sister and Sarah both rated making and playing with friends as easy for her. Sarah's teacher explained Sarah's difficulties with friendship in terms of her lacking empathy for other people and her being domineering. In contrast, Sarah's sister questioned why Sarah did not have more friends and explained it in terms of other children being less exciting and not as good at communicating as her.

SARAH'S SISTER: *she [Sarah] can go up to people and be really friendly and she will like be really nice to them but say, if they are not as confident as her then they probably won't react better, like won't be as nice to her back. Well, not not nice but I don't know how to explain it, just like, she is better at communicating with other people than maybe some people would be with her*

H: *Right okay. So do think people find her bit overwhelming? Then or or um*

SARAH'S SISTER: *I wouldn't say overwhelming but maybe a bit more exciting*

Sarah's sister's perception of Sarah's interactions with her friends as 'exciting' was different to my interpretation of her description of Sarah as 'overwhelming'. At this moment in the interview, I had imagined Sarah's confidence might be overwhelming to her peers. My use of the word 'overwhelming' suggests that I placed responsibility on Sarah for her exclusion from interactions with her peers and has led me to question again the assumptions I make in relation to children diagnosed with LI. Sarah's sister, on the other hand, placed responsibility for Sarah's exclusion from social interaction on the side of Sarah's peers. Within the interview, Sarah's sister described her enjoyment of her relationship with Sarah and her closeness to Sarah. She described Sarah's enthusiasm in her interactions with others using positive language. In Sarah's sister's view, any negativity or deficiency in Sarah's interactions lies with other children, not with Sarah. On numerous occasions, Daniel's mother also placed responsibility on other children and adults to accept and adapt to Daniel, rather than Daniel having to change himself.

DANIEL'S MOTHER: *why does Daniel have to do all the work, why can't these children learn to make allowances?*

Children's and families' experiences of LI highlight the importance of focusing support on all sides of children's relationships, rather than locating and targeting a problem within the child.

Language Impairment: Uncertain and Moving

There were divergent experiences and interpretations of children's behaviour by children's families, teaching staff, SLTs and friends. Professionals and families described children's behaviours in a variety of ways, such as impaired speech and language and social communication, social and emotional immaturity and egocentricity. They tended to make judgements about children's behaviour by comparing them to their peers and/or their expected development trajectory. They made judgements about how children differed from other children and expected norms and often, but not always, referred to medical diagnoses, such as specific language impairment (SLI) and autistic spectrum disorder (ASD). Parents and professionals also interpreted certain behaviours in terms of children's personal traits and perceived that children's personalities also influenced how other people responded to children's LI. One child's behaviours were interpreted as confirmation of parental neglect. Individuals' interpretations of children's behaviour were associated with their placement of responsibility for changing or improving relationships and situations.

Some teaching staff interpreted the unusual behaviour of a child negatively, whilst others did so with empathy and understanding and increased support in class. For example, Simon's teacher, LSA and friend all described how he interrupts and speaks out in class when he should not and how he does not see that he should share with others. Simon's teacher and LSA found him difficult to manage in class and described him as annoying, immature and egocentric.

> SIMON'S TEACHER'S diary:
> Immature
> Mood swings/stroppy
> Gets very down / silly / sulks
> Wants your undivided attention
> Self conscious
> Easily wound up

It is difficult to know how the negative language repeatedly used by Simon's teaching staff had become an accepted narrative amongst these staff. It is possible that their interpretation of Simon's behaviour may, in part, reflect a lack of confidence and agency to manage him within the classroom. There was little communication between Simon's mother, teachers and SLT and no formal space for communication to occur as Simon did not have a statement of SEN (a formal statement of the support needed to meet a child's needs until these are replaced by EHC plans between 2014 and 2018 (Children and Families Act 2014)).

In contrast to Simon, Sarah was described with warmth and affection by her teacher and thoughtfulness in response to her behaviour in class. Sarah understands that she makes mistakes at school, but she does not perceive this as failure. She is learning in a supportive, accepting environment and, unlike the other three children in the study, described enjoying lessons at school.

SARAH'S TEACHER: *she's nearly always putting her hand up to answer questions and things when I ask them. What I get back as answers very often doesn't make sense, it's like I've asked a question and she'll come back with something which is completely unrelated or just completely off the point to what I've asked....*

SARAH'S TEACHER: *[in front of the class] I just tend to take her ideas on board and say well that's a nice idea but and then, or however, and just explain that it's not quite what we were talking about and then and get it back to how it should be and take somebody else's point of view*

SARAH: *um [Sarah's teacher], he's my teacher of our class*

H: *is he? And what do you like about him*

SARAH: *he always um, understands if we make mistakes, he doesn't really shout out, um he doesn't care if we get thing wrong*

Differences in interpretations and explanations of children's behaviours were likely to reflect a number of different factors, including professional discourses and responsibilities, previous experiences, familiarity with children, family context and the formality of the situation or context in which participants experienced case children. Communication between participants was an important factor in the divergence of interpretations and explanations of children's LI.

The diverse interpretations of children's experiences and behaviours by children, parents, peers and professionals within this study echo Goodley and Roet's (Goodley and Roets 2008) poststructuralist view of impairment as uncertain and moving. The subjective experience of impairment is dynamic. It changes in different contexts and power relations. Goodley and Roet (2008) argue for researchers to challenge educational and medical practices, such as statements of SEN and medical diagnoses that create and recreate 'impairments'. They suggest that binary distinctions between people with and without impairments are problematic and unhelpful. Their arguments are supported by children and siblings within this study explaining experiences of LI in terms of other people's behaviours towards children, rather than children's own impairments and individuals experiencing and interpreting LI differently in various home and school contexts.

Language Impairment: Misunderstandings and Misunderstood

Misunderstandings between children and others were a common feature of the experiences of children and their families and professionals within the study. Parents and professionals recounted numerous examples of children's behaviour that they perceived as inappropriate, particularly in terms of speaking and sharing in turn in the classroom but also in terms of understanding the rules of games and in friendships. Children were sometimes unaware of misunderstandings between themselves and others. Tension existed between a child and other people in the child's world due to a mismatch between the child's understanding and subsequent action and other people's expectations of that child's understanding and/or action. Children's intentions were not taken seriously or were misunderstood by others, and others' misunderstandings of children's intentions were often described in negative terms.

Mismatches in understanding between children and others not only led to tension within relationships but were also frequently linked with fears about children's 'vulnerability' to being taken advantage of or bullied at secondary school. Children were seen as happy at present, but parents and professionals were fearful about children remaining happy due to the perceived challenges they envisaged for them as they get older.

SARAH'S TEACHER: *my worries is that they [Sarah and others like her] will just slip*
through the net and be seen as not successful academically
H: *right*
SARAH'S TEACHER: *and the more social issues will be swept under the carpet or*
brushed aside and not paid much attention to

H: *yeah*
SARAH'S TEACHER: *because I think, I don't know if I'm right on this but it seems to me as children get older, certainly into secondary school, those kind of problems, the social kind pastoral side of things does tend to fall away*

Incidents of bullying or teasing were described by participants in relation to all children in the study and included physical, verbal and relational bullying. The descriptions by participants suggested that children were vulnerable to bullying for several different, but possibly interlinking reasons. One commonly mentioned way in which children were described as 'vulnerable' to being taken advantage of or bullied was children's misinterpretation of situations and the intentions of their peers. Parents and professionals were particularly anxious about children being taken advantage of by others due to their naivety and trusting natures. It is possible that others' perceptions of children as naive or misunderstanding situations and intentions may place children as susceptible to relational bullying in particular.

Others' perceptions of children with LI, as unusual or strange, is another mechanism by which children may have been susceptible to name calling and other forms of bullying and social exclusion. Sometimes, children's unusual behaviours were interpreted in terms of children's personal qualities, rather than any physical or cognitive impairment. Goffman (1963) discussed social identity in terms of stigmatisation where 'normal' individuals view certain attributes of others as weak or dangerous. These attributes or 'stigma' devalue the other person. Goffman (1963) described three forms of stigmatisation: one relating to external deformations that are visible to others, one relating to deviant personal traits and another relating to a group of people in the minority with a particular ethnicity or religion. The children's language difficulties are not physically obvious or immediately visible. Therefore, the process of stigmatisation may be one relating to children's personal traits rather than visible attributes (Goffman 1963). For example, Simon's teacher and LSA described Simon in terms of his personal traits, as egocentric and babyish, and expressed little sympathy towards him when his peers were 'winding him up'. Pete's LSA is more protective of Pete and perceives it as her responsibility to keep Pete's peers from teasing Pete in class.

SIMON'S LSA: *they don't tease him just for the sake of teasing him*
H: *oh right*
SIMON'S LSA: *they tease him because of his behaviour, because he's normally doing*

	something babyish
PETE'S LSA:	*and it's easy for other children, especially those who have got a little bit*
	going on upstairs to work out how to wind up
H:	*oh right okay*
PETE'S LSA:	*when we're in the middle of a lesson and set him off and then he will get up and then that disrupt the whole lesson obviously*
H:	*did they do that a lot*
PETE'S LSA:	*no, they've done it a couple of times, but we stamped on it straightaway*

Of note were the differences in teaching staffs' attitudes towards classroom peers provoking children with LI and in the placement of responsibility for these incidents. Simon was reported by his LSA as having described himself as a baby to his peers. He had taken on the identity of the prevailing attitudes in the classroom around him. This has been explained as 'internalised oppression' (Reeve 2002), a form of psycho-emotional disablism where an individual incorporates and accepts the prejudiced views of those around them. Simon's accepting of and promoting himself as immature compared to his peers may also perpetuate social discourses surrounding his immature identity. These incidents serve as a reminder of the important role that teaching staff play in fostering an inclusive environment, and how they recognise bullying as teasing or dismiss such behaviour as 'winding up'.

Language Impairment: A Social, Relational Phenomenon

The multi-perspective study of children's LI provided a glimpse of the complex interplay between other people's interpretations of, and attitudes towards, children and their LI within social situations, and children's experiences of, and behaviours within, those situations and their developing identities. Problematic relational situations that professionals might attribute to a child's LI were not always experienced as 'impairment' by children and their families. For these children, impairment and disability were inextricably linked and were situational. The various explanations and interpretations of LI illuminated a shifting, relational phenomenon.

Implications for Practice

The research findings highlight a need for listening to and sharing perspectives and information between children, parents, teachers, LSAs and SLTs. For one of the children in the study, there was little communication between the family, school staff and the SLT, and consequently, teaching staff made assumptions about the child's life at home and linked this with his behaviour in school. In contrast, for other children in the study, there was more of a shared understanding of their needs between children's mothers and their teachers and SLTs. In the latter situations, the formal statement review process acted as an opportunity for professionals and parents to discuss and prioritise goals for intervention together.

Despite the formal review process, SLTs still described challenges around communicating with teaching staff directly and having time to discuss individual children. The introduction of education health and care plans in England, which aim to better integrate support and communication across health, education and social services (Department for Education 2011, 2012), provide an opportunity to improve communication and the development of a shared understanding between families, teaching staff and SLTs. The EHC plans also emphasise the importance of placing families and children at the heart of decision-making (Department for Education 2011, 2012) and provide an opportunity to encourage listening to children's experiences and views as a central part of the goal-setting process. Talking Mats and other arts activities proved useful communication tools within this study and could be used in a variety of school and SLT settings to listen to children with LI.

A Reflection on the Ethics of the Study

Prior to carrying out the interviews, I was confident that I had done everything I could to protect children within the research process and anticipate any harms of the research by talking to parents of children with additional needs and to my supervisors and relevant professionals about the study. My preparations facilitated the process of informing participants about the research and assisted my dealing with situations that arose during interviews, but they did not prevent real ethical dilemmas arising during the research process.

Exploration of children's lives, particularly their bad days led to children's disclosure of negative, sensitive experiences. Whilst I probed with sensitivity, it was difficult to know whether to give individuals space to expand on their experiences or move on to less sensitive topics if children became visibly emotionally distressed or withdrawn. One adult participant became upset talking about their child. I provided the option to stop the interview, but they wanted to continue and described finding the process cathartic.

One of the children had a strong reaction to my probe about his experience in the classroom. The child became upset about the audio recorder and who would be listening to the interview. The incident highlighted that the child had not fully understood the purpose and consequences of their participation in the research. I asked the child if they wished to stop the interview. They were happy to continue, so in response to their reaction, I changed the direction of the interview to a more light-hearted activity, which facilitated the child to lead the conversation and re-establish their confidence in the research interaction. For this child in particular, given their history of 'intervention' which I had learned about through interviews with family members, I was unsure whether the risk of harms of the research process outweighed the potential benefits. I discussed the child's participation with my supervision team and subsequently contacted the child's parent to check on the child's welfare and seek their wishes about the child's continued participation.

Each child reacted to and engaged with the research in different ways. Participation was a particularly positive experience for another of the children who spontaneously recalled the interview to their SLT with enthusiasm two years after it had taken place. The child expressed to their SLT that they had enjoyed telling me about their day-to-day experiences at home and at school.

Talking and listening to children, their families and the professionals that support them has given me a greater understanding and awareness of the disabling attitudes and social structures that create and recreate 'impairments'. This awareness has influenced my outlook on research and leaves me uncomfortable about research agendas that focus predominantly on children's difficulties or 'impairments'. The inherent tension between my agenda to conduct applied research that aims to improve support for 'impaired' children and the potential role of the very same research to perpetuate a process of labelling through identifying a child as the focus of special interest because of their LI is difficult to reconcile, particularly when impairment and disability are closely intertwined.

This tension not only exists in the context of research but also in the aims of professionals, family members and other individuals who wish to support and improve children's day-to-day lives. Listening to and understanding each other's perspectives, particularly children's perspectives in the context of the provision of support may help to prevent some of the negative consequences of labelling and assumptions that follow. Listening to teachers' and peers' perspectives is also important so that the focus of intervention is the relationship between a child and their teacher or a child and their peers, or a social context, rather than on an individual's impairments. As such, misunderstandings can be resolved and a shared understanding of expectations and intentions on both sides of a relationship can be realised. This may include improving the confidence of a teacher to manage a child in the classroom situation, working with a child's peers as well as working with the child themselves. Peer perspectives are an important part of a child's social world, and creative ways of working are needed to provide space for peer perspectives within the context of EHC plans and support for children with LI. EHC plans provide an opportunity for multi-disciplinary teams to place children's relationships and social worlds at the heart of support for children with LI.

References

Bishop, D. V. (2014). Ten Questions About Terminology for Children with Unexplained Language Problems. *International Journal of Language and Communication Disorders, 49*(4), 381.

Children and Families Act. (2014). London: The Stationary Office (c.6).

Clark, A., & Moss, P. (2001). *Listening to Young Children: The MOSAIC Approach.* London: National Children's Bureau/Joseph Rowntree Foundation.

Coad, J. (2007). Using Art-Based Techniques in Engaging Children and Young People in Health Care Consultations and/or Research. *Journal of Research in Nursing, 12*(5), 487.

Curran, T., & Runswick-Cole, K. (Eds.). (2013). *Disabled Children's Childhood Studies: Critical Approaches in a Global Context.* Basingstoke: Palgrave Macmillan.

Department for Education. (2011). *Support and Aspiration: A New Approach to Special Education Needs and Disability.* London: The Stationery Office (Cm 8027).

Department for Education. (2012). *Support and Aspiration: A New Approach to Special Education Needs and Disability: Progress and Next Steps.* London: The Stationery Office (Cm 8027).

Goffman, E. (1963). *Stigma: Notes on the Management of Spoiled Identity.* Upper Saddle River: Prentice-Hall Inc.

Goodley, D., & Roets, G. (2008). The (be) Comings and Goings of 'Developmental Disabilities': The Cultural Politics of 'Impairment'. *Discourse: Studies in the Cultural Politics of Education, 29*(2), 239–255.

Hambly, H. (2014). *Children's, Parents', Peers' and Professionals' Experiences of Language Impairment: A Multi-perspective Study to Identify Psychosocial Goals for Intervention* (Unpublished Doctoral Thesis). University of the West of England, Bristol.

Hodge, N., & Runswick-Cole, K. (2013). 'They Never Pass Me the Ball': Disabled Children's Experiences of Leisure. *Children's Geographies, 11*(3), 311–325.

McLeod, S., Daniel, G., & Barr, J. (2013). "When He's Around His Brothers He's Not So Quiet": The Private and Public Worlds of School-Aged Children with Speech Sound Disorder. *Journal of Communication Disorders, 46*, 70–83.

Murphy, J., Tester, S., Hubbard, G., Downs, M., & MacDonald, C. (2005). Enabling Frail Older People with a Communication Difficulty to Express Their Views: The Use of Talking Mats® as an Interview Tool. *Health and social care in the community, 13*(2), 95–107.

Reeve, D. (2002). Negotiating Psycho-Emotional Dimensions of Disability and Their Influence on Identity Constructions. *Disability & Society, 17*(5), 493–508.

Reilly, S., Bishop, D. V., & Tomblin, B. (2014). Terminological Debate Over Language Impairment in Children: Forward Movement and Sticking Points. *International Journal of Language and Communication Disorders, 49*(4), 452.

Roulstone, S., Coad, J., Ayre, A., Hambly, H., & Lindsay, G. (2012). *The Preferred Outcomes of Children with Speech, Language and Communication Needs and Their Parents*. London: Department for Education.

Smith, J., Flowers, P., & Larkin, M. (2009). *Interpretative Phenomenological Analysis: Theory, Method and Research*. London: Sage Publications Ltd.

Watson, N. (2002). Well, I Know This Is Going to Sound Very strange to You, but I Don't See Myself as a Disabled Person: Identity and Disability. *Disability & Society, 17*(5), 509–527.

Wickenden, M. (2010). *Teenage Worlds, Different Voices: An Ethnographic Study of Identity and the Life Worlds of Disabled Teenagers Who Use AAC* (Unpublished Doctoral Thesis). The University of Sheffield, Sheffield.

Helen Hambly has been working in health and psychology research since 2001. Her interest in language development and language impairments led to her joining the Bristol Speech and Language Therapy Research Unit in 2009, and she completed her PhD in the University of the West of England in 2014.

Resilience in the Lives of Disabled Children: A Many Splendoured Thing

Katherine Runswick-Cole, Dan Goodley, and Rebecca Lawthom

Key Points

- Traditional models of resilience have often suggested that disabled children cannot be resilient.
- Resilience is often conceptualised as an individual trait or quality of a human being.
- We understand resilience as the dynamic interplay of the human and a host of resources around them.
- Disabled children's resilience is boosted through their networks and access to a host of resources including community participation and acceptance which seek to promote positive identities.
- Disabled children experience their bodies and minds in ways that are deeply embedded in cultural scripts and societal stories of disability.
- In the context of economic crisis and austerity measures, resources that support disabled children's resilience are under threat.

K. Runswick-Cole (✉) • R. Lawthom
The University of Sheffield, Sheffield, UK

D. Goodley
Manchester Metropolitan University , Manchester, UK

© The Author(s) 2018
K. Runswick-Cole et al. (eds.), *The Palgrave Handbook of Disabled Children's Childhood Studies*, https://doi.org/10.1057/978-1-137-54446-9_27

Introduction

In this chapter, we question models of resilience that are built on the idea of individual normative development in spite of adversity or threat. We describe the limits of such an approach and its failure to take into account the cultural contexts in which resilience emerges. We further describe the ways in which traditional models of resilience have excluded disabled children from the category of 'resilient' child. We argue for a theoretical understanding of resilience underpinned by a social constructionist approach. A social constructionist approach to resilience allows us to recognise and celebrate resilience in disabled children's lives, as well as revealing the role that a range of resources play in enabling resilience. Finally, in a context of austerity, we argue that it is vital to contest models of resilience that attempt to locate responsibility for developing resilience (or lack of it) within individual children and families, and to focus on the wider cultural and societal contexts that enable or stifle disabled children's lives. Our work is informed by a research study, *Resilience in the lives of disabled people across the life course,* funded by the UK disability charity Scope (for information about the research visit: disability-resilience.wordpress. com. For information about the funder visit: https://www.scope.org.uk). Here, we focus on the experiences of disabled children and young people and their parents/family carers.

Childhood Resilience

In the global North, resilience is the popular contemporary term used to describe a person's ability to 'bounce back' or 'to succeed against the odds' (Runswick-Cole and Goodley 2013). Discussions about resilience are often held in reference to children's lives; indeed, childhood is constructed as a 'sensitive period' for the development of resilience (Masten 2001). A popular view dominates: children, when properly nurtured and parented, will build the resilience they need to cope with adversity in their adult lives (Lowe et al. 2015). At the same time, previous research indicates that it is important that children are not overprotected or completely shielded from risk and adversity as they may, then, miss the critical period in their development in which resilience must emerge:

> [i]ndividuals are not considered resilient if there has never been a significant threat to their development, there must be current or past hazards judged to have the potential to derail normative development. (Masten 2001: 228)

The hegemonic view is that resilience can be boosted by others but, simultaneously, one has to overcome hardship in order to be considered resilient. Hence, resilient children will make resilient (and productive) adults (Masten 2001). In a time of austerity and economic crisis, the call for children (and adults) to build their resilience has acquired a new sense of urgency. And so, in England, the government has placed a particular emphasis on 'character education' in schools, including resilience building (Department for Education 2015). To conceptualise resilience as an individual quality is a classic functionalist account of the child and disability. Popular conceptions and governmental conceptions merge to individualise notions of resilience, capacity, bounceability and resistance.

Such a view of resilience jars with our politicised understanding of disability and childhood. As we have suggested elsewhere (Runswick-Cole and Goodley 2013, 2014), the application of individual, trait-based models of resilience in disabled people's lives has often been problematic. Here, we rearticulate our call for a move away from traditional functionalist understandings of resilience, and draw, instead, on social constructionist models of resilience that view resilience as the product of social and environmental factors rather than individual (normative) development (Ungar 2004; Runswick-Cole and Goodley 2013, 2014).

The Problematic Relationship Between Disability and Resilience

Two accounts of disability and resilience dominate—both of which are problematic for disabled children and adults. On the one hand, there is the view that disabled people can only be considered resilient if they achieve (normative) goals *in spite of their impairments* (Runswick-Cole and Goodley 2014). These reports appear in the popular media in England as 'triumph over tragedy' stories (Swain and French 2000). The Paralympic Games provided the press with a glut of such stories where disabled athletes demonstrated their resilience by achieving sporting excellence in spite of their impairments (White 2012). Carr (cited in White 2012) describes such stories as 'inspiration porn' allowing non-disabled people to 'get off on' stories of disabled people's resilience. On the other hand, some disabled people are deemed unable to be resilient simply because they are (too) disabled—the presence of an impairment is enough to exclude them from the category of resilient (Runswick-Cole and Goodley 2014). For example, disabled children with complex needs are not seen, under trait-based and developmental models of resilience, as having the ability to bounce back or to triumph over adversity. Their impairments are conceptualised as inherently limiting; stifling the emergence of resilient behaviours and attitudes.

And yet, to add to the disability-resilience confusion, some disabled people are described as resilient simply because they have an impairment and are living 'ordinary' lives (Runswick-Cole and Goodley 2014). A story from our own experience illustrates this point well. We attended a conference with research partners to our current project *Big society? Disabled people with learning disabilities and civil society* (bigsocietydis.wordpress.com). The partners are members of a self-advocacy organisation who regularly deliver training to practitioners. At the end of their presentation, a member of the conference organising team came up to thank the presenters and said how 'brave' they were to have done their presentation. It seemed that the presence of the label 'learning disability' meant that there was an automatic assumption that the speakers had overcome some form of adversity (their learning disability) to deliver their presentation—despite the fact that presentations were part of their ordinary, day-to-day working life. There is something deeply patronising in the accreditation and identification of resilience.

We saw above that Masten argues that resilience can only emerge if a child has experienced 'past or current hazards', and that she goes on to say that those hazards must 'have the potential to derail *normative* development' (Masten 2001: 228 *our emphasis*). This positions disabled children, yet again, in an awkward relationship to resilience (Runswick-Cole and Goodley 2014). Often, disabled children acquire the label 'disabled child' precisely because their development has been judged to be non-normative—their development is 'delayed' or 'disordered'. Understandings of resilience premised on notions of 'normal' development mean that many disabled children are automatically denied entry to the category of 'resilient child'. Resilience research positions disabled children's lives and experiences outside of what is considered to be the natural variation (Michalko 2002) making it impossible for them to escape the normative shadows that haunt their lives (Overboe 2004; Curran and Runswick-Cole 2014).

The Consequences of Failing to Be 'Resilient'

A failure to meet the ableist standards set for entry into the category of 'resilient child' has potentially risky consequences for both children and their parents/family carers. As Ungar (2005: 91) points out, those individuals perceived 'to lack resilience' are often blamed for their 'perceived lack of inner strength to overcome "their lot in life"'. Children who 'lack resilience' are 'disruptive', 'disordered' and 'troubled'; while parents who fail to raise resilient children are deemed to have poor parenting skills and become the subjects of professional scrutiny and intervention (Lowe et al. 2015) as 'troubled families' (Department for Communities & Local Government 2012). A focus on resilience as an individualised character trait obscures the attitudinal, systemic and cultural factors that create difficulties in children and families' lives (Young et al. 2008). In a time of austerity, this approach to resilience serves those invested in rolling back state support, because it is individual children, young people and families that are held to account, rather than the actions of governments and the provision of services (Goodley et al. 2014). And yet, resilience, as Masten (2001) describes it above, can only be defined by reference to set of *culturally normal* behaviours (Ungar 2004). And so, the failure to pay attention to the different cultural contexts in which resilience emerges clearly undermines the coherence of individual, trait-based models of resilience.

In contrast to such models of resilience, Ungar (2005) offers an explanation that takes into account the social and cultural context. He argues that there are 'unique pathways to survival' (Ungar 2005: 91) and that the '[p]athways to resilience are a many splendoured thing' (Ungar 2007: 19) (a quote we rather love). The promise of 'unique pathways' to resilience conceptualised as a 'many splendoured thing' opens up the possibility that disabled children, notwithstanding their seemingly non-normative childhoods (Curran and Runswick-Cole 2014), might gain entry into the category of 'resilient child'.

Resilience as a Network of Resources

We follow Ungar (2004) in arguing that resilience can never simply be a matter of building individual capacity, it must also be a case of challenging social, attitudinal, cultural, economic and structural barriers which threaten people's lives (Young et al. 2008; Runswick-Cole and Goodley 2013). In this view, resilience is: 'the outcome from negotiations between individuals and their environments for the resources to *define themselves* as healthy amidst conditions collectively viewed as adverse' (Ungar 2004: 242; our italics). This relational understanding of the phenomenon of resilience sits far better with our postconventionalist approach to disability which seeks to understand the promotion of human capacities through interdependent networks of support (Goodley 2014).

Following Ungar (2004 cited in Runswick-Cole and Goodley 2014), we identify these resources as:

1. Material resources: this refers to access to financial, educational, medical and employment resources, as well as access to meet more basic needs such as food and clothing.
2. Relationships: here, the focus is on relationships with significant others, including peers, adults and children/young people including family members and people from the wider community.
3. Identity: identity refers to a personal and collective sense of self. Identity is concerned with purpose, self-appraisal of strengths and weaknesses, aspirations, beliefs and values, including spiritual and religious beliefs.
4. Bodies: these resources refer to the influence of one's body—including impairment—in relationships with others' people and resources;
5. Power and control: here, the focus is on the experiences of caring for one's self and others, as well as having a sense of being able to affect change in a person's own social and physical environment perhaps to access health, education and community resources.
6. Community

    (i) Community participation: refers to having the opportunity to take part in the local community through a host of activities including recreation and work.
    (ii) Community cohesion: refers to feeling a part of something larger than one's self whether this is a social or spiritual community.

7. Social justice: relates to having a meaningful role in community and a sense of social equality.

(Adapted from Runswick-Cole and Goodley 2014)

Each of these resources overlaps with and is interconnected with the others (Fig. 1):

Our exploration of resilience in the lives of disabled children and young people, described below, was informed by this theoretical understanding of resilience as a social construct.

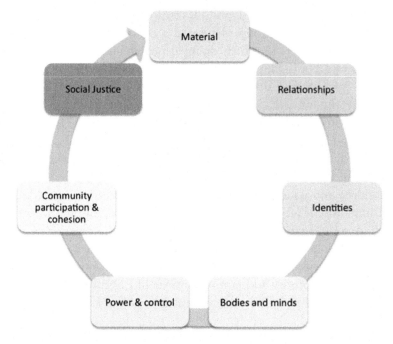

Fig. 1   A network of resilience

Methodology

As we have outlined above, this chapter discusses a study carried out at the Research Institute for Health and Social Change at Manchester Metropolitan University with Scope, the UK disability charity, called *Resilience in the lives of disabled people across the life-course* (2011–2012). The project had a number of aims:

1. to explore what resilience means to disabled people at different stages across the life course;
2. to explore how resilience, or a lack of it, has affected disabled people's ability to negotiate challenges and make the most of opportunities in their lives;
3. to understand what works in building resilience amongst different groups of disabled people;
4. to develop a toolkit for use by Scope's policy and services' functions that outlines what Scope means by resilience, what does or doesn't work in supporting people to become resilient and what we can do to build resilience in disabled people throughout the life course.

These aims were explored through four research phases: a literature review, a life story phase, a focus group phase and a community of practice phase (Lave and Wenger 1991) in which disabled people and researchers worked together to produce a toolkit for use by Scope in their service delivery. Full details of the project, recruitment, ethical approval, methods, findings and outputs from the project, including research reports, can be found at: disability-resilience.wordpress.com. This chapter reports on the findings from the life story phase that included 11 interviews with disabled children and young people and 11 interviews with parents/family carers, with reference to aims 1–3 of the research outlined above.

The children and young people in the study had already acquired a wide range of impairment labels. A life story approach was adopted in order to enable children and young people to participate in the research (Goodley and Runswick-Cole 2012). Life stories offer insights beyond children and young people's personal worlds, reflecting contemporary social, political, policy, service, community and family contexts in England as well as revealing the wider social, structural and cultural factors that shape disabled people's lives.

Ethics

Following the principles of disabled children's childhood studies (Curran and Runswick-Cole 2014), the research team took questions of voice seriously when listening to children and young people. We reflected on how we might respond sensitively and ethically to children and young people's concerns throughout the research project (Cocks 2006). We were constantly checking if the participant appeared to be tired or fed up, and if they were happy to continue. Participants chose their own pseudonyms in the stories below. We did not rely on modes of research production that were dependent on speech alone, instead using photos, maps, drawings and simply spending time 'being with' (Morris 2003) children and young people.

Analysis

Our approach to analysis was underpinned by a theoretical approach to resilience based on the social constructionist model of resilience outlined above and developed by Ungar. Life story interviews allowed us to explore with storytellers, the significance of resources for resilience in their lives as well as the ways in which resources interconnect with one another. We read and re-read the stories drawing on the network of resilience above, to guide our readings.

Below, we re-tell the children's stories in reference to the resources we identified above. We take each of the resources: material, relationships, identity, bodies and minds, power and control, community participation and cohesion and social justice, in turn.

Material Resources

> I am 10, live at home with my mum and brother and sister in Northwest town. I go to school there. I have a cat called Riley and love playing Minecraft [a computer game]. My favourite food is chicken. I am very shy and don't like noisy, crowded places. I pick things up quickly, but anxiety can make it difficult for me to talk to people. I don't like being given direct orders, asking is better! I like my laptop, or something I really wanted and got. I like...my cat Riley, my computer and playing Minescape [a computer game]. Familiar people, places and routine – family; home; school; feeling welcome, included and valued; being clever. (Mark, disabled child)

> My name is Annie, I am fourteen years old and I go to a special school. I live with my mum, dad and my brother who is eleven. My big sister, who is 23, lives nearby with her family. I love my mum and my dad and my sister and my brother very much. They say that I am happy go lucky, I smile a lot and that I teach them what the important things in life are. I like music – especially the Backstreet Boys and S Club 7 and Kylie Minogue to calm me down or the Eagles at night time. I like to try and take wet wipes out of their packet. I like throwing them behind me. (Annie, a disabled young person)

A safe and supportive home emerged as key conditions of a resilient life for disabled children and young people. While children and young people did not mention money, the benefit system nor the pressures of their parents' balancing finances, they did talk about a host of *material* conditions of everyday life. These included prosthetics, and adaptive devices, such as wheelchairs, augmentative communication and hoists. They and their families reminded us that these devices are expensive and difficult to get hold of. When such resources are denied to disabled children and young people, their resilience and that of their family is severely reduced. If the resources needed to be mobile or to communicate are unavailable, this clearly also impacts on disabled children and young people's sense of identity and self-worth.

Identity

Children and young people spoke to us about their developing a sense of being different from other children. While a disabled identity brings with it a sense of difference and otherness, children's *identities* were also intimately tied to specific interests and activities that they were involved in. Children's stories give a real sense of who they are through music, play and popular culture. At the same time, they remind of the complex ways in which ***identities*** are formed in a social world in which disabled identities are often viewed as lacking, deficient and Other. For many children, their encounters with notions of difference begins with the responses of other people to their *bodies and minds*.

Bodies and Minds

Childhood diagnosis may provide a functioning impairment label (Mallett and Runswick-Cole 2016) that allows services and professionals to respond to the needs of children. For others, diagnosis brings uncertainty.

> So she has global developmental delay. They should just write down a paragraph which says 'we have no idea what it is'! I've got a friend with cerebral palsy, I was sure Peppa had cerebral palsy too and I was banging on about it 'please can we scan her?' They scanned her and she doesn't have it. But my friend said she had thought that Peppa had CP as well. But a colleagues of hers had told her 'Oh well, of course, you've got cerebral palsy because when you were being diagnosed that's what they called anything they didn't understand and now they call it global developmental delay', so it's obviously it is just that same catch all the term! But we've got better scans now so we can look at them and say 'oh it's not CP, after all'. (Janice, a mother)

> We sat there and asked a couple more questions and with a big huff, the consultant said 'listen Mrs ***** I can't tell you if your daughter's got cerebral palsy or not, what I can tell you is…' and the words cerebral palsy drifted through the air, and at that point there was just this white noise and I could see her mouth moving, I don't know what she was saying after that point, I didn't listen…I didn't know what cerebral palsy was, I didn't know what it meant. I knew it was something drastic but I wasn't sure what. As we travelled back in the car, Chris [partner] was swearing, he was saying she didn't know what she was on about,

she was grasping at straws. When we got home Chris disappeared. I found him upstairs on the computer and he had put 'cerebral palsy diagnosis indicators' into the computer. (Cate, a mother)

These dealings with health professionals around diagnosis have been widely documented in the literature (Larson 1998). Diagnosis both gives a label to difference (which might be viewed as a way of accessing services and support and, therefore, as positive), whilst potentially pathologising the child (which can be felt as negative). As we saw above, labels can play a powerful role when decisions are made about which children are, and are not, categorised as resilient.

Growing *bodies* are often precarious bodies. As bodies change this creates difficulties for their parents in lifting children and places greater demands for expensive adaptations. Families are marked by the stress of operations, hospital visits and rehabilitation that drain resilience (Murray 2000, 2003). The body is often understood by medical, health and psychological knowledges in very negative ways, and, yet the body is, also, a key site for the development of a resilient identity: an *identity* that is aware of one's own *body* and the need for other people to respond supportively (Shildrick and Price 2009). Children were very much aware of their *bodies* and had clear ideas about how others should touch, respond and respect them:

I am very shy and don't like noisy, crowded places. I pick things up quickly, but anxiety can make it difficult for me to talk to people. (Mark, a disabled child)

I don't like it when people have cross or loud voices Being in a busy shop without my headphones in. It is OK for me to go in there if you remember to put my headphones on before we do! (Annie, a disabled young person)

Parents/family carers played crucial roles in enabling their children to develop a positive sense of *identity* and shaping what it was possible for their children to achieve.

Brian and June told us:

We just decided that we would give Gabby what we would give to any of our children so she went to brownies, guides, she learnt to play the piano, she did ballet and tap. Obviously her achievement levels were lower but that didn't matter, she was getting things back from it and she was learning. At six she started gymnastics and she went to her first games in Dublin when she was seven and she did gymnastics from seven to sixteen. She retired at sixteen but she still does swimming and fitness....she has been to Russia, Estonia, Denmark, Germany and the United States.

Her parents' support made it possible for Gabby to identify as an athlete.

As we can read from the visual network, the *body* is a key site through which a host of other resources are made visible from fighting for equipment (*social justice*), having an accessible shower room (*material*) and struggling to traverse inaccessible environments (*community participation*). The child's body can only be understood in its social, cultural, community and relational context. *Bodies* disrupt environments and demand cultural change to enable children's resilience to emerge.

Children's accounts of their bodies reveal that the body cannot be separated from the world in which it is situated: *bodies* become known, marked, felt, understood and reacted to *in relationships with others* (Michalko 2002), and these relationships are always imbued with issues of power, control and communication.

Power, Control and Communication

Being supported in their communication is key to children having a sense of *power and control* in their lives. Children complained that they were not asked for their opinions. Instead, as is often the case in childhood, their views were spoken via proxies.

> I do get involved in review [annual review of the statement of special educational needs] meetings, but it is hard to say when you are not happy with things, and they tend to have more meetings about me than with me. At the last review, there was some person on the list I didn't even know, the reviewing officer or some woman! I do join in, they do ask me what I would like to say but their stuff comes first and then they ask me. (Diane, a disabled child)

Asad told us, in contrast, that the fact that his parents spoke English as an additional language, meant that professionals had to speak to him:

> English is my first language but my mum and dad's first languages are Urdu and Punjabi. So generally, when we met with doctors and so on, I would communicate with the doctors because my parents didn't understand as much English as me. So professionals would explain it to me, tell me about where to get advice and so on and I would tell my parents. As I got older, my parents' English got so that they understood.

Asad's story reminds us of the importance of access to information in the lives of families of disabled children as a key resource in creating resilience (McLaughlin et al. 2008).

While acknowledging the limits of choice and autonomy afforded to (disabled) children, it is important to acknowledge the *power, control and communication* of parents and family members that is essential to supporting resilient childhoods: all the disabled children we spoke to cited their families as allies.

This raises important questions about advocacy and support in the lives of disabled children who do not live with their families or whose families are unable or unwilling to speak up for them for a variety of reasons, including the complexity of the systems and services on offer, living in poverty or the additional challenges faced if English is an additional rather than first language. If familial resilience undergirds the resilience of disabled children, then children without resilient families face significant threats. The importance of the role of wider communities in children's lives is revealed.

Community

The children were keen to share with us how they liked to spend their time. These activities indicate forms of *community participation* that encompass specialist and inclusive contexts including respite and short breaks, playing on the computer at home, watching DVDs in your bedroom, eating chocolate, digging in the garden, getting dirty, eating fish and chips, and dressing up.

Children shared with us what might be seen as quirky and unusual interests and activities as evidenced by Annie:

I like it when a spoon drops on the ground – whoops!!

Their accounts broaden our understandings of childhood participation, play and leisure. Some children preferred quiet and solitary activities. Others were more interested in being with a crowd:

My perfect day: I would be with my family. I would get up slowly and everything would be very calm. I would listen to music all day and have the mirror ball going. I would be in the sunshine and I would be able to go on the beach and put my feet on the sand. Then I would go in the hydro pool and splash about and I would have a bath too and splash about in there – I'd play splish, splash, splosh! And I would eat LOADS of food! When I came home, I would have my thigh massages and stay up late! (Annie, disabled young person)

Children described *community cohesion* as the willingness of others to support them in their activities. Parents, and family carers play a crucial role in educating others in their community, while, at the same time, children are themselves resilient agents of change demanding social justice.

Social Justice

Disabled children, through their very presence, demand social justice:

> We never used to complain, right letters, speak out, particularly, we aren't the sort of people that would necessarily say, this is wrong. We'd probably have a chat about it, put our names down on petitions every now and again but to be on the front line fighting, you know is a rally awkward position for me and Craig to be in, and we've had to learn to be in that position. The only way I think we've managed to do that is by thinking in many ways this is not for us, this is for Summer and Summer can't advocate for herself, and if we don't do it then her life will be undoubtedly disadvantaged. So that has been really, really hard I think, learning to fight, when it's not the actual kind of default kind of mode really. (Cate, a mother)

As the story above suggests, they have the potential to act as catalysts for the emergence of resilience on the part of their families and allies. The emerging resilience of children is enmeshed in their disabled identities and embodied differences. While children do not appeal to legislation or policy rhetoric, the underlying messages of rights-based practices and discourses were evident in their accounts.

As Annie put it:

> I need people who…Care about me; Listen to me and learn from my family; Take the initiative; Fit in with my family; Follow my routines with food and medication and sleep'. And so to remind you some of the things that are important to me:

- My family
- Learning about me and what my needs are
- Caring for me and about me
- Fitting in with me and my family
- Listening to me and my family

Clearly, the actions of all the adults in children's lives, not just family members, were important. Sometimes, children described the ways in which adults created barriers for disabled children participation in schools and communities:

> So I had a teaching assistant to support me in school from primary school until about Year 8 in high school, but I used to get really frustrated because the teaching assistants weren't helpful. They just said: 'you can be like everyone else if you just try harder' and I felt confused, because I didn't want to be like everyone else. I decided I had outgrown this sort of support. I don't want a teaching assistant any more. (Jim, a young person)

> At break time, I have to sit in a room with all the disabled children. I don't really know why because, well I used to have to go to the toilet at break, but I don't now. It seems like they're trying to club all the disabled children together, we're not ordinary friends, if I made an enemy of one of the people in there or something, if I had an argument with one of them, I'd still have to sit in there with them. (Diane, a disabled child)

These accounts demonstrate that all the adults in children's lives, family members and practitioners, have a role to play in enabling or stifling disabled children's resilience.

Conclusion

Childhood has traditionally been the site for research, exploring the nature and development of resilience. The ways in which resilience has often been characterised (normative development in spite of adversity) is clearly problematic in the lives of children who have often been defined as 'disabled' by virtue of their non-normative development.

However, if we adopt a theoretical framework of resilience that:

(i) accepts that resilience emerges when children and young people have access to the resources that allow them to *feel* resilient;

and

(ii) accepts that there a numerous pathways to resilience. (Ungar 2004, 2007)

It then becomes possible to think of disabled children as living resilient lives.

As the children, young people and parent/family members' stories here powerfully revealed, access to a range of resources builds resilience. In a context of austerity and every increasing cuts to services for disabled children, it is vitally important to resist attempts to locate responsibility for developing resilience (or lack of it) within individual children and families, and to defend the resources children and families need to lead resilient lives.

References

Cocks, A. (2006). The Ethical Maze: Finding an Inclusive Path to Gaining Children's Agreement to Research Participation. *Childhood, 26*(13), 247–266.

Curran, T., & Runswick-Cole, K. (2014). Disabled Children's Childhood Studies: An Emerging Domain of Inquiry? *Disability & Society, 29*(10), 1617–1630.

Department for Communities & Local Government. (2012). *Helping Troubled Families Turn Their Lives Around.* https://www.gov.uk/government/policies/helping-troubled-families-turn-their-lives-around. Date Accessed 20 Feb 2015.

Department for Education (DfE). (2015). *Character Education: Apply for Grant Funding.* https://www.gov.uk/government/news/character-education-apply-for-2015-grant-funding. Date Accessed 20 Feb 2015.

Goodley, D. (2014). *Dis/ability Studies: Theorising Disablism and Ableism.* London: Routledge.

Goodley, D., & Runswick-Cole, K. (2012). Decolonizing Methodologies: Disabled Children as Research Managers and Participant Ethnographers. In S. Grech & A. Azzopardi (Eds.), *Inclusive Communities: A Reader.* Rotterdam: Sense Publishers.

Goodley, D., Lawthom, R., & Runswick-Cole, K. (2014). Dis/ability and Austerity: Beyond Work and Slow Death. *Disability & Society.* http://dx.doi.org/10.1080/09687599.2014.920125. Date Accessed 20 Feb 2015.

Larson, E. (1998). Reframing the Meaning of Disability to Families: The Embrace of Paradox. *Social Science & Medicine, 47*(7), 865–875.

Lave, J., & Wenger, E. (1991). *Situated Learning: Legitimate Peripheral Participation.* Cambridge: Cambridge University Press.

Lowe, P., Lee, E., & Macvarish, J. (2015). Biologising Parenting: Neuroscience Discourse, English Social and Public Health Policy and Understandings of the Child. *Sociology of Health & Illness, 0*(0), 1–14.

Mallett, R., & Runswick-Cole, K. (2016). The 'Urge to Know' Normal: Theorising How Impairment Labels Function. In R. Mallett, C. Ogden, & J. Slater (Eds.), *Theorising Normalcy and the Mundane: Precarious Positions.* Chester: University of Chester Press.

Masten, A. S. (2001). Ordinary Magic: Resilience Processes in Development. *American Psychologist, 56*(3), 227–238.

McLaughlin, J., Goodley, D., Clavering, E., & Fisher, P. (2008). *Families Raising Disabled Children: Enabling Care and Social Justice.* London: Palgrave.

Michalko, R. (2002). *The Difference That Disability Makes.* Philadelphia: Temple University Press.

Morris, J. (2003). Including All Children: Finding Out About the Experiences of Children with Communication and/or Cognitive Impairments. *Children & Society, 17,* 337–348.

Murray, P. (2000). Disabled Children, Parents and Professionals: Partnership on Whose Terms? *Disability & Society, 15*(4), 683–698.

Murray, P. (2003). Reflections on Living with Illness, Impairment and Death. *Disability & Society, 18*(4), 523–526.

Overboe, J. (2004). *Articulating a Sociology of Desire Exceeding the Normative Shadows* (Unpublished PhD Thesis, Vancouver). The University of British Columbia.

Runswick-Cole, K., & Goodley, D. (2013). Resilience: A Disability Studies and Community Psychology Approach. *Social and Personality Psychology Compass, 7*(2), 67–78.

Runswick-Cole, K., & Goodley, D. (2014). You Don't Have to Be a Super-Crip: Reclaiming Resilience in the Lives of Disabled People. In C. Cameron (Ed.), *Disability Studies: A Student's Guide.* London: Sage.

Shildrick, M., & Price, J. (2009). Breaking the Boundaries of the Broken Body. In J. Price & M. Shildrick (Eds.), *Feminist Theory and the Body.* Edinburgh: Edinburgh University Press.

Swain, J., & French, S. (2000). Towards an Affirmation Model of Disability. *Disability & Society, 15*(4), 569–582.

Ungar, M. A. (2004). Constructionist Discourse on Resilience: Multiple Contexts, Multiple Realities Among At-Risk Children and Youth. *Youth Society, 35*(3), 341–365.

Ungar, M. A. (2005). Introduction: Resilience Across Cultures and Contexts. In M. Ungar (Ed.), *Handbook for Working with Children and Youth: Pathways to Resilience Across Cultures and Contexts.* Thousand Oaks, CA: Sage Publications.

Ungar, M. A. (2007). Contextual and Cultural Aspects of Resilience in Child Welfare Settings. In I. Brown, F. Chaze, D. Fuchs, J. Lafrance, S. McKay, & S. Thomas Prokop (Eds.), *Putting a Human Face on Child Welfare.* Toronto: Centre of Excellence for Child Welfare.

White, P. (2012). *Disabled People Divided About Paralympic Effects.* http://www.bbc.co.uk/news/uk-19428263. Date Accessed 20 Feb 2015.

Young, A., Green, E., & Rogers, K. (2008). Resilience and Deaf Children: A Literature Review. *Deafness Education International, 10*(1), 40–55.

Katherine Runswick-Cole is Chair in Education at The School of Education, The University of Sheffield, Sheffield, United Kingdom. Her research draws on critical disability studies approaches to explore the relationships between disability, childhood and families. Her research is informed by her experiences of mothering two young adult children, one of whom is disabled.

Dan Goodley is Professor of Disability Studies and Education at the University of Sheffield, United Kingdom. Recent publications include *Dis/ability Studies* (Routledge, 2014) and *Disability Studies* (second edition, Sage, 2016).

Rebecca Lawthom is Professor of Community Psychology at the Manchester Metropolitan University. She leads a Centre for Social Change and Community Well-being. She is a community psychologist and feminist. Her research interests include disability, migrants, community and feminist psychology, utilising qualitative participative methods that embrace marginality. She is co-editor for the *Community Work and Family* journal and co-author of the text 'Critical Community Psychology'.

Growing Up Disabled: Impairment, Familial Relationships and Identity

Key Points

- In the past, families of children with impairments have been harmed by ill-informed criticism, sometimes questioning parents' acceptance of their child. Such parents, who typically face immense structural disadvantage, need and deserve understanding and support.
- While acknowledging this, the following chapter aims to remind us that disabled persons, like others, are profoundly shaped by what happens in the family. Understanding the subjectivity of disabled adults must, therefore, allow for a careful yet critical examination of the ways in which impairment is responded to in the family context.
- The chapter draws on first-person experience of 'growing up disabled' in a family, highlighting how disability meanings are incorporated, both helpfully and unhelpfully, into formative relationships.

B. Watermeyer (✉)
University of Cape Town, Cape Town, South Africa

© The Author(s) 2018
K. Runswick-Cole et al. (eds.), *The Palgrave Handbook of Disabled Children's Childhood Studies*, https://doi.org/10.1057/978-1-137-54446-9_28

Introduction

As it is well known to readers of this book, the relationship between disability studies and psychology, especially in its applied form, has always been strained (Goodley and Lawthom 2006; Finkelstein and French 1993; Watermeyer 2002). Recent years, though, have witnessed the beginnings of a possible reconciliation (Watermeyer 2012a, 2013; Forshaw 2007; Simpson and Thomas 2015; Goodley 2014). In the context of disabled children's childhood studies, the worry that thinking psychologically will, as it has elsewhere in disability studies, render pathologizing and oppressive analyses is a perfectly justifiable one. We do not need such work, but we do need a psychology. The reason for this is simple. Talking about disabled childhoods means talking about the bedrock formation of adult disabled identities. Lifelong processes of socialization shape how disabled people engage with worlds of exclusion and with themselves (Watermeyer 2013).

As we shall see, a history of blaming parents, by practitioners who pay scant attention to oppressive structural realities, has quite appropriately evoked intense criticism. There is no doubt that families of disabled children need understanding and support, as well as material resources and social inclusion. But if we, as scholars of disability, are to understand the social position of disabled people, we must have the courage to examine family life, with its gifts and failings, its hopes and dreads.

The aim of this chapter is simply to demonstrate that, in families as elsewhere in society, disability is never simple, never sterile; always powerful. Both disability's gifts and its struggles show us that it is not a mere detail of human co-existence, but an evocative, influential force adding its varied colours to human relating. From a broadly psychoanalytic point of view, the nuclear family is our emotional hothouse, coalescing the felt histories of its members, their losses, longings and anxieties about belonging. Add to this disability, for many a harbinger of the unseen layers of the human state, of frailty and mortality, of the converse of all that modernity promises and demands (Frosh 1991; Lasch 1984; Marks 1999; Watermeyer 2013; Goodley 2014). Thinking about this should not, and need not, involve disrespecting 'disability families'; in many ways, it is their normality rather than their exceptionality, which I hope to highlight. Disability, in my experience and my view, can be both hard and mysterious. It calls everyone who it touches, and who is willing, to explore untrodden existential places which may be profoundly enriching but are almost never easy. The disability family is a crucible in which parents, whose task is formidable at the best of times, are required to digest a stew of rugged emotions, while managing stress and exhaustion, as well as any combination of forms of material adversity. It is in this crucible that the selves of disabled people—at least those with congenital impairments—are forged. Surely, we must be curious about this if we are to understand the existential place of disabled people in our societies.

To demonstrate these points, much of this chapter is devoted to a description of scenes from my own disability family story. I write this from many points of view simultaneously: I am a parent, a disabled person, a disability studies academic and a clinical psychologist. My intention is to provide an example of how the intermingling of disability with the evolving relationships of a family might be explored and considered, in a manner which neither idealizes nor denigrates. My familial experience, especially those aspects discussed here, was not a positive one. I do not imply that disability in families always, or even often, brings the sort of negative consequences it did in mine. Instead, my argument is that disability is always important, in ways which, although often intimately tied to material realities, also transcend these, as it structures and influences relationships that are elemental to human development. Naked impairment, if we can pretend for a moment that such a thing exists, collects its meanings, its emotional tone, its possibilities and limitations, in relationship. Further, disability's influences on the growing self are always interwoven with politics, with gender, familial hierarchies and sexuality, as the disability imago refracts and re-deploys all other identity signifiers.

While my story includes accounts of members of my family other than myself, it is my story alone. What this means is that I do not pretend to know about the interiority of my parents or siblings (except for M, who was consulted), but attempt, as honestly as I can, to describe how familial experiences settled within me. No matter how hard we try, if we do, to think about how our relating impacts on others, we will leave deep impressions on one another that we could not anticipate. I'm sure that such impressions were left by me, as well as upon me. I have grappled with the deep ethical questions at play here, wondering at the fairness or otherwise of my account. The solution I reach, albeit an unsatisfactory one, is that the ideas reflected here are a synthesis of experiences and signals which were, and remain, real and formative to me, notwithstanding the fact that I may have misunderstood the intentions of those around me. We are all social products and can only make meaning with what we have. Our responsibility as scholars, though, is to make that meaning with as much humility, integrity and intellectual responsibility as we can.

Disabled children's childhood studies, quite correctly, makes space for children who, notwithstanding their impairments, do not grow up believing they are disabled. Some may think of this as a sign of a family managing their disability scenario very well, and they would probably be right. But we would be doing this family a disservice if we assumed that disability was not an important factor in their familial life. The point I'm making is that studying the influential power of disability (incorporating both impairment and its socially constructed associations) in families does not equate to believing that disability always does harm; rather, that it is always influential in a mosaic of ways. Disability has the power to shape relational worlds, and thereby to weave itself into identities.

The approach I take is broadly psychoanalytic, applying the axiom that all behaviour is both rationally, that is consciously, and irrationally, unconsciously, determined (Frosh 2006; Hoggett 1992). Disability can resonate easily with unconsciously held human struggles, potentially rendering emotional currents which can complicate relationships and cloud cognition. As a trainer of child and family clinical psychologists, it is to me a reliable assumption that all parents, even abusive ones, hope, and endeavour, to do the best they can for their children. This view is my point of departure.

The chapter is structured from here as follows. I begin with remarks on key problems with historical theorizing on 'disability families', with particular emphasis on psychoanalysis. I then consider how such problems can be overcome, through an approach which is respectful, compassionate and curious. The balance of the chapter then comprises an account of how my own familial experience shaped my relationship with disability, and in so doing, with myself and the world.

Theorizing Disability in Families

As has been more thoroughly dealt with elsewhere (e.g. Watermeyer and McKenzie 2014; Watermeyer 2013), theorizing the psychological nature of disability in families is fraught with difficulty. For a start, the legacy of psychological work in this area is one which has, with some justification, been regarded as typifying the oppressions of the medical model (Goodley and Lawthom 2006). As we know, research from psychoanalysis has tended to avoid structural aspects of disablist oppression altogether, while describing the impact of disability on the family as always harmful, and often pathological. This narrow focus, and the discipline's tendency to bring human struggle, rather than resilience, into relief, contributes to a picture which is regarded by many as biased and by some as offensive (Ferguson 2001). An examination of the structural barriers faced by families, including a lack of essential services, educational exclusion, economic hardship and discrimination clearly directs us towards the need for support and advocacy, rather than the diagnosing of familial dysfunction. But as is evident in many domains of disability studies, the tension between a focus on structural factors and intra-psychic phenomena creates distortions on both sides of the argument. As psychoanalysis has ignored structure, so has materialism ignored psychology (Watermeyer and McKenzie 2014). Both positions are wrong.

Much psychoanalytic work on disability families from the second half of the last century focused attention on the impact of the arrival of an 'unexpected'—that is, disabled—infant. These accounts were almost always dire, detailing severe disturbances in attachment, repressed hateful feelings towards the disabled infant, families descending into 'chronic sorrow' and much else (e.g. Drotar et al. 1975; MacKeith 1973; Pinkerton 1970; Solnit and Stark 1961). Reading the literature, it is hard to see how any family might have felt helped by the interventions described. Interestingly, some writers view the mystifications of psychoanalytic theory as filling a defensive function for the practitioner or researcher, which actually prevents the uncovering of real experiences of parenting. Here, the development of new parental skills could be seen as evidence of avoidance or reaction formation, while an absence of overt expressions of conflict may be read as denial (Harris and Wideman 1988). At a minimum, if parents are to feel supported, they must be carefully listened to, and believed. But justifiable critiques of this sort of work have spilled, in my view, into a dangerous inference that the arrival and presence of childhood disability in families does not bring real and influential emotional reverberations, or, that when it does, these are not issues worth examining. I have been at pains to argue (Watermeyer 2012a, 2013, 2014, 2016; Watermeyer and Swartz 2016) that an essential part of overcoming disability inequality is the investigation of how lifelong processes of socialization shape the self-images and expectations of disabled people. To neglect this area is to pretend that the world of meanings about disability-difference that we are all immersed in somehow does not impress itself on the subjectivity of those it marks. Given the reality of how psychology and psychoanalysis have previously ridden roughshod over the lives of families in struggle, it is not surprising that disability studies scholars, including myself, are drawn to feeling protective. Anyone at all acquainted with how disablism can deprive and alienate will feel ready compassion for parents who, like any others, are simply trying their utmost to provide for their children. But what I wish to argue is that it is possible to think about disability in families in a way which is both critical and compassionate. In my own family, my parents spent their lives doing their best for their children, in the face of multiple forms of adversity, including financial strain and non-existent disability services. But like you and me, they were also complex individuals. This complexity and the structural and historical circumstances under which we lived and comingled, amplified and signified one another in ways that shaped me profoundly.

The Sacred Family

Many hurt and outraged responses to a perceived pathologization of disability families are penned by parents who take exception to relationships with their own children being viewed in a jaundiced light (e.g. Ferguson 2001). Insinuations that the birth of a child, who is an adult, might have brought sadness or anguish often feel like an affront to the sacredness of familial bonds. The almost accusatory tone of some psychoanalytic authors has not helped, galvanizing some parents into a blanket rejection of the relevance of examining the emotional milieu in which their children develop. I am a parent, and as such I find none of these responses difficult to understand. Most parents, notwithstanding their own possible histories of loss or trauma, give immensely to the task of supporting the development of their disabled child. And very often, the sacrifices this role exacts are significant. I would be the last to pass any judgement on a parent who, against this backdrop, found it difficult to think carefully about how emotional currents in his or her family may have shaped and delimited the subjectivity of a disabled child. Parenting is hard, and any parent can only do so much.

Besides being a parent, though, I am also a psychoanalytic psychotherapist and one who chooses to work with disabled people at every opportunity. In this work, I spend time accompanying disabled adults as they try to find self amid the confusions of a disablist society, refracted through the formative power of early familial experience. Everyone, disabled or not, has a family—that is, a set of key relationships which embed our unconscious sense of self and our place in the world. Some individuals come away with a solid foundation of self-worth, others with scars or limitations born of their parents' unresolved conflicts. Disabled people are no different to anyone else; indeed, I am discomforted by the insinuation that the families of disabled people should have some sort of 'special treatment'. In-depth-oriented psychotherapy one sees how trans-generational griefs and conflicts adhere, through unconscious processes, to aspects of the present in all families. We know as parents only too well how our styles of parenting reflect both conscious and unconscious responses to our own rearing; we do our best to avoid repeating our own early losses. Inevitably, in these efforts, we do enact repetitions of one kind or another, as painful old stories have an uncanny way of finding reiteration.

As an aside, let me acknowledge at this point that these positions are theoretical, reflecting a broadly psychoanalytic view of emotional life, and I do not imply that there are no other ways of seeing these matters. My use, here and there, of pronouns such as 'us' and 'we' is not intended to force my own beliefs on others, but to communicate my own theoretical view that it is reasonable to suggest some broad commonalities about human emotional life.

The past decade has seen elaboration of the argument that disability is especially evocative of unconscious material (Marks 1999; Watermeyer 2006, 2013; Goodley 2011). For reasons that are part culture, part mystery, disability speaks very directly to the more vulnerable layers of the human self, potentially sparking painful feelings and memories which we would rather forget. The air around disability is often thick with unconscious fantasies, evident in familiar worries and stereotypes about the 'damaged' lives of disabled people. This emotional valency exists in families as well. Why shouldn't it? The fact that a child's disability is evocative for us should not be a cause for shame; on the contrary, the more these feelings can be honestly examined, the less likely it is that some repetition of the trans-generational conflict that the impairment might signify will take place. Add to this the possibility that trauma is involved (Watermeyer and Swartz 2016). This may be in the form of shock at the birth of an 'unexpected' infant, through witnessing a child endure pain, hospitalization or invasive medical procedures, or the emotional consequences of a desperate, ongoing struggle for services and support. The psychoanalyst Robert Young (1994) describes how an experience of trauma can function as a 'homing device' which 'ransacks…the history of the victim until it finds a congruent, early experience' (p. 139). What this means is that traumatic events in the 'real' world can settle psychologically as confirmations of unconscious fears about the self, exposing one's most vulnerable parts. Far from existing purely as objective reality, trauma—like disability—is always experienced in terms of personal meanings, which are based in developmental history. The 'unexpected' arrival, therefore, along with possible subsequent traumatic experiences, will often evoke pre-existing personal conflicts in parents. There is nothing to be ashamed or embarrassed about regarding how one's inner, historically sedimented struggles can be touched upon by the unexpected events of life; it is nothing short of perfectly natural, perfectly human. But these possibilities have great implications for the selves of children growing up with disability.

It is axiomatic in psychoanalytic thinking, as well as in the theory of trauma and recovery (Herman 1997), that we will tend to enact, or repeat, that which we are unable to consciously digest. Thus, it is that a parent who has not had the support necessary, or the time, to fully process the grief of, say, physical and emotional neglect in early life, will tend to repeat part of this experience—in one way or another—with his or her own child. This could take the form of an anxious, even smothering preoccupation with the child's needs, an intense fear of failing the child emotionally which results in avoidance, or any of a range of other possibilities. What holds these scenarios together is that all are, in some way or another, a reaction to unconscious material—in this case, un-felt grief—which to some degree blurs perception of the here-and-now. Parenting a disabled child can present a sort of 'perfect storm', where (i) the arrival of a disabled infant evokes complex feelings, including anxiety, grief and ambivalence; (ii) experiences of trauma may further expose parents' personal struggles; (iii) the physical and emotional demands of parenting leave little energy or space for reflection and self-care; and (iv) guilty feelings arising from within and provoked by a world ready to criticize parents, discourage a compassionate reflection on one's own experiences, both positive and negative. These parents need our understanding, our compassion, for all facets of this predicament. Becoming a parent will involve a degree of psychological 'ransacking' for everyone. But what the circumstances above can create for parents of disabled children is a situation where that 'ransacking' is more profound, yet the space and resources for, and sense of entitlement to, compassion and support, may be lessened. As I have argued elsewhere (Watermeyer 2013), ironically, parents of disabled children may be less permitted to entertain 'complicated' feelings about their offspring than other parents.

Disability, Identity and Unconscious Repetition in My Family

What is to follow reflects my experience and understanding of members of my family and our shared history. But as I have stated, none of us can fully know the intentions of another, and so this account is a subjective one, purely reflecting the things which, in terms of my own unique positioning, left impressions on my life. As my brother M is a central part of this story, he has read it carefully, endorsed its contents and provided me with written permission for publication. My parents are long deceased, but I nevertheless believe that both of them would readily acknowledge and accept the importance of this inquiry. Note, too, that I am here only able to provide the quite broad strokes of key dynamics in my formative life, which may therefore appear a little fanciful. After more than 20 years of analytic inquiry into this story, I could provide much supporting detail if space permitted.

I am the youngest of seven sons, born into a family dominated by patriarchy and the valuing of physical prowess. My mother lost her only sibling and companion to cerebral malaria at the age of 14, a terrible loss which seems to have motivated her desire for a large family, as insurance against the loneliness she felt as a child. My father's early life was traumatic, involving being sent with his two brothers to a distant, militaristic boarding school; treatment for which he, in his own words, could never forgive his father. Significantly, girls were favoured in his family, and his two sisters were allowed to remain at home. My father described feeling deeply envious, perhaps even hateful, towards them. Each of my parents brought these and other losses to their relationship, and their children. For my father, it was reflected in his very limited ability to show love, as well as his precarious hold on a positive masculine identity. The prizing of girls in his family, and punitive relationship with his father, appeared to leave him with largely unconscious feelings of dislike towards maleness. In my understanding, he managed this painful reality by compensating psychologically with a gendered self-aggrandisement. This is a common dynamic in patriarchal systems, where grandiosity and the claiming of power are, in fact, a veneer-covering denigrating feelings about maleness; the control of women, and especially female sexuality, is its oppressive corollary. Indeed, a long tradition of psychoanalytic thought regards the ego—that part of the psyche that is visible as it relates to the world—as in large part shaped by its history of losses. In a sense, we are composed of emergent strategies of being which coalesce as a means of managing loss (Kohut 1972; Frosh 1991). The secret, envious idealization of the feminine showed itself in my family through my father's lifelong desire to have daughters; instead, and to his sadness, he had seven sons. My mother's early experience of abandonment led her to the familiar role of a wife and mother seeking to secure her belonging by caring for others; culturally condensed, unequal gender-typing routinely invite—or recruit—women into this positioning. To say this does not at all devalue the love she showed, but understanding her reparative persona involves recognizing that she struggled with lifelong feelings of low worth. Again, these are gendered dynamics not at all uncommon under patriarchy.

Myself and my next-to-youngest brother M were last-borns in a family dominated by a particular form of patriarchal hyper-masculinity, surrounded almost exclusively by male authority figures. Unbeknown to our child selves, we were soon to develop symptoms of an inherited degenerative disorder of the retina, which would progressively erode away our sight. Now settled down in South Africa (we were originally from colonial Zimbabwe), where (speaking here of the conservative white community) being a 'real' man required a denial of emotion, especially vulnerability, the prizing of physical strength, the punishment of weakness and the settling of conflict with domination. As with my father, though, this dominant male identity often only thinly covered shame and self-denigration, which in turn spurred further strivings for narcissistic purchase in the family and the world. My father's own struggles with self-worth and adequacy led him, in my mother's account, to criticize and discipline my elder brothers harshly, leaving them seeking vulnerable 'others' to dominate, in order to rescue their own battered sense of self. The ambivalence about gender in our family was never discussed, but evident in subtle and more overt ways. In one well-worn tale, my entire family, except my not-yet-born self, were walking along a busy street in Harare, when they met another family with whom my parents were acquainted. The family included a daughter of about four years old. My father declared that he would happily swap his six sons for this one little girl. As is often the case with such accounts, it is not the event itself which carried effects, but the way it was re-told, and the place it assumed in family mythology. I recall my mother murmuring in the kitchen about how it was not right for my father to speak that way. Such was the milieu into which M and myself began to appear as disabled children. Diagnosed at around age seven, we were both substantially sight impaired by our mid-teens. It should not be hard to see how disability, with its culturally condensed meanings of vulnerability and damage, was anathema to the mandatory toughness of our familial identity. The onset of our shared disability was met with a mix of outright denial and anxious silence. The knowledge that his two youngest sons were progressively to lose their sight seemed too much for my father, who dismissed the diagnosis as quackery. My elder brothers remained, at first, largely silent. In the face of this lack of support, it was left to my mother to hold the fear and anxiety for all.

As the youngest, I was particularly close to my mother who struggled with anxiety and depression. Some of my earliest memories are of serving prematurely as an emotional support to her. Since M was three years older than me, his diagnosis came first, and, among the men of the family, my mother had no one to talk to about this frightening new reality. So it was that I, at age five, was told the 'secret' by my mother that my brother M was to become blind; M was not told. I was, as any child, excited about being let into an important secret, but at a deeper level left feeling bewildered and scared. My own diagnosis came just two years later.

Any young boy in a family such as ours would have run the risk of authoritarian treatment. In circumstances where others need to wield power in order to feel legitimate, children are a very likely target. Neediness and vulnerability were projected onto M and myself long before disability became part of the picture; we were resented as the 'mollycoddled', 'weak', 'soft' young ones, who needed to be taught many hard lessons. But as we moved through our young lives, the symbolic power of disability would progressively add to these relational patterns in different ways for each of us.

M found school far more difficult than I, and was also diagnosed first. I was particularly, often hatefully, envied as the youngest and my mother's favourite. These factors and others added up to an almost psychotic split in my family's views of M and myself, where his disability came to be pityingly, stiflingly overestimated, while mine was virtually denied. Such cognitive distortions based on the defence of splitting are commonplace around disability, designating disabled people as either invalids or 'supercrips' (Watermeyer 2013). And so did the persistent narratives of our lives develop. M was damaged and vulnerable, presenting opportunities for others to intervene in ways which afforded the chance to feel both altruistic and powerful. His life was seen as hard, the epitome of Oliver's 'personal tragedy' (Oliver 1986). I, on the other hand, was regarded as having an inordinately charmed existence, perpetually devoid of the worries and responsibilities which should by rights characterize a life. And certainly devoid of anything as 'unfortunate' as 'real' disability. While unspoken expectations were, of M's life, being predestined as functionally limited, arid and difficult, I was still being handed newspaper articles to read more than a decade after I became fully print impaired.

One form which attitudes towards M took was a controlling over-involvement in matters regarding his education. After being informed, by letter no less, that M's disability rendered him no longer 'appropriate' as a pupil of his high school, my parents sent him to a residential special school. The experience was profoundly traumatic for him; he repeatedly ran away from the school, was moved to another and absconded again. The history of social responses to disability can, from one perspective at least, be summarized as the projection of human frailty into those designated 'disabled', followed by the exercising of various forms of domination and control aimed, unconsciously, at 'managing' and subduing the shameful psychic contents (Watermeyer 2013). This is what seemed to unfold in our family. Since M, in my understanding, carried emotional conflicts on behalf of my elder brothers, they evidently felt a need to forcefully control how these contents were materially dealt with in the world. They would not hear of his struggles at a special school which was rigid, pathologizing and neglectful, resolute in the negation of any emotional aspect of M's young life. Of course, they were also concerned for his education. But they seemed unable to listen to him, to hear him, at all. Treatment which was, in a manner deeply interwoven with disability, effectively Spartan and cruel, presented as responsible care.

As the younger brother, I watched these events with a mix of sadness and terror. I had been trained by my mother from a young age to manage, or *not manage*, my own emotional life by being overly concerned with others. Seeing my big brother hurting so much, and in ways so connected to disability—my own disability—sent deep reverberations of anxiety through me. My compromise, my 'solution', was to unconsciously take on my family's defence of seeing me as not only strong and fine but even 'fortunate'. Like Sally French (1993), I fell into convincing everyone, including myself, that if I was disabled at all, it was in a way which would have little impact on my 'happy life'. Still, in the values of patriarchal masculinity, I would never succeed. Freud's (1916) association of blindness with castration carries, in the disability symbolism of my family at least, real resonance. The onset of disability left me in a more extreme version of the quandary I had wrestled all my life; how to be a 'good enough man'. Disability mixes with gender here, as hyper-masculine dictates hatefully equate disability with femininity. In addition, the unconscious idealization of women and girls was only shallowly buried. My solution to both problems, in my early adulthood, was to take up the persona of a woman. I grew my hair very long and dressed effeminately, also appearing as a woman at every social occasion where I could pass it off as 'dressing up'. I did not understand my drive to do this at the time, but I saw later that it served to extricate me from the field of expectations directed at my young man self, while leaving male authority figures outwardly scornful but inwardly threatened and bamboozled. It was much easier to be a long-haired feminine man who struggled to see than a regular guy with a sight impairment. But all of this came at a cost. Disidentifying with one's own sex can mean losing parts of oneself, as these are jettisoned with unwanted aspects of gender. The symbolic violence, racism and denigration of women which were central to maleness in my family left me needing to hide and deny anything of myself which was masculine. This interfered, through my teens and early adulthood, with the development of my sexuality. Ironically, my rebellion was also somehow apologetic.

Through all of this, however, my anti-establishment ways only seemed to cement my elder siblings' view that I was carefree and spoilt and would 'never do an honest day's work in my life'; this, despite my accumulating several degrees and qualifying as a health practitioner. The part of me that could not help buying into this narrative distanced me from the lived realities of my own impairment.

The way in which disability is, or is not, talked about in the home has profound implications for how things go in the world 'out there'. For me, the shame and overwhelm communicated by the strand of silence in my family's response to me sent me into the world believing that acceptance was conditional on keeping my sight struggles to myself. I became the carefree, perfectly fine person of the stereotype, to avoid the embarrassment and with-drawal of others. In Sally French's (1993, p. 69) words, I did this to avoid 'spoiling other people's fun'; but as she and I both understand, it was also for our own security. It had never been, and simply could not be 'OK' to be someone who could not see properly. One among many problems associated with this stance involved meeting a possible girlfriend. If there was someone I was interested in, disclosure of my sight impairment (which I could then still disguise quite well), would, in my mind at least, spell rejection. But not disclosing felt like deceit, like I was offering a damaged product disguised as a pristine one. The spectre of 'going blind'—and I mean this more in terms of the stereotyped social role than the simple impairment—seemed far too explosive a secret to keep. It had been too much for my mother to keep to herself when I was five.

The narratives of tragedy and privilege created different dilemmas for M and myself, respectively. For M, it was a journey to find wholeness in the face of an unrelenting barrage of denigrating projections. His life and self were defined from without in the language of disability damage, leaving him with the immense challenge of finding lost parts of self which were not thus defined. For me, the challenge was to locate and allow my own vulnerability, to find a way to compassionately inhabit parts of myself which felt damaged and shameful and to grow in a faith that these could be shown and accepted by others. For M, the struggle was to find his identity outside of disability; for me, it was the converse. Both of us, now in our 40s, continue to live these dilemmas daily. Our family lives with disability are still very much with us, in us. My relationship with my sight impairment—its meanings and signifi-cance—is fundamentally interwoven with my formative familial experiences, and I am sure that, as a disabled person, I am not alone in this.

Conclusion

It is, in my view, difficult to overestimate the formative power of early famil-ial relationships, each with a profile of defences which bring some parts of reality into excessive relief, while obscuring others. I have written elsewhere on some of the ways in which anxieties provoked by disability can distort relational boundaries and entitlements to emotional experience (Watermeyer and Swartz 2008; Watermeyer 2009, 2012b). What we take from our fami-lies—our 'disability curriculum'—will be enacted in some form in subsequent relationships. According to Raphael-Leff (1994), all of us, whether we are growing up with disability or not, ingest layers of emotive meaning about the nature of our bodies—and hence selves—contained in how we see ourselves mirrored in the words, expressions and actions of others. She emphasizes that psychological representations of our bodies do not 'just spring from within', as some sort of solipsistic, biological formula (p. 13). Our feelings about our bodies are a complex amalgam of conscious and unconscious representations soaked up in our formative milieu. In Raphael-Leff's (1994) words 'we "learn" our bodies through the hands, faces and minds of significant carers and their bodily ministrations' (p. 16). The evocativeness of bodily difference means that the atmosphere around disability is often permeated with projections, all of which must find a home. There are so many things that, say, sight impairment can mean. What does it do? How might it feel? What is right for a sight-impaired person? What does he or she need? Is there place in society for such a person, or possibly a mate? The fantasied answers to all of these questions, constantly shifting with the unconscious emotional tide of the family, accumulated in my failing eyes and growing self over many years. Such meanings structure cognition, rather than composing it, and are therefore very hard to identify, let alone shift. We are speaking here of the very stuff of self-formation. Disability can powerfully shape relationships, and relationships shape people.

While it has not been the intention with this chapter to translate my reflections into recommendations, I will close with a few brief comments. Like society as a whole, each family will carry its own disability discourse, part known and part not. And like society, we in our families need to do all we can to understand, to unpack, our disability discourse. Most of the assumptions we communicate to our children about disability will be, firstly, hidden in the symbolic, and secondly, embedded in our own unseen, emotionally-based relationships with the body and its differences. We need to listen very carefully to children, doing our best to remain open to the meanings they make. But we also need to listen to ourselves, to one another, as we carefully and compassionately explore the parts of our histories which disability touches, triggers and mirrors. Disability draws all of us into an intimate and exacting encounter with what it means to be human. Both our physical and emotional frailty come into view, as searching questions are asked about what we truly value, and why. There are precious learnings to be had here, as engaging with life's less-travelled pathways, both inner and outer, can bring enrichment in relationships with oneself and others. But as any parent knows, this work is hard; any exploration must begin from a position of patience and compassion for the self.

References

Drotar, D., Baskiewicz, A., Irvin, N., Kennell, J., & Klaus, M. (1975). The Adaptation of Parents to a Birth of an Infant with a Congenital Malformation: A Hypothetical Model. *Pediatrics, 56*(5), 710–717.

Ferguson, P. M. (2001). Mapping the Family: Disability Studies and the Exploration of Parental Response to Disability. In G. Albrecht, K. Seelman, & M. Bury (Eds.), *Handbook of Disability Studies*. Thousand Oaks: Sage Publications.

Finkelstein, V., & French, S. (1993). Towards a Psychology of Disability. In J. Swain, V. Finkelstein, S. French, & M. Oliver (Eds.), *Disabling Barriers – Enabling Environments*. London: Sage.

Forshaw, M. (2007). In Defence of Psychology: A Reply to Goodley and Lawthom (2005). *Disability & Society, 22*(6), 655–658.

French, S. (1993). "Can You See the Rainbow?" The Roots of Denial. In J. Swain, V. Finkelstein, S. French, & M. Oliver (Eds.), *Disabling Barriers – Enabling Environments*. London: Sage.

Freud, S. (1916). Some Character-Types Met with in Psycho-Analytic Work: The Exceptions. In J. Strachey, A. Freud, A. Strachey, and A. Tyson. (Eds.), (1957) *The Standard Edition of the Complete Psychological Works of Sigmund Freud, Volume XIV (1914–1916): On the History of the Psychoanalytic Movement Papers on Metapsychology and Other Works*. London: The Hogarth Press.

Frosh, S. (1991). *Identity Crisis: Modernity, Psychoanalysis and the Self*. London: Macmillan.

Frosh, S. (2006). *For and Against Psychoanalysis* (2nd ed.). New York: Routledge.

Goodley, D. (2011). Social Psychoanalytic Disability Studies. *Disability & Society, 26*(6), 715–728.

Goodley, D. (2014). *Dis/Ability Studies: Theorizing Disablism and Ableism*. London: Routledge.

Goodley, D., & Lawthom, R. (Eds.). (2006). *Disability and Psychology: Critical Introductions and Reflections*. Basingstoke: Palgrave Macmillan.

Harris, A., & Wideman, D. (1988). The Construction of Gender and Disability in Early Attachment. In M. Fine & A. Asch (Eds.), *Women with Disabilities: Essays in Psychology, Culture and Politics*. Philadelphia: Temple University Press.

Herman, J. (1997). *Trauma and Recovery* (2nd ed.). New York: Basic Books.

Hoggett, P. (1992). *Partisans in an Uncertain World: The Psychoanalysis of Engagement*. London: Free Association Books.

Kohut, H. (1972). Thoughts on Narcissism and Narcissistic Rage. *Psychoanalytic Study of the Child, 27*, 360–400.

Lasch, C. (1984). *The Minimal Self: Psychical Survival in Troubled Times*. London: Norton.

MacKeith, R. (1973). Parental Reactions and Responses to a Handicapped Child. In F. Richardson (Ed.), *Brain and Intelligence*. Hyattsville: National Education Consultants.

Marks, D. (1999). *Disability: Controversial Debates and Psychosocial Perspectives*. London: Routledge.

Oliver, M. (1986). Social Policy and Disability: Some Theoretical Issues. *Disability, Handicap and Society, 1*, 15–17.

Pinkerton, P. (1970). Parental Acceptance of the Handicapped Child. *Developmental Medicine and Child Neurology, 12*(2), 207–212.

Raphael-Leff, J. (1994). Imaginative Bodies of Childbearing: Visions and Revisions. In A. Erskine & D. Judd (Eds.), *The Imaginative Body: Psychodynamic Therapy in Health Care*. London: Jason Aronson Inc.

Simpson, J., & Thomas, C. (2015). Clinical Psychology and Disability Studies: Bridging the Disciplinary Divide on Mental Health in Disability. *Disability and Rehabilitation, 37*(14), 1299–1304.

Solnit, A. J., & Stark, M. H. (1961). Mourning and the Birth of a Defective Child. *Psychoanalytic Study of the Child, 12*, 523–537.

Watermeyer, B. (2002). Blindness, Attachment and Self: Psychoanalysis and Ideology. *Free Associations, 49*, 335–352.

Watermeyer, B. (2006). Disability and Psychoanalysis. In B. Watermeyer, L. Swartz, M. Schneider, T. Lorenzo, & M. Priestley (Eds.), *Disability and Social Change: A South African Agenda*. Pretoria: HSRC Press.

Watermeyer, B. (2009). Claiming Loss in Disability. *Disability & Society, 24*(1), 91–102.

Watermeyer, B. (2012a). Is It Possible to Create a Politically Engaged, Contextual Psychology of Disability? *Disability & Society, 27*(2), 161–174.

Watermeyer, B. (2012b). Disability and Countertransference in Group Psychotherapy: Connecting Social Oppression with the Clinical Frame. *International Journal of Group Psychotherapy, 62*(3), 393–417.

Watermeyer, B. (2013). *Towards a Contextual Psychology of Disablism*. London: Routledge.

Watermeyer, B. (2014). Disability and Loss: The Psychological Commodification of Identity. *Psychology Journal, 11*(2), 99–107.

Watermeyer, B. (2016). 'I Don't Have Time for an Emotional Life': Marginalization, Dependency and Melancholic Suspension in Disability. *Culture, Medicine, and Psychiatry.* doi:10.1007/S11013-016-9503-X.

Watermeyer, B., & McKenzie, J. (2014). Mothers of Disabled Children: In Mourning or on the March? *Journal of Social Work Practice*, 1–12. doi:10.1080/02650533.2014.889103.

Watermeyer, B., & Swartz, L. (2008). Conceptualising the Psycho-Emotional Aspects of Disability and Impairment: The Distortion of Personal and Psychic Boundaries. *Disability & Society, 23*(6), 599–610.

Watermeyer, B., & Swartz, L. (2016). Disablism, Identity and Self: Discrimination as a Traumatic Assault on Subjectivity. *Journal of Community & Applied Social Psychology*. doi:10.1002/casp.2266.

Young, R. M. (1994). *Mental Space*. London: Process Press.

Brian Watermeyer is a clinical psychologist, disability activist, disability studies researcher and disabled person. He holds an M.A. (Clin.Psych.) from UCT, and a D.Phil (Psychology) from Stellenbosch University, and holds the position of Senior Research Officer, Disability Studies Division, within UCT's Department of Health and Rehabilitation Sciences. He has two published books and numerous journal articles and chapters in the field of disability studies, notably in the area of applying critical psychoanalysis to understanding all aspects of disability inequality.

Autistic Development, Trauma and Personhood: Beyond the Frame of the Neoliberal Individual

Damian Milton

Key Points

- This chapter critically explores notions of childhood development, particularly in regard to autism, reactions to traumatic events and the meaning of 'personhood'.
- The construction of the neoliberal individual is contrasted with that of personhood as experienced by an autistic person.
- Person-centred methods of engagement as outlined in this chapter can give opportunities for opening up a respectful discursive space where autistic development is not framed from the outset as 'disordered'.

Introduction

This chapter critically explores notions of childhood development, particularly in regard to autism, reactions to traumatic events and the meaning of 'personhood'. The chapter begins by looking at 'consensual normalcy' as a dominant thread throughout the history of Western philosophy and how contemporary neoliberal ideology constructs the individual. This idealisation of 'functional and productive' personhood is then contrasted with the experience of developing as an autistic person (conceived here as simply those who

D. Milton (✉)
London South Bank University, London, UK

© The Author(s) 2018

K. Runswick-Cole et al. (eds.), *The Palgrave Handbook of Disabled Children's Childhood Studies*, https://doi.org/10.1057/978-1-137-54446-9_29

identify or who are identified as 'autistic' and not to reify medical model notions of what autism is—see Milton 2012a, b). The arguments presented in this chapter have been influenced by a diverse range of theory, from Kelly's (1955) Personal Construct Theory (PCT), to Garfinkel's (1967) notion of 'breaching' and Derrida's (1988) methods of deconstruction, and goes on to explain how, through a number of projects, this theorising was implemented to help empower both myself and other members of my family who had experienced traumatic events in their childhood and/or sense of self/personhood. In conclusion, it is argued that autistic development can be seen as an affront to neoliberal notions of functional stages of child development, and yet person-centred methods of engagement as outlined in this chapter can give opportunities for opening up a respectful discursive space, where autistic development is not framed from the outset as 'disordered'. Of course, such a construing of autistic development as part of natural diversity is incongruent with the pathologising narrative of neoliberalism. In this sense, the 'double empathy problem' (or lack of mutual understanding and reciprocity) between autistic and non-autistic people (Milton 2012a, 2014a) is not only personal but political too. In accordance with other 'autistic voices' (Sinclair 1993; Sainsbury 2000), this chapter uses the descriptors of 'autistic person/people' and 'autistic spectrum':

> We are not people who "just happen to have autism"; it is not an appendage that can be separated from who we are as people, nor is it something shameful that has to be reduced to a sub-clause. (Sainsbury 2000, p. 12)

Western Society and Its Strong Drive Towards Central Coherence

One of the dominant psychological theoretical explanations of autism suggests that autistic people have a 'weak drive toward central coherence' (WCC) (Baron-Cohen 2008), depicted largely as a deficit or impairment compared to the 'neuro-norm'. According to the theory of WCC, autistic people may have a particular strength in processing details because of a lack in the ability to synthesise information quickly and gain meanings. It is an interesting exercise, however, if one reverses the gaze and considers the predominant typical neurotype, or at least its fanciful construction, as having a 'strong drive toward central coherence'. One can say there is a thread in Western philosophy connecting Plato's forms, Hobbes' views of the descent of man without civil society, Durkheim's collective conscience and the value consensus of Talcott

Parsons containing a desire for coherence and consensus. Some of these theorists noticed, however, that with this drive towards hegemonic normativity, one would always have those who do not fit: the pathologically dysfunctional deviant minority.

> The web of domination has become the web of reason itself, and this society is fatally entangled in it. (Marcuse 1964, p. 123)

Within current hegemonic norms, the notion of the fully independent, neoliberal functional individual, the social agent who is responsible for their actions, has become the ideal to which pathological deviance is contrasted, creating categories of those who can pass as 'normal', those who severely struggle to pass and those who cannot (and/or may not wish to). All could be said, however, to be constrained within these parameters. This form of 'individuality' does not allow for the celebration of diversity in all its forms and creates an 'us and them' mentality and 'othering' of an ever-increasing number of people.

Within the history of Western philosophy, there has also been a tradition that has not highlighted solidity, structure and consensus, however, but rather fluid and transactional processes. From Heraclitus to contemporary postmodernist theory, such a tension has existed. Postmodernist theorists, such as Foucault (1972, 1973) and Deleuze and Guttari (1972, 1980), reject notions of structure, massification, meta-narratives and conformity; individual identity is seen as in a state of constant becoming, and notions of difference and multiplicity not consumed by binary categorisations.

Fragmented Perception and Building an 'Aut-ethnography'

A popular technique within critical disability studies is that of the auto-ethnography. It is a method that focuses upon the writer's own subjective experience and reflects upon this to connect such situated understandings to wider cultural, political, and social meanings and discourse (Milton 2014b). A common feature of this interpretive method is the notion that one builds a coherent story of identity over time. Not only does this take on the hue of neoliberalism but it is also an experience that may not be applicable to some autistic ways of being in the world.

A number of cognitive psychological research studies have suggested that people on the autistic spectrum show a 'deficit' in the use and construction of personal episodic memory, yet an accompanying strength in semantic factual memory (Millward et al. 2000; Goddard et al. 2007; Crane and Goddard 2008; Goldman 2008). Rather than taking a deficit model of autism, one can view such differences in perception and memory construction as embodied differences that can impact on the social lifeworlds experienced by autistic people. However, such development as an autistic person could also be seen as an affront to the construction of the functional and productive independent neoliberal individual identity and notions of selfhood:

> An intensive trait starts working for itself, a hallucinatory perception, synesthesia, perverse mutation, or play of images shakes loose, challenging the hegemony of the signifier. In the case of the child, gestural, mimetic, ludic, and other semiotic systems regain their freedom and extricate themselves from the "tracing," that is, from the dominant competence of the teacher's language – a microscopic event upsets the local balance of power. (Deleuze and Guttari 1980, p. 15)

As an autistic person, my own sense of identity is not a coherent one, nor is it a completely fluid identity. For me, memories and sense of self are experienced as fragments, painstakingly structured and constructed to make patterns. Such patterns are movable, yet they shift and alter each time one attempts to view them (Milton 2013a). Personally, this is not a deficit to be remediated, but a difference to be acknowledged and worked with. Such a way of being in the world contains a tension between continuity and discontinuity and is more akin to a rhizomatic model of becoming, a milieu without boundaries, a continually evolving 'inter-being'. Thus, one might ask: what would an incoherent and nomadic 'aut-ethnography' look like (Milton 2013a, 2014b)?

What if One Has a 'Rhizomatic' Construct System?

It is not only autistic people who might have a fragmented experience of self-development over time. The construction of personal narratives can also be radically altered for those who have memory challenges following head injury or through reactions to personal trauma. In the construction of a personal narrative, there are a number of ways in which visual media such as photography can be utilised. This can include photomontage or collage (Ridout 2014), giving a camera to young participants in research to capture what is of meaning for them in a given situation, photo-sorting and Q-sort methodology (Milton 2014c), and many more. My own theorising in this area dates back to projects carried out with my mother (Milton 2002). These projects involved the use of photography with respect to individuals who struggled to compose personal narratives of self. These projects were influenced by a number of theoretical antecedents, the first of which is the PCT of George Kelly (1905–1967).

PCT developed as a pragmatic theory through Kelly's psychotherapy practice. At the time of conception, such therapy was dominated by two divergent schools of thought: Psychoanalysis and Behaviourism. Both perspectives were vastly different to one another, yet both took the standpoint that people were moved to act by forces largely outside of their own control. In contrast, PCT saw the person as an agent, making choices and decisions, and acting upon them. This conceptualisation would not divorce actions from the context within which people act, but for Kelly (1955), it was the constructions that an individual places on events that shape the meanings they form and the reactions they have to events. Thus, the starting point for PCT was the idiosyncratic ways in which people make sense of the world and how that leads to social action.

Such an approach to personal constructions draws heavily on a phenomenological approach, attempting to approach issues through the viewpoint of the individual experiencing them, rather than fitting them into a priori theories. Kelly (1955) used the term 'constructive alternativism' to suggest that there were many differing ways of perceiving and making sense out of the same thing or event, and rather than seeing any interpretation as 'correct', one should look pragmatically at how useful such a framing is to one's purposes. For Kelly (1955), following on from the work of Mead (1934), social roles were not fixed positions, but something navigated by an individual in their interactions with others. Importantly, in the context of autism, it involved placing oneself in the position of the other with whom one was interacting, so that one could adjust one's social performance accordingly:

> He [George Kelly] argued that there were two ways of treating other people. You can relate to others in the way that the early behaviourists thought normal, and treat them as 'behaving mannequins'. Only psychopaths do this, he claimed. The moral way to relate is to act in the light of the other person's view of things. In other words, taking their thoughts and feelings into consideration. (Butt 2008, p. 13)

Autistic people are often deemed to lack the ability to relate to others (Baron-Cohen 2008). Empathy is a two-way process, thus I would contend that to locate the 'deficit' in the autistic mind is an ableist theory. It is often autistic people who are the ones deemed (in this sense) to be 'behaviourist psychopaths', when all too often the theories of a lack of 'theory of mind' (Baron-Cohen 2008) combined with behaviourist ideology are used to frame the 'lifeworld' of autistic people from the outside, and consequently are often rejected by the way autistic people construe themselves (Milton 2012a, 2014a; Milton and Bracher 2013). Indeed, the current media tendency to equate autism with psychopathic behaviour (Park 2014) can be seen as a powerful construction being fed by notions of autistic people lacking empathy or as being empty vessels in need of behavioural remediation. Such constructions and ways of construing autism, as being defined by a lacking or deficient 'theory of mind', are dehumanising and disempowering, denying autistic people a voice in their own affairs. Indeed, rather than there being such a deficit in the minds of autistic people, I have previously argued that a 'double empathy problem' exists, that indicates an inherent difficulty for both parties to understand the way of being, construing and acting of the other (Milton 2012a, 2014a). One could even say that suggesting a deficit in theory of mind in autistic people is a form of projection of what is being done to autistic people. When conceived of in this way, the power differential with regard to who it is that produces knowledge about autism can be seriously questioned (Milton and Bracher 2013; Milton 2014a).

Kelly (1955) envisaged the personal construct to be ways of construing events along bipolar continuums, for example, from happy to sad, anxious to relaxed. This is not to say constructions are of the nature of either/or extremes, but they can be placed along continuums. Placed together, these constructions comprise a 'construct system'. In this sense, discourse tells us little about the actual event, but it tells us a lot about how someone is construing an event. Constructs are more than just conceptualisations, however, as they are both ways of reflecting upon phenomena and of motivating social action. Construing can also be seen as something that is an active process rather than something static that one 'has'. Therefore, a construct system is not a cognitive entity existing in a vacuum, but it is socially and discursively situated.

According to PCT, there is no such thing as a static 'self', as a cognitive entity made up of 'traits'. Equally, an individual is not seen as an empty vessel moved to act by outside forces alone, rather that there was a direction to a person's actions, or as later postmodernists may have said, a 'line of flight' (Deleuze and Guttari 1980). To make sense of this phenomenon, Kelly suggested that people develop 'core constructs' at the centre of their construct systems, which are therefore essential ways in which people construe the 'self'. In this conceptualisation, the 'self' is neither static nor fluid, not working with a psychological vacuum nor totally driven by external forces, but as a personally constructed 'clumping' of meaning-making activity (Milton 2013a, 2014a, b), a 'self-theory'.

Kelly (1955) and later theorists in the field produced a number of techniques and methods for investigating the meaning-making strategies and construct systems that people employ, the most famous of which being Kelly's own 'repertory grid'. This technique involves eliciting a number of 'elements' within a situation (for instance, particular people someone is associated with, or activities or organisations someone is involved with) and a number of constructs about these elements. One way in which this is elicited is to ask how two elements are similar to one another, but different to a third. This produces a grid, where the individual can rate on a numerical scale how much constructs relate to the various elements in question. What this technique does is produce a way of mapping how that individual is construing an event. The technique was not devised to be used in a mechanical way, but as a way of strategically enquiring about how someone is making sense of phenomena.

> The rules of logic do not apply in a person's phenomenology. Instead, we see an idiosyncratic psycho-logic in operation. (Butt 2008, p. 41)

Another technique developed utilising PCT was that of 'the Salmon line' named after its creator Phillipa Salmon (2003). This technique asks an individual to draw a line with words representing opposite extremes at each end (e.g. anxious to relaxed). The individual is then asked to place themselves along this line and where they would like to be in future. The individual is then asked to write or talk about how they think they will get from one point to the other. It is in this discursive space that for Salmon (2003), the learning experience takes place. Similar techniques have also been devised with regard to expressing a sense of 'real' and 'ideal' self-image (of course, with both being seen as constructions), or of the organisation one works within. Such techniques have helped inspire participatory work with autistic children (Moran 2006; Williams and Hanke 2007; Greenstein 2013).

It is also of great relevance to the understanding of the use of construct systems by autistic people that Kelly (1955) theorised that the construing and meaning-making process of human beings begins prior to language development. Thus, the construction of meaning and positionality in this view can be built upon sensory and emotional reactions to events without the need for linguistic interpretation, and yet it goes beyond the simple stimulus-response conceptualisation of behaviourism. This presents an interesting dilemma, however, as to how one might be able to build a dialogue with a less-verbal or non-verbal autistic person. The visual methods utilised by Williams and Hanke (2007) would not be accessible to all, yet through the use of 'talking mats', sorting photographs or building an interactional rapport with individuals, a 'map' of how an individual is construing the world may be built, however, incomplete that map may be. This should always be seen as an ongoing process of interaction though.

In previous chapters, I have argued that the construct system employed by autistic people may well be divergent from those of non-autistic people, due to differences in both neurological embodiment and cultural understanding (Milton 2012a, b, 2013a, b, 2014a, b). In this conceptualisation, autistic ways of being can be seen as being constructed as 'rhizomatic', a psycho-logic system that has no parameters, no hierarchy nor status, but seemingly endless connections. This can lead to a tendency to not 'fill in the gaps' in meaning-making by using previously learnt schema (Milton 2013b), or alternatively, a tendency towards building a concrete and rigid construct system as a defensive strategy, or constructing a fragmented construct system, which can mean anything from a contented 'embracing of the chaos' to a traumatic loss of a sense of self altogether (Caldwell 2014; Milton 2014b). As previously mentioned in this theoretical account, autistic people can sometimes have quite an incoherent sense of self over time (Milton 2014b). For some, expressions of one's personal construct system may be better suited to non-linear activities.

Childhood Trauma and the Personal Construction of Self

The initial theorising that began with my mother (Milton 2002) led to a number of projects involving the personal construction of self-following family trauma. The first of these was the construction of an alternative family album. This method involved collecting together photographs of family history, yet without the usual emphasis of the traditional family album, of presenting a happy and functional family unit. Instead, photographs were selected on the basis of the personal emotional impact of them, or 'punctum' (Barthes 1977). With each photograph, both my mother and I wrote descriptions of the personal relevance the photographs held. This was completed in isolation from one another and then compiled in chronological order and placed into a booklet. At the centre of the booklet were two blank pages, representing a traumatic event in our family history: that of a multi-car road traffic accident that led to my mother sustaining multiple severe injuries and serious psychological trauma to myself. This project opened up a space in which to talk about traumatic events of the past and how each of us had our own personal interpretations of these events, such a dialogue helped us both to communicate and express our own perceptions and understandings.

Following the road traffic accident, my previous set of beliefs and constructs about the world were shattered into tiny fragments. The mainstay of my previous existence being my mother, the construct of 'carer' was reversed and notions such as childhood and self-identity began to dissolve, leading to a very psychologically turbulent time through my teenage years (Milton 2014b). The alternative family album project, not only helped me and my mother to connect to one another but helped me to connect my new sense of self with that of my former childhood and find consistencies between them. Both my mother and I had to rebuild anew a sense of identity following the road traffic accident, as well as a mutual interdependency. This has been an ongoing process ever since, but one in which this project opened up a way of reflecting upon.

Such a linear narrative was, however, deconstructed in the next project my mother embarked upon entitled: 'Beyond the frame' (Milton 2002). Again, this project involved reflection upon a set of family photographs, exploring the tensions and traumas that the personal narratives contained. My mother discovered five photographs that had been taken of her and her sister in 1956. These photographs were taken on the day that my aunt was 'banished' (to live with their father in another country) since their mother was literally obliterating her existence from her social 'lifeworld' for having been born with brain damage. From that day, my aunt was never referred to or seen by her mother. This profound event could have caused an entire separation of the sisters; however, their childhood memories of that event proved to be extremely similar when they individually assessed their own memories of that fateful day, and, the act of my aunt's voice being heard and an equal partner in the project ensured a renewal of their bond. By the subversive act of bypassing the dominant voice, they were able to repair the emotional damage that further disabled my aunt and latterly my mother following 'the accident' and her own subsequent altered identity within family dynamics.

This project employed Derrida's (1988) concepts of deconstruction and discontinuity to explore the personal narratives of my mother and aunt concerning their separation as children and how they subverted the dominant narrative regarding disability, which came from their own mother, and was the reason for their initial separation. The focus of the project was to examine the trauma sustained to the psychological 'inner-self' through the domination of their mother's narrative regarding disability throughout their lives. One can therefore view these projects as being compatible with the concept of 'psycho-emotional disablism' (e.g. Reeve 2011), a concept that

I and others have since applied to the experiences of autistic people (Milton and Moon 2012). This concept is used to suggest that social oppression not only works at a public level but also at a personal level, affecting who people can be and what they can do. Such internalising of social oppression can lead to feelings of shame and worthlessness. This theorising of alienation caused by social othering and oppression, can be seen as reminiscent of interpretive social theories of labelling and the 'self-fulfilling prophecy' (Becker 1963), yet frames such a conceptualisation within wider social relations and discourse.

Through a collaborative process, my mother and aunt explored how disability and the 'othering' process produced fractures in our family history, and in doing so discovered an ever-changing sense of identity, one that could never be fully realised. Yet, through this process, they both reached a sense of mutual fulfilment in asserting their own voices regarding their own personal histories.

> Every memory and experience is unique to the individual, even if they share the 'same' event. (Milton 2002)

In this project, my mother expressed how meanings associated with historical traumas always escaped being fully captured and often lay 'beyond the frame' of the photograph. Thus, in the installation piece that my mother created from the project, influenced by Derrida (1988), she suggested that when engaging with the piece, there was something always unreadable in terms of meaning, what Derrida (1988) termed as the *parergon*. It is also interesting to note at this juncture, that it has also been argued that autistic people may struggle to read the subtext of the social interaction of others (Baron-Cohen 2008), being literal in interpretation. For some autistic people, it may be the case that the *parergon* lacks meaning and tangibility, being too ethereal to grasp (Milton 2013a, b). Influenced by these theories, my mother decided to crop and re-present aspects and details of the photographs. These fragments were then accompanied by fragments from two independently recorded monologues from my mother and aunt that had been triggered by their responses to the discovered photographs. This was placed within an installation piece set above a family mantelpiece. This multi-sensory experience disrupted assumptions of family life for those viewing it and the dominant family narrative that had led to the further disablement of both my mother and aunt.

> The wounds of trauma can be seen, openly exposed free from suppression…the unsettling exposure of hidden narratives. (Milton 2002)

This installation used deconstruction as a mode of questioning the visual narrative of photographic representation, and how such representations inhabit emotional and subjective experiences. By deconstructing the dominant family narrative, and by distorting and cropping images, interspersed by fragments of vocal narration from both sisters, this project was able to express the emotional impact of the childhood separation and trauma, giving 'voice' to the disabled other within the microcosm of family power dynamics.

Both projects looked into the notion of trauma, as a reaction and personal construing of an event that damaged some of the core constructs of selfhood for those involved. Trauma was thus conceptualised as a permanent discontinuity with a previous sense of self. The notion of 'breaching' (Garfinkel 1967) was also used, yet in the case of trauma, the 'natural attitude' is unable to quickly rebuild itself and in some cases is almost entirely fractured (Milton 2014b).

> What devastates one individual will not necessarily have the same effect on another…This is because different sense is made of the same event. Of course, this does not deny the massive effect of what is termed trauma. But it directs our attention to the sense-making process of personal construction. It makes us re-think the nature and definition of post-traumatic stress disorder (PTSD). (Butt 2008, p. 49)

What Butt (2008) suggests here is that the trauma comes from the meaning endowed onto an event rather than the event itself (which is, of course, still important to the reaction/creation of meaning). However, if anything were to breach or damage an individual's construct system, particularly at a 'core construct' level, it is potentially traumatising. Perhaps it is no wonder that the 'natural attitude' is to defend one's own core construct system at all costs. Some psychologists might conceive of such defensiveness as a form of 'cognitive dissonance' (Festinger 1957).

> Any construction is part of a system, a package deal, and change involves reverberation within that system. In this sense then, our freedom is not absolute, as Sartre would have it. It is always to be seen within the context of a personal construct system. (Butt 2008, p. 77)

And Butt (2008) continues:

> Behavioural regimes for tackling 'problem behaviour' frequently (but not always) involves the prospect of a wider disruption, and hence resistance on the part of the client. (Butt 2008, p. 95)

To add to Butt's formulation here, one can also locate the constructs that people utilise within a wider social and discursive dynamic too. At worst, behavioural regimes can be seen as a control mechanism employed by surveillance staff to discipline and punish those that have had their personhood 'othered' leading to further psycho-emotional disablement of their identity development (Milton and Moon 2012).

In the 'Beyond the frame' project, no simplistic resolutions to trauma were to be found, but a sense of fracture and incompletion. The othering of disability within the family itself caused fractures in the family narrative that simply are not 'resolvable'. Yet, by subverting the dominant narrative, a more fulfilled and empowering (yet incomplete) narrative could be constructed.

Both these projects were completed before my son and I were diagnosed as being on the autism spectrum, yet the notion of fragmentation and fracture became a construct that helped me to make sense of my own sense of self over time (Milton 2014b). In the figure below, you can see a collage that I created at a workshop at the Autscape conference (Milton and Ridout 2014). In this collage, there are two rhizomatic formations—on the left, my sense of self prior to self-identification as being on the autism spectrum, and on the right, my sense of self after that time (including being diagnosed) (Figs. 1 and 2).

Fig. 1 My sense of self prior to diagnosis, Autscape 2014

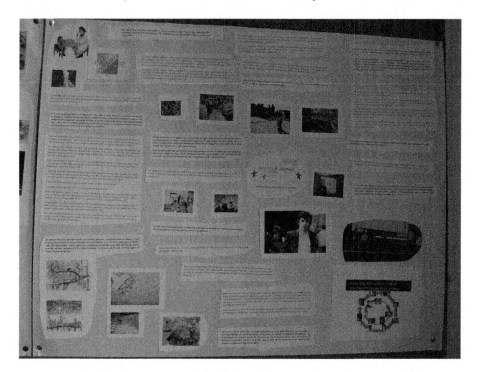

Fig. 2 My sense of self post-diagnosis, Autscape 2014

Some Final Remarks (for Now)

Autistic development could be said to be an affront to neoliberal notions of functional stages of child development leading to a 'healthy' and productive citizen, as 'nature's answer to 'over-conformity'' (Milton 2013c). Many of the 'interventions' designed to 'treat' autistic people are intimately embedded within ableist notions of normalcy and pathology. The subjectivities of autistic children and of autistic adults regarding their own childhoods are often trivialised in attempts to teach autistic children how to act less autistic (Milton and Moon 2012).

In order to redress the gap created by the 'double empathy problem' (or the mismatched salience of differing dispositions and constructions of the social lifeworld) between autistic and non-autistic people (Milton 2012a, 2014a), it is suggested here that autistic people be seen as having their own personal constructions of the world, and that methods deriving from PCT could be useful in building mutual rapport and understanding. All too often, however, the opposite is the case. I would also suggest that when utilising PCT, links need to be made between the personal constructions an individual utilises, whether in this case it be an autistic person, or a practitioner working with an autistic person, and the wider interpretive/discursive repertoires that they are drawing upon and employing to make sense of the world. In this sense, the double empathy problem can be seen to be deeply embedded within unequal power relations (Milton and Bracher 2013; Milton 2014a). Such methods do, however, give opportunities for opening up a respectful discursive space, where autistic development is not framed from the outset as 'disordered'. Of course, such a construing of autistic development as part of natural diversity is incongruent with the pathologising narrative of neoliberalism. In this sense, the double empathy problem between autistic and non-autistic people is not only personal but political too.

References

Baron-Cohen, S. (2008). *Autism and Asperger Syndrome: The Facts*. Oxford: Oxford University Press.

Barthes, R. (1977). *Camera Lucida: Reflections on Photography*. New York: Hill and Wang.

Becker, H. (1963). *Outsiders*. New York: The Free Press.

Butt, T. (2008). *George Kelly: The Psychology of Personal Constructs*. Basingstoke: Palgrave.

Caldwell, P. (2014). *The Anger Box*. Hove: Pavilion.

Crane, L., & Goddard, L. (2008). Episodic and Semantic Autobiographical Memory in Adults with Autism Spectrum Disorders. *Journal of Autism and Developmental Disorders, 38*(3), 498–506.

Deleuze, G., & Guttari, F. (1972). *Anti-Oedipus* (R. Hurley, M. Seem, & H. Lane (1977) Trans.). New York: Viking.

Deleuze, G., & Guttari, F. (1980). *A Thousand Plateaus* (B. Massumi (2004) Trans.). London: Continuum.

Derrida, J. (1988). *Limited Inc*. Evanston: Northwestern University Press.

Festinger, L. (1957). *A Theory of Cognitive Dissonance*. Stanford: Stanford University Press.

Foucault, M. (1972). *The Archaeology of Knowledge*. London: Pantheon.

Foucault, M. (1973). *The Birth of the Clinic*. London: Tavistock.

Garfinkel, H. (1967). *Studies in Ethnomethodology*. Englewood Cliffs: Prentice-Hall.

Goddard, L., Howlin, P., Dritschel, B., & Patel, T. (2007). Autobiographical Memory and Social Problem-Solving in Asperger Syndrome. *Journal of Autism and Developmental Disorders, 37*, 291–300.

Goldman, S. (2008). Brief Report: Narratives of Personal Events in Children with Autism and Developmental Language Disorders: Unshared Memories. *Journal of Autism and Developmental Disorders, 38*, 1982–1988.

Greenstein, A. (2013). Today's Learning Objective Is to Have a Party: Playing Research with Students in a Secondary School Special Needs Unit. *Journal of Research in Special Educational Needs, 14*(2), 71–81.

Kelly, G. (1955/1991). *The Psychology of Personal Constructs, Volumes 1 and 2*. London: Routledge.

Marcuse, H. (1964). *One-Dimensional Man*. London: Becon Press.

Mead, G. (1934). *Mind, Self and Society*. Chicago: University of Chicago.

Millward, C., Powell, S., Messer, D., & Jordan, R. (2000). Recall for Self and Other in Autism: Children's Memory for Events Experienced by Themselves and Their Peers. *Journal of Autism and Developmental Disorders, 30*(1), 15–28.

Milton, C. (2002). *Beyond the Frame [MA Project—Unpublished]*. Portsmouth: University of Portsmouth.

Milton, D. (2012a). On the Ontological Status of Autism: The 'Double Empathy Problem'. *Disability and Society, 27*(6), 883–887.

Milton, D. (2012b). *So What Exactly Is Autism?* London: The Autism Education Trust.

Milton, D. (2013a, September 4). *'Clumps': An Autistic Reterritorialisation of the Rhizome*. Theorising Normalcy and the Mundane 4th International Conference, Sheffield Hallam University.

Milton, D. (2013b). "Filling in the Gaps", a Micro-Sociological Analysis of Autism. *Autonomy: The Journal of Critical Interdisciplinary Autism Studies, 1*(2). Accessed from: http://www.larry-arnold.net/Autonomy/index.php/autonomy/article/view/7/html

Milton, D. (2013c). Natures Answer to Over-Conformity: A Deconstruction of Pathological Demand Avoidance. *Autism Experts*. Accessed from: http://autismexperts.blogspot.co.uk/2013/03/natures-answer-to-over-conformity.html

Milton, D. (2014a, March 17). Autistic Expertise: A Critical Reflection on the Production of Knowledge in Autism Studies. *Autism: The International Journal of Research and Practice (special edition 'Autism and Society')*, Onlinefirst.

Milton, D. (2014b). Becoming Autistic: An Aut-ethnography. *Cutting Edge Psychiatry in Practice* (4): Autism Spectrum Disorder, 185–192.

Milton, D. (2014c). *Educational Ideology and the Autistic Student: Findings from a Pilot Study Involving Q-sort Methodology* (pp. 84–90). Papers from the Education Doctoral Research Conference, Saturday 16 November 2013, University of Birmingham.

Milton, D., & Bracher, M. (2013). Autistics Speak but Are They Heard? *Medical Sociology Online, 7*(2), 61–69.

Milton, D., & Moon, L. (2012). The Normalisation Agenda and the Psycho-Emotional Disablement of Autistic People. *Autonomy: The Journal of Critical Interdisciplinary Autism Studies, 1*(1). Accessed from: http://www.larry-arnold.net/Autonomy/index.php/autonomy/article/view/9.

Milton, D., & Ridout, S. (2014, August 6). *Autistic Identity, Personal and Collective*. Autscape Conference.

Moran, H. (2006). A Very Personal Assessment: Using Personal Construct Psychology Assessment Technique (Drawing the Ideal Self) with Young People with ASD to Explore the Child's View of the Self. *Good Autism Practice, 7*(2), 78–86.

Park, A. (2014). *Don't Blame Adam Lanza's Violence on Asperger's.* http://time.com/19957/adam-lanzas-violence-wasnt-typical-of-aspergers/. Accessed 3 Sept 2014.

Reeve, D. (2011). *Ableism Within Disability Studies: The Myth of the Reliable and Contained Body.* Theorising Normalcy and the Mundane, 2nd International Conference, Manchester Metropolitan University.

Ridout, S. (2014, June 19). *Narrating Experience: The Advantage of Using Mixed Expressive Media to Bring Autistic Voices to the Fore in Discourse Around Their Support Requirements.* Paper presented at the 'Troubling Narratives: Identity Matters' Conference, University of Huddersfield, Huddersfield.

Sainsbury, C. (2000). *Martian in the Playground: Understanding the Schoolchild with Asperger's Syndrome.* Bristol: Lucky Duck.

Salmon, P. (2003). A Psychology for Teachers. In F. Fransella (Ed.), *International Handbook of Personal Construct Psychology* (pp. 311–318). London: Wiley.

Sinclair, J. (1993). *Don't Mourn for Us.* http://www.autreat.com/dont_mourn.html. Accessed 29 June 2014.

Williams, J., & Hanke, D. (2007). Do You Know What Sort of School I Want? Optimum Features of School Provision for Pupils with Autistic Spectrum Disorder. *Good Autism Practice, 8*(2), 51–61.

Damian Milton works for the National Autistic Society as Head of Autism Knowledge and Expertise and Researcher for London South Bank University. Damian's interest in autism began when his son was diagnosed in 2005 as autistic at the age of two. Damian was also diagnosed with Asperger's in 2009.

Part VI

Changing Practice and Policy

In this section the focus is on policy and practice. Discussions range from asking "Who is policy for?" to asking how policy and practice might be both imagined and enacted differently. Common themes of exclusion and marginalisation of the voices of disabled children and young people and their family members run through the chapters. Several authors reflect on their personal and professional experience in an attempt to imagine things otherwise for disabled children and young people's lives in the contested terrains of education, health and social care policy and practice in their local and global contexts. The authors outline current challenges but also possible opportunities for promoting enabling policies and practices for disabled children, young people and their families.

In the chapter "Making Policy for Whom? The Significance of the 'Psychoanalytic Medical Humanities' for Policy and Practice That Affects the Lives of Disabled Children", **Harriet Cooper** begins with a provocative question: Who are we making policy for? Harriet brings her knowledge of medical humanities and psychoanalytic approaches to reflect on her own experiences of growing up as a child with an impairment in England. She takes an autoethnographic approach drawing on her recently completed PhD study. Harriet acknowledges the tensions that exist between psychoanalysis and disability studies, before going on to explore the role of internalised oppression when thinking about 'the child's voice' in research. She asks: Is speaking of children the same thing as speaking for children? She concludes by challenging taken-for-granted assumptions about the benefits of rehabilitation in disabled children's lives and the implications this has for ethical policy and practice.

In the chapter "Disabled Children's Childhood Studies and Leadership as Experts by Experience' Leadership: Learning Activism in Health and

Social Care Education", **Tillie Curran, Ruth Sayers and Barry Percy-Smith** examine both their personal and professional experiences as they also reflect on a project working with service users who have become 'experts by experience' through their engagement with health and social care services. Through a series of workshops, participants reflected on their feelings of exclusion from the decision-making processes about their lives. They described how they were often asked to share stories about their lives by practitioners in the hope of improving services, but that they saw little evidence that this had effected change. The project looked at leadership from their experience, and, given that much of their experience is echoed by parents of disabled children, Tillie, Ruth and Barry ask how students in health and social care can learn from such supportive approaches to activism. They propose alternative forms of engagement with experts by experience in professional education and opportunities for students to learn how to make change happen together.

In the chapter "Being a Speech and Language Therapist: Between Support and Oppression", **Anat Greenstein** also engages in the process of reflection as she describes her personal narrative from her current standpoint as a lecturer in Learning Disability Studies in Manchester from her past experiences and practices as a speech and language therapist in Israel/Palestine. Anat examines the dis/abling practices of speech and language therapy, reflecting on them as mechanisms of power that constrain individuals. She critiques play-based approaches to practice, which are often used as a potent tool for normalization in the lives of disabled children. She concludes by arguing that she now understands the focus of her professional role as a speech and language therapist as being about engaging with children and young people to create meaningful interactions for their own sake and value.

In the chapter "You Say... I Hear...": Epistemic Gaps in Practitioner-Parent/Carer Talk", **Nick Hodge and Katherine Runswick-Cole** explore the thorny issue of parent/carer-practitioner partnerships in the context of education for children labelled with special educational needs and/or disabilities in England. Nick and Katherine reflect on a situation in which, despite the host of recent policy and practice initiatives in England, parent/carer-practitioner relationships remain fraught, focusing on the gaps in understanding that emerge in these relationships. Using Lipsky's (1971) notion of 'street level bureaucracy' to understand how these gaps emerge, they then draw on MacKenzie and Scully's (2007) concept of 'sympathetic moral imagination' to suggest ways forward to enable better partnerships between parents/carers, practitioners and children and young people.

Berni Kelly, Sandra Dowling and **Karen Winter** reflect on the experiences of disabled children living out of home care in Northern Ireland in the chapter "Disabled Children in Out-of-Home Care: Issues and Challenges for Practice". They trace the disabling contexts in which children have experienced neglect and abuse and lack of 'in-home' support. Drawing on a case study approach, they focus on the children's experiences as well as the challenges faced by birth parents, carers and social workers. They conclude by exposing the complexities of birth family relationships, the barriers to permanency, and the importance of listening to disabled children and young people.

In the chapter "Easy Targets: Seen and Not Heard—The Silencing and Invisibility of Disabled Children and Parents in Post-Reform Aotearoa New Zealand", **Rod Wills** describes the ways in which disabled children, young people and their parents have been silenced in the context of post-reform Aotearoa New Zealand. He reflects on his personal experience as a family member of the ways in which competitive individualism impacts negatively on family life. In the context of neoliberalism and globalisation, he explores the family as a site for resistance and for radical action and self-determination. He concludes by calling for families to speak out and to be heard as they way forward.

In the chapter "Family Voices in Teacher Education", **Peggy Gallagher, Cheryl Rhodes and Karen Lewis** describe a project focused on embedding families' voices in teacher education programmes. Writing from the United States, Peggy, Cheryl and Karen pick up on some of the issues raised in Nick and Katherine's chapter, including the problem of 'professional speak' that can create gaps in understanding between practitioners and families. They focus on the importance of listening to families' perspectives and offer advice on how to embed family voices within teacher education programmes.

In the chapter "Rights Not Needs: Changing the Legal Model for Special Educational Needs (SEN)", **Debbie Sayers** writes about the legal framework for supporting children identified as having special educational needs and/or disabilities (SEND) in England. Debbie challenges the deficit model of disability that continues to underpin policy and practice for children labelled with SEND in England. She explores how international law and rights-based perspectives might inform a shift in SEND policy and practice, and would allow a focus on the capacities of children and young people and their rights.

In the **concluding chapter,** "Concluding Thoughts and Future Directions", **Katherine Runswick-Cole, Tillie Curran** and **Kirsty Liddiard** review the themes that run through the studies. They reflect on how far studies help us to respond to Sara Ryan's aspirations for change, and develop further research questions and strategies for building research cultures to support those aims.

Making Policy for Whom? The Significance of the 'Psychoanalytic Medical Humanities' for Policy and Practice That Affects the Lives of Disabled Children

Harriet Cooper

Key Points

- This chapter considers the possible role of psychoanalysis in developing a theory of how oppression may be internalised by children during interactions with clinicians, social workers and researchers.
- How can the clinical encounter become a space for reflection? Can oppressive dynamics within the clinical encounter be altered?
- Psychoanalysis has often been viewed with suspicion within disability studies: this chapter explores what it might mean to become an 'ambivalent advocate' of psychoanalysis as a disability activist.

Introduction

How can clinicians, social workers and social researchers become more attuned to the voices and wishes of the disabled children with whom they work? How does the notion of the unconscious complicate an ethics of 'listening to the child's voice'? Moreover, if these 'voices and wishes' are already highly mediated by cultural responses to disability, and are embedded within

H. Cooper (✉)
University of East Anglia, Norwich, UK

© The Author(s) 2018   **481**
K. Runswick-Cole et al. (eds.), *The Palgrave Handbook of Disabled Children's Childhood Studies*, https://doi.org/10.1057/978-1-137-54446-9_30

a particular medical and familial context, how can we take account of particular 'voices and wishes' whilst also understanding the way in which internalised oppression—a sense of shame arising in connection with a low status identity—operates within such contexts?

These are big questions. Rather than seeking to find definitive answers to all of them, the purpose of this chapter is to point to the role of the humanities, and specifically the psychoanalytic medical humanities, in contributing to the debate on ethical issues affecting clinical encounters with disabled children. In particular, my focus in this chapter is on the notion of 'internalised oppression' and the ethical problems it poses. What does it mean for both the (medical-sociological) research encounter, and for the clinical encounter, if the child subject in question seems to offer no opinion, or agrees very easily to treatment which others might resist? Can clinicians listen out for the child's 'authentic voice', or is post-structuralist psychoanalysis right in engendering suspicion about the very notion of authenticity here (Lesnik-Oberstein 2011)? Via a discussion of the character and uses of what I call the 'psychoanalytic medical humanities', I debate these issues and argue that whilst there are no easy answers, there are opportunities to change the culture within which disabled children encounter medical professionals. In this chapter, I define internalised oppression as a person's sense of shame and dis-entitlement, which arises in the context of a long-standing connection with a low status identity category such as disability. Internalised oppression can be most pernicious when it functions unconsciously—that is, when the person in question is not very aware of having internalised certain beliefs about him/herself.

My argument in this chapter is not based on quantitative research. To the extent that my theorising here is evidence-based, it draws on my own personal experience of growing up with an impairment, of undergoing rehabilitation as a child, and of working towards freeing myself from internalised oppression via an engagement with psychoanalysis and with disability studies. I reflected on and analysed these experiences and processes in the auto-ethnographic writing I undertook in my PhD thesis (Cooper 2015). Although I make no claims to speak for the experience of others, I hope that the work I have done to integrate psychoanalytic thinking on internalised oppression into existing models of disability will speak to others. In mobilising these ideas within this chapter, it is my hope that they can become part of an ongoing dialogue between disabled children's childhood studies and health and social care policy. I use the term 'rehabilitation' to refer to my childhood experience, since the term 'habilitation'—used by the World Health Organisation (2011)—is not commonly used outside of a specialist context; however, in this chapter, I will not be discussing the experience of rehabilitation in adulthood for an acquired impairment.

As someone who has been able to find a political and academic voice partly through my engagement with psychoanalysis, I am an ambivalent advocate of this process. Although almost impossible to define as a single entity, psychoanalysis could be described as a set of ideas and techniques, first pioneered by Freud in the late nineteenth and early twentieth century and later developed by a range of other analysts, which seeks to understand the relationship between an individual's present-day suffering or inhibitions, and his or her unconscious beliefs and fantasies. Putting on one side the objections of disability studies that I am about to discuss, I am aware that disabled people do not always have emancipatory experiences of psychoanalysis: much will depend on the analyst's capacity to conceptualise disability in social-relational terms, and on the place of politics and critique in the analyst's practice. Furthermore, psychoanalysis is fraught with risk (Taylor 2014), and is a strange and paradoxical process that can (in my experience) repeat suffering before it feels as though it is doing any 'good' (see Cooper 2015). It is lengthy, expensive and rarely available via the National Health Service in the UK, meaning that it remains problematically inaccessible to most people (see Cooper 2015). For all these reasons, I remain an ambivalent advocate of psychoanalysis, yet in spite of—or perhaps more precisely because of—this ambivalence, I believe that psychoanalysis can be transformative not just to individuals but to society as a whole. What I want to say in this chapter is not 'disabled children need psychoanalysis' but rather 'we all need psychoanalysis', by which I mean that we need to understand what it is of ourselves that we cannot bear, and why it is that others—such as disabled children or other socially denigrated groups—are made to bear these aspects of ourselves for us (see Shakespeare 1997; Goodley 2011).

Psychoanalysis has often been understood as oppressive by disability studies, because of the way in which it appears to stand for the imperative for change, rather than accepting individuals as they are. As Goodley notes, it has been associated with 'normalising aims' (2011, p. 94). I open this chapter by addressing the tension which exists between psychoanalysis and disability studies. I then explain what I mean by the 'psychoanalytic' medical humanities, placing this sub-discipline within the context of medical humanities, which has emerged recently alongside disability studies. In the following section, I focus in on one particular idea, internalised oppression, and examine how the concept can be fleshed out via an engagement with the work of particular psychoanalytic theorists, notably that of Ferenczi. My discussion expands and develops Watermeyer's (2013) work on this theme, and, like Watermeyer, I seek to highlight the political and social value of working in this way. I consider the special relevance of internalised oppression within the context of medical encounters with children born with impairments.

Later in the chapter, I reflect on internalised oppression in relation to theoretical and ethical questions about what we mean when we talk about 'the child's voice': here I draw on the work of critical theorists of childhood, including Rose (1984), Lesnik-Oberstein (1994, 2008, 2011) and Caselli (2010). These authors identify a cultural tendency to reify the category of childhood, using it as a 'term of universal social reference' long after other identity categories have been deconstructed (Rose 1984, p. 10). This body of work invites us to question whether speaking of children is always, inevitably, speaking for children. Although it emerges out of a (deconstructive) psychoanalytic tradition, such work poses difficult questions of (psychoanalytic and other) theory that claims to know 'the child'. It does important work in interrogating what happens when someone is 'spoken *for*'. I conclude the chapter by examining the potential implications of my discussion for work which involves listening to children's voices and for childhood rehabilitation policy and practice.

Is Psychoanalysis Oppressive?

As Watermeyer (2013) notes, disability studies have struggled with the psychological realm as a whole. He observes that '[t]he problem which has daunted disability studies scholars is how to think about the psychological aspects of disability, which tug towards the individual, internal realm, while holding firm to a contextual analysis of structural barriers' (2013, p. 3). To engage with the psychological realm is seemingly to come dangerously close to a return to a medical model of disability, whereby disability comes to represent a tragic problem faced by the individual: it was this model that the early social model theorists sought to overcome (see, for example, Oliver 1983). There is an understandable suspicion of medico-psychological approaches, which are seen to contribute to disablement via the naming and classifying of impairments, and by imposing imperatives for disabled people to perform normative embodiment as best they can (see McRuer 2006). Having experienced this form of disablement in subtle ways, I am convinced that this view of disability is indeed dominant and pervasive in contemporary British society. Yet I am not convinced that the corollary of this experience is to disengage with the psychological realm or to assume that it has nothing to offer a critique of ableism; I follow Watermeyer's (2013) lead in wanting to engage with the psychological sphere, and, more specifically, in wanting to engage with psychoanalysis. I also follow

Shakespeare (2014) in feeling that the dominance of a 'strong' social model of disability has led to a failure to engage with healthcare issues in disability studies, and whilst the reasons for this are understandable, it nevertheless can be seen, from a certain perspective, as a loss for disabled people.

Both Watermeyer (2013) and Goodley (2011) allude to the rather strange disciplinary status of psychoanalysis with respect to the sciences and the social sciences. Watermeyer (2013, p. 3) points out that 'psychoanalysis is more often regarded in the social sciences as an oppressive anachronism than a subversive lens of social critique', while Goodley (2011, p. 94) suggests that '[s]ustained attempts by "scientific psychology" including cognitive psychology, to shut away psychoanalysis might make it appealing'. These two contrasting quotations frame psychoanalysis as, on the one hand, an outdated discourse of colonisation and oppression, and, on the other hand, a tool for radical critique and subversion. I believe that there is truth in both of these representations, in the sense that psychoanalysis is a powerful technique that can heal but which—as Taylor has noted—'can be hazardous' (2014, p. xiv). It is also true that certain psychoanalytic texts or schools have, or have had, a propensity to speak the language of medical discourse and 'pathologisation' (Watermeyer 2013, p. 2). I believe that more work needs to be done to develop a 'critical psychoanalysis' (Watermeyer 2013, p. 64), but I see this state of affairs as an opportunity to work in critical dialogue with psychoanalysis rather than to disavow its insights. I am interested in exploring what psychoanalysis has to offer disability studies but equally in what disability studies has to offer psychoanalysis. Like Goodley, I believe that a psychoanalysis which seeks to illuminate social phenomena has powerful radical potential (2011), and although I understand why Goodley warns against a 'deluded affiliation' with psychoanalysis (2011, p. 123), I share Watermeyer's (2013) sense that engagements with psychological phenomena in disability studies have been too tentative and that there are huge political and emancipatory gains to be made from a more thoroughgoing use of psychoanalysis in the field. Of course, the term 'emancipation' defies easy definition, and is, perhaps, a highly subjective concept. In this context, I use it to refer to liberation from a societal stigma that has been internalised and is enacted upon the self.

A psychoanalytic approach involves reflexivity. It involves opening oneself up to knowledge that it would be preferable to be able to ignore. For example, psychoanalysis leads us to rethink relationships between oppressor and oppressed, and to explore the ways in which we oppress ourselves and others, even when we regard ourselves as 'the oppressed'. The value of this way of working is its capacity to demonstrate that we are *all* susceptible to unconscious fantasies about the meaning of disability (Watermeyer 2013).

It paves the way towards a disability studies that is focussed on deepening our understanding of both ourselves and others. This is not to devalue our anger about ableism but rather to notice that ableism is not always something that comes at us from the outside (see Watermeyer 2013).

Medical Humanities and Psychoanalytic Medical Humanities

Whilst noting that the relationship between medicine and the arts is not new, Kirklin and Richardson (2001) locate the origins of the presence of medical humanities within medical education in the publication by the General Medical Council of the document *Tomorrow's Doctors* in 1993. The publication encouraged the development of 'arts-based courses' within the curriculum (Kirklin and Richardson 2001, p. 1).

Within university arts and humanities departments, the emergence of the field can be mapped alongside the turn to affect and to the body in the humanities. The field is 'diverse', as the Centre for Medical Humanities at Durham University notes on its website (2009). Seeking to define the field, the Centre observes that '[i]ts *object* is medicine as a human practice and, by implication, human health and illness, and the enquirers are, basically, people working from the perspectives of humanities disciplines' (2009). From a medical education standpoint, the enquirers might also be health professionals and trainees. Kirklin and Richardson argue that the field 'can be held to encompass any interaction between the arts and health' (2001, p. xv). Viney et al. (2015) have recently called for a project of 'critical medical humanities', highlighting the need for work in the field to be politically and socially contextualised. In my view, the 'psychoanalytic medical humanities' can contribute to a project of critical medical humanities which critically interrogates the psychosocial structures that empower and legitimise medical practice and discourse.

If to name is also to interpellate (see Butler 1997), then to speak of psychoanalytic medical humanities may be to bring something into being, as this is not the name of a well-established sub-discipline. The danger of so-naming a way of working is potentially to foreclose it, to reify it in such a way that a boundary is set up between what it is and what it is not. It creates the notion of a tribe, where perhaps there is none. My intention in using the term is not to cordon off such an approach from mixed- and multi-disciplinary ways of working in the medical humanities, which I see as highly generative, but rather to create a space in which to discuss the power and significance of psychoanalytic ideas as they apply to practices and dynamics in the medical consulting room.

Psychoanalysis is not a homogeneous body of ideas but rather a broad umbrella term encompassing a wide range of approaches and schools of thought. Whereas Goodley (2011, 2014) has tended to draw mainly, although not exclusively, on the work of Freud and Lacan, I tend to draw on object relations psychoanalysis, the school of thought associated with Klein and her heirs. Watermeyer notes that 'the emergence of Kleinian object relations theory [...] provided new concepts to connect the intrapsychic world with the social', going on to argue that:

> In Klein's model, bi-directional reverberating connections exist between an inner world of conflicting *objects*, and a real world of political battles. Actions on either terrain may be motivated by, and have consequences for, the other. [...] It is a misappropriation of Kleinian theory to portray these ideas as a reductionist pathologisation of individual political action. (2013: 56)

I am similarly convinced that object relations theory provides us with tools for a multi-layered analysis of the dynamics of social interactions.

In the UK, object relations psychoanalysis has a long-standing connection—albeit an ambivalent one—with the medical profession. In this sense, there is an existing connection between object relations theory and what we might call the psychoanalytic medical humanities. Winnicott—one of the most famous practitioners working in the object relations tradition—was a paediatrician as well as a psychoanalyst. Meanwhile, the psychoanalyst Balint, who was associated with the Tavistock Clinic, set up 'Balint groups' for general practitioners in the 1950s (Balint Society website 2012) which sought to facilitate a mode of practising medicine in which the complex interactions between mind and body, as well as the doctor-patient relationship, could be brought into the consulting room and explored as relevant to both diagnosis and treatment (see Balint et al. 1993). Balint was operating in a very different cultural and economic climate from today, which with hindsight could be understood as having facilitated the making of links between general practice and psychoanalysis—as Balint et al. observe:

> The National Health Service had only just started and the status of general practice was low. Psychoanalysts were only beginning to enter the field of general medicine and were not yet accepted – in many places they still are not – as respectable members of the medical team. (1993, p. ix)

These days, although the status of GPs is much higher, the National Health Service is ailing due to chronic under-funding, and psychoanalysis is still side-lined as an activity to be privately funded by those with disposable income: its ideas circulate outside of mainstream medical practice, as they did at the time of the publication of Balint's *The Doctor, His Patient and the Illness* (see Balint 1964). Nevertheless, the Tavistock Clinic, which has a history of combining psychoanalytic approaches with other medical approaches to illness, is still funded via the National Health Service (see Tavistock and Portman website 2015).

Having examined the disciplinary space within which this chapter is situated, I want now to turn to a specific concept—internalised oppression—and to consider how a psychoanalytic approach enriches our understanding of it. Although Ferenczi and Fanon are perhaps not, strictly speaking, object relations theorists, in that Ferenczi predates Klein and Fanon emerges in a different psychoanalytic tradition, the ideas I discuss in the next section are very compatible with an object relations approach.

Understanding Internalised Oppression with Ferenczi, Fanon and Wright

Internalised oppression is a key term in academic fields informed by identity politics. Watermeyer (2013, p. 155) locates its emergence in race theory and suggests that the idea has not been adequately explored in disability studies, although it is 'regularly quoted'. For Watermeyer, the concept of 'psycho-emotional disablism', coined by Thomas (1999) and developed by Reeve (see, for example, Reeve 2008) has helped to move disability studies towards a thorough interrogation of internalised oppression, but 'attachment to the disability-impairment binary means there is no suitable home for psychological phenomena' (Watermeyer 2013, p. 153). Although I find Watermeyer's discussion to be unduly critical, I do believe that there is a need for greater attention to the question of how oppression may be internalised by the individual over time, in a particular context, perhaps a childhood context (see Cooper 2015). A theory of internalised oppression can, in turn, help to develop a theory of resistance.

Watermeyer identifies a reluctance on the part of disability studies to identify 'difficultness' in the disabled person and his or her allies, contending that we should not be 'surprised' that 'lives of exclusion, denigration and distorted relationships shape personalities' (2013, p. 154). I find Watermeyer's uninterrogated use of terms such as 'difficult', 'distorted' and 'maladjusted' very problematic, as these terms imply an uncritical acceptance of normative and normalising labels: isn't 'maladjustedness' always a question of perspective? I do, however, think Watermeyer is right to suggest that, if we want to undertake psychosocial analysis, we must be prepared to turn the critical-reflexive gaze upon ourselves as disabled people and consider the ways in which we enact ableism upon ourselves. Furthermore, how can we reclaim 'difficultness' as part of an identity of resistance (see Ahmed 2014, for a discussion of 'willfulness')? Such work would be undertaken with the purpose of gaining a better overall understanding of the relational dynamics of oppression. It should not be understood as an exercise in self-blame or in retreating into a narrative of disability as personal tragedy, which Oliver (1983) recognised as being deeply disabling.

A key concept that expands our understanding of internalised oppression is Ferenczi's notion of the 'Confusion of Tongues between Adults and the Child' (1933): here, I argue that it can help to theorise aspects of the relational experience of diagnosis and rehabilitation for a small child. In order to think psychoanalytically about these medical practices, it is necessary first for them to be defamiliarised and reconceptualised through the eyes of a small child—perhaps a pre-verbal child or a child who is just coming into language. We cannot know what this child thinks and feels, we can only speculate. Of course, to do this is to universalise about a 'child' as though it were possible to speak of a unified child subjectivity, when we know there is not (Rose 1984; Caselli 2010; Lesnik-Oberstein 1994, 2008, 2011), and I shall discuss this issue in more detail in the next section. We should also be wary here of positioning psychoanalysis as a discourse which can provide the answers: Lesnik-Oberstein suggests that 'psychotherapy' should be regarded as 'a narrative whose meaning is constructed by therapist and patient together' (1994, p. 195). It is the role of psychoanalysis to imagine retroactively, based on the analysis of the transferences and countertransferences in the consulting room, when the adult who was once that child is present. Transference is the analysand's construction of himself or herself as he/she imagines it in the mind of the analyst. Countertransference refers to the feelings evoked by the patient in the analyst, which are also part of the relational world that the patient creates. As Lesnik-Oberstein (1994) notes, neither process permits access to an objective, stable truth. This is not, however, a reason to discount psychoanalysis. The act of working with a theory is always, to a certain degree, an act of assuming the provisional knowability of certain categories and actors.

In his 'Confusion of Tongues' essay, Ferenczi conjectures about the psychic worlds of children who grow up into adults who are unable to disagree with the interpretations of their analyst. Ferenczi is speaking of adults who have experienced some kind of (sexual) abuse as children—a point to which I shall return. He notes that '[o]ne would expect the first impulse [of the children] to be that of reaction, hatred, disgust and energetic refusal' (1933, p. 298). However, in fact, what Ferenczi finds is that the 'personalities [of the children] are not sufficiently consolidated in order to be able to protest, even if only in thought', and 'the overpowering force and authority of the adult [...] can rob them of their senses' (1933, p. 298). Ferenczi argues that what occurs in such cases is the 'introjection of the aggressor' such that 'he disappears as part of the external reality, and becomes intra- instead of extra-psychic' (1933, p. 299). This is important: Ferenczi's patients lack a sense of a self that might object to the Other's demands, but instead experience themselves as *one and the same* with the one who makes the demands. The Other's desire becomes the desire of the Self: there is no discernible difference between the two.

As noted, Ferenczi is speaking of cases of childhood sexual abuse. A programme of rehabilitative physiotherapy for the child is of course a very different thing indeed, in moral and ethical terms. It would be unacceptable to conceptualise a rehabilitation programme as 'aggressive' in the terms set out by Ferenczi: the programme is designed to help the child, to improve future prospects, not to harm the child—or so it seems at first glance. However, if we defamiliarise such a rehabilitation programme, and speculate about how it might be understood by a small child who does not have the conceptual and reasoned understanding of its social and symbolic meaning, isn't there a sense in which a rehabilitation programme could feel aggressive and intrusive, depending on how it is contextualised for the child? Isn't the risk of this greatest when the child in question lacks language (the conceptual framework) to interpret rehabilitation as useful? The Other who is seeking to help the child in terms of the adult world may be experienced as an aggressor by the child, even though this is not the intention. Whilst I would suggest that the rehabilitated child's experience might best be thought in terms of an 'introjection of the [Other]' rather than the 'aggressor', I nevertheless believe that it would be possible for a child undergoing rehabilitation, who is powerless to stop it, to be unaware of the desire to stop the rehabilitation, especially if the medical professionals directing the rehabilitation felt very strongly and unambiguously that the treatment was 'doing her good' and was 'for her own good'.

A comparison might be drawn with Fanon's (1970 [1967]) analysis of colonial education systems. Fanon observed that '[t]he black schoolboy in the Antilles [...] identifies himself with the explorer, the bringer of civilization, the white man who carries truth to savages – an all-white truth' (Fanon 1970 [1967], p. 104). According to this model, the education system is responsible for creating internalised racism, since it facilitates an identification between 'the black schoolboy' and 'the white man' about whom he is learning, in the absence of any black people in leadership roles to act as role models.

Analogies can be dangerous if they are misused, and we can note many differences between Ferenczi's concept, Fanon's concept and the scenario I am describing. Nevertheless, analogies can help to construct new ways of looking, which in turn make it possible to question what gets taken for granted as 'common sense'. These analogies can facilitate an interrogation of the cultural meaning of rehabilitation. In what sense is rehabilitation a form of education? What kinds of identifications does it propose? Oliver (1993, p. 15) sees rehabilitation as an ideological practice, noting that he is 'not suggesting that we can eradicate the influence and effects of power and ideology in rehabilitation, but that our failure to even acknowledge their existence gives rise to a set of social relations and a range of therapeutic practices that are disabling for all concerned'. Without wishing to take up an anti-medical position, I do think we need to attend to the way in which medical treatment might be experienced as a type of colonisation of the body or mind for a child who is not old enough to understand it otherwise. If I am unable to recognise the way in which I experience treatment as oppressive, because I have no conceptual framework within which to articulate this to myself, this is no longer straightforwardly 'oppression', but instead something that I identify with wholly as 'doing me good' (because becoming aware of the alternative perspective is not possible from inside this experience of identification with a dominant cultural position). Once such an experience becomes habitual, it is very hard to find a way back into ambivalence towards rehabilitation, even if a conceptual framework is later acquired—and this is why it is important to develop a diachronic understanding of internalised oppression. It is much easier, after an experience of 'identifying with the aggressor', to either reject rehabilitation outright or idealise it as a route to emancipation. Perhaps this binary thinking (which medical practice usually does nothing to discourage) goes some way towards accounting for the difficulty in healing the split in disability studies between the medical model and the social model of disability, although, of course, there are many other factors at play too.

Wright (1991) has framed this same discussion in terms of the child's internalisation of a particular quality of gazing relationship. Wright argues that the infant who experiences the parental gaze as cold, critical or unresponsive may associate this gaze with the thought that he/she, the infant, has done something wrong. The infant may conclude—unconsciously—that 'a behavior that so seriously jeopardizes the relationship with the mother must come to be avoided at all costs' and may identify a 'survival value' in 'seeing what the mother sees' (1991, p. 45). The child, in this situation, 'joins forces with this mother who looks, disowns the self [...], and thenceforward regards this threatening self as an Other' (1991, p. 46). Since, in the clinic, the critical gaze of the doctor upon the disabled child is heavily involved in the practices of diagnosis and rehabilitation, it is easy to understand how a child might come to identify with a gaze which perceives his or her body as being in need of correction and might take up the Other's position in order to survive what would otherwise be experienced as an attack on the self.

Is It Possible to 'Hear the Child's Voice'?

An important aspect of the concept of the 'introjection of the aggressor' is that it takes place unconsciously, and as long as it remains unconscious, it has the effect of maintaining and reinforcing internalised oppression. Ferenczi discovered it by realising that, when he made mistakes in the analysis of a group of his (adult) patients, they did not react with anger or by protesting but instead by agreeing with or accepting an erroneous interpretation that was actually further burdening them in some way (1933, pp. 294–295). He writes:

> Instead of contradicting the analyst or accusing him of errors and blindness, the patients *identify* themselves with him; [...] normally they do not allow themselves to criticize us, such a criticism does not even become conscious in them unless we give them special permission or even encouragement to be so bold. This means that we must discern not only the painful events of their past from their associations, but also – and much more often than hitherto supposed – their repressed or suppressed criticism of us. (1933, pp. 294–295)

Ferenczi's patients were unable to disagree because they were unable to know they disagreed, and this is what lies at the heart of internalised oppression as I see it.

Ferenczi's discovery has significant implications in terms of how we understand the voices of oppressed subjects, in both the clinic and the social research project. To my mind, it has particularly complex implications when it comes to thinking about the voices of disabled children. Curran and Runswick-Cole (2013a, b) observe that most studies of disabled children's lives focus on service provision or consider how specific impairments pose particular challenges in children's lives. Such studies are designed with an adult agenda in mind. They answer the questions that adults ask about disabled children. As Curran and Runswick-Cole (2013a, b) argue, the field of disabled children's childhood studies reframes the debate, posing a different sort of question altogether. What do disabled children want to tell us about their lives? My own research agenda is similarly committed to working with this important question, and this is why I believe that both the work of the research ethics committee and the work of the clinician need to take account of Ferenczi's concept of 'identification with the aggressor'. This idea complicates the project of listening to the other's narrative of self, of life, of experience. How do we deal with the fact that it is not just narratives, but experience itself, that is mediated (Lesnik-Oberstein 2008)? And are there additional ethical issues that are in play when the other is a child or a disabled child (see Goodley and Runswick-Cole 2012; Abbott 2013)? What does it mean to speak of childhood, from the vantage point of being an adult? These philosophical questions have important implications for ethics committees and clinicians, and it is precisely in this domain that the need for the humanities reveals itself. Collini (2012) argues that the humanities will always struggle to demonstrate their worth using quantitative indicators, because they are fundamentally about developing skills not for measurement, but for judgement and understanding. What can we learn from critical-theoretical work in the humanities on the figure of the child, and could such work ever be of use in the practical world of the clinic? It is to these questions that I now turn.

Lesnik-Oberstein has argued that academic work which researches and theorises 'the child' in both the social sciences and, to an even greater extent, the humanities, posits an essential 'real child' whose wishes and desires are assumed to be knowable (2011). Indeed, the problem of essentialism in relation to the child was observed as early as 1984, when Rose wrote that: 'Childhood […] serves as a term of universal social reference which conceals all the historical divisions and difficulties of which children, no less than ourselves, form a part' (1984, p. 10). The following quotation from Caselli implies that Rose's claim still holds true in the contemporary moment:

> it is still culturally accepted (and not only in everyday language) to refer in passing to what children are and what we should expect them to do, while – fortunately – more than one eyebrow would be raised if we were to state confidently what women are or what they ought to do. (Caselli 2010, p. 243)

It has been argued that work which constructs the child as real and knowable is seeking critical 'mastery' of the child by the adult (Rose 1984, p. 10; Lesnik-Oberstein 2011 p. 6). Rose suggests that we want to see childhood as situated firmly in the past, as 'something separate which can be scrutinised and assessed'; we are uncomfortable with Freud's notion of childhood as 'something in which we continue to be implicated' (1984, p. 13, p. 12). These ideas are important for an ethics of 'hearing the voice of the child' since they posit the fundamental impossibility—and indeed the undesirability—of such a project. Such a project will inevitably colonise the child, as long as it retains any attachment to the idea of 'knowing' the child, which includes 'knowing what (disabled) children are likely to need'. Where could such a project go from here? Is social research with disabled children always putting words in the mouths of disabled children—is it a colonising practice even when it aims to be the exact opposite? Do even the most empathic doctors 'colonise' the disabled children with whom they work? Furthermore, isn't there a sense in which the very theory used in this chapter is undermined by these ideas? Object relations psychoanalytic theory itself is grounded upon the stability of a notion of the child who grows up and develops into an adult. In spite of its investment in the idea of the unconscious—which problematises the very knowability of the self—this body of theory does propose particular (affective) connections between the child that I was and the adult that I am. As noted, psychoanalysis cannot be called upon to offer up a solution here, although, as Lesnik-Oberstein suggests, it is perhaps the fact that it continually seeks to engage with 'the interpretative and constructive process itself' which marks it out as different from some other kinds of discourse (1994, p. 199).

I believe that the work of Rose and Lesnik-Oberstein can and must contribute to the ethical project whose foundations I lay in this chapter. Doing this reading and thinking has led me to feel that all the groups of people that I am discussing—clinicians, social researchers and theorists in the humanities—need to be able to make contact with their desire for critical 'mastery' of the child (or whichever actors or texts they are studying) and to reflect on how this desire plays itself out in their work. In my opinion, diagnosing the desire for mastery is not an endpoint, as far as psychoanalytic medical humanities is concerned, but rather a starting point for self-reflexive work. Indeed, I suspect that all research projects—like the diagnostic projects of the clinicians whose work I would also like to influence—are invested in the desire to know, to find out and to locate.

Lesnik-Oberstein is, in my opinion, quite right to highlight the opposition that much social research sets up between discourse and experience, through which experience is privileged as primary and unmediated (2008): Ferenczi's discovery of his patients' identification with their aggressors reveals that what we experience consciously is itself constructed, it is a version of the world that is tolerable to us, which is often heavily distorted. Of course, the mention of 'distortion' here implies the existence of a recoverable 'real': Lesnik-Oberstein suggests that this is precisely the problem with the privileging of 'experience' and of the 'voice' in ethnographic work (2008, 2011). But what strikes me here is, whatever the status of the 'real', and its recoverability or otherwise, our experience is still our experience, it is still valid as material we can work with when understanding the subtleties of the clinical encounter. I am aware that my point here fails in that it is, in a certain sense, unethical to take ownership of 'experience' with a first-person plural pronoun, as I do in the previous sentence. Indeed, arguably Lesnik-Oberstein's œuvre as a whole highlights the ethical difficulties of adopting a first-person plural to speak of (and thus speak for) the child. This state of affairs does mean—I believe—that there is something inevitably 'colonising' in the clinical encounter and in the research encounter, and perhaps we would do better to acknowledge that rather than always striving to eliminate it. The desire of the researcher, author or clinician is—I would argue—always a contaminative force, projected into the subject of study in the yearning for mastery over it. In order for the clinician's act of diagnosis of disability to be grounded in a regard for ethical process, it should also remain attentive to the constant need to diagnose something else: the clinician's own desire and its workings in the consulting room. Since social researchers will continue to undertake social research, and medical practitioners will continue to diagnose, I would seek to foster an approach in which such 'contaminated' work can be celebrated, even as those authors who undertake it can develop an understanding of how their own subjectivity and desire is tangled up with their findings.

The notion of 'identifying with the aggressor' shows that it is all too easy to fail to attend to the otherness which works hard to hide its otherness from all, including from the self. Clinicians, researchers and social workers cannot be blamed if they fail to see it in action. Its very purpose as a defence mechanism is to ensure it is never identified; it measures its success by not being unmasked.

What Are the Implications of These Ideas for Medical Practice and Policy?

My chapter should be read as exploratory work, as work which poses questions, rather than providing definitive policy solutions. Furthermore, I want to be clear that I am not suggesting that social researchers and clinicians can or should attempt to take on the role of psychoanalyst, except perhaps in the sense that these professionals might benefit from psychoanalysing their own responses and interactions. Balint himself struggled with the ethical dilemma of how psychoanalysis should be used in general practice, and who should be trained to work in this way (see Balint 1964). I am speaking here not of change at the level of the individual but instead at the level of a culture.

In many ways, such a change is already underway, indeed, self-reflexivity is an important aspect of clinical training across the healthcare professions. Nevertheless, the problem of internalised oppression among disabled children (and adults) poses additional challenges that remain difficult to address, as I have been suggesting. To expand the discussion on this subject, I would seek to build on Hollway and Jefferson's (2013) work on the social research interview as a site of desire on the part of the researcher and also to think about the relevance of this work to the clinical encounter. The cultivation of the type of sensitivity discussed by Hollway and Jefferson could be developed through the reinstatement of Balint Groups, in which consultants working on the diagnosis and rehabilitation of disabled children would be encouraged to explore the relational dynamics of their clinical encounters, and think about the way in which their own feelings, including their own unconscious fantasies, might be impacting on the way they relate to children and to families.

Perhaps I am advocating the kind of change in clinical practice that cannot be enacted without huge structural and conceptual change in medicine. Balint spoke of a world in which all GPs were also psychotherapists as 'Utopia' (1964, pp. 282–293); it was a distant dream then and remains so. Nevertheless, for better or for worse, we do now 'live in a culture of therapy, where we demand to speak and know about ourselves and others' (Goodley 2011, p. 99). Goodley rightly describes this culture shift as 'pseudo-psychoanalytic' (2011, p. 99). Indeed, psychological therapies which do not subscribe to a theory of relationality often overlook their own contribution to an oppressive culture of self-management and the internalisation of norms. If this current of thought could move beyond the pseudo-psychoanalytic, perhaps there would be scope to work with it in order to bring about a culture change in terms of how disabled children are seen within services.

In order to take these ideas further, we need more research on disabled people's experiences of healthcare, an area that may have been neglected in disability studies because of understandable scepticism about the medicalisation of disability that such work could imply or entail (Shakespeare 2014). I think that in particular, we need more research exploring disabled adults' views of their childhood experiences of medical encounters. I would suggest that the psychoanalytic theories discussed here offer generative insights into the dynamics that may be at play in clinical encounters when disabled children are present, and that they should be a subject for further research and debate.

My chapter has sought to underline the need for an attentiveness to perspective in clinical and research practice. For a child who has been disabled since birth, rehabilitation may be an unwanted intrusion upon a body that feels fine as it is (Cooper 2015). Should 'success' in diagnostic terms only ever be linked to the discovery of pathology or disability, or could it come to play a more important role in the performative and human aspects of the practice? Should success in rehabilitative terms only ever be connected to regaining functionality? In this chapter, I hope to have thrown into question some of the 'taken for granted' aspects of policies and practices that affect the lives of disabled children.

Acknowledgements I am grateful for the financial support from Birkbeck's Institutional Strategic Support Funding from the Wellcome Trust, which enabled me to research and write this chapter.

References

Abbott, D. (2013). Who Says What, Where, Why and How? Doing Real-World Research with Disabled Children, Young People and Family Members. In T. Curran & K. Runswick-Cole (Eds.), *Disabled Children's Childhood Studies: Critical Approaches in a Global Context* (pp. 39–56). Basingstoke: Palgrave Macmillan.

Ahmed, S. (2014). *Willful Subjects*. Durham: Duke University Press.

Balint, M. (1964). *The Doctor, His Patient and the Illness* (2nd ed.). London: Pitman Medical Publishing.

Balint Society website. (2012). http://balint.co.uk/. Accessed 30 Aug 2015.

Balint, E., Courtenay, M., Elder, A., Hull, S., & Julian, P. (1993). *The Doctor, the Patient and the Group: Balint Revisited*. London/New York: Routledge.

Butler, J. (1997). *Excitable Speech: A Politics of the Performative*. Abingdon/Oxon: Routledge.

Caselli, D. (2010). Kindergarten Theory: Childhood, Affect, Critical Thought. *Feminist Theory, 11*(3), 241–254.

Centre for Medical Humanities website, Durham University. (2009). https://www.dur.ac.uk/cmh/medicalhumanities/. Accessed 30 Aug 2015.

Collini, S. (2012). *What Are Universities For?* London: Penguin.

Cooper, H. (2015). *Making the Disabled Child: Critical Disability Studies at the Intersection of Cultural Representation and Lived Experience* (Unpublished Doctoral Thesis). University of London, Birkbeck.

Curran, T., & Runswick-Cole, K. (2013a). Preface. In T. Curran & K. Runswick-Cole (Eds.), *Disabled Children's Childhood Studies: Critical Approaches in a Global Context* (pp. ix–xi). Basingstoke: Palgrave Macmillan.

Curran, T., & Runswick-Cole, K. (2013b). Concluding Thoughts and Future Directions. In T. Curran & K. Runswick-Cole (Eds.), *Disabled Children's Childhood Studies: Critical Approaches in a Global Context* (pp. 196–199). Basingstoke: Palgrave Macmillan.

Fanon, F. (1970 [1967]). *Black Skin, White Masks* (C. L. Markmann, Trans.). London: Paladin.

Ferenczi, S. (1933). Confusion of Tongues Between Adults and the Child (The Language of Tenderness and of Passion). In J. Borossa (Ed.), (1999) *Sándor Ferenczi: Selected Writings* (pp. 293–303). London: Penguin.

Goodley, D. (2011). *Disability Studies: An Interdisciplinary Introduction.* London: Sage.

Goodley, D. (2014). *Dis/Ability Studies: Theorising Disablism and Ableism.* Abingdon/ Oxon: Routledge.

Goodley, D., & Runswick-Cole, K. (2012). Reading Rosie: The Postmodern Disabled Child. *Educational and Child Psychology, 29*(2), 51–64.

Hollway, W., & Jefferson, T. (2013). *Doing Qualitative Research Differently: A Psychosocial Approach* (2nd ed.). London: Sage.

Kirklin, D., & Richardson, R. (2001). Introduction: Medical Humanities and Tomorrow's Doctors. In D. Kirklin & R. Richardson (Eds.), *Medical Humanities: A Practical Introduction* (pp. 1–6). London: Royal College of Physicians.

Lesnik-Oberstein, K. (1994). *Children's Literature: Criticism and the Fictional Child.* Oxford: Oxford University Press.

Lesnik-Oberstein, K. (2008). *On Having an Own Child: Reproductive Technologies and the Cultural Construction of Childhood.* London: Karnac.

Lesnik-Oberstein, K. (2011). Introduction: Voice, Agency and the Child. In K. Lesnik-Oberstein (Ed.), *Children in Culture, Revisited: Further Approaches to Childhood* (pp. 1–17). Basingstoke: Palgrave Macmillan.

McRuer, R. (2006). Compulsory Able-Bodiedness and Queer/Disabled Existence. In L. J. Davis (Ed.), *The Disability Studies Reader* (2nd ed., pp. 301–308). Abingdon/ Oxon: Routledge.

Oliver, M. (1983). *Social Work with Disabled People.* London: Macmillan.

Oliver, M. (1993). *What's So Wonderful About Walking?* Inaugural Lecture. University of Greenwich. Online at: http://disability-studies.leeds.ac.uk/files/library/Oliver-PROFLEC.pdf. Accessed Aug 2016.

Reeve, D. (2008). *Negotiating Disability in Everyday Life: The Experience of Psycho-Emotional Disablism* (Unpublished Doctoral Thesis). Lancaster University.

Rose, J. (1984). *The Case of Peter Pan, or the Impossibility of Children's Fiction.* London/ Basingstoke: Macmillan.

Shakespeare, T. (1997). Cultural Representation of Disabled People: Dustbins for Disavowal? In L. Barton & M. Oliver (Eds.), *Disability Studies: Past Present and Future* (pp. 217–233). Leeds: The Disability Press.

Shakespeare, T. (2014). *Disability Rights and Wrongs Revisited* (2nd ed.). Abingdon/ Oxon: Routledge.

Tavistock and Portman website. (2015). http://tavistockandportman.uk/. Accessed 1 Sep 2015.

Taylor, B. (2014). *The Last Asylum: A Memoir of Madness in Our Times*. London: Hamish Hamilton.

Thomas, C. (1999). *Female Forms: Experiencing and Understanding Disability*. Buckingham: Open University Press.

Viney, W., Callard, F., & Woods, A. (2015). Critical Medical Humanities: Embracing Entanglement, Taking Risks. *Medical Humanities, 41*, 2–7.

Watermeyer, B. (2013). *Towards a Contextual Psychology of Disablism*. Abingdon/Oxon: Routledge.

World Health Organization (WHO). (2011). *World Report on Disability*. Geneva: World Health Organization.

Wright, K. (1991). *Vision and Separation: Between Mother and Baby*. London: Free Association Books.

Harriet Cooper Researcher, completed her PhD in cultural disability studies at Birkbeck, University of London, in 2015. She is now working on a qualitative health sociology project entitled 'Rights-based Rehabilitation' at the University of East Anglia, and is building an interdisciplinary career within and between the social sciences and the humanities.

Disabled Children's Childhood Studies and Leadership as Experts by Experience' Leadership: Learning Activism in Health and Social Care Education

Tillie Curran, Ruth Sayers, and Barry Percy-Smith

Key Points

- People with experience of using health and social care who contribute to its development and those in disabled children's childhood studies call for social justice.
- In both these groups, people voice their anger at being seen by professionals as the source of 'the problem', and at the failures of professionals to see how decisions made, without their involvement, result in crises.
- Sharing experience, generating knowledge and engaging practitioners across professional boundaries to *really* listen, are approaches used by families and individuals to counter exclusion.
- We explore critical pedagogy for students to develop skills in activism as core to developing their professional role and commitment to social justice, and we discuss our activist roles as academics and Experts by Experience in those approaches.

T. Curran
University of the West of England, Bristol, UK

R. Sayers
McPin Foundation, London, UK

B. Percy-Smith
University of Huddersfield, Huddersfield, UK

© The Author(s) 2018
K. Runswick-Cole et al. (eds.), *The Palgrave Handbook of Disabled Children's Childhood Studies*, https://doi.org/10.1057/978-1-137-54446-9_31

The impetus for writing this chapter arose from our recognition of exclusion as a theme that cut across our different involvement in participation initiatives with young people, families and people contributing their own experience of using services to improve the experiences of others. The term 'Expert by Experience' is used here to describe the various roles that service users and carers have taken up to develop health and social care, but also a deliberately more active and empowering stance based on a recognition of strengths rather than perceived vulnerability. The contributions of Experts by Experience to professional education, policy and service development is informed by their own immediate experience and is extended through links with others sharing such experiences. In this chapter, we want to explore the relevance of ideas concerning Experts by Experience to disabled children's childhoods and the way in which professionals engage with disabled children.

We took part in a project that aimed to explore and develop leadership practices with Experts by Experience in the context of health and social care. In response to the exclusion from professionals' decision-making that disabled children and their families and Experts by Experience reported, we wanted to explore the potential of activist learning or learning to be activists in professional education. By 'activist' we mean a role that explicitly aims to challenge established taken for granted professional orthodoxies and bring about change in the systems and actions that create barriers to civil liberties and opportunities for childhood and adult life.

The first aim of this chapter is to share some of the experiences of exclusion that have been voiced at disabled children's childhood studies conferences and by a wider group of Experts by Experience. Families and individuals told us how they have been made to feel as though *they* are the source of 'the problem'. For some, such negative events have acted as an impetus to speak out as 'Experts by Experience' to bring about change for themselves and for others in the future. The second aim is to identify the principles and strategies used by people involved in disabled children's childhood studies and Experts by Experience in those initiatives. In particular, we discuss a project that we facilitated around leadership in the role of Expert by Experience and highlight the networks created for immediate mutual support, critical dialogue and collective action. The third aim is to consider how professional education might provide opportunities for students to engage with the perspectives of disabled children, families and others in the role of Experts by Experience and to share their commitments to change. We explore critical pedagogy as an approach for students in health and social care that encourages learning for creative engagement with disabled children and the skills for sustainable activism. We end with discussion of the different roles that the approach suggests for us. Through our work together we have been challenged and inspired from learning from Experts by Experience, but all come to this chapter from different contexts. We therefore felt it important to exercise a degree of reflexivity with respect to this chapter so will begin by introducing ourselves to explain why we have written this chapter together.

Tillie is a social work lecturer at the UWE involved in disabled children's childhood studies and the participation of Experts by Experience in professional education. Ruth is an expert by experience of using psychiatric services and is involved in user-focused research and professional education. Barry is a professor in childhood studies and participatory practice with experience in facilitating participatory learning and change in public sector service. We came together when Tillie invited Ruth, Jon and Barry to co-design and facilitate the leadership project discussed in this chapter. Jon, a senior lecturer at the UWE, has since left his post and chose not to co-author. We aim to reflect his contribution in the discussion of our joint work below. The project and the writing of this chapter provided further learning for us and we return to our own perspectives at the end of the chapter.

Tillie

Since the 1990s as a social worker and academic, I have supported the principles of participation of people using services in decisions, development of provision and professional education as central to anti-oppressive practice (Curran 1997). The disability civil rights movement was highly critical of welfare as an individualizing system perpetuating rather than transforming inequality, and the social model of disability was advanced to recognize disability as an oppressive social relation requiring societal change informed by the experiences of disabled people (Oliver 1991). The authority derived from the claim that the knowledge is objective and value free was also challenged and participatory approaches such as action research were favoured where research is explicitly focused on achieving experience-based social change (e.g. Reason and Bradbury 2001). Oliver (1991) explained that a focus on an individual's impairment was a form of methodological individualism that asks what is wrong with that person and argues that a social model approach should instead ask disabled people what is wrong with society and what action is needed. Anti-oppressive practice draws on civil rights campaigns advancing an advocacy role for professionals towards social justice (Dalrymple and Burke 2006), and in social work Experts by Experience have been increasingly involved in policy, practice and professional education. Social justice continues to be presented as a core focus for the profession:

> *The social work profession promotes social change, problem solving in human relationships and the empowerment and liberation of people to enhance well-being. Utilising theories of human behaviour and social systems, social work intervenes at the points where people interact with their environments. Principles of human rights*

and social justice are fundamental to social work. (BASW 2012, The Code of Ethics for Social Work, http://cdn.basw.co.uk/upload/basw_112315-7.pdf: p6)

As a social worker working with disabled children and their families and then as an academic, I used action research to work with social workers around listening to disabled children (Curran 2010). During this research, I began to doubt the emancipatory ideals and recognize how such liberatory discourses could act as strategies of power. The techniques of governmentality discussed by Tremain (2006, 2015) produce the 'disabled person' in terms of 'impairment' and that, she explains, is a social practice. The splitting of 'impairment' from the 'social' that is so key to the social model of disability, she argues, limits the focus of campaigns to service eligibility rather than societal change. The alternative to liberal discourses of empowerment or participation that Tremain proposes focus on the formation of alternative desires without adopting individualised forms of 'disabled' subjectivity.

In disabled children's childhood studies, we have sought to move away from such welfare forms of subjectivity. We reject the deficit discourses where disabled children are portrayed as having or being problems rather than having childhoods and contest modern discourses of childhood and disability, the 'ideal child' and the normative nosology of 'the life span' (Curran and Runswick-Cole 2013, 2014). Our alternative focus is childhood experience and desires, and what needs to change in practice and society. In this chapter I wish to respond to the anger voiced about professional practice. As an academic in professional education I wish to explore the potential of critical pedagogy for students to have direct experience of activism and opportunities to critically discuss professional statements around 'involvement', 'empowerment' and 'participation'.

Writing this chapter entailed further learning for me and I reflect on the following questions at the end. To be part of activist learning, I consider how I might discuss my identity and how the above concerns around authority and my attachment to social justice also link to my childhood. How might I engage openly with students in discussions around with 'vulnerability' and how might this strengthen co-working with Experts by Experience without replicating stigmatizing practices?

Ruth

As a lecturer in sociology, part of my work research and teaching focused on inequalities in power, social capital and the development of equal opportunities. These interests influenced my responses to how I experienced treatment when I became stressed at work, sought support for my mental health, and was diagnosed *with serious mental illness. Four experiences of hospitalization, including being subjected to sectioning under the Mental Health Act, gave me extreme experiences of disempowerment, surveillance and humiliation and have subsequently contributed to my interest and increasing work in mental health activism and user-focused research. Those experiences of exclusion and disenfranchisement also, paradoxically, enabled me to recover my mental health as I determined that I would never be forced to undergo similar treatment in future.*

Along the way I joined with other people who defined themselves (or accepted the definition from others) as service users and carers, and who ached to change the responses of services to their needs (and often especially the needs of others in the future) for the better. Many of these people then found positions where they could act to promote or provoke change in a wide range of ways—through service user and carer participation in evaluating and inspecting existing services, commissioning new ones, training professionals, researching people's experiences and develop better forms of treatment and care (see Pilgrim 2005). In every setting where we are working as activists and advocates we rely on being accepted, welcomed and heard by people defining themselves as professionals and other forms of gatekeeper. We seek to contribute our knowledge and understanding from lived experience to discourses that seek to create new forms of knowledge and changes to the services provided. For example, the emerging interdisciplinary field of Mad Studies challenges and contextualizes the dominant psychiatric perspective of madness, by listening to people's own experiences of and points of view of madness (Burstow et al. 2014).

When Tillie proposed working together on a practical project to explore and enhance the qualities of leadership amongst people, I had been working alongside and with other activist Experts by Experience, I was enthused to join what appeared to be a fresh and probably long overdue endeavour.

I have recently been inspired by learning more about Peer Supported Open Dialogue (Open Dialogue 2016), which is a way of responding to mental health crises of psychosis by creating a space for all the significant members of the person's network to share their feelings, fears and find solutions, supported by professionals. Open Dialogue uses some of the same methods as our Knowledge Cafe approach explained below, and allows time for a deeper and more revealing level of discussion than current mental health services in England can provide. Open Dialogue present evidence internationally that indicates the approach is more effective over the longer term and can cut waste in terms of anti-psychotic medication, use of psychiatric services and wasted lives (Open Dialogue 2016). I am interested in how students can best learn about these ways of working—probably by experiencing such processes for themselves, and how academics also share in and support this.

Barry

Narratives about ability/disability, inclusion/exclusion often struggle to be translated into lived realities in practice. In part this is a result of prevailing assumptions about the relative merits of professional knowledge over other forms of knowledge such as knowledge of Experts by Experience. In turn there is inertia in systems, practices and approaches to learning and change that perpetuates professional knowledge at the expense of 'other' voices. This appears true for children and young people as generational groups as it does for children in particular situations such as children in care, children with mental health issues, children from minorities as well as disabled children. Yet post-positivist approaches to research and development (Gibbons et al. 1994; Reason and Bradbury 2001), which acknowledge with integrity (rather than tokenistically) the value of such groups as genuine partners, are increasingly being recognized as effective alternatives to service improvement.

My interests have focused predominantly on the participation and empowerment of children and young people in matters that affect them. Construction of alternative narratives of involvement and participation in the field of children's participation has in turn begun to change attitudes and practices concerning children themselves. Participatory approaches to learning for change reconstruct hierarchical and oppressive relationships and in turn highlight the agency of such user groups. Equally children's participation concerns the empowerment of children themselves in ways that offer more meaningful opportunities for participation in everyday life contexts as autonomous social actors rather than just in relation to professional agenda. This empowerment is perhaps more important for disabled children in realizing a sense of agency and inclusion where everyday forms of participation and inclusion maybe less easily realized.

The developments in thinking and practice this chapter focuses upon I feel are imperative in translating innovation in thinking into meaningful change in the way service users and carers are treated. I therefore bring to this chapter a curiosity and desire to explore how we might make sense of critical discourses of disabled children's childhoods in relation to issues of power and empowerment, whilst simultaneously seeking to understand better the perspectives and possibilities of Experts by Experience as activists in catalyzing professional learning and new discourses of social care and in turn social change.

The discussion of disabled children's childhood studies, in the next section, identifies some of the concerns raised by families and highlights their strategies towards change. The concerns and formation of mutual support networks were also evident in the project we facilitated with Experts by Experience set out in the second section. We look at critical pedagogies in the third section as we each have roles in professional education. At the end, we comment briefly on our learning from working together on this chapter.

Disabled Children's Childhood Studies

Disabled children's childhood studies emerged through the voices of disabled children and young people and their families through a series of Child, Youth, Family & Disability Conferences held in the UK that originated in Manchester Metropolitan University in 2008 (Curran and Runswick-Cole 2013). The conference titles convey the agenda for change (Time for Change 2013; Building Understandings 2014; There is no Them! 2015; and Ethical Participation? 2016). There is a clear message given that service evaluation or studies of health conditions are not accepted as studies of disabled children's childhood (Curran and Runswick-Cole 2014). To keep this focus on disabled children's childhoods, the guidance the conference team provides sets out three principles: a focus on disabled children's childhood experience and voice; open discussion of ethical issues and location of the study in the global context. Disabled young people, disabled adults, family members, allies and activists from a range of voluntary-sector projects have contributed. Professions represented include social work, nursing, paediatrics and physiotherapy, education, and music therapy; and academic disciplines include disability studies, sociology, critical psychology, geography and cultural studies. The Child, Youth, and Family Disability Research Network South West & Wales was formed by conference participants in 2014 to share and develop research questions from this perspective. Social media has been used to discuss these events internationally and many people involved contribute to international events hosted by other networks also shifting the focus to disabled children's perspectives.

At the conferences, dissatisfaction with professional intervention has been strongly expressed by parents, both mothers and fathers. Professionals, we have heard, individualize a 'crisis' as if it was about the individual child or family's coping ability, whereas from parents' perspectives, crisis is reached through the negative impact of professional interventions, the exclusion of children, young people and their families from decisions about their lives, the lack of options offered and the hostility of others in the wider community. Children, young people and their families told us that vulnerability did not stem from the child's impairment or carers' coping capability, but through processes of exclusion (see Coles 2015). It was the impact of exclusion that provided the impetus for participants in the project discussed in this chapter to speak out as a matter of survival. Specifying the location of each study helped us to understand these individualizing interventions as an effect of systems sustaining inequality in a global context through post-colonial relations (see Chataika and McKenzie 2013; Grech 2013). Burman et al. (2015) call upon us to reject deficit-generalizing views of the Global South; to contest the 'good' of interventions, and to critique post-colonial conditions. For example, Mills and Fernando (2014) critique the Global Mental Health field and movement as a strategy that produces generalized claims about normal and abnormal health that boosts profit in the Global North through increased export of medication to the Global South. The medication, they warn is subject to scrutiny in terms of its efficacy, but its proliferation also distracts attention from the practical changes needed to address poverty as a major factor underlying poor health.

The (re)energized collective networks in disabled children's childhood studies stand in contrast to the individualizing practices experienced by disabled children and their families and the same contrast is voiced by Experts by Experience in the leadership project discussed in the next section. As such, critical reflection on the experiences of both of these groups is valuable as part of the development of a critical pedagogy for professional learning in Health and Social Care.

Leadership as Experts by Experience in Health and Social Care

The 'leadership as Experts by Experience' project was developed in response to concerns raised informally to the chapter authors by the service users and carers involved in social work education, and in many other health and social care initiatives in both the region and nationally. The personal energy demanded of Experts by Experience in the range of roles held was considerable. Organizations gained credibility from their involvement, but Experts by Experience voiced their concerns about the lack of visible impact from their contributions to training and service development. Having been invited to contribute to change and then having no feedback from service providers that any changes occurred, left Experts by Experience feeling marginalized and disrespected (Curran et al. 2015). In response to these feelings of marginalization, we designed a project to explore and develop leadership as Experts by Experience. A series of three workshops took place over three months with the aim of enhancing and evidencing the impact of Experts by Experience in health and social care improvement. The leadership project adopted a Knowledge Café approach (Brown 2001) using principles of participatory action inquiry (Reason and Bradbury 2001). The Knowledge Cafes aimed to create a space for service users and carers to explore and make sense of their roles as Experts by Experience whilst developing their own practice as 'leaders'. We approached the interpretation of the idea of 'leadership' broadly to allow for participants to ascribe their own meanings emerging from their inquiries into their roles. Fourteen Experts by Experience from around the region enrolled, bringing a range of experience as carers and service users including experience of disability, learning disability and mental health service provision.

The Knowledge Café inquiry process began with participants' sharing stories from experience and, through informal conversations, identifying issues and questions that they felt were important in making sense of their role and engaging in inquiry in response to their experiences of exclusion. In the first workshop, *Exploring and valuing our leadership by experience*, participants shared how they became Experts by Experience and identified themes around 'leadership'. In preparation for the second workshop, *Deepening ways of thinking about leadership*, participants were invited to create 'rivers of experience' posters (Percy-Smith and Walsh 2006) mapping their journeys from service user or carer to becoming an Expert by Experience. Participants reflected on these learning journeys and reanimated their experiences using a different lens identifying times when they felt they had exercised 'leadership' and how that was manifested. In the third workshop, *Deepening our impact in health and social care*, activities were designed to hone the knowledge generated and to develop skills to evaluate their impact when involved in education and service development. The facilitators had developed ideas for the focus for each workshop a priori and then revised these at the end of each session in light of issues emerging in the knowledge cafes.

Three dimensions of leadership practice were identified during the workshops and consent to share them was agreed in the final workshop and individually after the workshops ended (Curran et al. 2015). These interpretations and enactments of leadership emerged organically out of their own sense-making of their experiences and reflected notions of agency, self-determination and empowerment as articulated through their everyday actions and orientations in their roles. The three dimensions of leadership as Experts by Experience are as follows:

i) Loving into action.
ii) Networking together and across organizations.
iii) Two-way listening towards positive impact (Curran et al. 2015).

Loving into Action

Loving, having a deep regard for family members or compassion for oneself, was identified as the source of participants' strength and energy, the impetus to take action and the tenacity to keep going. This bond was contrasted with professionals' commitment who they felt usually saw them as 'the problem'. Consequently, the meaningfulness of their distress went unrecognized or was labelled 'challenging behaviour'. 'Blame stops understanding and leads to alienation' one participant commented (Curran et al. 2015: 626). This alienation was also characterized by a sense that professionals failed to recognize and value the integrity of their roles. Participants felt they were expected to be deferent and commented that provision appeared to exist for practitioners' convenience rather than to support them. Instead, their own articulations of leadership as self-initiated action in providing compassionate care and unconditional commitment provided the basis for self-respect and value in support roles.

Networking Together and Across Organizations

Networks were seen as central to surviving inequalities through developing a sense of solidarity, entailing support for other carers and service users, reaching a clear shared purpose and pulling resources together. Challenging each other was seen as key to listening and necessary to explore and make visible what was happening. Experts by Experience described how they provided mutual support and generated understanding together, especially at points that were reaching crisis. The style and practice of leadership therefore arose from, and were grounded in, specific contexts, 'developing as a leader from within a situation, not from personal inclination' (Curran et al. 2015: 627).

Two-Way Listening Towards Positive Impact

As is the case with disabled children, in seeking greater acknowledgement and respect for their 'expertise by experience', service users and carers argued that professional relationships, and therefore provision of services and support, needed to be based on two-way listening, characterized by dialogue and mutual respect. Experts by Experience also felt it was essential to know what impact their contribution (e.g. teaching professionals) had in and on practice, and for the evaluation not to be limited to feedback forms, but developed through continuing dialogues. Experts by Experience encouraged practitioners *really* to listen and to share their values so that they too openly recognize the inadequacy of services and would then share the goal to bring about change. Two-way listening was regarded as key and the communication skills that participants demonstrated and promoted were the same skills found in professional literature. Two-way listening therefore entails professionals shifting their practice from that of 'expert' to a more 'interpretive' role in which professional responses are based on listening, learning and joint decision-making. This entails building in critical reflexivity into their engagement with service users and carers; being open to challenging their own assumptions with respect to service user experiences, and open to changing practice in response to that learning (Weil 1997; Percy-Smith and Weil 2003). When practitioners did listen with openness effectively, it was very much appreciated.

In keeping with the Knowledge Café process, the literature around 'leadership' was discussed towards the end of the project and we identified links with collaborative theories. Contemporary theories generally shift from the traditional individual notion of a 'leader' who imparts vision and direction to followers in favour of strength-based concepts involving collaborative learning and development (see Ladkin 2008; Gronn 2002; Uhl-Bien et al. 2007). We also found endorsement in the UK Professional Capabilities Framework for Social Work, where 'professional leadership' is defined in terms of influence through learning and development and that includes the involvement of service users and carers (The College of Social Work 2012). In addition, the advancement of the 'learning organization' in social work includes co-production initiatives with service users (Gould 2004). In service user participation literature, the impact of Experts by Experience networking, as well as disabled children in their 'struggle for recognition' and respect, is recognized as a process of knowledge co-production (Beresford and Branfield 2006) and, in the field of participatory inquiry, communicative action is promoted (Kemmis 2001) to signify collaborative learning and recognize validity and impact. It is these processes of networking, mutual support and reciprocal learning identified in both disabled children's childhood studies and the Experts by Experience project that appeared to contrast so sharply with the accounts of professionals' individualizing practice. The contrast in values and approaches raised the following questions for us:

- How might professionals join and support change initiated by Experts by Experience?
- If change can occur through networking processes, how might professionals develop networks?

- How might professional education providers in health and social care make opportunities available for students to explore and develop their understanding and skills for changing practice?

These questions do not imply that all professionals work in the ways described above, or are responsible and to blame for the systems they encounter. Indeed many practitioners are themselves also often silent in the systems they work and need support to voice their concerns as part of their professional role. Developing practice through interpretations of leadership as outlined above can thus be generative for practitioners as well as service users and carers. In the next section, we consider the value of critical pedagogy approaches for understanding and practicing activism.

Critical Pedagogy and Activism

Pedagogy is the theory and practice of education. Critical pedagogy challenges the individual 'banking' model of education that takes for granted expert knowledge claims in favour of experience-based participatory learning towards social justice (Saleebey and Scanlon 2005). Though the current 'business' context of higher education in the UK makes the option of critical pedagogy appear unlikely, Saleebey and Scanlon (2005) suggest that it is precisely because of that context and the welfare austerity measures faced by families, that critical pedagogy becomes an imperative. Austerity measures in England are particularly impacting on disabled children and their families escalating existing inequalities (Office of the Children's Commissioner 2014).

Critical pedagogy has its roots in critical theory and its traditions include Marxist, feminist and post-structural perspectives. Friere (1972) promoted learning through sustained conversation and critically reflective learning with students, teachers and community to investigate social (dis)location together. Honneth (1995), in focusing on the centrality of 'struggles over recognition' in service user and carer engagement with professionals, similarly pursues alternative professional practice discourses in terms of love, rights and solidarity (see Thomas 2012 for application of Honneth to understanding participatory relations with children). From a constructivist perspective, Preston and Aslett (2014) advance activist pedagogy to build a community of activist learners and educators in the classroom. Razack (2009) is critical of 'international social work' as it has tended to (re)produce 'the problem' as the Global South and the 'ideal' as the Global North. He discusses de-colonial and post-colonial pedagogy for students to have the opportunity for dialogue and deep engagement in order to analyse the geopolitical context together in the classroom. The common themes are around sharing experience as the starting point for building understanding, and through critique of context, identifying and developing ways to bring about change together.

In relation to disability, Beckett (2015) offers anti-oppressive pedagogy for disabled and non-disabled pupils in schools to learn about disability equality that we can apply here to professional education. She stresses the importance of considering carefully what the learning objective is if pedagogy is aiming to address oppression. The first objective, learning about and celebrating the 'other', she explains, might dispel stigma, but it can also promote essentialist differences and take our attention away from the social practices that generate stigma. It puts pressure on disabled pupils to tell their story for the benefit of non-disabled pupils and can be an exposing and exploitative relation where any empathy may become romantic sympathy. 'Celebrating' can imply a normalization 'they are just like us', or give rise to inspirational discourse. A second learning objective asks how 'othering' happens—focusing on how systems, practices and privileged groups subordinate disabled people as 'other'. Beckett suggests this objective is more in line with the social model of disability and Freire's aim of 'conscientization'. Students learn to understand ideology and power in capitalism, recognize dehumanizing practices, and locate their own socio-economic position in order to act on that system. Links are made to other structures of exploitation. 'Voice' from this perspective is about the experience of oppression and what needs to change, but why, Beckett asks, would the dominant group seek to disempower themselves?

Beckett (2015) favours 'post-critical pedagogy' for learning about and transforming power relations between disabled and non-disabled people. Versions draw on Foucault, post-colonialism (and a number of other post-structural theories) where power is not only seen as coercive and somewhat fixed, but positive, discursive and involving resistance. For Kumashiro, (2000 in Beckett, 2015), students are encouraged not to repeat harmful statements but to construct disruptive, different discourses including disruption of the 'normal' from the self. They need support to do this labour. Drawing on Deleuze, Beckett explains the aim is not to replace the oppressor's truth with the truth of the oppressed, but to 'think otherwise', and for some (especially those more privileged) that can become a vulnerable space and crisis results. It is at that stage that new possibilities can emerge as normalcy and otherness (and all other binary oppositions) are transgressed. Again there is no guarantee that students will participate or take action. Beckett proposes a central role for disabled people and their organizations to engage in dialogue with other academics to critique neo-liberal discourse and its erosion of equality policy.

It follows that the involvement of Experts by Experience is developed for critical discussion and not reduced to a consumer quality assurance discourse, and, that academics are prepared to transform their own relationships with disabled people as we discuss further. It is important to recognize relations with disabled academics and to include the significance of intersectionality.

From a survivor's perspective, there is another important point to make in relation to the role of academics. The above model certainly contrasts with the frequent occasions where people designated as 'service users' or 'carers' are invited to tell students about their experiences, while the academics and professionals involved can present themselves as 'non-service users' and 'non-carers', without or detached from the vulnerability those labels imply. The questions about which services, why use arises or what the label feels like are rarely addressed or formulate the basis of discussion which includes all of those involved in this dichotomy. Our foray into the use of action inquiry in this initiative suggest there is considerable value and potential in using the participative paradigm to challenge power inscribed in roles and discourses and open up possibilities for challenging pre-eminent professional discourses by engaging the professional in reflecting on their own position and practices in relation to the systems and rhetoric that frame the reality of service users and disabled children. The academic environment, however, does not easily encourage such challenges from the less-powerful category of service users, who may indeed feel privileged and grateful to be invited to enter the portals of the university. However, these approaches are not necessarily addressing the academics' identity and without that, the power relations and identity dichotomy will continue to be modelled to the students in ways that perpetuate power inequalities. Academics need courage, compassion and openness to expose themselves to such potential challenges from those they have a role to 'support' or 'help'. It follows that practitioners will need this too.

The sharing of feelings and emotions, the critical discussion of vulnerability and labels, is not to be conflated with the therapy discourse promoted in the consumer neo-liberal discourse in education. Amsler (2011) suggests that disinterest and disbelief in social change occurs through individualization and consumerism in education just when the need to act towards social justice becomes an imperative. Education is reduced to a form of therapeutic relief rather than opportunities for consciousness raising and learning for change. Therapy culture, Amsler (2011) explains, draws on notions of 'positive psychology' and becomes a form of education throughout schools and services for those deemed to be in need of intervention to be 'well', to learn to manage their emotions or 'simply' to cope with the social reality they are confronted with. In higher education, the students must be happy, satisfied with the standardized offer and may be so invested in an individualized goal, that any other goal would amount to self-destruction. Amsler (2011) turns to the 'pedagogy of discomfort' (Zembylas and Boler's 2002 in Amsler 2011) and suggests a post-structural framework in which emotions are explored together as discursive practices of comfort and discomfort. The task is to locate the power strategies, investments, resistances involved:

> *the fundamental task is therefore not to teach people what to feel about themselves or others in particular, much less in a determined way and it is not necessarily connected to immediate feelings of 'wellbeing'. Rather, the aim is to enable people to understand why they have certain feelings, desires and needs; why, perhaps, they do not have or are not 'supposed' to have others: and to critically imagine conditions in which radical alternatives might be possible.* (Amsler 2011: 58)

To explore, debate and reimagine feelings would appear to re-energize a core professional commitment to experiential learning and social justice. Identifying the sources of professionals' comfort and discomfort in the encounters discussed above by disabled children's families and Experts by Experience might lead to a readiness to consider radical alternatives rather than the comforts sought in defence and blame of families.

Critical pedagogy transgresses the oppositions of learning and action, and the dominant normalcy discourse of individual achievement that characterizes the foundations of modern education. For Goodley (2007), a socially just pedagogy is about the ever-changing learner and reconfiguration of the normative classroom and the adversarial divide between learning and activism is transgressed. Drawing on Deleuze and Guattari, Goodley presents the rhizome visualization of a person, the productive, becoming, with multiple links and directions, weaving rather than coding or fixing. Disabled students for instance are not other, or lacking, or exceptional, in need of inclusion, but productive with desires. Concepts are then understood not as being based on fixed claims to expertise, but as dynamic, in a state of evolving and continuing practices. Goodley (2007) explains that the professional role is no longer fixed and preoccupied with control; the relationship is to be constructed through fluid, learning-based interactions to find connections with disabled people and others, in which critical reflexivity is imperative (see also Percy-Smith and Weil 2003).

Further Reflections

We suggest academics need to provide students in health and social care with the opportunities for creating critical networks with professionals, service users and activists—to provide new spaces for debating comfort and discomfort and forming different relationships. However, providing the space is not enough if academics repeat the power relations of detachment and othering in their behaviour to Experts by Experience. We end with our thoughts about how to directly engage with vulnerability, labels and learning that we have had through writing this chapter together.

Ruth

For me, the role of expert by experience involves complex decisions about how I present and manage my identity. During my training as a teacher and previous work as a lecturer, I had to develop at least an appearance of being expert and not vulnerable—invulnerable expertise. However, in order to use my experience of using services (as an expert by experience) to prompt professionals to think about my perspective as a service user more deeply or openly, I need to expose myself as a vulnerable person—a person with mental illness. My mental health identity is stigmatised—as in Goffman's (1963) 'spoiled identity'—and I need to manage carefully how far I expose it with other people. Sharing this identity within an 'expert' role involves taking risks. I have periods of illness when I wish I could hide under a stone, to be invisible, when I am unable to talk openly, or appear in a public forum. I have to be feeling relatively well to feel comfortable about revealing my personal life in a classroom.

However, my role as expert by experience seems to works best when I feel able to reveal my weakness and vulnerability—to be fully visible to strangers. Talking when I am feeling closest to the edge stimulates the most thoughtful and sensitive responses from students, but also requires me to move as far out of my comfort zone as I dare at that particular time, with that particular group. To keep myself as safe as possible I need to feel my way into the situation on the day and estimate how much of myself I can reveal.

I know that I need to be visible to have any effect, but I need to balance my desire to influence understanding, and therefore change, with the opposing pull to dissemble and disappear, between a status of 'expert' and a 'spoiled identity', an 'ill person'.

So returning to the role of trainer or educator is most difficult and often impossible when I am enclosed and stuck within my stigmatised identity—as someone needing mental health support.

Developing work on Leadership for Experts by Experience has also been challenging. Often I was feeling less capable and more vulnerable than many of the workshop participants who have developed substantial spheres of influence. Taking on a training role involved being in touch with my own feelings of weakness and vulnerability at the same time as recognising my own strength and accumulated experience.

Tillie

Ruth challenged me to share my vulnerability in my academic practice, and changing the detached academic/vulnerable person opposition is clearly encouraged in the critical pedagogy approaches discussed. But, I said, I have not experienced multiple encounters with health and social care professionals; indeed I gain privilege from individualized discourses of achievement. I can share that I built my attachment to social justice from my second-generation experience of deportation, exile and, after invasive mental health intervention, repatriation to East Europe. It is not surprising to me that I had doubts about the authority of experts, institutions and their dominant forms of knowledge from an early age, and for that I feel fortunate. As I grew up, I found some affirmation in alternative education and later anti-oppressive social work practice, but had further doubts about those narratives as discussed above. Ruth asks me a more direct question. 'What do I do when I am stressed?' Could I share what I do when I am stressed in teaching to normalize mental health and, when co-working together, to change our relationship? For me such critical conversations are at the heart of sustaining everyday activism and critical conversations are what I really like when I am stressed! I have a fresh appreciation of the critical network around me to encourage me to resist therapy culture in education and to go beyond familiar oppositions. This year new social work students were welcomed with a café approach, fruit and cake, a space to get to know each other, offer a context for learning activism and share their passions about possibilities for bringing about change. Experts by Experience and other members of the programme team shared their passions for change. We talked about learning together and introduced the possibilities of the ever-changing learner.

Barry

Struggle and vulnerability are not the preserve of certain groups, rather are symptomatic of the human experience cutting across social structures and divisions. Reflecting on our own stories and experiences may offer possibilities for connection, rediscovering our shared humanity and provide a basis for mutual engagement in ways that frees up rather than controls and restricts human interaction, learning and change. Within increasingly instrumentalised professional worlds there appears to still be scope for and indeed an increased imperative for re-searching and discovering or rediscovering our own agency and sense of empowerment to stake a claim and act on underlying human values that may not normally gain expression in contemporary professional roles, but may hold the seeds of change in professional work and a move towards social justice. Kemmis (2001) draws on Habermas to argue that through dialogue and contestation, interactions between professionals (systems) and service users (lifeworlds) can offer spaces for creativity in developing alternative social realities and relations through inquiry and social learning as re-animation of ascribed labels and meanings. Our experience through the Expert by Experience work reinforces my views about the value of participatory social learning in that endeavour.

In response to the anger about the dehumanizing, detached behaviour of professionals voiced by parents of disabled children and by Experts by Experience, we have critiqued dominant models of professional practice and education as well as neo-liberal conceptualizations of user involvement as an essentialized view of vulnerable otherness. Instead we have pursued an inquiry into the possibilities of developing a discourse of leadership as Experts by Experience involving the development of an alternative approach to professional education involving a radical pedagogy of learning activism. In such pedagogy, emphasis is focused on a practice of listening, sharing and knowledge co-construction based on relationships of mutual learning and respect. We suggest education is to some extent reconfigured when students are described by Ruth as thoughtful and sensitive and see this as a very different form of professional practice to the unwanted response to a 'person needing mental health support'. Thoughtful and sensitive professionals also differ markedly from the experiences of disabled children's families who were seen as 'the problem'. Thoughtful and sensitive responses from professionals provide opportunities for open dialogue and *really* listening. Hopefully such critical conversation acts the springboard for sustainable connected everyday activism that better understands the experiences of disabled children and their families and aims to promote the life opportunities they desire. In an era of ever increasing control and prescription in public services based on normative assumptions and instrumental professional roles, the challenge for professionals, educators and students in developing critical pedagogies has never been more important.

References

Amsler, S. (2011). From 'Therapeutic' to Political Education: The Centrality of Affective Sensibility in Critical Pedagogy. *Critical Studies in Education, 52*(1), 47–63.

BASW. (2012). *The Code of Ethics for Social Work*. http://cdn.basw.co.uk/upload/basw_112315-7.pdf

Beckett, A. E. (2015). Anti-oppressive Pedagogy and Disability: Possibilities and Challenges. *Scandinavian Journal of Disability Research, 17*(1), 76–94.

Beresford, P., & Branfield, F. (2006). Developing Inclusive Partnerships: User-Defined Outcomes, Networking and Knowledge – A Case Study. *Health & Social Care in the Community, 14*(5), 436–444.

Brown, J. (2001). The World Café: Living Knowledge Through Conversations that Matter. *The Systems Thinker, 12*(5), 1–5.

Burman, E., Greenstein, A., & Kumar, M. (2015). Editorial: Frames and Debates for Disability, Childhood and the Global South: Introducing the Special Issue. *Disability and the Global South, 2*(2), 563–569.

Burstow, B., LeFrancois, B. A., & Diamond, S. (Eds.). (2014). *Psychiatry Disrupted: Theorizing Resistance and Crafting the (R)evolution*. Quebec: MQUP.

Chataika, T., & McKenzie, J. (2013). Considerations of an African Childhood Disability Studies. In T. Curran & K. Runswick-Cole (Eds.), *Disabled Children's Childhood Studies: Critical Approaches in a Global Context* (pp. 89–104). Basingstoke: Palgrave Macmillan.

Coles, B. (2015). A 'Suitable Person': An 'Insider' Perspective. *British Journal of Learning Disabilities, 43*, 135–141.

Curran, T. (1997). Power, Post Modernism and Participation: Mental Health Education. *Social Work Education, 16*(3), 21–36.

Curran, T. (2010). Social Work and Disabled Children's Childhoods: A Foucauldian Framework for Practice Transformation. *British Journal of Social Work, 40*(3), 806–825.

Curran, T., & Runswick-Cole, K. (2013). *Disabled Children's Childhood Studies: Critical Approaches in a Global Context*. Basingstoke: Palgrave Macmillan.

Curran, T., & Runswick-Cole, K. (2014). Disabled Children's Childhood Studies: A Distinct Approach? *Disability and Society, 29*(10), 1617–1630.

Curran, T., Sayers, R., & Percy-Smith, B. (2015). Leadership as Experts by Experience in Professional Education. *Procedia – Social and Behavioral Sciences, 186*, 624–629. doi:10.1016/j.sbspro.2015.04.005.

Dalrymple, J., & Burke, B. (2006). *Anti-oppressive Practice and the Law* (2nd ed.). Open University Press. ISBN 9780335218011. Available from: http://eprints.uwe.ac.uk/1458

Friere, P. (1972). *Pedagogy of the Oppressed*. New York: Herder & Herder.

Gibbons, M., Limoges, C., Nowotny, H., Schwartzman, S., Scott, P., & Trow, M. (1994). *The New Production of Knowledge: The Dynamics of Science and Research in Contemporary Societies*. London: Sage.

Goffman, E. (1963). *Notes on the Management of Spoiled Identity*. London: Penguin.

Goodley, D. (2007). Towards Socially Just Pedagogies: Deleuzoguattarian Critical Disability Studies. *International Journal of Inclusive Education, 11*(3), 317–334.

Gould, N. (2004). The Learning Organisation and Reflective Practice – The Emergence of a Concept. In N. Gould & M. Baldwin (Eds.), *Social Work, Critical Reflection and the Learning Organisation* (pp. 1–11). Hants: Ashgate.

Grech, S. (2013). Disability, Childhood and Poverty: Critical Perspectives on Guatemala. In T. Curran & K. Runswick-Cole (Eds.), *Disabled Children's*

Childhood Studies: Critical Approaches in a Global Context (pp. 89–104). Basingstoke: Palgrave Macmillan.

Gronn, P. (2002). Distributed Leadership as Unit of Analysis. *The Leadership Quarterly, 13,* 423–451.

Honneth, A. (1995). *The Struggle for Recognition* (J. Anderson, Trans.). Cambridge: Polity Press.

Kemmis, S. (2001). Exploring the Relevance of Critical Theory for Action Research: Emancipatory Action Research in the Footsteps of Jurgen Habermas. In P. Reason & H. Bradbury (Eds.), *Handbook of Action Research: Participative Inquiry and Practice* (pp. 91–102). London: Sage.

Ladkin, D. (2008). Leading Beautifully: How Mastery, Congruence and Purpose Create the Aesthetic of Embodied Leadership Practice. *The Leadership Quarterly, 19,* 31–41.

Mills, C., & Fernando, S. (2014). Globalising Mental Health or Pathologising the Global South? Mapping the Ethics, Theory and Practice of Global Mental Health. *Disability and the Global South, 1*(2), 188–202.

Office of the Children's Commissioner. (2014). They Still Need to Listen More. In *A Report About Disabled Children and Young People's Rights in England.* London: Office of the Children's Commissioner.

Oliver, M. (1991). *The Politics of Disablement.* London: Macmillan.

Open Dialogue. (2016, September 16). http://www.mindfreedom.org/kb/mental-health-alternatives/finland-open-dialogue

Percy-Smith, B., & Walsh, D. (2006). *Improving Services for Children and Families: Listening and Learning, Report from a Systemic Action Inquiry Evaluation Process.* Northampton: Children's Fund Northamptonshire/SOLAR.

Percy-Smith, B., & Weil, S. (2003). Practice-Based Research as Development: Innovation and Empowerment in Youth Intervention Initiatives Using Collaborative Action Inquiry. In A. Bennett (Ed.), *Researching Youth.* London: Palgrave Publishing.

Pilgrim, D. (2005). Protest and Co-option – The Voice of Mental Health Service Users. In A. Bell & P. Lindley (Eds.), *Beyond the Water Towers: The Unfinished Revolution in Mental Health Services 1985–2005* (pp. 17–26). London: The Sainsbury Centre for Mental Health.

Preston, S., & Aslett, J. (2014). Resisting Neoliberalism from Within the Academy: Subversion Through an Activist Pedagogy. *Social Work Education: The International Journal, 33*(4), 502–518.

Razack, N. (2009). Decolonizing the Pedagogy and Practice of International Social Work. *International Social Work, 52*(1), 9–21.

Reason, P., & Bradbury, H. (2001). *The Handbook of Action Research: Participative Inquiry and Practice.* London: Sage.

Saleebey, D. S., & Scanlon, E. (2005). Is a Critical Pedagogy for the Profession of Social Work Possible? *Journal of Teaching in Social Work, 25*(3–4), 1–18.

The College of Social Work. (2012). *Professional Capabilities Framework.* http://www.tcsw.org.uk/pcf.aspx. Accessed 10 Sept 2014.

Thomas, N. (2012). Love, Rights and Solidarity: Studying Children's Participation Using Honneth's Theory of Recognition. *Childhood, 19*(4). http://journals.sage-pub.com/doi/abs/10.1177/0907568211434604

Tremain, S. (2006). On the Government of Disability: Foucault, Power and the Subject of Impairment. In L. J. Davis (Ed.), *The Disability Studies Reader* (2nd ed., pp. 185–197). New York/Abingdon: Taylor and Francis Group.

Tremain, S. (2015). *Foucault and the Government of Disability* (2nd ed.). Ann Arbor: University of Michigan Press.

Uhl-Bien, M., Marion, R., & McKelvey, B. (2007). Complexity Leadership Theory: Shifting Leadership from the Industrial Age to the Knowledge Era. *The Leadership Quarterly, 18*, 298–318.

Weil, S. (1997). Rhetorics and Realities in Public Service Organisations: Systemic Practice and Organisational as Critically Reflexive Action Research (CRAR). *Systemic Practice and Action Research, 11*(1), 37–61.

Tillie Curran Senior Lecturer in social work at the University of the West of England (UWE), has developed her approach to disabled children's childhood studies from The Children Act 1989 which brought disabled children into 'children's' legislation for the first time and required that their wishes were heard. Disabled young people and their allies lead on changing policy, practice and public understanding and Tillie is interested in how practitioners can respond, support and make those changes happen.

Ruth Sayers is an expert by experience of using psychiatric services and is involved in user-focused research and professional education. She is interested in how students can best learn about these ways of working—probably by experiencing such processes for themselves, and how academics also share in and support this.

Barry Percy-Smith is Professor of Childhood and Participatory Practice and Director of the Centre for Applied Childhood Youth and Family Research at the University of Huddersfield, UK. He has extensive experience of research with children and childhood professionals. His main interests are in children's participation and participatory learning and change in children's services.

Being a Speech and Language Therapist: Between Support and Oppression

Anat Greenstein

Key Points

- Speech and language therapy can support disabled children and their families in developing better communication.
- Sometimes the process of diagnosis focuses on deficits and difficulties and may lead to people feeling disempowered.
- Speech and language therapy sometimes focuses on getting disabled children to satisfy developmental norms instead of looking at what the children themselves want to achieve.
- This chapter explores why these things happen and how therapy can be made more supportive and less oppressive.

Introduction

This chapter is a reflection upon my past practice as a speech and language therapist in Israel/Palestine. From a very young age, I have always wanted to change the world and make it a better place. In my youth that commitment had translated into political activism in anti-occupation, anti-militarist and feminist movements. In 1998, when I had to decide on a career path, becoming a speech and language therapist seemed like a good option for having a

A. Greenstein (✉)
Manchester Metropolitan University, Manchester, UK

© The Author(s) 2018
K. Runswick-Cole et al. (eds.), *The Palgrave Handbook of Disabled Children's Childhood Studies*, https://doi.org/10.1057/978-1-137-54446-9_32

523

'practical' profession, while still making the world a better place and supporting people to live a full life. Yet as I started practicing, I began to realise that the professional interventions I had to offer, while often supporting disabled children to participate in social, educational and familial situations, were doing so by making children fit better the rules and norms of oppressive social systems (such as, for example, the expectations that children will automatically obey teachers without hesitation, or that they will always maintain eye contact during communication (see Greenstein 2015)). For eight years, I moved between different provisions in health and education, looking for a place where I can use my professional practice without taking part in oppressing my clients. One day, while searching on the internet, I encountered the social model of disability (Oliver 1990), which explores how social structures and environments enable certain people to participate while disabling others. This was an 'ah-ha' moment that (within a couple of years) resulted in moving to the UK to research and teach in the field of disability studies.

Reading some of the literature and theories in disability studies (e.g. Davis 1995; Goodley 2011) and critical psychology (e.g. Burman 2008) has enabled me to phrase in words some of the difficulties and dilemmas I experienced during my practice. It is these dilemmas that I refer to in the subtitle of this chapter as situated 'between support and oppression'. The chapter will focus on some of the ideas behind different therapeutic approaches, specifically exploring the kinds of positions these approaches construct for children and for therapists. Other important issues, such as the role of families, schools, social institutions and services, as well as the ways disability is understood within the specific context of the settler colonial state of Israel, are beyond the scope of this work.

The Cognitivist Approach

The basic approach to speech and language therapy is rooted in the models of cognitive psychology. In my first year as a student of speech and language therapy, every introductory lecture opened with a slide presenting what is known as 'the speech chain' (Dense and Pinson 1993) which is supposed to represent the full context of a 'communication event' (ibid). The speech chain diagram shows a 'speaker', illustrated as a brain, a mouth and an ear floating in space; and a 'listener', only comprised of a single ear and a brain. Arrows and squiggly lines are drawn between these disembodied organs to represent nerves, muscles and sound waves. Communication, it was explained to us, first-year students, is seen as a natural and direct connection between two individual minds or subjects, taking place through a series of translations where meanings are transformed by the brain into words (the linguistics level), articulated through movements of the tongue, the mouth and the vocal cords (the physiological level) which create sound waves (the acoustic level), which are transmitted through the ear to be translated back into words and meanings in the brain of the listener. While some cognitive theories of communication do consider other issues and questions—about the dependence of communication on a shared social system and a context, or about how metaphors and humour are understood—these questions are relegated to a marginal position while the possibility of direct transmission is given priority. This understanding of language, as a transparent and neutral 'vehicle' of meanings that exists objectively and independently, necessitates a notion of the subject (and its object) as pre-existing and unproduced by their social context and location (Easthope 1990).

People, according to this model, are understood as the sum of many discrete rational processes of thought, each of which can be subjected to scientific study, analysis and treatment. The 'normal' person is conceived as a hyper-reasoned, conscious and reasonable individual, against which all individuals are universally ranked and judged. It is an offspring of the modernist Cartesian distinction between body and mind—reflected in the image of the speaker and listener as lacking a body, comprised of brain, mouth and ear only—and the distinction between inner world and external 'reality' (Goodley 2011). According to this approach, the main focus of speech and language therapy should be therefore on those intrinsic individual components rather than on any external factors. Further, cognitivism and its epistemological ally positivism enliven cognition but rarely touch on feelings and often render anonymous the very people it studies (Turner 2008, pp. 232–233 cited in Goodley 2011). As students of speech and language therapy, we were taught about emotions and emotional aspects of behaviour, but that was not because emotions were valued as a major part of what it means to be human. We studied about emotions and their role so that we could manipulate them—by pacifying 'negative emotions' which may impede learning, and by finding effective ways to 'lure' children into therapy and training.

I must admit, I was fascinated by the 'discoveries' of this scientific discourse, growing evermore hidden and complex—it was not just performance that could be trained, measured and ranked (mostly for accuracy, rarely for creativity), but also 'speed of processing', with fractures of seconds separating 'normal' from 'impaired'. I was particularly drawn to the 'little surprises' of science, like the story of poor H.M., a young man who after having brain surgery could not remember any new events, people or facts, but could learn new skills through practice; or the surprising ways in which a few rules of grammar are used to produce infinite number of sentences and meanings. It was only when I started practicing that I realised the oppressive and restrictive effects this scientific discourse has on its subjects—both clients and professionals.

At many times, I enjoyed being a speech and language therapist. I enjoyed drawing on my knowledge of language and cognitive psychology to interact better with my clients and to support their learning. I did that by using my knowledge of grammar to simplify my speech, and advising families and teachers about simplifying their speech; by using drawings and pictures to support memory and communication, and so on. What I found interesting, enjoyable and helpful in my practice was finding out the specific and unique ways in which a child communicates. But that was contradictory to the cognitivist and positivist model my discipline was based upon. Under this model, my individual clients were to be understood through their specific sum of skills and processes—phonological awareness, vocabulary, short-term memory span, and so on. Each of these skills was first examined on a large number of individuals, under strictly imposed conditions, measured and averaged, until it 'transcended' the state of an indexical, specific and personal occurrence and morphed completely into an 'objective truth', 'objective' meaning that it is not true of anyone in particular and hence true (or desirable) of everyone in general.

The process of diagnosing speech and language difficulties involves administrating a set of standardised test questions, under highly formalised conditions (e.g. many tests include specific instructions regarding how many times a question can be repeated or what forms of support and clues can be provided), followed by calculating the scores of the child against the population's norm and standard deviation (one of my favourite expressions—even deviancies are standardised), what Davis (1995) calls a statistical model of normalcy. Supporting a child by, say, repeating the question is considered to invalidate the diagnosis, as it provides a kind of support that cannot be calculated in advance and compared across the population. Although identifying effective ways to support a child's communication may be much more beneficial to the therapeutic process than arriving at a numerical score, the professional discourse of diagnosis defines ability as residing within a unitary, bounded individual (Venn 1984), manifesting itself in independent and unaided performance. Regardless of its stigmatising potential, speech and language diagnosis is pathologising because it assumes a view of individual rather than distributed competence (Booth and Booth 1990), independence rather than interdependence (Kittay et al. 2005).

The standardisation of skills and its use in the process of differential diagnosis gives speech and language therapists a finite repertoire of standard practices that are applicable to a limited set of contingencies or perceived client needs. As such, the practice can be described as a form of 'pigeonholing', a process in which the therapist matches a presumed client need to one of the standard practices in her repertoire (Skrtic 1995). An incident in an after-school service for students with reading difficulties, where I worked, clearly demonstrates this. As part of a reform to improve services, each professional team (speech and language therapists, occupational therapist and special needs teachers) was asked to prepare a list of possible therapeutic goals, which would then be used to plan individual therapy by selecting the appropriate goals for each student. This was said to increase the service's efficiency by constructing therapy around a set of clearly defined and **measurable** goals. This would allow closer monitoring of students' progress and faster referral to 'better-suited services' (e.g. special classes or special schools) if progress is too slow or insignificant. Table 1 shows a one-page segment of this five-page document prepared by the speech and language therapy team at that service (translated from Hebrew by the author).

Continuous measurement of performance, judging and ranking the potential of individuals, and allocating them to different spaces according to test

Table 1 An excerpt from the SLT goals document

Level of proficiency	Vocabulary
1 2 3 4 5	Expressive vocabulary
1 2 3 4 5	Comprehension voc.
1 2 3 4 5	Categories
1 2 3 4 5	Conjunctives
1 2 3 4 5	Prepositions
1 2 3 4 5	Adjectives and adverbs
1 2 3 4 5	Time concepts
1 2 3 4 5	Spatial concepts
1 2 3 4 5	Emotions
1 2 3 4 5	Distinguishing registers
1 2 3 4 5	Naming strategies

results, all evident in this initiative, are described by Foucault (1977) as the main mechanisms by which disciplinary power constitutes and constrains individual subjects. I have only come to this understanding several years later, and therefore could not express such concerns at the time. I did, however, oppose this initiative in team meetings, if to no avail, for what I perceived as distorted relationships between theory and practice. Under this initiative we were not expected to first meet clients, getting to know their needs and aspirations, their interests and activities, their strengths and difficulties, the barriers they face and their sources of support, and only then draw on theory and professional knowledge to support their communication and learning. Instead we were asked to start with the theory, use it to define a priori a possible set of problems and solutions, and then view our clients only through those 'theoretic slots', rendering any other aspect of their lives irrelevant. Defining therapeutic goals a priori means viewing disabled children in terms of deficit—in vocabulary, in grammar or narration. Goals such as supporting a student's understanding by speaking slowly to them and teaching them or their families to ask others to speak slowly, or providing a student with a whiteboard to draw on when they forget a word, are impossible to chart in advance, but may be much more helpful than trying to speed a child's 'rate of processing'.

Play-based Approach

After a couple of years of practice I joined a child development centre, and started working with very young children (my youngest client was 14 months old when we began therapy). It was there that I encountered child-centred and play-based approaches to developing speech and language therapy, such as Greenspan's Developmental, Individual-Difference, Relationship-Based model (DIR®) and Floor-Time (Wieder and Greenspan 2003). Unlike cognitivist approaches, these approaches highlight the importance of interactions between child and caregivers. They consider internal states of the child and encourage caregivers to identify the child's preferences and follow them, aiming at mutual enjoyment. The DIR method is based on spontaneous Floor-Time sessions, during which the therapist (and caregivers) are encouraged to follow the child's free play 'utilizing affectively toned interactions through gestures and words to move the child up the symbolic ladder' (Wieder and Greenspan 2003, p. 425).

This focus on play felt like a breath of fresh air compared to the highly standardised and quantifiable approach of cognitivism. I remember the wonderful feeling I had when I entered the centre for the first time. Closets packed with toys—building blocks, dolls' houses and furniture, balls, cars, farm animals, kitchen equipment, and so on. I'm going to play with all that and get paid for it?! I felt like a child walking into a huge toy shop being told she can have anything she wants. Promoting free play, mutual enjoinment and following the child's own interest carried with it greater respect to children's choices and curiosity, drawing on naturally occurring situations rather than on regimented tasks. The centrality of play to child development echoes psychoanalytic understandings of the role of play and 'potential space' (Winnicott 1971) in the development of the 'self'.

Winnicott (1971) critiqued classical psychoanalysis' focus on the inner world and its relationship with the outer reality, and claimed that the subjective experience is created through a third space, which he called the potential space, in which the distinction between inner and outer worlds is blurred, such as in instances of play, fantasy and creativity. For example, consider a child playing swords with his mother (see Burman (2008) for a critical discussion of how mothers are positioned through developmental psychology discourses) and triumphantly declaring 'I killed you!' to which the mother responds by playing dead. This experience does not take place under the rules of 'outer reality'—the mother is not dead and the child knows that. More than that, knowing that the mother won't really die is crucial for enjoying the situation. But the experience is also not located within the inner world of the child—if the mother hadn't responded to the child by playing dead, but would have instead said 'no, you didn't' or 'killing is bad!'—it would have been a whole different experience. While Winnicott locates the roots of this potential space in the merger of baby and mother to an inseparable dyad, play works to incorporate the potential space into the child's individual subjectivity as part of the process of 'normal' or 'healthy' development.

The goal of such 'healthy' development is to create a self that can successfully incorporate the inner and outer reality. This is not simply achieved by satisfying the rules of external reality, but by using them in new and creative ways, filling them with the emerging content of the inner world (Amir 2008; Bion 1966). You are 'normal' as long as you successfully balance between the emergent and the continuous dimensions of the self. The emergent self includes those dimensions of experience that are unique, constantly changing and impossible to chart or pin down along lines of past-present-future, cause and effect. The continuous self includes those dimensions of experience that are similar, predictable and understandable through knowledge of causality in continuous space and time (Amir 2008).

This vision of filling dreary rules with emergent meanings is indeed highly compelling. Yet, during the course of therapy only certain meanings were accorded value. In the child development centre, speech and language therapists were examining children's play, ranking it and trying to push it to 'the next level', under the assumption that some forms of play are better than others. If a child chose to play with cars, we were to follow her lead and play with the car. But playing by spinning the wheels of the car or sorting the cars by colour was deemed 'autistic' play, and we were to change it to 'symbolic' play such as moving the car around while making motor sounds. The implicit logic of this 'therapy' is such, in play the child manifests his inner representations of the world; by changing play behaviour, we can change those inner representations, making them more 'normal'. Understanding a small and motorless piece of plastic as 'a car' and therefore playing by moving it around is valued as symbolic ability. Understanding it as 'yellow' is undervalued and must be changed. It is interesting to note here that organising things by colour does not always seem pathological to development professionals. As part of the developmental evaluation that children attending the centre must undertake, it was common to ask them to complete a colour-sorting puzzle (see Fig. 1). Thus, in one context organising objects by colour is perceived as an important developmental milestone, while in other contexts it is seen as a sign of pathology.

Play therapies such as DIR, while using play as a route to the inner world of the child, do not simply seek opportunities for connection and mutual understanding. Instead they aspire to use play as a potent tool for normalisation, potent in that it carries the promise to normalise not only overt behaviour but also the child's very subjectivity and inner world (Shelly and Golubock 2007).

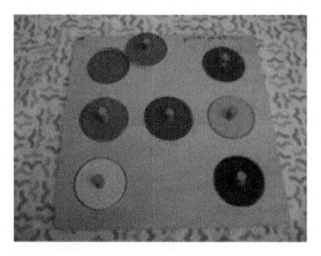

Fig. 1 Colour-sorting puzzle used for developmental evaluation

Similarly, Goodley and Runswick-Cole (2010) have argued for the need to emancipate disabled children's play, understanding play as valuable in its own right rather than as an area of deficit or a therapeutic tool.

Focusing on the Interaction

Growing increasingly frustrated with the normalising, and what seemed to me even manipulative, aspects of play-based approaches, I started moving away from trying to create meaningful interactions with children as a tool for achieving developmental milestones. These practices, while according value to interactions and mutual enjoyment, still focus on *individuals* in interaction. Interactions are seen as created through two (or more) bounded selves, with their private interests, needs, motivations and deficits. Instead, I began to understand my professional role as engaging with clients to create meaningful interactions for their own sake and value.

Using my current theoretical knowledge, I can map this focus on interaction to Deleuze and Guattari's (1980) metaphor of the rhizome rather than trees to describe human societies. This metaphor comes from biology in which rhizomes are horizontal forms of plants that send out roots and shoots from their different nodes. If a rhizome is cut into pieces, each piece will be able to give rise to a new rhizomatic plant. Deleuze and Guattari use this metaphor to explore the human life. Unlike Freudian psychoanalytic models that focus on the task of an individual to become separate from others and sees desire as a consequence of some lack the individual experiences, Deleuze and Guattari understand humans as rhizomes—that is, not discrete and separate individuals but involved in a contestant process of becoming through connection and separation. This shifts the focus of development from a journey to build an individual, separate and self-sufficient self, to a model focusing on linkage and proximity. In this model, desire is the energy that drives the constant process of becoming, thus understood as productive and ever present, rather than oriented at fulfilling a certain lack. In this model, people do not exist in the world as separate entities, but are in continuous and shifting relationships with the physical environment and with others in it. We exist beyond the boundaries of our skin, merging with other part subjects, part objects. Becoming a rhizome can be exemplified by the deep pain and anger one might feel when seeing a helpless dog being beaten with a stick, forcing her body to act against her better judgement and challenge the bully. It is the deep emotion one might feel when listening to a favourite piece of music that takes hold of the body and mind. It is the different roles we play in different relationships, or in different instances of the same relationship that allows desire to flow between people, animals and objects; that allows for new things to be produced in different forms and competences.

Several writers have pointed to the profound implications of a rhizomatic model of existence on our understanding of, and responses to disability and impairment (e.g. Goodley 2007; Overboe 2009; Shildrick and Price 2006; Slater 2012). These researchers seek to problematise notions of the conscience, bounded agentic self who has full control over body and mind. They offer instead a world of rhizomes, sites for connectivity and linkage:

> *In a model in which corporeality is no longer to be thought in terms of given and integral entities, but only as engaged in ever dynamic and innovatory linkages, bodies are neither whole nor broken, disabled nor able-bodied, but simply in a process of becoming. [...]It is not the agency of a self embodied in a complete and integrated organic unity that is the driving force, but the flows of energy that bring together part objects – both living material and mechanic – to create surprising new assemblages.* (Shildrick and Price 2006, np.)

Interaction, then, is a surprising new assemblage, that does not have to be guided towards some linear trajectory of development or conform to fixed roles and identities of 'professional' and 'client'. This approach has enabled me to try and interact with clients, enjoying the interaction and following its surprising paths, without necessarily trying to harness it towards specific linguistic goals. This meant that I engaged with children in conversations about different subjects and experiences, often willing to give up on an opportunity to expand a child's vocabulary or linguistic structures if I felt it was impeding the flow of the interaction. When a school child came to our meeting upset and said she and her classmates were unfairly punished, we spent the session writing a letter to the teacher explaining her arguments. When a boy was heartbroken by the loss of his cat, we showed each other picture of our pets and shared our mutual love for them.

It was liberating and fairly easy to do so with children who were happy to share their experiences or initiate certain games, even if they relied on my linguistic support or used non-verbal communication. It was clear to see how our joint abilities and interests merged together to create these surprising new assemblages filled with enjoyment and meaning. These interactions were not just tools to expand the children's skills and improve future social participation, but were, in themselves, valued moments of social participation and connection. Yet those children can still be seen to fit what Masschelein and Simons (2005) call the entrepreneurial self. Under neo-liberal discourse,

Masschelein and Simons explain, the developmental goal has shifted from achieving independence to creating individuals who use entrepreneurial behaviours to satisfy their needs, be it by acting 'independently' or by facilitating others. This discourse is not only about an active and ongoing creation of conditions and control of entrepreneurial behaviour, but it also ensures that everyone is willing to establish an entrepreneurial relation to the self, is willing to invest in one's own life, willing to offer their social or material capital, willing to profit from their competencies and knowledge and willing to invest in learning, health and security.

But there was one child that utterly confused me. To my usual approach of being unstructured and waiting for the child to initiate (I referred to it as using 'natural' interactions, but are they really so natural?), he reacted with frustration, refusal and anger. It was only when I used highly structured tasks that he was happy to participate and seemed to draw a sense of satisfaction and fulfilment from our interactions. For a whole year we were playing the same board game (snakes and ladders) to which I've added different mechanical linguistic tasks, such as counting the sounds in a word or making a sentence with a specific number of words. At the beginning of every meeting, I had asked him to choose between snakes and ladders and another game. For the first eight months, he always chose snakes and ladders. After that he started choosing other games in one out of every four or five meetings, but has always asked to return to snakes and ladders at the following meeting, and sometimes even during the course of the same meeting.

I was baffled, even shaken. On the one hand, the 'interactionist' in me was happy. We were both enjoying the interaction that, though constituted around the same game with the same outcome (his victory and my defeat, through a little twist in the rules), seemed to offer a site for many new and surprising events. As Grosz interpreting Deleuze says: 'repetition is never the generation of the same but the motor of the new' (1999, p. 5). I was happy about those repetitions; felt that they were empowering and enabling, an area of strength to build upon. But on the other hand, the little speech and language therapist in my head kept whispering, 'This need for repetition is not **normal.** It's a sign of **pathology**, of learning disability'. I was always pleased when he chose a different game, always slightly disappointed when he came back to the snakes and ladders. At the same time that I saw the repetition as a strength, as a driving power in our interactions, I was also secretly hoping that he would 'outgrow' the need for repetition, as if playing different board games was somehow superior to playing the same one.

I was also unsure about the linguistic tasks that I set. I have moved a long way from this isolated structured notion of speech and language therapy, and there I was practicing it again. What was I doing? Indeed we had a few discussions about game strategies, a small conversation here and there, but they were rare, most of the speech in the room was generated through those tasks. It seemed that without such structured tasks we would spend most of our time in silence. Is there room for silent speech and language therapy or is this just a waste of time and money?

Conclusion

I explored in this chapter different approach to the role of professional knowledge in speech and language therapy and how this works to construct certain subject positions for (dis)abled children and for the therapists who work with them. These positions, I argue, constantly shift between offering support and reifying oppression. I certainly recognise that professional knowledge can be used to improve the life experiences of disabled children in several ways. First, the 'specialised' cognitivist knowledge acquired through speech and language therapy training can often be drawn upon to analyse a child's linguistic needs and abilities, the areas they are struggling with and the effective strategies to support them. This can increase opportunities for communication both by building the child's skills and by changing the environment to a more linguistically accessible one. Yet it is important to note here that using cognitivist or developmental knowledge in ways that support access rather than underscore deficit, goes against the basic epistemological assumptions that produce such knowledge. Instead of seeking an 'objective' diagnosis that compares performance to average population norms, we should look for the particular ways children make meaning of the world and what strategies can be used to support them. Therapists should be looking at what children can do when most supported, and draw on professional knowledge to analyse how such support works and how it can be implemented in other contexts rather than seeking to capture their unaided abilities and point to areas of deficit.

Second, the experiential knowledge gained through numerous interactions with children with a diversity of communication styles, needs and preferences is an important professional tool speech and language therapists can and do draw upon to facilitate meaningful interactions. I have argued that such interactions should be valued in their own right rather than merely as an opportunity to get children up an assumed developmental ladder. Understanding interactions as rhizomatic sites, areas where meaning is created through linkage and separation can help move away from deficit models and allow for surprising and new assemblages and encounters. Yet a model that stresses blurring boundaries and roles can raise anxieties (and some very real questions!) about professional knowledge and roles. When a child is 'entrepreneurial' enough to identify areas that are of interest to them, it is possible to draw on experiential knowledge of interaction and theoretical knowledge of language and cognition to follow a child's lead, supporting them in setting and achieving their goals. But when a child resists those entrepreneurial conventions, when they are not willing or able to readily identify their own needs or interests, to communicate and share their experiences, is there a place for a *professional* (read paid) interaction with a speech and language therapist?

Bibliography

Amir, D. (2008). *On the Lyricism of the Mind.* Jerusalem: Magnes Press.

Bion, W. R. (1966). Catastrophic Change. *Scientific Bulletin of the British Psychoanalytical Society, 5,* 12–24.

Booth, T., & Booth, W. (1990). Making Connections: A Narrative Study of Adult Children of Parents with Learning Difficulties, *8.*

Burman, E. (2008). *Deconstructing Developmental Psychology* (2nd ed.). l: Routledge.

Davis, L. J. (1995). *Enforcing Normalcy: Disability, Deafness and the Body.* New York: Verso.

Deleuze, G., & Guattari, F. (1980). *A Thousand Plateaus.* London: Continuum.

Dense, P. B., & Pinson, E. N. (1993). *The Speech Chain: Physics and Biology of Spoken Language* (2nd ed.). New York: Freeman.

Easthope, A. (1990). "I Got to Use Words When I Talk to You": Deconstructing the Theory of Communication. In I. Parker & J. Shotter (Eds.), *Deconstructing Social Psychology* (pp. 76–87). London: Routledge.

Foucault, M. (1977). *Discipline and Punish: Birth of the Prison.* London: Penguin Books.

Goodley, D. (2007). Towards Socially Just Pedagogies: Deleuzoguattarian Critical Disability Studies. *International Journal of Inclusive Education, 11*(3), 317–334. doi:10.1080/13603110701238769.

Goodley, D. (2011). *Disability Studies: An Interdisciplinary Introduction.* London: Sage.

Goodley, D., & Runswick-Cole, K. (2010). Emancipating Play: Dis/Abled Children, Development and Deconstruction. *Disability & Society, 25*(4), 499–512. doi:10.1080/09687591003755914.

Greenstein, A. (2015). *Radical Inclusive Education: Disability, Teaching, and Struggles for Liberation.* London: Routledge.

Grosz, E. (1999). An Introduction. In E. Grosz (Ed.), *Becomings: Explorations on Time, Memory and Futures* (pp. 1–11). Ithaca: Cornell University Press.

Kittay, E. F., Jennings, B., & Wasunna, A. (2005). Dependency, Difference and the Global Ethic of Longterm Care*. *Journal of Political Philosophy, 13*(4), 443–469. doi:10.1111/j.1467-9760.2005.00232.x.

Masschelein, J., & Simons, M. (2005). The Strategy of the Inclusive Education Apparatus. *Studies in Philosophy and Education, 24*(2), 117–138. doi:10.1007/s11217-004-6527-4.

Oliver, M. (1990). *The Individual and Social Models of Disability.* Paper Presented at Joint Workshop of the Living Options Group and the Research Unit of the Royal College of Physicians. Retrieved December 10, 2009, from http://www.leeds.ac.uk/disability-studies/archiveuk/Oliver/in soc dis.pdf

Overboe, J. (2009). Affirming an Impersonal Life : A Different Register for Disability Studies. *Journal of Literary and Cultural Disability Studies, 3*(3), 241–256. doi:10.3828/jlcds.2009.3.

Shelly, S., & Golubock, S. (2007). If Not a Cure, Then What? Parenting Autistic Children. In *Autreat Conference* (pp. 1–20). Retrieved from http://www.solashelly.org/IfNotaCure.pdf

Shildrick, M., & Price, J. (2006). Deleuzian Connections and Queer Corporealities: Shrinking Global Disability. *Rhizomes, 11/12.* Retrieved from http://www.rhizomes.net/issue11/shildrickprice/index.html

Skrtic, T. M. (1995). *Disability and Democracy: Reconstructing (Special) Education for Postmodernity.* New York: Teachers College Press.

Slater, J. (2012). Self-Advocacy and Socially Just Pedagogy. *Disability Studies Quarterly, 32*(1). Retrieved from http://dsq-sds.org/article/view/3033/3061

Turner, B. (2008). *The Body and Society* (3rd ed.). London: Sage.

Venn, C. (1984). The Subject of Psychology. In J. Henriques, W. Hollway, C. Urwin, C. Venn, & W. Walkerdine (Eds.), *Changing the Subject: Psychology, Social Regulation and Subjectivity* (pp. 115–147). London: Methuen.

Wieder, S., & Greenspan, S. I. (2003). Climbing the Symbolic Ladder in the DIR Model Through Floor Time/Interactive Play. *Autism, 7*(4), 425–435. doi:10.1007/s13398-014-0173-7.2.

Winnicott, D. W. (1971). *Playing and Reality.* London: Tavistock Publications.

Anat Greenstein is a Senior Lecturer in Inclusive Education and Disability Studies at Manchester Metropolitan University. Her main research interests include using creative methods to work in partnership with disabled children and adults, exploring processes of oppression and marginalisation and searching for more inclusive and libratory society.

"You Say… I Hear…": Epistemic Gaps in Practitioner-Parent/Carer Talk

Nick Hodge and Katherine Runswick-Cole

Key Points

- Policy guidance has often focused on the need for strong partnerships between parents/carers and practitioners to support the learning of children labelled with Special Educational Needs and/or Disabilities (SEND).
- Despite this policy focus, relationships between parents/carers and practitioners are often difficult.
- This chapter explores the nature of these difficulties drawing on the work of Lipsky (1971) and McKenzie and Scully (2007).
- In conclusion, there are suggestions for how partnership working between parents/carers, practitioners and children might be developed.

Introduction

The past two decades have seen a focus in educational policy in England on the development of more effective practitioner-parent relationships (Department for Education and Skills (DfES) 2001, 2004). Yet, parents continue to report feeling marginalised and excluded within these relationships (Hodge and

N. Hodge (✉)
Sheffield Hallam University, Sheffield, UK

K. Runswick-Cole
The School of Education, The University of Sheffield, Sheffield, UK

© The Author(s) 2018
K. Runswick-Cole et al. (eds.), *The Palgrave Handbook of Disabled Children's Childhood Studies*, https://doi.org/10.1057/978-1-137-54446-9_33

Runswick-Cole 2008). Clearly, different ways of thinking about, understanding and engaging within these relationships are required if practitioner-parent partnership is to become more than just policy rhetoric. In this chapter, we draw on the theoretical and philosophical concepts of "epistemic gaps" (MacKenzie and Scully 2007) , shared biographical standpoints (Ashworth 2016) and street-level bureaucracy (Lipsky 1971) to expose and to explore some of the problematic communications that arise between parents and practitioners in their talk in the context of the SEND system. The focus of this chapter is on partnership within education and related services. Practitioner therefore refers to all those employed to offer educational and related health and care services to disabled children and young people and their families. In brief, we propose that epistemic gaps arise when each of the parties in a communication exchange has significantly different life experiences from each other; they do not share the same biographical standpoint. We explore the nature and impact of these epistemic gaps on parents and their children in more detail below before then positioning them within the wider systemic context. We suggest that a discussion of how epistemic gaps emerge within practitioner-parent communication is timely, given the changing policy context for SEND following the passage of the Children and Families Act 2014 (DfE 2014) through the British Parliament. The Children and Families Act (2014) brought in fundamental changes to provision for children and young people with SEND in England. Parts of the Act also apply to Scotland, Wales and Northern Ireland. Drawing on a discourse analysis approach, we examine practitioner-parent talk to reveal the gaps between the epistemic positions of practitioners and parents. We then identify some of the systemic barriers that create and maintain epistemic chasms. Our discussion concludes with a consideration of how MacKenzie's and Scully's (2007) concept of "sympathetic moral imagination" might be a useful tool for enabling more informed and shared understandings of biographical standpoints between practitioner and parent. Knowledge and appreciation of these different standpoints might then act as bridges over epistemic chasms that allow practitioner-parent partnerships to flourish.

The Current Policy Context in England: Practitioner-Parent Partnership

The new "Special Educational Needs and Disability Code of Practice: 0 to 25 years" has been recently published (DfE 2014). The SEND Code of Practice sets out the services that education and health services in England must provide for disabled children and those with special educational needs, 0–25 years, and their parents/carers. This Code is a revision of the "Code of

Practice on the Identification and Assessment of Special Educational Needs" (DfES 2001) and responds to a raft of changes in provision for children with SEND and their families set out in the Children and Families Act 2014 (DfE 2014). A key area of focus in the original "Code of Practice" (DfES 2001) was practitioner-parent partnership. The new Code (DfE 2014: 14) has taken up this theme and claims to offer "a clearer focus on the participation of children and young people and parents in decision-making at individual and strategic levels". It reaffirms that local authorities must have regard to "the views, wishes and feelings of the child or young person, and the child's parents" (DfE 2014: 19) and that they must support the participation of parents and children in decision-making (DfE 2014). Local authorities in England are the councils that provide services for local areas.

Local authorities are required to support the child or young person and their parents to achieve the best educational and other outcomes, "preparing [children] effectively for adulthood" (DfE 2014: 19). The Code is a reiteration of the policy discourse advocating practitioner-parent partnership that has characterised special education policy in England over the last 30 years (DES 1978). Following the changes in the Children and Families Act 2014 (DfE 2014), local authorities are now required to include, "fully" children with SEND and their parents in the process of developing education, health and care plans. Education, health and care plans detail the provision that a child or young person will receive across these three services. These set out the provision needed to support the child and replaced the previous system of statements of special educational needs. Furthermore, local authorities are required to consult parents on changes to provision for the child. The Code describes parents' views as "important" (DfE 2014: 21) and states that education providers should ensure that they "give them [parents] confidence that their views and contributions are valued and will be acted upon" (DfE 2014: 21). However, this continued emphasis on the need for parents' views to be taken seriously in the SEND process is balanced by a focus on the requirement to prioritise the views of the child. Indeed, in the Code, when a child reaches 16, there is a significant change in how parents are positioned, as the focus shifts to making the views of young people a priority:

> The Children and Families Act 2014 gives significant new rights directly to young people once they reach the end of compulsory school age (the end of the academic year in which they turn 16). **When a young person reaches the end of compulsory school age, local authorities and other agencies should normally engage directly with the young person rather than their parent**, ensuring that as part of the planning process they identify the relevant people who should be involved and how to involve them. (DfE 2014: 21) (**our emphasis**)

While the Code maintains the view that families will continue to play a "critical role" (DfE 2014: 21) and recognises that "[m]ost young people will continue to want, or need, their parents and other family members to remain involved in discussions and decisions about their future" (p. 21), it remains unclear, as yet, how these changes will impact on practitioner-parent relationships.

In our previous writing about practitioner-parent partnership, we have acknowledged the tensions in practitioner-parent relationships including disagreements between parents and practitioners about what constitutes "knowledge" about a child. Often practitioner knowledge of syndromes and impairment is privileged over a parent's expert knowledge of their child. Of course, tensions also occur in particular over the delivery of services and available budgets (Runswick-Cole 2007; Hodge and Runswick-Cole 2008). Parents and practitioners disagree about a host of things: diagnosis, intervention, support and school placements to name but a few (Hodge 2005; Runswick-Cole 2007; Hodge and Runswick-Cole 2008). The day-to-day reality of practitioner-parent partnership fails to live up to the policy rhetoric. The fact that a high number of parents continue to register appeals with the Special Educational Needs Tribunal (3600 in 2012/13 (MoJ 2013)) is evidence that conflict in the system remains. This conflict was acknowledged by the coalition government (The Government in England and Wales that was in power at the time of the development and passing of the Children and Families Act 2014 and other related legislation) in England and Wales and the publication of "Support and Aspiration: A New Approach to Special Educational Needs" (DfE 2011) and the passage of the subsequent Children and Families Act (DfE 2014) sought, in part, to address conflict within the system. Edward Timpson, the then minister for children, argued that the Act was intended to address what had become an entrenched and adversarial special educational needs system:

> For too long, families who face big enough challenges already have also found themselves facing – as one mother put it – "an unending battle" with a system that's supposed to be on their side. (Timpson 2014, np)

It can be seen therefore that even though the nature and experience of practitioner-parent partnership in education has been widely researched and discussed by policy makers, practitioners and parents still struggle to work in partnership. In the context of continued tensions and a changing policy landscape, practitioner-parent partnership remains an important area of inquiry for anyone interested in the lives of children, young people and families engaged in the SEND system. New understandings of what enables or disables these relationships are vital to developing more positive ways of working for everyone.

Epistemic Positioning

As authors of this chapter, we share an interest in and some of the same understandings of how disability impacts upon the lives of children "with SEND" and their families. This is reflected in some of our previous joint research and publications (Hodge and Runswick-Cole 2008, 2013; Runswick-Cole and Hodge 2009). We conceptualise SEND premised on sociological understandings of disability that locate the "problem" of disability in society, not in the individual child or family (Mallett and Runswick-Cole 2014). Moreover, we share an "epistemic position" (MacKenzie and Scully 2007) as researchers who locate our work in the fields of critical disability studies and special educational needs. We both hope that by supporting greater understanding between practitioners and parents, we can contribute to more enabling practices in special education. However, despite our shared positions, we have often found that our different life experiences can often lead us to interpret the experiences of parents, children and young people and practitioners very differently. Within social theory, the term "biographical standpoint" is used to capture how our own particular life experiences, including the cultural, social, political and personal, shape a unique understanding of the world (Ashworth 2016). Education research has illustrated how in schools, "issues of ethnicity, race and socio-economic class inform the shifting power play..." (Lumby 2007: 221). As white middle-class academics, we will have shared some privileged experiences of engagement with schools that are likely to be very different from those from other biographies and experiences of social economic power. But even within our own shared position, our individual characteristics and unique experiences mean that we arrive at disability and schools from both shared and distinct epistemic positions.

It is from our biographical standpoint, therefore, that we then interpret all that happens to us. Different biographical standpoints lead to different understandings of situations and interpretations of social exchanges. So for the authors our different biographical standpoints cause at times an epistemic gap to open up between us. Intersubjectivity is the term that is used to conceptualise shared understandings of being in the world between distinct subjects (Crossley 2005). The authors have a collective standpoint through our shared interest in disability and so respond similarly to some events. However, our distinct biographies, detailed in brief below, contain our individual and unique lived experience of disability. These sometimes then lead us to interpret exchanges between parents and practitioners quite differently.

Nick came to research as part of his practitioner development as a former teacher and as a lecturer. Katherine came to her research as a former early-years teacher but also as the mother of a disabled child, and she was simply "bloody furious" with a system that was letting her and her son down. These different positions and experiences mean that despite the many experiences and understandings we share, we often see things differently from one another. We are still sometimes surprised by each other's reactions to and interpretations of experiences. For example, Katherine shared a story with Nick of a parent who did not know any of the other parents at her son's primary school. This resulted from teaching assistants (TAs) asking the mother to stand in a different place from everyone else at home time so that she could be there to take immediate responsibility for her son as soon he left the classroom. Nick was amazed this could happen and while he exclaimed that: "You see, the teaching assistants just wouldn't know that the mother felt like that". Katherine felt that the TAs should have worked that out for themselves. Nick, however, wondered why the mother had not told them. Another example occurred recently, Nick remembered a mother telling him about a time when she had collected her son from his first day at secondary school. The young man started to show signs of agitation. "Oh", said the teacher to the mother, "he's been fine until now. He is just doing this because you are here". For the mother this was a devastating encounter. Already anxious about her son and how he had managed a new larger and busier school on his first day, the mother reported that the teacher's comment then made her feel as though she herself was a source of tension for her own son. A devastating thought for a parent. The mother was distressed and perplexed as to why a teacher might make such a hurtful comment to a parent. On hearing this account, Katherine agreed emphatically with the mother, the actions of the teacher made no sense to Katherine either. For Katherine, the teacher should have known the effect that such a comment would have on a parent. Nick, on the other hand, when told of this encounter by the mother, had felt an immediate sympathy with the teacher. Nick's own experience as a teacher informed *his* understanding of this encounter between the mother and the secondary school teacher. Nick remembered how worried he would sometimes feel as a teacher that a parent would think badly of his school if their child showed signs of distress when the parent came to collect their child. Nick may well have said these same words himself on occasion, thinking that they would offer reassurance to the parent. Knowing how this mother reacted to the words however then helped Nick to see that his own words might not always have been received as positively as he had intended. This incident illustrates our different epistemic positions but more crucially it demonstrates how practitioner-parent relationships can develop from "day one" into antagonistic polar lines of defence.

Despite our shared roles as researchers, our positions as "practitioner" and "parent" mean that we can struggle to know what it means to have lived the life of the other. We want to identify and understand better where, how and why the gaps in understanding and communication occur between practitioners and parents when in theory they should be on the same side and working together in the best interests of the child. We see this as essential because we know that children, young people, parents and practitioners can all fall down these gaps with damaging and sometimes devastating consequences for those involved (Runswick-Cole 2007).

We decided to explore these gaps through a focus on parent-practitioner talk. In doing so, we sought to explore what these micro-level interactions could reveal about the macro-nature of parent-practitioner relationships within the current policy context. We also wondered what some of the wider messages that society gives out about SEND might be revealed in such talk. In focusing on talk, we draw on a long tradition of discourse analysis (Parker 2002). Discourse analysis pays attention to what language, or discourse, *does*. Discourse analysts argue that language does not merely describe what is there: it also constructs it. The ways that things or people are described impact on how people perceive and think about them. In the context of the SEND system, we take the phrase "the special needs" to illustrate the point (Runswick-Cole and Hodge 2009). Gale (2000) quotes a parent who, within a research project in Australia, spoke of the experiences of her daughter whose personhood was taken from her the moment that she was categorised as "a 6", the highest level of disability on the Australian school assessment scale: "If your child is a 6 the teachers go into the next room and say, 'Okay, who is going to take this 'level 6?'" (p. 261). Similarly, we have identified in our own research that children are sometimes referred to as "the special needs" as, for example, in "we're taking the special needs to the supermarket tomorrow" (Runswick-Cole and Hodge 2009: 3). When this happens, it is not just a description of a category of children. Rather, the language used here constructs "the special needs" and defines the limits for what disabled children are allowed to be: they become non-children, different from and, implicitly, lesser than other (normal) children. In becoming "the special needs" these children are therefore denied their humanity. Where these discourses dominate, they also proliferate and are adopted by other members of the school community. So, for example, we have heard one pupil say to another: "is your brother a special need?" (Runswick-Cole and Hodge 2009: 3).

Crucially, for our analysis of parent-practitioner talk, discourse analysis suggests that the meanings of language change constantly, rather than having one meaning and being fixed (Burman and Parker 1993). We accept that the interpretations that we offer below are highly contested and that different accounts and analyses of the talk by readers with different epistemic positions arising from different biographical standpoints could be offered. However, the purpose of drawing from discourse analysis here is that it allows us to reflect on what people say and what this might reveal of the meanings within the detail of the talk and the nature of the wider society in which we live.

Illustrating the Problem

The following examples that we use to illustrate some of the problems within practitioner-parent talk come from our own experience or have been reported to us by participants within the different research projects that we have been involved with. We have heard a number of these examples in similar form from many different parents over the years. We are particularly interested in examples of talk where the practitioner was giving a message to a parent and in how that message was understood. An example of this from Katherine's own experience occurred when a social worker said, "I'm sorry I've not got back to you I've been really busy". Katherine, as a parent, heard this as: "Other families are more important than ours".

We have shared our analysis of these encounters at conferences with practitioners and parents. Conference delegates tell us that they recognise many of these examples from their own experiences. The practitioners who have made such statements to parents themselves have revealed that they had not anticipated that the comments might be received so differently from how they were intended. Although once reflected upon the potential for different understandings becomes apparent. The examples are presented below. We first report something that a practitioner has said to a parent and then we describe how that parent told us they had interpreted the statement.

You Say ... I Hear ....

You say...	I hear ...
Head teacher: Have you thought about going back to work?	**Parent:** She thinks I'm an over anxious mother with too much time on my hands.
Teaching Assistant: She was really tired when she came in this morning.	**Parent:** We never go out because of her difficulties with fatigue, we never do the things other families do, and just for once, when we do, you have a go at me! You're telling me off.
Doctor: What's your job?	**Parent:** What does it matter what my job is? You are judging me.
Occupational therapist: I didn't tell you about Disability Living Allowance: a welfare benefit for disabled children and adults because I knew your partner had a good job.	**Parent:** You shouldn't be claiming benefits.
Teacher: He has said he doesn't want to go to work for experience. You can overrule him at home but I can't, he's 17.	**Parent:** Adult services won't look after my child properly.
Teacher: His teaching assistant reads with him. I have 29 other children in the class to think about.	**Parent:** The teacher doesn't see my child as her responsibility.
Inclusion officer: You are not entitled to a Rolls Royce service. We have limited resources that we must allocate fairly.	**Parent:** You are a greedy, pushy and selfish parent.
Teacher: I know he's lashing out but that is what children with autism and epilepsy do.	**Parent:** You don't see my son, you don't recognise him as an individual.
Speech and language therapist: Your daughter is making really good progress.	**Parent:** Hey! She's still really struggling – oh no, they are about to discharge her!
Speech and language therapist: I'm sorry but your child doesn't meet the criteria for our service. There are some spaces on the anger management classes for parents.	**Parent:** You think I have a problem with anger and I can't parent my child.
Receptionist at LA offices: [Hands over phone so slightly muffled] It's Mrs Smith on the phone, are you in?	**Parent:** The whole office thinks I'm a problem.

Bridging the (Epistemic) Gap

The accounts above reveal the gaps between parents and practitioners in their everyday talk. They are uncomfortable, but they are, perhaps, familiar extracts. We suspect that readers may have their own examples of when these sticky moments have emerged in their talk with parents and/or practitioners.

What we are interested in here is how far is it possible to bridge these gaps in understanding between parents and practitioners? A discussion like this is one starting point. The recognition of a fracture in parent-practitioner partnerships and a desire to understand how and why this might occur open up the possibility of developing new understandings. Ashworth (2016) notes that within phenomenology, it is argued that people can achieve a "reciprocity of perspectives" (p. 26). This occurs when one party in communication adopts the mental perspective of another. Husserl (1931) identifies empathy as one route to doing so but neither Husserl nor Ashworth detail how exactly this might be achieved across significantly different lifeworlds. To offer one possible explanation for how this might occur, we have drawn on the work of two philosophers MacKenzie and Scully (2007). MacKenzie and Scully (2007) have explored what they describe as the epistemic gap between non-disabled people and disabled people in relation to quality-of-life issues. We use their ideas to explore parent-professional talk in the analysis below.

How Would *You* Feel?

A simple, common-sense response to all of the encounters above is to say that parents and professionals should ask themselves how they would feel if someone said that to them. So, for example, in the last of the examples above, we could ask the practitioner: "how would *you* feel if *you* rang up to ask for information and overheard someone checking whether the person who is supposed to help you wanted to or not?" Just simply imagine that *you* were in the *parent's* place. If *you* wouldn't like it then, chances are *they* wouldn't either. Implicit in this advice is that it is easy to imagine how another person might be feeling, simply do unto others as you would have them do unto you (MacKenzie and Scully 2007).

In this example, imagining how *you* would feel if *you* made the phone call seems straightforward and good advice, but it does not perhaps capture the full complexity of the encounter. *You* did not make the phone call, an(other) parent of a child with SEND did. To understand this phone call more fully, there needs to be what MacKenzie and Scully call (2007: 339) "perspective shifting". In other words, simply projecting your own experiences may not be enough for you to understand the parent's feelings about the phone call.

What is needed is for you to make "imaginative adjustments" (MacKenzie and Scully 2007: 339) in order to understand the encounter, not as if it happened to *you* but from the perspective of the parent caller; a failure to do this may mean that we simply put *ourselves* in the place of an *other,* rather than responding to the *other's* experience.

It could be suggested that what is needed is something more like what Peter Goldie (cited in MacKenzie and Scully 2007: 341) calls "in-your-shoes-imagining". This requires us to imagine, not that the event is happening to *us* but to someone else; we have to imagine that *we* are that person—as if *we* were that parent caller. But this, it turns out, is no simple task. As MacKenzie and Scully (2007) point out, our ability to do this depends on two factors: first, the pool of our own experiences we have to draw on. Our own experiences of making phone calls or asking for information will influence how we understand the parent's experiences. If we have never made a phone call asking for help or for information on behalf of a child, then this will be more difficult to imagine. Second, it will also depend on what we already know about that *particular* parent. From the account, we know very little, but we can *imagine* that she has phoned before, that she is known in the office and that she is someone that people find difficult to talk to and that the people in the office have stopped caring whether or not she knows this (though we do not know the reasons why).

Let us take another example from the encounters above: "she was really tired when she came in this morning". At face value, this is a simple statement of fact. We do not know if the TA in this story is a parent her (him) self who has struggled to get her own child to bed at night or to wake her up in the morning. The TA may feel that she is duty bound to tell the parent every aspect of the child's school experience—good or bad. The TA may not intend that the parent act on the information, only that she has it. We do not know from this conversation how well the TA knows the child and if she understands what the parent describes as "fatigue issues", and the TA probably does not know that this was the first night out the family had been on for ages. It seems that the TA is not engaging in "in-your-shoes-imagining". But as we have already noted, depending on your own knowledge and experiences, this is a difficult thing to do.

In her doctoral study, Broomhead (2013) looked at the judgement teachers and TAs made about whether children could control their behaviour, and she asked how these judgements were influenced by the label or diagnosis a child had been given. She found that children labelled with Behavioural, Emotional and Social Difficulties (BESD) were more likely to be thought as those able to control their behaviour than children labelled with autism, for example, who, because of people's understandings of autism, were thought to be unable to control their behaviour. As part of the study, one of the parents of a child with the label of BESD worked with trainee teachers to describe her life as the mother of a child with BESD. She talked about what life was like outside of school for her and her child. Following the session, one of the student teachers remarked that she had never really thought about what happened to children before or after school. This lack of "in-your-shoes-imagining" is a striking example of the epistemic gap between parents and practitioners and between practitioners and pupils. And yet, as MacKenzie and Scully (2007) suggest, the dangers of "in-your-shoes imagining", in this situation, are that we simply project our own experiences and prejudices onto the situation: "if I had a child with fatigue, I'd get a baby sitter, if I wanted to go out late…" So something more is required than "in-your-shoes imagining" if reciprocity of perspective is to be achieved. Mackenzie and Scully (2007) suggest that this might be Sympathetic Moral Imagination.

Sympathetic Moral Imagination

> In sympathetic moral imagination one does not try to imagine being the other from the inside. Rather, one recognises that the other is different from oneself, one imaginatively engages with her perceptions and experiences, as she represents them, and one responds emotionally to her perspective and her situation. (MacKenzie and Scully 2007: 347)

Sympathetic moral imagination involves recognising that a person is different from ourselves but trying to identify how an event is experienced by that actual person rather than how we think we would experience it if it happened to us. Let us return to another example from the parent-practitioner talk to explore how this might work:

Teacher: I know he's lashing out but that is what children with autism and epilepsy do.	*Parent:* You don't see my son. You don't recognise him as an individual.

Here, the epistemic gap is clearly visible. The practitioner is drawing on his (her) "expert" knowledge of children with "autism and epilepsy" to inform a parent that the child's behaviour is "normal" for a child with that label. In stark contrast, the parent is invoking her (his) own knowledge of the child as an individual with fears and frustrations that can be triggered by external stimuli and to which the child sometimes lashes out. The parent may have experienced many times previously her child's behaviour just being explained away by practitioners as "just what children with autism and epilepsy do" without anyone really giving thought to whether there are other reasons why the child might feel the need to resort to lashing out. The claim that "lashing out" is what children with autism and epilepsy "do" seems yet another attempt to close down the conversation. It demonstrates a reluctance to engage with the parent's concerns, thoughts and experiences at an emotional level. It fails to recognise the long shared history of the parent and child in negotiating the behaviour with the child and with other practitioners. The appeal by the teacher to the labelling discourse is an attempt to "fix" the meaning of the child's behaviour and firmly to locate the difficulty within the child. This kind of discursive positioning is difficult for a parent to resist. Their knowledge of their child as an individual is made irrelevant; any challenge might seem to deny the teacher his/her expert knowledge and status. What might a response from a practitioner look like that involved "sympathetic moral imagination"? An approach that draws on sympathetic moral imagination would encourage the practitioner to open up the conversation, to ask about what the behaviour means for the parent, the issues that arise for the parent because of it and how the shared history of parent and child might inform the development of a support strategy. Yet the opportunity for either parent or practitioner to engage in such conversations at the school gates at the end of the day or in a multi-professional meeting seems limited. Applying sympathetic moral imagination is essential but the sharing of experience requires protected time and space.

We have argued therefore that the notion of biographical standpoint suggests that the practitioners may not always have the intuitive capability to understand what it means to be a parent of a disabled child. However, we would not want to position the responsibility for ruptures in communication entirely with individual practitioners: they do not operate within a vacuum and are part of a system that dictates many of their practices and which promotes a particular view of disability. Individual practitioner responses are situated therefore within wider systemic barriers that often work against achieving informed and shared understandings between practitioner and parent.

Systemic Barriers

Habermas, a sociologist and philosopher, argues that the system makes objects of the people that it serves rather than valuing them as partners working together to achieve the goals of its members (Burns and Früchtel 2014).

In doing so the system substitutes the equality of shared, reciprocal and negotiated support between people within the lifeworld with the structured, contracted and paid service delivered by the system. Lifeworld is used here in the sense of the everyday lives of people where caring about and for each other takes place within informal social networks. Within this process empathy becomes a tool of instrumental rationality (Weber 1964 cited Burns and Früchtel 2014) in the sense that it is reduced to a method that enables the practitioner to solve the problem of the parent and restore order to the system. Practitioner empathy as controlled by the system is different to the empathy of the lifeworld. In the lifeworld, empathy arises usually out of an informed and detailed understanding of what it means to be the other person and how she (he) feels about what is happening in her life. This understanding might arise from a long-standing relationship with the other person and/or through sharing a similar life context and experiences. Practitioner empathy however is more distanced, measured and controlled without the genuine felt emotional connection that can arise from a shared history of experience. Empathy is utilised to achieve the goals of the organisation rather than to recognise and appreciate the effect of the system on families.

This is not to suggest that practitioners are emotionally cold, cynical manipulators of parents of disabled children. Of course, we know that the majority of child educators and practitioners in related services are deeply committed to enabling and supporting the lives of disabled children and their families. But we are all subject to the insidious workings of the system that often without us recognising it; the system shapes how we respond within the customs and practices of the workplace. Lipsky (1971) proposed the notion of "street-level bureaucracy" to make explicit some of these embedded cultural work practices that inhibit practitioners from effectively bridging epistemic chasm between staff and "clients". Lipsky's ideas, although conceived over 30 years ago, are still utilised by social science researchers (Ellis 2007, 2011) and are a helpful support here when theorising why epistemic chasms might erupt between practitioners and clients.

Lipsky argues that practitioners experience stress as a result of being the front-line representatives of a system that will never provide for all the requirements of those compelled to use its services. The pressure of time constraints, the requirement to distribute extremely limited resources and the pressure to meet performance targets produce defensive reactions in practitioners. These include desisting from fully appreciating clients as people and being on constant guard against negative reactions from clients. Lipsky proposes that one mode of reaction to these stresses is to adopt "simplifications" (p. 395). An example of a simplification might be to think of parents who accept instruction or advice without question as "good parents" and those who challenge practitioners as "difficult parents". Both categories of course act to de-personalise the parent and prevent practitioners from coming to fully developed understandings of the parents as people. Lipsky also identifies defence mechanisms that practitioners resort to in order to manage these stresses. One of these is to conceptualise certain groups as being outside of their remit of care. So, disabled children and their parents may be thought of as "special", different and more suited to medical or psychological intervention than to education and so therefore really beyond the skills and responsibility of the education practitioner. Lumby (2007) argues that within the school system, the voice of parents "is not given epistemic equality with that of staff" (p. 222). Using the Lipsky model, this could also be conceived of as a defence mechanism: the dismissal of parental concerns over provision and practices as misinformed or the unfounded worries of overprotective parents excuse educators from critically examining their own practices, and the work of the school can then continue untroubled.

For Lipsky, what is critical is that these issues are brought into the light and reflected upon so that practitioners come to recognise these as views that they hold and accept that they too are part of the problem. This can lead to the realisation that breakdowns in communication are not just the result of special or difficult parents or an under-resourced system but also because of how practitioners are choosing to engage with their clients. Lipsky suggests that clients are likely to have greater confidence and trust in those practitioners to whom they can best relate to, those who most seem to understand and appreciate their experience. These may not always be the most highly qualified or most experienced staff and so schools and related services need therefore to be alert to where successful relationships are developing between their staff and parents and to reflect upon and learn from these successes.

Conclusion

In this chapter, we have argued that practitioner-parent talk often works against the forming of positive partnerships. We have illustrated this through the provision of examples from the experiences of parents to highlight the damage that talk can do. Sometimes, this occurs through miscommunication when one party hears a message that the other did not intend. However, often parents accurately "hear between the words" of practitioners talking messages of criticism and rejection. We argue here that these destructive communications often arise from the gaps between the epistemic positions of practitioners and parents that result from their different biographical standpoints. They arise because practitioners have not appreciated what it means and feels like to be that parent at that time in that situation. We have identified some of the structural barriers that prevent the street-level bureaucrat from having the time, space, confidence and permission to try and bridge these epistemic gaps. But many practitioners are committed, skilled and resourceful and once alerted to the problem will find ways to address it. We have suggested here that one way of bridging these gaps is through the employment of sympathetic moral imagination. If practitioners were better able to understand the emotional and physical impact of their talk on parents, then they are likely to be more careful with the messages they convey. However, MacKenzie and Scully (2007) acknowledge that being able to imagine the experience of another is a challenging task. Clearly, this is difficult enough between practitioners and parents but the Code of Practice also requires local authorities and other agencies to engage directly with young people. Epistemic gaps exist within all communications and the further apart the biographical standpoints, the wider the chasms are likely to be. Accessing the lived experience of disabled children and young people and understanding the impacts of this on their being will challenge even the most empathetic of non-disabled practitioners. Sympathetic moral imagination is a skill that all practitioners need to develop if they are to bridge the epistemic divides between themselves and those whom they support.

Sympathetic moral imagination relies upon a focused attendance to how a parent (or child, young person) is representing that experience:

> In sympathetic moral imagination one does not try to imagine *being* the other from the inside. Rather, one recognises that the other is different from oneself, one imaginatively engages with her perceptions and experiences, as she represents them, and one responds emotionally to her perspective and her situation. (p. 347)

Practitioners may often feel that they do not have the ability, the time or sufficient contact with a parent to be able to develop this degree of intimacy with a parent's particular situation. Nor would we want parents to be expected to reveal to practitioners all aspects of their lives. So the question remains as to how practitioners might develop sympathetic moral imagination. Turning again to MacKenzie and Scully (2007: 347), they suggest how this might be enabled:

> There are a variety of ways in which moral imagination can be cultivated and stimulated, including talking to those whose perspectives one is trying to understand, informing oneself about their situation, reading fictional representations of their lives, watching films that represent the world from their point of view, and so on.

Acknowledging and talking through these issues with colleagues is, perhaps, one way to develop sympathetic moral imagination. More critical is hearing representations from parents themselves. Many parent and carer groups provide information and training sessions for practitioners about a range of experiences related to being the parent or carer of a disabled child: these should become a critical part of any practitioner development programme. Learning generically about experiences of parents may not always enable practitioners to know exactly how life might be for a particular parent, but it will make practitioners more aware of the epistemic gaps. And the best way to avoid falling into a gap is to know it is there.

Acknowledgements The authors would like to thank the parents, carers and practitioners who have shared their experiences and permitted us to represent them here. We would also like to thank members of the Disability Research Forum at Sheffield Hallam University for their feedback on a presentation of this work and Jack Levinson, City University New York, for directing us to the work of Lipsky.

References

Ashworth, P. D. (2016). The Lifeworld – Enriching Qualitative Evidence. *Qualitative Research in Psychology, 13*(1), 20–32.

Broomhead, K. (2013). *Socio-Emotional Aspects of Home-School Relationships Between Parents of Children with Special Educational Needs and Educational Practitioners; Perceptions of Blame, Stigma, Partnership and Empathy* (PhD Thesis). University of Lancaster, Lancaster.

Burman, E., & Parker, I. (Eds.). (1993). *Discourse Analytic Research: Repertoires and Readings of Texts in Action.* London: Routledge.

Burns, G., & Früchtel, F. (2014). Family Group Conference: A Bridge Between Lifeworld and System. *British Journal of Social Work, 44*, 1147–1161.

Crossley, N. (2005). *Key Concepts in Critical Social Theory.* London: SAGE.

DES (Department of Education and Science). (1978). *Special Educational Needs: Report of the Committee of Enquiry into the Education of Handicapped Children and Young People (The Warnock Report).* London: HMSO.

DfE (Department for Education). (2011). *Support and Aspiration: A New Approach to Special Educational Needs and Disability – A Consultation.* http://media.education.gov.uk/assets/files/pdf/g/green%20paper%20presentation.pdf. Accessed 25 Aug 2015.

DfE (Department for Education). (2014). *Children and Families Act.* London: HMSO.

DfES (Department for Education and Skills). (2001). *The Code of Practice on the Identification and Assessment of Special Educational Needs.* London: HMSO.

DfES (Department for Education and Skills). (2004). *Removing the Barriers to Achievement: The Government's Strategy for SEN.* London: DfES.

Ellis, K. (2007). Direct Payments and Social Work Practice: The Significance of 'Street-Level Bureaucracy' in Determining Eligibility. *British Journal of Social Work, 37*(3), 405–422.

Ellis, K. (2011). 'Street-Level Bureaucracy' Revisited: The Changing Face of Frontline Discretion in Adult Social Care in England. *Social Policy and Administration, 45*(3), 221–244.

Gale, T. (2000). Rethinking Social Justice in Schools: How Will We Recognise It When We See It? *International Journal of Inclusive Education, 4*(3), 253–269.

Hodge, N. (2005). Reflections on Diagnosing Autism Spectrum Disorders. *Disability and Society, 20*(3), 345–349.

Hodge, N., & Runswick-Cole, K. A. (2008). Problematising Parent-Professional Relationships. *Disability and Society, 23*(6), 637–647.

Hodge, N., & Runswick-Cole, K. (2013). "They Never Pass Me the Ball": Disabled Children's Experiences of Leisure. *Children's Geographies, 11*(3), 311–325.

Husserl, E. (1931). *Cartesian Meditations* (D. Cairns, Trans.). Dordrecht: Kluwer.

Lipsky, M. (1971). Street-Level Bureaucracy and the Analysis of Urban Reform. *Urban Affairs Quarterly, 6*, 391–409.

Lumby, J. (2007). Parent Voice: Knowledge, Values and Viewpoint. *Improving Schools, 10*(3), 220–232.

MacKenzie, C., & Scully, J. L. (2007). Moral Imagination, Disability & Embodiment. *Journal of Applied Philosophy, 24*(4), 335–351.

Mallett, R., & Runswick-Cole, K. (2014). *Approaching Disability: Critical Issues and Perspectives.* Abingdon: Routledge.

MoJ (Ministry of Justice). (2013). *Tribunals Statistics Quarterly – July to September 2013- Includes SEND Information for the Academic Year 2012–13.* https://www.gov.uk/government/uploads/system/uploads/attachment_data/file/265148/quarterly-tribs-q2-2013-14.pdf. Accessed 25 Aug 2015.

Parker, I. (2002). *Critical Discursive Psychology.* Basingstoke: Palgrave.

Runswick-Cole, K. A. (2007). The Tribunal Was the Most Stressful Thing: The Experiences of Families Who Go to the Special Educational Needs and Disability Tribunal (SENDisT). *Disability and Society, 22*(3), 315–328.

Runswick-Cole, K. A. (2008). Between a Rock and a Hard Place: Parents' Attitudes to the Inclusion of Their Children with Special Educational Needs in Mainstream Schools. *British Journal of Special Education, 35*(3), 137–180.

Runswick-Cole, K. A., & Hodge, N. (2009). Needs or Rights? A Challenge to the Discourse of Special Education. *British Journal of Special Education, 36*(4), 198–203.

Timpson, E. (2014, July 10). *An Address to the Association of Directors of Children's Services (ADCS).* https://www.gov.uk/government/speeches/edward-timpson-talks-about-special-educational-needs-reforms. Accessed 25 Aug 2015.

Nick Hodge is a Professor of Inclusive Practice, Sheffield Institute of Education, Sheffield Hallam University. Prior to becoming an academic, Nick (@goodchap62) supported disabled children and their families in schools for 15 years. Nick's research focuses on the education and well-being of disabled children and their families. Nick's work challenges deficit-led models of disability that mark children and young people as disordered and other.

Katherine Runswick-Cole is Chair in Education at The School of Education, The University of Sheffield, United Kingdom. Her research draws on critical disability studies approaches to explore the relationships between disability, childhood and families. Her research is informed by her experiences of mothering two young adult children, one of whom is disabled.

Disabled Children in Out-of-Home Care: Issues and Challenges for Practice

Berni Kelly, Sandra Dowling, and Karen Winter

Key Points

1. Child protection practice with disabled children should be grounded in a commitment to their right to be safeguarded and protected from significant harm.
2. Holistic and sensitive assessments of risk are required when responding to safeguarding concerns for families with disabled children with a careful balance between interventions to protect disabled children and support to enable parents to more effectively protect and care for their disabled child.
3. A greater range of out-of-home placements is required for disabled children and young people to increase their opportunities for permanency in out-of-home care. More flexible service boundaries would also help to recognise the multiple needs of disabled children who have been separated from their birth parents and improve their access to therapeutic, advocacy and specialist support when required.

B. Kelly (✉) • K. Winter
Queen's University Belfast, Belfast, Northern Ireland, UK

S. Dowling
The University of Bristol, Bristol, UK

© The Author(s) 2018
K. Runswick-Cole et al. (eds.), *The Palgrave Handbook of Disabled Children's Childhood Studies*, https://doi.org/10.1057/978-1-137-54446-9_34

4. Disabled children and young people in out-of-home care need consistent, caring relationships with carers, social workers and other professionals who should be familiar with their needs and preferred communication styles.
5. Professionals must engage directly with disabled children in out-of-home care to ascertain and address their views and feelings. Such participatory practice is particularly important when safeguarding, and placement decisions are being made based on the best interests of disabled children.

Introduction

Historically, institutionalisation and segregation have been key features of out-of-home care for disabled children and young people (Oswin 1978; Schmidt and Bailey 2014). However, with the policy shift towards family support and community care, alongside growing recognition of the rights of disabled children and their families, we have witnessed a move from institutional care to family-based care in the community (Burrell and Trip 2011; Cantwell et al. 2013). This policy and practice shift is welcomed by both disability activists and those caring for disabled children and young people.

Whilst most disabled children and young people grow up safe and happy within their birth families, there is also evidence to suggest that disabled children are at greater risk of abuse or neglect (Morris 1999; Stalker and McArthur 2012; Sullivan and Knutson 2000). Disabled children are reported to be vulnerable to abuse or neglect due to assumptions about their inability or lack of opportunity to disclose abuse, reduced physical mobility and exposure to a greater range of adult personal carers (Westcott and Jones 1999; Morris 1999; Jones et al. 2012). Disabled children are also more likely to live in families facing external stressors such as poverty and social deprivation (Emerson 2010), stigma and social isolation (Akrami et al. 2006), and parental stress or illness (McConkey et al. 2004; Philips 1998). However, the greater risk of abuse or neglect for disabled children also indicates a fundamental denial of their basic human right to experience adequate care and protection in childhood.

Reflecting on increased vulnerability to abuse, there are also concerns that disabled children and young are over-represented in public care systems (Lightfoot et al. 2011; Hill et al. 2015). Factors that can lead a disabled child to come into care are complex and interwoven. A range of the risk factors outlined above combined with insufficient 'in-home' support may lead to family breakdown and a decision to place a disabled child in an out-of-home placement.

However, despite consistent evidence of the higher numbers of disabled children in care and knowledge of the multiple factors that may precipitate their entry to the care system, there has been a notable gap in research into the reasons for their over-representation in public care and limited reporting of the views and experiences of these children and their families (Dowling et al. 2013). Existing research tends to focus on abuse prevalence rates with only a few small-scale studies focusing specifically on the experiences of disabled children and young people who have been abused or have been subject to child protection procedures (Franklin et al. 2015; Taylor et al. 2015). Similarly, there is a dearth of research with disabled children and young people living in out-of-home care (Baker 2007; Cousins 2006). Our study sought to address this gap in knowledge by investigating the over-representation of disabled children in the public care system in Northern Ireland (NI) and their experiences of living in out-of-home care.

Background to the Study

The three-year study on which this chapter is based was funded by the NI Government, the Office of the First Minister and Deputy First Minister. The study aimed to investigate the over-representation of disabled children and young people in public care in NI; however, the findings are also pertinent to the experiences of disabled children in out-of-home care in other jurisdictions. The study had three main stages: a review of literature and policy (Dowling et al. 2013; Kelly et al. 2014); a survey to profile the characteristics of the population of disabled children in out-of-home care (n = 323), including their demographic background, reasons for being in care and placement experiences (Kelly et al. 2015); and 15 case studies involving case file reviews and interviews with disabled children and their parents, carers and social workers (Kelly et al. 2016). This chapter focuses predominantly on key themes from the case study stage of the research, prioritising the views and experiences of disabled children and young people but also exploring some of the challenges for birth parents, carers and social workers in their efforts to meet the ongoing needs of disabled children in care.

The case study below is used to illustrate the key themes emerging from the research findings. It is an anonymous fictional case based on a mosaic of the common features of the case studies undertaken as part of the third stage of the research study. The use of a fictional case illustrates the experiences of disabled children and their families whilst protecting individual children's personal identities. Anonymised quotations from interviews with children and their social workers also are used to illustrate key points, alongside images drawn by disabled children who gave their consent for them to be used in any write-up of the study findings.

Erin's Story Erin is a 12-year-old girl who likes playing with dolls, watching TV and singing. She has experienced multiple out-of-home care placements since she was 4 years old and is currently living with a non-relative foster carer. Shortly after Erin's birth, she was diagnosed as having a severe cognitive impairment and a range of additional health needs, including epilepsy and respiratory problems that can necessitate tube feeding. Her mother is a single parent of four children. Her father separated from her mother shortly after her birth and has no contact with Erin or her mother. In Erin's early years, hospital staff and health visitors expressed safeguarding concerns, including parental failure to administer necessary medication, repeated missed medical appointments and Erin's failure to thrive. Her mother told the health visitor that she found it difficult to cope and in response to her request for support, she was allocated to a low level of short break services. When Erin started school, a number of referrals were made to social services regarding her unkempt appearance and poor hygiene, culminating in a referral regarding unexplained bruising. During the child protection investigation, Erin's mother informed social services that she could no longer cope and wanted to put Erin into care. Although further support was offered at that point, her mother insisted that she was afraid that she would harm Erin so she was voluntarily admitted to care. Due to a shortage of longer-term specialist foster care placements, Erin stayed in three different short-term foster homes over the course of 6 months. During this time, her mother re-married and decided she could look after Erin with support from her new partner. Following a social work assessment of risk and parenting capacity, Erin returned home with a more intensive family support care package. However, 6 months later a member of the public reported witnessing Erin's mother and step-parent physically assaulting Erin in a local shop. Following a child protection investigation, social services applied for a Care Order and Erin was taken into care again, being placed in another short-term foster home. This foster carer had prior nursing experience but lived some distance from Erin's birth family. As social services cannot identify a long-term placement, Erin has remained in this placement with additional provision of monthly short break support. She has a close attachment with her carer who is considering looking after her on a long-term basis. Erin has contact with her siblings (who, following a social work assessment of risk, remained in their mother's care) and her mother at monthly supervised family contact meetings but would like to see them more often.

Journeys into Care

In Erin's case, initial safeguarding concerns were responded to with a protection plan that incorporated short break support to enable her mother to take a break from the caring role and provide adequate care for her at home. This was a common approach in cases where there were concerns regarding low-level or persistent neglect, rather than an actual incidence of abuse. In many of these cases, parents reported high levels of stress and ongoing unmet support needs. Indeed, Erin's mother was only given access to low levels of short break services in response to her request for support. Eventually, she could no longer cope and agreed to Erin being voluntarily accommodated. It was only at this point, when an appropriate care placement for Erin could not be identified, that her mother was offered more intensive support. Similarly, in our study, we found some cases where high levels of short breaks were provided to support non-relative foster carers to care for a disabled child despite these services not initially being made available to their birth parents when the early signs of breakdown became apparent.

However, Erin's case also raises the issue of varying approaches to safeguarding decisions and child protection planning for disabled children at risk. For example, would the same response to the early professional concerns for Erin's well-being be made for a non-disabled child? It is possible that Erin's failure to thrive was related to the impact of her additional health needs (e.g. respiratory or malabsorption conditions), and missed medical appointments reflected the stress of managing appointments with a wide range of professionals in contact with a disabled child with multiple health needs. However, it is important that social workers question their assumptions about impairment effects and critically reflect on their empathy with parents to ensure they apply the same thresholds of significant harm to a disabled child as they would a non-disabled child (Kelly and Dowling 2015). Whilst parental stress is a feature of this case, Erin's right to be safeguarded should be a paramount consideration (Taylor et al. 2015). As evident in this case, Erin was then exposed to physical abuse ultimately leading to her long-term placement in out-of-home care under a court order. Similarly, Morris (1999) highlighted that the neglect and abuse of disabled children is not always recognised when professionals' preoccupation or ignorance regarding impairment potentially masks abuse and leads to minimal efforts to spend time with disabled children to ascertain their views and experiences as part of a holistic assessment of strengths, needs and risk (Murray and Osbourne 2009). This leads to concern that child protection procedures may not be sufficiently responsive to the needs of disabled children and, indeed, that disabled children may not be subject to the same levels of protection as non-disabled children.

Reflecting on Erin's story, some disabled children in our study had been in out-of-home care from a young age whereas others came into care in their mid-childhood or adolescence. Neglect, often in combination with parents not coping or emotional abuse, was the most common reason for being in care. One-third had witnessed domestic violence and just over a quarter had been subject to physical abuse. A smaller proportion (9%) had experienced sexual abuse. Parental (both fathers and mothers) substance abuse and mental health issues were also commonly reported. Whilst these are many of the same reasons why non-disabled children enter the care system, it was also clear that additional factors were underlying in child protection issues for disabled children. The qualitative data from the case studies showed that limited support for families under pressure, delayed diagnosis and lack of access to specialist disability services also played a part in family breakdown and compromised parenting. Whilst social workers acknowledged the effects of parenting under additional stress, including high-level care demands, fatigue and limited economic or social resources, they also highlighted the danger of applying differing thresholds of risk of significant harm for disabled children. Indeed, one senior manager emphasised the following core question for child protection workers responding to families with a disabled child which demonstrates a need to refocus on the rights of the child: '*Is this a child abuse, child protection issue or is this an absolutely stressed and exhausted parent?*' Clearly, early intervention is essential to provide structured support for parents when their children are young or to prevent escalation of low-level need to higher levels of need or risk. Such early intervention incorporating multi-agency support is critical for disabled children deemed to be on the edge of care and can play a key role in enabling parents to more effectively protect and care for their disabled child.

In relation to the experience of coming into care, some disabled children in our study could recall the reasons why they came into care, including memories of life before coming into care and recollections of their experience of being taken into care. For example, one child illustrated how he felt confused and 'a wee bit shocked' at leaving his birth mother's home and coming to live with foster parents, where he still resides.

Another young person described their memory of coming into care and their realisation that they were not returning home:

> *I'm not too sure what happened… I came down to the stairs finding both of them arguing and then… my memory went blank after that. And then the next thing I*

was in a police car... then a few days later the social workers came and took me up
to here. And I came walking into the kitchen and I could remember sitting down
wondering why am I here for a visit? And then whenever she went away I realised
that I was here for good.

This young person's narrative highlights the importance of providing explanations for disabled children so they are clearly informed about the decisions
that are being made to keep them safe and have an opportunity to express
their wishes and feelings about such life-changing events. Indeed, a further
young person reflected on how they wished things had turned out differently,
feeling powerless to effect change:

Actually I would say that sometimes it felt really nice being away from home and
some not nice... 'cos I really didn't want to be with my mum at the time... but now
I do and I can't leave here 'cos the social workers think that it's a good place.

Such findings emphasise the importance of counselling and therapeutic
support for disabled children taken into care as they begin to build a picture
of the reasons why they have been separated from their birth families and renegotiate their sense of identity and belonging.

Permanence for Disabled Children

Whilst movement to and from home and various foster care settings provided
an opportunity for Erin to be returned home, it also created instability during
her formative early years and delayed decision-making about her long-term
care. The disabled children and birth parents we interviewed were clear that
they wanted every opportunity for children to be cared for at home; however,
in some cases, removal from the family home was necessary to protect the
disabled child.

Like Erin, many disabled children in our study experienced multiple placement moves, sometimes coming into care more than once following repeated
efforts to support them at home with birth parents or in kinship care arrangements. Some children also had multiple moves to different care placements.
Indeed, our profiling survey found that almost two-thirds of the disabled children in care had been subject to placement moves, with 38% experiencing three
or more placement changes. For example, one 9-year-old drew the following
picture as she described the six homes she had lived in during her time in care.

Similarly, another young person explained:

I was shipped about an awful lot. I lived in a foster placement, another foster placement, my mummy, a foster placement, then mummy, then back into care, another residential home and then here, this home.

Placement disruption meant moving to new carers, neighbourhoods and perhaps schools which was substantially challenging for some disabled children and young people. Multiple placement moves were also the result of difficulties associated with finding appropriate long-term foster care placements for disabled children, as was the case for Erin, who was eventually placed out of area. This was also the experience of some of the disabled children in our study, with a small number of disabled young people being placed even further away from home in England and Scotland. Placements out of area are usually sought to meet the specialist or complex needs of some disabled children; however, the need to place a child out of area also clearly indicates a lack of specialist service provision in their own local authority, including opportunity to access more intensive supports within the family home. The negative impact of out of area placements by local authorities on disabled children's connection with their local communities, schools and extended families should not be underestimated. In addition, birth family contact can be difficult for parents and professionals to organise and sustain over time for disabled children in out of area placements.

Relationships with Birth Families and Professionals

The disabled children in our study had varying levels and forms of contact with their birth families but consistently emphasised the importance of birth families in their lives, despite ongoing challenges associated with family contact. For example, one child drew the following picture of his birth family contact visit placing his birth mother as the largest, central figure with everyone holding hands.

In Erin's case, contact is regular and supervised. This was often the case for disabled children in the study; however, contact often also required supervision or support to make it meaningful and positive and to ensure disabled children were protected from negative parental behaviour. Children and young people separated from their birth families also require support to negotiate their personal and family identities as they make sense of the reasons why they are placed in care and work towards a positive construction of their self-identity. This is true for both disabled and non-disabled children coming into the care system. However, only a few disabled children in our case study sample had benefited from life story work, helping them to explore identity issues and understand their experiences of family relationships and loss. Disabled children's limited access to life story work could indicate a general lack of such therapeutic services for children in out-of-home care but may also be due to impairment-related assumptions that disabled children would not have the capacity to understand family dynamics or engage in life story work. Such therapeutic work, however, was of much benefit to those who accessed it and could also include consideration of psycho-emotional aspects of disability identity, particularly in cases where disabled children's siblings remained at home and they received messages that they were in care because of their impairment or because their parent could not cope with their particular needs.

Disabled children also highlighted the importance of consistent positive relationships with carers and professionals. Many children reported close and loving relationships with their carers and talked of aspects of their foster care placements that they particularly enjoyed; as one child explained:

> It's cool here; come in. We have lots of food in this house.

Most children and young people described a positive relationship with their social worker and described the activities their social worker engaged in, including listening, home visits and outings, for example:

> I get on well with my social worker… we are actually really close… usually I tell her if something is starting to annoy me.
> If I text her and I'm like 'listen I need a bit of help, this is getting too much', she's there… she would take me out when I am a bit stressed and she would talk to me and try to tell me like just to try and pull myself back and try and not let it get to me.

Social workers were also key sources of support at significant times of change in the lives of children and young people, such as, placement change and transitions when leaving care. However, children and young people could also identify social workers who were less effective at building good working relationships. Another young person compared the positive relationship with her current field social worker with the lack of connection with previous social workers:

> I had another social worker before and I didn't like her so I asked for her to be changed. She was not very good, like we would ask her to… speak to someone, to do something – she would never do it and then she was off for like a year and a half and I didn't have anyone!.

Multiple staff changes impacted on opportunities to develop working relationships with social workers and left some children feeling that they were missing out on support or had no one who knew their case to advocate for them. One young person explained their frustration about staff turnover:

> They were good but the girl… just got up and moved and then the [other] girl just left and didn't come back one day and didn't contact me again… when I was like ten and I really liked the girl and then it just annoyed me.

Being Heard

A key priority issue for disabled children and young people in out-of-home care is the importance of having an opportunity to voice their wishes and feelings and to contribute to decisions affecting their lives. Interestingly, none of the disabled children and young people in the study had given evidence in court regarding their experiences of abuse or neglect. Once in out-of-home care, there is a range of structured processes in place to facilitate the inclusion of the perspectives of children in care including care planning, reviews of placements and individual meetings with social workers. Many of the disabled children and young people in our study were aware of these processes and forums where decisions about their lives were taken, however, few attended care planning or review meetings. Overall, children and young people gave mixed reports as to whether or not they felt listened to or had a say in decisions. A small number of young people reported being involved in decisions, for example, moving on to a new placement; however, some also reported not being listened to:

Some social workers never listened, they never listened to a word you said and that made it worse… People not listening to me is one of the biggest things that pushes my buttons.

Another young person reported that while she was listened to, she was rarely asked for her opinion, saying:

Sometimes you don't get a choice… like people do listen, but sometimes they don't ask.

Given their experiences of abuse or neglect and ongoing issues whilst in care, it is important to consider who disabled children and young people have to turn to if they need someone to talk to. Young people identified various people in whom they could confide or go to if they had a problem. They mentioned teachers, social workers, foster carers and birth parents. However, only two young people in our case studies had accessed formal counselling services and only one of these young people felt these services met their needs. In addition, although disabled children and young people were rarely attending meetings, none of those in our case studies had accessed independent advocates to represent their needs or wishes at such decision-making forums.

Access to Support

Disabled children and young people in the study were engaged with a range of disability, mental health and children's services, including diagnostic assessment, short break services and therapeutic support. For example, like Erin, some children use short breaks to support foster care placements. Short breaks gave foster carers a break from the caring responsibilities but they should also meet the needs of the disabled child. A few children in our study found the experience of going to short breaks quite stressful, often due to the experience of repeated separation from carers:

> I got real homesick. I was phoning the house demanding to come back here. I had to go there but I could not go away… I could not live anywhere else… The plan was to stay there for two days full, and I could not do like twelve hours.

A balance needs to be struck between supporting care placements and responding to the views and needs of disabled children, who may well have already experienced much change in their young lives, as is the case for Erin.

Some disabled children and young people had struggled to access specialist mental health services at an early stage when their emotional well-being began to deteriorate. Other young people were receiving targeted interventions, for example, anger management courses. However, one young person recalled how she had not benefitted from such a course:

> I've been to anger management, but I've never really liked it because I suppose I don't really understand what they're talking about and it's so much stress and people telling you do this and try that… plus nearly every way you can think of to cope with your anger I would have tried already.

Often lack of access to specialist services was a result of an imposed service identity. For example, once a child was known to disability services, it was usually assumed that psychiatric assessment and treatment would be provided by the disability service. However, disabled children and young people often had emotional and mental health needs linked to their prior traumatic experiences of abuse, neglect or separation/loss (needs that were clearly unrelated to their impairment) and required accessible, specialist child or adolescent mental health support. Thresholds for access to disability and mental health services are also high, resulting in some disabled children with low-to-moderate levels of need or undiagnosed impairments failing to access necessary specialist services. These findings suggest a need for more flexibility in service arrangements as disabled children and young people cross service boundaries including child, disability, mental health and transition services.

Key Messages for Practice

The findings of our study indicate key areas for the development of practice and research with disabled children and young people in out-of-home care. In relation to practice, firstly, there is a need to ground child protection and care practice in a commitment to the rights of disabled children and young people to be safeguarded and protected from significant harm—protection should be prioritised as a right of all children. Social workers need further training on the application of thresholds for intervention of disabled children in the context of the ongoing support needs of parents (Murray and Osborne 2009). Responses to safeguarding concerns should include both intervention to protect disabled children from harm or abuse and consideration of the supports available to enable struggling parents to maintain adequate standards of care for their disabled children. Many parents of disabled children require additional practical and emotional supports that may be difficult to access in the context of government resource constraints and local service cutbacks. Holistic and sensitive assessments of risk and need are required to enable professionals working with disabled children and their families to make decisions in the best interests of the disabled child.

Secondly, a greater range of alternative placements is required for disabled children and young people. Erin's movement to multiple placements is a common feature of cases in our study, often due to a failure by service commissioners to invest in the training and recruitment of an adequate range of suitable foster carers. The resulting over-reliance on short-term carers to provide long-term placements is also a critical issue requiring robust review and further efforts to develop long-term care placements offering permanency for disabled children and young people.

Thirdly, consistent, caring relationships are important for any child or young person. For disabled children and young people, this is particularly important as carers, social workers and other professionals in their lives should be familiar with their particular needs and preferred communication styles. Linked to this theme of relationship, professionals must be supported to make more concerted efforts to engage with disabled children and young people to ascertain their views and respond to their feelings and wishes as decisions affecting their lives are made. Disabled children and young people want professionals and carers who are interested in their lives and perspectives and who take time to develop relationships with them. Given our findings on the lack of involvement of disabled children and young people in formal review processes, it is also important to extend the availability of targeted independent advocacy services for disabled children in care.

Finally, in terms of implications for practice, there is a need to move beyond the constrictions of service-imposed master identities for disabled children and young people. Their lives are characterised by a multiplicity of experiences and needs that stretch across traditional service boundaries and require a more flexible approach. Social services have a critical corporate parenting duty to disabled children and young people who have been removed from their birth families and, as such, these children and young people should be prioritised in decisions about access to specialist, therapeutic interventions and services beyond the traditionally restrictive boundaries of diagnostic or eligibility criteria. Overall, we need more critically reflexive approaches to working with disabled children and young people growing up in out-of-home care which question existing service structures and shift usual working practices towards more inclusive and participatory practice cultures.

Key Messages for Research

The findings from our study provide useful pointers for further research with disabled children and young people in out-of-home care but we still have much more to learn about disabled children's experiences of child protection services and out-of-home care. As this study was situated in one UK jurisdiction, it would also be helpful for further research in other countries to explore the diverse experiences of disabled children and young people in a range of out-of-home placements in varying cultural contexts, globally. This study also encourages us to incorporate the multiple experiences of disabled children and young people into our theorising of disabled childhoods. The disabled children and young people participating in this study present with a range of identities over time and context as they move to and from their birth families and engage with a range of services and care environments. Their narratives of growing up as a disabled child in the care system offer a unique perspective on the heterogeneous lives of disabled children that highlights the need to further explore the psycho-emotional effects of childhood abuse/neglect and birth family separation on disabled children and the diverse identities of disabled children growing up in out-of-home care including ethnicity, sexuality and gender. Critical childhood disability theory can inform our understanding of the construction of disabled childhoods in the care system and the impact this has on safeguarding and pathways to permanency in out-of-home care for disabled children and young people.

Conclusion

This chapter has explored the experiences of disabled children and young people who are removed from their birth family home and live in out-of-home care. Erin's story highlights some of the key issues for these disabled children and young people including the complexities of birth family relationships, the barriers to permanency and the importance of listening to disabled children and young people. The intersections of growing up disabled and in out-of-home care are also highlighted, including disabled children's engagement with professionals and areas for further research and service development. As there is a paucity of research with disabled children and young people in out-of-home care, this chapter raises awareness of the priority issues for these children and the challenge for professionals and carers aiming to protect and care for disabled children and young people. There is also a challenge for researchers engaged in disabled children's childhood studies to further investigate these issues and the everyday life experiences of disabled children and young people in out-of-home care in a global context.

References

Akrami, N., Ekehammar, B., Claesson, M., & Sonnander, K. (2006). Classical and Modern Prejudice: Attitudes Towards People with Intellectual Disabilities. *Research in Developmental Disabilities, 27*, 605–617.

Baker, C. (2007). Disabled Children's Experience of Permanency in the Looked After System. *British Journal of Social Work, 37*, 1173–1188.

Burrell, B., & Trip, H. (2011). Reform and Community Care: Has De-institutionalisation Delivered for People with Intellectual Disability? *Nursing Inquiry, 18*(2), 174–183.

Cantwell, N., Davidson, J., Elsley, S., Milligan, I., & Quinn, N. (2013). *Moving Forward: Implementing the United Nations Guidelines for the Alternative Care of Children.* Glasgow: Centre for Excellence for Looked After Children in Scotland.

Cousins, J. (2006). *Every Child Is Special: Placing Disabled Children for Permanence.* London: British Association for Adoption and Fostering.

Dowling, S., Kelly, B., & Winter, K. (2013). *Disabled Children and Young People Who Are Looked After: A Literature Review.* Belfast: OFMDFM and Queen's University Belfast.

Emerson, E. (2010). Deprivation, Ethnicity and the Prevalence of Intellectual and Developmental Disabilities. *Journal of Epidemiology and Community Health, 68,* 218–224.

Franklin, A., Raws, P., & Smeaton, E. (2015). *Under Protected, Over Protected: Meeting the Needs of Young People with Learning Disabilities Who Experience, or Are at Risk of, Sexual Exploitation.* London: Barnardo's.

Hill, L., Baker, C., Kelly, B., & Dowling, S. (2015). Being Counted? Examining the Prevalence of Looked-After Disabled Children and Young People Across the UK. *Child and Family Social Work.* doi:10.1111/cfs.12239.

Jones, L., Bellis, M. B., Wood, S., Hughes, K., McCoy, E., Eckley, L., Bates, G., Christopher, M., Shakespeare, T., & Officer, A. (2012). Prevalence and Risk of Violence Against Children with Disabilities: A Systematic Review and Meta-analysis of Observational Studies. *The Lancet, 380*(9845), 899–907.

Kelly, B., & Dowling, S. (2015). *Safeguarding Disabled Children and Young People: A Scoping Exercise of Statutory Child Protection Services for Disabled Children and Young People in Northern Ireland.* Belfast: Safeguarding Board NI.

Kelly, B., Dowling, S., & Winter, K. (2014). *A Review of the Legislative and Policy Context in Relation to Looked After Disabled Children and Young People in Northern Ireland.* Belfast: OFMDFM/Queen's University Belfast.

Kelly, B., Dowling, S., & Winter, K. (2015). *Profiling the Population of Disabled Looked After Children and Young People in Northern Ireland.* Belfast: Queen's University Belfast/OFMDFM.

Kelly, B., Dowling, S., & Winter, K. (2016). *Addressing the Needs and Experiences of Disabled Children and Young People in Out-of-Home Care.* Belfast: Queen's University Belfast/OFMDFM.

Lightfoot, E., Hill, K., & LaLiberte, T. (2011). Prevalence of Children with Disabilities in the Child Welfare System and Out of Home Placement: An Examination of Administrative Records. *Children and Youth Services Review, 33,* 2069–2075.

McConkey, R., Nixon, T., Donaghy, E., & Mulhern, D. (2004). The Characteristics of Children with a Disability Looked After Away From Home and Their Future Service Needs. *British Journal of Social Work, 34*(4), 561–576.

Morris, J. (1999). Disabled Children, Child Protection Systems and the Children Act 1989. *Child Abuse Review, 8,* 91–108.

Murray, M., & Osborne, C. (2009). *Safeguarding Disabled Children: Practice Guidance.* Nottingham: DCSF.

Oswin, M. (1978). *Children Living in Long-Stay Hospitals.* London: Spastics International Medical Publications.

Philips, R. (1998). Disabled Children in Permanent Substitute Families. In C. Robinson & K. Stalker (Eds.), *Growing Up with Disability.* London/Philadelphia: Jessica Kingsley Publishers.

Schmidt, V., & Bailey, J. D. (2014). Institutionalization of Children in the Czech Republic: A Case of Path Dependency. *Journal of Sociology and Social Welfare, 41,* 53.

Stalker, K., & McArthur, K. (2012). Child Abuse, Child Protection and Disabled Children: A Review of Recent Research. *Child Abuse Review, 21*(1), 24–40.

Sullivan, P. M., & Knutson, J. (2000). The Association Between Child Maltreatment and Disabilities in a Hospital-Based Epidemiological Study. *Child Abuse & Neglect, 22*, 271–288.

Taylor, J., Cameron, A., Jones, C., Franklin, A., Stalker, K., & Fry, D. (2015). *Deaf and Disabled Children Talking About Child Protection*. Edinburgh: University of Edinburgh & NSPCC.

Westcott, H. L., & Jones, D. (1999). Annotation: The Abuse of Children. *Journal of Child Psychology and Psychiatry, 40*, 497–506.

Berni Kelly is a Senior Lecturer in Social Work and Co-Chair of the Disability Research Network at Queen's University Belfast. Her main research interests are child and youth disability studies and disabled children's experience of child care and protection services. Berni also has an active interest in participatory research with disabled children and young people.

Sandra Dowling is a Lecturer in Disability Studies at the Norah Fry Centre for Disability Studies, University of Bristol. She has a particular interest in childhood disability research including projects focused on disabled looked after children and young people and safeguarding disabled children. She is also interested in identity and has developed inclusive methods for engaging disabled children and young people in research.

Karen Winter is a Lecturer in Social Work. Her research and publications centre on children and young people known to social services. Projects have focused on children's rights; social worker relationships and communication with children, professionals and carers; children's educational and social wellbeing; and early intervention support services.

Easy Targets: Seen and Not Heard—The Silencing and Invisibility of Disabled Children and Parents in Post-Reform Aotearoa New Zealand

Rod Wills

Key Points

- Families are positioned by services, professional knowledge and media.
- Disability charity organisations and support groups have taken on the roles previously associated with state-funded institutions.
- Families become consumers rather than navigators steering their own course.
- De-institutionalisation had taken over two decades to achieve, the model of managerialism and reform was implemented in less than 12 months.
- Print media discourse maintains a negative regard of disabled people, children and their parents.
- The provision of care by families is linked to the view that disability is an individual's burden.
- In contemporary society, the ethos of individualism and choice often displace disability rights.

This chapter takes a critical view of the experience of families caring for a child or adult identified as disabled. The analysis and commentary is framed within multiple contexts. Family experiences and caregiving demands of the 1960s offer a starting point. While much has changed, little appears to have altered in the power relations between families and the professionals and services in place to support them and their family member. The analysis of this lack of change and an exploration of the emergence of the new models of

R. Wills (✉)
University of Auckland, Auckland, New Zealand

© The Author(s) 2018
K. Runswick-Cole et al. (eds.), *The Palgrave Handbook of Disabled Children's Childhood Studies*, https://doi.org/10.1057/978-1-137-54446-9_35

575

disability support are framed within an account of the policies and politics of neo-liberal reform and disability in Aotearoa New Zealand.

Introduction

Families in Aotearoa New Zealand, who have a member with an intellectual disability are 'positioned' by regulations, service practice, the impact of professional knowledge and media reporting. Often, these elements combine to shape, filter or silence their voices. I start this exploration in the context of the extended family of which I am a part. I then offer analysis of the impact of government reform, examine media discourse from samples I have gathered and explore mechanisms of control, before reflecting on future challenges and actions needed for children, young adults and parents to be heard. I have explored in many ways how the 'personal is political'. Although the attribution is debated (Hanisch 2006), it is inescapably this phrase that best connects the larger social and political structures with the personal experience of disability in Aotearoa, New Zealand, today.

While the ideas of choice and consumerism play well with the drivers of competitive individualism now predominant in our lives, there are other vulnerable members of society for whom these approaches may be less effective.

Where identity and role cannot be readily altered, Davis (2013) suggests that the biocultural era creates a question of the validity of a person who differs in body or mind from others. The processes established to deliver what had been regarded as good and necessary for the individual, because of their deviance or deficiency, have often silenced families. Along the way, little time is given to understanding what is best. My concluding remarks close the cycle where the chapter began, seeing the family itself as the site for action and self-determination (Fig. 1).

Prologue: One Family—Three Generations

The ethics panel reported that they were not prepared for me to introduce the family snapshot, made in 1941, into the material that I was researching. The photograph was regarded as creating 'inadvertent subjects' who were then categorised as being vulnerable, and furthermore one of the infants in the photograph had a disability, he needed protection. However, they said if I was to disguise the identity of the subjects, then the issues that caused them concern would be addressed. I spoke at length with the twin brother

Fig. 1 The anonymised twins (Rod Wills)

of the young child with Down syndrome who had died in 1976. He had no problem with his image being used, and all things considered felt it was appropriate for his twin to be shown too. Our conversation had been about the work and struggle of their mother in raising them and their four siblings in the provincial town they lived in. Following medical advice, the twin with Down syndrome was institutionalised. His mother maintained contact with the hospital authorities, some 500 kilometres away, and was increasingly concerned for her child. She made the journey south to the institution before her son turned five to see for herself and disturbed by the situation where he was being cared for, brought him back home. Community participation became a significant issue for this family. He attended the local primary school for some time; a situation that in the late 1940s was regarded as too difficult for the teachers. He stayed home, and his mother provided basic tuition while raising him with his siblings. Dissatisfied with the only government care available being at the institution in the South Island, his mother joined with other parents and established a branch of the Intellectually Handicapped Parents' Association in their town. Forty-four years later, her granddaughter, my wife, gave birth to the eldest of our three daughters. Sophie had Down syndrome too. Both families' pathways have been similar; education for the child at the local school, their living at home and a future with siblings in an extended family arrangement. The two women taking roles was highly visible to the neighbours and residents of their communities, in supporting other families and advocating for the everyday lives of disabled children.

Much had changed in the intervening years, but in some respects, little has altered. There was a struggle for mothers to be heard by specialists and practitioners, to be respected without question by officials in order to readily access the range of supports and services to live a good life in the community. The last of the institutions closed in 2006, and in their place, a collection of statutory and voluntary organisations had established themselves as disability service providers.

Disability: Children and Families

The government response to intellectual disability in New Zealand had seen a policy of segregation and isolation accepted by the public. Families and communities were removed, at least in part, of the 'burden' of care. Up until the 1960s, institutionalisation was evident to a level that when compared saw 'nearly four times as many children and three and a half times as many adults as the United Kingdom' (O'Brien et al. 1999: 6) being placed in the lunatic asylums, psychiatric hospitals and psychopaedic hospitals throughout New Zealand.

The physical institutions are no longer used, some have been demolished and others have been repurposed, as the government policy of providing institutional care has ended; however, the power of ideas and practices associated with the institutions remains largely intact. A shift is evident where over time the nature and function of the major disability charity organisations and parent support groups have taken on many of the functions and much of the influence associated with the former institutions. The impact this has had on disabled children and families appears in the most part to be overlooked.

With the continued mimicry of approaches borrowed from abroad, assumptions remained in place that practitioners were experts, and that families best remained as the subjects of their intervention. While such a response can be readily understood as a demand associated with reliance upon a teleological model, seen as a cure-all or necessity in reaction to a disabling condition, such a stance would often be insufficient in offering the understanding needed to look beyond the particular characteristics and features of impairment. A much more critical regard of systems may have helped to see and understand the paradigm shifts needed as part of the achievement of inclusion sought by government policy. However, looking through an introspective lens would not enable a clear understanding to develop and in all likelihood will lead to a reductionist position. By way of contrast, a systems-thinking approach as contemporised by Peter Senge counteracts an otherwise narrowing vision.

'We are taught to break apart problems, to fragment the world. This apparently makes complex tasks and subjects more manageable, but we pay a hidden enormous price. We can no longer see the consequences of our actions' (Senge 1990: 6). Consequently, the lack of critical vision has left disabled children and their parents as easy targets for service systems which continue to engage with families, as consumers, but not necessarily as navigators steering their own courses over the lifespan of the disabled child.

The influence of international policies and economic arrangements associated with globalisation are evident in New Zealand as the politics of neoliberalism. They cast a shadow across the less well off in communities and across society in general, and they shape the political economy of disability. Accounts of the broad and rapid changes enacted by successive governments of both left and right political leanings have been detailed elsewhere. The most accessible and comprehensive account is offered by Kelsey (1997) in her work *The New Zealand experiment: A world model for structural adjustment?*

My analysis arises from my professional practice in the formal welfare, disability and education sectors, and a much longer engagement in voluntary community roles in the same domains. These activities have been, and continue to be, intertwined within the context of the government agenda of reform. My views are coloured by our experiences as parents, and as a family where disability has often dominated our focus and future vision. The monitoring of media commentary and reporting in these areas broadens my observation of 'life from the inside' as the published messages about human difference bring echoes of earlier eugenic concerns. The parallels between the experiences of two women, my wife and her grandmother were strong in similarity; both families having had several members involved in the education sector, and with what we call in Aotearoa New Zealand, the 'number eight wire approach' of problem-solving. Meaning that many things are possible with a hands-on approach and a can-do attitude and that with simple tools and materials (number eight wire is used in farm fences) a lot can be achieved. And it is from these points of comparison, and looking across our own journey of the last 30 years, that I anchor my concerns. We had witnessed and participated in much of the change surrounding the education of disabled children and the development of structures to provide support for families in the local community (Wills 1994, 1997; Wills and Chenoweth 2005).

The present systems, services and groups operating to provide support have brought a stifling of voices, identity, individual choice and influence. The silencing and loss of 'real identity' of children, young adults and their parents, where a family member has a cognitive dependency, comes about from the interweaving of three sets of factors:

- The first element is the maintenance of stereotypic identities by media process.
- The second element is the emergence of disability charity organisations and their reach into the service sector.
- The third element arises from the second, with the proliferation of small provider groups within the disability sector.

The mechanisms used by government ministries and agencies follow the business practices of contracting with pricing control and quality monitoring through measured outcomes. Where an organisation is registered as a charity, they are subsequently prohibited from any advocacy or lobbying activities deemed to be political. These purchase and advocacy controls have brought about a culture that muffles and silences the voice of families, just as much as it enables instrumental support. As a consequence, the overwhelming impact of these three elements is the dis-juncture between the multiple functions of sector organisations and the solutions sought by families to meet their individual child's need.

In times of fiscal restraint since the global financial crisis of 2008, rather than enabling change for the better, many sector groups and charity organisations lean towards continuation of the status quo. This often means that children identified as disabled, and their families, are propelled down a pathway of dishuman experience. This is shaped by the crude binaries of distinction, 'dis/ability' and 'disa/abled' where the subjugation into the role and identity of 'other' and 'less than' is the norm when receiving services or support and alterity is assured, leaving individuals positioned as outliers in the societal mainstream.

Government Reform: The New Agenda

The reforms deployed by successive governments—the New Zealand 'model' had their genesis in the Treasury briefing following the general election in 1987. *Government Management* 'catalogued the weaknesses of the existing administrative order and provided the analytic framework' for correction and subsequent changes (Boston et al. 1996: 3). The model presented broad objectives to be achieved, key principles or doctrines to be followed and the specifics of policies that formed the whole model. Amongst the principles was the position that 'The government should only be involved in those activities that cannot be more efficiently and effectively carried out by non-governmental bodies (e.g. private businesses, voluntary agencies, etc.)' (Boston et al. 1996: 6). Increasingly, the provision of disability services and support had moved from being the domain of the state, to a mix of providers, over a range of settings.

This new combination of state, voluntary and for-profit sectors constituted a market for disability support and enabled independent service providers, specialist professionals, voluntary groups and not-for-profit trusts to transact in the field. The boundary distinctions, characteristics and differentiations that previously operated had become blurred by the contracting approach. The suggestion that a 'tension field' approach which examined the nature of these relationships was made by Scott (2003: 299) in considering the need to understand the 'interacting, brokering challenging and dynamics' between the organisations that occupy these positions.

A Tool for Change

The agenda for reform was particularised. Amongst the stated objectives of the health reforms was the desire to 'encourage efficiency, flexibility and innovation in service delivery; widen consumer choices' (Upton 1991: 137). The purpose of the change in funding and implicitly, accountability, was presented with this underscoring 'the government's strategy of trying to make individuals, their families and their local community responsible for their own wellbeing, rather than the state' (Rudd 1997: 252). Serendipitously, the reform goals and the process of deinstitutionalisation aligned with the changes in the health services. The move to a market model was swift. The debate around the philosophies of models for disability service provision had brought impetus to institutional closure, albeit in a somewhat piecemeal fashion that would eventually take 15 years amongst the health authorities and the district health boards to reach completion. The change to the model of service funding and management approach took place in less than 12 months.

> The central feature of the health reforms introduced in July 1993 was the splitting of the roles of purchaser and provider ... this required the integration into a single budget of funds for primary, secondary and disability support services, ... all of which had previously been funded by different funding streams. (Ashton 1999: 135)

This change commenced in the Auckland region, the largest population centre—with an already greater percentage of disabled people living in the community than in other cities. Throughout the institutional closure processes critical commentary and dissent accompanied the planned changes. The media rhetoric, particularly that in the local community press, fuelled disdain and nimby-ism (not in my backyard) that reflected a level of bigotry not often expressed towards other community groups. Twenty-five years after the closure of the psychopaedic hospital in Auckland, the daily press continued to be the vehicle for a discourse that readily maintained discrimination against disabled people, disabled children and their families.

Populist Views: Media Discourse

Language often reinforces the dominant culture's view of disability, contributing a blend of understanding, shaped by a range of influences from a variety of sources. Bignell (2002) maintains that 'linguistic codes used in newspapers are not all the same. Particular linguistic signs, narrative forms, and mythic meanings deriving from a news source' (Bignell 2002: 89). In the Aotearoa New Zealand society of 2015, a convergence of influences associated with media, charity and medicine came into play—when considering disability, these brought forward a series of messages to the public, politicians and the state sector; all those who had influence over policymaking.

The examples of text found as headlines in the online edition of the largest metropolitan daily newspaper, *The New Zealand Herald*, exemplified the way in which the media constructed or framed people with impairment as a social group. The mechanism of framing relied on the 'presence or absence of certain keywords, stock phrases ... and the use of sentences that provided thematically reinforcing clusters of facts or judgments ... to ... makes certain terms more salient or memorable for their audience' (Haller 2010: 50); these set in place a populist commonsense or 'truth'. The headlines presented relied upon and reinforced readers' existing knowledge, even where this had been mediated and shaped by the writer or the sub-editor of the 'story'. Publishing practice with its emphasis on multi-format publishing broadened the platform of the reporter from the traditional print edition of the publication, to variants accessed through the Internet, of multiple media forms.

To build a record of the media discourse of disability, a sampling method was adopted. Every day for the ten-month period until the end of August 2015, the front page of the online version of the NZ Herald was checked for stories about disability, the paper had an audited daily print circulation of 140,600 (ABC 2015), and in 2014, it had reported a combined daily print and online audience of 844,000 readers. The articles may have been opened from the front page, or their headline presented in a section on the page with the rest of the story opening once the headline had been selected. Each story was printed and a copy saved for future analysis. With the exception of one account, the stories were about events occurring in Aotearoa New Zealand, a total of 33 items were gathered. Their captions are grouped thematically with the headlines presented as they appeared in the publication. The headings in Table 1, which follows, have been clustered under six themes, four of which are the subject of specific government policy provision—education, health,

Table 1 Press headlines: NZ Herald November 2014–August 2015

Education: troublesome—a bother to the rest of the school
Special needs plan a 'cruel' change
Take back bad pupils schools told
Green Bay High fights to keep boy with Asperger's out
He's owed a huge apology says mother of expelled boy with Asperger's
Funding pitiful for schools with needs
School gets $4M for 11 kids

Health: sick and diseased
Unborn baby tests fail to take off
Paracetamol link to ADHD
Disabled Kiwis dying up to 23 years before others
System-failing offenders with alcohol-related brain disability
Treating ADHD with games
Passed fit for school

Carer payment: a price to be paid
Pay family as caregivers Turia urges
Bureaucratic hurdles means few parents get paid to care for disabled children
Human tragedy lost in cash rush
Voucher system sparks fear of privatisation

Risk: a group to be avoided
Report slams dysfunctional care provider
Auckland police in search for missing autistic man
Home criticised after autistic resident harmed
Disabled teen drowns in bath
Roommates show others how it's done

Employment: not real workers
KFC policy lets it ditch disabled
KFC gives way for the disabled
KFC calls back disabled staff
Disabled staff forced out of a job

Social identity: others not like us
Families of Down Syndrome children respond to Laws' remarks
Shop's Facebook post made fun of people with Down Syndrome
Disabled people must have a voice
Dating show with a heart an antidote to franchise hell

Social identity: Weird—freaks
The Cystic Sisters spread good deeds to raise awareness
Man who froze dead cats receives ban
Disabled man eats himself to death
Lone Ranger anger over evil birth defect

employment and carer payment. The other headings of risk and social identity are also areas of policy or regulatory concern. These mainstream media stories are indicative of the understanding and expression of disability constructed by the press. Overwhelmingly, the message from this sample presented a discourse that disabled people should be noticed for their cost, risk and dangerousness to society.

The disability charity sector organisations would argue that their purpose, in part, was to counter these views; however, their reliance on government-funded contracts for service delivery and the controls on advocacy regulated by the Charities Act (2005) all too often silences the voices they had previously been a conduit for.

Disability Charity and Funding

The establishment of the major disability charity organisations is well documented. Through the accounts of Millen (1999), Newbold (1995) and New Zealand CCS (1995), the development of the impairment-specific support groups can be traced. These groups offered support and links between parents and families in their communities. The larger charity organisations had become sophisticated in their multi-pronged fundraising strategies, while the small parent support groups often relied on funds from their local government authority through the Community Organisation Grant Scheme and may have supplemented this by way of Lotteries Grants Board funding or donations from philanthropic and charitable sources, alongside community fundraising ventures. While the Gaming and Lotteries Act (1977) required the return of 20 cents in every dollar back to the community, through the Lottery Grants Board, the 1991 legalisation of electronic gaming increased the level of funding to the community which made a real difference for the operation of disability support groups. The Casino Act (1990) required that 37% of the takings of electronic gaming machines be returned back to groups whose activity was of benefit to the whole, or a section of, the community.

Service Purchase

With the process of deinstitutionalisation, completed by 2006, the disability charity organisations and the smaller support groups had become the disability sector service providers. Alongside the funding from the re-distribution of gambling takings across the community, many of the groups and organisations negotiated contracts for service with the Ministries of Health, Social Development and Education (Beatson 2000). These contracts prescribed and specified the range of activities and services to be delivered within the broader legislative framework for government-funded providers and the particular requirements of the Health and Disability Services Act (2000). Where organisations had previously enjoyed less formal arrangements, they were subjected to the rigour and controls applied to all state-funded services. Restructuring was to follow as many of the traditional arrangements and supports were no longer purchased. Local variation would occur where other providers were able to contest and win contracts for specific 'outputs' as part of the service mix determined by the funder for the population of disabled adults and children in any particular community or region.

Regulating Advocacy

A further control mechanism, felt across the sector, but particularly by the smaller parent support organisations, was the application of the registration standards and controls of activities stipulated in the Charities Act (2005). The requirement that organisations had exclusively charitable purposes and the use of definitions and tests of their activities was prescribed by the legislation. A Supreme Court ruling on the activities of the Greenpeace organisation impacted directly on the advocacy activities of all registered charities and specifically that defined as political action. In essence, a group could not utilise the funding or income it had generated through support or service delivery to subsidise its lobbying for legislative or regulatory change, or to maintain the adoption of a political stance in disagreement with government policy.

Lessons from Education: Rights and Needs but Not Collective Concerns

In some Western nations, there had been an attraction to follow a pathway of rights assertion, supported by statute and aided by litigation. In New Zealand, the few instances of these approaches and the subsequent outcomes, failed to signal to families that stepping down the legal pathway would bring resolution to disputes. Court actions undertaken in the domains of education and family carer support and payment had both led to rulings at appellate level that left unresolved questions for others who may have wished to follow a similar route.

The most publicised case associated with educational rights arising from disability had been conducted over a sustained period. The significant cost and stress associated with the court hearings had, no doubt, acted as a dissuading factor for other parents considering the legal route to challenge decisions and seek remedy to their disputes. The lack of a fully funded legal and advocacy service has contributed to the fact of there being only three actions through the High Court.

The earliest case has been illustrative of the complexity of juridical process in this area of law. The court rulings arising from the action commenced by a group of 16 parents of disabled students at the beginning of 2000, Daniels v. Attorney-General, have been discussed 'as to their ultimate impact on the enforceable right of a disabled child to an inclusive education in local schools' (Wills 2014: 93). The sequence of hearings firstly in the High Court in 2002, the subsequent appeal by the Ministry of Education and a further hearing by the Court of Appeal in 2003, had presented two opinions with differing content and application. The outcome has 'left judicial review as an all but hollow remedy in terms of enforcing the right to education in New Zealand' (Ryan 2004: 746).

A casualty of the changes linked to state reforms had been a weakening of the sense of duty and obligation to others as a stance of competitive individualism had emerged. As the state is rolled back the policies of privatisation impacted heavily upon the traditional infrastructures and social fabric. These were weakened, and the caring networks of families and community struggled to fill the gaps created. As Kemshall (2002: 115) suggested, 'Social capital – that is, trust, civic obligation and social solidarity – does not exist in sufficient measure to replace state welfare'. Where in the past civil society prevailed, a care 'market' had evolved. The neo-liberal critique would suggest that this could be expected as community responsiveness is eroded by 'moral dependency and the moral hazard of welfare' (Kemshall 2002: 115). While the state had answered the concerns of political legitimacy in leaving a mechanism in place to enable a welfare response to care needs, the political economy of disability had sharply re-focused care provision as a parental task as disability was re-configured as an individual burden. Sector providers, seeing an opportunity to establish lines of influence, developed an organisational response to the needs of carers across the range of health and disability organisations.

Carers NZ: A Service Lobby

The voluntary disability sector with its multiple arms of engagement left a confusing presence for the public. Organisations associated with supporting families, and aiding children and adults with disabilities were among the major 'players' in the disability service marketplace. In 2007, the Minster for Disability Issues and Minister for Senior Citizens, Hon Ruth Dyson, announced the *Carers' Strategy*. The *Strategy* was identified as being 'part of a wider Government process to improve the choices of parents and other informal carers so they can better balance their paid work, their caring responsibilities and other aspects of their lives' (Ministry of Social Development 2008: 4).

The announcement detailed the history of the approach from the NZ Carers Alliance group, a consortium of 45 national not for profits representing most of the sector groups responding to disability and chronic illness. While some operated at the grassroots level in communities, others were national providers. Carers NZ, a parallel umbrella organisation, acted as both a secretariat of the Alliance and a provider of information, advice, learning and support for its individual members. Additionally, it provided the constitutional support for three other carer sector groups and indicated on its website that its network extended to 50,000 carers nationally.

Alongside the objective of providing support to family carers, the organisation stated its primary role to promote the interests of its members to decision-makers in health, education, employment, social services and other relevant areas. A 70-page magazine was produced quarterly in both print and electronic formats. While giving the appearance of being a representative body carrying forward ongoing concerns of the broad constituent membership, the establishment of the organisation, the umbrella website, magazine production and support centre operation, was all primarily the work of one person. Subsequently the collective funnelling through this single point, and the consolidation of information and issues by The Carers Alliance is likely to filter individual's stories and any impact they may have had upon policymakers, as the primary function became that of the representation of the interests of the provider sector members who funded the costs of the operation.

Policymaking

The policymaking environment in New Zealand may be described as one of disjointed incrementalism (Lindblom 1979); the approaches this engenders are characterised as muddling through. Bureaucrats and officials in departments and ministries have responded to disability in areas of education, community participation and family support through the promotion of solutions to problems rather than a shift in values. Pragmatism, feasibility and a level of consensus amongst interest groups had been factors to be considered. Often policy trials would be a feature, and consequently, implementation varied as many participants and groups responded by re-interpreting the mix of policy goals and values being brought forward. The loss of sight of the impacts of policy decisions upon individuals and their families had been a feature of the policy landscape for some time. The effect of their distantiation easily overlooked by officials often isolated from the impacts of changes upon individuals, families and communities. Many times, issues were exacerbated by historical patterns of service provision no longer matching population distribution. And in the case of the largest population centre, the Auckland region, the cultural diversity and migrant population concentrations created conditions not found elsewhere. While the situation existed within the framing of an understanding of rights in which 'in the case of international human rights law, the state has a *duty* to ensure that the right is protected' [emphasis in original] (Geiringer and Palmer 2007: 15); this was no guarantee of outcomes. Contemporary society in Aotearoa New Zealand, alongside the framing of rights was seeking an even stronger ethos of individualism and choice, even when the consequences of choice making were not fully understood.

Choice and Possibilities

Davis (2013) reiterates, 'welfare and social well-being are viewed as products of individuals choice … within a free market economy' (10). What jars in this re-framing is the notion that identity might be something that is chosen too, and in many instances, this seems to be accepted. However, the extension of the lived experience of disability into this model does not work, 'disability just doesn't fit into this concept of lifestyle choice' (Davis 2013: 11). One feature of the reform agenda of the government had been the repositioning of the family as consumers of disability support services. This role should be understood as part of the construct of a market model, with the intersections between the range of services, as illustrated in Fig. 2.

However the expectation that family choice and responsibility would go hand in hand is illustrative of the differences that existed between the care market and the typical experience of purchasing consumer items. In the market of disability support, service and care, it is often the supplier who decides upon the quantum and range of goods produced. As the supply is usually linked directly to resources allocated by the state, gaps can develop between supply and demand created by family 'wants'. As Cheyne et al. (2000) pointed out 'Choice is determined by the resources available and the decisions of the professionals, not … by the consumer' (192). The problem emerged when the logic was extended to the position that by the making of a choice the consumer was then responsible for the outcomes and consequences of their decisions.

New Zealand disability data provided a backstory of significant disparities where the educational achievement, comparative income levels and life expectancy of disabled youths and adults varied from that of other New Zealanders.

- Students with high or very high support needs have a significantly lower achievement rate in National Certificate in Educational Achievement (NCEA) qualifications than the general population. Eighty-five per cent of the teenagers receiving special education support will achieve below the standards of their same-age peers (Treasury 2015: 20).
- A total of 80% of the population with an intellectual disability as living below the poverty line and '18% of children with a disability living in families with an income less than $30,000 per year' (IMM 2014: 88).

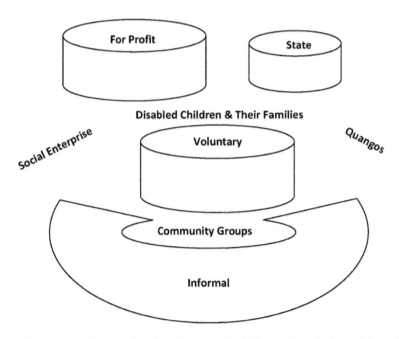

Fig. 2 The complex intersection in reformed disability services (Adapted from Scott 2003)

- Women with an intellectual disability having a life expectancy 23 years less than that of women without such a condition. Men with an intellectual disability are expected to live 18 years less than men without such impairment (Ministry of Health 2011: xi).

The ability to respond to this data from a policy and service basis appears to be hampered by sector lobbying and provider capture that clouds the development of innovative responses to better address the situation.

Government Planning and the Future

The inability of the sector to provide workable advice to the government had been signalled. A Disability Data and Evidence Working Group, co-facilitated by the Office for Disability Issues and Statistics New Zealand, was established during 2015. They would 'Identify the current high priority areas to support the monitoring of and reporting on the Convention on the Rights of Persons with Disabilities, the New Zealand Disability Strategy and the Disability Action Plan 2014–2018; and ensure informed decision-making supports the development of disability policy and service planning to accommodate the needs of disabled people' (Hon Nicky Wagner, Minister for Disability Issues June 2015).

The pointed observation was made two years after Sophie was born, and the reflection remained as valid today; 'The industries in our field are political, defensive, organized, and less interested in the public good than they should be' (Blatt 1987: 216) as they are still reliant upon disabled children, adults and families as consumers of their services. For data and evidence to be real and hold sway over policymakers and their processes, individuals need to be known as members of families and a part of their local communities, not as anonymous service consumers. To achieve this, a new challenge prevails.

Individual Voices

The health, disability and research protocols that currently 'protect' disabled children, their parents and disabled adults, by making them anonymous, have a range of unintended consequences. For individuals seeking to retain or reclaim agency in their lives, the use of their name moves them closer to a point of dignity and control, when much of everything else may have been removed as a feature of their care. For disabled children, the substitution of a label for their true identity readily allows their being rendered as someone who is less. A new identity is substituted for people like Sophie and her second cousin, something akin to that arising from Fig. 3, if they are regarded as vulnerable and dependent and not really known for whom they are. Other voices are being heard, increasingly speaking against a similar loss of agency. Of late, these have been individuals whose identities have been suppressed on the order of a law court, to protect them as individuals who have been abused or whose family member had committed suicide. They too have been silenced, and now their desire to speak out and generate public debate finds the mechanism of their protection leaving them as victims without a voice of their own.

It is evident that at times the acceptance and maintenance of some principles may be wrong. This is not a popular position to adopt and will provoke anger from those who hold the view and belief of what is declared to be the best for others. Nevertheless when this position is upheld without question, difficulty and power imbalance remains. The position taken by the community organiser Saul Alinsky demands consideration:

> … there is a constant danger that our own complete acceptance and passionate devotion to a cause may preclude that very cause from any critical scrutiny. It is that strange paradox that the things we primarily take for granted are the last to be questioned. (Alinsky 1946: 33)

Fig. 3   The socially acceptable disabled person (Rod Wills)

Being in Action: A Necessary Response

The policy sociologist Stephen Ball (1995) proposed that while theory may offer a way forward or an understanding, this might be neither straightforward nor obvious, and it may 'upset the applecart'; how excellent! Much of what families encounter arising from their child being called disabled, following on from Ball's position needs a sound application of theory:

> Theory is a vehicle for 'thinking otherwise'; it is a platform for 'outrageous hypotheses' and for unleashing criticism. Theory is destructive, disruptive and violent. It offers a language for challenge, and modes of thought, other than those articulated for us by dominant others. It provides a language of rigour and irony rather than contingency. The purpose of such theory is to de-familiarise present practices and categories, to make them seem less self-evident and necessary, and to open up spaces for the invention of new forms of experience. (Ball 1995: 266)

Speaking out and being heard becomes the next step for disabled children and parents in post-reform Aotearoa New Zealand. Their present silencing and invisibility as easy targets—seen and not heard—has done little to change the fundamental experience arising from being called disabled.

References

ABC Audit Bureau of Circulation. (2015, August 31). newspaper.abc.org.nz, downloaded.

Alinsky, S. D. (1946). *Reveille for Radicals*. Chicago: University of Chicago Press.

Ashton, T. (1999). The Health Reforms: To Market and Back? In J. Boston, P. Dalziel, & S. St John (Eds.), *Redesigning the Welfare State in New Zealand: Problems, Policies, Prospects* (pp. 134–153). Oxford: Oxford University Press.

Ball, S. J. (1995). Intellectuals or Technicians? The Urgent Role of Theory in Educational Studies. *British Journal of Educational Studies, 43*(3), 255–271.

Beatson, P. (2000). *The Disability Revolution in New Zealand: A Social Model*. Palmerston North: Massey University.

Bignell, J. (2002). *Media Semiotics: An Introduction* (2nd ed.). Manchester: Manchester University Press.

Blatt, B. (1987). *The Conquest of Mental Retardation*. Austin: Pro-Ed.

Boston, J., Martin, J., Pallot, J., & Walsh, P. (1996). *Public Management: The New Zealand Model*. Auckland: Oxford University Press.

Cheyne, C., O'Brien, M., & Belgrave, M. (2000). *Social Policy in Aotearoa New Zealand: A Critical Introduction* (2nd ed.). Auckland: Oxford University Press.

Davis, L. J. (2013). *The End of Normal: Identity in a Biocultural Era*. Ann Arbor: University of Michigan Press.

Geiringer, C., & Palmer, M. (2007). Human Rights and Social Policy in New Zealand. *Social Policy Journal of New Zealand, 30*, 12–41.

Haller, B. (2010). *Representing Disability in an Ableist World: Essays on Mass Media*. Louisville: Avocado Press.

Hanisch, C. (2006). *The Personal Is Political: The Women's Liberation Movement Classic with a New Explanatory Introduction*. http://www.carolhanisch.org/CHwritings/PIP.html. Date accessed 14 Feb 2016.

Independent Monitoring Mechanism. (2014). *Making Disability Rights Real: Second Report of the Independent Monitoring Mechanism*. Aotearoa: Author.

Kelsey, J. (1997). *The New Zealand Experiment: A World Model for Structural Adjustment?* Auckland: Auckland University Press and Bridget Williams Books.

Kemshall, H. (2002). *Risk, Social Policy and Welfare*. Buckingham: Open University Press.

Lindblom, C. E. (1979). Still Muddling, Not Yet Through. *Public Administration Review, 39*(6), 517–525.

Millen, J. (1999). *Breaking Barriers: IHC's First 50 Years*. Wellington: IHC New Zealand Inc.

Minister for Disability Issues. (2015). *Press Release*. Wellington: Parliamentary Services. http://www.beehive.govt.nz/release/new-zealand-world-leader-disability-issues

Ministry of Health. (2011). *Health Indicators for New Zealanders with an Intellectual Disability*. Wellington: Author.

Ministry of Social Development. (2008). *The New Zealand Carers Strategy*. Wellington: Author.

New Zealand CCS. (1995). *On the Move: A Celebration of 60 Years of New Zealand CCS* (A Pictorial History). Wellington: Author.

Newbold, G. (1995). *Quest for Equity: A History of Blindness Advocacy in New Zealand*. Palmerston North: Dunmore Press.

O'Brien, P., Thesing, A., & Capie, A. (1999). *Living in the Community for People with Intellectual Disabilities Who Moved Away from Long-Stay Care*. Auckland: Auckland College of Education.

Rudd, C. (1997). The Welfare State. In B. Roper & C. Rudd (Eds.), *The Political Economy of New Zealand* (pp. 237–255). Oxford: Oxford University Press.

Ryan, E. J. (2004). Failing the System? Enforcing the Right to Education in New Zealand. *Victoria University Wellington Law Review, 35*(29), 735–768.

Scott, D. (2003). The Role of the Voluntary and Non-governmental Sector. In J. Baldock, N. Manning, & S. Vickerstaff (Eds.), *Social Policy* (2nd ed., pp. 293–324). Oxford: Oxford University Press.

Senge, P. M. (1990). *The Fifth Discipline: The Art and Practice of the Learning Organisation*. New York: Double Day.

The Treasury. (2015). *Using Integrated Administrative Data to Identify Youth Who Are at Risk of Poor Outcomes as Adults*. Wellington: Author.

Upton, S. (1991). *Your Health and the Public Health*. Wellington: Ministry of Health.

Wills, R. (1994). It Is Time to Stop. In K. Ballard (Ed.), *Disability, Family, Whānau and Society* (pp. 247–264). Palmerston North: Dunmore Press.

Wills, R. (1997). Up Against It! Quality of Life and Families. In P. O'Brien & R. Murray (Eds.), *Human Services: Toward Partnership and Support* (pp. 293–305). Palmerston North: Dunmore Press.

Wills, R. (2014). The Problematics of Inclusive Education. In R. Wills, M. Morton, M. McLean, M. Stephenson, & R. Slee (Eds.), *Tales from School: Learning Disability and State Education After Administrative Reform* (pp. 91–108). Rotterdam: Sense Publishers.

Wills, R., & Chenoweth, L. (2005). Support or Compliance. In P. O'Brien & M. Sullivan (Eds.), *Allies in Emancipation: Shifting from Providing Service to Being of Support* (pp. 49–64). South Melbourne: Thomson Dunmore Press.

Rod Wills is a senior lecturer at the University of Auckland, New Zealand. He is the parent of a woman with a disability and has been involved in the disability sector for over 25 years. His current research explores learning about disability, individual narratives and the re-imagining of disability through the arts.

Family Voices in Teacher Education

Peggy Gallagher, Cheryl Rhodes, and Karen Young Lewis

Key Points

1. Building parent-professional partnerships begins with listening to families.
2. The voices of family members represent diverse perspectives and experiences.
3. Family members have an investment in supporting the child with disabilities and can be utilized in teaching others how to best interact with the child with disabilities.
4. A variety of strategies and resources are available to assure that family voices are shared while training teachers and other professionals who work with children with disabilities.

P. Gallagher (✉)
Georgia State University, Atlanta, GA, USA

C. Rhodes
Marcus Autism Center, Atlanta, GA, USA

K.Y. Lewis
Children's Healthcare of Atlanta, Atlanta, GA, USA

© The Author(s) 2018
K. Runswick-Cole et al. (eds.), *The Palgrave Handbook of Disabled Children's Childhood Studies*, https://doi.org/10.1057/978-1-137-54446-9_36

Introduction

Family voices are not always heard in teacher education. Yet, family members are valuable partners in the education of those with disabilities. They truly know the child best because they are with the child day in and day out, year after year. Their voices must be heard. This chapter presents an introduction to the practice of embedding family voices in teacher education in the U S, beginning with an overview of the importance of listening to families. Then, a brief overview of several theoretical frameworks of families with children with disabilities and specific suggestions for including family voices in teacher education are highlighted. While the theoretical models are from the research literature, the parent stories are included to illustrate the ideas. Parent stories have been collected by the authors from parents of children with disabilities and are used herein with permission. Next, techniques and tips for working with family members are outlined. Resources are also included. Resources and ideas from the broader global context are included where possible in hopes that these ideas can be shared and utilized across the world.

As teachers and other service providers, it is valuable to acknowledge family members as true partners in the well-being of the person with disabilities. Recognizing the parents' or siblings' knowledge, along with the perspective of the person with the disability, adds their important voices. For the purposes of this chapter, the voice of the person with disabilities will not be addressed, but it is acknowledged herein as the most important voice to hear when teaching and learning about persons with disabilities. The self-advocacy and self-determination movements (www.ngsd.org; www.autismspeaks.org; www.pacer.org/transition/; Gallagher et al. 2010) are invaluable in addressing the voice of the person with disabilities. Please note that "person first language" is used in this chapter (i.e., the person with disabilities, rather than the disabled person) to denote the importance of viewing people with disabilities first, as persons.

Often listening and learning from parents and family members begins at birth, especially for newborns in the Neonatal Intensive Care Unit (NICU). Karen, a mom whose son received early intervention services and later volunteered to share her story with program providers, recalls this perspective. "I learned other important lessons while there – listening was key, but also the art of conversing with professionals. During the first 8 months my son was listed as 'failure to thrive', but the first 5 months were his most critical. He had numerous surgeries and after each, his conditioned worsened. My son had different neonatologists making rounds; they took meticulous notes for each other to follow and since I was at his bedside daily, I began reading these charts to keep abreast of anything that happened when I was not present. One reoccurring theme I began to question was why his condition worsened after each surgery even though most were considered routine. The reports noted that usually a day after the surgery his condition would change to critical, but I remembered that after one particular surgery he fared better. The doctors listened to my concern and discovered the diuretic typically administered to patients was actually causing my son more harm. This doctor actually took the time to listen and the issue was corrected. The point I am making was that these were professionals at the top of their game giving exceptional care, but they listened and treated me as a peer – a partner in my son's care. In turn I listened and absorbed everything they told me. This has carried me through the 9 years of my son's life and has helped me in partnering with my son's teachers at school as well".

Imagine a teacher candidate hearing Karen tell her story. How powerful would that be in helping professionals to be more sensitive to the importance of listening to and learning from parents and other family members, as well as helping them understand the journeys that parents have often gone through with their child with significant disabilities.

Listening to Families

"Professional speak" is a term we use to describe the communication and understanding gap that can occur between parents and therapists, teachers, doctors, or other professionals. It is important that professionals be careful not to use professional jargon or acronyms without explaining them to the family members. Hearing a story such as the one below can bring to life the value of listening and partnering with family members as well as the importance of non-verbal communication. Such family stories are a "powerful way to develop relationships among parents and professionals", and as a result, have the potential to lead to change (Gabbard 1998, p. 1).

"At times these professionals speak on levels that families do not completely follow – what is being said is translated internally different to the recipients. This phenomenon goes both ways. One of the best examples of this situation happened when my son's physical therapist asked my opinion on a situation she was involved in. She noticed a family she was seeing had become distant, defensive, and seemed to have schedule conflicts sometimes when she wanted to visit. By her account, the family was originally very friendly, open, and involved in their child's progress. When asked what occurred on her last visit before everything changed, she said that she informed the parents that they needed to consider ordering a wheelchair for their son since he would soon turn three. I smiled and told her not to explain anything else (I had listened as a parent.) What I think the family heard was that their son would not learn to walk. Shocked, the therapist said that she would never say something like that to a parent and could not figure out how the parents jumped to that conclusion. My advice was for her to go back to the parents and explain the reason behind getting a wheelchair. For example, did you tell them that he is required to have a wheelchair in school if he could not walk? How that wheelchair would be essential if ever there was a fire at the school? That it is school policy that if a child is to be transported by school bus a chair is required? Did you relate the reason using everyday life examples? Did you explain how helpful it would be if the family decided to go shopping at a mall or any other place that required distance?"

On the flip side, many breakdowns in communication happen when parents speak to professionals. This story was shared with students in a class on collaboration with families and professionals:

"As a parent I have concluded that while the situation is new to me, these professionals who constantly work with children that have special needs can become desensitized because they see the diagnosis/situation and work with it daily. Usually the most mundane concern can become escalated. Parents may then be labeled as in denial, defensive, or even not understanding. A quick example comes to mind. I had a strained relationship with one of the first Occupational Therapists that saw my son during home visits. Her thoughts were that I was over protective because of my input. (She was the specialist and I needed to learn.) That was basically true, but I was simply trying to convey that my son was legally blind in his left eye and that maybe he was not progressing because she needed to adjust his therapy to accommodate the vision issue, not because he couldn't. This was not a listening relationship and eventually came to an end".

Communication must be a "two-way" street. Parents and professionals, while both wanting what's best for the child, do not always communicate well. A parent shared the story below of her perspective on her relationship with her son's school teachers:

"I will admit I was very reluctant to have my son enter into the school system at age 3. He was tracheid, nonverbal, fed through a G-Tube, had cortical visual impairment, severe sensory issues, and could not hold things effectively with his hands or even crawl. This was a new environment for me. But my son thrived and I learned to communicate and understand at yet another different level.

His first three years in pre-school he had the same teacher. He was the only child in class with medical issues as well as severe global delays. The school district's policy was to have a one on one nurse present at all times for a tracheid child. I described situations that may need attention to the nurse but I quickly realized that giving a medical report was not sufficient. My son would exhibit unexplainable behaviors and because I was not with him I could not help. The teacher and I had to develop better communication. Every child came home with a daily report (green = good, yellow = okay, and red = bad day). For him, she started including bowel movements, eat times, how much he ate, to paint a clearer picture of his day or what could have elicited behaviors. She wanted to know what I knew. Tears or certain behaviors were out of the ordinary. For example, banging his head on a toy meant that the switch was not on and he needed someone to activate the toy – not that he was having a melt-down. Hitting himself under his chin meant he was having gas or intestinal issues, swinging his arm up hitting his head meant stress, laughing uncontrollably and profuse sweating could be the onset of a seizure and seizure/seizure like behavior was usually followed by illnesses. Sudden shrill or loud sounds –sounds that you or I are accustomed to in everyday life – could lead to hysterics for hours. Turning away from the group or looking away at a task did not necessarily mean disinterested, it was a cortical issue. Sadly whenever I received a report of 'exceptional' behavior and a mellow child, I knew he was coming down with an illness (Now his teachers are able to detect if he is becoming sick)". A final example of an extended family story is included in Appendix A.

Theoretical Frameworks

Voices of family members come from many perspectives. Parents of course are major players in their children's development, but siblings, grandparents, aunts, uncles, and cousins are some of the many others whose voices also must be heard. Turnbull et al. (2011) describe family systems theory in which they focus on the importance of family members in the lives of children with disabilities. They remind us that the family is a system that incorporates many subsystems such as the sibling relationship or the parental relationship. They also describe the various functions that families serve including affection, daily care, education, spirituality, socialization, economics, and recreation, all of which are impacted with a person with disabilities. The Turnbulls also discuss the various stages of a family life cycle such as the birth of a child or discovering and coming to terms with the disability that are important to consider when looking at family members and their experiences. Another important foundational theorist for thinking about family voices is Uri Bronfenbrenner (1977). His bio-ecological model describes a child within a series of concentric circles, each of which is ever widening to include extended family members plus the broader community, all supporting the child and family. It is helpful to think of the family in a broad context, which includes parents, but also grandparents, brothers and sisters (Gallagher et al. 2006; Kresak et al. 2009), cousins, aunts, uncles, and so on. All these family members have a stake in supporting the child with disabilities and should be recognized as important partners who can be utilized to maximize opportunities for learning and support in informal settings.

Including Family Voices

Parents have been included in medical education and physician training for many years. Project Delivery of Chronic Care (DOCC) (Appell et al. 1996; Vaidya et al. 1999) uses family faculty to train residents and fellows in pediatrics and family medicine programs in the US and Australia (www.projectdocc. org). Developed in 1996 by parents of chronically ill children, the model uses three strategies, including home visits, parent interviews, and presentations, to teach doctors, nurses, and health educators about children with disabilities from a parent's perspective. In addition to providing a unique opportunity for medical professionals to learn about everyday life for families living with children with disabilities, family faculty report personal benefits from the program through having their experiences valued, gaining an understanding of the physician's view, and learning new skills (Appell et al. 1996).

Project DOCC also helps parents learn narrative advocacy, literally storytelling for policy advocacy, which connects unique personal experiences with larger issues. "This skill of strategic communication and advocacy is ideally developed when the child with special needs is very young, so that it will serve the parent and families throughout the educational process" (http://www.projectdocc.org/index.php/main-menu-narrative-advocacy). To assure successful inclusion of family members, it is important to consider several factors such as selection, preparation and training, feedback, and compensation.

Selection

Identify parents or other family members such as siblings or grandparents who are able to tell their story in a way that includes others. With parents, one suggestion is to target those whose own child was diagnosed several years prior, thus giving them a bit of distance and objectivity so that they may be at a point where they are comfortable sharing personal information and answering questions from the audience. As the program expands, experienced parents are excellent resources for recruiting and training new parent trainers.

Preparation

Giving parents and other family members clear guidelines and opportunities to practice telling their story is crucial to success. Since most presentations are part of a larger presentation, being able to share information concisely and in a way that captures the audience's attention makes a difference. Some programs provide written materials; video samples; in-person training ranging from several hours to a full day or more, with additional training through annual meetings; conference calls; and post-training debriefing to help family members learn to share their stories. Some common pitfalls to avoid are overwhelming the audience with too many details (getting lost in the story), using jargon (since medical terms and acronyms can be confusing or distracting), or not connecting with the audience. Having family members prepare their story (write it out), practice presenting the story (be sure to time it), and then solicit feedback from the audience (review it) help parents develop effective and interesting presentations.

Feedback

The parent or instructor can ask for feedback immediately following the presentation. Alternatively, written feedback can be shared with the parent or family member at a later date. Parents can reflect on their own presentation by requesting feedback from the instructor. If a participant evaluation form is used for the class or event, it should include questions about the impact of the parent presentation. Feedback from the co-trainer, verbally or in writing, is recommended.

Compensation

Although most family members do not seek compensation to share their story, many programs provide a stipend, gift card, or honorarium to recognize the value of the parent's time and cover or offset costs such as travel, parking, or child care. In a study evaluating the impact of parent trainers in resident training, parents were paid a US$50 stipend for each parent interview or home visit (Kube et al. 2012). Parent trainers in an early intervention training program were paid an honorarium each time they shared their story or attended the annual trainer meeting.

Strategies

We present a few of the many strategies to assure that family voices can be shared while training teachers and other professionals who work with children with disabilities. One important way is to co-teach a course or workshop with a parent or other family member. Another is to include guest lectures by family members. Students training to be teachers can also avail required visits to family homes, interviews with parents or siblings or grandparents. They can also gain a family perspective from required tasks during field placements such as attending meetings and considering them from a family perspective or interviewing teachers about their communication with family members. They can watch videos by siblings on what it was like to grow up with a family member with disabilities or read required articles that share the family perspective and experiences. Doctors and nurses, as well as hospital social workers and/or chaplains, can also benefit from hearing the voices of family members since they are often important team players in services for students with disabilities.

Co-teaching a Class

Co-teaching a class with a professional and family member can be a powerful way to show students how valuable family perspectives are. In a graduate class for masters' level students in Early Childhood Special Education, for instance, a faculty member co-taught a class on collaboration with families and professionals with a mother of a child with disabilities. This occurred over the course of eight years with two different mothers who were paid as an instructor. The parents were involved in developing the syllabus such that students would gain understanding of the strengths but also the challenges in families raising a young child with disabilities. The parent was present for every class and shared family scenarios and examples on various topics such as communication, setting up team meetings, family involvement in the schools, and so on. Parents read over student journals from visits with family members and commented from a family perspective.

Likewise, during in-service professional development workshops, parents can co-train with professional trainers. For example, one state's early intervention system required module training workshops on assessment, typical and atypical development, evaluation, teaming, and family systems included a paid family trainer along with the professional trainer. The parents gave their perspective on each of the important topics, including stories about their individual child to make the content meaningful and real world. Quotes from participants in these workshops supported the positive nature of the family voices and included the following: "I'm going to work on how to be more sensitive to families' beliefs"; "It was particularly strong that we learned about the dynamics of a team and how it's important to begin building the relationship with parents by letting them know they're the experts on their child"; "I loved having the parent trainer present and hearing her perspective"; "Learned more about communicating with the family"; and "Thoroughly enjoyed the parent trainer—great source of knowledge".

Guest Lectures

Guest lectures by family members can also be valuable in sensitizing students to the strengths and needs of family members, as well as the broader definitions of families. For instance, in a course on characteristics of young children with disabilities, having a mother (and sometimes her son and/or husband) attend class to share the journey of her son's premature birth and subsequent year's stay in an NICU of the hospital proved important in getting the students to understand why parents may seem overly protective of their child with disabilities or why they are sometimes frustrated that progress doesn't happen more quickly for their child. Representative quotes from both graduate and undergraduate teacher education candidates who have experienced guest lectures follow.

"…I was so moved by the guest speaker at class Tuesday night. So real and honest and inspiring. What an amazing yet involuntary journey she has taken alongside her fighter of a son, Cyrus. To hear a real story, live and in person, from a mother who has lived both dreams and nightmares in the medical and real world with her special boy, is an experience that will stay with me forever I hope".

"The best advice the mother shared with educators was to listen to the parents. When both the parents and educators communicate effectively the child reaps the benefits".

"When PARENT read the piece 'Where are the Parents' [S. Stuyvesant, https://www.child-autism-parent-cafe.com/where-are-the-parents.html], I immediately related that to my classroom parents. It's so important as a teacher not to place any pre-judgments on any family. Every family has their own dynamics".

"Her story reinforced the point that parents are truly the experts on their own children".

"I now understand how important it is to consider the family as a whole and the child as a whole. I will always remember the mother and son who visited the class. They taught me to remember the capability a child has no matter how fragile, and to listen to parents' hopes and dreams for their child".

"As a future special education teacher, her best advice for me was about communicating with parents. She spoke about how much she appreciates honesty and candidness when talking about her son's progress. I think it will be challenging to balance being realistic with parents while also keeping the tone positive".

"The most profound take-away from the lecture was to not ask parents to give up hope. It was really impacted by the personal story she shared about how her daughter's occupational therapist said she would never be able to write her name. This made me realize that as a teacher, I may have to get creative with how students reach their goals, but I can never stop believing in them".

"It was very refreshing to hear different parents discuss their perspectives on the IEP process. Teachers need to be mindful of parents' concerns as well as making the parents feel comfortable and free to ask questions. I loved how PARENT talked about how every parent takes on their own unique and on-going journey. As teachers, we have to be compassionate and empathetic with these families".

Home Visits

Another constructive way to enable students to understand families and their perspectives is through required home visits as part of a class requirement. The instructor must have relationships with families such that he/she can facilitate these visits. In one example, a faculty member requires graduate-level students to make three home visits to a family of a child with disabilities over the course of the semester. The syllabus states that "the goal of this assignment is to observe first-hand the everyday experiences associated with parenting a child with special needs. You will spend 6 hours over the course of the semester with the family, at times that are convenient for the family, and participate in whatever the family is doing during this time. The time should be spread out over 3 sessions with no visit being less than one hour. On each visit, you are to participate in whatever the family is doing during the time you are there. This might include meals, playtime, homework, family outings, recreation activities, grocery shopping, etc. You are to participate in the activities to the extent that you and the family feel comfortable. You should never be left alone with the child with disabilities (or any other children)—this is not a babysitting situation. You are also not there to provide help, consultation, or advice to the family. You are the one learning in this situation. Your goal is to see how the family interacts with the child and how the child interacts with his or her family and in the community. You are also there to learn what is is like to have a child with a disability—to learn the aspects of family life that are the same across all families and the unique challenges involved in including a child with disability into family routines and community environments" (Gallagher, EXC 7000; Spring 2015). A series of probe questions are reflected on by students after each visit. Student quotes below support the value of assignments such as these:

"Prior to meeting the family, I was a little nervous to be walking into someone's home without knowing anything about them and them not knowing much about me. However, I was immediately welcomed by the whole family. After meeting the family I realized how much having a child with a disability can affect simple tasks and everyday living. From meal times to simple errands, an even attending church, this family had to be constantly thinking ahead and worried if CHILD would have a meltdown".

"I think the biggest take away from this assignment was to be able to see the pains a family may experience living and taking care of a child with a disability. The mother was able to share her pains with me and shed some light on how incredibly frustrated she was and how she felt alone".

"From my experiences with PARENT and his family, I have become more empathetic and understanding of parents with children with more severe disabilities".

"I realized that family routines are common, and here the mother is in charge of many things, and disability or not, it is obvious a stay-at-home mom wears many hats.

Although I felt nervous about the first meeting, things did get easier after being there just a few minutes. Each visit got more and more comfortable. This experience taught me to be more sensitive and open when meeting parents of a child with a disability. Each family has a different story, and I feel it is important as a teacher to be open and listen to parents about concerns, scheduling conflicts and challenges. I was never truly aware of how much time, stress, and effort went in to caring for a child with a disability. I knew it was hard work prior to this experience, but after talking with the mother and seeing all the details I was so unaware of, I now understand better how much work goes into every day. I have such a high level of respect for these families and I will truly never forget this experience".

Field Assignments

Another fruitful way to understand family perspectives is through assignments in field or clinical placements that help students think about families. Requirements such as attending an Individualized Education Plan (IEP) meeting with professionals and families in attendance and then reflecting on it from the parent's perspective, or doing an interview with the teacher on all the ways she communicates with families, can be effective in helping students remember the perspectives of families. Students can learn so much from assignments, where they talk to family members. Several examples of student reflections from our own classes are below:

"She places more expectations on her child without a disability and she fears this is disrupting their relationship. She is aware of the challenges… I hope this mom can begin to take care of herself more".

"She said it can be difficult for other people to grasp and it is hard for some of her friends and family to understand what really goes on at home. She talked about the hours that parents like her spend in therapy sessions with their child, and how it can be tiring and overwhelming. One of the themes that came from our conversation was the reality of loneliness for a parent of a child with special needs. I told her how meaningful it had been to talk with her. Even though I have only had a small glimpse into STUDENT's life, I feel like I have gained a really valuable perspective. Our conversation made me think about how teachers can come along side parents in truly helpful ways. I've come away from this visit with a deeper understanding of the importance of listening to families".

"This experience really helped me grow as an individual and professional. It was so amazing to hear all of the hard work that goes into their everyday lives. Each family is different but I do feel every parent puts forth the effort for their child the best they can".

And another quote from reflections on field work in schools:

"I have seen that parents are quite involved in the activities at the school and I frequently see parents at the school. There were parents at both field trips. All teachers set up a parent-teacher conference schedule and meet with the parents during the year. For the Head Start program, teachers are required to complete home visits. STUDENT's mother and younger brother were at the team meeting also. The school holds coffee chats with the principal for parents throughout the year. The school also recently held a Family International Night. Each classroom represented a different country and families from the represented countries prepared food to share".

Readings, Videos, Internet Sites

When time or availability prevents family participation, the family experience can be represented through journal articles, parent blogs, videos, and handouts. *Welcome to Holland* (Kingsley 1987) is a good resource that is widely referenced and frequently used as it eloquently describes the initial reaction of a parent when she received her child's diagnosis of Down syndrome. Several alternate versions have been written by parents to describe their personal experiences with other disability conditions, some of which are not as positive as Kingsley's original essay. Parent-created videos, including many versions of *Welcome to Holland,* can be shared with students (see resources). Ensure that you preview these for length, appropriateness for students, and technical quality. Essays written by parents of children with disabilities can also be used to highlight themes, perspectives, or a specific disability (Klein and Schive 2001). For instance, the Denial article by Gallagher et al. (2002) can stimulate great class discussions (http://yec.sagepub.com/content/5/2/11.full.pdf). Parent websites and blogs (*10 Blogs for Special Needs Parents* www.sheknows.com/parenting/articles/816188/10-blogs-for-parents-of-kids-with-special-needs-1 and www.child-autism-parent-cafe.com; *Where Are the Parents* http://www.child-autism-parent-cafe.com/where-are-the-parents.html and http://www.danasview.net/where.htm) are good sources for poems and essays written by parents. Some essays and poems are heartfelt or gut wrenching, while others are funny and optimistic, revealing strengths such as humor, love, patience, and resilience. Students in our classes were most positive about their experiences with these types of assignments. Representative quotes follow:

"Last week we watched videos on how other children cope and handle living with a sibling that may require more attention, be able to get away with things, and at times, be embarrassing. I do not think that I had really thought about how living with a child with a disability would affect siblings. The video expressed how the typically developing child may feel towards their 'different' sibling".

"I wish I had a relationship with my siblings like they have. I think that it is hard to have a sibling with a disability because you always feel a responsibility for them, more so than a typical sibling".

"I do not want to be the educator who knows nothing about her students' home lives and only communicates with families in the form of newsletters. I want to directly connect with them and discuss their plans for their child together".

"I think that as I learn to become a professional I need to know that parents are often my greatest asset in helping children, and I need to not only have empathy for them but try to truly understand where they are coming from in order to successfully collaborate with them".

Tips for Family Professional Collaboration

Instructors should prepare for working with the family member. Regardless of the amount of parent participation, the instructor is responsible for communicating with the parent in a supportive, non-judgmental manner to make the parent feel welcomed and respected while modeling effective parent-professional collaboration. Sometimes this is easier said than done. The professional must be comfortable and accepting of different perspectives and willing to give up some control. Even with adequate preparation and discussion of key "talking points", the presentation may not go as planned. Parents sometimes give too much information on their own family or friends and may need to be gently reminded of confidentiality issues. It may be helpful to prepare them by saying "You may get asked questions that you find too personal. You don't have to answer every question; you can say, 'that's not something I want to talk about today'".

Additionally, the professional instructor should consider how to respond if a parent challenges something said by the instructor or a student or if they offer opinions or information that differs from what had been discussed previously in class. It will be helpful to discuss in advance the instructor's role and class interaction. For example, "You may hear some things in class that are new to you, that differ from your experience or that you disagree with. If you do, please ask me". Or, "Please feel free to comment but if you do, please be respectful of other perspectives, as we are all here to learn from each other".

Tips for Family Trainers: Preparing Your Story (See Appendix A for an Example)

- Know your message. What is the purpose of this story? Write it down. Start with an outline of no more than three to four major points.

- Know your audience. Will your story engage the listener? Tailor to your audience.
- Create an opening sentence that will get the listener's attention and end leaving the listener wanting for more. Tell your story succinctly. Don't try to fit in every fact or detail.
- Time and re-write the speech until you are satisfied that it fits the allotted time, reads well, and will engage the listener. If you stumble over pronunciation of certain words, such as medical terms, practice until you feel confident delivering the content.
- Rehearse to yourself—don't read the speech to yourself—say it out loud, using the speed and intonation you will use when speaking to a large group.
- Be creative. Use props or technology to make your presentation interesting and memorable. Perhaps prepare a slide presentation to enhance your talk; insert video clips and photos to introduce your child. Ask the instructor if you need help with technology. A parent of a preemie started her presentation by showing her baby's tiny first hat, socks, and diaper. Another described her multiple roles and responsibilities by filling a basket with hats to represent cook, worker, advocate, coordinator, teacher, and so on. And a tech-savvy parent made a video with her favorite music and pictures.

Tips for Family Trainers: Presenting Your Story

- Be present. Before you begin your talk, take a moment to look out at your audience, "plant" your feet, and take a few deep breaths.
- Project your voice. If you are speaking to a large group or your voice does not project, consider using a microphone.
- Make eye contact with your audience. Frequently "sweep" the room, looking from side to side to connect with participants in all parts of the room.
- Add humor if appropriate to illustrate a point or lighten the mood. Stick to personal anecdotes and avoid sarcasm or teasing.
- Don't read, but do stick to the talk you prepared in advance.
- Be open to questions. Participants usually don't mean to offend you; sometimes, they just really may not understand something. Take their questions in stride and answer what you want to answer.

While it's the stories that help people connect and have the power to change lives, preparation will promote confidence, enhance connection with the audience, and enhance efficacy as a storyteller and change agent.

Conclusions

The power of family voices for both the listener and the presenter has been documented through research, student self-reflections, and course evaluations. Family voices have the ability to connect people and experiences. We recognize the importance of the family in the education of children with disabilities; as life-long caregivers, the family has a role to play in educational decision-making, future planning, and self-determination. Bringing family voices into teacher education, as well as the education of other providers, has the potential to produce long-term benefits for the learner and the family members. Not only do these experiences offer an interesting way to present information but hearing and reading about family stories and insights also offer the learner a unique perspective and more personal connection to the material, such as in the example of Karen's story of a family's journey with a child born with a serious medical condition. Parents report feeling supported and empowered when they feel heard and can use their own experiences to make a difference. Finally, the opportunity for parents to learn new skills and have a forum to practice narrative advocacy, that is, telling their story to effect change, is an important benefit (Appell et al. 1996).

It is important to acknowledge that the voices of families must come from all cultural and socioeconomic contexts. Our experiences come from parents who are Caucasian, African American, and Hispanic in the US, many of who were at lower income levels. While some family members may feel comfortable presenting their information using a slideshow through technology, others may only want to tell their story to a small group. We also inquired of colleagues in China, India, Peru, and Sri Lanka about their experiences of having family members as teachers, and they all noted that they had not seen nor heard of that in their country. It will be important to embed these ideas into the cultural context of each country for future use and research. Additionally, most of our insights have come from mothers of children with disabilities, and it will be important in the future to hear more from fathers and other family members as well.

Appendix A

Example of a Parent's Story. (Permission is hereby granted to reprint this story for educational purposes citing the chapter and book.)

On July 27, 2006, at 25 weeks, my husband Jeff and I welcomed our son—Cyrus Stephens Lewis—our little macro preemie. He weighed one pound ten ounces. Five days later, he was transferred to Children's Healthcare of Atlanta (CHOA) where he started his long slow journey before finally making it home.

I still vividly remember my first days at CHOA. If you are like me, or most people for that matter, you have little to no experience with hospitals—nor do you want to. It is a foreign place, but a needed place that parents pray they will never have to use for their child. But I was there, and as I rushed through the hospital trying to navigate my way to my son, the first thing I noticed was the friendliness of the staff that I encountered on the way to the Neonatal Intensive Care Unit (NICU) and the smiles from the nurses in the unit. As I left that night, I felt confused, frustrated, and angry with the world. I distinctly remember turning to my husband and complaining, saying, everyone there was "too darn happy". I was irritated and did not want my child there. I wanted him back at his birth hospital and being taken care of by the nurses that I knew.

To put it into context, imagine going to a new school (in a different country with a different language.) There are friendly faces, but you know no one. You are prepared not to like anyone and find fault. You don't understand what they are talking about or their "culture". Looking back, I would consider myself closed off (not rude), but difficult. Naively, I just wanted the doctors and nurses to miraculously "fix" my little son. As days turned into weeks, then months, my emotions ran the gamut—angry, confused, hurt, hopeful, delusional, resigned…but the nurses steadfastly stood by my side and supported me. The relationships that were forged as my son spent time in NICU were a lifeline to my sanity.

Cyrus is my first and only child, and I was determined to focus all of my time and energy into him. If he was going to be there, then I decided I would be a fixture there as well. The nurses let me work through my issues, and as I gradually calmed down, I started noticing all the support they were providing. It was the little things that let me know that they cared not just for my child, but for me and my family. Each person added a different dynamic to my "healing".

The nurses, bless them, were on the frontline. They encouraged me to ask questions, to talk, to refocus my energy. As busy as they were, they listened. The chaplain would always find me or leave me a note to let me know she stopped by. The ladies at the checkout register in the cafeteria would always ask about my son and would notice if my husband and I did not stop in to eat. There was the receptionist in the front lobby who would always greet me with a smile. She even came to visit him when she got off work one day. Even the custodians who cleaned the NICU area would always greet my son as "King" in reference to his first name.

The caring also extended to the doctors following my son. One doctor would always gently admonish me to take care of myself. Once when I was feeling light headed, he asked when was the last time I had eaten (I had missed lunch). He threatened to send me to a "grown up" hospital if I became sick. With another doctor, I had gotten it my head that I was going to help discover why it was taking my son so long to get better. Each day after I left the hospital, I would pore over medical journals and the internet. The next morning, I would confidently present my list of theories or questions that could be the reason for his slow progress. This doctor did not become angry or remind me that he had spent years in his field becoming a doctor, but kindly and patiently listened to everything I presented. It got to the point that if my son was on his rotation, whenever he saw me, I could just hand him my written list of questions/assumptions. He would go down the line answering each one with "Yes; Yes; No, you have asked me that before and (the most hilarious answer) No, you only see that if the child would have been born in this region or country". I learned that the doctors were human and they were patient.

But what finally completely melted my heart was the respiratory therapist who would stop by my son's bedside each day. He worked to let my son hold his finger. At that time, my son's hand was so tiny that it could not completely wrap around one finger. That little boy grasped anyone's finger that came near his hand—nurses, doctors—it did not matter to him, and they all let him. I learned that everyone was doing everything humanly possible for my son.

That solidified what I already knew—the level of care and compassion my son was receiving was beyond comparable. These people were not just lab coats and scrubs, but breathing human beings who truly cared. If my son had found a way in his little body to trust and form a bond, then maybe his mom could also. After a while, my relationships grew from being one sided to noticing my surroundings. I relaxed (as much as a mom could whose son is in NICU) and knew that my son was in good hands. His ups and downs were their ups and downs. I begin to realize that not only were these people my son's lifeline but mine as well. I wanted to know about the person behind the scrubs.

As the holidays rolled around, I started celebrating by decorating my son's bedside. The staff became my extended family. We shared holidays together at the hospital and celebrated milestones together.

The relationships I built with other families will always be what I cherish the most. Our reasons for being in the NICU varied, but we shared our pain, frustrations, and our hopes and dreams with each other. That bond is still strong to this day.

But as I write this, I do not wish to mislead people to think everyone meshed together immediately and easily. What I want is for people to take away that it is a road to building those relationships, and you have to be open to accepting them. It was not always easy—especially when life or death is involved. Communication derailed at times, and I became frustrated more than I want to remember. I realized that my personality would not always click with everyone and that was okay. Not once did anyone's behavior alter as I navigated my way through my emotions. But I will say that on that road, I found some lasting friendships.

When I look back, I cannot say enough good things about everyone I encountered even though I could not see or appreciate it at the time. The staff was friendly, helpful, smiling, welcoming, and willing to assist at every turn. For that, I am eternally grateful.

References

Appell, D. J., Hoffman, M. W., Speller, N. B., Weiner, P. L., & Meryash, D. L. (1996). Parents as Teachers: An Integral Component of a Developmental and Behavioral Pediatrics Curriculum. *Journal of Developmental and Behavioral Pediatrics, 17*(2), 105.

Bronfenbrenner, U. (1977). Toward an Experimental Ecology of Human Development. *American Psychologist, 32*, 513–531.

Gabbard, G. (1998). Family Experiences: Ways to Lead Change Through Telling Your Story. *Early Childhood Bulletin*, Spr 1998. http://ectacenter.org/~pdfs/pubs/famexp.pdf

Gallagher, P. A., Fialka, J., Rhodes, C., & Arceneaux, C. (2002). Working with Families: Rethinking Denial. *Young Exceptional Children, 5*(2), 11–17.

Gallagher, P. A., Powell, T. H., & Rhodes, C. A. (2006). *Brothers and Sisters: A Special Part of Exceptional Families*. Baltimore: Paul Brookes Publishing.

Gallagher, P. A., Schober-Peterson, D., & Rhodes, C. A. (2010). Collaboration with Families. In R. P. Colarusso & C. M. O'Rourke (Eds.), *Special Education for All Teachers* (5th ed.). Iowa: Kendall Hunt.

Kingsley, E. P. (1987). *Welcome to Holland*. http://www.our-kids.org/Archives/Holland.html

Klein, S. D., & Schive, K. (2001). *You Will Dream New Dreams: Inspiring Personal Stories by Parents of Children with Disabilities*. New York: Kensington Books.

Kresak, K., Gallagher, P. A., & Rhodes, C. (2009). Siblings of Infants and Toddlers with Disabilities in Early Intervention. *Topics in Early Childhood Special Education, 29*(3), 143–154.

Kube, D. A., Bishop, E. A., Roth, J. M., & Palmer, F. B. (2012, September 18). Evaluation of a Parent Led Curriculum in Developmental Disabilities for Pediatric and Medicine/Pediatric Residents. *Maternal and Child Health Journal*, Published online. http://projectdocc.org/images/pdf/ProjectDOCC.pdf

National Gateway to Self-Determination Web Portal. *A Clearinghouse for Resources, Training, and Information on Promoting Self-Determination.* www.ngsd.org.

Opening Doors to Self-Determination Skills, Wisconsin Department of Public Instruction. Retrieved December 29, 2015., from www.autismspeaks.org

Pacer's National Parent Center on Transition and Employment. http://www.pacer.org/transition/

Turnbull, A., Turnbull, R., Erwin, E. J., Soodak, L. C., & Shogren, K. A. (2011). *Families, Professionals, and Exceptionality.* Boston: Pearson.

Vaidya, V. U., Greenberg, L. W., Patel, K. M., Strauss, L. H., & Pollack, M. M. (1999). Teaching Physicians How to Break Bad News: A 1-Day Workshop Using Standardized Parents. *Archives of Pediatric Adolescent Medicine, 153*(4), 419–422.

Selected Resources

Websites

Pacer's National Parent Center on Transition and Employment. www.pacer.org
Project DOCC (Delivery of Chronic Care). http://www.projectdocc.org/index.php/main-menu-narrative-advocacy

Poetry

Where Are the Parents? www.parentcafe.

Videos

A Minority Parent's Perspective on Autism (Kennedy Krieger Institute). *Mom Describes Her Experiences as an African-American and Mother of a Child with Autism.* https://www.youtube.com/watch?v=W3fBogCoilQ

Canadian Institutes of Health Research. The multiple sides of autism: A parent's perspective *Father of a 15 year old and member of Canadian Parliament talks about raising a child with autism.* https://www.youtube.com/watch?v=tkBgooP36No

Cincinnati Children's Hospital Medical Center. www.cincinattichildrens.org

Dreams of Our Children—Autism—A Caribbean Parent's Perspective. *A Perspective from Parents of a Four Year Old Child with Autism.* https://www.youtube.com/watch?v=ARKQCW7I6hc

Families with Special Needs. *Thoughts on Having a Child with Special Needs from a Mother of a Child with Down Syndrome.* https://www.youtube.com/watch?v=etUfZjAE08Q

Raising a Child with Autism & Special Needs. https://www.youtube.com/watch?v=6H6tpsqXqFQ

Tell Me a Story Video Library contains 127 brief videos of parent stories. Examples: *Challenges of Spina Bifida Unite Fifth-Grader's Family, Bringing Nora Home (twin, heart defect and Down syndrome), and Special Needs Change Family's Look at Life*

UK Resources

Caudwell Children. www.caudwellchildren.com

Disability in the Family Series

Family stories from the perspectives of father, mother, and sibling (brother)

Contact a Family (UK). www.cafamily.org.uk

Parent Stories: A Mother's Experience (*mother of a 22 year old son with autism*) https://www.youtube.com/watch?v=-C30M83aSt0

Parent Stories – Away with the Fairies *(9 min. documentary describes experience of a family caring for their 10 year old daughter with multiple disabilities)* https://www.youtube.com/watch?annotation_id=annotation_639409&feature=iv&src_vid=-C30M83aSt0&v=roeqzXWhcOs

Parent Stories: Me and My Disabled Child

Part 1: Before the News; Part 2: The Early Years; Part 3: A Different Family Life; Part 4: Finding Support https://www.youtube.com

Welcome to Holland Resources

Holland Schmolland by Laura Krueger Crawford. http://www.asasb.org/PDFs/AccessGuide/VoicesofExperience.pdf

Welcome to Beirut (Beginner's Guide to Autism) by Susan F. Rzucidlo. http://www.bbbautism.com/beginners_beirut.htm

Welcome to Holland (print). http://www.our-kids.org/Archives/Holland.html

Welcome to Yellowknife: A Subarctic Autism Awareness Day Analogy *(Blog—mom's experience of living with autism)*. http://www.blogher.com/subarctic-autism-awareness-day-analogy?page=full

Videos

Holland, Beirut, Holland Schmolland (uplifting story of one family's experience raising a son with autism). https://www.youtube.com/watch?v=YlQlOG6sxkg

Welcome to Holland—(Parent Story Describing Prematurity and Physical Disabilities). https://www.youtube.com/watch?v=Tehcysu03EI

Welcome to Holland (Performed by British Dad). https://www.youtube.com/watch?v=RqGQjoTn2xY

Welcome to Holland—Raising a Child with a Disability Video (Young Girl with Autism). https://www.youtube.com/watch?v=CfDXxOBohn4

Peggy Gallagher is Professor Emerita at Georgia State University and has 30 years of experience in Early Childhood Special Education. Her research interests include families of children with disabilities, inclusion, and personnel preparation. She wrote a book on siblings of children with special needs and has served as a Fulbright Scholar to Sri Lanka.

Cheryl Rhodes is Director of Care Coordination at Marcus Autism Center and has 35 years of experience with children with disabilities and their families. Her interests include family support, early intervention, and impact of disability on families, especially siblings and grandparents. As the mother of a daughter with disabilities, she co-authored a book on siblings.

Karen Young Lewis is the mother of a child with complex medical issues and developmental delay, Parent Resource Coordinator for Early Intervention, and Parent Mentor at Children's Healthcare, Atlanta. She serves on boards and committees to give insight on parents' perspectives, benefits of early intervention/inclusion, transitions, and lengthy hospital stays.

Rights Not Needs: Changing the Legal Model for Special Educational Needs (SEN)

Debbie Sayers

" ...You want answers?"
"I think I'm entitled!"
"You want answers?!"
"I want the truth!"
"You can't handle the truth!"
A Few Good Men (Columbia Pictures; 1992)

Key Points

- The chapter considers the current legal model for SEN and the problems it creates. This model is not rights based and lags behind the disability equality model reflected by the Equality Act (EA) 2010 (HMSO 2010).
- It explores how international human rights obligations and the EA could provide a legal imperative to reconceptualise SEN as an equality rights issue. It proposes that a rights-based approach, and the use of the language of human rights, could shift the focus from servicing 'needs' to building the capacity of individuals to understand, claim and fulfil their rights.

The author is a qualified solicitor and runs the legal research consultancy, interalia.org.uk. The author is also a co-founder and executive committee member of the Educational Rights Alliance.

D. Sayers (✉)
Interalia, Salisbury, UK

© The Author(s) 2018
K. Runswick-Cole et al. (eds.), *The Palgrave Handbook of Disabled Children's Childhood Studies*, https://doi.org/10.1057/978-1-137-54446-9_37

Introduction

What is the truth about special educational needs (SEN) law in England? The Coalition Government's (2010–15) self-proclaimed 'landmark' (DfE, Press release, 13 March 2014a) Children and Families Act 2014 (CFA) (HMSO 2014a) has prompted considerable discussion about how best to support pupils who are identified as having SEN. The term SEN was introduced over 30 years ago following the Warnock Report (DES 1978) and was enshrined in the EA 1981 (HMSO 1981), but little has changed in the thinking behind the law's approach since then. Indeed, despite recent reform, the statutory SEN process still centres on the issue of need defined through a process of assessment, largely premised on meeting adults' perceptions of the child's 'deficits'. Its methodology is paternalistic, often with expectations of normality. This may encourage the idea that children and young people (CYP) with SEN are 'others' (i.e. 'not one of us'). As a lawyer and a parent, the unchanging legal approach in this area concerns me greatly because I believe it perpetuates institutional inequality.

In this chapter, I hope to explore the possibility of an alternative legal approach. In doing so, I will:

- consider the current legal model for SEN and the problems it creates. This model is not rights based and lags behind the disability equality model reflected by the Equality Act 2010 (EA) (HMSO 2010);
- explore how international human rights obligations and the EA could provide a legal imperative to reconceptualise SEN as an equality rights issue;
- propose that a rights-based approach, and the use of the language of human rights, could shift the focus from servicing 'needs' to building the capacity of individuals to understand, claim and fulfil their rights.

Two further points should be made. First, although it is impossible to undertake an academically valid comparative study of SEN legal models within the constraints of this chapter, reference is made to the international norms where appropriate. Additionally, I have provided space for the voices of those engaged on the front line: teachers, parents, special educational needs coordinators (SENCOs), teachers with specific responsibility for SEN issues in schools. Their evidence is anecdotal (further research is required) but their truth is deserving of a wider audience.[1]

Special Educational Needs Law in England

Having an "inclusion department" is like having a "not racist" department. Shouldn't it go without saying that everyone is included? (SENCO Nicole Dempsey of Dixons Trinity Academy)

The more complex and 'special' you make something sound, the more likely it feels disconnected from the general experience. The evolution of SEN law in England is the history of a law apart: generally disconnected from the development of education and equality law and, perhaps, from the broader experience of teaching and schooling. A 'specialist' subject with its own jargon buried in a labyrinth of opaque and often illegal local authority (LA) policies designed to gate-keep financial resources.

The development of SEN law began with the Warnock Report (DES 1978) which led to the creation of a new system with the Education Act 1981 (HMSO 1981). The 1981 Act gave parents new rights in relation to SEN, urged the inclusion of children in mainstream classes, introducing the system of 'statementing' to provide special educational support. It was envisaged that the term SEN would be a fluid concept and that, while a small group of children would require specialist provision via a statement of needs, others (around 20%) may only need support from time-to-time in school. A SEN Code of Practice (DfE 1994) was issued in 1994 providing statutory guidance on practice.

The Education Act 1996 (HMSO 1996) developed the SEN system further by establishing a graduated approach to SEN that recognised a continuum of need which might require increasing action by a school. Under s. 312 (1), a child had SEN if s/he had learning difficulty which called for special educational provision to be made. The system was based on securing the 'provision' (support such as teaching assistants, special materials or aids, etc.) appropriate to meet the individual 'needs' of the pupil. 'Needs' were intended to be assessed on an individual basis and not according to what a LA could afford.[2] There were three levels of intervention for pupils with SEN: School Action (where a school decided to provide support for a child which was additional to or different from the school's usual differentiated approach), School Action Plus (where access to external services were required) and a Statement of SEN (where the child required support beyond that which the school could provide). In the case of a statement, a LA was legally obliged to arrange the provision set out in it. Without a statement, a school had only to use its 'best endeavours' to put the provision in place (a situation that remains with the Children and Families Act 2014), that is, effectively 'to do their best'.

A significant development was the Special Educational Needs & Disability Act (SENDA) 2001 (HMSO 2001) which connected the legal concept of disability discrimination to the issue of SEN for the first time. SENDA strengthened the right to mainstream 'inclusion'. A revised SEN Code of Practice followed in 2001. However, by 2008, Baroness Warnock had described the SEN system she had helped to create as 'needlessly bureaucratic' while calling for the establishment of a new enquiry (TES 2008). There was a growing feeling that the system was not fit for purpose and that an irreconcilable conflict had been created by making LAs responsible for the assessment of need and the funding of provision to meet it. Further reports by the House of Commons Education and Skills Committee (HoC 2006) and Brian Lamb (Lamb 2009) created an impetus for change, noting high levels of parental dissatisfaction with the system and continuous poor outcomes for children. A Green Paper, *Support and Aspiration: Better Outcomes for Children and Families* (DfE 2011), proposed changes to the law and led to the introduction of the Children and Families Act (HMSO 2014a).

There are many different aspects to the CFA and I do not intend to provide a detailed assessment of them here (see, for example, DfE 2015c; CDC 2014; Duff and Patel 2015; Holt 2015). This chapter focuses on the system for ensuring that children are supported within schools. The CFA creates a single school-based stage of 'SEN Support' which replaces School Action and School Action Plus. It also creates Education, Health and Care Plans (EHCPs) which will set out the health and social care services as well as the educational provision a child needs. Without an EHCP, a child continues to rely solely on the school's legal duty to use its best endeavours to meet the pupil's SEN (s.66). This means that many children have limited legal rights to any type of SEN support (around 1.2 million pupils (12.6% of all pupils) receive 'SEN support' (DfE 2015b: 1)). It has long been the case that only a tiny fraction of pupils (2.8%) have legally enforceable provision via statements of SEN or an EHCP (DfE 2015b: 1).

In attempting to secure an EHCP, a Needs Assessment will be undertaken under s.36 of the CFA which will include education, health and social care: previously, statements only set out educational provision (see also HMSO 2014b). An EHCP will also set out the outcomes the delivery of the SEN provision is expected to produce. However, it is important to note that, even if an EHCP is obtained, the provision set out for health and social care (the lack, or its inadequacy) cannot be challenged at the First-tier Tribunal (SEN and Disability) as educational provision can. We must also consider whether, given the reality of austerity,[3] obligations to assess and arrange health and social care provision will result only in fewer children being identified as having those needs to prevent them from becoming legally enforceable.

Problems with the Current Legal Model

In terms of general legal approach, three key points can be made about the current state of the law:

(i) the legislative emphasis remains on 'needs'. Thus, the opportunity to create a new SEN model based on the language of rights has been missed;

(ii) the efficacy of law is also about its context. Context is important as it can explain why law fails to protects rights despite its substance; and

(iii) the CFA continues the 'othering' of present 'special education'.

Needs Not Rights

Alongside the evolution of SEN law, at international level, two key documents have influenced the direction of travel: the United Nations Convention on the Rights of the Child (UNCRC 1989) and the Salamanca Statement (UNESCO 1994). The latter sets out that 'the fundamental principle of the inclusive school is that all children should learn together, wherever possible, regardless of any difficulties or differences they may have' (UNESCO 1994: 11). The UNCRPD was then adopted at international level in 2006 and ratified by the UK in 2009. Article 24 of the UNCRPD guarantees all disabled learners a right to participate in all forms of mainstream education with appropriate support.

The CFA does not incorporate (i.e. give effect to) this international human rights framework in the UK law. It does not change current thinking about inclusion and, in fact, refers to inclusion only once (in securing the general presumption in law of mainstream education). The definition of SEN (s. 20) remains basically the same as that set out in the Education Act 1996 and the test for an EHCP remains the same as that for a statement. Oliver (2014: 176) notes that the 'feeling from much of Part 3 of the 2014 Act is that it is the same as before but simply repackaged'. Consequently, developments in disability rights, and the broader human rights context, remain largely outside the current SEN paradigm. This is important as there is significant overlap between disabled children and those with SEN. The SEN Code of Practice (DoH and DfE 2015) notes that many children and young people who have

SEN may have a disability under the EA 2010 (DoH and DfE 2015: 16). There are different definitions of disability but, for the purposes of the EA, disability is 'a physical or mental impairment which has a long-term and substantial adverse effect on their ability to carry out normal day-to-day activities' (s.6). The Code acknowledges that this definition 'provides a relatively low threshold and includes more children than many realise: "long-term" is defined as "a year or more" and "substantial" is defined as "more than minor or trivial"' (DoH and DfE 2015: 16). It includes sensory impairments and long-term health conditions such as asthma, diabetes, epilepsy and cancer.

We, therefore, have two potentially distinct models which have not been effectively connected. First, the disability equality model (recognised by the EA) underpinned by a social model of disability which identifies disability not solely with impairments but with the limitations experienced by individuals in society. This is more in keeping with the international human rights framework. Second, we have SEN law. This does not reflect existing models of disability rights. It continues to identify any 'learning problem' as belonging to the student. This distinction may cause people to overlook the connection between the two forms of law. Additionally, SEN law, in its current guise continues to be seen in terms of the medical model of disability rather than the social model: that is, in terms of 'personal troubles' not 'public issues'. As Gareth Morewood, SENCO, consultant and researcher told me:

> The majority of schools and politicians like to try and 'medicalise' the SEN and Disability (SEND) issues into processes.

This can lead to the personalisation of the difficulty in a way which promotes exclusion and isolation rather than inclusion. Sociologist C Wright Mills described the distinction thus:

> When, in a city of 100,000, only one man is unemployed, that is his personal trouble, and for its relief we properly look to the character of the man, his skills, and his immediate opportunities. But when in a nation of 50 million employees, 15 million men are unemployed, that is an issue, and we may not hope to find its solution within the range of opportunities open to any one individual. (Mills 1959: 9)

In comparison to a disability rights model, the SEN model feels dated: individuals may be pitied for their difficulties and parents for their 'burdens'. Obstacles are not seen as the outcome of structural or political arrangements. The talk is of 'care' and 'co-production' and 'support': it is not of human rights.

Peacey (2015: 3) argues that, while the reforms enhance aspects of the previous SEN framework, they 'do not have adequate safeguards for introduction into an educational environment which is in many ways hostile to inclusion and equality' and they 'fall short of the highest international standards on difference and disability, particularly those set out in the [UNCRC] and on the [UNCRPD]'. This may be compounded by the way schools approach their legal SEN duties. Barney Angliss, SENCO told me:

> SEND is another tricky area in the way a school is judged (Performance Measures, league tables). It's also one of the few areas for which there is still a legal duty to have a policy (on top of the SEN Information Report on the school's website). So SEND is seen in terms of duties and measures rather than equality and rights.

The current SEN framework's commitment to inclusion is further watered down by the inclusion 'opt-out'. Section 33 (2) of the CFA continues the Education Act 1996's (HMSO 1996) conditional promotion of mainstream education requiring it 'unless [it] is incompatible with: (a) the wishes of the child's parent or the young person, or (b) the provision of efficient education for others'. Does this affect the promotion of rights and the responsibilities of schools to ensure equality of education? There is no research on this point but, anecdotally, it is very common to hear parents and teachers talk of schools being inclusive or non-inclusive as if inclusion were a choice rather than a legal imperative. This may create the perception that society is tolerating disabled children and permitting them to be involved as long as they do not create too much disruption. The concern is that, once we make inclusion a matter of choice, we take away its egalitarian force and divert attention from the centrality of the individual's right to education. We make it about the decision-maker rather than the child.

In such a context, inclusion becomes less about where a child is placed than whether the child's rights are respected. The issue is far more complex than the physical placement of a child. The number of pupils with statements of SEN placed in special schools has been rising (from 40.2% in 2010 to 43% in 2015) (DfE 2015a). The DfE predict that the number of special schools will increase by 30% in the next five years (DfE 2015a). Arguably, the continued use of special schools demonstrates the failure to increase the capacity of mainstream schools and staff to provide an inclusive education to SEN and disabled pupils (CRAE 2014, 28) and certainly many parents take the view that the mainstream schools simply do not welcome their children (OCC 2014). However, we need to be honest. We are currently very far from the human rights ideal of inclusive education as 'a dynamic approach of responding positively to pupil diversity and of seeing individual differences not as problems, but as opportunities for enriching learning' (UNESCO 2005: 12). Thus, presently, just being physically *placed* in a mainstream school is not enough to secure a child's educational rights and may at times be damaging. There is exceptional work being done by many special schools and their dedicated and skilled staff who work hard to encourage aspiration and create opportunities for inclusion in society beyond school. When we consider the failings of the current situation, the child and their fundamental rights, must remain our core focus, in the short and long term.

Problems with Content and Context

The law cannot be divorced from its social and economic context. Over the last four years, families with disabled children have been particularly adversely affected by many of the Government's changes to the benefits and tax system (CAF 2014). I can see no evidence that the reform of the SEN system has been any more benevolent in effect or that it has created 'a cultural, as much as a legislative, revolution' (Council for Disabled Children (CDC 2013: 1), the Government's Strategic Reform Partner). Indeed, lawyer Edward Duff told me that the transition from statements to EHCPs has caused chaos and entailed substantial costs:

> Lack of funding has led to significant difficulties. Figures are unclear, but it seems that around £200 million has been put towards the SEND reforms. A significant point of the SEND reforms was to empower parents and young people so that they are involved in the SEND system and get access to support more readily. £200 million is, unfortunately, not enough to achieve this. Estimates of the costs of just moving every child from a Statement to an EHCP are around £1.2 billion.

When evaluating the success of these reforms, it is notable that £1.2 billion would have paid for many individual hours of occupational therapy, educational psychology or speech and language therapy. Yet Oliver (2014: 176) contends that 'the contents of the [EHCP] do not seem to be much more than a rehashing of a statement of SEN under a different name'. Whether the transfer from statements to EHCPs constitutes anything more than an opportunity to tighten access to SEN provision under the guide of expensive rebranding seems doubtful.

There are also practical problems with the implementation of the new law. First, no mandatory national EHCP 'template' exists and there has been no national evaluation of consistency. This is important as it is in the implementation of law that the real problems arise. For example, legally, EHCPs, like statements, are required to set out SEN provision in a specific and quantifiable way: *L v Clarke and Somerset* (1998) ELR 129. This makes the provision in a statement legally enforceable provision. Under the Education Act 1996, parents frequently had to battle LAs to ensure that statements were specified and quantified and therefore enforceable. Has this changed with the transfer to EHCPs? One parent (who wishes to remain anonymous) who works as an advocate, specialist teacher and a parent representative told me:

> In regards to specification and quantification, there's always been problems gaining therapies but what I am now seeing/hearing is that many LAs are using the reforms to state that 'hours are no longer needed', which is contrary to existing case law........The story appears to be pretty much a postcode lottery.

Second, under the old law, it was not uncommon for parents to have to take judicial review proceedings to force LAs to arrange the provision in their child's statement (*N v North Tyneside Borough Council* [2010] EWCA Civ 135 N). There is no evidence that this has changed.

Third, there has been little independent evidence considering the actual implementation of the reforms to date. The Government's own evaluation of the pilot schemes which trialled aspects of the CFA before its implementation was not particularly favourable (DfE/SQW 2015: 98) confirming that '[d]espite the improvement around the process, there was no statistical change in the extent to which families thought the decisions reached were fair. Around 20 per cent remain dissatisfied'. This is particularly concerning given that the sample group for the evaluation was self-selected by LAs (as confirmed by SQW—the research consultance delivering the project). Even the use of a biased sample group could not produce more positive results.

Fourth, the context to the reform is significant. The reforms have taken place in a climate which may be seen as hostile to disability and vulnerability (e.g. Duffy 2014). This has manifested itself in several ways. First, we have witnessed a significant number of children wiped from the SEN figures (DfE 2015d: 5). The possible reasons for this give cause for alarm. Government data confirms that, in January 2015, the number of pupils with SEN decreased from 1.49 million pupils (17.9%) in January 2014 to 1.30 million pupils (15.4%). It claims '[t]his may be due to more accurate identification of those with SEN following implementation of the SEN and disability system reforms'. But this seems to be little more than political speculation.[4] The DfE has however confirmed that the primary need of 'Behaviour, Emotional and Social Difficulties' was removed in the reform process "to reflect that behaviour issues are not necessarily related to SEN" (email to me of 6 November 2015: cited with permission). This reflects assertions made by Government Ministers during the reforms 'that those most deserving of help often find it difficult to get adequate support while too many are wrongly placed on the register' (Telegraph 2012). The DfE's email also confirms that 'those with this primary need in 2014 were not all expected to move to the new category of "Social Emotional and Mental Health" (SEMH) in 2015'. Thus, it appears that the Government's intention was always to remove some children from the SEN register despite writing to parents to confirm that 'the new law does not change the definition of SEN' (DfE 2014b). The removal of a tranche of children from the data is mirrored by the equally worrying 'disappearance' of people with learning disabilities from official statistics and services designed to support people with learning disabilities (Duff 2015). Hatton (2015) notes, we are 'seeing an officially sanctioned (if implicit) shrinkage of who counts as a person with learning disabilities, with people with "mild" learning disabilities being written out of the picture and state support reserved for "protecting" the most "vulnerable"' which could consign 'generations of people to a fight for survival in education, employment, housing, health and social contexts that are anything but conducive to a flourishing life'.

Removing labels removes the obligation to provide support. Curran suggests that the reduction in numbers of the SEN register could be the result of pressure on school resources and states that some school staff 'suggested that the government's changes were a way for schools and local authorities to reduce the number of SEND children being supported, and the costs of this support. Some even indicated that they thought this was the reason behind the reforms' (Curran 2015). The drive to remove labels is also working because many schools lack the capacity to distinguish between 'unwanted behaviour' and diversity or the underlying learning difficulties which may create 'differences' in behaviour. Tomlinson (1982: 80) has pointed out that teachers may be willing to accept the 'bright, brave child in a "wheelchair" but are less receptive to the "average" child with special needs – "the dull, disruptive" child'. Institutional intolerance to difference may be compounded by perspectives such as Ofsted's[5] report in 2014 entitled 'Below the radar: low-level disruption in the country's classrooms' which claimed the existence of widespread low-level disruption caused by 'inappropriate' student behaviour. The report makes no mention of SEN or disability or the EA, yet much of the 'low-level disruptive behaviour' identified reads like a SEN or disability checklist, for example 'talking and chatting', 'disturbing other children', 'calling out', 'fidgeting or fiddling with equipment' and 'not having the correct equipment'. This type of approach may undermine efforts at inclusion as it may encourage schools, parents and children, to view pupils with different needs as being inconsistent with a productive learning environment.

The Effect: The 'Othering' of Pupils with Special Educational Needs

In placing SEN law within the CFA, as distinct from an Education Act, the current Government has again side-lined SEN from the main education debate. SEN remains the responsibility of a 'Children and Families' Minister and pronouncements from the Education Secretary or shadows are rare.[6] The development of niche, SEN law facilitates the side-lining of SEN issues away from broader education and political debate. Through the autumn of 2015, in preparation for this chapter, I contacted several leading national education commentators for their thoughts on this issue but none felt willing or able to comment. Yet, without mainstreaming these issues (i.e. ensuring that disability perspectives and the goal of disability equality are central to all activities, policies and decisions), and without the language of human rights, SEN remains a matter for the specialists and is therefore hidden away from mainstream education debate which is generally a 'hot' political topic receiving substantial media coverage. It is clear that 'SEND needs to move up schools', policy makers' and the emerging middle tier's agendas' (Driver Reform Trust 2015, 50).

The side-lining of SEN issues from mainstream education debates is accompanied by the development of 'an expanded and expensive SEN industry' (Tomlinson 2014: 56). It could be said that the development of this 'industry' encourages the perception of SEN as a highly specialist issue. The consequence is that SEN is not a matter of concern for many 'ordinary' teachers, head teachers, political commentators, activists, parents or politicians. Teachers may feel the topic has become too complicated for them to access and may leave 'SEN' issues to SENCOs. Barney Angliss, a SENCO who himself has Asperger's Syndrome, told me:

> [SEN] is regarded as specialist, politically sensitive, emotive, costly, a legal minefield... That's why we have a SENCO. That person over there, across the staffroom, he/she deals with that. Go talk to them....

Nancy Gedge, teacher, parent and blogger spoke to me in similar terms:

I think it would be fair to say that many people in schools see the field of SEND as one for the specialist, namely the SENCO. All teachers have the best interests of their students at heart, but they haven't necessarily been given the skills and training to do this for children with SEND, and therefore they can fall back on old fashioned and outdated ideas. Leaders in education need to get informed – and pass that information on to their teachers.

Those in special schools may find themselves even further disconnected from the main education debate. Simon Knight, a deputy head of a special school and Associate Director at National Education Trust, told me that political disinterest in the education of children with learning disabilities is shown in the absence of appropriate teacher training routes so that this 'political ambivalence, becomes pedagogical ambivalence'.

The consequence of this state of affairs is that the interests of children with SEN are excluded from broader political and education debate. This matters and not just because side-lining the interests of any group is wrong. It matters because it may have dramatic consequences on children and young people. Pupils with SEN are often facing multiple disadvantages. For example, they are more than twice as likely to have the income levels low enough to be eligible for free school meals (FSM) than those without SEN (28.2% compared to 12.8%) (DfE 2015b). Childhood disability is associated with disadvantaged family circumstances, such as family poverty (Parsons and Platt 2013: 3). Further, Lupton et al. (2015) found that in 2014, the GCSE performance of children with SEN on FSM dropped, in comparison to the 2013 results, by 32.8%. This is unacceptable when disabled people are already more likely to live in poverty, to have fewer educational qualifications and experience more problems with hate crime or harassment (Johnson and Kossykh 2008). To make matters worse, a substantial number of qualitative accounts already suggest that bullying is a pervasive experience in the daily lives of disabled children and young people (Connors and Stalker 2002; Norwich and Kelly 2004). 'Indeed, bullying can be represented as one of the means by which children with impairments or particular needs become "disabled"' (Chatzitheochari et al. 2014: 4).

The current situation only fosters isolation and exclusion. Peacey (2015: 5) has noted that, when confronted with issues concerning minorities, 'governments often prefer approaches that emphasise the "special" and "different" features of individuals and groups, rather than starting with changes to environments and attitudes'. The problem with this is that the use of 'special' becomes a pejorative way to define a group of individuals as different from the 'normal', that is, 'abnormal' in comparison with the dominant group. It also aids the development of what has been described as 'othering' (Wendell 1996), that is, that the individual or group is 'not one of us'. 'Othering' language and attitudes can lead to social exclusion where people outside the main group are viewed as being 'laced with strangeness' (Stevenson 2008: 201). It means that disabled people are represented as distinct and apart from the assumed normality as well as apart from the 'normal' and the 'natural' majority (Wendell 1996, 60–61).

The language of 'special needs' certainly carries negative connotations (Martin 2011). Runswick-Cole and Hodge, (2009: 13) argue for the abandonment of the special needs discourse claiming that it has, in fact, led to exclusionary practices within education. They advocate for the adoption of the phrase 'educational rights' and suggest that the positive impact of such a linguistic turn would be significant for the lives of children currently described as having 'special educational needs'. Law reform could have made a dramatic break with the exclusionary and paternalistic language of the past by replacing 'needs' with rights. It did not and the failure to challenge the language and practice around disability in schools is inexcusable. SENCO Nicole Dempsey puts forward a damning summary of the failure of the current model which many will recognise. She described to me what she calls an 'internal-segregation-as-inclusion' paradigm which is worth setting out in full:

> For me, many of the barriers faced by those with disabilities – both in education and in society as a whole – stem from the same, chronically overlooked problem; the current educational inclusion paradigm is actually a form of internal segregation and does not represent social justice. I believe that the common artefacts of inclusion as we know it – Teaching Assistants (TAs)[7], withdrawal intervention, SENCOs and SEN/inclusion departments, corridors, rooms etc. – all result in a segregation of space, service, expectation and experience and, ultimately, schools are *designed* to get the best out of and for their students; what does it mean for a child to sit even slightly outside of that design?

> What does the current 'internal-segregation-as-inclusion' paradigm tell SEND students about themselves? What does it teach a child about their place in society if they always sit slightly outside of the systems? Especially if 'their space' is inferior in quality, such as learning spaces away from the knowledge hubs and unqualified, non-specialist staff. And especially if that segregation instils an 'us and them' or even culture of fear between the SEND and non-SEND students, such as inclusion areas (oh, the irony) and 'safe spaces' for vulnerable students.

By segregating students with additional needs and/or disabilities, what are we teaching our non-SEND students? What are we telling them is the right way to support diversity and vulnerability in our communities? That it is someone else's problem? And, surely, we are denying them the opportunity to value and learn about diversity and what it can bring to the community. These students will go on to be the potential employers of ability diversity.

In combination, these unintentional by-products of our current approach to inclusion perpetuate the unequal society paradigm that exists way beyond childhood and education. We inadvertently teach our SEND students that they are 'other' and should expect 'less'.

Law reform needed to challenge this dysfunctional paradigm to create real progress on disability equality. It did not.

A Rights-Based Approach to Special Educational Needs Law

The term 'special educational needs' exists in most EU countries (European Agency for Special Needs and Inclusive Education 2012). Internationally, definitions vary and it has been said that the 'use of the terms "inclusion" and "inclusive education" and their associated meanings vary a great deal among different countries and also among different regions within the same country' (European Agency for Special Needs and Inclusive Education 2014b). A comparative analysis of legal systems is beyond the scope of this chapter but it seems clear that, despite ratification of the key UN Conventions, EU Member States face similar issues in relation to a human rights-based approach to SEN. For example, a pan-EU publication on the key terms used in all EU SEN systems (European Agency for Special Needs and Inclusive Education 2014a) makes no mention of the words 'right' or 'rights' save for reference to the UNCRPD. Further, recommendations aimed at all EU Member States urge policy-makers to review their national legislation and education policy to ensure that they are consistent with and actively support the principles of both the UNCRC and the UNCRPD (European Agency for Special Needs and Inclusive Education 2014b: 22).

The development of law and practice based on human rights principles may offer a more inclusive approach. Human rights law can promote legal and cultural change because human rights norms can be used to challenge the existing status quo. However, change will always be constrained by the limits of our socio-economic system, so we should not assume that a human rights-based approach alone will provide the sort of structural challenge needed to target the inherent inequities produced by the current system (Marks 2011). We must, therefore, be conscious that human rights can provide 'both a distraction from the necessary diagnosis and the necessary remedy' (Moyn 2015: 168). In terms of a 'necessary remedy', the value of a human rights-based approach lies in the re-envisaging of a problem with the individual at its centre and the moral and legal obligations this creates. To explore this further, we must start with a working idea of what is meant by a rights-based approach. People may talk of 'rights' when they are in fact talking about legal entitlements (e.g. the right to apply for an EHCP). Rights in this sense are different from those legal norms considered to be human rights. Freeman (2007: 7) explains that the importance of the distinction is that:

> Rights are important because they recognise the respect the bearers are entitled to. To accord rights is to respect dignity: to deny rights is to cast doubt on humanity and integrity.

This is where the critical distinction between the language and legal enforcement of rights and needs may become important in practice. A needs-based model may aim to protect people by providing basic minimum services, but it holds no capacity for empowerment. A need which is not fulfilled may be considered to be a frustration: a human right may carry more weight as the violation of a legal norm. A rights-based model may transform the paradigm from individual 'need' to recognition of specific and fundamental legal rights by the entire society. This approach also specifically reinforces the obligations of duty bearers (in this case statutory decision-makers) to understand, respect, promote and guarantee these rights.

The legal imperative of human rights may help achieve this change because rights are ultimately moral trump cards (Dworkin 1978). Human rights allow legitimate claims to be articulated with a moral authority that other approaches lack (Boesen and Sano 2010). Fortin (2009: 297) further contends that a rights-based approach is more transparent and that it may be more child centred. A rights-based approach implies accountability of those with duties or obligations in fulfilling, respecting and protecting the right to education. It requires outcomes to be measurable (UNESCO/UNICEF 2007). Other principles that inform a rights-based approach include equality and non-discrimination, participation and inclusion, empowerment and respect for the rule of law.

International legal norms exist to promote disability equality in schools and legislative reform should begin with an understanding of the human rights commitments made by States and how central they should be to the development of legislation. Any legislation relating to inclusion within the education system should be underpinned by the fundamental commitment to ensuring every learner's right to inclusive and equitable educational opportunities. The CFA does not incorporate international treaties or make reference to the human rights framework. The EA is referred to only in respect of SEN Information Reports (s. 69) and applications to the Tribunal for breaches of it (ss. 58–60). However, despite this missed opportunity, we can still use existing law to promote a rights-based approach to SEN issues. We must start with the recognition that disabled children have human rights in three ways: children's rights; disabled person's rights; and rights by virtue of being a human. The international human rights framework thus provides general and distinct protection for children and disabled people above and beyond SEN legislation.

Presently, in terms of the general human rights framework, the rights set out in the European Convention on Human Rights (ECHR) are domestically incorporated (made part of English law) and actionable by the Human Rights Act 1998 (HMSO 1998). These rights include the right to education (Article 2 of Protocol 1) and the right not to be discriminated against in the exercise of one's rights (Article 14). In terms of distinct rights, the UNCRC sets out rights which are particularly relevant to the SEN system. For example, it requires that all decisions should be taken in a child's best interests (Article 3) and that a child's views must be taken into account in decision-making where a child is of the age and maturity to express them (Article 12). This can be a complicated issue and is beyond the scope of this chapter. It also prohibits discrimination in enjoyment of their rights (Article 2) and obliges State Parties to provide children with the right to life and the right to develop to their full potential (Article 6). The CRC also confirms that children have rights to health care and to a full and decent life under Articles 23 and 24 and a specific right to education under Articles 28 and 29. Statutory guidance has been issued on the UNCRC (DfE 2014c) and LAs must have regard to it. Additionally, Article 7 of the UNCRPD obliges States Parties to ensure that 'children with disabilities have the right to express their views freely on all matters affecting them, their views being given due weight in accordance with their age and maturity, on an equal basis with other children, and to be provided with disability and age-appropriate assistance to realize that right'. Article 24 sets out the right to inclusive education.

Incorporation signals more clearly a government's genuine intention to realise the rights in a treaty. However, treaties can impact on national law and practice in the UK even when unincorporated as case law confirms that treaties like the UNCRC and UNCRPD still provide critical policy impera-tives as well as guidance for state action (e.g. *R v Secretary of State for the Home Department, ex parte Brind* [1991] 1 AC 696). The current SEN Code of Practice makes direct reference to these Conventions (DfE 2015e: paras 1.2 and 1.26) but there should be a clearer and more systematic approach to their application to law and practice. This appears to be a problem encountered throughout Europe as the European Agency for Special Needs and Inclusive Education (2014b: 9) has noted that 'the UNCRC (Articles 23(3), 28 and 29(1a)) and the UNCRPD (Article 24) should be considered to ensure that both age and disability dimensions are included in legislation and policy, as countries move on from debating the meaning of inclusion to a focus on a whole education system that leads to a more equitable and just society'.

Additionally, even when included in the law, we need to ensure that human rights obligations are actually complied with. Too often, obligations in relation to disabled children are considered a low priority or an 'optional extra'. How do we ensure they are implemented in practice? This is a critical issue because the answer is not always more law, or even better law, but more effective implemen-tation of the law: it is the *operation* of the law in practice that is core to any genu-ine promotion of rights. Over a hundred years ago, Roscoe Pound (1910) made the distinction between the 'law in the books' and the 'law in action'. 'Law in the books' refers to a law as it should be, as it is made and appears in Acts, and so on. This is contrasted with the 'law in action' which refers to the extent to which legal principles are implemented in any given justice system. Empirical research (research based on the study of the law in practice) can look at the gap between the 'law in the books' and the 'law in action' and suggest possible ways to bridge this gap. Without this research, we may produce more law, but it may have little or any real impact. SEN is an area of law ripe for this type of study not least because an understanding of the social construction of disability is essential to our understanding of how to eradicate barriers and reduce disadvantage. Without empirical legal research examining the barriers preventing lawful prac-tice and impeding disability equality, any legal reform is built on shaky founda-tions and remains subject to unevidenced political claims of effectiveness.

Empirical legal research and human rights-based reform are long-term goals but we can make more immediate changes with the effective implemen-tation and enforcement of the EA 2010 and the existing human rights frame-work. This may help reframe the debate in terms of rights and positive duties. The EA may encourage a change in the use of language to promote a focus on the rights of the individual. The Code acknowledges that 'the Equality Act 2010 and Part 3 of the Children and Families Act 2014 interact in a number of important ways'. However, this, it says is because 'they share a common focus on removing barriers to learning' (DfE (2015e), para 1.33) and because the 'Equality Act 2010 provides protection from discrimination for disabled people' (DfE (2015e), para 1.26). Yet, equality is about something far more fundamental and culturally significant than 'learning barriers' and 'non-discrimination'. So what could the EA bring us as the basis of a different approach to SEN?

The EA (reflecting the international obligations under the ECHR, Article 14 and EU legislation on non-discrimination) imposes clear legal obligations which create a binding imperative towards equal opportunity and genuine inclusion. Under the Act, schools, early years providers, post-16 institutions, local authorities and others must:

(i) not directly or indirectly discriminate against, harass or victimise disabled children and young people (ss. 13 and 19);
(ii) not discriminate for a reason arising in consequence of a child or young person's disability (s. 15);
(iii) make reasonable adjustments to procedures, criteria and practices and by the provision of auxiliary aids and services to ensure that disabled children and young people are not at a substantial disadvantage compared with their peers (s.20). This duty is anticipatory—it requires thought to be given *in advance* to what disabled children and young people *might* require and what adjustments might need to be made to prevent that disadvantage.

The EA embeds the legal principle that prohibiting discrimination is not enough to achieve equality because positive steps may be needed to achieve a level playing field. This is further reinforced by s. 149 of the EA which imposes a duty known as the public sector equality duty (PSED). This requires relevant public bodies (including schools) to have due regard to three specified matters when exercising any of their functions. Those matters are the need to:

(i) eliminate discrimination, harassment, victimisation and any other conduct that is prohibited by or under the Act;
(ii) advance equality of opportunity between persons who share a relevant protected characteristic and persons who do not share it; and
(iii) foster good relations between persons who share a relevant protected characteristic and persons who do not share it.

The EA (Specific Duty) Regulations reinforce s. 149 by imposing specific duties on public authorities to ensure better performance of the PSED (HMSO 2011). The Regulations seek to achieve this by requiring public bodies to prepare and publish objectives, setting out what they intend to achieve in order to further the aims of the duty, and to publish information annually to demonstrate their compliance with the duty. Objectives must be specific and measurable. These statutory duties are important because they do not just require policies: they require action and records of action to promote individual rights. They require target setting, and publication and information and engagement: genuine target setting cannot take place without real engagement ('nothing about us without us'). They require disabled pupils to be considered when *all* functions are exercised and *all* decisions are made (*R (ex p. Brown) v Secretary of State for Work and Pensions and Others* 2008). They constitute a key protection against disadvantage. The EA also forms part of the human rights framework.

In addition to these duties, schools have other legal duties:

(i) They must publish accessibility plans setting out how they plan to increase access for disabled pupils to the curriculum, the physical environment and to information (Equality Act, Sched. 10);
(ii) They must establish a policy on supporting pupils with medical needs (Children and Families Act 2014, s.100); and
(iii) Governing bodies must ensure that arrangements are in place in schools to support pupils at school with medical conditions. They must also ensure that school leaders consult health and social care professionals, pupils and parents, to ensure that the needs of children with medical conditions are effectively supported.

These legal obligations exist to protect the right to equal treatment for disabled children, so let us start by implementing them properly. Presently the Government has made no efforts to monitor compliance with the EA in schools but Ofsted committed itself to ensuring compliance in its Common Inspection Framework:

> 15. Inspectors will assess the extent to which the school or provider complies with relevant legal duties as set out in the Equality Act 2010 and the Human Rights Act 1998, promotes equality of opportunity and takes positive steps to prevent any form of discrimination either direct or indirect against those with protected characteristics in all aspects of their work. (Ofsted 2015a)

Head teachers and governors are heavily influenced by Ofsted's inspection regime. Effective action by Ofsted could have a dramatic effect. Sadly, despite the clear commitment above, there is scant evidence in published Ofsted reports that schools are being assessed for compliance with these statutory duties (ERA, 2015). Indeed, Ofsted has stated that 'marking a school down for not publishing information [as required by law], where it is evident in practice the school is doing well for all groups of people, could be seen as unfair and disproportionate' (Ofsted 2015b). In view of the fact that Ofsted inspectors are in schools for a day, it is hard to understand what evidence inspectors could obtain that could make legal compliance with a mandatory statutory obligation an irrelevance. It is also difficult to comprehend the legal rationale behind Ofsted's approach as it has no power to pick and choose which laws schools must comply with. This laissez-faire attitude to the law is not good enough. An accountability system must set the standards and promote equality. Children deserve nothing less.

Conclusion

This chapter is not intended to be a guide to the EA or any other human rights law. Recourse to individual legal action is important and can create pockets of change but generally it empowers the few and results in isolated or individual successes. Additionally, individual legal action places the burden on the backs of parents. Profound social and cultural change requires political action. Certainly cultural change will not happen with the CFA in its current form as Peacey (2015: 20) explains:

> The ultimate arbiters of its [CFA] creation did not know or did not care sufficiently about the United Kingdom's commitment to international rights conventions or about the research literature which all points in the same direction: to enhance the education and well-being of minority groups in the streets, homes or classroom you must start by enriching the environment and experiences of all, across and within institutions, extending universally designed provision as necessary in individual cases.

We can start immediately by changing from the language of 'needs' to the language of legal 'rights'. Freeman (2007: 6) argues that '[t]he language of rights can make visible what has for too long been suppressed' and that it can lead to 'different and new stories being heard in public'. These stories need to be told and empirical research needs to be undertaken if we are genuinely to address the failure of the current SEN system and construct reforms which work in practice. We need to move away from a model where:

> Children who, because they have a learning disability, because they have additional needs, are expected to place a high visibility vest over their head for playtime in the name of 'Inclusion'. Because nobody knows any better. (Simon Knight)

The present system is not working and the CFA does not have the potential to create radical, long-lasting change. We must also break away from the idea of the 'needy' and the 'deserving'. The use of the language and authority of human rights law must be used to de-stabilise a system which perpetuates inequality: the law must be used to create an imperative for mainstreaming. Nicole Dempsey puts the challenge this way to me:

> I believe that a big contribution to our reluctance to move on from this step on the journey towards justice is that we have somehow persuaded ourselves that this approach is a good thing. Like having an inclusion department with a load of TAs, withdrawal interventions and escape from the mainstream is a benevolence. Like we are doing those with disabilities a favour by putting a ramp up to a side entrance so they can get in to our able spaces. It's patronising. The school with the biggest SEND departments is the *least* inclusive, not most.

Pupils with SEND are the 'canaries in the mine' in an inequitable education environment dominated by an increased 'emphasis on competition and comparison, prompted by a market ethos' (Corbett 1996). The tenor and tone of mainstream education reform creates a negative backdrop of competition which must be challenged. Gareth Morewood told me:

> The momentum with 'inclusion' from the 90s has been overridden with a 'traditional' educational discourse that adds weight to this increased inequality and 'lack of appetite' for equality as a prominent discourse.

We do not have to accept this. We can advocate for real change. First, we must demand empirical research to explore the reasons why the law fails to protect disabled children's rights. Second, we must make this a political issue. We need overtly political dialogue and we must demand that disability equality issues are raised in political debate: they must be mainstreamed. Third, we need to consider how the existing human rights framework can be applied immediately, for example through the effective implementation of the EA. To this end, we should challenge schools, governors and LAs to demand that its basic requirements are implemented throughout schools. Fourth, we should secure an effective oversight system for schools. Ofsted should be required to implement its own framework and ensure compliance with the law as a basic necessity. Finally, we need to recognise that while talks and conferences and blogs are important to raise awareness, discussion will not solve the problem. Put simply, if we do not connect the fight for disability equality to the fight against broader inequality in our schools and in our society, then any change will be short lived. The obstacles preventing equality are profoundly connected to the way political power marginalises, disempowers and scapegoats minorities generally. Are we ready to handle that truth?

Notes

1. I approached a variety of leading education figures from different fields: parents, head teachers, lawyers, SENCOs and asked them about SEN and equality. Their answers were provided by email correspondence. All views are cited with permission.
2. Local Authorities are the organisations responsible for key public services such as education and social services in their local government area.
3. Austerity policies in the UK have involved policies to reduce government spending in order to try and reduce government budget deficits.
4. In November 2015, I asked the Department for Education (DfE) to provide evidence to support its assertions but none has been forthcoming at the time of writing.
5. Ofsted is the Office for Standards in Education, Children's Services and Skills. They inspect and regulate schools, amongst other services.
6. All main political parties were contacted in relation to this chapter in November 2015 but, at the time of writing, the author has received one specific response to questions about mainstreaming. Labour Party Shadow Minister for Children, Sharon Hodgson responded at some length explaining the extensive work she had done, alone, and with colleagues, to highlight SEND issues and to ensure these matters were mainstreamed. Ms Hodgson explained (and this is cited with consent) that she had family experience of the SEN world and agreed that "the lack of support for children with SEND [was] an issue of equality as when provision does not address issues of those with SEND then they are being failed by the system in reaching their utmost potential". Ms Hodgson also explained that the distinction between the briefs for Education and SEN was down to a replication of Government posts but she stressed that this did not stop colleagues working together across briefs.
7. Teaching assistants support children with their learning activities in and outside the classroom. They are frequently used to support children with SEN in schools in the UK.

References

Boesen, J. K., & Sano, H.-O. (2010). The Implications and Value Added of a Rights Based Approach. In Andreassen, A. & Marks, S.P. (Eds.), *Development as a Human Right, Legal, Political and Economic Dimensions*. London: Harvard University Press.

CAF. (2014). *Counting the Costs*. London: Contact a Family.

CDC. (2013). *Council for Disabled Children Digest,* Summer 2013 Issue 34. http://www.councilfordisabledchildren.org.uk/media/360617/digest_june_2013.pdf?dm_i=6N7,1KNXR,PNJTV,5ER29,1. Accessed 17 Nov 2015.

CDC. (2014, June 25). *Summary of the Children and Families Act.* London: Council for Disabled Children.

Chatzitheochari, S., Parsons, S., & Platt, L. (2014, June). *Bullying Experiences Among Disabled Children and Young People in England: Evidence from Two Longitudinal Studies* (Working Paper, No. 14–11). Department of Quantitative Social Science.

Connors, C., & Stalker, K. (2002). *The Views and Experiences of Disabled Children and Their Siblings: A Positive Outlook.* London: Jessica Kinglsey Publishers.

Corbett, J. (1996). *Bad-Mouthing: The Language of Special Needs.* New York: Routledge.

CRAE. (2014). *Children with Special Educational Needs and Disabilities, State of Children's Rights in England 2014.* London: Children's Rights Alliance for England.

Curran, H. (2015). *SEND Reforms 2014 and the Narrative of the SENCO: Early Impact on Children and Young People with SEND, the SENCO and the School.* BERA Conference, 15–17th Sept 2015, Belfast, Northern Ireland.

DES. (1978). *Warnock Committee Report.* London: HMSO.

DfE. (1994). *Special Educational Needs Code of Practice 1994.* London: HMSO.

DfE. (2011). *Support and Aspiration: A New Approach to Special Educational Needs and Disability.* London: HMSO.

DfE. (2014a). *The SEN Reforms Led to What Has Landmark Children and Families Act 2014 Gains Royal Assent.* Press Release, 13 March 2014.

DfE. (2014b). Letter to Parents, 1 Sept 2014. https://www.gov.uk/government/uploads/system/uploads/attachment_data/file/348842/Parents_letter_Aug_2014_final.pdf. Accessed 7 Jan 2016).

DfE. (2014c). *Listening to and Involving Children and Young People,* January 2014. London: HMSO.

DfE. (2015a). *National Pupil Projections: Trends in Pupil Numbers –* July 2015. (SFR 24/2015). London: HMSO.

DfE. (2015b). *Statistical First Release*: January 2015. (SFR25/2015). 27 July 2015. London: HMSO.

DfE (2015c, September), *Transition to the New 0 to 25 Special Educational Needs and Disability System.* London: HMSO.

DfE. (2015d, November). *Special Educational Needs: An Analysis and Summary of Data Sources.* London: HMSO.

DfE. (2015e). *Special Educational Needs and Disability Code of Practice: 0 to 25 Years.* London: HMSO.

DfE/SQW. (2015, July). *The Special Educational Needs and Disability Pathfinder Programme Evaluation, Final Impact Research Report.* London: HMSO.

DoH and DfE. (2015). *Special Educational Needs Code of Practice 2015.* London: HMSO.

Driver Reform Trust. (2015). *Joining the Dots: Have Recent Reforms Worked for Those with SEND*. London: Driver Reform Trust.

Duff, E. (2015, July 24). *Where Did All the Children with SEN Go?* http://www.sen-expertsolicitors.co.uk/news/where-did-all-the-children-with-sen-go/#sthash.cW7zE5h1.dpuf. Accessed 17 Nov 2015.

Duff, E. and Patel, L. (2015, October 9–11). Special Educational Needs: All Change! *Ed. L.M.*

Duffy, S. (2014). *Counting the Cuts*. Sheffield: Centre for Welfare Reform.

Dworkin, R. (1978). *Taking Rights Seriously*. Harvard: Harvard University Press.

ERA. (2015). *Inspecting [in]equalities Part 2: Ofsted, Schools and the Law*. 23 October 2014. http://educationalrightsalliance.blogspot.co.uk/2015/10/ofsted-schools-and-law-inspecting.html. Accessed 17 Nov 2015.

European Agency for Special Needs and Inclusive Education. (2012). *Special Needs Education Country Data*. Odense: European Agency for Special Needs and Inclusive Education.

European Agency for Special Needs and Inclusive Education. (2014a). *Thematic Key Words for Special Needs and Inclusive Education*. Odense: European Agency for Special Needs and Inclusive Education.

European Agency for Special Needs and Inclusive Education. (2014b). *Organisation of Provision to Support Inclusive Education*. Odense: European Agency for Special Needs and Inclusive Education.

Fortin, J. (2009). *Children's Rights: The Developing Law* (3rd ed.). Cambridge: Cambridge University Press.

Freeman, M. D. A. (2007). Why It Remains Important to Take Children's Rights Seriously. *International Journal of Children's Rights, 15*, 5–23.

Hatton, C. (2015, November 2). *The Disappeared*. http://chrishatton.blogspot.co.uk/2015/11/the-disappeared.html. Accessed 17 Nov 2015.

HMSO. (1981). *Education Act 1981*. London: HMSO.

HMSO. (1996). *Education Act 1996*. London: HMSO.

HMSO. (1998). *Human Rights Act 1998*. London: HMSO.

HMSO. (2001). *Special Educational Needs & Disability Act 2001*. London: HMSO.

HMSO. (2010). *Equality Act 2010*. London: HMSO.

HMSO. (2011). *Equality Act (Specific Duty) Regulations SI 2011/2260*. London: HMSO.

HMSO. (2014a). *Children and Families Act 2014*. London: HMSO.

HMSO. (2014b). *Special Educational Needs and Disability Regulations*. London: HMSO.

HoC. (2006). *Education and Skills Committee, Special Educational Needs*, HC 478-I, Third Report of Session 2005–06.

Holt, E. (2015). Special Educational Needs: Implementation of SEND Reforms. *Education Law, 16*(1), 6–7.

Johnson, P., & Kossykh, Y. (2008). *Early Years, Life Chances and Equality: A Literature Review*. London: Equality and Human Rights Commission.

L v Clarke and Somerset. (1998). ELR 129.

Lamb Inquiry. (2009). *Special Educational Needs and Parental Confidence*. London: HMSO.

Lupton, R. et al., (2015). *The Coalition's Record on Schools: Policy, Spending and Outcomes 2010–2015* (Working Paper 13). Social Policy in a Cold Climate.

Marks, S. (2011). Human Rights and Root Causes. *The Modern Law Review, 74*, 57–78.

Martin, N. (2011). Brief Reflections on Disability Theory, Language, Identity, Equality and Inclusion. http://blogs.lse.ac.uk/diversity/2011/05/brief-reflections-on-disability-theory-language-identity-equality-andinclusion/N. Accessed July 2017.

Mills, C. W. (1959). *The Sociological Imagination*. New York: Oxford University Press.

Moyn, S. (2015). A Powerless Companion: Human Rights in the Age of Neoliberalism. *Law and Contemporary Problems, 77*, 147–169.

N v North Tyneside Borough Council. (2010). EWCA Civ 135 N.

Norwich, B., & Kelly, N. (2004). Pupils' Views on Inclusion: Moderate Learning Difficulties and Bullying in Mainstream and Special Schools. *British Educational Research Journal, 30*(1), 43–65.

Office of the Children's Commissioner (OCC). (2014, April). *It Might Be Best If You Looked Elsewhere*. London: Office of the Children's Commissioner.

Ofsted. (2015a). *The Common Inspection Framework: Education, Skills and Early Years*. London: Ofsted Publications.

Ofsted. (2015b). Letter Dated, 8 December 2015. http://educationalrightsalliance.blogspot.co.uk/2015/10/ofsted-schools-and-law-inspecting.html. Accessed 4 Mar 2016.

Oliver, S. (2014). A Sea Change or Simply a Reshuffle? A Comment on the Children and Families Act 2014, Part 3. *Education Law, 15*(3), 175–179.

Parsons, S., & Platt, L. (2013, November). *Disability Among Young Children Prevalence, Heterogeneity and Socio-Economic Disadvantage* (Working Paper Nov 2013). Centre for Longitudinal Studies.

Peacey, N. (2015, August). A Transformation or an Opportunity Lost? The Education of Children and Young People with Special Educational Needs and Disability Within the Framework of the Children and Families Act 2014. *Research and Information on State Education*. http://www.risetrust.org.uk/pdfs/SEND%20Discussion.pdf. Accessed July 2017.

Pound, R. (1910). Law in Books and Law in Action. *American Law Review, 44*, 12.

R (ex p. Brind) v Secretary of State for the Home Department. (1991). 1 AC 696.

R (ex p. Brown) v Secretary of State for Work and Pensions and Others. (2008). EWHC 3158 (Admin).

Runswick-Cole, K., & Hodge, N. (2009). Needs or Rights? A Challenge to the Discourse of Special Education. *British Journal of Special Education, 36*(4), 198–203.

Stevenson, S. (2008). (M)Othering and Autism: Maternal Rhetorics of Self-Revision. In M. Osteen (Ed.), *Autism and Representation*. New York: Routledge.

TES. (2008, May 11). *Warnock Calls for Rethink*.

The Telegraph. (2012, May 15). *Thousands to Be Struck Off Special Needs List.* http://www.telegraph.co.uk/education/educationnews/9265948/Thousands-to-be-struck-off-special-needs-list.html. Accessed 7 Jan 2016.

Tomlinson, S. (2014). *The Politics of Race, Class and Special Education: The Selected Works of Sally Tomlinson.* London: Routledge.

UNCRC. (1989). *United Nations Convention on the Rights of the Child.* London: UNICEF.

UNCRPD. (2006). *United Nations Convention on the Rights of Persons with Disabilities.* New York: UN General Assembly.

UNESCO. (1994). *The Salamanca Statement and Framework for Action on Special Needs Education.* Paris: UNESCO.

UNESCO. (2005). *Guidelines for Inclusion: Ensuring Access to Education for All.* Paris: UNESCO.

UNESCO/UNICEF. (2007). *A Human Rights Based Approach to Education for All.* New York: UNESCO.

Wendell, S. (1996). *The Rejected Body: Feminist Philosophical Reflections on Disability.* New York: Routledge.

Debbie Sayers is a qualified solicitor and owner of the legal research consultancy Interalia.org.uk. She has a PhD in Human Rights Law and works as a freelance legal researcher. Her research interests encompass all aspects of human rights, including access to justice and children's rights, equality and non-discrimination issues, and specifically the implementation of rights.

Concluding Thoughts and Future Directions

Kirsty Liddiard, Tillie Curran, and
Katherine Runswick-Cole

Introduction

In this chapter, we draw together four main themes that run across many of the Handbook studies. We identify the first theme as focusing on **the voices of disabled children and young people** and consider what can we learn from their experiences and those of their families and supporters in different situations and contexts. This theme informs the second, **re-orientating research inquiry** where we draw out the creativity and sensitivities involved in listening to disabled children and in generating meaningful impact from research. The third theme, **thinking and theory,** runs throughout the Handbook with authors highlighting the significance of questioning, activism and speaking out in order to critique assumptions and to broaden understandings of disabled children's lives. These three themes are brought together in a final theme around **re-imagining research, policy and practice** in terms of *what* needs to change and considerations for the future. In each of the sections below, we identify limitations and areas for further attention making links with other

K. Liddiard (✉)
School of Education, The University of Sheffield, UK

T. Curran
University of the West of England, Bristol, UK

K. Runswick-Cole
School of Education, The University of Sheffield, UK

© The Author(s) 2018
K. Runswick-Cole et al. (eds.), *The Palgrave Handbook of Disabled Children's Childhood Studies*, https://doi.org/10.1057/978-1-137-54446-9

643

supporting approaches including Mad Studies and Global Disability Studies. We end the chapter with some comments in response to Sara Ryan's Preface.

The Voice of Disabled Children and Young People

The voices of disabled children are written throughout the Handbook. The chapters that seek to present disabled children and young people's voices directly give us insight into children's lived experience and the ways in which they contribute to their communities as family members, workers, activists and more. In the Handbook, we hear directly from disabled children and young people, often with the support of those closest to them. A unique feature of the Handbook is that we also hear from disabled adults reflecting back on their childhoods in ways that offer crucial insights into contemporary attitudes and practices in disabled children's lives. The Handbook also includes studies that explore children's experiences in and of community and services, and show the significance of children's views to inform change and to imagine alternative futures for disabled children and young people.

Contributors to this book take the call to listen to children seriously. **Heloise Maconochie,** in chapter "Making Space for the Embodied Participation of Young Disabled Children in a Children's Centre in England", shows us how to recognise and support the rights of children who express their choices in embodied ways, and she illustrates the value of reflective practices that we need in order to listen, check our understandings and respond. **Debby Watson, Alison Jones and Helen Potter** (chapter "Expressive Eyebrows and Beautiful Bubbles: Playfulness and Children with Profound Impairments") also explore disabled children's embodiment as they call upon us to understand and encourage children's playfulness as part of everyday life—playfulness as childhood. Too often, disabled children's play has been dominated with goals of treatment and therapy, but **Dawn Pickering,** in chapter "'The Embodiment of Disabled Children and Young People's Voices About Participating in Recreational Activities': Shared Perspectives", re-orientates traditional understandings of recreation that are focused on treatment and health to see recreation as social and, above all, fun. However, the continued exclusion of disabled children from access to play is vividly described in **Wendy and Jamie Merchant's** chapter (chapter "'What Can I Say?'").

The chapters written by disabled adults reflecting on their childhoods illustrate changes to some of the barriers they encountered but powerfully show the need to challenge the everyday experiences of marginalisation and exclusion that continue into the present. Crucially, these chapters teach us that disabled children's experiences stay with them, throughout their lives and into adulthood, in both disabling and enabling ways, showing how important it is to imagine and re-imagine futures for disabled children and young people. The professionals in their lives are not short-term transient conveyors of policy decisions; rather, children and their families live with their practices in the long term. Another aspect of these accounts is the agency demonstrated by disabled children, the verve and daring actions taken to shape childhood and adulthood. **Jo Skitteral** in chapter "Being a Disabled Woman and Mum: My Journey from Childhood" demands us to unsettle notions of a 'normal' life course to motherhood. In the re-imagining of the idea of 'burden' by **Sophie Savage** in chapter "The Heaviest Burdens and Life's Most Intense Fulfilment: A Retrospective and Re-understanding of My Experiences with Childhood Liver Disease and Transplantation", burden becomes a meaningful source of self from which to reflect upon and to tackle the normative behaviours of others in ways that make different contributions to understandings of health and well-being.

The authors writing from a close proximity to disabled children and young people, as parents and family members, challenge the reader to re-imagine Western normative notions of heterosexual nuclear families. Fathers have often been characterised as a 'hard-to-reach' group in the studies of disabled family life, but **Joanne Heeney** listens to fathers, in chapter "Intersectionality Theory in Research with the Fathers of Children with the Label of Autism", who contest assumptions around gender and disability, appealing for change to enable fathers' and young people's participation in personal and community life. **Luke Jones** and **Kirsty Liddiard,** in chapter "A Diversity of Childhoods: Considering the Looked After Childhood", reflect upon the external forces that contour both the lives of disabled children who are looked after by the Local Authority in Britain (Looked After Children) and the impact of this on the relationships that Othered children can have with those close to them. **Sandra Dowling, Roy McConkey** and **Marlene Sinclair** share the experiences of young people who have had a life changing injury in chapter "My Friends and Me: Friendship and Identity Following Acquired Brain Injury in Young People" and focus on the ways in which they re-construct friendships in their lives.

Blair Manns, in his 'texting project' with his mother **Sarah Manns**, presents his choices and sources of enjoyment. He says he likes horses because they are calm and don't judge. 'Being judged', he explains, means being judged on every aspect of his life. The reach of wider culture is vivid in this intimate conversation. As **Rebecca Whitehead** (chapter "My Sister, My World: From Second Mum to Nurse") also shows, personal voices are not context free.

Young people's everyday endeavour to shape their futures requires energy and entails taking risks, as we saw in the chapters above. The voices of disabled children and their families in service settings in England are discussed by **Jennifer McElwee, David Cox, Tony Cox, Rosemary Holland, Thomas Holland, Theresa Mason, Chloe Pearce, Caroline Sobey, Julie Bugler, Andy James and Beverley Pearce** in chapter "The Tree of Participation: Our Thoughts About Growing a Culture of Participation Between Young People, Parents and Health Team Staff" but are also explored by **Peggy Gallagher, Cheryl Rhodes and Karen Young Lewis** in chapter "Family Voices in Teacher Education" as a way of developing teaching practices. 'Participation' and 'inclusion' have often been criticised for being limited or tokenistic, but we see here how small beginnings can be sustained to develop far beyond initial service-led expectations. Participants bring their concerns but they also come to recognise exploitation and to challenge providers to take responsibility for their role and practice. In the context of participation, **Ben Whitburn** (chapter "The Kids Are Alright: They Have Been Included for Years") alerts us to the significance of children's silence, their capacity to resist and the power exercised when refusing to participate. As **Tillie Curran, Ruth Sayers** and **Barry Percy-Smith** in chapter "Disabled Children's Childhood Studies and Leadership as Experts by Experience' Leadership: Learning Activism in Health and Social Care Education" show, sharing experience with service providers, policymakers and professionals can be a powerful form of leadership for change but is also demanding, with little evidence of impact on the unacceptable forms of practice children and families describe. Curran et al. propose critical pedagogies for professionals to take up their role in activism and, in chapter "Normalcy, Intersectionality and Ableism: Teaching About and Around 'Inclusion' to Future Educators", **Jenny Slater** and **Elizabeth Chapman** also consider different pedagogies to address ableism as the problem. They explain that the inclusion agenda in education can be individualised so that stories of children's and families' experience serve to support, rather than to challenge, injustices.

We are mindful that by merely listening to children, and failing to act on what they say, this is yet another form of exploitation and exclusion. Stories of experience can at first appear positive and hail the exceptional, or the inspirational, but as Peers (2015) in her 'auto-ethnography of a super crip' shows us, such stories can endorse the norms of 'achievement' and repeat hostile valuations of 'who counts' as a person. We are also mindful of the importance of issues of intersectionality and the context of oppressions regarding sexuality, age, gender and ethnicity. Authors have included discussions of how disabled children and young people are infantalised or dis-gendered by others and how their sexuality and intimate lives are erased. 'Race', ethnicity and the global context is also made invisible through the unreflexive claims of universal childhood and disability theory.

The voices of disabled children, young people and families provide the impetus for change and build understandings that expose norms.

Re-orientating Research Inquiry

Re-orientating the research inquiry has meant starting with the concerns of disabled children, young people and those who support them. This has entailed the development of research methods that are accessible and sensitive, and the development of methodologies that value personal experience as rich data to be analysed. We have chapters using a play, text messages, life writing and deconstruction, and **Nick Hodge and Katherine Runswick-Cole** (chapter "You Say… I Hear…": Epistemic Gaps in Practitioner-Parent/Carer Talk") use examples of conversation to illustrate the different epistemic positions and deconstruct these to illustrate the power relationships at play in parent-professional partnerships. Research studies have also brought together people working in different disciplines to give a wider view of life and to re-orientate the focus to children's experiences. **Helen Hamby** in chapter "A Relational Understanding of Language Impairment: Children's Experiences in the Context of Their Social Worlds" is not looking at speech and language problems but the experiences of children, as they struggle to be heard. **Anat Greenstein** (chapter "Being a Speech and Language Therapist: Between Support and Oppression") also re-orientates research around speech and language difficulties to focus on concerns about children's experiences of oppression.

In the context of research, universities and funders both require researchers to set out any ethical concerns and the steps that they will take to mitigate risk at the start of a research project. However, the studies in this Handbook show how important it is to respond creatively *throughout* the research process if researchers are to sustain aims of listening as an ethical practice. **Sumaira Nasseem** (chapter "'Just Sumaira: Not Her, Them or It'") shows us the difference between ethical involvement and exploitation in research, reminding us that simply obtaining consent, albeit informed and accessible, can amount to exploitation. She describes how research can be experienced as objectification and questions the justification of research on the basis that it may, one day, be of some future benefit to other children.

Research by parents about their own experiences has often drawn on auto-ethnography, and authors have reflected on the ethical complexities of writing about their children. They have shown how important it is to work through the ethical issues in order to protect the identity and voice of family members. **Liz Thackray** clearly sets out the considerations researchers need to attend to in telling their own story in chapter "Anonymity, Confidentiality and Informed Consent: Exploring Ethical Quandaries and Dilemmas in Research with and About Disabled Children's Childhoods" to avoid telling another's story when both lives are fully linked. **Barbara Coles,** chapter "Personalisation Policy and Parents: The Formalisation of Family Care for Adult Children with Learning Disabilities in England", discusses her parent and researcher roles without sharing details of her son's life or that of the adult children of the parents in her study by presenting the impact of systems in the lives of families. **Tania Watson** (chapter "The Construction of Life Trajectories: Reflections, Research and Resolutions for Young People with Behavioural Disabilities") makes the decision not to share her own experiences and that of her children but discusses the considerable emotional labour entailed when the experiences of others resonate with the author's own life. **Brian Watermayer,** writing in chapter "Growing Up Disabled: Impairment, Familial Relationships and Identity", reminds us of the sensitivity required to draw in and upon one's own childhood, which is always situated in the lives of close others. **Jill Pluquailec,** in chapter "Thinking and Doing Consent and Advocacy in Disabled Children's Childhood Studies Research", shares the need to question set procedures around ethics such as 'consent' and to critique these orthodoxies for the lives of disabled children and young people.

Chapters in the Handbook tend not to draw on what is now called 'big data'—research drawn from large-scale questionnaires with large numbers of participants. This is, in part, because the studies in the Handbook are, for the most part, generated by people in close contact with disabled children and young people and so have taken experience as the starting point. However, the authors are also, perhaps, aware of the limitations of research drawing on science-based disciplines, such as medicine and psychology. Often, the goal of such research is to discover universal truths and deviant norms within a population, to isolate significant variables and identify correlations towards causal explanations or to simply count 'them'. We agree with Oliver (1991) who described the use of this positivist paradigm as methodological individualism that seeks to point to what is wrong with individuals rather than what is wrong with society. The studies here purposefully focus on the context of disabled children's childhoods, in their local, temporal and global locations.

However, we can see some potential for disabled children's childhood studies in moving into quantitative research but only if we can re-orientate research inquiry away from 'professional concerns' to focus on the hopes, dreams and aspirations of disabled children and young people. We need to consider how big-data questions might be inspired by disabled children's childhood studies.

Theory and Thinking About Disabled Children's Childhoods

Disabled children's childhood studies is unique in its desire to delve into the life worlds of children and their families and to understand lived experience through the lenses of emotion, intimacy, love, care and proximity. We have encountered this desire across the chapters of this Handbook. Many chapters have used emotion as the register through which to understand material, social and cultural realities within the lives of disabled children and young people and their families. For example, many chapters in the Handbook speak of the copious emotional work and labour that come from surviving disablism and living through ableism. From endlessly negotiating with multiple professionals, systems and policies to performing disability in ways that enable resources and from support and advocacy to managing the psycho-emotional consequences of being marked as Other, the affective politics of disability are brought to bear in ways seldom considered in other ways of knowing and theorising childhood.

Kirsty Liddiard and **Luke Jones** (chapter "A Diversity of Childhoods: Considering the Looked After Childhood") centre emotion in their analysis of family foster caring. In their chapter, they expose 'the team around the child' as a mechanism that can disrupt familial intimacy and closeness. Yet, being family foster carers also means being part of this very team. This involves significant emotional and relational labour, much of it mundane and every day. In contrast, the emotions of hate and indifference that children experience in **Sandra Dowling, Roy McConkey and Marlene Sinclair's** chapter expose the subtle violence of ableism. **Katherine Runswick-Cole** and **Dan Goodley** critique traditional normative notions of resilience and their casting of disabled children as weaker and Other (chapter "Resilience in the Lives of Disabled Children: A Many Splendoured Thing"). **Harriet Cooper's** contribution (chapter "Making Policy for Whom? The Significance of the 'Psychoanalytic Medical Humanities' for Policy and Practice That Affects the Lives of Disabled Children") thoroughly explores the place of psychoanalysis in disability studies and builds connections beyond common oppositions.

While ableism, or assumptions of able-bodiedness, is not always directly referenced in every chapter in this book, taken as a whole, the chapters rage against the presumptions of an able-centric world in which failure to live up to the idealised myth of abled embodiment results in marginalisation and exclusion. **Berni Kelly, Sandra Dowling and Karen Winter** in chapter "Disabled Children in Out-of-Home Care: Issues and Challenges for Practice" present the context where disabled children are in need of safeguarding and expose the layers of lost opportunities to support children, their families and carers and how 'distant' 'specialist' services are then rationalised as the only options. When professionals are operating amongst such partial levels of investment, we are minded of Butler's work on legal violence (see https://www.youtube.com/watch?v=coBcQajx18I), where a population is divided and subdivided to the point that inequality of attention to the survival of 'other' is normalised. In other words, the formal practice of categorising 'vulnerable' groups is dangerous. **Debbie Sayers** (chapter "Rights Not Needs: Changing the Legal Model for Special Educational Needs (SEN)") also questions the category of 'needs' as a barrier to 'rights'. If disabled children's rights were met, needs would also be met, but if needs are the focus, rights do not become the focus. In short, engagement with disabled children and young people's voice, their lives, their childhood and youth and re-imagined futures is a key action against hate and othering practices.

Disabled Children's Childhood Studies aims to draw in and upon the global—to situate geopolitically disabled childhoods in their wider global contexts. This has been a central tenet of Disabled Children's Childhood Studies since its inception, to both contest global norms around disability, childhood, family, bodies, and community, while at the same time disrupting the dominance of Global North accounts and Euro-American ethnocentric understandings of what constitutes both 'childhood' and 'disability'. We have sought to avoid the routine reification of Western understandings of childhood and invited authors to locate their studies not only in terms of geographical location but also in terms of geopolitical context. However, we acknowledge here that this Handbook is dominated by analyses of primarily Western childhoods. It is important to mark this for two reasons: first, to make visible the childhoods that this excludes and second, in order to openly acknowledge that there is much work to be done to shift the dominance of the Global North within our understandings of disabled childhoods.

There are, of course, exceptions and these offer opportunities to understand ableism, disablism and normalcy as global forces and ones which are inherently shaped by historical and contemporary global economies, histories and supranational policies. For example, in chapter "Supporting Families in Raising Disabled Children to Enhance African Child Development", **Tsitsi Chataika and Judith McKenzie** write about support in African childhoods. They argue that disabled African children cannot be seen as distinct from their families, especially in situations of poverty. The necessary materialisation of what they call 'disability families' offers ways to negotiate and celebrate disability while staying mindful of the fact that threats to disability families can be found in increasing Westernisation, a process they suggest draws disability out of the family and community and into structure and services. However, in theorising *through* disabled children's childhood studies framework, all chapters have rubbed up against the global, even if they haven't contextualised their analysis within it or spoken explicitly about global issues. This subtlety affirms both the labour and commitment required of all us interested in the intersections of disability and childhood to think beyond our own borders, binaries and boundaries.

If we are not to be complicit with individualised accounts and if we are to reject the export/profit goals of 'development' work, Grech (2013) suggests we begin by being open about those goals and the futility of seeking universal concepts of childhood and disability:

> *it is perhaps more important for any analysis to start off by understanding what surrounds the child, what it means to be a 'full' child and a 'full' person, because this is what disability is positioned along/against and how it is defined and interpreted by both disabled people and those around (p. 95).*

Grech (2013) illustrates the hybrid relations in his study about disabled children and young people, their families and community in Guatemala, pointing to gendered relations, family and community relations in context. From his critique of Western discourses of individual 'rights', he proposes exploration of 'community rights'.

In the same vein, another 'absent-presence' within the Handbook is that of mental health, well-being and illness. Authors have critiqued the significant psychologisation of everyday life in advanced neoliberal-ableism, as mental health literacy enters our schools, workplaces and families, and we come to know and rework ourselves through the dominant psy-knowledges of psychology and psychiatry. Authors have discussed well-being and illness, labels and experiences, systems of governance and their cultural impact and introduced alternative starting points. **Damian Milton** in chapter "Autistic Development, Trauma and Personhood: Beyond the Frame of the Neoliberal Individual" alerts us to the different perspectives around labels and re-imagines the 'aut' critiquing the impact of neo-liberalism. **Kristin Snoddon** and **Kathryn Underwood** in chapter "The Social Relational Model of Deaf Childhood in Action" analyse the social relations of deafness and show how the lives and communities of deaf people have been impacted by regimes imposed to normalise.

Globally, we are told that children and young people are in significant emotional distress and therefore are always at risk of—or are already experiencing—mental illness. In the West (and increasingly in the Global South), this is marked by the psychologisation and psychiatrisation of childhood and youth, with biochemical responses ensuring what Mills (2014) calls neurochemical childhoods as childhood, in contexts of poverty, becomes a pathological state.

As an emerging field, disabled children's childhood studies seek to be critical friends with studies of critical mental health and Mad Studies. This is in order to deindividualise, contextualise and politicise mental health and well-being in contexts of disability and childhood. Mad Studies is a growing academic discipline that has emerged from Mad and Psychiatric Survivor movements, primarily in Canada and Scotland (LeFrancois et al. 2014). Importantly, it shares many values with disabled children's childhood studies: contesting normalcy, medicalisation, oppressive structures, and the dominance of the expert, towards privileging the voices and histories of Mad people, and including their contributions in its research, teaching and writing, as **Ruth Sayers** discusses in chapter "Disabled Children's Childhood Studies and Leadership as Experts by Experience' Leadership: Learning Activism in Health and Social Care Education". In the current time of global austerity, where supports are systematically being removed from disabled children and their families, it is important to politicise distress and resist the routine psychiatrisation of poverty (Mills 2015).

Relatedly, in this Handbook, we have made attempts to draw upon the intersectionality of disabled lives. Intersectionality, as **Slater and Chapman** suggest in their 'three key concepts' in chapter "Normalcy, Intersectionality and Ableism: Teaching About and Around 'Inclusion' to Future Educators", relates to the intersections of disability with race, class, gender, age, sexuality and nationality: an acknowledgement of the heterogeneity of the disability experience and a means through which to understand the intricacies and complexities of multiple and intersecting oppressions in the lives of disabled children and young people and their families. For example, **Jo Skitteral** (chapter "Being a Disabled Woman and Mum: My Journey from Childhood"), **Kim Davies** (chapter "Going 'Off Grid': A Mother's Account of Refusing Disability") **Katherine Runswick-Cole and Dan Goodley** (chapter "The 'Disability Commons': Re-thinking Mothering Through Disability") centre the gendered politics and realities of mothering and motherhood. In chapter "Being a Disabled Woman and Mum: My Journey from Childhood", **Jo Skitteral** recounts her experiences as a disabled woman on the road to motherhood and reminds us of the extent to which parenting while disabled is filled with barriers from childhood and beyond. More than this, she shows the complex intersections of disability and gender through the paradox of being expected, as a girl, to undertake childcare responsibilities for siblings, while at the same time actively being written off as future woman and mother because of disability. Motherhood, due to the assumed asexuality and incapability to parent that dis/ableism can often mean for disabled women. Jo tells a story of not just becoming a mother but becoming a mother in the minds and under the gaze of professional others, showing that disablism is always lurking, even when normative gender roles are adhered to. Such gendered stories of disability and parenting are seldom heard, even within disability studies (Ignagni et al. 2016).

As we turn to our final theme, **re-imagining research, policy and practice,** we reflect upon change. Throughout this Handbook, there is a call for recognition, not of difference and disorder but of the capacities and potential of disabled children and young people. These capacities and potentials are not clouded by the shadow of the norm; rather, they disrupt such ways of thinking and offer alternative possibilities for all children and young people. The Handbook reveals that there is a need for a fundamental shift in research, policy and practice away from a deficit model and towards a celebration of disabled children's disruptive potential to re-orientate understandings of childhood, youth and adulthood.

Concluding Comments in Response to Sara Ryan

The key strength of this book, however, is the imaginations it both evokes and demands. The denial of an imagined future has, for too long, been the default position for too many people

As Sara Ryan comments in her preface, this book is about (re)imagining. The chapters in the book demand us to think differently about the lives of disabled children and young people across the globe. They demand us to expect more of and for disabled children and young people, to see their potential and to celebrate their lives.

We hope that readers will take up the messages in this book to always seek to (re)imagine the lives of disabled children and young people so that they can fulfil their potential and live the lives they want to lead.

References

Grech, S. (2013). Disability, Childhood and Poverty: Critical Perspectives on Guatemala (Chapter 8). In T. Curran & K. Runswick-cole (Eds.), *Disabled Children's Childhood Studies Critical Approaches in a Global Context* (pp. 89–104). Basingstoke: Palgrave Macmillan.

Ignagni, E., Fudge-Schormans, A., Liddiard, K., & Runswick-Cole, K. (2016). Some People Aren't Allowed to Love: Intimate Citizenship in the Lives of People Labelled with Intellectual Disabilities. *Disability and Society*. doi:10.1080/09687599.2015.1136148 OPEN ACCESS.

LeFrancois, B. A., Menzies, R., & Reaume's, G. (Eds.). (2014). *Mad Matters: A Critical Reader in Canadian Mad Studies*. Toronto: Canadian Scholar's Press.

Mills, C. (2014). *Decolonizing Global Mental Health: The Psychiatrization of the Majority World*. London/New York: Routledge.

Mills, C. (2015). The Psychiatrization of Poverty: Rethinking the Mental Health-Poverty Nexus. *Social and Personality Psychology Compass, 9*(5), 213–222.

Oliver, M. (1991). *The Politics of Disablement*. Basingstoke: Macmillan.

Peers, D. (2015). From Inhalation to Inspiration: A Genealogical Auto-ethnography of a Supercrip. In S. Tremain (Ed.), *Foucault and the Government of Disability* (pp. 331–350). Ann Arbor: University of Michigan Press.

Kirsty Liddiard is a research fellow in the School of Education at the University of Sheffield. Her research spans disability, gender, sexuality and intimacy and youth, with a particular interest in how disablism and ableism both inform and shape these experiences in the everyday lives of disabled people. She tweets at @kirstyliddiard1. To read more about Kirsty's work, please visit kirstyliddiard.wordpress.com

Tillie Curran, Senior Lecturer in Social Work at the University of the West of England, has developed her approach to disabled children's childhood studies from The Children Act 1989 which brought disabled children into 'children's' legislation for the first time and required that their wishes were heard. Disabled young people and their allies lead on changing policy, practice and public understanding, and Tillie is interested in how practitioners can respond, support and make those changes happen.

Katherine Runswick-Cole is Chair in Education, The School of Education, The University of Sheffield, Sheffield, UK. Her research draws on critical disability studies approaches to explore the relationships between disability, childhood and families. Her research is informed by her experiences of mothering two young adult children, one of whom is disabled.

Index[1]

---

¹Note: Page number followed by 'n' refers to notes.

© The Author(s) 2018
K. Runswick-Cole et al. (eds.), *The Palgrave Handbook of Disabled Children's Childhood
Studies*, https://doi.org/10.1057/978-1-137-54446-9

Printed by Printforce, the Netherlands